# ADAPTING INSTRUCTION TO ACCOMMODATE STUDENTS IN INCLUSIVE SETTINGS

### Judy W. Wood
*Virginia Commonwealth University*

**Merrill Prentice Hall**

Upper Saddle River, New Jersey
Columbus, Ohio

**Library of Congress Cataloging-in-Publication Data**
Wood, Judy W.
  Adapting instruction to accommodate students in inclusive settings / Judy W. Wood.—
4th ed.
     p. cm.
  Includes bibliographical references (p. 667) and index.
  ISBN 0-13-091068-6
     1. Inclusive education—United States. 2. Handicapped students—Education—United
States. 3. Socially handicapped children—Education—United States. 4. Mainstreaming in
education—United States. I. Title

LC1201.W66 2002
371.9—dc21                                              2001044532

**Vice President and Publisher:** Jeffery W. Johnston
**Executive Editor:** Ann Castel Davis
**Editorial Assistant:** Keli Gemrich
**Production Editor:** Sheryl Glicker Langner
**Production Coordination:** Lea Baranowski, Carlisle Publishers Services
**Design Coordinator:** Diane C. Lorenzo
**Cover Designer:** Rod Harris
**Cover Photo:** Corbis/Stock Market
**Production Manager:** Laura Messerly
**Director of Marketing:** Kevin Flanagan
**Marketing Manager:** Amy June
**Marketing Coordinator:** Barbara Koontz

This book was set in Helvetica by Carlisle Communications, Ltd. It was printed and bound
by Maple Vail Book Manufacturing Group. The cover was printed by Phoenix Color Corp.

Pearson Education Ltd., *London*
Pearson Education Australia Pty. Limited, *Sydney*
Pearson Education Singapore, Pte. Ltd.
Pearson Education North Asia Ltd., *Hong Kong*
Pearson Education Canada, Ltd., *Toronto*
Pearson Educación de Mexico, S.A. de C.V.
Pearson Education—Japan, *Tokyo*
Pearson Education Malaysia, Pte. Ltd.
Pearson Education, *Upper Saddle River, New Jersey*

Merrill
Prentice Hall

10 9 8 7 6 5 4 3 2 1
ISBN 0-13-091068-6

This book is lovingly dedicated to the following persons who exhibit courage for life, love for others, and an endless drive for making a difference

Pastors Vicki and Lowell Qualls—whose faith brought a miracle.

Paula Friedrich and Debra Gibson—my daughters of choice.

A special appreciation to my lifelong friends and sisters: Beth Bloxham, Pat Feola, Dr. Cynthia Bryant, Carolyn Tomlin, Carolyn Hamada, Dr. Alta Harvey, Dr. Don Collins, Dr. Cheritta Matthews, Patsy Glover, Donna Wanner, and Kay Christian Morse.

John and Sue Wheal—my parents of choice.

Appreciation is expressed to the faculty of Spring Branch Middle School, Houston, Texas; Christian Friedrich; and Ashley Black.

Tommye Boyd, President, Texas Association of Secondary School Principals.

My sons **EDDIE, SCOTT,** and **JASON.**

And my loving husband and best friend, **DAVID A. DUNCAN.**

And to the memory
of
Charlotte Anne Christian.

# PREFACE

Adapting Instruction to Accommodate Students in Inclusive Settings has been written and developed for use in survey, inclusion, and/or mainstreaming courses, method courses (general and special education), as well as for inservice classes. This text is a **complete package** written to provide instructors, graduate, and undergraduate students with a practical, user-friendly, easy-to-follow text. The major focus of this text is to assist general educators, special educators, administrators, and other support personnel in providing appropriate services for students with disabilities and for students at risk for failure in general education settings. The text is designed around a semantic map that helps students to see the whole text visually and each specific chapter as covered.

## ORGANIZATION OF THE FOURTH EDITION

The text is divided into two parts. Part 1, Chapters 1 through 5, builds the foundation for the "road to responsibility." Included in this part is coverage on the legal foundation for inclusion; the functions, roles, and responsibilities of the multidisciplinary team; teaching the culturally diverse and bilingual student; how to identify the various characteristics of students at risk; and a description of the continuum of placement for students and informations on transitions.

Part 2, "Including All Students," introduces the reader to the two-step procedure of inclusion. In Chapter 6, the first step—the **process**—teaches "how we do inclusion" with a focus on collaboration and its various models, including coteaching. Chapters 7 through 16, focus on step two—the **content**—or "what we do in inclusion." These 10 chapters discuss the content segment through the use of the research-based model developed and tested extensively by the author.

## THE "SAALE" MODEL

Developed over the past several decades and class-tested by teachers from all over the country, the SAALE model (**S**ystematic **A**pproach for **A**dapting the **L**earning **E**nvironment) expands on the model of mainstreaming introduced in the earlier editions. The first component of the model is a transition/intervention checklist to identify student problems in the general class setting. Following this, the student is shown how to use the model to accommodate and individualize within the specific chapters on adapting the learning, behavioral, and physical environments. Chapters covering lesson planning, formatting of content, and media technology follow. The model concludes with chapters on evaluation and grading.

# SUPPLEMENTS TO THE TEXT

*Adapting Instruction to Accomodate Students in Inclusive Settings* offers a complete ancillary package for the instructor. The following are available:

*Instructor's Manual*—The manual includes chapter outlines, key concepts and terms, activities, test questions, suggested homework and classroom assignments, handouts, resources, and overhead black-line masters.

# ACKNOWLEDGMENTS

Appreciation is extended to the talented, patient, and dedicated staff members at Merrill/Prentice Hall Publishing: Ann Castel Davis, editor; Lea Baranowski, production editor at Carlisle Communications, and Michelle Lulos Livingston, copy editor.

I am indebted to the reviewers who provided valuable comments and suggestions that helped guide me on my journey: Georgine Steinmiller, Henderson State University (AR); Bill McInerney, University of Toledo (OH); and Kai Yung Tam, The City College of New York.

Several wonderful, talented writers assisted me in bringing new ideas and research to this work: Rachel Wise; Debra Gibson; Paula Friedrich; Paul and Pat Feola; Gary Meers; Deborah Wilson; Samir Haddad; and Jerry Fouchey.

Because of an injury during the development of this text, many gifted physicians worked with me on my difficult journey to recovery. I will be forever grateful to Dr. Leslie Kryzanowski; Dr. Leslie Rose; Dr. John O'Bannon; Dr. William White; and Dr. Donlin Long of Johns Hopkins Medical Center in Baltimore, Maryland.

A special gratitude is extended to the hundreds of educators who provided invaluable suggestions and field tests, and to the children, youths, and adults who live daily with disabilities and educational needs and so proudly continue the journey. Lastly, to the professionals who strive to teach reality and to the students who will carry the educational torch; thank you for your courage.

# DISCOVER THE COMPANION WEBSITE ACCOMPANYING THIS BOOK

## THE PRENTICE HALL COMPANION WEBSITE: A VIRTUAL LEARNING ENVIRONMENT

Technology is a constantly growing and changing aspect of our field that is creating a need for content and resources. To address this emerging need, Prentice Hall has developed an online learning environment for students and professors alike—Companion Websites—to support our textbooks.

In creating a Companion Website, our goal is to build on and enhance what the textbook already offers. For this reason, the content for each user-friendly website is organized by chapter and provides the professor and student with a variety of meaningful resources.

## FOR THE PROFESSOR—

Every Companion Website integrates **Syllabus Manager™,** an online syllabus creation and management utility.

- **Syllabus Manager™** provides you, the instructor, with an easy, step-by-step process to create and revise syllabi, with direct links into the Companion Website and other online content without having to learn HTML.

- Students may log on to your syllabus during any study session. All they need to know is the web address for the Companion Website and the password you've assigned to your syllabus.

- After you have created a syllabus using **Syllabus Manager™,** students may enter the syllabus for their course section from any point in the Companion Website.

- Clicking on a date, the student is shown the list of activities for the assignment. The activities for each assignment are linked directly to actual content, saving time for students.

- Adding assignments consists of clicking on the desired due date, then filling in the details of the assignment—name of the assignment, instructions, and whether or not it is a one-time or repeating assignment.

- In addition, links to other activities can be created easily. If the activity is online, a URL can be entered in the space provided, and it will be linked automatically in the final syllabus.

- Your completed syllabus is hosted on our servers, allowing convenient updates from any computer on the Internet. Changes you make to your syllabus are immediately available to your students at their next logon.

## FOR THE STUDENT—

- **Chapter Objectives**—outline key concepts from the text
- **Interactive Self-Quizzes**—complete with hints and automatic grading that provide immediate feedback for students

After students submit their answers for the interactive self-quizzes, the Companion Website **Results Reporter** computes a percentage grade, provides a graphic representation of how many questions were answered correctly and incorrectly, and gives a question-by-question analysis of the quiz. Students are given the option to send their quiz to up to four email addresses (professor, teaching assistant, study partner, etc.).

- **Web Destinations**—links to www sites that relate to chapter content
- **Message Board**—serves as a virtual bulletin board to post—or respond to—questions or comments to/from a national audience
- **Chat**—real-time chat with anyone who is using the text anywhere in the country—ideal for discussion and study groups, class projects, etc.

To take advantage of the many available resources, please visit the *Adapting Instruction to Accommodate Students in Inclusive Settings,* Fourth Edition, Companion Website at

**www.prenhall.com/wood**

# CONTENTS

**PART TWO**     **Including All Students: The Process and the Content   164**

**CHAPTER   6**   *The Process of Collaboration   166*

**CHAPTER 14**   *Adapting Multimedia Approaches: Assistive Technology and Technology Applications in the Information Age Classroom   510*

*Note:* Every effort has been made to provide accurate and current Internet information in this book. However, the Internet and the information posted on it are constantly changing, so it is inevitable that some of the Internet addresses listed in this textbook will change.

# PART ONE

# Building the Foundation for Serving Students in General Education Classrooms

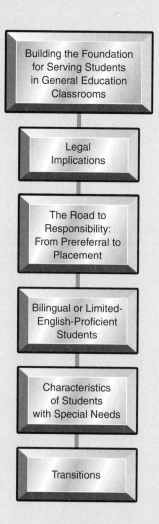

Building the Foundation for Serving Students in General Education Classrooms

Legal Implications

The Road to Responsibility: From Prereferral to Placement

Bilingual or Limited-English-Proficient Students

Characteristics of Students with Special Needs

Transitions

Our journey started before many of you were born. But some of you were already young children; others, who are older, can easily remember and relate to historical change. In 1975, landmark federal legislation began a national movement that gave students with disabilities the right to an education with their nondisabled peers. This movement, called *mainstreaming,* became the impetus for numerous changes in education. Preservice standards at the university and college levels were modified, state certification requirements were altered, and inservice education topics began to change.

Public schools were presented with new challenges. Students with disabilities, previously served in self-contained classes or denied a public education altogether, were now knocking on the doors of general education classes. As the doors began to open and special students took their seats in the general class, other problems surfaced. General education teachers realized that they needed additional skills to teach these students. Special education teachers found that their roles had to expand from providing direct services to children in self-contained settings to working as consultants with general educators, at times even team teaching with their colleagues. Special education students were now faced with an unfamiliar curriculum, and students with disabilities were frequently not achieving success in the educational mainstream. Parents also had new roles as advocates for their children within general education. They now had to become knowledgeable about not only their rights and those of their children but also the general education curriculum. Many questions were raised that had no easy answers: Why is my child failing? What can be done? Whose responsibility does this become?

The year 1975 was a good one—a threshold for changes in education, although society did not realize the impact of what was to come. At last, students with disabilities would have educational rights equal to those experienced by other children. But another fact soon became clear: Even though the right to an equal education was made available, the education was not always equal.

This book, now in its fourth edition, will take you on a brief journey from 1975 to the present. Its main focus will be on adapting instruction for students with mild disabilities and those at risk who are served in general education environments. The book's guidelines and suggestions for instruction can be applied to all students who are experiencing problems within the education system. Educators will find that the ideas presented may also be used with all children within the instructional process.

The concept of providing intervention via accommodations has become the hot conversation of many educators. The third edition of this text felt the growing impact of interventions. Now, four years later, interventions are here and will remain. Children will be given every opportunity in general education. This reality is changing the focus of (a) attitudes, (b) curriculum, (c) instruction, and (d) testing.

Part 1 includes five chapters that set the stage for the remainder of the text. Chapter 1 will take the reader on a journey from 1975 to the present and point out major legislation that has affected the lives of students with special needs. Chapter 2 will briefly continue our journey on the pathway that children may follow when educators are seeking special services for them. Chapter 3 presents information for educators when working with bilingual children. Chapter 4 takes an in-depth look at the specific characteristics of disability areas and offers a model for possible placement options. It also tells us how this information affects the classroom. Chapter 5 is a delightful addition to the text. Written by Dr. Gary Meers of the University of Nebraska-Lincoln, this chapter follows transition as it unfolds into the remaining chapters of the text. Dr. Meers highlights transitions in all areas of the SAALE Model.

# CHAPTER 1

## *Legal Implications*

*Contributions by Debra Gibson*

```
┌─────────────────────────┐
│ Building the Foundation  │
│  for Serving Students    │
│ in General Education     │
│      Classrooms          │
└─────────────────────────┘
            │
┌─────────────────────────┐
│        Legal             │
│     Implications         │
└─────────────────────────┘
            │
┌─────────────────────────┐
│     The Road to          │
│   Responsibility:        │
│ From Prereferral to      │
│      Placement           │
└─────────────────────────┘
            │
┌─────────────────────────┐
│  Bilingual or Limited-   │
│  English-Proficient      │
│      Students            │
└─────────────────────────┘
            │
┌─────────────────────────┐
│   Characteristics        │
│    of Students           │
│ with Special Needs       │
└─────────────────────────┘
            │
┌─────────────────────────┐
│      Transitions         │
└─────────────────────────┘
```

**Chapter-at-a-Glance**

Section 504 of the Rehabilitation Act (1973)

Education for All Handicapped Children Act (1975)

Education of the Handicapped Act Amendments (1986)

Individuals with Disabilities Education Act (1990)

Americans with Disabilities Act (1990)

Individuals with Disabilities Education Act, IDEA (Revisions 1997)

By looking at history, we know that persons with disabilities have always existed. Society has attempted to hide, shun, and even persecute persons with disabilities. Gradually, society began to offer protection, and from protection, eventually "equal treatment under the law." There is a long history of special education and services for children with special needs or those at high risk in society. Table 1.1 outlines the events that created special education as we know it. These events are also the foundation for major legislation that has changed the tone of education in the United States. Today we find that special education has begun to affect education as a whole and is affecting our society totally. Education for any student is no longer in isolation; it is a team effort.

Because of legislation and societal support, the numbers of students crossing from special education into general education are increasing. In 1995–1996, 95 percent of students with learning disabilities ages 6 through 21 were educated with their general education peers. For this same period, 46 percent of the students with learning disabilities were removed from their general class placements for 21 percent of the day.

**TABLE 1.1**
Historical events in the field of special education.

| | |
|---|---|
| Renaissance and Reformation | Individuals with disabilities were cruelly treated—tortured, killed, or placed in workhouses. |
| Period of Christianity | Residential institutions were established. |
| 1700s–1800s | Special schools were established in Europe. |
| Late 1800s–early 1900s | The Industrial Revolution created jobs and helped Americans focus on child abuse in factories and the fair treatment of all individuals. |
| Early 1900s Mental measurement movement | Alfred Binet and Theodore Simon developed the first intelligence quotient (IQ) scale. This was also the beginning of the environment (nurture) versus heredity (nature) debate. |
| World War I–post-World War I | People focused on rehabilitating wounded soldiers. Specialized rehabilitation hospitals were established. |
| 1960s Civil rights movement | There was a call for the basic right of access to equal opportunities. |
| 1970s | The normalization movement called for services for persons with mental retardation that more closely paralleled services for individuals without disabilities. |
| 1980s | The regular education initiative called for regular education to increase the number of students with mild/moderate disabilities served in general/regular education classrooms. |
| 1990s | The full inclusion movement advocated that all students attend the school they would otherwise attend if they were not identified as disabled. Education would be provided in age- and grade-appropriate general education classrooms. |
| 2000s | The debate over full inclusion continues. Educators begin to focus on educating all students. National and State testing is high focus and high stakes. |

Twenty-nine percent went out of general education classes for 21 percent to 60 percent of the day for special or related services, whereas only 22 percent of these students with special needs were served outside general education for 60 percent of the day (U.S. Department of Education, 1998). The "push" to give students with disabilities access to the general curriculum is growing as well as the need for additional teachers to provide these services.

# PUBLIC LAW 93-112: SECTION 504 OF THE REHABILITATION ACT OF 1973

Over the years, attention to the individual rights of persons with disabilities has continued to grow. Section 504 of the Rehabilitation Act of 1973, also known as Public Law (PL) 93-112, included provisions to prevent the exclusion of any person with a disability from vocational programs receiving federal funds. In 1974, section 111a of PL 93-516 amended the Rehabilitation Act to require any recipients of federal funds to provide equal employment services for persons with disabilities. Section 504, although only a brief paragraph in the text of the law, has and continues to have a significant impact on the lives of individuals with disabilities. This law applies to all Americans with disabilities, regardless of age. Therefore, it applies to all children with disabilities, ages 3 through 21, with respect to their public education.

Section 504 states the following:

No qualified handicapped person shall, on the basis of handicap, be excluded from participation in, be denied benefits of, or otherwise be subjected to discrimination under any program or activity which receives or benefits from Federal financial assistance. A recipient, in providing any aid, or service, may not, directly or through contractual licensing, or other arrangement, on the basis of handicap:

1. Deny a qualified handicapped person the opportunity to participate in or benefit from the aid, benefit, or service;
2. Afford a qualified handicapped person an opportunity to participate in or benefit from the aid, benefit, or service that is not equal to that afforded to others;
3. Provide a qualified handicapped person with an aid, benefit, or service that is not as effective as that provided to others;
4. Provide different or separate aid, benefits, or services to handicapped persons or to any class of handicapped persons unless such action is necessary to provide qualified handicapped persons with aid, benefits, or services that are as effective as those provided to others;
5. Otherwise limit a qualified handicapped person in the enjoyment of any right, privilege, advantage, or opportunity enjoyed by others receiving an aid, benefit, or service. (34 CFR CH 1, July 1, 1992)

Within the public schools, section 504 provides additional rights for students with disabilities and includes students who need assistance but are not covered under PL 94-142 or its amendment, IDEA. (These laws will be discussed later in the chapter.) According to Huefner (1994), these children may be classified into three groups. First are age-eligible children who have physical or mental disabilities that limit a major life activity such as seeing, hearing, breathing, walking, speaking, caring for themselves, or learning. Within this category are children with AIDS, attention-deficit disorder, and asthma or those who are temporarily homebound. Second are children with a history of physical or mental disabilities (for example, leukemia). Third are children whom society wrongly regards as disabled (for example, those with epilepsy, facial disfigurements, and so on).

In postsecondary settings, section 504 has opened doors that have traditionally been closed for students with disabilities. Recruitment, admission, and postadmission treatment must be nondiscriminatory, and "reasonable adjustments" must be made. Modifications necessary for academic performance must be provided. These could include more time on tests, oral reading of tests, and copies of class notes. Modifications are needed because tests may not measure a student's achievement and may be discriminatory due to the disability. Auxiliary aids may also be necessary so that students with disabilities can receive the same education as their nondisabled peers. These can include taped texts, interpreters, and readers. All campus programs and activities must be accessible.

From 1950 to 1975, litigation brought about by advocacy groups built a framework for the educational future of persons with disabilities. As laws were passed, educational opportunities began to open for children with disabilities, and the basic individual rights of these children soon became a major national concern in public education. As litigation continued, the need grew for a federal mandate that would have significant ramifications for the education of children with disabilities. This movement culminated in PL 94-142, the Education for All Handicapped Children Act, which President Gerald Ford signed into law on November 29, 1975.

## PUBLIC LAW 94-142: EDUCATION FOR ALL HANDICAPPED CHILDREN ACT OF 1975

Recognized as a landmark in legislation for education, the Education for All Handicapped Children Act, basically, was the first step in providing a free and appropriate public education for individuals with disabilities. According to the Council for Exceptional Children (CEC, 1989), PL 94-142 had four major purposes:

1. To guarantee the availability of special education programming to handicapped children and youth that require it
2. To assure fairness and appropriateness in decision-making about providing special education to handicapped children and youth
3. To establish clear management and auditing requirements and procedures regarding special education at all levels of government
4. To financially assist the efforts of state and local government through the use of federal funds (p. 2)

### Major Components of the Law

PL 94-142 had a tremendous impact on our education system. "Whom must we serve?" "When must we serve?" and "How must we serve?" are all questions that surfaced after its passage. Basically, the law has five major components that affect the classroom and instruction:

- A right to a free appropriate public education (FAPE)
- Nondiscriminatory evaluation procedures
- Procedural due process
- Individualized education programs (IEPs)
- The least restrictive environment (LRE)

By law, all children are guaranteed a *free appropriate public education* at no expense to parents or guardians. Historically, many children with disabilities were denied this basic freedom. As a result, they received no education, were charged tuition for private services, or were unable to obtain services. The passage of PL 94-142 established the fundamental right of a free appropriate public education for children with disabilities. As of September 1, 1978, this right was afforded to children with disabilities between the ages of 3 and 18. Incentives were provided for states to extend the availability of this right from ages 3 to 21 by September 1, 1981. Subsequent legislation provided additional incentives for states to extend this service from birth to age 21 by 1991. Students with special needs could no longer be denied the right to attend school. They must be provided with an education equal to that of general education students and the support services necessary for an education.

In an attempt to eliminate errors in the classification and placement of children with disabilities, PL 94-142 provides procedural safeguards. Historically, evaluation procedures were limited and frequently discriminated against a child's culture or physical or perceptual disabilities. The establishment of *nondiscriminatory evaluation* procedures in the law requires that testing and evaluation materials and procedures used for the evaluation and placement of children defined as disabled must be selected and administered so as not to be racially or culturally discriminatory (*Federal Register,* August 23, 1977, pp. 42496–42497). The law requires that, at the minimum, all state and local educational agencies ensure the following:

1. Trained personnel must administer validated tests and other evaluation materials, and provide and administer such materials in the child's native language or other mode of communication.
2. Tests and other evaluation materials must include those tailored to assess specific areas of educational need and not merely those designed to provide a single general intelligence quotient.
3. Trained personnel must select and administer tests to accurately reflect the child's aptitude or achievement level without discriminating against the child's disability.
4. Trained personnel must use no single procedure as the sole criterion for determining an appropriate educational program for a child.
5. A multidisciplinary team must assess the child in all areas related to the suspected disability.

*Procedural due process* extends the basic rights of all U.S. citizens to children with disabilities and their parents. Due process provides certain procedural safeguards to guarantee fairness during educational evaluation and placement:

1. Written parental permission is necessary before a child can be evaluated for special education services.
2. Written parental permission is necessary before special education placement, and this permission may be withdrawn at any time.
3. Parents have the right to examine and question all relevant records concerning their children.
4. Parents have the right to request an independent evaluation of their child's present level of performance.
5. Confidentiality must be maintained.
6. Parents and school authorities have the right to a due process hearing and the right to present evidence, call and confront witnesses, and have a lawyer present during the hearing.
7. Parents and school authorities have the right to an appeal.

The *individualized education plan* (IEP) refers to a written education plan that must be developed annually for all children with disabilities who are receiving special education or related services. Functioning as a road map for instruction, the IEP is the one safeguard that parents have to ensure that their children receive instruction designed to meet their unique educational needs. Before a child can be placed into a special education program, a selected committee holds a meeting to write and sign the IEP. The committee is composed of a representative of the school system, the child's teacher, one or both of the child's parents, the child (if appropriate), and other individuals at the discretion of the parent or the school system. Even though the IEP is revised once a year, the IEP team may be reconvened at any time. A complete and updated assessment of the child is required at least every three years.

From state to state and locality to locality, the format of the IEP may vary. However, certain basic components appear on all IEPs. A fundamental knowledge of these components will help the general classroom teacher not only instruct children with disabilities but also understand the total special education program. Table 1.2 contains basic information about all the components common to IEPs.

When developing a student's IEP, it is important to keep in mind that it represents only a *written* description of a student's total educational program. The actual program, when carried out, stretches far beyond the limits of the written document. While an examination of an IEP may reveal that it includes all of the required components, this does not necessarily mean that the document constitutes an appropriate educational program for that child, one that has the potential for meeting the student's individual learning needs.

**TABLE 1.2**
Components of an IEP.

| Component | Description |
| --- | --- |
| Present level of educational functioning | Information obtained from norm- or criterion-referenced tests; gives actual level and skill at which a child is functioning |
| Annual or long-range goals | Projection of how far teachers think a child can progress during the school year; each present level of educational functioning will have a projected annual goal |
| Short-term instructional objectives | Objectives, written in behavioral terms, listing the intermediate steps between the present level of performance and the annual goals |
| Beginning and ending dates | Projected dates for initiation of services and anticipated duration of services |
| Objective criteria and evaluation procedures for short-term objectives | Statement of criteria and evaluation procedures for completion of short-term objectives |
| Special education services | Type of specific service the child is receiving |
| Related services | Any service outside of special education required for appropriate education |
| Regular classroom participation | Curriculum areas and amount of time each day the student will spend in the regular classroom |
| Projected dates for assessment | Must be reviewed at least annually by the IEP committee to determine whether short-term instructional objectives are being achieved |
| Course of study* | Must be started/described for students 14 yrs. or older |
| Transition plan | Describes and plans the set of activities for a student which promotes movement from school to postschool activities for the student by the age of 16, and younger when appropriate |
| Committee members present | Must be signed by all committee members |
| Parental signature | Parents present at IEP meeting are asked to sign IEP at their discretion |

*Added under IDEA, 1997.

It is important to remember that the amount of special education or related services indicated on a student's IEP should reflect the student's needs and should not be dictated by administrative convenience or limits imposed by professionals' caseloads. For example, if a secondary student needs speech-language therapy twice weekly, but the speech-language therapist visits the high school only once a week, services should be scheduled to reflect the student's needs, with modifications made in the therapist's schedule as necessary. Likewise, the dates when services are to be initiated should not be modified to accommodate waiting lists. If a student is found to need a particular service at the time that an IEP is written, the student should begin to receive that service as soon as possible—that is, without undue delay. The best practice for IEP service is within a few days after the IEP is written. In some instances, the team may decide that it is in the best interest of the student to delay initiation of services, as in the case of a major program change to be initiated close to a long school holiday, but such cases should be an exception to standard practice.

One critical guideline to keep in mind when writing a description of a student's present level of performance is that it must be described adequately and accurately. In this section of the document, standardized tests as well as performance and observational data should be described in language that all IEP team members, including parents, can understand. Thus, it is helpful to report standard scores in age or grade equivalences whenever possible and to translate terms such as *cognitive level, auditory processing,* or *peer interaction* into familiar terms. A frequent weakness in this section is a focus on the student's deficits rather than a balanced view of his or her strengths as well as areas targeted for growth or improvement. This may be the most important area for parental input into the IEP. Because parents observe their children in many different situations and in response to many different individuals, their input is essential to ensure an accurate and realistic description of the student. The importance of developing a realistic description of the student is underscored by the fact that this description will be the basis for the goals and objectives, which in turn will provide a blueprint for lesson plans for classroom activities. If the goals and objectives are based on an inadequate or inaccurate description, they will probably not be effective in identifying and meeting a student's unique learning needs.

While the goals and objectives written on IEPs are usually adequate, weaknesses are frequently found in the specification of the evaluation criteria and the procedures and schedule used to determine whether goals and objectives have been met. One signal that evaluation criteria may not be delineated appropriately is the use of the same criterion for every objective on a student's IEP. A "95% or greater accuracy rate" may be ideal, but it may not be realistic for the skills involved in each objective or be the easiest or most logical means of measurement. Similarly, if each evaluation procedure on an IEP reads "teacher-made test," the student may not be given an opportunity to demonstrate accomplishments in various ways. As we discuss in greater detail in chapter 13, there are a variety of valid means of assessing student performance, and these should be reflected in each student's IEP. If the evaluation schedule reads "end of school year" for each objective, this may not take into account that a student's timetable for acquiring skills across curriculum areas may vary significantly. Again, this may serve as a red flag, indicating that the IEP has not been individualized.

In summary, for an IEP to be effective in meeting a student's needs, each stated objective should be matched with individualized evaluation criteria, evaluation procedures, and a timetable for evaluation. Chapter 2 presents an IEP and shows the reader at which point within the process the IEP is developed.

The *least restrictive environment* (LRE) clause of PL 94-142 placed responsibility on the school district to educate children with disabilities in the same settings and programs as nondisabled children to the maximum extent appropriate. The child's needs, as indicated on the IEP, determine placement in the least restrictive environment, which may vary from child to child. The concept of the least restrictive environment is based on the premise that many creative alternatives exist to help the general educator serve children with learning or behavior problems within the context of a general class setting.

As students with disabilities have been progressively placed in general education classes, the concept of mainstreaming evolved. Students with disabilities who *proved* that they could compete with students without disabilities were granted the privilege of sitting in general education classrooms. However, individualization of content was not as much of a factor as physical placement. In the 1980s the regular education initiative (REI) was an organized effort to blend general and special education or diminish the physical and curricular boundary between general and special education. The responsibility of all students, general or special, would become a shared responsibility among general and special teachers. The invisible but solid boundaries established over many years would hopefully now diminish.

According to Rueda, Gallego, and Moll (2000), rethinking of the least restrictive environment is in order. The least restrictive environment promotes greater success for students with disabilities within general education. The regular education initiative "seeks to restructure general education so that it accommodates the needs of students with disabilities. Inclusion, on the other hand, is seen as promoting the restructure of general education so that all students are educated in that setting from the beginning of their school careers (p. 76)."

## The Regular Education Initiative

The general education/special education initiative goes by many names: collaborative teaching, cooperative teaching, supported education, prereferral intervention, mainstream education, and, most commonly, the regular education initiative (REI) (Miller, 1990; Robinson, 1990). The REI calls for a restructuring of special and general education to create a partnership among educators from both disciplines to serve all students better. Typically, the REI focuses on two groups of low-performing students: those identified as mildly disabled and those at risk for school failure due to disadvantaged economic or social backgrounds. If carried out in its purest form, the REI would result in a seamless web of education services in which all students would receive individualized services in the general education environment without giving a label or special designation to any student (Robinson, 1990). Ideally, the REI would combine effective practices from special, general, and compensatory education to establish a general education system more inclusive of students with learning needs (Reynolds, Wang, & Walberg, 1987).

The REI most likely began at the local level when teachers, administrators, and parents began to realize the shortcomings of a segregated special education system.

It was legitimized in a 1986 policy statement by Madeleine Will, then assistant secretary for special education and director of the Office of Special Education and Rehabilitative Services of the U.S. Department of Education (Robinson, 1990). Some people criticized Will's statement, calling it a reflection of Reagan-Bush economic policies aimed at decreasing federal support for education. Yet the proposal focused national attention on the lack of an interface between general and special education students (Chauffeur, 1989; Robinson, 1990). Since that time, professional educators have debated at length about the relative strengths and weaknesses of the REI.

Numerous factors served to fuel the REI movement. Proponents for reform made several charges (Anderegg & Vergason, 1988; Gersten & Woodward, 1990; Kauffman, 1989; Reynolds et al., 1987; Robinson, 1990):

1. Special education had become a dumping ground for students who were not truly disabled but only difficult to teach.
2. A lack of consistency was evident in defining categories of students with disabilities, especially for the category of learning disabilities. This resulted in a great discrepancy between and within school divisions and the state regarding which students were eligible for special education services.
3. Unnecessary barriers were created that excluded students with special needs from becoming fully integrated into school and community life. This was a disadvantage for students both with and without disabilities.
4. There was a lack of compelling evidence about the validity of categories and other special education requirements in promoting expected educational outcomes.
5. Educators were disenchanted with tracking systems in general. Special education was viewed as one of the most rigid tracks.
6. There was a lack of standardized curriculum in pullout programs (for example, the resource room). In cases where such a curriculum was used, it was not linked to the core curriculum in the general classroom.
7. Requirements for excessive and oppressive paperwork existed without evidence of direct benefit to the students served.

Not surprisingly, calls for reform of the existing dual system have met with resistance. Two major sources of resistance to the REI can be traced to its roots. First, the REI originated in the field of special education. Because special educators, who are perceived as outsiders, have called for reform of the general education system, they have not always been welcomed by general educators, who lack a sense of ownership in the movement. A second source of resistance is the perception of the reform as a top-down approach. While the need for increased collaboration between general and special educators had become evident to many schools and school districts before Will's proposal, calls for reform from the federal and state levels alienated practitioners at the local level, who were already frustrated by a perceived lack of control over programs in their own buildings and classrooms.

Both special and general educators have raised legitimate concerns in response to the REI, including these:

1. The rights of students with disabilities would be jeopardized if existing categorical labels were changed or eliminated.
2. The rights of students with disabilities to an equal educational opportunity could not be ensured if options for education outside the general class were eliminated (Kauffman, 1989).
3. General educators have not yet fully embraced the idea of mainstreaming. Not all teachers are adequately prepared to meet the special learning needs of all students, nor are they willing to assume even more responsibility (Gersten & Woodward, 1990; Kauffman, 1989).
4. Unable to meet the curricular demands of the general classroom, students with disabilities would exhibit increased frustration levels and behavioral problems and decreased self-esteem.
5. The differences between elementary and secondary schools (for example, curriculum demands, skill-level plateaus at secondary levels, and organizational structures) could prevent successful wholesale application of the REI at the secondary level (Schumaker & Deshler, 1988).
6. The placement of students with special learning needs in general education classrooms may adversely affect other students because teachers must devote more of their time to the students with disabilities.
7. Combining general and special education budgets would decrease special education services available to students with disabilities who need special services (Kauffman, 1989).
8. Special educators would be relegated to advisory roles, and their specialized skills and training would be wasted.

In the 1990s, the concept of placing students with special needs into general education classes began to be known as *inclusion.* According to Lombardi (1994), "it is generally agreed that inclusion involves a commitment to educate each student with a disability in the school and, when appropriate, in the class that child would have attended had the child not had a disability. . . . [The] guiding principle behind inclusion is to bring the services to the student, rather than the student to the services" (p. 7). This definition parallels our definition of special education: a service, not a place. Although greatly debated and widely defined, *inclusion* is becoming the term of choice and relies greatly on individualization for effective implementation. In reality, you will see inclusion implemented differently in different areas of a state or the country. British Columbia, Canada, implemented total inclusion in the purest sense of the phrase. By 1990 *all* students were returned to general education settings.

There are many opinions about inclusion—what it is, where it occurs, how it is implemented, and so on. Let's look at a three-level plan for inclusion designed by

**Level I Inclusion**

| | |
|---|---|
| Irregular | Some schedule coordination |
| Spontaneous | Few, if any, modifications |
| Teachers are often friends | Short time periods |
| Usually extra-curricular | Exceptional students usually go to regular class |
| Informal | Children participate in their own way |
| Little teacher planning | |

**Level II Inclusion**

| | |
|---|---|
| Regular (hour or day) | More schedule coordination |
| Planned | Some team teaching |
| May include core subjects | May include reverse mainstreaming |
| Closer working relationships | Teachers share ideas and work |
| More formality and structure | |

**Level III Inclusion**

| | |
|---|---|
| Daily regularity | Same schedule for most subjects |
| High degree of planning | Students have the same classroom |
| Close working relationship | Groupings based on interest, skill, or need |
| Teachers share ideas and work | High level of instructional coordination |
| Inservice needs | All teachers and aides available to all students |

**FIGURE 1.1**
Characteristics of inclusion levels.

*Source:* Fitzgerald, M. A., Glodoski, J., Knox, H., McCaskill, Y., Pelzek, K., Szopinski, E., & Toshner, J. (1992). Inclusion of special education students in general education classes. *LD Forum, 18*(2), 14–16.

Fitzgerald, Glodoski, Knox, McCaskill, Pelzek, Szopinski, and Toshner (1992). Level 1 refers to limited inclusion; level 2, moderate inclusion; and level 3, full inclusion. The characteristics of each level are presented in Figure 1.1.

Whatever term is used, it is a reality that students with special needs and those at risk will at some level receive instruction in the general education setting. Thus, teacher training at the college/university level will change. No longer can a general educator leave the system unprepared to teach *all* children; no longer can special educators expect to be segregated into their own classrooms. Both programs must begin to look at ways of training together and working together. In the process, administrators will begin to see the importance of their role as the instructional leaders of the school. The inclusive model must be explored, and instructional, physical, and emotional support for teachers must be provided. Inclusion will be a shared effort regardless of the model of implementation chosen.

# THE SIX FACES OF INCLUSION

The concept of inclusion may be thought of as six parts comprising the total concept, inclusion. Students may be "included" by the definition of inclusion, "promoting the restructure of general education so that all students are educated in that setting from the beginning of their school careers" (Rueda, Gallego, & Moll, 2000, p. 76). However, they may also be excluded socially, emotionally, behaviorally, physically, academically, and/or by assessment standards.

## Social Inclusion

Any student can be placed within general education and not be accepted. The appropriate social skills for social integration are not taught or have not been taught.

## Emotional Inclusion

After a student has received a majority of his or her education separated from general education and is returned to general education, an emotional shock from change may arise. Rules, routines, procedures, and so forth are different. Classwork and assignments are new. Grading and evaluation procedures vary. Not only do these factors impact the student but the teacher as well. How do the teachers feel about the sudden change of student numbers in the class or ability levels?

## Behavioral Inclusion

New behaviors are expected as environments change—both for students and teachers. Many students' behaviors become "misbehaviors" when inclusion occurs. Learning "how to behave for the new teacher" or how to accept the new student's behavior becomes a major focus.

## Physical Inclusion

This face of inclusion probably was the first concept for inclusion and relates to the mandate of least restrictive environment. Where do we put or place the student? So many times the physical placement (inclusion) really meant "exclusion" of a student. The placement met the concept of the law but may not have allowed for an appropriate education.

## Academic Inclusion

Are we teaching the student at the appropriate grade level? Do we set appropriate interventions? Does the educator realize what tasks are important and should become an instructional priority? Physical inclusion is common. Academic inclusion needs growth.

## Inclusion by Assessment Standards

Assessment has moved to the front of educational conversations. How to assess? How to grade? Who takes the state test? Who takes an alternate test? Do I do something differently for this student? Or do I continue business as usual? The inclusion by assessment standards have become a front-runner in issues of inclusion.

In summary, since the 1975 passage of PL 94-142, children with mild disabilities have moved from being almost totally excluded from general classrooms to being almost totally included. Although attempts to amend and weaken the law occurred in 1981, pressure from advocacy groups defeated such efforts. The right of a child with a disability to a free and appropriate education in the least restrictive environment remains guaranteed by law. This right became even stronger in 1990 and was reaffirmed in 1997.

# PUBLIC LAW 99-457: EDUCATION OF THE HANDICAPPED ACT AMENDMENTS OF 1986

Numerous sections of PL 94-142 (1975) were amended when President Reagan signed into law the Education of the Handicapped Act amendments of 1986. Provisions of these major amendments include the following:

- All the rights and protections of PL 94-142 (part B) were extended to children with disabilities ages 3 through 5 years in the school year 1990–1991. To support the achievement of this objective, the Preschool Incentive Grant Program (PL 94-142, section 619) was revised to reflect authorization of a dramatic increase in the federal fiscal contribution for this age group.
- A new state grant program for disabled infants and toddlers (ages birth through 2) was established for the purpose of providing early intervention services for all eligible children as defined by the legislation. This program appears as a new part H of the existing Education of the Handicapped Act (EHA).
- The proven components of the EHA (part C, early education authority) were retained and refined to maximize support toward achieving the objectives of the new early intervention and preschool initiatives (CEC, 1989).

PL 99-457, unlike other amendments, focuses not only on the child with disabilities but also on the family. This law shifts from a child-centered, single-agency planning effort to a family-focused, multidisciplinary planning effort. Among the required components of part H, the Individualized Family Service Plan (IFSP) is of paramount importance to the child and family. Specific concerns that must be addressed in this family-tailored plan include the following (Hale, 1990, pp. 14, 17):

- A statement of the child's present levels of physical development, cognitive development, language and speech development, psychosocial development, and self-help skills, which is based on professionally acceptable objective criteria

- With the concurrence of the family, a statement of the family's strengths and needs related to enhancing the development of the child

- A statement of major outcomes expected to be achieved for the child and family; the criteria, procedures, and timelines used to determine the degree to which progress is being made; and whether modification or revisions are necessary

- A statement of the specific early intervention services necessary to meet the unique needs of the child and the family to achieve the outcomes, including the frequency, intensity, duration, and method of delivering the services, and the payment arrangements, if any

- Other services and the steps that will be undertaken to secure those services

- The projected dates for initiation of the services and the anticipated duration

- The name of the case manager who will be responsible for implementing the IFSP and coordinating the agencies

# PUBLIC LAW 101-476: INDIVIDUALS WITH DISABILITIES EDUCATION ACT OF 1990

In October 1990, President Bush signed into law the amendments that reauthorized discretionary programs and made certain changes to several parts of the EHA. A major change in this legislation was renaming the EHA, which is now known as the Individuals with Disabilities Education Act (IDEA). Other significant changes included the following:

- All references to *handicapped children* were changed to *children with disabilities.*

- Two new categories of disabilities were added: autism and traumatic brain injury.

- The definitions of *assistive technology device* and *assistive technology service* were added.

- *Transition services* were added and defined as a coordinated set of activities for a student, designed within an outcome-oriented process, which promotes movement from school to postschool activities, including postsecondary education, vocational training, integrated employment (including supported employment), continuing and adult education, adult services, independent living, and community participation.

The coordinated set of activities should be based upon the individual student's needs, taking into account the student's preferences and interests. Activities include instruction, community experiences, the development of employment and other postschool adult living objectives, and, when appropriate, acquisition of daily living skills and functional vocational evaluation.

Perhaps the most significant change brought about by these amendments is the emphasis on "person first" language. In other words, we now refer to a person *with* a disability rather than a disabled person.

# PUBLIC LAW 101-336: AMERICANS WITH DISABILITIES ACT OF 1990

A major breakthrough for persons with disabilities, the Americans with Disabilities Act (PL 101-336) was signed into law in the summer of 1990 by President Bush. This law prohibits discrimination against any persons with disabilities and has four major focus areas:

1. Employers of 15 or more employees may not refuse to hire or promote a person with a disability because of that disability when the person is qualified to perform the job.

2. An employer must make reasonable accommodations for a person with a disability if that accommodation will allow the person to perform the essential functions of the job. (Examples of reasonable accommodations include making existing facilities accessible, part-time or modified work schedules, modification of equipment devices, or provisions of qualified readers and interpreters.)

3. New vehicles bought by public transit authorities must be accessible to persons with disabilities. One car per train in existing rail systems became accessible on July 26, 1994.

4. It is illegal for public accommodations (businesses that people use every day, such as hotels, restaurants, dry cleaners, grocery stores, schools, and parks) to exclude or refuse persons with disabilities. Auxiliary aids and services must be provided (for example, large-print materials, tape recordings, and captioning) unless doing so would be too disruptive or burdensome for the business.

The purposes of the act are as follows:

- To provide a clear and comprehensive national mandate for the limitation of discrimination against individuals with disabilities

- To provide clear, strong, consistent, enforceable standards addressing discrimination against individuals with disabilities

- To ensure that the federal government plays a central role in enforcing the standards established in this act on behalf of individuals with disabilities

- To invoke the sweep of congressional authority

# PUBLIC LAW 105-17: INDIVIDUALS WITH DISABILITIES EDUCATION ACT OF 1997

On June 4, 1997, President Clinton signed into law the Individuals with Disabilities Education Act (IDEA, 1997). With this action he stated, "It reaffirms and strengthens our national commitment to provide a world class education for all of our children."

Revisions to PL 94-142 took almost 3 years of debates and negotiations between bipartisan working groups, 4 months of almost daily meetings, and weekly meetings with the public. It was the first comprehensive change to PL 94-142 in 22 years. Many persons involved felt that it was a compromise bill where no one was completely satisfied. There were three main reasons its reauthorization was delayed: (a) discipline of students with disabilities; (b) funding issues; and (c) achievement and accountability. The federal government contributes fairly little to state and local governments to offset the cost of special education services. This is one of the reasons there has been some backlash about special education. In several states, there have been court cases about the amount it costs to educate a student with special needs as compared to a nondisabled student.

## Background Behind the Reauthorization of IDEA

The subcommittees in the Senate and House of Representatives preface the law with their findings that help us understand what the new law tried to encompass. They wanted to focus on "improving educational results" for children with disabilities. They identified barriers that have prevented children with disabilities from receiving the maximum benefit from education. They included in the law statements that PL 94-142 had been "successful in ensuring children with disabilities . . . access to a free appropriate public education." It had, however, been negatively impacted by "low expectations and an insufficient focus of applying applicable research on proven methods of teaching and learning for children with disabilities." They referenced 20 years of research about high expectations and strengthening the role of parents to participate in the education of their children. The law reiterated that special education should be a service provided rather than a place where children are sent. The increasing population of minorities is addressed and how this might impact special education. The preface of the law includes information on the need to prevent the mislabeling and dropping out of school of minority children as well as to provide incentives for "whole-school" approaches and prereferral intervention to reduce the need to label children as disabled in order to address their learning needs.

There is growing concern about students with disabilities dropping out at a rate higher than their nondisabled peers. Research has shown that students with disabilities are more likely to be unemployed or underemployed. Therefore, emphasis is placed on providing educational experiences that will prepare them for employment and independent living while considering a student's assistive technology needs, his/her communication needs, and other considerations addressed later in this chapter.

## Highlights of the New Law

- Emphasizes education results and access to the general curriculum
- Increases parental participation and required reporting to parents
- Improves individualized programming in the IEP
- Expands stricter discipline provisions for students carrying weapons or guns

- Prohibits the cessation of education services due to suspensions/expulsion
- Increases the inclusion of students with disabilities in state assessments
- Requires an alternate assessment for students that are not involved in the state assessment
- Increases reliance on mediation between parents and school systems to settle disputes, thereby, hopefully, decreasing the amount of money/time spent on costly and lengthy legal due processes
- Adds the inclusion of behavioral supports in the IEP if a child's behavior disrupts his/her learning or the learning of others
- Requires that the IEP team consider if and how a child's limited English proficiency affects their program or need for other services

As mentioned previously, one of the main reasons that the reauthorization of IDEA took 2 years longer than anticipated was due to disagreement over the discipline section of the law. In the end, compromise was necessary on the parts of all parties. The new law introduced a new concept, an Interim Alternative Educational Setting (IAES). In the past, if a student with very dangerous behavior or in possession of weapons or drugs was facing a possible suspension, a causal hearing (now called a Manifestation Determination Review) was held to determine if the disability and misbehavior were related. If they were, the child would not receive the same consequence for the behavior. If they were not related, the team could recommend a change in the child's placement. A catch 22 existed in that, if a parent did not agree to change the child's placement (i.e., to an alternative setting or a more restricted setting, etc.), the only recourse for a local division was to appeal to a judge for an injunction which, in essence, would prevent the child from returning to the current setting. This process was lengthy. The change to IAES allows the school division to place a student in an IAES in the case of weapons or drug use up to but no longer than 45 days. The IAES must (a) allow the child to participate in the general curriculum, (b) continue to receive special education services and modifications that enable the child to continue the goals of the IEP, and (c) include specific services designed to teach alternatives to the behavior that caused the IAES placement.

Also, under suspensions, either before or not more than 10 days after taking disciplinary action that results in a temporary change in placement, a district must convene the IEP team. If a functional behavioral assessment of the student's behavior and a behavior intervention plan has not been previously conducted and developed, this must be done. The IEP team must explore and consider the need for strategies and support systems to address any behavior that may impede the learning of the child or the learning of his/her peers. This will include (a) looking at what function the behavior is serving for the student; (b) looking at what will help the student to eliminate the inappropriate behavior; (c) teaching an alternative behavior that will satisfy the need but is more socially acceptable; and (d) providing the supports to ensure continuation of appropriate behavior.

Lastly, a big change under the new law is identification of "Age of Majority." States may choose to enact laws that will transfer the rights afforded to parents to the child when the child turns 18. This requires informing students one year prior to their 18th birthday that they have this right. Parents would continue to receive any notice from school related to the child's special education program. There is a process parents can follow if they think their child cannot understand or give informed consent about educational decisions.

# HOW LEGISLATION HAS AFFECTED OUR SOCIETY AND THE COMMUNITY

For individuals with disabilities, change has been slow. Even though laws have been passed, it was not until 1990 that legislation was in place to provide comprehensive and equal opportunities for persons with disabilities. Parents and students are more aware of their rights. This change has had a significant impact on both the classroom for persons with disabilities and employment opportunities.

Restructuring within the schools means that the community as a whole must be re-educated about the changes. It must now begin to create job opportunities for a diverse population of students existing in the system. Businesses are becoming more involved within the schools and as a result more involved with students with disabilities. Business partnerships exist that are reciprocal in nature, exchanging ideas, resources, and facilities. Years ago individuals with disabilities were not integrated into the community. Now, however, the community is encountering persons with disabilities, which means preparing emotionally as well as practically for them. Communication between the community and the schools has become even more important. Some school systems are placing students in jobs with job coaches or in assisted employment situations and providing support to the employer as problems or situations arise. Some of these same students retain their employment with the companies after graduation.

What follows is a brief description of the practical and ethical implications as well as the changes in educational practice. How legislation has created change for students, educators, families, community and in the anticipated future are mentioned.

## Practical Implications

The implications of these legislative mandates range from the practical to the ethical, and often the difference between the two is finely drawn. Traditional goals of the school systems have changed. Teaching to the standardized test has become the norm. Discipline standards and methods have changed. Students as well as parents know their rights, which cover an array of areas, including housing, the removal of architectural barriers, civil rights regarding institutionalization, and rights to a free and equal education. Funding uncertainties have become real. How will states and local school districts fund mandates that have little to no funding provisions?

Employment is now more accessible due to acts such as the Job Training Partnership Act and the Fair Labor Standards Act. Training is more readily available, and employment is a reality. Individuals with disabilities now have the ability to get to jobs as a result of acts that mandate more accessible transportation measures.

Within the classroom, the differing abilities of students have changed teaching methods, materials, and training. Technology has become a way of life for many people and a way of survival for many persons with disabilities.

## Ethical Implications

Ethics, more than anything else, has been affected by legislation for individuals with disabilities. Better health and nutrition services are now available. Social services are wider in scope. An education that is equal, free, and appropriate is now within the reach of persons with disabilities. They have been denied educational rights for so long, but now these rights extend from early childhood throughout adulthood.

Legislation has brought multicultural diversity concerns and issues to the forefront. Not only are we more aware of differences among people, but we are also more understanding of these differences. A wider acceptance of individuals with disabilities has meant a broader acceptance of differences in general.

The gap between the "haves" and the "have-nots" has narrowed, and awareness of differences has led to greater tolerance. People as a whole are more willing to share what they have with those who have less. Today, ignorance is no excuse for the mistreatment of any individual because the knowledge base about differences has expanded. This has been made possible by the passage of laws establishing rights and by the growing visibility of the community of persons with disabilities. Assessment outcomes are changing. More holistic measures of evaluating individuals are coming to the forefront of educational practice. Expected outcomes are individualized and human tolerance has expanded within the outcomes.

As a result of legislation, persons with disabilities are better prepared for competitiveness in a global workplace. New roles and employment opportunities will be available, and individuals with disabilities will be better prepared to meet the challenges of life.

But there is a dark side. Often, people with the least knowledge are making educational delivery and curriculum decisions. State mandates are set and standards passed down that are not only inappropriate but also unreasonable for developing programs at the local level. In addition, certification requirements for teacher-training programs are established and mandated by state boards that may be composed of members without current knowledge of education. These requirements establish what future educators will learn and, in turn, how they will teach. Ethically, we owe it to all students to make sure that the very best standards are established by qualified persons.

# CHANGES IN EDUCATIONAL PRACTICE

Legislation has far-reaching implications for the classroom, both practically and ethically. These implications have produced changes in educational practice for students, educators, the family, the community, and the future.

## Changes for Students

Nothing in the history of our country has influenced students' lives more than legislation resulting in educational changes and practices within our schools. This debate extends beyond the classroom into the community. Legislation has made possible the education of students with disabilities in a setting with their nondisabled peers. What impact has this had on these two groups of students?

*Effects on nondisabled students.* Through contact with students with disabilities, students without disabilities acquire a realistic view of a heterogeneous society. At an early age they learn that physical, intellectual, and emotional differences are a reality, and this information helps produce mature adults who are more accepting of individual differences. Nondisabled students learn more tolerance of others and develop a greater acceptance of their own differences. Although research is limited on the effects of students with disabilities on their nondisabled peers, available literature indicates that this influence does not harm nondisabled children and in many cases benefits them (Staub & Peck, 1995). Peck, Carlson, and Helmster (1992) found that nondisabled students do not absorb undesirable behavior from students with disabilities.

*Effects on students with disabilities.* Students with disabilities now have the opportunity to remain in settings with their peers without disabilities and participate in typical school activities. Benefits include improved academic achievement and social and emotional growth (Wood, 1993). Evidence from the past 15 years has shown that segregating students with disabilities is detrimental to their academic growth and social adjustments (Baker, Wang, & Walberg, 1995).

Accountability for students with special disabilities has definitely been a positive outcome of legislation for students with disabilities. Educators and society can no longer claim that a lack of appropriate programs accounts for little or no progress among students with disabilities. Society is now accountable for the education and treatment of persons with disabilities. This will be addressed more in the chapter on evaluation.

Related services, once completely out of reach, are now an everyday part of life for many students with disabilities. Occupational and physical therapy and psychological, medical, health, counseling, and transportation services are available as needed at no cost to students with disabilities and to their families. Speech-language pathology, social work services, recreation therapy, parent counseling, and training, as well as assistive technology devices and services, are a reality (National Information Center for Children and Youth with Disabilities, 1991).

# Changes for Educators

Legislative mandates for individuals have had sweeping effects on the members of the educational field. Administrators, general education teachers, special education teachers, and support personnel have all felt massive change.

Administrators are faced with finding money for unfunded mandates and allocating the necessary resources, materials, and manpower to support educators. New technology and teaching curricula must be investigated. Business as usual can no longer exist. Administrators are faced with changes in the emotional climate of the school as students with disabilities are increasingly being integrated into general education settings. The focus of inservice programs must change; encouraging work for the benefit of the child is a high priority. Communicating administrative support to all parents, students, teachers, and the community is necessary considering the growing number of mandated changes. In addition, accountability for student learning outcomes has become a focus, and restructuring is a necessary element now that general and special education have become alienated.

General education teachers have specific roles in assisting in developing materials, individualizing for all students, and diagnosing and modifying curricula. A new relationship is forming between general and special education teachers. As team teaching becomes more common in the schools, general educators must often share their rooms. Emphasis is on *how* information is taught rather than *what* is being taught. Teaching is based on various evaluation tools, such as learning styles, instruments, and so on. Communication skills become necessary as general educators work more closely with special education teachers and parents of children with special needs. Resistance to change makes the work more difficult. Job satisfaction has also become a factor because of job burnout, an increase in class load, and new instructional responsibilities.

However, on the positive side, general education personnel are benefiting from the strategies they learn from special education teachers. These strategies are helpful to all students, many of whom would have received no help without the movement to place students with special needs into general class settings.

Special education teachers have roles that have radically changed, almost overnight. In one period in our history, the special education teacher mainly taught children with disabilities in self-contained classes or resource (pullout) placements. The special education teacher is now moving into general class settings, providing assessment and instructional planning, conducting remedial and tutorial instruction, team teaching with the general education teacher, and communicating with parents. In many situations the special education teacher is called upon to help all students. Modifications of lesson plans have become a major focus. Providing the general education teacher with medical information about the students, helping him or her become aware of all available resources and services, and being ready to listen and provide reinforcement and suggestions for change are daily tasks.

## Changes in the Family

Having a child with a disability makes a huge impact on a family. Just imagine what this impact was like when there was no legislation available to support children and families. Education was denied. Physical accessibility was often impossible. Networks were unavailable or nonexistent. Many families now have computers that provide "hot-off-the-press" information on special education and new techniques or strategies.

The impact of legislation on the daily and long-term lives of families has been extremely important. Parents now have the right to their child's records as well as procedural due process rights. They must also be notified and give permission before their child can be removed from a general class setting and placed into a special setting. The quality of education for the child has vastly improved, giving everyone in the family the hope of a higher quality of life. Parents are now part of a team for developing a plan for their child. They offer feedback on the child's progress and have an opportunity to become involved in his or her education. Family plans are developed early, and the whole family learns to address the needs of the special child.

## Changes for the Future

As the spirit of the laws becomes an everyday way of life, a good future for individuals with disabilities will be the norm instead of the exception. We hope that understanding of, and tolerance for, persons with disabilities will also be integral parts of society.

In the future, schools will move away from merely learning facts to learning *how* to learn because facts are constantly changing. Reasoning and higher-order thinking skills will be necessary elements of the educational system. Accommodations for individuals with disabilities will result in greater and more progressive technological advances.

## CONCLUSION

The inclusion of students with special needs within our schools is now a reality. The concept has developed over several hundred years and has slowly been supported by major legislation. Since 1973, with the passage of section 504, special-needs students and students at risk have progressed closer toward receiving the rights enjoyed by all individuals.

PL 94-142 and IDEA have brought us closer to providing a free, appropriate, public education to children with disabilities. Now that you have learned about the history and the legislation, we will continue our journey down the road to responsibility. Chapter 2 looks at how students are selected for special classes, who these students are, and the different placement options available for special students.

# CHAPTER 2

## The Road to Responsibility: From Prereferral to Placement

*Contributions by Debra Gibson*

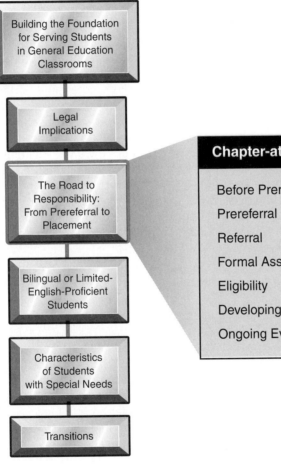

Building the Foundation
for Serving Students
in General Education
Classrooms

Legal
Implications

The Road to
Responsibility:
From Prereferral to
Placement

Bilingual or Limited-
English-Proficient
Students

Characteristics
of Students
with Special Needs

Transitions

**Chapter-at-a-Glance**

Before Prereferral

Prereferral

Referral

Formal Assessment

Eligibility

Developing the IEP

Ongoing Evaluation

Some 30 years ago, legislation was the impetus that began the long process of including students with disabilities in public education. It paved the road so that students with disabilities and those at risk could receive a more appropriate education with their nondisabled peers, if appropriate. In the years that have followed, teacher attitudes, along with research into best practices and the emphasis on "access to the general curriculum," have hopefully made the process more than just what's required by law. In this chapter we follow the path from the initial point of concern to the student's final designation.

This process is called *prereferral to placement*. During the process the disability category is identified (if any) and a plan of action is established. The journey has seven steps that help teachers assist students to be successful in general classes even if they are having difficulty with the class work or with behavior and/or emotional issues. If further assistance is needed, the process continues: the student's specific concerns are noted, and he or she may be evaluated and identified as having a specific disability. It will be determined if the student requires special services or accommodations. An individualized education plan (IEP) is developed and a placement in which to receive services is identified. While this chapter takes a close look at identification (who are these children?) and placement (where will services be provided?), we will wait until chapter 4 to examine the characteristics of different disabling conditions and placement options. We are still on our journey.

Figure 2.1 offers an overview of the seven major steps that students may go through between prereferral and ongoing evaluation. Naturally, each step can become quite involved. However, for the purposes of discussion, we will make each one as simple as possible.

## STEP 1: BEFORE PREREFERRAL

The general classroom teacher uses many methods of informal assessment for instructional intervention. These methods are used with all students in the class. They include tests that are a part of a curriculum series, teacher-made tests using curriculum content, student work samples, homework, and systematic classroom observation. These methods aid the teacher in classroom planning and the adaptation of instruction. The teacher may determine, for example, that the pace of instruction is too rapid or too slow for a particular group of students. The teacher may need to check the instructional materials for readability levels or for the use of complex vocabulary terms. Information gathered about these types of learning problems may be used to modify instruction for all students in the class.

An environmental assessment of the classroom will give the teacher insights that he or she can use in planning instruction. The physical variable of the classroom setting may be evaluated by using an instrument such as the transition checklist (see appendix A). A student may have difficulties in the classroom that can be attributed to such external variables. Therefore, if the teacher modifies some of these variables, he or she can improve the student's academic success.

**FIGURE 2.1**
Prereferral to placement.

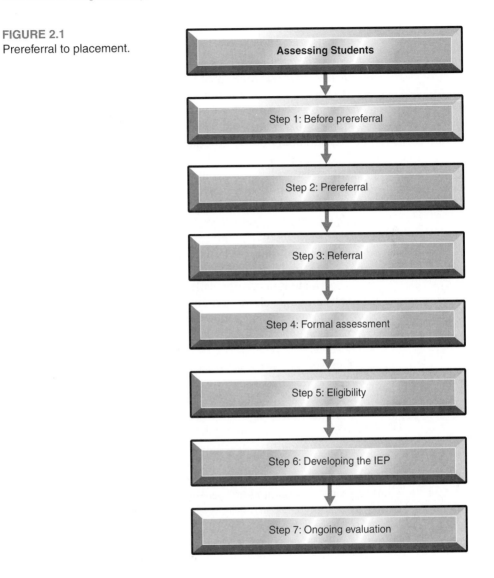

The general classroom teacher should also assess teaching methods to determine if the strategies that provide structure, guidance, and reinforcement of skills or content are best for all students, and particularly suitable for students who may be at risk for academic failure. Many teachers find it helpful to ask for suggestions at this point. There are many persons in a school building who can fulfill the need for an objective look at the classroom. An administrator, peer observers, or guidance counselors can observe the classroom, not a particular child at this point, and offer suggestions of things to try that might be beneficial.

# STEP 2: PREREFERRAL

If a student continues to have difficulty after all variables of classroom setting, instructional methods, behavioral management, and curriculum have been assessed, the classroom teacher may need to take a closer look at the student's ability to master the curriculum. For example, a student may have difficulty with the appropriate grade-level math curriculum. The same student may not complete class assignments or math homework. If the student continues to perform poorly on teacher-made math tests, the teacher may need to determine which skills have not been mastered, for example, by analyzing the student's errors to locate specific difficulties in the mathematics operations. Once the target errors are identified, the teacher can prepare additional probes to test the specific errors. The student may provide insight by explaining the process or steps used to solve the math problem. The teacher may observe the student trying to work the problem to identify process errors. These methods of informal assessment may be used with all students in the general classroom to aid in instructional planning and intervention.

When a student appears to have difficulty mastering content or skills at the appropriate grade level, the teacher may use curriculum-based assessment to pinpoint the area of difficulty. An error analysis may provide the information necessary to make educational interventions. The interventions may include adapting instruction according to the individual student's learning style or organizing the classroom or the lesson presentation in a different format. General guidelines such as Overton's (1992) adapted classroom teacher observation guidelines may help the classroom teacher with the prereferral process (see Figure 2.2).

The classroom teacher consults with the members of a prereferral committee. The role of the teacher during the referral/assessment process is illustrated in Table 2.1. Some members of the prereferral team may also make up the multidisciplinary assessment team, such as the school psychologist and the school social worker. Other team members may be professionals who are not active members of the multidisciplinary assessment team. For example, the prereferral committee, sometimes called child consultation team, or a child study committee, may include additional general classroom teachers of the same grade or various grades, the school principal, special education teachers, school counselors, or members of the school curriculum committee. These members may observe the student in different environments, analyze student-teacher interactions, or review the curriculum used to locate possible instructional interventions. A prereferral intervention plan is designed with suggestions for the classroom teacher. The prereferral committee members may suggest changes in the classroom arrangement, behavior management strategies, or curriculum and teaching methods as instructional interventions. The teacher should attempt a variety of instructional interventions and document the changes in the student's behavior or learning that occur as a result of these interventions. One excellent source for identifying "points of intervention" in the classroom is the intervention checklist (Wood, 1998) that will computer generate intervention strategies.

Name of Student _____

Concerned Teacher _____

Briefly describe area of difficulty:

1.    Curriculum evaluation

_____ Material is appropriate for age/grade level

_____ Instructions are presented clearly

_____ Expected method of response is within the student's capability

_____ Readability of material is appropriate

_____ Prerequisite skills have been mastered

_____ Format of materials is easily understood by students of same age/grade level

_____ Frequent and various methods of evaluation are employed

_____ Tasks are appropriate in length

_____ Pace of material is appropriate for age/grade levels

2.    Learning environment

_____ Methods of presentation are appropriate for age/grade levels

_____ Tasks are presented in appropriate sequence

_____ Expected level of response is appropriate for age/grade level

_____ Physical facilities are conducive to learning

3.    Social environment

_____ Student does not experience noticeable conflicts with peers

_____ Student appears to have adequate relationships with peers

_____ Parent conference reveals no current conflicts or concerns within the home

_____ Social development appears average for age expectancy

4.    Student's physical condition

_____ Student's height and weight appear to be within the average range of expectancy for age/ grade level

_____ Student has no signs of visual or hearing difficulties, such as asking teacher to repeat instructions, squinting, holding papers close to face to read

_____ Student has had vision and hearing checked by school nurse or other health official

_____ Student has not experienced long-term illness or serious injury

_____ School attendance is average or better

_____ Student appears attentive/alert during instruction

_____ Student appears to have adequate motor skills

_____ Student appears to have adequate communication skills

**FIGURE 2.2**

Classroom teacher observation guidelines.

*Source:* From Overton, T. (1992). *Assessment in special education: An applied approach* (p. 10). Upper Saddle River, NJ: Merrill/Prentice Hall. Adapted by permission.

**TABLE 2.1**
The classroom teacher's role in the assessment process.

| Steps in the Assessment Process | Regular Classroom Teacher's Role |
| --- | --- |
| Before referral | Use informal assessment methods to monitor daily progress, curriculum-based assessment, and behavioral observations; consult with team members; implement educational interventions |
| | Consult with parents |
| Identification of disabled student | Recognize behaviors and characteristics of students with disabilities so that these students can be identified, evaluated, and served if appropriate |
| | Recognize behaviors and characteristics that are indicative of cultural or linguistic differences and do not warrant special education services |
| Referral to placement process | Use data collection of student work samples, behavioral observations, teacher-made tests, and other informal measures to identify educational strengths and weaknesses |
| | Consult with team members |
| | Consult with parents; determine their level of understanding of the referral and assessment process; provide answers to questions and any materials requested |
| | Complete necessary referral documents |
| | Attend child study committee meetings and present appropriate data collected on student progress and behaviors |
| | Participate during development and implementation of IEPs for students in regular class settings |
| Uses of test data | Use IQ and other norm-referenced tests appropriately |
| | Respect parents' rights and confidentiality of all test/identification materials |
| | Be aware of specific tests and what they do and do not measure |
| | Carefully read test interpretations and question how results can help plan educational interventions |

The use of prereferral intervention strategies has been found to increase consultation among the general classroom teacher and members of the multidisciplinary team, while decreasing the number of students tested and placed in special education (Graden, Casey, & Bonstrom, 1985). When prereferral intervention strategies seem inadequate, the teacher's documentation of which strategies were tried and the results of each may be beneficial to the team members in both diagnosis and educational planning.

After multiple educational interventions have been implemented and the student continues to struggle educationally, the general classroom teacher may wish to consult with the multidisciplinary team for advice. This team may suggest further prereferral intervention strategies or want to observe the student in the academic setting. If the student continues to have difficulty making progress, the team may suggest that the student be referred for a comprehensive educational assessment. This process begins with completion of a formal referral form and notification of the student's parents.

# STEP 3: REFERRAL

The general classroom teacher will have the documentation necessary for a formal referral if the prereferral plan was in place. He or she may use the observations and documentation of changes in behavior or learning, or the lack of significant changes, as a basis for the referral. All referrals should be written in an objective format, addressing specific academic or behavioral concerns. These concerns should be further supported by quantitative data whenever possible. For example, if there was a prereferral plan to decrease both the number and level of math problems for homework, supporting data may be used to state that the student was able to complete only 30% of the assignments correctly.

Referrals for behavioral problems should also be stated objectively. A student who seems to bother other students and does not complete tasks may be referred using observational data that reveals that she is out of her seat 75% of the class period, initiates inappropriate conversation during 50% of her peer interactions, and completes a maximum of 20% of her assignments. The following examples illustrate appropriate and inappropriate referral statements written for a fifth-grade student.

### Inappropriate

John has been a terror in the fifth grade. He seems to enjoy making trouble, and I can't remember the last time he turned in homework. He needs to be in a different class.

### Appropriate

Prereferral strategies include small-group instruction, a new seating arrangement, and slower-paced adapted curriculum.

Talking out of turn: 60 percent of classroom interactions

Completed assignments: 35 percent

Completed homework: 0 percent

Identified areas of difficulty: math, reading, spelling—all below grade level

During the prereferral and referral periods, the parents will become involved in the process. Members of the prereferral and assessment team as well as the classroom teacher, should contact the parents from time to time since parents hold valuable information about a child's background, nonacademic strengths/weaknesses, likes, dislikes, and so on.

Figure 2.3 shows a student evaluation/placement assurance checklist used for each student once the referral has started.

Name of student_____ Birthdate_____

Name of parent/guardian_____ School_____

Home address_____ Grade_____

Home telephone_____ Work telephone_____

Maximum date for completion of case study and MDC _____

Date      Initials

_____  _____    1.  Date of case study referral and its source

_____  _____    2.  Referral source informed of decision to conduct or not to conduct a case study evaluation

_____  _____    3.  Parents notified of intent to conduct case study

_____  _____    4.  Parent consent received

_____  _____    5.  Parent/guardian notification of rights

_____  _____    6.  Determination of student's language-use pattern, mode of communication, and cultural background

_____  _____    7.  Notification of language-use pattern in student's temporary record

_____  _____    8.  Case study evaluation components:

_____  _____        a.  Interview with student

_____  _____        b.  Consultation with parents

_____  _____        c.  Social developmental study, if required

_____  _____        d.  Assessment of adaptive behavior

_____  _____        e.  Assessment of cultural background

_____  _____        f.  Medical history/current health status, if required

_____  _____        g.  Vision screening within 6 months

_____  _____        h.  Hearing screening not prior to consent, but prior to eligibility

_____  _____        i.  Review of academic history and current educational functioning

_____  _____        j.  Educational evaluation/achievement/learning processes

_____  _____        k.  Assessment of learning environment/observation

_____  _____        l.  Psychological evaluation

_____  _____        m.  Speech/language evaluation, if required

_____  _____        n.  Other specialized evaluations

_____  _____    9.  Notation of any missing component(s) in the student's temporary record

_____  _____   10.  Parent notification of multidisciplinary conference (MDC)

_____  _____   11.  MDC to formulate program and service options

_____  _____   12.  Written report of multidisciplinary conference

_____  _____   13.  Parent notification of decision not to place student in special education, if applicable

_____  _____   14.  Parent notification of IEP meeting (if different from item 11)

_____  _____   15.  IEP developed

_____  _____   16.  Parental consent for placement

_____  _____   17.  Parent notification of special education placement

**FIGURE 2.3**

Student evaluation/placement assurance checklist.

# Parental Involvement

PL 94-142 and IDEA specifically include parents at all levels of the referral/assessment/placement process. Parental permission for the comprehensive evaluation must be secured before administering any tests used to determine eligibility. This consent is further defined in federal regulations as informed consent and means that parents are to be informed about which tests will be used and what these tests are designed to measure. Parents may revoke their consent at any time.

Federal regulations also provide for parental participation during eligibility and the formulation of the IEP. It is especially important that the special education teacher and the general classroom teacher work with the parents during the writing of the IEP. Parents were very involved in the reauthorization of IDEA. However, there are parents who are passive in the process. They may not, for whatever reasons, choose to participate in assessment, contribute to the eligibility decision, or share in the development of the IEP. IDEA "insists" that school divisions ensure parent participation and attendance. Meetings are to be held only after reasonable attempts to have the parents present, without success, have been documented. A definition of "reasonable attempts" is not provided in the law; however, many school divisions practice documenting inviting the parent to the meeting by using certified or registered mail if the parent fails to show for the first meeting. If phone calls and subsequent letters do not get the parent in, then the meeting is held. For some parents the time of the meeting or lack of transportation is the primary reason they do not attend. Schools need to be as accommodating as possible. This is where the school social worker or school guidance counselor could be helpful. It is especially important to have parental insight into a student's home and cultural background. This may be one method of decreasing the possibility that students from different cultures are overrepresented in special education. When the child study committee determines that a student needs a comprehensive evaluation, federal regulations require that parents must grant informed consent before the assessment process. However, the regulations also state that parents may revoke their consent at any time. They are to be informed of their rights and the procedural safeguards, in their native language or mode of communication (for example, in a manual communication system). Many states have parents' rights information presented at the beginning of the evaluation process, and the parents are asked to sign a form indicating that they have been informed of their rights. The general or special classroom teacher, acting as a liaison or parent advocate, should be certain that parents are clearly informed and understand their rights. A disadvantage of informing the parents of their rights through a written format is that the readability level of the materials may be questionable. In addition to readability levels, these materials may contain highly complex legal vocabulary. Parents' rights information that is presented in a different language may become confused in the translation. The special education teacher and the general classroom teacher, perhaps with an interpreter, can help the parents understand complex concepts.

## Screening of Referrals

The screening committee may be made up of the same professionals as the child study committee or prereferral committee. These educators review the child's educational history and prereferral intervention plan. They discuss the formal referral and consider it thoroughly. The committee members may suggest alternatives before submitting the case to the multidisciplinary team. For example, members may consider placement in a different classroom of the same or lower level. Sometimes the at-risk student may be assigned to remedial programs or placed in a classroom one grade lower for difficult subjects. A third-grade student may be placed in a second-grade class for reading but remain in the general class for other subjects. The effects of such actions on a child's self-esteem would have to be closely considered and monitored.

When prereferral instructional strategies are not effective in changing the student's learning or behavioral difficulties, the committee may believe that a student needs to be assessed to determine if a specific disability exists that may require special services. The parents are consulted for permission to evaluate and determine which evaluation components will be conducted, and the process begins.

## STEP 4: FORMAL ASSESSMENT

The primary purpose of assessment is to obtain information that will be useful in determining if the child is a child with a disability. It is useful as well in making educational decisions about interventions that may be necessary for optimum educational achievement. The general classroom teacher should be prepared to ask questions and seek information that will aid in educational planning. Test data on the student's intellectual, perceptual, language, and academic functioning can be useful for educational planning.

Norm-referenced tests of intelligence and academic achievement are used to compare a student with the age or grade norm group. The comparison is made to determine if the student deviates significantly from what is expected of the age or grade level. Scores are expressed in a standard format such as an IQ or cognitive ability score, which may have an average of 100, percentiles, or grade or age equivalents. Using standard scores based on an average of 100 and a standard deviation of 15, a student may be compared with the expectations of the grade or age level and may be reported as being one or two standard deviations below the norm. A student who scores two standard deviations below peers would probably be considered eligible for special education services in the specific academic area. If the scores are reported as percentiles, a student scoring in the 60th percentile is believed to be functioning better than 60% of the norm group.

Once parental permission has been obtained, the comprehensive assessment process begins (see Figure 2.4). PL 94-142 stipulates that the comprehensive evaluation must include assessment of all areas of suspected disability. These may include academic, intellectual, emotional, perceptual, motor, visual, auditory, language, and physical abilities. The assessment involves a professional team, each

## The Road to Responsibility: Referral to Placement

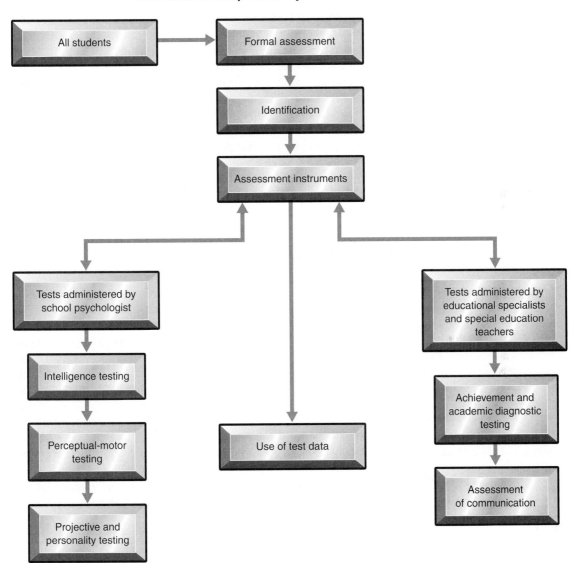

**FIGURE 2.4**
Formal assessment.

of whom will assess in a specific area of expertise. Team members design an assessment plan for each student who is to receive a comprehensive assessment. The responsibilities of the team members are listed in Table 2.2.

A safeguard intended to prevent misdiagnosis and promote nondiscriminatory assessment is the provision that the local educational agency use a variety of

**TABLE 2.2**
Who's on the multidisciplinary team?

| Team Member | Responsibilities |
| --- | --- |
| School nurse | Initial vision/hearing screening, checks medical records, refers health problems to other medical professionals |
| Special education teacher | Consultant to regular classroom teacher during prereferral process, administers educational tests, observes in other classrooms, helps with screening and recommends IEP goals, writes objectives, suggests educational interventions |
| Special education supervisor | May advise all activities of special education teacher, may provide direct services, guides placement decisions, recommends services |
| Educational diagnostician | Administers norm-referenced and criterion-referenced tests, observes student in educational setting, makes suggestions for IEP goals and objectives |
| School psychologist | Administers individual intelligence tests, observes student in classroom, administers projective instruments and personality inventories, may be under supervision of a Ph.D.-level psychologist |
| Occupational therapist | Evaluates fine motor and self-help skills, recommends therapies, may provide direct services or consultant services, may help obtain equipment for student needs |
| Physical therapist | Evaluates gross motor functioning and self-help skills, living skills, job-related skills necessary for optimum achievement of student; may provide direct services or consultant services |
| Behavioral consultant | Specialist in behavior management and crisis intervention; may provide direct services or consultant services |
| School counselor | May serve as objective observer in prereferral stage; may provide direct counseling services, group or individual counseling, schedule students, help with planning of student schedules |
| Speech-language clinician | Evaluates speech-language development, may refer for hearing problems, may provide direct therapy or consultant services for classroom teachers |
| Audiologist | Evaluates hearing for possible impairments, may refer students for medical problems, may help obtain hearing aids |
| Physician's assistant | Evaluates physical condition of student and may provide physical exams for students from a local school system; refers medical problems to physicians or appropriate therapists |
| Home-school coordinator, school social worker, or visiting teacher | Works directly with family; may hold conferences, conduct interviews and/or administer adaptive behavior scales based upon parental interview; may serve as case manager |
| Regular education teacher | Works with special education team, student, and parents to develop environment that is appropriate and as much like that of nondisabled students as possible; implements prereferral intervention strategies |
| Parents | Active members of special education team; provide input for IEP, work with home/school academic and behavioral programs |
| School administrator | Oversees activities that team members from his/her building are responsible for |

*Source:* Overton, T. (1992). *Assessment in special education: An applied approach* (p. 10). Upper Saddle River, NJ: Merrill/Prentice Hall. Adapted by permission.

assessment tools and strategies to gather relevant functional and developmental information. With the revision of IDEA, there is a new emphasis on enabling the child to be involved in and progress in the general curriculum, or, for preschool children, to participate in appropriate activities. Local school divisions are instructed to not use any single procedure as the sole criterion for determining whether a child is a child with a disability, as well as to use technically sound instruments that assess cognitive and behavioral factors, in addition to physical and developmental factors. This encourages the use of both formal and informal assessment techniques. Informal assessment information may be collected by the general classroom teacher, a special education teacher, the school psychologist or educational diagnostician, or the speech-language therapist. The intent is to gather enough information to provide a true picture of the whole child rather than to base educational decisions upon a single score, such as an IQ score. Even an "appropriate" assessment is only a small picture or window into the whole child, and this is why other information is so important in the assessment process.

Another safeguard for nondiscriminatory assessment is the regulation requiring that all assessments be conducted in the child's native language or mode of communication unless it is clearly not feasible to do so. Tests used to assess a child are to be selected and administered so as not to be racially or culturally discriminatory. The general classroom teacher can provide assistance in the assessment process by informing the diagnostic team about the child's native language.

## Use of Test Data

Teacher and parents may feel more comfortable with scores that are reported as age or grade equivalents. It is important for the classroom teacher to remember that grade equivalents do not represent a grade level of functioning. These equivalents merely represent the number of items answered correctly by the norm group at each grade level rather than mastery of content at a particular grade. For example, a student who obtains a score of 4.5 (fourth grade, fifth month) may not have mastered the skills required of the mid-fourth-grade year, but the score means that the student answered the same number of items correctly as did the norm group of fourth graders. One should not assume, therefore, that this student has mastered half of the fourth-grade curriculum.

Classroom teachers who feel unsure about the educational implications of test interpretations should consult the person who administered and interpreted the instruments. Because tests represent small samples of behavior at a given time, the teacher needs to understand exactly what the test measured and how it was measured. For example, often a teacher may question the results obtained on a particular instrument because of knowing the child's performance level in areas of academic instruction. The teacher may believe that the student is capable of successfully completing fifth-grade-level reading assignments, yet the test results indicate a third-grade reading level. By questioning the diagnostician, the classroom teacher may learn that the score was obtained in only one area of reading, such as decoding nonsense words, while the reading comprehension score was significantly higher. Diagnostic testing is presented across many specific areas using many different formats. By understanding what each specific score represents, the teacher can make the necessary academic program or curriculum changes.

The teacher will be able to use the scores obtained from norm-referenced assessment as a basis for further criterion-referenced or curriculum-based assessment. These types of assessment will provide information about the student that will be used to develop the goals and objectives of the IEP.

## Assessment Instruments

There are thousands of commercially produced assessment instruments available. The assessment team members are trained to select instruments designed to assess skills or abilities in their specific area. Each student to be tested for the purpose of determining eligibility for special education should already have an individual assessment plan. Team members decide on this plan after careful examination of the student's prereferral and referral information, the student's cumulative records, and any other information the child study team provides. Examples of these informal types of instruments as well as commercially produced instruments are listed in Table 2.3.

Tests are administered by school psychologists. Many assessment instruments used for eligibility decisions are complex norm-referenced standardized tests. They include intelligence (IQ) tests, perceptual motor tests, behavioral inventories, and projective personality tests. The administration of these tests is often restricted to personnel with advanced training in assessment, such as school psychologists or educational diagnosticians. Intelligence tests are perhaps the most frequently used types of instruments.

Because testing represents a small sample of behavior observed at a specific time, care should be taken not to overemphasize the importance of the scores obtained on an intelligence quotient (IQ) or cognitive ability test. Analysis of items contained on intelligence tests reveals that many of the questions or tasks measure learned material or achievement rather than innate intellectual ability. Cultural fairness of many of the test items has also been questioned.

Most intelligence instruments contain several subtests designed to measure traits or skills thought to be indications of intelligence. For example, subtests may measure auditory short-term memory, understanding of language concepts, and perceptual motor speed. School psychologists may interpret the tests in a manner that reflects subtest analysis. These interpretations are useful in educational planning. For one student, the results may indicate a short attention span or a tendency to be easily distracted. For another, the results may indicate that the student has significantly higher perceptual motor or visual motor skills than verbal comprehension skills. This type of information is much more helpful to a teacher than a single numerical value such as an IQ score.

School psychologists may use the scores obtained on a test measuring cognitive ability or IQ to determine the existence of a specific learning disability. The extreme variance in scores on the test, together with other indicators on other mea-

**TABLE 2.3**
Assessment instruments.

| Type of Instrument | Examples |
| --- | --- |
| Informal | Teacher-made tests, observations, curriculum-based tests, student work samples, student interviews or self-reports |
| Criterion-referenced tests | Brigance Diagnostic Inventory of Basic Skills; KeyMath—Revised |
| Norm-referenced academic screening tests | Wide Range Achievement Test—3d; Peabody Individual Achievement Test—Revised; Kaufman Test of Educational Achievement: Brief and Comprehensive Forms |
| Norm-referenced academic achievement tests | Woodcock-Johnson—III: Standard and Supplemental Tests; Kaufman Test of Educational Achievement: Comprehensive Form; Wechsler Individual Achievement Test—III |
| Norm-referenced academic diagnostic tests | KeyMath—Revised; Woodcock Reading Mastery Tests—Revised; Test of Mathematical Abilities |
| Norm-referenced perceptual motor tests | Motor-Free Test of Visual Perception; Bender Visual-Motor Gestalt Test; Auditory Discrimination Test; Detroit Test of Learning Aptitude—Primary & 2 |
| Norm-referenced language tests and written expression tests | Peabody Picture Vocabulary Test—Revised; Test of Word Finding; Test of Language Development—2; Test of Adolescent Language—2 |
| Norm-referenced intelligence tests | Wechsler Intelligence Scale for Children—Revised; Woodcock-Johnson—III; Kaufman Assessment Battery for Children; Stanford-Binet Intelligence Scale |

sures, may signal possible processing difficulties. Cognitive processing difficulties may result in learning problems and low achievement in academics.

Intelligence test scores may also be used as an indicator of subaverage functioning. If a student has subaverage intellectual functioning, subaverage adaptive behavior, and low academic functioning, the student may be diagnosed as having mental retardation.

Scores obtained on different measures of intelligence may vary from time to time. The student may perform better on one day than another, or a change in a student's score may represent actual developmental growth, maturity, and achievement. In other words, scores on IQ measures are not permanent and should not be viewed as such.

The Wechsler Intelligence Scale for Children—Revised, the Stanford-Binet Intelligence Scale, and the Woodcock-Johnson—Psycho Educational Battery Revised, Tests of Cognitive Ability are some commonly used intelligence test instruments. Each test takes approximately an hour or more to administer and will provide the examiner with a sample of how the student responds to a variety of tasks. Other instruments, such as the Slosson Intelligence Test, are designed for use as a quick screening test. Screening tests are not appropriate for use in eligibility decisions.

An examiner may want to determine how the student best perceives and responds to information. There are instruments that measure auditory memory, auditory discrimination, visual memory, visual discrimination, visual-motor responses or fine motor skills, and other areas. These are considered measures of perceptual or perceptual-motor abilities. Although these assessments may provide insight for the teacher in program planning, these tests alone will not provide enough information to determine if the child is eligible for special education services. "In 1986, the Council for Learning Disabilities recommended a moratorium on perceptual assessments until research support for this approach was available (McLoughlin & Lewis, 1990, p. 233). Nevertheless, using the results of perceptual-motor assessments to plan educational strategies continues to be a helpful and common practice for designing instruction around a child's strengths.

If the teacher is not certain about a child's best learning modality, informal assessment in the classroom may be conducted. The teacher may ask the student to copy different designs or words from the board or a sheet of paper, repeat a series of words or numbers, or perform simple visual-motor or auditory tasks. The teacher may ask the student questions such as "Would you rather learn about something new by reading about it in a book or by someone telling you about it?" These types of informal measures may provide the teacher with additional insight about how the student prefers to learn. Often, the student knows how he or she can be most successful in learning new material. The student may say, "I say it over and over until I remember," or "I draw myself a picture or write down words that help me." In fact, the teacher may find it useful to determine the learning styles of all students in the class rather than only those students referred for, or receiving, special services.

The administration of tests to assess personality disorders is usually restricted to psychologists with advanced training. A projective test may consist of showing a stimuli picture card and asking the student to interpret what is happening in the picture. The psychologist attempts to find a trend or pattern in the verbal responses given by the student. Many school psychologists prefer to use informal classroom observation or systematic observation and clinical interview as a basis for assessing personality disorders. Classroom teachers may be asked to collect behavioral observation data to assist the school psychologist in determining how frequently certain behaviors occur. Educational specialists and special education teachers may give many measures of academic achievement. These instruments may be norm-referenced or criterion-referenced tests. Some of these tests may not require much advanced training to administer; however, the examiner should become familiar with the test and the test manual and should practice test administration several times before administering the instrument to a student. If possible, he or she should consult with someone who has had experience in the administration of the instrument.

The test data obtained from achievement testing and diagnostic academic assessment are probably the most useful to the teacher. The scores represent how the student performed at that particular time when material was presented in a specific standardized format. The presentation of the material as well as the response mode required of the student may make a difference in the way the student performs. For example, most spelling curricula include testing of spelling on a general basis, often weekly. Here is the format: The teacher says the word, reads a sentence using the word, and repeats the word; the student writes the word on a piece of lined note-book paper. The spelling subtest presented on the Peabody Individual Achievement Test—Revised is quite different. On this subtest, the examiner says a word, and the child selects the correct spelling of the word from four choices. As the words increase in difficulty, the discrimination becomes more difficult as well. A student who has poor visual memory or poor visual discrimination may find the subtest a much more confusing measure of spelling, which the obtained score may reflect. This may make a difference in the way the information obtained from this subtest is used.

Teachers should also be aware that the name of a test or subtest may be deceiving. The reading subtest of the Wide Range Achievement Test—Revised is actually only a measure of word recall and contains no measure of reading decoding or comprehension. This test should be used for screening only, not for educational planning.

The better achievement tests are those that provide a variety of items and subtests to measure many types of skills and content. One such test is the Woodcock-Johnson Psycho-Educational Battery—Revised Tests of Achievement. This instrument contains standard and supplementary batteries that measure several areas of academics. It may be used to measure skills from the preacademic ages to college and adult levels. The student will be assessed in topics such as reading comprehension, decoding, word recognition, math computation and concepts, applied math, science, social studies, and humanities.

The speech-language clinician or therapist may also administer a variety of assessment instruments. These tests may measure articulation, auditory discrimination, verbal expression, receptive language, language concepts, or word-finding ability. Language assessment may be formal or informal. Many of the language areas can be assessed informally in class. The teacher may collect written documentation of the child's ability to construct sentences. Vocabulary development is part of the language arts curriculum and can be assessed naturally. The teacher should note students who have a limited vocabulary, do not seem to have a command of language, or do not know how to use complex concepts for communication.

## Identification

The various disabling conditions defined in IDEA are identified through the assessment process and will be discussed in detail in chapter 4. Some of these disabling conditions, such as deaf-blind, are low-incidence disabilities not found in many schools. Individual student needs can be so involved that the students may be served in special day schools or in residential facilities. Other conditions such as learning disabilities or emotional disturbances are more common, and students with these conditions are likely to be found in most schools.

The general classroom teacher may have students with milder learning problems in the regular classroom to receive all or part of their instruction. For example, a teacher may have a student with a language impairment for the entire day, another student who has specific learning disabilities in reading for most of the day, and a third student with mild mental retardation for art and physical education only.

Because the greatest number of students receiving special education are those found to have mild learning problems, the chances are great that the general classroom teacher will have such students in his or her classroom.

## Issues in Assessment

The classroom teacher should keep important issues of assessment in mind during the entire prereferral-to-placement process. These issues have been the basis for legal actions in some states and represent areas of education that may change in the future.

One of the most important issues to consider is the overrepresentation of minorities in special education. We hope that, with parental involvement and improved nondiscriminatory test practices, the number of misdiagnosed students will decrease. Prereferral intervention strategies are changing the focus of the assessment team from a test-and-place sequence to a consultation-and-prevention sequence. This change may also prevent the overrepresentation of minorities in special education.

Such minority overrepresentation has been documented in the literature (Reschly, 1988; Tucker, 1980). It occurs when the percentage of a minority population in the special education setting is greater than the percentage represented naturally in the geographic region. For example, if a geographic school district includes a Hispanic population of 12%, and 35% of the special education population in that district is composed of Hispanic students, that particular group is overrepresented in special education. It is extremely important that general education teachers do not misinterpret behaviors that represent cultural or linguistic differences as indicative of learning problems. The teacher who is not certain of cultural or linguistic differences should consult with the prereferral committee or the parents.

The issues in Assessment have become far reaching. Initially, focus was on equal assessment during the evaluation for placement testing process. Assessment issues now extend nationally. In chapter 14, *Evaluation,* alternate assessment, state standards, and high stakes testing is discussed.

## Exit Criteria

Another issue of concern for assessment practice is exit criteria. It seems that much of the time spent in assessment is devoted to testing with the goal of placing students into special education rather than putting them back into the mainstream of education and therefore society. Classroom teachers may help reverse this tendency by designing objectives for special education students with the ultimate goal of returning those students to the mainstream.

## STEP 5: ELIGIBILITY

Assessment data will be used to determine eligibility and placement. The decision of eligibility should be a group decision, and team members should not reach a decision before the meeting. Test reports may include service or placement recommendations that may be considered; however, the actual decision will be made by all members of the group. A placement decision should be reached only after considering all possible alternative placements or settings. The parent should be a part of all of these discussions and decisions.

The multidisciplinary team closely follows each case as it progresses through prereferral to placement. The team is responsible for reviewing case study evaluation/reevaluation, determining a disability, identifying adverse effects, identifying educational needs, and determining eligibility for special education.

## STEP 6: DEVELOPING THE IEP

Once the decision has been made for the eligibility of services, the multidisciplinary team and the parents discuss the type of services that are needed and how/where they will be provided. At this point in the process, the team becomes responsible for reviewing current program and performance levels, developing program goals and objectives, considering the need for an extended school year, considering the need for a transition plan, considering the need for a behavior management plan, determining necessary related services, determining general education participation, considering placement options, and determining least restrictive placement. These are decisions that will impact the child's future and education and should not be made hastily and without careful consideration.

Too often the team, unconsciously or consciously, appears intimidating to the parents, who are sometimes apt to accept whatever the other team members develop. If parents feel confident about their role from the beginning, they will be active participants throughout the IEP development.

Chapter 1 described the individualized educational plan (IEP), and a sample of an IEP appears in Figure 2.5. The important components are the amount of special education and/or related services to be provided in the least restrictive environment, a description of the student's present level of performance, and a statement of goals and objectives that may be decided at the eligibility meeting. Because much of the information used in making eligibility decisions is gathered from norm-referenced sources rather than informal assessment, the eligibility meeting is not the ideal time to write the educational goals and objectives. It is better to write the IEP objectives after the classroom teacher completes further assessment to measure specific skill levels. Therefore, after the determination of eligibility and placement, a second meeting with the student's parents must be arranged when the teacher has completed the assessment. This meeting and the writing of all educational goals and objectives must be completed within 30 days of the determination of eligibility (Federal Register, June 4, 1997).

## Educational Goals and Objectives

During the meeting to develop the IEP goals and objectives, the long-term goals of the educational program are discussed by teachers, special education professionals, and parents. Since the passage of the Education of the Handicapped Act amendments of

Name  Pam Smith

Date of birth  8-12-82                    Grade  Fifth                    Date  9-14-92

Summary of present levels of performance:

According to results from the Woodcock-Johnson—Revised Tests of Achievement and teacher reports and work samples, Pam is functioning as expected in all academic areas with the exception of math calculation and applied problems. Pam has difficulty with multiplication concepts and facts. Language arts areas are strengths for Pam, and she enjoys all other subjects.

Continuum of services

Pam will receive all instruction in the regular fifth-grade classroom. Resource room support for math will be available for independent work. Curriculum will be adjusted by Randy Jones.

Committee members

Martha White—principal
Randy Jones—special education teacher
Cynthia Murray—fifth-grade teacher
Tim Brown—educational diagnostician
Linda Smith—parent

Individualized Education Plan

Name  Pam Smith                                        Date  9-17-92

Annual goals:

Pam will be able to complete third-grade math curriculum materials and begin fourth-grade materials by May 1993.

| Short-term objectives | Beginning and ending dates | Evaluation methods and criteria for objectives |
|---|---|---|
| 1. When given multiplication problems for the facts 1–10, Pam will be able to write the correct responses. | 9-17-92 | Daily probes, teacher-made tests using math curriculum, end of chapter tests<br>Criteria: 80% accuracy |
| 2. When given multiplication homework for the facts 1–10, Pam will complete assignments. | 9-17-92 | Homework assignments will be completed 9 out of 10 days |
| 3. Pam will be able to complete applied math problems from the third-grade math text. | 9-17-92 | Daily probes, teacher-made tests using applied problems from the third-grade math curriculum<br>Criteria: 85% accuracy |

**FIGURE 2.5**
An individualized educational program (IEP).

1990, long-range planning has been emphasized in the IEP, with a new focus on transition services: that is, planning for the student's future after public education. These amendments include the requirement that a student's IEP include "a statement of the needed transition services for students beginning no later than age 16 and annually thereafter (and, when determined appropriate for the individual, beginning at age 14 or younger)" (CEC, 1990, p. 1).

Teachers and parents should discuss the long-range plans of each student because such thinking will aid in the formulation of annual educational goals. For students entering middle school or high school, the guidance counselor may provide insight about which subjects or courses the student should take to graduate and meet entrance requirements for college or postsecondary training, if that is the long-range goal. If the parents and teacher envision the student entering the world of work following high school, a different curriculum or subject sequence may be followed. In many cases, it is appropriate for the student to be involved in such long-range planning.

With the long-range plans in mind, the special education teacher or another team member will write the annual educational goals. These goals will be targets for the student to move toward during the academic year. The educational objectives will be founded on these goals.

In order for the teacher or special education teacher to write effective short-term objectives, it is necessary to test the student using criterion-referenced or curriculum-based assessment. Some published curriculum materials provide placement tests that give the teacher a breakdown of skills mastered. These tests may be used to target specific skills for educational objectives. If the curriculum materials do not provide such an analysis, the teacher may need to task-analyze materials or break the skills into very small steps. Next, the teacher will design a test that includes items for each of the small steps in the task. If the teacher uses items from the curriculum material, the test is a form of curriculum-based assessment. For the initial test, several items for each small step should be included. The teacher administers this teacher-made instrument and analyzes mastery of items or errors made by the student. The errors represent skills or content that the student needs to master and will therefore be used as a basis for short-term objectives. The skills mastered may represent areas of strength and should be considered in educational programming. Continued assessment using the curriculum materials will allow for close monitoring of progress.

The teacher must determine the criterion to use in measuring student mastery of an objective. This criterion may be expressed as a percentage of accuracy or frequency of correct responses (for example, 9 out of 10 correct responses). A criterion-referenced test will be designed to measure the attainment of the objective. For example, a teacher may write an objective stating that the student will decode three out of five consonant clusters and then design a posttest with the five clusters included. When the student is able to decode three out of the five correctly, the criterion has been met. The teacher then changes or adapts the objective.

The short-term educational objectives serve as steps toward meeting the annual goals. The objectives should be written in observable and measurable terms.

Doing so will help the teacher determine when the objectives have been met so that new objectives may be written. The following examples illustrate the difference between behaviorally stated, measurable objectives and unmeasurable ones:

The teacher will know when Sue reaches the two objectives in the first column because a measurable criterion is given for each of the objectives. Close monitoring by using curriculum-based and/or criterion-referenced assessment will provide the teacher with information necessary to write new educational objectives.

All other components required by IDEA have to be considered prior to concluding the IEP meeting. These include consideration of the parents' concerns and strengths of the child, any evaluation data, whether or not the child's behavior impedes his/her learning or the learning of others, and if so, provide for the supports like a behavior intervention plan or additional goals and objectives. The team must also consider (a) if the child requires assistive technology devices, (b) his/her communication needs, and (c) inclusion in state and district level testing.

## STEP 7: ONGOING EVALUATION

Under 94-142, students receiving special education services were required to have a comprehensive evaluation at least every 3 years. Now the IEP team can consider what evaluations, if any, need to be completed to determine if the child is progressing, and if he/she requires to be eligible for services. Teachers or parents who feel a program adjustment is needed during the 3-year period may request that the multidisciplinary team reconvene to examine the student's progress.

Student progress can best be monitored through ongoing evaluation by the classroom and/or special education teacher. Ongoing assessment is composed of many types of informal assessment. The teacher will use classroom observation, teacher-made tests, curriculum-based assessment, criterion-referenced assessment, work samples, student self-reports or interviews, homework assignments, and daily work to monitor student progress.

The monitoring of student progress should prompt the teacher to watch closely for the mastery of short-term objectives. The teacher may amend the IEP by updating the short-term objectives. These changes in instruction, not in educational programming, do not warrant an IEP meeting. The short-term objectives should be changed as often as the student masters an objective. In this sense, the IEP is a working document for the teacher. The short-term objectives should be considered daily as the teacher plans for instruction. Student strengths should be used to plan activities of enrichment or reinforcement. With the mastery of each objective, the student moves closer to the attainment of annual goals, and progress is evident.

General educators and special educators must work closely together to ensure successful programming for a student. Special education teachers should share all student data, especially the IEP. Many times general education teachers have remarked that one of their students had a disability, but that teachers were never informed. Sharing information among all persons involved is critical for successful planning, instruction, and evaluation of students with special needs. Figure 2.6 summarizes our exploration of the prereferral-to-placement process.

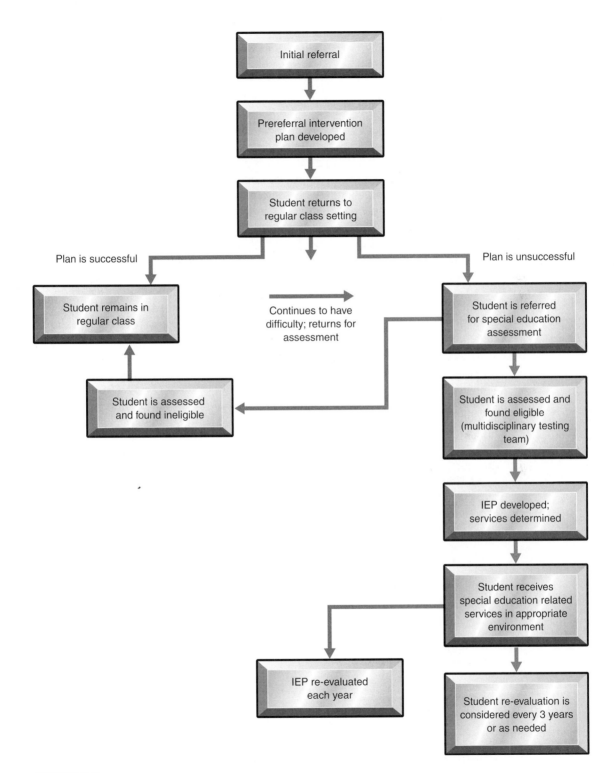

**FIGURE 2.6**

From initial identification to eligibility determination and placement in special education services.

*Source:* Wood, J. W., & Lazzari, A. (1997). *Exceeding the boundaries: Understanding exceptional lives.* Fort Worth, TX: Harcourt Brace Jovanovich. Reprinted with permission.

# CONCLUSION

Classroom teachers can contribute to the assessment in many ways. The purpose of assessment is to make educational interventions necessary for academic success. Classroom teachers can aid the multidisciplinary team by making certain that referrals are a last resort rather than a first-choice strategy. Teachers can also monitor student progress and behaviors carefully to ensure that students are referred only for significant academic weaknesses rather than cultural or linguistic differences.

Classroom teachers can become experienced in collecting data in an objective manner to document academic and behavioral concerns. The teacher should work closely with the parents, assuring them that they make vital contributions of useful information. At all times the teacher needs to make certain that the parents understand the assessment procedure.

Assessment data should be employed in making educational decisions. To make the best possible decisions, the teacher should understand what each test measures and how this information can be used in planning. The teacher should become an active and interested member of the multidisciplinary team.

The classroom teacher should keep in mind the issues that concern special educators when working with any at-risk student. The teacher should stay informed and updated on the legal issues surrounding assessment. The teacher should remember that the primary goal is optimum academic achievement for all students. Ongoing evaluation through informal assessment provides both the teacher and the student with realistic goals and expectations to promote progress.

It is imperative that classroom teachers be aware of the process covered in this chapter; not only be aware, but be comfortable and familiar with the terminology used. Educating all children requires the time and involvement of many persons. It must be a team effort with knowledgeable team members committed to doing what is best (and legal) for each child.

# CHAPTER 3

## Bilingual or Limited-English-Proficient Students

*by Deborah Wilson, Samir Haddad, and Jerry Fouchey*

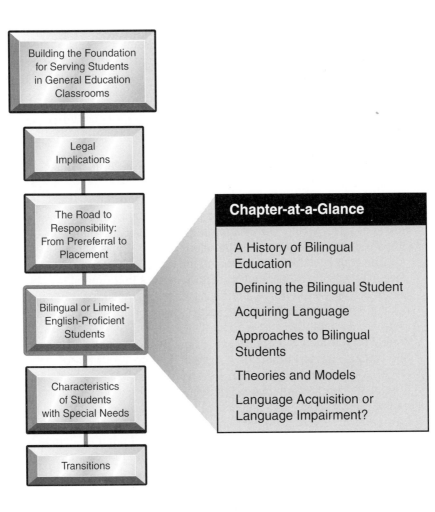

Building the Foundation for Serving Students in General Education Classrooms

Legal Implications

The Road to Responsibility: From Prereferral to Placement

Bilingual or Limited-English-Proficient Students

Characteristics of Students with Special Needs

Transitions

**Chapter-at-a-Glance**

A History of Bilingual Education

Defining the Bilingual Student

Acquiring Language

Approaches to Bilingual Students

Theories and Models

Language Acquisition or Language Impairment?

During the 1990s there was a dramatic increase in the number of students in our public schools who were limited-English-proficient (LEP). Nationally, this number was more than 70% higher than it was in the 1980s. Because researchers predict that the number will continue to grow, more and more teachers are faced with the challenge of providing an equitable education for a group of students that they are not well prepared to teach. Colleges of teacher education are notably deficient in their willingness to require coursework in bilingual education. Nevertheless, providing appropriate instruction for these students, although not prescribed in the same way that special education programs are, is required by law.

This chapter will provide an overview of relevant topics in bilingual education, discuss how the SAALE model applies to bilingual students, and explain some modifications to the SAALE interventions that are uniquely effective with bilingual students.

## THE ROOTS AND RIGHTS OF BILINGUAL EDUCATION: A HISTORICAL PERSPECTIVE

Diversity is a unique and marvelous characteristic of the United States. Unfortunately, current controversies evolving from the intersection of politics, language, and culture have resulted in legislative proposals for English-only instruction in our schools. Such an approach is naive because it ignores a significant portion of the research base, which demonstrates the value of bilingual education (using students' native language) as a foundation for later English acquisition.

The impact of this controversy on the future of bilingual education has yet to be determined. But a quick study of history reveals that American schools in the 19th century routinely offered academic courses in languages other than English. Numerous immigrant communities were studying and speaking languages such as German, Finnish, Italian, Swedish, Dutch, and Spanish. Diverse groups vied for control of local institutions and for the right to name cities and land forms and to define various strata of American culture in the late 1800s.

This was also a time when European nationalism was flourishing here and abroad. Its rapid growth helped to define a new role for public schools: to "Americanize" immigrants. This linguistic homogenization began when many states passed laws requiring English-only instruction. A far more invasive program was the forcible removal of Native American children from their homes to placement in boarding schools, where speaking their native languages was forbidden.

This trend continued until well after World War II, when the shortage of foreign-language skills among Americans proved to be a weakness in our effort to advance the United States as an international power. Foreign-language instruction was dramatically expanded when the National Defense Education Act (NDEA) of 1958 provided federal money to promote a foreign-language policy for the sake of "improving international relations and national security." Even today, negotiating the delicate balance between the development of a pool of multilingual citizens (a valuable natural resource) and the insistence on English-language instruction for immigrants remains a challenge for state and federal governments.

When increasing numbers of immigrants began arriving in the 1950s and 1960s, English-as-a-second-language (ESL) instruction was advanced as a strategy. Here, immigrant children competed with native English speakers in academic courses without bilingual support. But many students did not succeed with this strategy, so some local districts decided to establish bilingual schools long before the first federal legislation required bilingual education.

## BILINGUAL EDUCATION AND LEGAL COMPLIANCE

Under the leadership of President Lyndon B. Johnson, Congress passed the Civil Rights Act of 1964. Title VI of this act states:

> No person in the United States shall, on the ground of race, color, or national origin, be excluded from participation in, be denied the benefits of, or be subjected to discrimination under any program or activity receiving federal financial assistance.

The title VI requirements protect students with limited proficiency in English because interpretations of the law have defined failure to provide services to the LEP student as "denying them equal access to an education." Denied access because of a linguistic barrier, they are unable to participate in or benefit from regular or special education programs.

During the late 1960s, the Office of Civil Rights (OCR) became aware that many school districts were making little or no provision for LEP students even though a substantial number of these students were enrolled. This led to the development of a memorandum officially titled "Identification of Discrimination and Denial of Services on the Basis of National Origin," issued by the Department of Health, Education, and Welfare. The memorandum was distributed to school districts that had a population of international minority children greater than 5% of the total. This memorandum, which is informally referred to as the "May 25th Memorandum," states:

> Where the inability to speak and understand the English language excludes national origin minority group children from effective participation in the educational program offered by a school district, the district must take affirmative steps to rectify the language deficiency in order to open its instructional program to these students.

In 1974, a landmark U.S. Supreme Court decision (*Lau v. Nichols*) unanimously upheld the May 25th Memorandum based on the provisions of the Civil Rights Act of 1964. The court concluded that 1,800 Chinese students in the San Francisco area were not being provided with equal educational opportunity compared with their English-speaking peers. The Lau remedies were issued as suggested guidelines for complying with title VI.

Title VI compliance is ensured by the OCR, which routinely investigates complaints of discrimination against state and local districts. Although the May 25th Memorandum does not mandate, specify, or prescribe the steps a district must take to ensure "effective participation in the educational program," the OCR examines some important issues, including the following:

- Has a district identified all LEP students who need special language assistance?
- Has it ensured the placement of LEP students in appropriate programs?
- Has it provided a special language assistance program for all LEP students who need such a program?
- Has it taken steps to modify a program for LEP students when that program is not working?
- Has it ensured that LEP students are not misassigned to classes for mentally handicapped students because of their inability to speak and understand English?
- Has it ensured that parents who are not proficient in English are provided with appropriate and sufficient information about all school activities?

Because there are significant differences in student populations, and the needs of bilingual students vary from state to state and district to district, the OCR allows districts broad discretion about what provisions may be taken to ensure an equal educational opportunity. For more information about the specific provisions for bilingual education in your state, contact your state department of education.

## THE DEFINITION OF A BILINGUAL STUDENT

There are many myths and misconceptions about who can actually be classified as a bilingual student. To comply with the specifications of the May 25th Memorandum, school districts must identify and assess students who are potentially eligible to receive bilingual services. Typically, each state department of education has developed a questionnaire or home language survey designed to identify the home language. These surveys may be modified at the district level to satisfy local needs, but they generally focus on questions in two areas: Does the student speak a language other than English? Is there a language other than English spoken in the home? Based on the answers to these questions, students may fall into one of the following six categories on the language-acquisition continuum and thus be considered bilingual:

1. A non-English-speaking student who is monolingual in his or her home language
2. A limited-English speaker who is fluent in a language other than English
3. A student who speaks both English and a language other than English fluently
4. A student who is limited in both English and a language other than English
5. A student who speaks English fluently but is limited in a language other than English
6. A student who speaks English fluently but does not speak another language

As we stated earlier, there are many myths and misconceptions about the classification of a student as bilingual. It may be obvious that a foreign-born student who speaks little or no English but is fluent in his or her native language qualifies for bilingual services. Similarly, a child who communicates well in two languages is readily viewed as bilingual. However, many people wonder why a student who speaks only English can be considered bilingual. Furthermore, educators are often reluctant to believe that an apparently fluent English speaker can have a bilingual issue based on mixed-language experiences, which may interfere with his or her reading comprehension. Some assume that a non-English- or limited-English-speaking student could not have been born in the United States.

# LANGUAGE ACQUISITION

If you have never personally experienced a bilingual home, the classifications discussed in the previous section may seem confusing and even illogical. They become much clearer and more useful when we explore the complex process of language acquisition. The following example illustrates just one example of a bilingual home from which a student classified in category 6 might come. We have chosen this illustration because this type of bilingual student, who has a mixed language background and is fluent but not yet proficient in English, is most misunderstood by general educators.

Imagine the following scenario. You enter a bilingual home where the children are watching television in the living room. The phone rings, and the mother answers in English: "Hello?" As soon as the caller is identified, she begins speaking in her native language. Distracted by the noise, the mother asks the children to turn off the television in her native language. The children understand her request but answer in English, telling her that the program is almost over and they want to watch for a few more minutes. Soon visitors arrive at the home and greet the children in their native language. The visitors' children go off to play with their hosts, and the adults have coffee in the living room. The adults speak their native language, but the children speak English. When the adults speak to redirect the children, they use their native tongue. The children understand these directions but respond in English.

Based on this scenario, can we conclude that the language development of these children is distinctly different from the language development of children raised in a home where English is the only language spoken? Do the children from these two environments hear the same or similar modeling of vocabulary and speech patterns? Will this difference affect their school performance in terms of their ability to respond to oral directions, comprehend lectures, and extract information from academic textbooks?

Sometimes the impact is quite significant. Too often, the bilingual child may be unsuccessful if asked to explain concepts in either English or the native language and is then assumed to have some type of language impairment. Yet this skill deficit is most accurately attributed to the complex mixture of productive and receptive language to which the child has been exposed. Such misunderstanding can lead to the inappropriate placement of LEP students into special education programs.

There are many levels of language acquisition in bilingual children. The strongest and first language of a child is usually labeled L1, and the second language is L2. Interestingly, sometimes English is not L1, even for the child who was born and raised in the United States. This is very important for educators to understand because without this awareness many inappropriate decisions and assumptions could be made for children. The issue of language acquisition must be a point of focus when choosing instructional interventions that best match the student's instructional needs.

To understand this important framework for responding to bilingual students, let's go back to the previous scenario: The children are watching television; the adults are speaking one language and the children another. The children would be considered to have productive and receptive language in English but only receptive language in the mother's native language. It is also possible that the older children in the family did not speak English fluently when they began kindergarten but did speak the mother's native language. One of these children may be in fourth grade and having a great deal of difficulty understanding academic content. Let's assume that this child spent a vast percentage of her learning energy in the primary grades understanding the routine of the school day, learning English to meet her survival needs, memorizing common songs, understanding the stories she heard, and making friends at play. Is it possible that she might not have learned all the upper and lowercase letters and sound-symbol relationships as fast or as easily as students who spoke only English?

Extending this scenario even further, consider a child who has developed in one language until age 5 and then suddenly arrests that language development in favor of English. Language foundations such as sentence structure, vocabulary, and concept development have been partially formed in the native language. The student then transfers whatever concepts she knows, such as requesting basic needs and understanding the names of colors and foods, into English words and structures. From now on, all future concept building must be done in the new language. The student must learn not only a concept but learn it in her least-competent language.

Over time, this child "forgets" her first language. But the specialized vocabulary used in school for directions, literature, science, and social studies is unknown to her. She may have a vague idea of what is being studied, but in first and second grade the books have lots of pictures, and the language is not too demanding cognitively. Many hands-on experiences, context clues, and 3 years in an English environment have led staff members to the erroneous conclusion that the student is a proficient user of the English language. Then third grade begins, with its attendant increase in content-area curricular demands. All of the sudden, the student who looked pretty good and performed fairly well seems to fall apart. Can we begin to understand why?

Students with prior knowledge of concepts in one language can quickly transfer labels or vocabulary into another language and then learn phrases for explaining conceptual processes if they know these concepts and terms in their strongest language first (L1). Prior knowledge in L1, the native language, is among the factors that can be used to predict faster and more successful academic language learning. Collier (1987) studied the amount of time it took immigrant children to become proficient in English relative to the age they arrived in the United States. The study looked at three groups of students: those arriving between the ages of 5 and 7, 8 and 11, and 12 and older.

Most people would assume that the youngest students would be the most successful, but they were not. There is a prevalent misconception that younger children are better language learners. The reasons for this misconception are twofold: Young children learn English without an accent, and the speech and cognitive processes expected of a 5-year-old are less complex and easier to produce than those of older students.

Collier found that the 8- to 11-year-olds experienced the fastest success because of their ability to read, write, and process in the first language and because of their prior knowledge and experience in using language in academic contexts. This age group had experienced school language in L1 and could transfer that experience to the new language. In addition, academic language in third, fourth, and fifth grade is less cognitively demanding than language at the secondary level.

The oldest group of students (12 and older) also benefited from having prior knowledge in their native languages, which may lead you to believe that high school students might be the first to acquire language proficiency. We should clarify, however, that Collier's study was examining the fastest learners, not the learners who would be better off in the long run. Recall that academic language and content demands are significantly easier at the elementary levels than they are at the secondary levels. Therefore, high school students, who are developing both basic interpersonal communication skills and the development of cognitive-academic language in more complex contexts, frequently graduate before those processes are complete. Nevertheless, many of them eventually do remarkably well and move on to higher education.

Other factors influence the rate and ease with which a student becomes proficient at academic language and experiences success in school. Students whose home language uses the same alphabet as English may go through some initial interference in the reading process, but the similar alphabet, directionality of text, and cognates from one language to another greatly influence this process. Languages with similar word order (syntax), parts of speech, and sounds are also easier to learn because prior skills can be transferred.

However, consider the challenges faced by a Chinese student, who initially learns to read in columns from top to bottom and turns pages from left to right. The student must also memorize thousands of characters that "picture" each word or concept. Wouldn't this student see phonics as a task with no clear purpose? Chinese has no past tense but uses a linguistic mark to indicate the past. How could past-tense verb forms be an intelligible concept for a Chinese student who is beginning to read English?

Second-language acquisition theories are less mysterious and more understandable when they are compared to learning a first language. Babies first learn language by listening to and observing the modeling of their family members, caregivers, and even strangers in public places. People speak to babies as if they understand. Language is used in context. Parents do not overcorrect their children when they begin to speak but show excitement and encouragement while modeling corrections of their children's mistakes. Among young children, there is a natural desire to communicate, and parents are the very best language teachers.

Let's consider some examples. A mother and her 18-month-old child are shopping. They go down the aisle in a toy store.

The baby says, "Ball," and points to a ball.

The mother may pull the ball off the shelf and smile, repeating, "Yes, ball, ball. You said, 'Ball.' That's a ball. Isn't it a nice ball? Do you want the ball?"

The child smiles and claps, saying, "Ball." The ball goes into the cart.

Later, a woman walks by and comments to the mother about how cute the baby is. She asks the child's age. The mother replies. The woman looks at the baby and says, "What's your name?"

The baby stares blankly at the woman.

The mother says, "Her name is Caroline."

The woman comments, "What a lovely name!" and moves on to continue her shopping.

Can you begin to see the subtle process of language acquisition? This child has just experienced a rich language lesson delivered within a natural, contextualized approach. Again, think about the vast difference in the number of hours of English language experience shared by the bilingual student versus the native English speaker.

## SECOND-LANGUAGE ACQUISITION: KEY CONCEPTS

While it is important to note that there is an abundance of theories on second-language acquisition, there are identifiable key concepts that teachers of English language learners (ELL) should know in order to effectively teach these students in the regular classroom. These key themes have been extracted from the various theories on second-language acquisition.

It is also significant to note that while specific student training in second-language acquisition, provided by support staff, is very important in educating English language learners (ELL), regular classroom teachers positively impact these students when they become knowledgeable about these key concepts. The language acquisition process can not be effectively facilitated through bilingual or English-as-a-second-language (ESL) instruction that is not supported through regular classroom practice.

These concepts, abstracted from the various theories on second-language acquisition, will be delineated and followed by implications for classroom application.

### 1. Language Acquisition Is a Process the Human Brain Does Well

We are social creatures with a complicated system of communication. The human brain is essentially "wired" for language acquisition. We naturally acquire our first language without consciously thinking about it. Parents do not go out of their way to teach their children how to use the language. This is evidenced by examples of the complex language that young children can produce. A 3-year-old child can construct a sentence using the past-perfect continuous tense without a single grammar lesson. Parents do provide the rich environment and climate necessary for language acquisition to occur.

### Implication for the Classroom

Teachers should provide an environment conducive to language acquisition that is rich in stimulus and interaction, free of threat, and that provides ample opportunities for communication among students.

## 2. Students Learn a Second Language in Different Ways and at Different Paces

Although there are similar pathways students travel when acquiring a second language, there are also notable individual differences. These differences can be due to a number of factors, including learning style, language background, educational experience, native language proficiency, linguistic aptitude, motivation, and personal history, among others. These differences can be a source of genuine frustration for teachers. This is especially true when students do not meet the benchmarks that teachers have come to expect from English language learners.

### Implications for the Classroom

Teachers can work to accommodate individual differences in student learning patterns and should be flexible in setting benchmarks. Some students will start verbalizing within weeks, while others might take months or longer.

## 3. Language Acquisition Is Not Easy for Children

Learning a second language is no small task. Contrary to conventional wisdom, it is not necessarily easier for children to acquire a second language (Collier, 1989; Genessee, 1987). Unlike adults, children can generally acquire a second language without an accent, but adults can become proficient at a much faster rate. This is probably due to many factors, the most important of which is the proficiency level within the native language. Adults need linguistic labels for concepts with which they are already familiar, while children need to learn the concepts as well as the language associated with them.

### Implications for the Classroom

- Teachers should encourage their students to keep, use, and further develop their first language.
- Teachers should modify lessons to accommodate English language learners.
- Teachers should not assume students will just acquire the language without support.

# 4. Learning a Second Language Takes Time

Research has demonstrated that second-language acquisition might take up to 7 years to accomplish (Hakuta, 2000). Oral fluency alone can take from 3 to 5 years to develop, while academic proficiency can take 4 to 7 years. Other research studies have indicated that the process might take as long as 10 years (Garcia, 1998). Obviously individual differences exist and are influenced by many factors like ability, motivation, and readiness. Access to effective instructional practices can also change the length of the process.

### Implications for the Classroom

- Teachers should be patient with second-language learners.
- Lack of English proficiency does not necessarily indicate a disability or a deficit.
- Teachers should provide students with instruction that promotes English acquisition.
- Students can be provided with additional support from specialized programs within and outside the classroom environment.

# 5. Proficiency in a Native Language Supports Second-Language Acquisition

Studies have consistently demonstrated that the ease with which students acquire academic proficiency in a second language is directly related to the strength of the native language (Krashen & Biber, 1998). Other research (Collier & Thomas, 1989) has concluded that English language learners who have had schooling in their native language first become proficient with English much faster than do students who have not had any schooling in their native language. Cummins (1989) has drawn an analogy between the experiences of a bilingual student who is learning a second language and a person who is riding various kinds of bikes (Figure 3.1). If we imagine that each wheel of the bike represents a language, then the student who is monolingual regularly travels on a unicycle. He can get places and the ride is interesting, but some terrain is inhospitable. Riding the old-fashioned two-wheeler with the big front wheel is like having one strong language and another that is not as strong but still helpful. You can travel over a broader range of territory with less risk than you can on the unicycle. But if you have two good-sized wheels that are nicely balanced and fully inflated, you can go much further and faster. Riding this effective and efficient two-wheeled bike is like having two strong languages. The options for the traveler are much broader. However, a haphazard approach to second-language acquisition could result in a two-wheeled bike whose wheels are not fully functional. Students who are not provided with the experiences necessary to develop at least one strong language first are severely limited. Such a vehicle will not get the traveler very far at all.

One wheel can get you places…

So can a big wheel and a little wheel…

However, when your wheels are nicely balanced and fully inflated you'll go further…

Provided, of course, the people who made the wheels knew what they were doing…

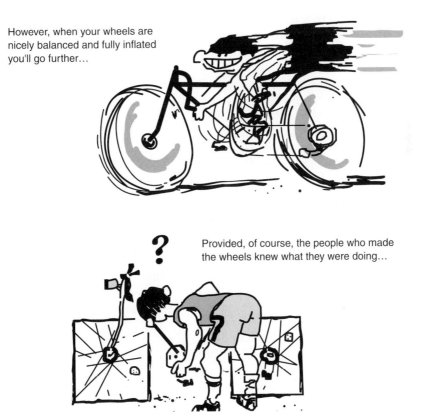

**FIGURE 3.1**
The bicycle analogy.

*Source:* Cummins, J. (1989). *Empowering minority students* (p. 43). Sacramento: California Association for Bilingual Education.

Implications for the Classroom

- Encourage the student's use of the native language. Use native language speakers when available.
- Encourage the use of native language materials when available.
- Encourage parents to continue to use the native language in the home.
- Staff should learn survival vocabulary in the native language when possible.

# 6. Students Acquire Language in Stages

Students develop a second language in stages. Different labels have been given to the different stages by various researchers. Krashen's stages have been widely used, and, in the writers' opinion, provide teachers with the clearest and most useful labels.

*I. Pre-production Stage:* The pre-production stage is often known as the "silent period." It may last up to 1 to 2 years or could end within weeks. The speed of language acquisition can be impacted by the student's level of comfort and development of social language. During this period the child is actively inputting language and developing patterns of interaction at a primarily nonverbal level. During this time the child should be assessed on listening skills alone, preferably in a manner that is not language dependent. Peer interaction is important at this stage and supports the development of language to help negotiate the meaning of more difficult concepts later.

*II. Early Production Stage:* This stage may begin within weeks of arrival in the new setting or may be delayed several months. At this stage the child begins to manipulate the language he or she has acquired to communicate his or her needs. A great deal of input is still necessary. Responses will be short one- or two-word phrases. The student will find abundant written and spoken models beneficial. Peer interaction is still critical, and many of these interactions become increasingly complex verbally. There is a need for increased attention to demonstrations of concepts and the language that accompanies them. Early literacy skills are being acquired, and the child may become somewhat adept at decoding but have negligible comprehension skills.

*III. Speech Emergence Stage:* At this stage the child becomes a risk taker and much more verbal. Development in this stage, where academic language begins to take hold, is dependent upon comfort level, motivation, prior literacy level, support, and input. Language and written expression at this point may show numerous errors, but corrections should be modeled examples rather than overt corrections. The child may begin to read for pleasure, and book selection should be guided to age and language-appropriate levels. High expectations can increase motivation, but should remain realistically flexible.

*IV. Intermediate Fluency Stage:* The child becomes more capable of dealing with academic language and producing independent language. Written expression can be more individualized and creative. Spoken language nears fluency, which can be distracting to the observer who notes variations and inconsistencies in skill level.

Implications for the Classroom

- Lesson plans should be aligned with the identified stage of language development.
- When testing children it is important to note that any content area test is a language test as well for English language learners.
- Preview lessons for English Language Learners using support staff when available.
- Set appropriate expectations for classroom participation.

## 7. Silence Is Sometimes Needed

Some English language learners go through the silent period mentioned previously. During this time, the learner is inputting language but is not ready to output it. Some teachers are uneasy with the silent period when they assume that they are not reaching the student. This assumption can put undue pressure on both the teacher and student and may result in a longer silent period. The period can last days, weeks, or in some instances months. At times, a silent period can be generated by challenging events within or outside the classroom.

Implications for the Classroom

- Teachers should allow the students to experience the silent period if necessary.
- Teachers should provide a risk-free environment where students feel free to make mistakes and try things.
- Teachers should make other students aware of the needs of English language learners.

## 8. Fluency on the Playground Does Not Indicate Proficiency in the Classroom

The distinction between language fluency and proficiency is also an important consideration for teachers who are assessing bilingual students. A student who demonstrates fluency in English during peer interactions will not necessarily be proficient in classroom discourse. Social interactions are important and sometimes complex, but they do not approach the level of complexity required for classroom-based academic learning. Students who are fluent on the playground may require 4 to 6 years of additional English study before they will attain the level of proficiency required to be regularly successful in the classroom (Collier, 1987). Because of their fluency in the language these students are sometimes mislabeled as special education students, when what they lack is academic proficiency. Some districts have developed procedures to guard against such misplacements (see Figure 3.4 on page 84 for an example).

Implications for the Classroom

- Teachers should get to know their students at a deeper level.
- Do not assume proficiency because students sound like native English speakers.

## 9. Students Need Content to Learn English

Language is best taught through meaningful content. It is more effective to use social studies or literature to teach English than to use drill and practice. Teaching becomes much more effective if what is taught is meaningful to the learner because it draws on concepts the student already knows or past experiences. Studies on the Canadian Immersion programs (Genessee, 1987) have documented that students become more proficient in the language when they are immersed in meaningful content.

Implications for the Classroom

- The study of academic content can't wait until students become proficient in the language. Content and language acquisition go hand-in-hand.
- Use modified instruction to deliver content to English language learners.

## 10. Students Need Meaningful Interaction with Native Speakers to Learn a Second Language

Language learning is enhanced and accelerated when opportunities to use the language are provided. When situations requiring communication are present, students are compelled to learn and use the language. Learning a language means learning to do the things you want to do with people that speak that language.

Implications for the Classroom

- Teachers should provide conscious and consistent opportunities for English language learners to interact with native speakers in the classroom. This can be accomplished through cooperative learning, group projects, literature circles, and so forth.

## 11. Errors in Language Productions Indicate Progress

As with first-language acquisition, errors indicate progress (Zehler, 1994). A child learning his first language might make a mistake like, "He goed to the store." When this happens it indicates that the child has internalized the need for a grammatical structure regarding past tense and is working to implement it. Such errors are almost always effectively corrected through modeling. "You mean to say, 'He went to the store.'" When errors occur with second-language learners it should be thought of as a necessary stage in language acquisition. It should be dealt with through modeling and not direct correction.

Implications for the Classroom

Teachers should be tolerant of mistakes and work to model and have fellow students model the correct form of the language.

## 12. Receptive Language Skills Are Usually More Advanced Than Productive Skills

As with the first language, receptive language skills are almost always more advanced than productive skills. We normally understand more vocabulary terms than we are generally able to use effectively. This presents a set of issues for teachers of second-language learners, especially in assessment situations. Students can't fully express their thoughts because of limited working vocabulary and language structures.

Implications for the Classroom

- Modify assignments and use alternative assessments.
- Consider the use of group assignments.

## APPROACHING BILINGUAL STUDENTS

Bilingual programs throughout the United States vary significantly from place to place because of the varying demographic characteristics of specific communities. There are two basic approaches: an English-as-a-second-language approach (ESL) and a bilingual approach. Both have the common goal of providing effective instruction in an environment that comfortably supports a student in his or her new culture and promotes literacy in English. These two approaches work best when used in combination with the inclusion model delineated in the other chapters in this book.

The ESL approach uses an English-only framework to teach students without native language instruction. A bilingual approach uses native language instruction to teach reading, writing, and important concepts. Students are also taught English orally, but reading instruction in English follows after reading proficiency in the native language has been established.

During the early 20th century, immigrant children in the United States had no special provision for instruction. A strategy known as *submersion*—the "sink or swim" approach—meant that students who could not speak English were placed into regular classrooms without modifications under the assumption that they would just pick up the language. However, most students failed or dropped out of school as a result of this approach. Submersion is no longer legal or appropriate in an age of sophisticated technology and high-speed communication. Please note that submersion is not the same as inclusion.

Bilingual instruction is usually provided by bilingual paraprofessionals or certified bilingual teachers who speak the native language of the students. Most states offer a bilingual or ESL endorsement on teaching certificates, which indicates specialized teacher training in ESL instruction and theories of language acquisition. The bilingual endorsement requires proficiency in the language of endorsement.

When state departments of education and local school districts are deciding on the best approaches for teaching bilingual students in their particular setting, they must consider demographics. If districts have a substantial portion of their bilingual population from the same or similar culture group, all speaking a common language, bilingual approaches are more prevalent. Districts with wide diversity among the bilingual population tend to follow an ESL approach. However, if there are large groups of bilingual students in a diverse bilingual community, you may find a strong combination of both bilingual and ESL approaches. The bilingual component is invaluable because it relates to the comfort of students and the effectiveness of instruction. The additional support provided by a bilingual approach is significant for students, teachers, and parents when they communicate with each other about language and culture.

Although there is conflicting evidence about the effectiveness of any single approach, long-run success seems most dependent on three factors: (a) the consistent use of strategies and techniques that are research-based and identified as best practice; (b) the appropriate match of language-delivery strategies (with L1, L2, or both) with the students' needs; and (c) the inclusion, acceptance, and interaction of the bilingual student in the school and culture.

The following chart compares an ESL approach delivered through two very different sets of strategies and approaches.

| *Best Practice* | *Worst Practice* |
| --- | --- |
| Students learn words and concepts in thematic units. | Students learn words and concepts randomly. |
| Students are taught using higher-order thinking and metacognitive strategies. | Students are taught through rote learning with lots of drill and practice. |
| Reading, writing, listening, and speaking are integrated. | Listening and speaking are taught separately from reading and writing. |
| Culture is a constant consideration when interacting with students, and components of culture are used in instructional units. | Culture is downplayed and undervalued. Students are forbidden to speak their native language. |
| Students are encouraged to use their native language with peers. | Students are isolated from and not encouraged to interact with native-English-speaking peers for much of the school day. |
| Flexible grouping in experiential activities allows for much interaction with native-English-speaking peers. | |

The integration of approaches should also match the intervention with the student's level of language acquisition in L1 or L2. If a bilingual student is strong in L1 (his or her native language), bilingual instruction would best serve that student as opposed to an entirely English system of instruction. If the student is more fluent in English, an ESL approach or inclusion with modifications in instruction as needed would best serve the student. Willingness to value and integrate aspects of each approach will give educators more opportunities to match the needs of students with the interventions that would benefit them most.

In the past, as with other specialized programs such as gifted and talented and special education, service to bilingual students was usually compartmentalized and coordinated separately from the regular classroom. The delivery of service typically took place outside of the classroom. As more and more research drives educators toward an inclusive philosophy, bilingual education will be advanced by the integration of inclusion strategies.

A final note regarding approaches for bilingual students: Sometimes temporary arrangements are made to accelerate English language development for students who have little or no English language proficiency. The reason for this is obviously because there is a limit to the accommodations and modifications that can be done in the regular classroom. If a school district registers a significant number of non-English-speaking students, intensive English language instruction may be provided while mainstreaming students in other courses. It is critical that these students interact with English-speaking peers for a significant portion of their day.

## THE IMPORTANCE OF CULTURE

Everything we do is influenced by our culture. Culture pervades our ways of thinking, behaving, believing, and valuing. It is reflected in what we choose to eat, wear, read, listen to, and watch. How we spend our time, where we work, who we visit, how we worship, and what we do for fun are also affected by culture.

Like the components of a sophisticated camera, these aspects of an individual's culture serve to define the aperture through which he or she views the world. The curve of the lens, the size of the opening, and the character and quality of the filters all contribute to the nature of the world view held by the individual. This is as it should be when a culture is homogenous and shares deeply rooted ideals about how life is conducted. This is part of the vehicle that conveys the characteristics of a culture from one generation to another. The challenge emerges when people from different cultures focus their cameras on the same image and get snapshots of life with radically different interpretations. For example, a veteran teacher may have acquired some specific ideas about child behavior based on study and broad experience with students from a majority culture. Then, when observing a student from a minority culture, the teacher could form judgments and reach erroneous conclusions about a student's performance because the student's behavior is culturally influenced in a way that the teacher's camera does not recognize. As another example, avoiding eye contact during conversation may be interpreted by American teachers as rude or, perhaps, an admission of guilt. Yet in many cultures this behavior is encouraged as a sign of respect shown for superiors. Similarly, from the perspective of some students from minority cultures, the behavior of handing something to another person with the left hand, as opposed to the right, is an insult. Others are mystified about why American teachers don't like to be addressed respectfully as "teacher."

The generalizations a teacher might make regarding child development, from experience with students of the majority culture, do not always apply to students from minority cultures. What might be considered normal verbal interactions between children and adults in one culture could be considered either disrespectful or developmentally delayed in another. Assumptions made about the set of experiences a student has had prior to school will frequently not match the reality, whether it is content-related issues like understanding the meaning of terms such as fireworks or snow or skill-related issues like having spent time shopping in a superstore or playing a video game.

Social conventions frequently do not translate well for bilingual students or their parents. For example, something many American educators do not understand is that the delineation of roles and responsibilities between school and home is largely culturally determined. Many parents of LEP students have cultural barriers that prevent them from being active participants in their child's education. This is not based on ignorance or lack of concern but on experiences in the native culture. For example, in middle-eastern educational systems, there is no provision for parents to be involved with the school. The school is considered the absolute authority, and even though parents care very much about their children's education, they may have never entered the school building. When these parents emigrate to the United States and fail to attend parent conferences, their actions are often misinterpreted as "not caring" rather than the result of a cultural barrier. Some parents avoid conferences because they do not understand their purpose, fear that their English is too poor, or worry that the teacher will scold them for speaking their home language with their children. Further, the use of educational jargon, which is often challenging for native-English-speaking parents, has the effect of setting up additional hurdles for minority parents to negotiate.

Language and culture cannot be separated. Many immigrants intuitively understand this and consciously teach and reinforce the home language to their children, knowing that "if you lose the language, you lose the culture." To understand and value a student's culture, we must value and seek to understand some of the subtleties of his or her language and its role in shaping behavior.

A theory called *contrastive analysis* describes the transfers made from one language or dialect to another (Dulay, Burt, & Krashen, 1982). Because students write what they say, aspects of accent, grammar, and syntax will appear in their writing. Students will need time to make the transition to all the conventions of English. (For more information on aspects of the home language and comparisons, contact the Center for Applied Linguistics; see Table 3.1 for the address.)

It would be impossible to construct a list of all the potential culturally determined mismatches a teacher might encounter. The key to success is developing a willingness to learn about the cultures of the students in our classrooms and the many perspectives they bring to school. We can do this by adjusting the cameras with which we view the world. Effective cameras need wide-angle lenses, broad openings, and few filters. Such action will no doubt result in more understanding, communication, and success.

**TABLE 3.1**
Adaptive materials for English as a second language.

| Company | Comments |
| --- | --- |
| Addison-Wesley Publishing Company<br>Reading, MA<br>(800) 552-2259 | Addison-Wesley ESL, Longman catalog (Longman is a division of Addison-Wesley)<br>Longman Classics Set of Rewritten Literature |
| Children's Press<br>(a division of Grolier Publishing)<br>Danbury, CT<br>(800) 621-1115 | Children's Press catalog<br>Rookie Readers and Rookie Biographies |
| Ballard and Tighe<br>Brea, CA<br>(800) 321-4332 | Thematically approached elementary ESL series with excellent literature integration |
| Prentice Hall<br>Old Tappan, NJ<br>(515) 284-6751 | Side by Side series for ESL middle and high school organized by themes, grammar, and functions<br>Expressways series especially for adult-oriented situations |
| Alemany Press<br>Division of Prentice Hall<br>Silven Ave., Route 9, West PHR Building<br>Englewood Cliffs, NJ 07632 | Classroom Teacher's ESL Survival Kit #1 |
| Dorling Kindersley<br>Family Learning, Inc.<br>(407) 857-5463 | Excellent resource for providing content with outstanding visuals; well organized and includes picture dictionaries and books about children and culture |
| Center for Applied Linguistics<br>1611 North Kent Street<br>Arlington, VA 22209 | |
| National Clearinghouse for Bilingual Education (NCBE)<br>(800) 321-NCBE<br>E-mail: askncbe@ncbe.gwu.edu<br>BBS: (800) 752-1860 | Resource for research, information, and instruction for bilingual students |

# THEORIES AND MODELS

The following theories and models offer a brief overview of the most important research on bilingual students and provide a framework for understanding the students' instructional needs.

## Comprehensible Input

Founded on the premise that second-language acquisition must parallel first-language acquisition, Krashen's (1989) theory of comprehensible input insists that language must be taught through meaning and context. Using visuals, preteaching academic lessons in the native language, and providing alternative textbooks written at an appropriate level of language challenge are examples of curricular modifications of content-area material that make it more accessible to the LEP student.

An important phenomenon of second-language acquisition is the silent period (Krashen, 1982). Just as very young children frequently go through periods when they do not speak, even though their parents know that they understand, bilingual students may not speak for up to 6 months. This has been observed more frequently among students who are introverted, less confident, or fearful. Factors such as risk taking, perfectionism, and affect also play a role.

The silent period is frequently misunderstood by educators. Like very young children, LEP students need to spend time first in receptive language learning. Some even learn to read during this period, but all eventually speak when they have reached the needed comfort level supported by their increased language acquisition. They may jump from single words before the silent period to complete sentences following it. In contrast, many outgoing and confident students will begin speaking immediately and make steady progress from words to phrases to sentences.

Pervading all of the discussion in this chapter is the belief that limited-English-proficient students should be held to the high expectations established for all students. When these expectations are addressed through thoughtful instruction that builds on their previous education and current language proficiency levels, we increase the probability that the students will find the instruction more user-friendly. A variety of factors in the affective domain, including personality, culture, and feelings of acceptance, can greatly affect the ability of a student to acquire a second language. Much research has been done on this topic. Cummins (1981) and Krashen (1982) have also examined the role of acceptance of the LEP student by the target language culture as it relates to effective language learning. Remaining sensitive to this affective domain factor is critical to the success of all LEP students regardless of age or experience.

More and more, current research replaces the LEP (limited-English-proficient) acronym with the more positive ELL (English language learner). Focusing on the positive, the strengths of students, and the goal will promote greater teacher expectation and student success.

Language will develop over time. Teachers must understand that mistakes indicate progress, that transfers will eventually be made from the native language, and that the emphasis of instruction should remain on clear communication. Paying attention to what is being said, as opposed to how, will enhance the affective domain.

## The SAALE Model

The SAALE model provides numerous instructional accommodations and a systematic approach that can be adopted for bilingual students. Although bilingualism is not an impairment, many of the tools identified in the SAALE model (such as the note-taking strategies designed for the hearing impaired) work well with bilingual students when appropriately matched to the students' needs. Furthermore, the inclusion options discussed in the SAALE model have tremendous application for teachers within the context of the bilingual approaches previously described.

Collaboration among teachers as described in the SAALE model provides the opportunity for a valuable exchange of ideas and materials, which empowers the regular classroom teacher to provide an equitable education for LEP students. ESL and bilingual teachers, who are language-acquisition and culture experts, cannot also be experts in all content areas at all grade levels. Regular classroom teachers are needed to provide the clarity and richness of concepts and vocabulary in the curriculum.

ESL and bilingual teachers, along with bilingual paraprofessionals, can suggest modifications of language and materials to ensure that the curricular content is consumable by the bilingual student. They can also provide better communication about the school and classroom for parents with limited English. ESL/bilingual staff have insights into the cultural factors that may influence bilingual students in areas such as prior knowledge, holidays, customs, and religious beliefs. These insights may enable them to work with students and parents to facilitate change of some erroneous perceptions based on language and cultural differences.

Inclusion provides the bilingual student with more time in the classroom to interact with his or her English-speaking peers. Because students learn English to communicate and participate in activities with other English language speakers, peer interaction is essential for language development. The lack of meaningful interaction among bilingual and native-English-speaking students has been a major criticism of bilingual programs in the past.

Together, classroom teachers and support staff can use the SAALE model to assess a student's skill level, set goals for themselves and the students, select appropriate strategies for delivery of instruction that match the student's, and monitor the student's progress. All the information and strategies delineated in this text regarding the inclusion model in the special education setting can be applied to bilingual education. Again, the only modifications needed in the SAALE model are related to the unique aspects of bilingual students and speakers of nonstandard English.

Several approaches and models that bilingual educators particularly employ to deliver curriculum and teach ESL are confluent with SAALE. They are the natural approach, active learning, and CALLA (the cognitive academic language learning approach). Many of the same excellent strategies and modifications are woven throughout each approach because all are research-based best practices and consequently good teaching practices.

## The Natural Approach

This approach (Krashen & Terrell, 1983) mirrors the early-language acquisition of young children and is designed to nurture personal communication skills in both the oral and written streams. The basic personal communications goals are generally discussed in terms of situations (such as the grocery store), functions (such as locating items), and topics (such as low-salt canned vegetables). The emphasis of this approach is not academic learning or grammatical accuracy but using a thematic approach that builds the students' ability to understand the meaning of their communication. In addition to emphasizing topics for communication, this approach has several other guiding principles: (a) comprehension precedes production; (b) production is allowed to emerge in stages, and students are not compelled to speak until ready; (c) speech errors that do not interfere with communication are not corrected; (d) instructors must pay attention to the affective filter when assessing the relevancy of topics; and (e) a low-anxiety environment is essential.

The SAALE model's socioemotional component completely fits this approach, so ESL and bilingual teachers will immediately grasp the benefits that bilingual students will enjoy with teachers who are already implementing this functional language-learning strategy. Not only does this component make language more comprehensible in a meaningful environment; it also helps the student to know exactly what is expected and eases the culture shock that many students face. (For examples of differences in school culture faced by students from foreign countries, consult *The Classroom Teacher's ESL Survival Kit #1* [Claire & Haynes, 1994]).

As long as teachers remember to make minor accommodations in pace and regular comprehension checks of vocabulary, bilingual students will benefit significantly from role plays and video demonstrations of learning when acquiring language in context. Additionally, translating and adapting the comprehensive SAALE checklist and educating parents about the culture of American schools and classrooms can be helpful.

## Active Learning

Active learning is based on the cognition theories of Paolo Freire (1981) and L. S. Vygotsky (1978). Freire's theory promotes the notion that effective learning is situated within a student's own knowledge and world view. Vygotsky's "zone of proximal development" supports the idea that students learn best when new information is just beyond the reach of their present knowledge. Active learners share responsibility with the teacher for their classroom experiences and their learning, and what could be more relevant and closer to the world view of the learner than the classroom? The SAALE model's socioemotional component also addresses the ineffectiveness of content that is either too easy or too frustrating for the student.

A method related to active learning is total physical response (TPR). Developed by J. J. Asher (1977), TPR is useful for both children and adults in the early stages of second-language acquisition. When following this method, the teacher gives commands to the students and then models the physical movements necessary to carry out the commands. At first, the students focus on listening and responding with appropriate physical movement. Later they begin speaking the command themselves and eventually move to reading and writing. This total physical response increases access to long-term memory.

# Cognitive Academic Language Learning Approach

The cognitive academic language learning approach (CALLA) (Chamot & O'Malley, 1987) is an instructional model for modifying content-area instruction for bilingual students using cognitive, social-affective, and metacognitive strategies. It was developed in response to the research on BICS (basic interpersonal communication skills) and CALPS (cognitive academic language proficiency skills) (Cummins, 1980) in an effort to reduce the amount of time it would take bilingual students to acquire CALPS. It is also based on research that concludes that higher-order thinking strategies and student awareness of learning strategies make instruction more effective. Again, there is much confluence and overlap with the SAALE model, with only minor modifications needed for bilingual students.

Both CALLA and SAALE emphasize the need for increased sensitivity to the learning needs of specific learners when teachers analyze curriculum and materials, present the curriculum, and assess a student's need for modifications. Other strategies such as incorporating higher-order thinking, helping students organize information with outlines and graphic organizers, adapting textbook assignments and assessments, using visuals, adapting note-taking strategies, and listening to books on tape are also shared by the models. Cooperative learning and peer tutoring are included as strategies by both CALLA and SAALE.

Because CALLA has been specifically designed for English-language learners, it gives more attention to assessing the student's prior knowledge and preteaching lesson vocabulary and content than the SAALE model does. This shift in emphasis increases the instructional effectiveness and relevance for bilingual students in the actual presentation of the lesson. Many content lessons have a cultural component, and without more attention to background differences, bilingual students will be confused or lost. For example, it is important for science teachers to understand that many students from the rain forest region of South America know (correctly from their prior knowledge and experience) that frogs live in trees rather than ponds. Furthermore, depending on their country of origin, students will have very different notions about geographic concepts, such as the number of continents on Earth.

Creating, identifying, and using adapted materials is an important consideration for bilingual students. A lower reading level alone is not always helpful, often because of cultural differences embedded in the text, idioms expressed, or unknown vocabulary. There is, however, an excellent set of rewritten literature classics from Longman Publishers that uses very common vocabulary. For example, *miniature* in the original text is replaced with *very small* in the rewritten version. Although the eventual goal is for students to read rich and colorful language fluently, they must first develop comprehension and fluency in the language. These books advance skills and build confidence by not bogging down the bilingual student with complex vocabulary and language forms until some fluency has developed. The texts are written at four levels of difficulty, with each level increasing the vocabulary challenge by about 500 of the most frequently used words in the English language.

Using visual texts, such as the books available from Dorling Kindersley also helps bilingual students understand concepts. There are also several good series for teaching English thematically and relatively naturally. A few are listed in Table 3.1.

## DIFFERENTIATING BETWEEN BILINGUAL AND SPECIAL EDUCATION

Many teachers wonder if reporting concern about a student's progress is a bilingual or a special education issue. We hope you now have a better grasp of the many factors within culture, affect, and language development that can help you make thoughtful decisions about interventions needed for students.

A student may need both bilingual and special education support. However, when there has been a mismatch or an inappropriate placement of bilingual students, they actually regress and lose ground in language acquisition.

Careful collaboration among informed professionals in special and bilingual education should help sort out teacher questions and student behaviors. The lists in Figures 3.2 and 3.3 will help staff members examine the linguistic experiences of such students and the implications for language acquisition in both the native language and English. Further, Figure 3.4 illustrates one school district's process for decision making. This information, used in conjunction with the SAALE checklist, can provide a comprehensive picture of instructional options for the student (see Appendix A).

Answers to the following questions will provide important information for assessing student and parent language circumstances to determine instructional strategies and translations needed.

**General Background**

1. Student's full name _____
2. National origin of the student _____
3. National origin of the student's father _____
4. National origin of the student's mother _____
5. Countries other than the United States where the student resided and at what ages the student lived there _____
6. Legal guardians of the student _____
7. Birthdate of the student _____
8. Siblings and their ages _____

**Linguistic Background**

9. Language(s) spoken in the home

   Adult to adult _____         Child to adult _____

   Adult to child _____         Sibling to sibling _____
10. Language(s) used in videos, music, or reading material in the home _____
11. Language(s) in which the student is literate _____
12. Is the student a beginning or fluent reader in this/these language(s)? _____
13. Language(s) in which the parent(s) are literate _____
14. Are the parents beginning or fluent readers in this/these language(s)? _____
15. Home language(s) used to help with homework _____

**Educational Background**

16. Student's initial level of English proficiency in kindergarten

    Non-English _____         Limited _____         Fluent _____
17. Country(ies) and/or school districts for each grade of instruction and the language of instruction:

    K _____         3 _____

    1 _____         4 _____

    2 _____         5 _____


    6 _____         9 _____

    7 _____         10 _____

    8 _____         11 _____
18. Reasons for any grades not attended or significant absenteeism ____ _____
19. Level of education attained by

    Mother _____ Father _____ Older siblings _____

**FIGURE 3.2**
Building a student's linguistic profile.

The Bilingual Oral Language Development (BOLD) Inventory was developed for elementary school children. The form can be used to record observations of the child's performance in both the native language and English. A plus (+) should be recorded for each communicative behavior that is performed effectively; a minus (−) should be recorded for each communicative behavior in which a deficiency is noted. The behaviors listed on the inventory are described below.

1. *Comments on own actions.* The child comments on personal actions while these actions are taking place. Example: "I'm working fast."

2. *Comments on others' actions.* The child comments on actions of others in the environment. Example: "He broke the pencil."

3. *Describes experiences accurately.* The child is able to give an accurate description of personal experiences.

4. *Describes events sequentially.* The child describes a sequence of events in the order in which they occurred.

5. *Attends to the speaker.* The child allows communicative partners to speak and shows appropriate listening behavior.

6. *Follows directions.* The child follows directions presented in the classroom setting.

7. *Initiates interactions.* The child initiates conversations with classmates.

8. *Takes turns during conversation.* The child alternates appropriately as speaker and listener during conversations with peers.

9. *Maintains topic.* The child is able to maintain a topic of discussion over a series of utterances during interactions with peers.

10. *Answers questions.* The child gives appropriate responses to simple questions.

11. *Requests attention.* The child uses language to seek the attention of others.

12. *Requests information.* The child asks questions to obtain information about people, actions, events, and so on.

13. *Requests action.* The child uses language to direct the actions of others.

14. *Requests clarification.* The child requests clarification when verbal statements made by others are not understood.

15. *Expresses needs.* The child uses language to inform others of personal needs.

16. *Expresses feelings.* The child uses language to express feelings such as joy, fear, and anger.

17. *Describes plans.* The child describes plans for events that will take place in the future.

**FIGURE 3.3**

Inventory of bilingual oral language development (BOLD).

*Source:* Mattes, L. J., & Omark, D. R. (1984). *Speech and language assessment for the bilingual handicapped.* San Diego: College-Hill. This form may be reproduced for nonprofit educational use.

18. *Supports viewpoints.* The child expresses personal opinions and is able to provide a logical rationale for those opinions.

19. *Describes solutions.* The child describes solutions for simple problem situations.

20. *Expresses imagination.* The child uses language to express imagination through drama, story-telling, puppet shows, and so on.

**Bilingual Oral Language Development**

Child's Name:

Birthdate:

Child's First Language:

Child's Second Language:

| Communicative Behavior | First Language | Second Language |
| --- | --- | --- |
| 1. Comments on own actions | 1. | 1. |
| 2. Comments on others' actions | 2. | 2. |
| 3. Describes experiences accurately | 3. | 3. |
| 4. Describes events sequentially | 4. | 4. |
| 5. Attends to the speaker | 5. | 5. |
| 6. Follows directions | 6. | 6. |
| 7. Initiates interactions | 7. | 7. |
| 8. Takes turns during conversation | 8. | 8. |
| 9. Maintains topic | 9. | 9. |
| 10. Answers questions | 10. | 10. |
| 11. Requests attention | 11. | 11. |
| 12. Requests information | 12. | 12. |
| 13. Requests action | 13. | 13. |
| 14. Requests clarification | 14. | 14. |
| 15. Expresses needs | 15. | 15. |
| 16. Expresses feelings | 16. | 16. |
| 17. Describes plans | 17. | 17. |
| 18. Supports viewpoints | 18. | 18. |
| 19. Describes solutions | 19. | 19. |
| 20. Expresses imagination | 20. | 20. |

Due to the increasing diversity in the Farmington Public School District, issues related to excellence in education for all students are increasing in number and complexity. One of those issues is the number of referrals of Bilingual Students for evaluation for Special Education Services. Research has shown that many factors used to identify learning disabilities in students often resemble the characteristics of children developing proficiency in a second language. For that reason, the Bilingual Department and Special Education Department, in collaboration with General Education and Administration, formed a committee to further investigate these issues, and created a procedure for Special Education referrals of English Language Learners. It is hoped that this process will facilitate identification and appropriate programming for the students, provide uniformity across buildings in dealing with such cases, and lead to further collaboration between the two departments.

E.L.L. Student Pre-Referral Process

*April 2000*

*English Language Learner

STEP 1—Someone reports that an E.L.L. student is experiencing difficulty

STEP 2—Is the problem academic, behavioral, physical, or language based in nature? Investigation of language proficiency characteristics similar to the characteristics of learning disabilities should be examined, and can be obtained through the Bilingual Department, or independent research.

STEP 3—All interventions and support provided to the student should be explored. Has the child had or is he or she eligible for, bilingual support, inclusive support, literacy groups, extended learning opportunities (C.L.A.S.S., Camp Read a Lot, etc.), Reading Recovery, or other interventions? Once support has been determined and/or provided, the impact and results of the support should be investigated.

At this point, the results of any language testing that has been administered by the Bilingual department should be obtained by contacting the Bilingual Teacher Consultant at centrex #3609. *A person is to be designated on each Building Committee Team to make this contact.*

STEP 4—If a problem still exists, further examination of the student's educational environment and language proficiency should be explored. If the student has scored NES (Non-English Speaking) or LES (Limited-English Speaking) on the IDEA Oral Proficiency Test, further Bilingual Support is indicated.

STEP 5—A consultation between the Bilingual Staff* and the classroom teacher may help to determine some appropriate classroom interventions prior to a child study being initiated. Additionally, a socio-cultural survey should also be implemented in order to gather pertinent data regarding language and culture issues that can impact learning. This survey should become a part of the student's file, and may be administered as a cooperative effort by the teacher, Special Education Staff** and Bilingual Staff*.

STEP 6—A building team meeting is convened according to building procedure, to include input from the Bilingual Staff*, in order to seek further information about the difficulty. A referral for Special Education Evaluation may be the outcome of this process, or the team may choose to continue to seek further support and/or input from the Bilingual Staff.

*The term 'Bilingual staff' may indicate the Director, Teacher Consultant, or their designee*

**The term 'Special Education Staff' may include Resource Room Teacher, Student Assistance Program Personnel, Social Worker, Psychologist, Speech Pathologist, or other support persons identified by the building*

FIGURE 3.4

Farmington Public Schools: Special education procedures for English language learners.

*Source*: Developed by The Bilingual and Special Education Departments of the Farmington Public Schools, May 2000.

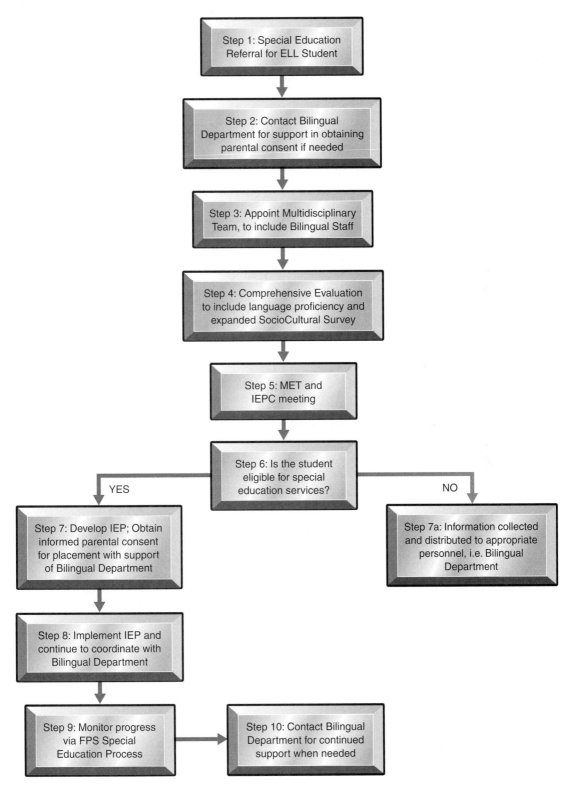

**FIGURE 3.4**
*Continued*

Administered/Coordinated by: _____

Date: _____

# Socio-Cultural Student Variable Survey

- Student's Name _____ Age: _____ Grade: _____
- Native language _____
- Language spoken in the home _____
- Country of birth _____

**Experiential Background**

- How long has the student been in the U.S.? _____ In Michigan? _____ In Farmington? _____ In current school? _____
- Has the student's attendance at school been inconsistent? _____

  _____

- Has the transiency of the family affected school attendance? _____
- Was the child placed appropriately upon registration? _____
- What is the quality of prior instruction, if known? _____
- Are there unique features regarding the family's lifestyle? _____

  _____

- Was there any interruption in the child's schooling? _____
- Is the student literate in his/her native language? How do you know? _____
- Have the following been administered and/or reviewed?

  Hearing test? _____ date _____ Vision Test? _____ date _____
- What are the student's or his/her parents' goals in terms of learning and education? _____

  _____

- Are parents literate? _____
- Is the child supervised after school? _____
- Are there any special or unique household routines? _____
- What are the student's interests, hobbies, or talents? _____
- Who is responsible for discipline in the home? _____
- Do expectations differ at home and at school with regard to academics? _____ If so, how? _____

**FIGURE 3.4**
*Continued*

**Culture**

- What is the structure of the student's family? _____
- If known, are there religious factors that may affect the child's learning? _____
- Does the child have contact with the homeland? _____
- What was the reason for immigration? _____
- Is the student's behavior culturally appropriate in the native culture? _____
  In Farmington? _____
- To what degree has the child assimilated or acculturated? How willing is the student to assimilate or acculturate? _____

**Motivational Influences**

- Is the student's self-concept enhanced by school experiences? _____
- Does the student experience academic and social success? _____
- Does the school community communicate a respect for culture and language? _____
- Do the child's classmates communicate a respect for culture and language? _____
- Is schooling perceived as relevant and necessary for success in the student's family and community? _____

# CHAPTER 4

# Characteristics of Students with Special Needs

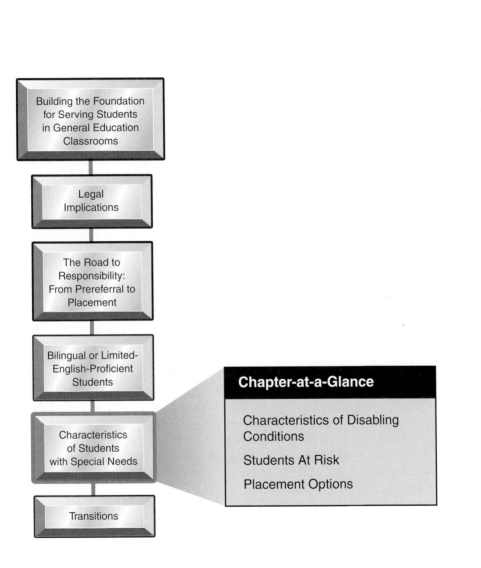

Building the Foundation for Serving Students in General Education Classrooms

Legal Implications

The Road to Responsibility: From Prereferral to Placement

Bilingual or Limited-English-Proficient Students

Characteristics of Students with Special Needs

Transitions

**Chapter-at-a-Glance**

Characteristics of Disabling Conditions

Students At Risk

Placement Options

This chapter examines the characteristics of various disabling conditions, offers tips for the classroom teacher, and presents possible placement options.

# CHARACTERISTICS OF VARIOUS DISABILITIES

Over the years, students have been labeled for numerous reasons. Initially, students with special needs were labeled for funding purposes: that is, if a school district had *x* number of students with mental retardation, a class was established and a teacher was hired. Labels have also helped schools develop curricula for specific categories. Nevertheless, labels can have negative effects, and a child can be labeled for life.

Today, many states still divide their special population into areas of mild, moderate, and severe disabilities. However, numerous states continue to use categorical labels. We will discuss each category as defined under PL 94-142 and IDEA. But remember, your state may organize these categories without using labels. Moreover, different states may recognize categories using different terms. For example, students with mental retardation may be called mentally disabled or developmentally delayed. Learn your state's term of choice.

## Mental Retardation

It is difficult to list characteristics that are found in all children who are educable mentally retarded (EMR). No single child has all of these characteristics because some characteristics are peculiar to only a certain group. The definition of mental retardation has been challenged since 1992 by the American Association on Mental Retardation. The AAMR proposed classifying persons with mental retardation based on the level of support that is needed to function as independently as possible. However, after eight years, this idea has not been adopted by the policy and decision makers. The Federal Register and IDEA continue to use the term *mental retardation.* The word *retardation* is an emotionally charged word, and therefore many school systems have chosen to use the label *mentally disabled.*

From the 1930s to 1992, the definition of mental retardation has been revised and expanded. By 1992 the definition included 10 specific adaptive skill areas and read as follows:

> Mental retardation refers to substantial limitations in present functioning. It is characterized by significantly subaverage intellectual functioning, existing concurrently with related limitations in two or more of the following applicable adaptive skill areas: communication, self-care, home living, social skills, community use, self-direction, health and safety, functional academics, leisure, and work. Mental retardation manifests before age 18. (American Association on Mental Retardation, 1992, p. 1)

The following four assumptions are essential to the application of the definition:

1. Valid assessment considers cultural and linguistic diversity as well as differences in communication and behavioral factors.
2. The existence of limitations in adaptive skills occurs within the context of community environments typical of the individual's peers and is indexed to the person's individualized needs for supports.
3. Specific adaptive limitations often coexist with strengths in other adaptive skills or other personal capabilities.
4. With appropriate supports over a sustained period, the life functioning of the person with mental retardation will generally improve. (American Association on Mental Retardation, 1992, p. 1)

## Classification System

Mental Retardation A classification system is basically a way to sort categories of persons to place them in a group for informational purposes. Individuals with mental retardation were traditionally classified by causes. This system assisted medical fields better than educational ones. The newer system for classifying individuals with mental retardation is a system developed according to the levels of support they need within their environments, not their IQ scores. Since both systems, traditional and new, are used in the literature, you should become acquainted with both. Table 4.1 presents the traditional classification system for individuals with mental retardation.

The newer system allows an individual to move up and down levels. This system is not as lock-stepped as the traditional system. The levels of support include:

1. *Intermittent.* Does not require constant support, but may need support on a short-term basis for special occurrences, such as receiving help finding a new job
2. *Limited.* Requires certain supports consistently over time, such as with handling finances, or may need time-limited support for employment training
3. *Extensive.* Needs daily support in some aspects of living, such as long-term job support
4. *Pervasive.* Requires constant, high-intensity support for all aspects of life

## Characteristics of Mental Retardation

There are numerous characteristics of students with mental retardation, including:

- Deficits in cognitive skills
- Difficulties in focusing and maintaining attention
- Difficulties in learning due to slowness
- Inferior social skills
- Delayed or impaired communication skills

TABLE 4.1

Traditional Classification System for Individuals With Mental Retardation

| Level | IQ Test Score | Explanation |
|-------|---------------|-------------|
| Mild | 50–55 to approximately 70 | • May not be identified until school age<br>• May be initially placed in self-contained settings (classrooms)<br>• Can function well in regular class settings<br>• Should have curriculum that stresses reading, writing, arithmetic<br>• Develop social and communication skills in a similar manner as students without disabilities<br>• Can be functionally independent in adult life<br>• Blend into traditional society after completion of school |
| Moderate | 35–40 to 50–55 | • Will exhibit developmental delays prior to entering school; discrepancies between this group and individuals without disabilities tend to increase with age<br>• Usually start out in self-contained classes and may remain there<br>• Are the focus of a national movement to place these students into regular education classrooms<br>• Need more support than those with mild retardation<br>• Should have curriculum emphasizing self-help and daily living skills; academics limited to functional activities such as learning "survival" words (*danger, stop, restroom,* etc.), counting, and making change<br>• Will need supervision as adults |
| Severe<br>Profound | 20–25 to 35–40<br>Below 20–25 | • Typically are identified at birth<br>• Historically, have significant probability of medical complications<br>• In the past were kept almost exclusively in institutions<br>• Today may live at home and be served within their local schools<br>• Can be taught simple life tasks<br>• 24-hour supervision is necessary<br>• Severe: May become semi-independent by adulthood<br>• Profound: Will need constant supervision |

*Source:* Wood, J. W., & Lazzari, A. M. (1997). *Exceeding the Boundaries—Understanding Exceptional Lives* (p. 433). Fort Worth, TX: Harcourt Brace College Publishers.

Understanding the characteristics of individuals with disabilities assists in identification and educational practice. Figure 4.1 presents additional characteristics of individuals with mental retardation, implications for educators, and ideas for parents. Understanding characteristics of a population assists in teaching. For example, if the self-concept is weak, lots of praise is needed.

**Characteristics**

- A person with mental retardation functions academically 3 to 4 years behind his or her age peers.
- The student has a short attention span or lack of concentration and participation.
- The student has a low frustration tolerance level, which may cause behavioral problems.
- More often with the younger population, mental age as opposed to chronological age determines the EMR child's interest level.
- At the end of the student's formal school career, his or her academic achievement will probably have reached second- to sixth-grade level, depending on his or her mental maturation or special abilities.
- Any failures in unskilled occupational tasks are generally related to personal, social, and interpersonal characteristics rather than an inability to execute the task assigned.
- Frequently, EMR students have met with failure during the early years. Because they expect to fail at difficult tasks, they develop a failure set. To escape further frustrations of failure, they set lower aspirations and goals than are appropriate.

**Implications for Educators**

- Use concrete materials that are interesting, age-appropriate, and relevant to the student.
- Teach these children, whenever possible, in the same school they would attend if they were not mentally retarded.
- Teach tasks or skills that students will use frequently in such a way that students can apply the tasks or skills in settings outside of school.
- Remember that tasks that many people learn without instruction may need to be structured or broken down into small steps or segments.
- Stress success.
- Provide prompt and consistent feedback.
- Focus on the child's strengths and accomplishments as well as his/her deficit areas.
- Present new information in concrete terms, providing tangible models and real-life examples.
- Plan lessons that stress functional skills and concepts.
- Advocate for your students to be included in all aspects of school activities.
- Seek parents' input regarding objectives and approaches best suited for their child.

**Ideas for Parents**

1. Look for and celebrate small successes.
2. Give your child responsibilities at home, just as you do with your other children.
3. Don't be afraid to allow your child to try and fail.
4. Provide opportunities for your child to interact with other children in the neighborhood and community outside of the school setting.
5. Be an advocate for early vocational planning for your child.

FIGURE 4.1
Students with mental retardation.

### Causes of Mental Retardation

Many persons are concerned with "Why is this child mentally retarded?" Causes may be maternal infection, maternal substance use and abuse, genetic causes, maternal malnutrition, prenatal anoxia, substandard and deprived environments, or metabolic disorders. Understanding causes certainly assists with prevention.

## Learning Disabilities

Children with learning disabilities display many atypical characteristics that tend to interfere with their learning behavior and performance. Children with learning disabilities demonstrate a discrepancy between their ability and their achievement. They often possess processing disorders as well. Of the characteristics listed in Figure 4.2, any combination might be found in any one child. Seldom will a single child have all of them. Because students with learning disabilities appear in great numbers in general education classes, the following tips will give teachers additional support:

1. Have children work at their own ability level in each academic area. Levels may vary in reading, spelling, language, and math, with one or more areas lower than the others.

2. Plan and provide a number of successful experiences because tolerance for failure is low.

3. Provide clear instructions and recognize that, even if children appear to understand, they may be confused. Avoid instructions involving more than two steps at a time.

4. Consider special physical arrangements in the classroom to decrease overstimulation and distractibility. A cubicle or a desk placed away from distractions may help a child pay attention to learning tasks, but make it clear to the child that this is not a punishment.

5. Be alert to signs of emotional disturbance or behavioral problems. If problems exist, recommendations for children with emotional handicaps may be applicable.

6. Use multisensory (auditory, visual, tactile [touch], and kinesthetic [movement]) approaches to instruction whenever possible.

7. Communicate with the resource teacher to discuss which methods seem to be most successful.

8. Sequence learning tasks into steps that children can successfully achieve. Reinforce successful achievement of each step.

9. Use short assignments. If an entire worksheet (such as one filled with math problems) appears frustrating, cut the worksheet into strips, allowing the child to complete one at a time.

10. In reading, children frequently confuse similar words (can/ran, talk/walk, was/saw). Ask them to spell the confusing word orally and then repronounce it.

## Characteristics

- The student with learning disabilities may exhibit a deficit in perception—that is, in using the senses to recognize, discriminate, and interpret stimuli. Specific perceptual areas include visual perception, visual discrimination, visual memory, auditory perception, auditory discrimination, and auditory memory.
- Fifty percent of individuals with learning disabilities have language and speech problems that reflect deficient skills in oral expression and listening comprehension.
- The student with learning disabilities lacks the ability to begin tasks immediately or sustain tasks for long periods of time and may avoid the task completely.
- Students with learning disabilities may be inconsistent in their abilities. What they can do today, they may not be able to do tomorrow.
- Many students with learning disabilities have poor self-concepts and experience social rejection.
- Students with learning disabilities may have difficulties with reading, writing, and spelling, as well as difficulty in performing arithmetic functions or comprehending basic concepts.

## Implications for Educators

- Use short sentences and a simple vocabulary.
- Directions should be short and given one or two at a time.
- Provide highly structured activities and clear expectations.
- Use self-correcting material that provides immediate feedback without embarrassment.
- Capitalize on students' strengths and provide opportunities for success in a supportive atmosphere. Positively reinforce appropriate social skills at school and home.
- Use flexibility in classroom procedures, such as allowing the use of tape recorders for note taking and test taking when students have trouble with written language.
- Use computers for drill and practice and for teaching word processing.
- Help students with learning disabilities connect new information with previously learned concepts. Make the connections explicit using directions or graphic aids to illustrate.
- Help students with learning disabilities organize ideas and concepts using semantic maps, flow-charts, outlines, study guides, and other visual representations of knowledge.
- Strategically seat students with learning disabilities to minimize distractions, provide peer assistance, and provide proximity to the teacher.
- Use learning strategies such as mnemonic devices, paired association, and verbal rehearsal to provide assistance with memorization of factual materials in class.
- Provide opportunities for students with learning disabilities to demonstrate their understanding in ways that use their strengths; for example, allow an oral report or a poster drawing of a written book report.

## Tips for Parents

- Break tasks down into shorter steps. For example, instead of saying "clean your room," explain the steps to be included in the task: Specify picking up all the dirty clothes as the first step; followed by putting away all books, toys, and papers; then emptying the trash; dusting; making the bed; and sweeping.
- Help your child develop strategies for organizing homework—establishing a time and place to do homework, a system for writing down assignments, the means for obtaining assistance, and a plan for prioritizing assignments and tasks.
- Provide extra practice and assistance with memorization tasks such as spelling words, math facts, and maps. For example, practice the multiplication tables while driving in the car, spend 15 minutes before going to bed to study maps, or recite the spelling words at breakfast.
- Provide opportunities for your child to discover and demonstrate areas of strength at home. For example, a youngster who has a good sense of visual organization might make a good family photographer or may be particularly helpful organizing cupboards or bookshelves at home.
- Provide honest and genuine feedback to your child. Point out errors and shortcomings in an honest, respectful, and straightforward manner and give praise when your child is correct.

**FIGURE 4.2**
Students with learning disabilities.

11. Record progress in graph or chart form. Share this with each child so that he or she can see the progress.

12. Design teacher-made games for individual or small-group activities to reinforce skills that are being developed.

13. Structure and consistency in the classroom environment as well as a daily routine are extremely important. If changes in schedule are to occur, prepare the child ahead of time and reemphasize the change periodically.

14. Use cross-age, peer, and volunteer tutors.

### Causes

Little is known about the causes of learning disabilities. The pendulum has gone from speculation of cause (maybe a brain trauma, unknown causes, language and learning problems) to possibly emotional stress. As technology improves, perhaps the cause of learning disabilities will emerge. Today the focus on what to do appears to be the best course of action.

## Emotional/Behavioral Disorders

The causes of emotional disturbances have not been adequately determined. Although heredity, brain disorder, diet, stress, and family functioning have been suggested, research has not shown that any of these factors is the direct cause of behavior problems. Until 1997, *seriously emotionally disturbed* was used as the term or label for these children. With IDEA, the word *seriously* was dropped from use. Just like any of the categories mentioned in this chapter, cases range from mild to severe. Children with the most serious emotional disturbances exhibit distorted thinking, excessive anxiety, bizarre motor acts, and abnormal mood swings and are sometimes identified as having severe psychosis or schizophrenia. Many children who do not have emotional disturbances may display some of these same behaviors at various times during their development. However, when children have serious emotional disturbances, behaviors continue over long periods of time and thus signal that they are not coping with their environment or their peers.

Students eligible for special education services under the emotional/behavioral disorders category often have IEPs that do not include psychological or counseling services, although these are legitimate related services mentioned in the law (CFR 400.14). Often school districts suggest that families should take their children to a mental health center for therapy. However, an increasing number of state education and mental health agencies have reported collaborative efforts to make mental health services (particularly school-based mental health services) more available to identified students. Sometimes these services include short-term therapy; more often they are defined as consultations with teachers and families, which are available during crisis. There is growing recognition that families with seriously troubled children need support, respite care, intensive case management services, and a multiagency treatment plan, which is now available through a federal program called the Child and Adolescent Service System Program (CASSP). Such efforts work best when school and mental health professionals work collaboratively.

Families of children with emotional/behavioral disturbances may need help in understanding their children's conditions and learning how to work effectively with them. Help is available from psychiatrists, psychologists, and other mental health professionals in public or private mental health settings. Sometimes children may need an out-of-home placement. They should be provided with services based on their individual needs, and all persons who are involved with these children should be aware of the care they are receiving. It is important to coordinate all services, with open communication among home, school, and the therapeutic community. Figure 4.3 lists some characteristics, implications for educators, and parent tips to consider when working with students with emotional/behavioral disorders.

---

**Characteristics**
- Impulsiveness
- Hyperactivity
- Aggression/self-injurious behavior: acting out, fighting
- Withdrawal: failure to initiate interaction with others, retreat from social interaction, excessive fear or anxiety
- Immaturity: inappropriate crying, temper tantrums, poor coping skills
- Learning problems: academically performing below grade level
- Short attention span

**Implications for Educators**
- Educational programs for children with behavioral or emotional problems should include attention to mastering academics, developing social skills, and increasing self-control and self-esteem.
- Career education (both vocational and academic programs) is rapidly becoming a major part of the secondary education of these children. Career education should be part of every adolescent's IEP.
- Behavior modification (shaping behaviors with positive reinforcement) is one of the most widely used approaches to helping children with emotional/behavioral disorders. However, while students can learn to meet classroom expectations, questions have been raised about how much the learning transfers to other situations.
- A number of schools are trying different strategies to help students take responsibility for their thoughts, feelings, and actions. It is important for teachers to focus on academics and opportunities for their students to develop social skills in addition to working on behavioral control.

**Tips for Parents**
- Understand your child's behavior and events leading to and resulting from behavior episodes.
- Be an active part of your child's planning committee.
- Work closely with the school in carrying out behavioral plans.

---

**FIGURE 4.3**
Students with emotional/behavioral disorders.

### Causes

Just like a learning disability, a behavioral/emotional problem is a causal puzzle. Physicians look to medications, psychologists to insight, and educators to strategies which work. In 1997, the interpretation of IDEA underlined specifics of a functional behavioral assessment and behavior plan for children with emotional/behavioral problems. Chapter 8 provides an example and explanation of the plan.

## Autism

Autism was added as a disability category in 1990, when IDEA was revised (see chapter 1). "The half century that has passed since the syndrome of autism was first identified has seen great changes in perspectives and approaches concerning the disorder" (Wood & Lazzari, 1997). Remember that autism includes a wide spectrum of disorders. There is no such thing as a "typical" child with autism. Figure 4.4 lists information helpful to the category of autism.

### Causes

As with the two previous categories, the causes of autism are foggy. Some think the cause of autism may be a structural neurological dysfunction (something chemical). Research is ongoing and autism remains a puzzle.

## Traumatic Brain Injury

Like autism, the category of *traumatic brain injury* (TBI) was added to IDEA in 1990. It is one of the fastest growing disability categories in the United States. More and more children are surviving head injuries from accidents involving vehicles, motorbikes, water sports, playground equipment, abuse and assault, infections of the brain, and car accidents. In such cases, a relationship with the hospital's education program facilitates a child's reentry into the school setting. Figure 4.5 lists characteristics and educational implications relating to students with head injuries.

## Attention Deficit/Hyperactivity Disorder

In 1990, when autism and traumatic brain injury were added to IDEA as disability categories, parents were eager to have attention deficit/hyperactivity disorder (AD/HD) added as a separate category to be served under the law. When the federal government did not add this category, grave concerns began to arise. In 1992 lawmakers finally ruled that AD/HD students could be served under section 504 and have a 504 plan that includes classroom accommodations. In cases where the child's AD/HD significantly interferes with his/her education, a child may qualify as "Other Health Impaired" under IDEA, and as such would have an IEP. Figure 4.6 lists characteristics of this population and educational implications for teaching them.

## Characteristics

- Difficulty relating to people, objects, and events
- Repetitive movements such as rocking, spinning, finger snapping, or hand flapping
- Insistence on sameness in the environment and in following routines; marked distress over changes in trivial aspects of either
- Avoidance of eye contact
- Impaired communication skills, both verbal and nonverbal
- Unconventional use of toys and objects
- Impairment of social interaction and abnormal social play
- Restricted range of interests and preoccupation with one narrow interest
- Cognitive problems in attention, organization, and sequencing

## Implications for Educators

- Structure the learning environment so that it is predictable and consistent. This includes the physical structure of the classroom as well as routines, schedules, and teacher behavior.
- Design instructional programs to provide ways to help children learn to communicate. Remember that verbal communication is only one way to communicate; provide students with alternatives such as signing, writing, or using the computer or facilitated communication (assisted communication using a typewriter, letter board, or other keyboard to spell out messages while a person who serves as the facilitator supports the student's forearm).
- Because students with autism have difficulty managing their own behavior without structure, develop individual and group behavior plans that stress positive behavior management and set forth clear instructions, rules, and consequences.
- Work closely with the family to ensure consistency among school, home, and other settings in approaches, methods of interaction, and response to students.
- Organize the classroom layout so that it's clear which kinds of activities are supposed to occur in which areas; use pictures or written labels or signs to mark different areas.
- Use pictures or written schedules to provide information and predictability to students concerning what is going to be happening, when, with whom, and so forth.
- Present verbal instructions and directions in a brief, clear manner.
- Determine whether verbal, visual, or physical prompts are most effective with particular students, and use them as appropriate.
- Break tasks to be taught into smaller, more manageable steps, and then combine them to develop more complex activities and routines.
- Do your best to provide parents with relevant and helpful sources of information (e.g., books, newsletters, pamphlets) on their legal rights and their child's disability.

## Tips for Parents

- Visit and participate in your child's classroom often.
- Maintain ongoing communication with the teacher via notes, phone calls, and informal and formal meetings.
- Get involved with agencies and organizations, which may be of help to you and your child (e.g., local chapter of the Autism Society of America).
- Remember that you will always be the primary constant in your child's life.

**FIGURE 4.4**
Students with autism.

### Characteristics
- Physical Impairments
    - Problems with speech, vision, or hearing
    - Headaches
    - Seizure disorders
    - Paralysis
    - Motor coordination problems
- Cognitive difficulties
    - Distractibility
    - Short- and long-term memory problems
    - Confusion
    - Shortened attention span
    - Poor concentration
    - Difficulty remembering recent events
    - Slowness of thinking skills
    - Difficulty with language comprehension and expression
    - Problems with reading, writing, and math skills
    - Irritability
    - Fatigue
    - Impulsiveness
    - Decreased tolerance for frustration
- Social/emotional problems
    - Sudden mood changes
    - Self-esteem problems
    - Difficulty in relating to others
    - Apathy
    - Poor motivation
    - Self-centeredness
    - Sadness and depression
    - Loss of inhibition
    - Agitation and fatigue
    - Threatening self-destructive acts

### Implications for Educators
- Encourage the student to reread directions more than once, underlining important elements.
- Ask the student to repeat instructions verbatim before beginning an activity.
- Verify the student's comprehension of the instructions by requesting that they be restated in different words (paraphrased).
- Remind the student to proofread assignments carefully before turning them in, checking for completeness and accuracy.
- Ask the student to describe aloud the correct versus incorrect aspects of the work so that he or she can understand when instructions have been misunderstood or misinterpreted.

### Tips for Parents
- Provide repetition and consistency.
- Provide hands-on experiences.
- Avoid figurative language.
- Reinforce attention span tasks.
- Keep areas distraction free.

FIGURE 4.5
Students with traumatic brain injury.

**Characteristics**

- Fidgets with hands or feet or squirms in seat; in adolescents, may be limited to subjective feelings of restlessness
- Has difficulty remaining seated when required to do so
- Easily distracted by extraneous stimuli
- Has difficulty waiting for his or her turn in games or group situations
- Blurts out answers to questions before they have been completed
- Has difficulty following through on instructions from others, such as failing to finish chores; this is not due to oppositional behavior or failure to comprehend the instructions
- Has difficulty sustaining attention during task or play situations
- Shifts from one uncompleted activity to another
- Has difficulty playing quietly
- Talks excessively
- Interrupts or intrudes on others
- Does not seem to listen to what is being said directly to him or her
- Loses items necessary for tasks or activities at school or home
- Engages in physically dangerous activities (not for the purpose of thrill seeking and without considering possible consequences)—for example, running into the street without looking
- Ratio of males to females vary 4:1 to 6:1

**Implications for Educators**

- Place the student away from distracting situations.
- Provide structure for instruction as well as for transitioning from one activity to the next. For example, provide study guides before a test, use graphic organizers for delivering class instruction or for assisting the student in writing essays, and provide a checklist of tasks that the student is to complete before viewing a movie or video.
- When giving the class information or directions for tasks, use a multimodality approach. Use transparencies to emphasize major points or lecture topics, provide an outline for note taking before lectures, and use as many hands-on activities as possible.
- Seat work or individual tasks should be carefully monitored. Give students a checklist so that they will know exactly what tasks are to be done during seat work time. Give the student a peer helper. Check the student frequently to reinforce on-task behavior. Be sure that the assignment or task is designed to be completed within the student's time frame for attention.
- When giving homework assignments, be sure that the student can complete the amount given. Break it down into short segments; give only a small section to be completed at home; and, most important, be sure that the assignment will result in success and not failure. These students have poor self-esteem and need positive reinforcement.
- Alternate class activities so that a long period of sitting will not be required. Give students alternatives so that they can physically move without being considered inappropriate. For example, provide a class chore such as collecting papers or running an errand for the teacher.
- Note taking may prove difficult. Provide copies of notes, allow students to tape-record information, use a graphic organizer for note taking, and provide a note-taking buddy.

(*continued*)

**FIGURE 4.6**
Students with attention-deficit/hyperactivity disorders.

**Implications for Educators—*continued***
- Allow students to record answers to tests instead of writing them. Be sure that tests are short; avoid lengthy tests. Split long tests in half. Limit the number of distractors on multiple-choice items.
- Use a means of evaluating student performance other than traditional tests.
- Remember that these students are overly sensitive to criticism; therefore, frequent praise is necessary.
- Be consistent. Students with AD/HD deal poorly with change. They need a sense of external structure because they lack a sense of internal structure.
- Help manage the students' time. Their time clock consists of plenty of time or no time.
- Avoid placing students at tables with a large number of children.
- Use colors and shapes to help with organization.
- Remember, many are visual learners.
- Don't take their behavior personally.

**Tips for Parents**
- Avoid distracting stimuli.
- Surround your child with good role models.
- Practice exercise breathing.
- Try to remain calm.
- Make eye contact when speaking to your child.
- Keep punishment brief. For young children, start fresh everyday; for teenagers, keep punishment time under a week.
- Kitchen timers are excellent for dressing, time out (never make time outs long), going to bed, study breaks, and so on.
- Praise your child frequently.
- Use "I" statements: I feel, I would, and so forth.
- Ask "feelings" questions: "How did you feel when . . . ?"
- Problems always belong to more than one person. Watch blaming.
- Watch for teenagers' reactions in hormonal fluctuations, depression, risks associated with driving, substance abuse, and so on (Nadeau, 2000)

**FIGURE 4.6**
Continued.

### Causes

Both genetic and environmental causes are reported for AD/HD. Without question, heredity is a causal factor. The disorder is passed genetically by a parent to about half of his/her children. Certain pre/perinatal injuries may create AD/HD symptoms, such as hemorrhages, ischemia toxemia, lead, alcohol, cocaine, marijuana, and pesticides.

## Sensory Disabilities

Language, communication, visual, and hearing impairments are all considered within the category of sensory disabilities. You will find that many students receive services for language and communication; however, hearing and visual impairments occur less frequently.

## Speech, Voice, and Communication

The broad area of communication disorders may be further divided into disorders of speech, voice, and language. Causes of communication problems may range from organic and emotional to environmental. This category of disabilities is the one seen most frequently in children, and the one for which help is most readily available. Figures 4.7 and 4.8 provide information for educators and parents who work with students with communication disorders.

## Visual Impairments

Visual impairments include partial visual loss and loss of vision. Students with visual impairments will often have partial sight; however, their vision may be blurred, cloudy, spotty, or double. Most students who are identified as legally blind do have some measureable vision or light perception. To be considered legally blind, a person must have corrected vision that is limited to a narrow field of less than 20 degrees, or his/her corrected vision must be no better than 20/200; that is, seeing at 20 feet what the average person sees at 200 feet. Problems associated with visual impairments are also apparent. Visual impairments may cause students not to see or comprehend written material which may include announcements of test dates, procedural information, and content of the examination itself. Figure 4.9 provides characteristics, implications, and tips (Chang, Richards, & Jackson, 1996).

## Hearing Impairments

Communication is obviously a major problem. Hearing impairments may cause students not to hear or comprehend rapidly spoken information, such as instructions, directions, questions posed by other students, and answers given before the actual test begins.

The two major ways that students with hearing impairments communicate are oral (speech or lip reading) and manual (sign language). Speech (lip) reading is the understanding of spoken language by watching lip movements of speakers, and sign language is the translation of oral communication into manual communication by an interpreter. Persons who communicate in the oral method use a combination of speech and speech reading.

Students who communicate using the manual method use the American Sign Language (ASL) system. This is a system of hand and arm movements, positions, and gestures that translates the spoken word into visual representations. ASL is a short-cut version and is not equal (verbatim) to the English language. Finger spelling may be used in place of the signs in case there are not equivalent signs for the words. This frequently happens when technical or subject-specific vocabulary is used.

Certainly, speech (lip) reading (see the definition above) is one solution for some students with hearing impairments. However, the problem is that students

**Characteristics**
- Approximate age of sound development

  | Age | Sounds |
  |-----|--------|
  | 3 | p/m/h/n/w |
  | | b/k/q/d |
  | 3½ | f/y |
  | 4 | t/ng |
  | 4½ | r/l |
  | 5½ | s/ch/sh/z/ju |
  | 6 | th |
  | 7 | zh |

- Remember that children's development varies, and approximately only 90% of children consistently produce these sounds by age 7.
- Aphasia is a central nervous system processing disorder that may limit the child's ability to be able to use oral language expressively or receptively. Speech may be jibberish or telegraphic.

**Implications for Educators**
- Become acquainted with the aims and objectives of the speech/language therapy program.
- Help other children develop an attitude of acceptance.
- Reinforce good speech and language performance during classroom activities to establish the importance of using what is learned during the therapy sessions.
- Work cooperatively with the therapist in providing integrated therapy to students, if appropriate.
- Help the speech-language pathologist evaluate progress at different stages of the therapy program.
- Assist the disfluent child by letting him or her talk without interrupting or making suggestions:
     Don't tell the child to hurry up.
     Don't tell the child to speak more slowly.
     Don't tell the child to stop and start over.
     Don't tell the child to take a deep breath before speaking.
- Accept the child's disfluencies as his or her way of talking without showing disapproval, fear, embarrassment, irritation, or surprise.
- Help the pupil follow his or her treatment program, especially if the child is to avoid abusing his or her voice or be on vocal rest.
- Realize that the child with a cleft palate or lip may require special academic help for those extended periods of time he or she must miss school due to surgery or doctor visits.
- Become aware of strengths and weaknesses and help to develop these strengths to the fullest.

**Tips for Parents**
- Do your homework in seeking services for your child. Start with the school.
- Remember that the law requires that all children receive services through the age of 21.
- Model good speech for your child.
- Younger children may stutter. This is normal. Be patient and don't rush your child's speech.
- Give your child ample time to answer questions.
- Make eye contact when speaking to your child.

FIGURE 4.7
Students with speech and language impairments.

**Characteristics**

Children with communication impairments are said to have defective speech or language. Defective speech interferes with communication, causes the child to be maladjusted, or calls unfavorable attention to itself. If language is affected, the communication impairment can interfere with or limit the ability to formulate, express, receive, or interpret oral language.

Communication problems may vary in degree from mild (the child is understandable, although errors are noted in his or her speech) to severe (the pupil is completely unintelligible). Speech and language problems may be exhibited in one, or in combinations, of the following disorders and may have a functional or organic base. Communication problems may be present alone or with other conditions such as mental retardation, a learning disability, or emotional disturbance.

Lesley Jernigan of the Department of Speech and Hearing Sciences at the University of Southern Mississippi has compiled the following list:

- *Articulation disorder.* The youngster may omit, distort, or substitute one speech sound for another.
- *Delayed language.* The child is confused about how to form words and to put them in the right order and cannot properly use language symbols as tools to assist in organizing and expressing visual, auditory, tactile-kinesthetic, and other sensory experiences. It is frequently present with other speech problems.
- *Disfluency (stuttering).* This is a disorder of rhythm in which the child's flow of speech is interrupted.
- *Voice disorders.* These frequently result from vocal abuse and may require medical attention in addition to speech therapy. Voice disorders may involve quality, pitch, or loudness. The speech may be hoarse, harsh, nasal, breathy, or inappropriate for the pupil's age or gender.
- *Cleft palate or lip.* These are incomplete formations of the oral structures. They may be of several types and degrees of involvement. Repair of the cleft condition begins early and should be almost completed during the primary grades. This condition frequently causes the speech to be nasal. Articulation errors and voice disorders also may be present.
- *Hearing-impaired.* This is affected by the severity and type of hearing loss present. The speech pattern may be too loud or too soft.

Refer to Figure 4.7 for Implications for Educators and Tips for Parents.

**FIGURE 4.8**
Students with communication impairments.

who rely on reading lips can at best read 30 percent of the sounds of spoken English. Teachers can help the situation in the following ways:

- Face the student directly when speaking.
- Speak normally and naturally rather than exaggerating lip movements when speaking.
- Speak clearly and concisely.
- Speak at a normal speed rather than too fast.
- Speak directly to the student, not to the interpreter, if an interpreter is used.

**Characteristics**
- Appearance
  - Red-rimmed, encrusted, or swollen eyelids
  - Inflamed or watery eyes
  - Frequent sties
  - Eyelids in constant motion
- Behavior
  - Rubs eyes often
  - Shuts or covers one eye, tilts head, thrusts head forward, blinks more often when reading
  - Difficulty reading or in work requiring close use of eyes
  - Stumbles over small objects
  - Holds book close to eyes
  - Squints eyelids together or frowns
  - May be slower than other students to develop motor skills
  - May be unaware of things to the side of, above, or below him- or herself
  - Seems to listen closely to sounds
- Complaints
  - Eyes itch, burn, or feel scratchy
  - Cannot see well
  - Dizziness
  - Headaches
  - Nausea
  - Blurred or double vision

**Implications for Educators**
- Flexible seating arrangements
- Furniture that fits
- Getting as close as you have to
- Good lighting; needs may differ
- Nonglare work surfaces and paper
- Participation in demonstrations
- Verbalizing board work and demonstrations
- Familiarizing student with room, building, equipment, and materials
- Allowing for extra time
- Choosing representative problems (quality, not just quantity)
- Comprehension questions, performance tasks
- Magnification
- Physical education, playground activities, student projects
- Orientation clues about finding information on maps, charts, diagrams (help develop a systematic search pattern)
- Short work periods for visual tasks
- Using felt-tip pens or light photocopies; underlining important areas

FIGURE 4.9
Students with visual impairments.

**Implications for Educators—*continued***
- Vertical positioning of materials (desk, stands)
- Board work pages at desk
- Pictures that are bold, simple, highly contrasted, with not too many small details
- Examining texts and work sheets for contrast, importance, and size of detail
- Manipulative materials
- Parts tied together
- Multisensory clues, visual clues (color, size, details, shape, movement, relationship to parts)
- Tachistoscope; block paper for structure
- Find ways for students to touch instead of look at things, such as tactile charts and diagrams.
- Students with visual impairments need to be shown and told about the new locations if furniture and equipment had to be moved around in the classroom or lab.
- Many students use adapted versions of the texts used in their classes. The two major types of adapted versions of the texts are enlarged books and books produced on microcomputer disks. Enlarged books are heavy and bulky. Books on disks can be viewed on a computer screen. The size of the type can be adjusted. Any page of the book can be printed out on paper and in Braille. Instant voice-to-print and print-to-voice translations of documents are possible.
- The print in standard text can be enlarged on a closed-circuit television. Such modifications are essential for most students with glaucoma, congenital cataracts, or nystagmus. For students with good central vision but a limited visual field, enlargements may be a hindrance. For those students, audiocassette versions of textbooks may be a better choice. (Smith & Luckasson, 1995)
- Use personal readers.
- Arrange for a special edition of the examination (tape, individually read, large print, or Braille).

**Tips for Parents**
- Express your expectations openly to educators involved in the education of your child.
- As with any disability, thoroughly understand the nature of your child's disability.
- Join support groups.
- Be aware of the tendency to be overprotective.
- Encourage independence.
- Become knowledgeable of technology developments useful to your child.

**FIGURE 4.9**
Continued.

- Avoid talking as much as possible as you write on the board with your back to the student.

- Provide lecture notes to the student.

- Make arrangements with a student in the class who takes good notes and who is willing to help the student with hearing impairments by making a copy of the lecture notes.

- Allow the student with hearing impairments to videotape the lecture.

- When students with hearing impairments are using lip reading and sign language, teachers should avoid, as much as possible, blocking the area around their mouths with their hands or other objects while talking.

- List major topics of the lecture or discussion on the board or overhead projector. The use of an overhead projector enables the teacher to continue facing students while talking and presenting materials.
- Use handouts extensively.
- Students may be given written instructions or information ordinarily read aloud by the examiner.
- The oral or sign language interpreter may translate oral instructions and information.
- Write on a piece of paper or on the board when it is necessary to communicate with students with hearing impairments.
- Consider using visuals—charts and graphs.
- If movies without captions are shown, written summaries or outlines of the movies are most helpful.
- Verbal assignments, due dates, exam dates, and changes in the normal class schedule may be missed by students with hearing impairments. Written instructions should be given.
- Select a seat that gives the student a direct line of vision to the teacher, the board or screen, and the interpreter.
- Students with hearing impairments not only watch lip movements, but also facial expressions, gestures, and other body language to communicate. Do not stand in front of a major light source such as a window. Shadows on the face make speech reading difficult.
- Only one person should talk at a time. Students with hearing impairments should face the speaker at all times.
- Appropriate use of facial expressions, gestures, and other body language is helpful in conveying the message.
- A hearing aid is virtually ineffective if the speaker is more than 3 to 8 feet from the hearing aid receiver. Furthermore, in many situations, persons having hearing impairments, even with an appropriate hearing aid, may have difficulty in understanding speech due to competing background noise. Shortening the distance between the speaker and listener and minimizing background noise as much as possible are much more effective than raising the voice. Never shout at hard-of-hearing persons who use hearing aids. They are sensitive to loudness and background noises. Noises are amplified by the hearing aid and interfere with the hard-of hearing persons' communication. Figure 4.10 provides the reader with additional information.

## Physical Disabilities and Special Health Problems

This category is very broad. It may include children who have cerebral palsy, spina bifida, muscular dystrophy, cystic fibrosis, juvenile rheumatoid arthritis, HIV infection,

**Characteristics**

- No response to a voice from more than 10 feet away
- Not following simple directions appropriately
- Impaired or unclear speech
- Attentive to faces during conversations
- Avoids situations that require talking and listening
- Shy, withdrawn from other children
- Shows joy and pleasure through silent laughter or a high-pitched screeching sound
- Very sensitive to bright colors and objects
- Very aware of change in decor, furniture, bulletin boards, and so on
- Unusual reactions to loud, dull noises (slammed door, dropped books); may respond to vibrations of low-flying airplanes or heavy trucks

**Implications for Educators**

- Accept the child as an individual. An awareness of assets as well as limitations is needed. Capitalize on the assets but do not overprotect.
- Remember that most children with hearing impairments possess normal intelligence.
- Encourage the child's special capabilities and help him or her experience success and achievement in some special task.
- Remember that no child with a hearing impairment can understand everything all of the time.
- Use as many visual aids as possible. Demonstrate what you want the child to understand. Use gestures.
- Use the chalkboard as much as possible. Do not talk while writing on the board or otherwise turn your back to the class.
- Use a normal tone of voice, a normal rate of speech, and a normal intensity of voice. Do not yell.
- Speak clearly and distinctly but do not exaggerate lip movements. Project your speech. Guard against talking with your lips closed or having your hand or a book in front of your face while speaking.
- Speak with the light on your face. Allow the light to be behind the child.
- Rephrase questions and repeat key words. Try to avoid walking while dictating problems or pronouncing spelling words.
- Seat the child where he or she can see your face (the second or third row if possible). Try to have his or her better ear toward you and the class.
- Write key words, new words, and new topics on the board. Say them to the class so that the child may also see them on your lips.
- Whenever possible, preview new work with parents so they can discuss the topic at home.
- Do not assume that a hearing aid will make the child's hearing normal.
- Discuss with class members the problems of the child with a hearing impairment and those associated with wearing a hearing aid.
- Encourage the child to ask for repetition.
- Remember that all noise is made louder by an aid, and the child will have difficulty understanding when there is excessive noise in the room.
- Remember that soft or voiceless sounds such as *f, s, th, k,* and *sh* may not be heard or may be greatly distorted. He or she may also distort those sounds in speech.

*(continued)*

**FIGURE 4.10**
Students with hearing impairments.

**Implications for Educators—*continued***
- Remember that many speech defects are caused by defective hearing.
- Remember that a hearing loss can occur or recur at any time, especially if the child has a cold, an allergy, a sore throat, or an earache.
- Children often daydream because they do not hear you. Always get the child's attention, then make your statement.
- Children fatigue easily because they are straining to perceive with their eyes what is written and what is being said.
- Teach the child to use the dictionary pronunciation key.
- Encourage the child to participate in musical activities. They stimulate residual hearing and add rhythm to the child's speech.
- Encourage and promote active participation in school and social functions.
- Seek professional help and advice from qualified persons and agencies.
- Phrase your thoughts in simple, easy-to-understand language, but always speak in complete sentences.
- Longer words or phrases are sometimes better than short ones.
- Don't be overly critical if the child talks to neighbors in class. He or she may ask another student to confirm information.
- Remember that children with almost identical hearing losses may function very differently and cannot be lumped into one generalized category for teaching purposes.
- Encourage a buddy, or buddies, to help the child with directions, assignments, or notes.
- Don't make the child feel inferior by protecting him or her from speaking assignments, but try to maneuver the presentation so that it is shorter and within his or her range.

**Tips for Parents**
- Face your child when speaking.
- Learn to communicate with your child in all methods he or she is learning.
- Be involved in your child's educational process.
- Encourage your child to wear hearing aids during all waking hours to receive optimum benefit.
- Create a hearing environment where your child can listen to different sounds.
- Observe your child and seek medical help if you suspect a hearing difficulty.

**FIGURE 4.10**
Continued.

and AIDS. Schools are also experiencing an increase in cases of asthma, diabetes, and childhood cancer. Physical impairments are due to a variety of causes including spinal cord injury, cerebral palsy, severe arthritis, amputation, and multiple sclerosis. One common result of many of these disabilities is paralysis or the loss of voluntary motor function. There are several types of paralysis, including monoplegia (partial or complete paralysis of one limb), triplegia (partial or complete paralysis of three limbs), tetraplegia (partial or complete paralysis of both arms and legs), paraplegia (partial or complete paralysis of the lower part of the body), and hemiplegia (partial or complete paralysis of an arm and a leg of either the right or left side of the body). Another frequent result of these types of disabilities is a loss of control over voluntary muscles in the arms, legs, tongue, or eyes that, in turn, result in awkward movements,

**Characteristics**
- Tires more quickly than others in class
- Excessive absences due to medical appointments
- Difficulty performing gross motor tasks
- Difficulty completing manipulative activities (holding a pencil, cutting, drawing, stringing beads)
- Difficulty distinguishing differences in size, depth, and spatial relationships (a common characteristic in children with cerebral palsy)
- May be socially delayed due to lack of interaction with other children

**Implications for Educators**
- The contributions of related services such as physical, populational, and speech and language therapy are often central to the education of children with physical disabilities. The greatest progress is achieved when therapy suggestions are consistently applied in the child's home as well as in school. This carryover strengthens appropriate feeding, positioning, and language stimulation patterns.
- Architectural factors must be considered. Section 504 requires that programs receiving federal funds make their programs accessible. This could mean structural changes (for example, adding elevators or ramps) or schedule or location changes (for example, offering a course on the ground floor).
- Sometimes the nature of the child's disability requires changes in school equipment or curriculum. In the same way, a student's placement should be the least-restrictive one appropriate for him or her; the day-to-day school pattern also should be as normal as possible.
- Physical disabilities can have profound effects on children's emotional and social development. Parents and teachers should avoid overprotection and encourage children to take risks within limits of safety and health. Teachers and classmates should also understand that, although children with physical disabilities and health impairments may be physically disabled, they are more like their classmates than different from them.
- Technology holds great promise for making the life of a child with a disability more normal. Computerized devices, for example, can help nonvocal, severely physically involved children communicate for the first time.
- Students who require recurring or long-term hospital care may need special services such as tutoring or homebound instruction to keep up with their class. Depending upon the nature and severity of the condition, counseling for the entire family may be helpful.

**Tips for Parents**
- Alert school personnel of any medical emergencies which could arise.
- Seek counseling for siblings who may have responsibility for caring for the child who is disabled.

**FIGURE 4.11**
Students with physical disabilities or special health problems.

irregular gait, facial grimacing, or drooling. Other physical manifestations of these disabilities might be difficulty with breathing, shortness of breath, and frequent coughing. Technology is continually changing for persons with physical disabilities. Figure 4.11 lists some general characteristics and educational implications for students with physical disabilities or special health problems. However, individual disabilities may vary greatly. One relatively common issue in the general classroom is epilepsy. Therefore, it is wise to be alerted before the child joins your class. You should also be

prepared to handle a seizure. There are two varieties of seizures: grand mal and petit mal. Petit mal seizures may go totally unnoticed; the student may simply stare into
space for a few seconds. When back on task, the student will have lost the train of
thought in the lesson. Petit mal seizures may occur many times during the day. The
Epilepsy Foundation of America offers the following suggestions for teachers with
students who have epilepsy:

1. Be sure to obtain and read current literature on epilepsy.
2. Remember that epilepsy is a very common condition and is no disgrace.
3. Most people with epilepsy can become seizure-free if they take medication as
   prescribed by their doctors.
4. If a grand mal seizure should happen in class, the teacher must remain calm.
   Students will follow the teacher's emotional lead.
   a. Try to prevent the student from striking his or her head or body against any
      hard, sharp, or hot object.
   b. Do not try to revive the student. Let the convulsion run its course.
   c. Do not try to restrain the student's movements or put anything between the
      teeth or in the mouth.
   d. Turn the student's face to the side and make sure that his or her breathing
      is not obstructed.
   e. Carefully observe the details of the seizure for a subsequent report to med-
      ical personnel.
   f. On the rare occasion when a seizure continues for more than 10 minutes,
      call the child's doctor for special instructions.
   g. Do not be frightened if the person in a seizure momentarily appears not to
      be breathing.
   h. Remember that a seizure cannot hurt the onlookers.
   i. When the student regains consciousness, he or she may be incoherent or
      very sleepy. The child should have the opportunity to rest.
   j. Proper persons (for example, parents) must be notified.
5. Turn a grand mal seizure during class into a learning experience, where accurate information, wholesome attitudes, and understanding (not pity) are the end
   results. Such an experience need not be frightening.
6. Remember that, given proper treatment, most children with epilepsy can live
   like any other children.
7. Do not pamper a child with epilepsy for fear that he or she may have a seizure.
   Do not let the child rule the roost.
8. Remember that someday you or a member of your family may have a seizure.
9. Treat students with epilepsy as you would have others treat you or your child
   under similar circumstances.

# NEW DIRECTIONS: THE AT-RISK POPULATION

The inclusive movement has opened many doors for another vast and frequently overlooked population of students: those at risk for school failure. Consider the following statistics:

- More than 24% of children age 4 and under are poor. During their early years, which are crucial to development, nearly one fourth of all U.S. children lack medical, nutritional, and early-learning resources (Reed & Sautter, 1990).

- More than 12.6 million American youngsters—nearly 20 percent of all children under age 18—are poor (Reed & Sautter, 1990). "A large percentage—more than 45 percent—of culturally diverse families live in poverty" (Wood & Larrazi, 1997).

- More than 1 million children are abused or neglected by their parents each year; for every case of child abuse that is reported, two additional cases go unreported.

- More than 25 percent of all high school seniors in the United States do not graduate (Olson, 1987).

- In the three decades between 1956 and 1986, the suicide rate in the United States among the 15–24 age group increased from 4.5 to 12.4 deaths per 100,000 (Guetzloe, 1989).

- A 1989 national survey revealed that at least 4 million Americans are homeless and that families with children comprise the fastest-growing segment of the homeless population (National Coalition for the Homeless, 1989).

What are the implications of these overwhelming statistics for educators? Even a cursory glance at these figures shatters the image of the rosy-cheeked student who cheerfully beckons to us from the back-to-school advertisement—a student who is healthy, carefree, well nourished, and supported and nurtured by two loving parents. Today, as a result of demographic shifts and changes in societal rules and practices, the face of the student population has changed. Students at risk for educational failure comprise the fastest-growing student population. As such, they are the focus of growing concern among a cross-section of general and special educators, in both rural and urban settings (Council of the Great City Schools, 1988; Helge, 1989a).

Exactly how is a student placed in the at-risk category? Must a student belong to one or more of the statistical groups I have just noted to be considered at risk? Historically, other labels have been used to identify this same population: culturally deprived, marginal, underprivileged, low performing, low achieving, remedial (Presseisen, 1988). While there is no clear consensus regarding an exact definition of students at risk, current definitions have been extended beyond those factors imposed solely by poverty or cultural deprivation. Helge (1989b) identified 16 characteristics most frequently associated with at-risk students (see Figure 4.12). Typically, students will meet one or more of the conditions, which are frequently related to one another.

**FIGURE 4.12**

Characteristics associated with at-risk students.

*Source:* Helge, D. (1989). Rural (at-risk) students—Directions for policy and intervention. *Rural Special Education Quarterly, 10,* 10. Copyright 1989 by *Rural Special Education Quarterly.* Adapted by permission.

- Substance abuse
- Involvement with crime
- Suicide attempt/depression/low self-esteem
- Child abuse (physical, emotional, verbal, or sexual)
- Poverty
- Child of alcoholic or substance abuser
- Child in a dysfunctional family system
- Illiteracy/English as a second language
- Migrant
- Disabling condition
- School dropout
- Sexually active/pregnant
- Minority and poor
- Health problem
- Performance significantly below potential
- Residence in a rural or remote area

The Iowa Department of Education (1989) has adopted a broader definition of the at-risk student: Any identified student who is at risk of not meeting the goals of the educational program established by the district, not completing a high school education, or not becoming a productive worker. These students may include, but are not limited to, dropouts, potential dropouts, teenage parents, substance users and abusers, low academic achievers, abused and homeless children, youth offenders, the economically deprived, minority students, culturally isolated students, those with sudden negative changes in performance due to environmental or physical traumas, and those with language barriers, gender barriers, and disabilities.

As Table 4.2 shows, this definition includes three distinct categories of at-risk students identified by specific, observable criteria.

Although differences exist in the type and number of factors that may be used to place a student in the at-risk category, a conservative estimate of the percentage of students who are seriously at risk for school failure is one fourth to one third of the total school population (Frymier, 1989). In rural areas, the prevalence of at-risk students may be even higher, with some rural states such as Wyoming reporting that as many as half of their children could be classified as at risk (Helge, 1989b).

The effects of individual risk factors and combinations thereof will differ from one student to another. However, the earlier that children are exposed to conditions that place them at risk, the greater the likelihood of a long-term negative effect on their development and academic achievement. Children who enter the public school system without a grasp of basic concepts and self-help skills and with limited abilities to listen, attend, and follow directions will begin to lag behind the achievement levels of their peers by the end of kindergarten. Without early detection and intervention, this discrepancy in ability and performance will continue to grow.

**TABLE 4.2**
At-risk categories and specific criteria for identification.

| Not Meeting Goals in Education Program | Not Completing High School | Not Becoming a Productive Worker |
|---|---|---|
| Low achievement scores; below the 30th percentile or 2 years or more behind | Pregnancy | No identified career interests |
| Inability to cope with a full class schedule; low grades in one or more classes (below a *C,* or 2.0 on a 4.0 scale) | Teen parent | Course selection is random, leading toward no specific postschool training or career choice |
| Poor attendance; missing 1 day per week | Dropout | |
| | Culturally or geographically isolated; not able to interact with students of a different race or socioeconomic background | No reasonable career plans upon graduation or beyond graduation |
| Suspended or expelled 2 or more times | No extracurricular involvement | No specific plan for post-high school training |
| Lack of friends | Substance use or abuse; unhealthy physical appearance | Low motivation to seek employment |
| Dislike for school; frequent mention of not belonging | Inability to adjust to transition steps in the education process (elementary to junior high/ middle school, or junior high/ middle school to high school) | Inability to keep employment; unacceptable work behavior |
| Sudden negative changes in classroom performance or social interaction | | Unfamiliarity with and inability to use community service agencies |
| Poor organization of study habits; can't find homework; lacks necessary materials | Homeless | Low aptitude/skills for competitive work |
| | Frequently tardy | |
| Inability to pay fees, lunch tickets, transportation, materials | Transient (moves from school to school within and outside the district) | |
| Limited English proficiency | Suicidal tendencies | |
| Disabled and not succeeding as expected after being given support services by special education staff | Negative peer influence (social crowd of dropouts, delinquents, or poor achievers) | |
| Difficulty meeting long-term goals | Victim of overwhelming peer harassment | |
| Low motivation to complete assignments | | |

*Source:* Iowa Department of Education. (1989). *Guidelines for serving at-risk students.* Des Moines: Author. Copyright 1989 by the Iowa Department of Education. Adapted by permission.

The body of research on the positive effects of preschool education in pre-venting later scholastic failure among children at risk leads to the inescapable con-clusion that high-quality, comprehensive, early childhood programs must be made available to all children, especially those who are disadvantaged or at risk (Mitchell, 1989; Schweinhart & Weikart, 1980). Funding is a critical factor in accomplishing this end. With the exception of Head Start, which continues to be funded with small annual increases, federal support for early childhood programs has declined in real dollars during the 1990s. Some states, however, have begun to develop and fund programs for young at-risk children, and many state departments of education are beginning to initiate prekindergarten programs in local public school districts. More recently, some federal interest in early childhood programs appears to have been renewed, as evidenced by the creation in 1988 of Even Start, a joint parent-child education program with the dual goals of improving adult literacy and providing ed-ucation to children between ages 1 and 7 (Mitchell, 1989).

The importance of establishing and maintaining programs for young at-risk children to prevent later academic failure and school dropout cannot be overem-phasized. Still, the need to continue similar efforts beyond the preschool years is also critical. No longer can early childhood educators (grades K–4) in public schools rely on curriculum approaches and methods designed for students with en-riched backgrounds. As increasing numbers of children exposed to one or more risk factors enter elementary school, techniques must be available to identify and meet their unique needs. For many children, this will entail educating their parents along with them. For others, specialized instruction blending approaches from general early childhood education, special education, and compensatory education will best meet their needs. For all children, early identification and intervention are key factors that will increase their chances of school success as they progress through the upper elementary grades.

As students enter middle school, critical factors in adolescent development (such as development of coping skills and dealing with issues of identity, indepen-dence, self-esteem, and self-image) may become unduly complicated when a stu-dent is already affected by, or becomes involved with, one or more of the risk fac-tors listed in Figure 4.12 (Helge, 1989b). Because of societal pressures and the compounded nature of many risk conditions faced by adolescents, curricular mod-ifications are needed at the middle and secondary levels to meet the changing needs of students. A greater emphasis on life skills, including training in problem solving, interpersonal communication, and the development of coping skills, can help all students meet and overcome the challenges of daily living imposed by risk factors. Redick and Vail (1991) use three descriptors to categorize the characteris-tics of students at risk: environmental, behavioral, and individual. Environmental descriptors include various conditions.

- Young people in poverty represent approximately 49.5% of American poor. With poverty comes lack of food, clothing, medical help, recreation, and so on.
- Stress affects everyone, especially the adolescent.

- Homelessness greatly affects our children. Every night between 68,000 and 500,000 children are without a home (Children's Defense Fund, 1991).

- Many young people are abused and neglected, and many are academically disadvantaged. Homes lack books, newspapers, or money to enrich the academic environment.

- Young people from dysfunctional families crowd our schools. Medical problems, alcohol, and unemployment are a few of the factors affecting many children's lives.

Behavioral descriptors such as eating disorders, chemical dependency, and sexual activity also place students at risk. Homosexual youths are harassed and humiliated. Young people with sexually transmitted diseases are increasing daily. More and more students become pregnant and step into parenthood during their early teenage years, and many schools have established day care facilities so that young parents can continue their education. Delinquent youth, youth in gangs, young members of satanic cults, and school dropouts are all at high risk. Sechler and Crowe (1987) believe that dropouts are 6 to 10 times more likely to become involved in criminal acts compared with students remaining in school. Drug use and unemployment are also higher among these students. As technology progresses, dropouts will continue to fall further behind within society.

Individual problems can put young people at risk, including mental illness, disabilities, and loneliness and disengagement. Therefore, you probably are beginning to see that this text speaks to all students and to all educators. The skills we have developed for use with students with disabilities can also help us with other students. The development of collaborative teaching is one technique that helps all children in the classroom.

Here is my own definition of a student at risk, which covers all children and adolescents who are having difficulty within the system:

Any student

At any time

Who is not succeeding

Educators can no longer work in isolation in their attempts to provide interventions for problems facing at-risk children and youth. Nor can they be expected to bear the full burden of overcoming social and economic inequities with limited personnel and fiscal resources (Reed & Sautter, 1990). It is critical for educators to form partnerships with parents and community leaders in accessing community resources (such as community mental health agencies and comprehensive community health services) and developing in-house resources (such as after-school care and family literacy training) to help overcome the multitude of problems associated with at-risk conditions.

When the growing statistics about at-risk groups are considered along with the increasing numbers of individuals, families, and communities affected by one or more risk conditions, it becomes clear that no school, classroom, or teacher can escape the influence of these risk conditions. All educators, including general and special education teachers and administrators, must develop new strategies to serve heterogeneous student populations and meet the diverse needs of at-risk students in the general education environment. Here are a few practical hints for teachers to share with parents of at-risk students (a special thanks to Shirlene Allen for sharing these ideas):

Encourage your child to:

- Accept responsibility for chores or activities.
- Listen to adult suggestions.
- Follow directions.
- Always follow safety rules.
- Take care of equipment and return materials after use; put everything in its proper place.
- Complete chores independently.
- Be trustworthy.
- Control mistakes; always proofread.
- Participate in organized activities outside of school and home, such as sports, scouts, dancing, music, and so on.

As a parent:

- Let your child know that you love and respect him or her.
- Accept your child as he or she is and become knowledgeable about the child's strengths and weaknesses.
- Be consistent with discipline, demands, and expectations; all children need to know their restrictions as well as the consequences for certain behaviors and actions.
- Ask for details, such as who, what, when, and where, when your child is trying to tell you something but is confused.
- Keep your child's decision making as simple as possible.
- Set a schedule or routine for bedtime, homework, meals, and chores; all children, especially those with learning problems, need the security of definite routines, schedules, and expectations.
- Keep a chart of job tasks and times for doing them.
- Have the child keep a record of when a chore has been completed, but don't give credit for sloppy work (like a half-made bed).
- Encourage independence.
- Understand that a good job attitude and responsibility for completing tasks are important.

- Avoid putting your child under time pressure.
- Do not assume that your child has heard something unless you have the child verbally repeat what he or she thinks you said.
- Make eye contact or call your child by name before talking to him or her about something.
- Let your child help you with projects around the house (yard work, washing the car, painting a room, and so on).
- Break directions into steps for complicated tasks.
- Increase job tasks from one to two or three activities.
- Use positive reinforcement for jobs well done; children with learning disabilities often need more praise and reinforcement than others because of so much past failure.
- Set up successful situations for your child as frequently as possible to help build self-image.
- Be decisive and stick to your decisions; don't argue or bargain after a decision has been made.
- Be firm and handle each situation immediately; don't fall back on "Wait until your dad gets home!"
- Always follow through, and don't make promises or threats you can't or won't keep.
- Keep your child's room organized, not cluttered; and let him or her be responsible (this is especially important for kids with learning disabilities).
- Encourage open communication and free conversation; be sure to do a lot of listening.
- Be open and honest about your child's strengths and weaknesses, and be sure he or she understands why certain teaching methods may not work with him or her; show your child that learning in a different way is really no different from wearing glasses to help weak eyes.
- Do not compare children within the home or classroom; each has the right to be him- or herself.
- Do not bug him or her about bad and good days at school.
- Never take for granted that a child knows even very simple concepts such as up, down, under, on, front, and back.
- Work with your child's teacher; consistency between home and school is a real asset.

Remind your child that he or she is not alone with this problem, that famous people who have contributed greatly to the advancement of the human race have shared it. Albert Einstein didn't speak until he was 4 years old and didn't read until he was 7. We continue to use the inventions of Thomas A. Edison, even though one of his teachers said, "He's too stupid to learn." Be sure your child knows that the great statesman Winston Churchill failed sixth grade. And tell them about the newspaper editor who was quick to fire a young man whose talents he could not admire. The editor said that the young man did not have one good idea and was void of potential. That young man was Walt Disney.

# MODEL FOR INCLUDING ALL CHILDREN

Models for the integration of students with disabilities into general class settings fill the professional education literature. A basic assumption is that a student with disabilities is placed into a model displaying an array of educational alternatives, ranging from the least restrictive to the most restrictive. Another basic assumption of many of the models is that a student will be placed into an alternative setting for varying degrees of time during the school day.

The model in Figure 4.13 focuses instead on the numerous instructional options that can be found within general education. The general education class functions as the home base for all children regardless of the difficulties they might be experiencing. The emphasis is on providing different instruction within the general class or close to its parameters rather than different physical placement. On the left side of the model, four options are available within the general class setting for all students. The right side of the model presents eight options available to a student when the options on the left do not work, which are considered only after the student has been through the formal assessment procedures.

## General Education Class Placement

All students should begin their educational experience within a general education class unless extenuating circumstances make this impossible. Some young children with disabilities or those who are significantly developmentally delayed are located and identified during their preschool years and will receive direct intervention or support services during that period. The vast majority of children who are at risk educationally may go unnoticed until the elementary years. In the past, if a student experienced noticeable difficulties academically or socially within general education, the child would be identified as disabled, and the long process to find an appropriate placement would begin. Many times, the student would continue to experience failure until a placement decision was made.

Educators now realize that we cannot afford to lose this precious time with students. Educational problems can and should be addressed within the general class before formal assessment, which often becomes unnecessary as a result. Steps 1 through 4 of the model offer viable alternatives for the general education teacher to pursue and investigate for each child before formal assessment.

*Step 1:* General class placement with instructional interventions. At-risk students remain in the general class with their peers, and the teacher informally assesses the problem, providing an appropriate intervention. Chapter 2 provides information on the teacher's role in the process of informal assessment. Frequently, adaptations or interventions involving teaching technique, materials, or testing procedures within the general classroom provide all the adjustments a student needs

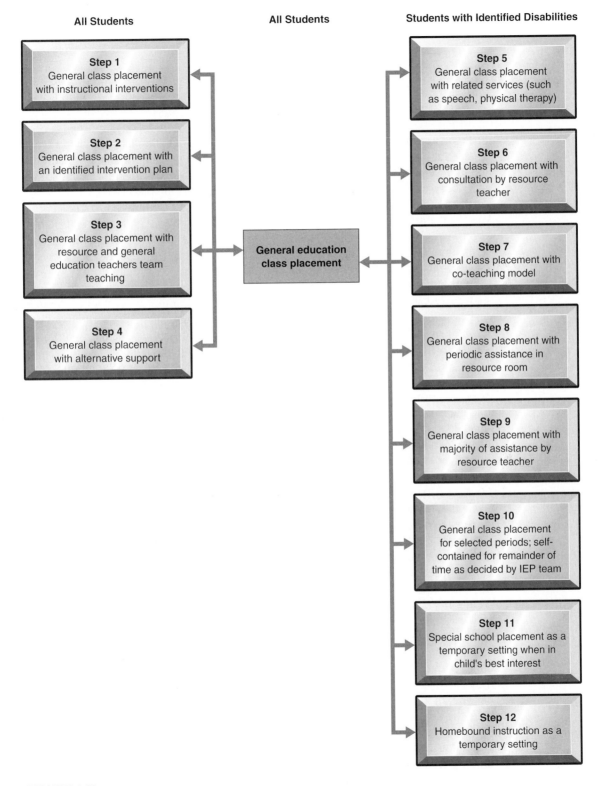

All Students

**Step 1**
General class placement with instructional interventions

**Step 2**
General class placement with an identified intervention plan

**Step 3**
General class placement with resource and general education teachers team teaching

**Step 4**
General class placement with alternative support

All Students

**General education class placement**

Students with Identified Disabilities

**Step 5**
General class placement with related services (such as speech, physical therapy)

**Step 6**
General class placement with consultation by resource teacher

**Step 7**
General class placement with co-teaching model

**Step 8**
General class placement with periodic assistance in resource room

**Step 9**
General class placement with majority of assistance by resource teacher

**Step 10**
General class placement for selected periods; self-contained for remainder of time as decided by IEP team

**Step 11**
Special school placement as a temporary setting when in child's best interest

**Step 12**
Homebound instruction as a temporary setting

**FIGURE 4.13**
Possible placements for children with special needs and at-risk students.

to succeed. If teachers make step 1 a natural component of their instruction, they will find that referral for formal assessment becomes reserved for students with more severe difficulties.

*Step 2:* General class placement with an identified intervention plan. The teacher seeks assistance among peers for the child who is at educational risk. Within the assessment process, this step is called *prereferral.* The prereferral process allows a teacher to go to a team of peers, discuss a child who is experiencing difficulty within the class, and, with the team's help, develop an intervention plan.

*Step 3:* General class placement with resource and general education teachers team teaching. Step 3 is rapidly becoming a preferred option for helping all children within general education classes. Traditionally, the resource teacher remained in the special class and was not allowed to teach a student unless that student had been identified as having a disability and had a valid IEP. Educators are now realizing that a valuable resource—the special education or resource teacher—is not being used. Programs are being implemented that allow the general and resource teachers to work collaboratively within the general class setting, with both teachers helping all students. Instructional interventions are used during this step, with both teachers sharing the responsibility for educating all children.

*Step 4:* General class placement with alternative support. At-risk students may move out of the general class to receive additional services. Some models bring these services, provided in reading and math for students performing in the bottom quartile, into the classroom. Chapter I or Title I programs are a common alternative. A visit to the guidance counselor, school nurse, or school psychologist also helps support many children. In some areas, a foster grandparent program brings senior citizens into the school for reading or one-on-one time, benefiting both students and volunteers.

General educators may use steps 1 through 4 continuously to provide educational options for students who have difficulty with traditional education. When these alternatives have been exhausted, the formal assessment process may become necessary, leading to steps 5 through 12.

*Step 5:* General class placement with related services. IDEA defines related services as those that are necessary to assist the child to benefit from special education (Federal Register, June 4, 1997). Related services include physical therapy, occupational therapy, guidance counseling, and speech-language therapy. Students must be formally identified as needing a related service. At times, the service will be provided as a support to services provided by a special education or resource teacher. In other cases—for example, a student with a language delay—a related service may constitute the student's primary and only special education service and be provided as an adjunct to a general class placement. The student may leave the general class for a short period at varying times to receive a related service, or it may be delivered in the general class. Regardless of the type of service, the student's home base remains in general education.

*Step 6:* General class placement with consultation by resource teacher. The student with special needs receives general class instruction with nondisabled students. This step does not involve resource room placement. However, when the student with disabilities is experiencing instructional or behavioral problems, the general class teacher can summon the special education resource teacher for instructional adaptation and modification suggestions. The special education teacher can then prescribe educational alternatives to general class instruction. Thus, the student receives services without being moved to a special class setting.

The clear advantages of resource consultation include less obvious labeling of students, less stress on teachers, less crowding of special education classrooms, and the help it provides to struggling students that are not identified. For example, even though students with disabilities must be screened, evaluated, and placed for special education consultation services, they remain more "alike" than "different" because they are still integrated with their peers in the general class setting. In addition, the overworked general classroom teacher has a support teacher to help with instructional modifications. Finally, keeping students with disabilities on consultation whenever feasible keeps special class space available for those students in definite need of such placements.

This step also serves as a phasing-out option for students who have previously received instruction from the resource teacher outside the general class. The consultation step is a popular choice for students who need a label to receive services, while teachers observe carefully to ensure that they can succeed without direct support.

*Step 7:* General class placement with co-teaching model. Step 7 is probably one of the most popular inclusive approaches because all students benefit from the co-teaching model. It allows the student with special needs to remain in the general class for instruction and socialization. Chapter 5 will discuss this approach in detail.

*Step 8:* General class placement with periodic assistance in resource room. Other situations require that a student with disabilities, although still in a general class setting, receive part-time services in the resource room. For example, a student may need special assistance in reading or require extra time for social studies. The adaptations and modifications in the appropriate instructional program for these students require a more concentrated effort by the special resource teacher. The student may go to the resource room for as little as one class period a day or for as much as half a day. The student's IEP dictates the amount of time to be spent as well as the subjects to be studied in both the resource room and the general classroom. The main difference between steps 6 and 7 is that in step 6 the student never leaves the general classroom for instructional purposes, whereas in step 7 the student may leave for one to several periods per day.

*Step 9:* General class placement with majority of assistance by resource teacher. For varying reasons, both academic and nonacademic, some students with disabilities may need intense instruction or attention from the special education resource teacher. This instruction may occur in either the general class or a special class. The intensity of the student's needs and the preference of the parent or student may dictate the specific locations where services will be provided. Integration of the student occurs as much as possible.

*Step 10:* General class placement for selected periods; self-contained for remainder of day as decided by IEP team. This placement is usually considered restrictive for students. Although not often supported as an alternative placement, the self-contained class is still a model used within schools.

*Step 11:* Special school placement as a temporary setting when in child's best interest. This point in the continuum reflects a change in emphasis from the student with mild disabilities to the student with more severe difficulties. A student served at this step needs a concentrated program because the general class setting, even with modifications and adaptations, fails to meet the instructional needs of the child. This service option should be viewed as only temporary while every effort is made to return the child to the general class setting.

*Step 12:* Homebound instruction as a temporary setting. Sometimes children need to receive educational services at home. A child recovering from surgery may need such services for only a short period of time, whereas a more seriously ill child may require homebound instruction for an extended period. In any case, a visiting teacher travels to the student's home and provides instructional services. Occasionally, a school uses a two-way communication system when services are required for an extended period of time. This approach, if used during school hours, provides contact between child and classroom, between child and teacher, and between child and peers, thus providing a simulated educational environment for the disabled student.

## MODEL SUMMARY

Presently, an array of service options is available for all children served within the schools. Services that historically were available only for a student with an identified disabling condition are now open to any child experiencing instructional difficulties. Equally important, opportunities that were once available only for the nondisabled student are now open to students with special needs as well. Educators are beginning to see that they must share the responsibility for the education of all children. Professionals and parents speak of integrating special students; however, if special students are never segregated, integration will become unnecessary. They will never have left the regular class! We need to think of special education as a service rather than a place, not a "life sentence." From the moment a child is found eligible for services and an IEP is developed, we need to think of what we want as outcomes for the student, and then focus on teaching compensatory strategies in the hopes that the day will come when the student will be dismissed from services.

## Transition Planning for Special Needs Students

*Written by Dr. Gary Meers*

*"If we always do what we have always done, we will always get what we have always gotten."*

Source unknown

Building the Foundation for Serving Students in General Education Classrooms

Legal Implications

The Road to Responsibility: From Prereferral to Placement

Bilingual or Limited-English-Proficient Students

Characteristics of Students with Special Needs

Transitions

## Chapter-at-a-Glance

Historical Development of Transition

Transition Planning and the IEP

Transition of Bilingual Children

Characteristics of Students with Special Needs

Persons Involved in the Transition Process

Using the SAALE Model in Transition

Transition Attitude Boundaries

Adapting the Behavioral Environment

Adapting the Physical Environment

Adapting Lesson Plans

# INTRODUCTION TO TRANSITION

There is comfort in staying with the known. It is the basis of all recipes. A cup of this, a teaspoon of that, and bake for 20 min at 350° as called for in the recipe. The outcome will always be the same. When the recipe is changed a little here and there, a pinch of this and a splash of that is used, the outcome is not known and the results will vary. Sometimes the product will be greatly enhanced and might even be a national winner of a bake-off contest; on the other hand, the results may be a substance that can be called hazardous waste. It is the challenge of experimentation and the unknown that makes cooking exciting. Transition services often encounter this same situation. Each IEP transition component has to be student centered and is unique to that student. Transition planners have certain federal laws and state/local guidelines to follow. But, beyond that, it is an experimental process based upon experience, expertise, and best judgment. Transition planners must ask a number of questions as they start the process:

1. Is the transition component student-centered?
2. Are all of the stakeholders involved?
3. Has a team been created for the planning process?
4. Are all of the support services available?
5. Are all components of transition being addressed?
6. What has been done previously?
7. What are the realities of opportunity?

The third edition of the *American Heritage Dictionary* defines the word *transition* as: 1. Passage from one form, state, style, or place to another. 2.a. Passage from one subject to another in discourse. b. A passage connecting two themes.

Transitions of varying degrees of importance happen in everyone's life. Some of these transitions are standard, while others tend to be more situational and may not pertain to everyone's life experiences. The standard transitions are called *lifespan developments* (vertical transitions), and they relate to major life events, such as the onset of school, graduation from school, and/or growing older. The situational transitions (horizontal transitions) refer to the movement from one situation or setting to another. The process of a person changing from being single to being married is an example of a horizontal transition. Regardless of the type of transition being experienced by an individual, it is best to have a plan so that the stress generally associated with the transition or change is mitigated (Blalock & Patton, 1996).

*Transition* is a term being used with more and more frequency within the disability community. It is reflective of the ongoing evolution of services needed and required by individuals with disabilities as they complete their secondary training and look to take advantage of postsecondary opportunities. Transition became a byword of planning as a result of the outcome from other programs for students with disabilities. With the requirement of a free and appropriate public education (FAPE), an individualized education program (IEP), and a least restrictive environment (LRE) for all students with disabilities, it was only a matter of time before comprehensive planning would be required for post–high school opportunities. Students with disabilities were getting better content, greater opportunity, and realistic planning for their educational journeys. Some process had to be created that would assist them as they reached adulthood. This process became known as *transition planning*. A brief review of some of the impacting legislation and historical perspectives will assist in developing an understanding of how the transition process came about.

# HISTORICAL DEVELOPMENT OF TRANSITION

The early history of the transitioning process can be traced to the roots of special education in Europe. Before the 17th century, minimal effort was devoted to training individuals with disabilities. The first formal efforts to educate and rehabilitate people with disabilities occurred in the 1600s. These first efforts were chiefly devoted to techniques designed to enrich the lives of blind and deaf individuals. Also at this time, persons with mental illness began to receive more humane treatment, but any effort to educate and rehabilitate these people was not considered a worthwhile endeavor (Szymanski, Hanley-Maxwell, & Asselin, 1992).

By the 1700s, great strides were made in the education and rehabilitation of individuals with disabilities. Special schools were set up for blind and deaf persons. Moreover, one of the contemporary doctrines of special education was established by the French philosopher Jean-Jacques Rousseau. Rousseau felt that an individualized education was an avenue in which a person could attain a productive and useful life. Lastly, the 1700s ended with the groundbreaking work of Itard and the "Wild Boy of Aveyron" in France. His work with this boy enabled Itard to set up training procedures that successfully improved the social and language skills of a person with considerable mental challenges (Szymanski et al., 1992).

The United States followed the European model of using asylums in New England for the people with severe disabilities or who were blind. This model of treatment and service was used until the mid-1800s. The Civil War era brought about a number of changes in the services and treatment of persons with disabilities as a result of two major movements. A concern for the treatment and welfare of slaves extended to persons with disabilities. Also, with the return of soldiers who had been maimed in war, a need to include them within the community structure developed. Special schools and programs were established to assist persons with disabilities to gain additional social and academic skills.

Later in the 19th century, a social concern was raised about crime and degeneracy. Grave new concerns emerged about morality. Information emerged that led to the identification of a disability as not only the punishment for presumed behavior transgressions but also a heritable trait (Dugdale, 1910; Goddard, 1912).

The first steps in creating the transition process were found in a movement during the early 1900s. Children with disabilities had two principles applied to them as part of their educational planning: (a) the principle of opportunity and (b) the principle of proof. The principle of opportunity simply meant that any child should be allowed to enroll in any class open to other children, with no prior restriction placed on participation. The principle of proof provided that continuance in a class, school experience, or school activities would be contingent on meeting the standard used to determine satisfactory performance. The principle of opportunity gave entrance, but the principle of proof gave schools and educators a way of keeping students with disabilities out of many programs, since they were not able to meet the qualitative expectations of the class or program. A start toward transition began, but only in theory (Sitlington, Clark, & Kolstoe, 2000).

With the end of WWI, another major shift in societal perceptions and schooling for students with disabilities came about. The returning soldiers carried with them many different forms of disability as a result of their injuries, which caused many people to question that disabilities were a heritable trait. The soldiers had acquired their disabilities as a result of defending their country, and thus should receive some type of training and support to allow them to "transition" back into civilian life. They were entitled to that much. Also during this time, the use of IQ tests (the Army Alpha and Beta tests) revealed that the number of persons with scores below what was thought to be "normal" was much larger than originally expected (Anastasi, 1976). Collectively, society wanted to help these individuals, so a wide variety of services were provided.

These helping programs were primarily segregated in nature. Residential schools were established in almost all of the states, and they generally served the blind, deaf, and mentally retarded. Many people felt that students could most benefit when living and being educated among others with the same disability. Where residential schools did not exist, self-contained classes were created. Students with disabilities were given a so-called equal opportunity to acquire the academic and life skills needed for adult success. As is known, adult success for the vast majority of persons with disabilities meant working in segregated settings with persons with similar disabilities. Deaf persons, for example, were channeled into the printing industry, where the noise of the presses and hot lead machines would not hurt their hearing. The positive aspect of this is that persons with like kinds of disabilities came to dominate certain industries where they could earn reasonable salaries and be gainfully employed. Other disabled persons, unfortunately, were directed to institutions where they would spend the remainder of their lives in sequestered settings or remain in their homes.

During this time an interesting piece of federal legislation was passed that created a contradiction and yet paved the way for vocational training of persons with disabilities many years later. The Smith-Hughes Act of 1917 was passed as the first piece of legislation to set forth vocational training opportunities for young adults. Within the legislation was the creation of the Federal Board for Vocational Education. The Federal Board was to administer and oversee both the establishment of vocational educational programs and vocational rehabilitation service delivery systems. Yet, the Federal Board for Vocational Education had this to say about the education of students with disabilities:

The Federal Board desires to emphasize the fact that vocational schools and classes are not fostered under the Smith-Hughes Act for the purpose of giving instruction to the backward, deficient, and incorrigible or otherwise subnormal individuals; but that such schools and classes are to be established and maintained for the clearly avowed purpose of giving thorough vocational instruction to healthy, normal individuals to the end they might be prepared for profitable and efficient employment. Such education should command the best efforts of normal boys and girls. (Meers, 1987)

Thus, in 1917, both vocational education training and vocational rehabilitation services were under the same administrative umbrella, but it would be many years later before there was a joining of effort, philosophy, and programming for persons with disabilities. Together, separate, together, separate—a seemingly repeated pattern of educational reform.

During the 1950s and early 1960s, major changes started to occur within the social fabric of the United States. A sense of unrest was developing because not all sectors of society were being included in the growing prosperity of the country. The groundwork was being laid for the coming civil rights movement. A hint of the coming opportunities for persons with disabilities was revealed in the passage of the Vocational Education Act of 1963 (PL 88-210). This act was the first piece of federal legislation that identified the importance of providing monitory assistance to individuals with special needs so they could have a chance to achieve fulfillment in regular vocational education programs. Furthermore, PL 88-210 allowed federal funds to be used for programs giving occupational training to individuals who had disabling academic, socioeconomic, or other conditions which would hinder them from flourishing in regular vocational settings. Still, the Vocational Education Act of 1963 did not dictate that the use of these funds had to go specifically to the betterment of individuals with disabilities. Thus, the services provided to individuals with disabilities were arbitrarily funded and poorly organized (Colby, Wircenski, & Parrish, 1987). In 1964 the Civil Rights Act (PL 88-352) was passed. Although the act did not specifically address the educational and vocational needs of people with disabilities, it did empower these same individuals with the sense that they possessed the same fundamental rights as all other Americans (Colby et al., 1987).

As can been seen, a momentum was building to include all sectors of society, yet not one group or organization was quite sure how to do it. There was a stirring of need, but no plan of implementation. The word *transition* had not yet been created in relation to the application that is made today. The 1960s were a decade of turmoil. Societal classes were changing, organizations of advocacy were being created, and school reform was being discussed without a clear agenda. A next step was needed. The Vocational Education Amendments of 1968 (PL 90-576) were passed. These amendments to the Vocational Education Act of 1963 (PL 88-210) attempted to rectify the difficulties of funding and of organizing special needs programming. America was in an era of building the "Great Society" and to do so everyone had to have a part in the process. PL 90-576 apportioned federal funds especially for the purpose of endowing persons with disabilities a vocational education.

The act broke the special needs population into two separate categories: (a) disadvantaged students and (b) students with specific disabling conditions. These two categories of individuals were allotted funds in a manner that the states would provide at least 15 percent of their core vocational funds to the former group and at least 10 percent of their core vocational funds to the latter group. The Vocational Education Amendments of 1968 also brought into vogue the notion that a more individualized vocational educational experience would be in the best interest of the students and that these students should be assimilated into the regular vocational programs with the provision of the necessary support networks (Meers, 1987).

For the first time, this piece of federal legislation "set aside" money to be used for the vocational training of students with disabilities at a time when little or no structure existed to do so. There were no IEPs, no transition components, and no student-centered teams to help in the planning process. It was a time of experimentation to see what worked. Many comprehensive and unique programs were established at this time. Much of the program development was based upon best practices as shared between and among fellow educators. In 1972, a professional organization was created to facilitate in the sharing of this much needed information. The organization, the National Association of Vocational Educational Special Needs Personnel (NAVESNP), started a journal, a newsletter, and regional conferences to help with information exchange. Educators working in this area had a resource to go to during this developmental time.

Also during this time, there was opposition from the general education and vocational communities concerning the integration of students with disabilities into vocational training programs. Vocational education had long been seen as a "dumping ground" for students who lacked the intellect to succeed in regular subjects. To put special needs students into these classes would serve to reinforce the previously held misconceptions. In addition, special needs students would create a safety issue, force the lowering of standards and would slow entire classes down with their inability to read, all of these being barriers to integration. Through demonstration of student performance and advocacy on the part of special and vocational teachers, these fears were slowly put to rest. The best argument that could be made was that of success. Through demonstrating student program completion and positive work experiences, programs were able to show that the voiced fears were unfounded. At times, this issue still surfaces and educators have to show that their students have the abilities to succeed in vocational classes and community work experience programs.

## DECADES OF DEVELOPMENT

Another piece of federal legislation that was to continue the momentum of equality or persons with disabilities was the passage of the Vocational Rehabilitation Act of 1973 (PL 93-112). This act afforded civil rights protection for the disabled, and decreed affirmative action hiring practices would be in place for them as well. The two key components of PL 93-112 are: (a) section 503 and (b) section 504.

Section 503 helped make it easier for individuals with disabilities to find employment in public and private jobs. More specifically, section 503 states that any employer who receives federal assistance in the form of contracts for $2,500 or more is mandated to implement an affirmative action plan to help in the recruitment, hiring, training, and advancement in employment of individuals with disabilities. Additionally, companies receiving federal contracts of $50,000 or more and having 50 or more employees are prescribed to have an affirmative action program within 120 days that plans for specific policies and procedures with regard to the employment of persons with disabilities. These same employers are also bound to make reasonable accommodations to meet the needs of workers with disabilities.

Section 504 of PL 93-112 outlawed employment discrimination of a person having a disability by programs and activities receiving and/or benefiting from federal financial aid.

The following points were stipulated in section 504:

1. Discrimination is prohibited with regard to providing health, welfare, and other social services.
2. Discrimination in admissions into higher education is banned.
3. Children of school age with disabilities are enabled to have a free and appropriate education.
4. Employers are mandated to give equal opportunities and compensation to persons with disabilities.
5. All new public buildings are bound to be accessible to individuals with disabilities.

The Vocational Rehabilitation Act of 1973 also set up the federal-state vocational rehabilitation program still in use today. Moreover, later amendments to PL 93-112 earmarked money for supported employment services for people with severe disabilities with the intent of increasing their employment, independence, and integration into the work force and community.

The groundwork was laid to fit the pieces of the transition puzzle together, remembering that, as of yet, the term *transition* was not in use either in policy or legislation. In place were federally funded vocational training programs, nonexclusion policies, and reasonable accommodation requirements. A comprehensive piece of legislation that would attempt to tie all of these loose ends together into one source of information for educational planners was needed. The passage of the Education for all Handicapped Children Act of 1975 (PL 94-142) brought this about. PL 94-142 was monumental because it required state and local education agencies to provide free and appropriate public education to persons between the ages of 3 and 21 with disabling conditions. In addition, schools had to provide assessment of student ability, due process, and individualized education programs (IEP) that were free and appropriate. Students with disabilities were to be educated in the least restrictive environment and mainstreamed into regular classrooms wherever possible. To develop the required IEP, a team of stakeholders was created. The team consisted of educators, administrators, adult service providers, parents, and the student. The IEP was to be developed and reviewed annually with services being provided in differing ways as the maturity and needs of the student dictated—another major step to implementing transition planning.

The passage of the Individuals with Disabilities Education Act (IDEA) of 1990 (PL 101-476) gave transition planning the guidelines and formality needed to complete the planning process. IDEA required the arrangement of transitional services for students in special education who were 16 years old and older. This then provided transition opportunities from age 16 until 21 or until graduation from high school, which was a definite window of opportunity for planning. This law also gave a clear legal definition of transition.

> Transition services means a coordinated set of activities for a student, designed within an outcome oriented process, which promotes movement from school to postschool activities, including postsecondary education, vocational training, integrated employment, including supported employment, continuing adult education, adult services, independent living, or community participation. The coordinated set of activities shall be based upon the individual student's needs, taking into account the student's preferences and interest and shall include instruction, community experiences, employment development, and other postschool adult living objectives, and when appropriate acquisition of daily living skills and functional vocational evaluation. (PL 101-476)

The definition of transition was given, the age of implementations was stated, and guidelines were shared as to how the family, student, and/or school personnel were to be involved. Transition was coming together philosophically and programmatically.

Also in 1990, the Americans with Disabilities Act (ADA) was passed. The ADA covered a number of issues that had been facing the disabled community. Specifically, no longer would discrimination be allowed in the areas of public transportation, public accommodations, and employment. Employment issues were covered through two very clear definitions: reasonable accommodations and essential job functions. Employers had to make reasonable accommodations for persons with disabilities. These accommodations were designed to not impose unreasonable requirements upon the employer, while providing persons with disabilities the opportunity to be gainfully employed. The essential job functions called for the employers to clearly define the job descriptions and duties to be performed by the workers. These definitions could then be used by the perspective employees and employers to see how a "best" fit could be made. This law provided a major entryway for youth leaving school and wanting to enter the workforce.

Another part of the transition puzzle was completed—transition was defined, age requirements given, and adult opportunities provided. Progress had been made legislatively.

In addition, the previous decade had given educators much experience in the development and refinement of career planning processes. This experience was of much benefit in refining how IEPs could be developed. One additional component needed to be added. In 1997, the Individuals with Disabilities Education Act Amendments (PL 105-177) were passed. This new law kept the definition of transition but broadened it in a number of ways. One of the expanded points was in the area of co-ordinated activities, which could include related services, such as transportation, and support services, such as speech and language pathology and audiology services, psychological services, physical and occupational therapy, recreation, social work services, counseling services (including rehabilitation counseling), orientation and mobility services, and medical services (for diagnostic and evaluation purposes).

A significant change in the law was made related to when transition planning must begin for students. PL 105-177, section 614, states: *"For each student with a disability, beginning at age 14, and updated annually, a statement of the transition service needs of the child under the applicable components of the child's IEP that focuses on the child's course of study (such as participation in advanced-placement courses or a vocational education program)"* (PL 105-177). The 1997 amendments retained the requirement that the transition components of the IEP for a student 16 years of age must include the statement of interagency responsibilities or any needed linkages. The age 14 planning requirement is intended to give the student, parents, and school officials time to plan courses and support services leading up to implementation of transition components at age 16 and beyond.

A student with a disability can receive services from birth through age 21. During this period of time, educational planning helps to dictate the free and appropriate public education the student will receive. As the student reaches different levels of chronological maturity, different services will be provided. All of these services are to be coordinated in such a fashion that upon graduation, or at 21 years of age, the student will have the experiences desired. This is the goal of transition planning.

An interesting side benefit of the transition movement has been the realization that transition planning is needed for all students. The 1994 School-to-Work Opportunities Act was designed to provide career planning for all students. The act created and funded a number of programs and activities to assist all students in making the transition from school to the community and adult life. The three components outlined within the law are school-based activities to illustrate to students the relevance of what they are studying in class, community-based activities to show students how the real world functions, and connecting activities to show how classroom activities and teachings can be connected to the community. This act is a direct reflection of the transition process.

# TRANSITION PLANNING AND THE IEP

## Setting the Stage

Transition to adult and community living revolves around competence within three major career areas:

Career as a homemaker

Career as a community participant

Career in gainful employment

A career as a homemaker involves gaining independent living skills to the maximum degree possible. Everyone is a homemaker to one extent or another. Whether living alone, in a group home, or with someone, the individual helps make up the home. The home may be a bedroom decorated and maintained based upon personal preference, a shared setting with the need for caring about others' feelings, or one's own residence. Living alone in an apartment without the skills to maintain the home will make for a very unsuccessful experience. However, if the individual has the skills to cook, clean, launder, and decorate the apartment, then satisfaction will be forthcoming, leading to a contented maker of the home.

Independent living skills are based upon the individual and the support network available. An example of a transition component on developing independent living skills is the school district leasing an apartment in which students could practice and develop independent living skills.

Students age 14 to 16 would go to the apartment and spend a few hours during which they would clean the premises, do laundry, and prepare a snack. As time and maturity allowed, the students would expand the time spent in the apartment. Responsibilities would be expanded as well until the students spent the entire day. During the day, they would completely maintain the apartment and prepare lunch and dinner.

The ultimate goal of the program would be for the students to progress until, before leaving the secondary school setting, they would have spent a month living in the apartment. Supervision of the students and the apartment would be shared between the school and adult service providers. This sharing of supervision serves two purposes: The students get to meet and become familiar with adult service providers who will eventually be their adult case supervisors, and the school officials become familiar with the next steps in the lives of their students.

Parents also play a critical role in the process as they are seeing their children gain independence while being supported as needed. Parents become familiar with the next steps of their children's lives, and they learn how to plan for their children's independence, whatever form it might take.

A career as a community participant involves being able to use the resources that are in the community. Skills are needed to help the students be able to get around the community via public transportation, driving, or other means. Other community needs are shopping, voting, and using recreational facilities. The 14 to 16 transition component could include the development of a training program for the students, such as an in-school program for developing navigating skills within the building. The 16 and beyond transition services would include the above-mentioned skill development in using public transportation, getting a driver's license, using recreational facilities, purchasing, and so on.

Training for a career in gainful employment would include students' securing the experience necessary to make choices about what they like and dislike in relation to work settings. Exploration, such as job shadowing, would be a major part of the needed transition services. As the students mature, the transition service needs would be changed to include paid employment with supervision by job coaches. Prior to leaving the formal school setting, the students would be working in some form of employment with minimum supervision.

## Legislative Transition Planning

The outcome of any quality educational program is the ability of the graduate or completer to go to the next level of opportunity, be it further training or employment. The previously discussed laws all have as their ultimate goal the successful integration of students with disabilities into the adult community. Public Law 105-17, the Individuals with Disabilities Education Act (IDEA), has as a primary purpose to "ensure that all children with disabilities have available to them a free appropriate public education that emphasizes special education and related services designed to meet their unique needs and prepare them for employment and independent living" (34 CFR§ 300.1(a)).

This statement in its entirety should ensure that students with disabilities are properly educated and supported in their transition efforts. Unfortunately, this has not been the case, as supported by research.

A follow-up study has shown that students with disabilities do not enjoy the same success rate as their nondisabled peers. A large proportion of students with disabilities do not go on for further training after high school. Additionally, it has been found that they do not receive the postschool supports and services needed (Blackorby & Wagner, 1996; Wagner, 1991; Wagner, 1993).

In order for transition planning to be successful, it must contain many different options to ensure that students are given ample opportunity to meet their individual needs as they approach and enter into adulthood. These options must be carefully considered by all the service providers in conjunction with students' self-determination. This complex task must be completed over a period of time when students are maturing physically and emotionally. Students are in the process of finding and defining their independence in relation to their disability, which translates into a very challenging time for all the stakeholders.

## Finding Their Way in Transition

Students with disabilities must also find a path for themselves within the school curriculum. Schools traditionally offer three paths for students to follow:

1. General education—preparation for life with a set of general basic skills
2. College preparatory—preparation for a four-year postsecondary setting
3. Vocational preparation—preparation for employment upon leaving secondary school

Students with disabilities must be assisted in the planning process to enable them to find a location on one of these paths or to create a combination of paths to ensure that they are in fact receiving the most appropriate and suitable educational program. A combination of legal understanding, collective team planning, and community-based experiences must be coordinated through the IEP transition components to ensure that students with disabilities are being provided with transition opportunities.

The IEP has been the primary vehicle through which educational and career planning and services have been provided. This vehicle has been strengthened even further through the 97 amendments to IDEA, which are summarized in the following list:

- Require earlier transition planning
- Help to start the student and parents thinking about the long-term future
- Create a picture of the student's needs, interests, and preferences
- Refine current student performance
- Identify the support and services the student needs for success
- Ensure that the student learns to the maximum extent appropriate within the general curriculum and environment
- Assist the IEP team in setting goals and objectives yearly that will culminate in positive postsecondary experiences

With the IEP as the planning instrument, transition components must be refined in such a way that they give early opportunities for exploration and later opportunities for specific training and/or postsecondary preparation. The following are the two *primary* required components of transition, as covered within the IEP:

(b)(1) For each student with a disability beginning at age 14 (or younger, if determined appropriate by the IEP team), and updated annually, a statement of the transition service needs of the student under the applicable components of the student's IEP that focuses on the student's courses of study (such as participation in advanced-placement courses or a vocational education program); and

IDEA 97 (34 CFR § 300.347)

(2) For each student beginning at age 16 (or younger, if determined appropriate by the IEP team), a statement of needed transition services for the student, including, if appropriate, a statement of the interagency responsibilities or any needed linkages.

As can be noted, the wording is very similar for both requirements. To try to reduce the level of confusion, the two requirements will be separated and discussed in depth.

*Transition service needs of students age 14 (or younger, if determined appropriate by the IEP team)* means that not only must the IEP team fulfill the requirements of the IEP, but they must also provide "transition service needs" components. Transition service needs may take the form of courses of study or a multiyear description of course work to achieve the students' desired postschool goals. The transition service needs are intended, through early planning as Congress stated, "to augment, and not replace" the later planning that must occur with 16-year-old students.

An example of an employment development transition service need would be as follows.

*Goal:* With preferred job cluster areas of interest selected, students will explore a variety of career options.

Students will:

- Job shadow three businesses.
- Participate in two volunteer work experiences.
- Interview a worker.
- Tour a supported employment program.
- Complete work samples.
- Enroll in career class and participate in related work experience.
- Attend career days.

All of the experiences are exploratory, giving students experiences and a knowledge base from which decisions can be made later in terms of specific career preferences. These transition service needs are being met to allow the students choices and to give parents additional information about their children's career preferences. Without meeting these needs it would be very hard for students to progress to the needed services stage due to the lack of exposure to opportunities.

Starting at age 16 (or younger, when appropriate) the IEP must incorporate *needed transition services.* These services are to be specific to the career plans of the students. An example of needed transition services would be as follows.

*Goal:* Students will secure employment.

Students will:

- Write/update resume.
- Practice interview skills.
- Contact and apply to three businesses.
- Keep records of job search.
- Develop a career portfolio.
- Secure employment.
- Secure needed support services.

The age 14 transition service needs for students give an experience base from which the age 16 transition service needs can be expanded and developed as students progress through the educational system. IDEA 97 also states "The statement of needed transition services . . . includes instruction, related services, community experiences, the development of employment and other post-school adult living objectives; and if appropriate, acquisition of daily living skills and functional vocational evaluation" (34 CFR §300.29(a)(3)). In addition, the statement of needed transition services must also include "a statement of the interagency responsibilities or any needed linkages" (§ 300.347(b)(2)). As can be seen in the previous example, needed linkages or support services are a part of the transition planning process. There are two major reasons for the linkages: (a) the students need the linkages to progress transitionally, and (b) the linkages are needed to provide adult services, such as transportation and housing.

# Creating Effective Transition Components within the IEP

The IEP is designed to be an individual educational process that leads students to successful completion of school training and movement into the adult community. Careful and comprehensive planning of the transition components will help to ensure that the IEP is both effective and efficient. To help with this planning process, the following steps are suggested.

### Get a Clear Picture of the Students' Postschool Goals

The IEP team needs to learn from the students what they want to do beyond school. Is it further education, technical training, employment, or the military, for example? How and where do the students want to live? An apartment, family home, or group home? Do they understand the concept of independent living? In what ways do the students want to take part in the community? Will they be involved with public transportation, recreation, or community activities?

The development of a clear picture of the students' postschool goals is based upon their preferences, needs, and interests. Many students will not have any idea of what they want out of their school career. The IEP team can help this process by having a long-range vision in mind and by allowing the students to continue to have input in the IEP planning process over the years. Maturity and experience will help to more realistically define the long-range goals. Many adults do not know what they want to do nor what they want out of life, so students with disabilities are not the exception. The students, though, have a team of concerned stakeholders helping them with their life plan.

Being realistic is a concept that is hard to grasp by many students and their IEP team. Everyone dreams about a career that is glamorous, pays well, and does not involve extensive work. The reality is that there are not many careers that offer this. Instead, students must be able to explore their dreams while being exposed to a dose of reality. By providing exploration opportunities, students can discover for themselves what they can and cannot do or what additional training or education they must have to enter their career choice. These experiences can be secured through job shadowing, work experience, and career interview, for example. The students, as they progress, will start to develop a sense of reality about what they want out of their transition experiences.

### Clearly Describe the Students' Present Levels of Educational Performance (PLEP)

IDEA 97 requires that the IEP include *"A statement of the child's present levels of educational performance, including how the child's disability affects the child's involvement and progress in the general curriculum (i.e., the same curriculum as for nondisabled children)"* (34 CFR §300.347(a)(1)(I)). By having the student's PLEPs, the IEP team will have a database from which more realistic planning can emerge.

Inviting students to participate in their IEP meetings creates a sense of self-determination. This assists not only the students but the parents as well. The parents will start to see the maturation process beginning to take place in their children's lives. Whether the students attend the IEP meetings does not matter. It is the invitation that is important because it demonstrates that their interests, preferences, and needs are still being considered. Depending upon their abilities, a level of self-advocacy will start to emerge as a result of this process. Their present level of educational performance will serve to highlight when and where certain career and transition components should be introduced.

The PLEP discussions that take place in the IEP meetings should move beyond the discussion of special education eligibility and focus on the supports and services the students need now and in the next few years. As the next few years are expanded into long-range planning, the PLEP becomes more important with each year's assessment, during which the long-range goal is retained but modified based upon student needs and changing life goal preferences.

### Design Transition Service Needs Statements

As has been previously discussed, the transition service needs must be identified and included in the IEP by age 14 or earlier if needed. These statements must include listings of courses that will lead the students to graduation or completion of a school program. The statements must also include a list of needed supports that will assist students in successful completion of their education, employment, and independent living goals. As always, the long-range vision is kept foremost in the minds of the IEP team.

### Design Needed Transition Service Statements

The IEP team is in the process of finalizing the transition process for the students when the needed transition service statements are developed. These statements generally include the following:

- A complete "outcome-oriented" plan for adult life. This would be reflective of all the previous experiences the students have had as well as the last several years of IEP planned training.

- The transition components, which are still a part of the long-range thinking by the students and parents where the students' needs, preferences, and interests are kept in the forefront of the planning.
- Coordinated activities that include instruction, related services, community services, employment, postschool training, and daily living skills.

### Coordinate Support Services

Bringing other involved individuals or agencies into the planning process in a formal way is addressed in IDEA 97: "At the discretion of the parent or the agency, other individuals who have knowledge or special expertise regarding the child, including related services personnel as appropriate" (334 CFR §300.344(a)(6)). Further, "The public agency also shall invite a representative of any other agency that is likely to be responsible for providing or paying for transition services" (34 CFR §300/344(b)(3)(i)). Adult service providers need to be generally involved as the first transition components are introduced at age 14. At age 16, the general involvement changes to specific ways the adult service providers will be delivering services for the students. All of the stakeholders need to be part of the process. Some of the transition planning will involve service providers who are directly involved in vocational evaluation and employment training, such as vocational rehabilitation, and others, such as developmental disabilities agencies, may be involved in planning for adult day programs or residential accommodations. As students mature and make career plans, it becomes critical that a continuum of services be created to ensure that appropriate services are identified and delivered. Also, as students reach the latter part of their secondary education, issues of who will pay for certain adult services start to surface. By having agency representatives involved in the long-range planning process, many of the payment issues can be resolved before the actual need for paid services occurs. This will do much to reduce the eligibility lag that often occurs in dealing with a multitude of service providers.

## SUMMARY

Effective and efficient IEP development is dependent upon full participation by all those affected by the outcomes of the plan. Students must have as much input as they can in developing their long-term goals and objectives. Parents, special education teachers, regular education teachers, and adult service providers must be outcome oriented while being respectful of the students' needs, interests, and preferences. The transition services must progress from being identified to being delivered in a sequential way that will maximize the opportunity for students to move from school to adult postschool settings with minimum disruption in their life plans.

## TRANSITION OF BILINGUAL CHILDREN

Transition planning for children from bilingual homes depends greatly upon the educational background and English language command possessed by parents. If the parents are conversant in English and have an understanding of the educational process, then transition planning should proceed in the same way it does for monolingual students and their parents. Chapter 2 discusses this procedure in length.

Children from bilingual homes are often first-generation students that are dealing with a new culture, education, language, and their disability. All of these challenges make transition planning very complex. Educators must be aware that students and their parents are facing several barriers that must be overcome, such as:

- English language understanding
- Cultural understanding
- School process understanding
- IEP planning understanding
- Knowledge of career options

Transition planning becomes complex when bilingual students come from a first-generation family that is striving to understand the culture and options presented within the United States. By law, IEP notices and meetings must be presented in the language of the student and parents. This requirement also includes the transition components.

IEP team members presenting transition information and components must be sensitive to the students and parents when completing this process. They must make sure that the parents are understanding the process of developing the IEP. Once that is clear, then the transition components can be introduced into the meetings.

In many cases the students are much more familiar with the educational process, school culture, and career planning than their parents. This can make for an awkward setting when meeting with the parents. The IEP team must ensure that the parents understand what is meant by *transition* and how planning for postschool opportunities works. Parents who have recently come to the United States are in the process of creating economic and residential stability for their children. They, in many cases, are not aware of the career opportunities that exist for their children. In addition, they may not have the academic skills to process all of the information that is being shared with them, or language translation may not be clear or complete. These issues can serve to complicate transition planning.

Transition planning for these parents must be developed in small increments of information. The parents must be educated on the planning process and how career opportunities can be explored. A clear picture needs to be created that shows that their children are being provided experiences that will give them choices and opportunities that may not have been a part of their backgrounds.

An example of this would be a deaf Spanish-speaking middle school student from a newly arrived immigrant family. The parents understand their child is deaf and have developed a method of communicating with the child that involves facial expressions and certain signs. The child enters school and is being taught American Sign Language with Spanish components. The child develops expertise in using this newly acquired form of communication, which is shared with the parents.

They learn a few of the signs, but basically rely upon the previously developed home-based form of communication. At the IEP meeting, school officials share with the parents the various components of transition and the recommendations that they have. The parents in the meantime are trying to understand the options that have been presented while seeing a gap between themselves and their child. They question whether or not they are clearly understanding what is being presented for their consideration. They feel that they have to make choices without total understanding of what the choices really are.

Through incremental delivery of information and many illustrations, school officials can do much to increase their understanding. Graphic representations of options, in addition to examples and testimonials from other parents and their children, can do much to set the parents' minds at ease. The parents must be made to feel as comfortable as possible in the meetings so that they feel they are making the right decisions with and for their children. Because the transition planning process will be refined each year as the child progresses through the system, the parents will be able to develop a more comprehensive understanding of what is happening within the educational program of their child. The child matures while the parents expand their knowledge base. Transition planning becomes more realistic and focused for the child and supportive for the parents.

# CHARACTERISTICS OF STUDENTS WITH SPECIAL NEEDS

## Adjudicated Youth with Disabilities

The number of adjudicated youth with disabilities in school systems has been increasing in the past few years. The magnitude of problems associated with juvenile crime and gang-related activities and the burden they place on our society cannot be exaggerated. Unfortunately, these problems have grown dramatically over the past 25 years. Serious crimes committed by male juveniles have increased 25 percent; female juvenile crime has increased by more than 120 percent during this time period (National Center for Juvenile Justice, 1997). With the increase of more-defined special education services and better assessment, adjudicated youth with disabilities are being identified more accurately. The majority of adjudicated youth with disabilities are learning disabled, behaviorally impaired, and mentally challenged (Pollard, Pollard, & Meers, 1995). These students are facing a number of challenges in relation to transition planning. These challenges involve:

- Society's understanding of services for adjudicated youth
- Schools' responsibilities to these students
- Safety for the general student populace
- Effective educational programs for these students
- Coordinated services for these students
- Understanding of the impact the disability has on the student

- Parents' role in supporting their children
- Community influences on students' behavior

Education is viewed, by many, as the channel through which troubled youth who deviate from the beliefs of our society can acquire the necessary social, academic, and vocational skills needed to succeed. For some adjudicated youth, education takes place within a correctional environment; for others, alternative school provides their training. No matter the site, comprehensive transition planning is required. Not only must they have a carefully planned and coordinated IEP, plus appropriate transition components, but they also require unique support services to enable them to remain in the school setting. These support services may come from the courts and probation offices, creating a blend of support personnel.

While juvenile delinquency is commonly thought of as antisocial behavior, delinquency can also be described as social behavior in that it typically occurs among groups of youths of similar age and social characteristics. While the recent focus has been on gangs and gang-related activity, delinquency is most often a spontaneous activity that occurs in ordinary peer groups (Goldenstein, 1990; Huff, 1990). Gangs merely represent a more structured peer group with acknowledged leadership.

Of course, the odds of engaging in delinquent behavior are much greater for youth with delinquent friends than those without such acquaintances. Youths asked to report on how they initially got involved in delinquency are likely to mention friends and peer pressure (Jenson & Rojek, 1992; Quay, 1987; Sagatun, 1991).

Although, delinquent friends consistently emerge as critical in explaining and understanding delinquency, the acquisition of delinquent associates is most often influenced by the degree of attachment to family and success in school. Conversely, the influences of parental and school attachment appear to be the most effective components in deterring delinquency (Wiatrowski & Anderson, 1987).

Longitudinal and cross-cultural studies on moral development have determined that individuals progress through a series of age-related stages, from a preconventional stage (essentially egocentric in nature) to stages characterized by concern for others and an adherence to rules that regulate desired behavior. Not surprisingly, a strong correlation between an individual's stage of moral reasoning and delinquent behavior has been found in a number of studies (Arbuthnot & Gordon, 1988; Blasi, 1980; Chandler & Moran, 1990; Nelson, Smith, & Dodd, 1990; Quay, 1987). Typically, delinquents are portrayed as preconventional reasoners who have not developed desired sociomoral reasoning skills. Adjudicated youth, especially those with disabilities, have not responded well to traditional teaching methods. They are characterized as having poor morale and low self-esteem that results from a history of frustrating educational experiences. This at-risk population performs better within an environment that emphasizes the application of learning to real situations (Leon, Rutherford, & Nelson, 1991; Pollard & Kaufman, 1994).

Although the instruction of this at-risk group continues to be one of the biggest educational challenges today, a more customized curriculum tailored to the unique learning needs of this population has been successful for many students (Coffey, 1987; Krogstad, 1987; Rutherford, 1988). An individually based, achievement-oriented curriculum providing both basic academic skills and vocational training is advocated. The focus should be not only on the acquisition of vocational skills but on the development of transition and job-related skills, including proper work habits, interpersonal communication, social, daily living, and job search skills, as integral components within a more functional curriculum (Leon et al., 1991; Pollard & Kaufman, 1994; Pollard et al., 1994).

Exemplary educational programs provide a continuum of educational services designed to meet the needs of adjudicated youth in diagnosing, placing, and providing appropriate services. Such programs advocate the development of an individual career plan (ICP) that provides a full spectrum of services from attainment of necessary job-related skills to a successful transition to any number of postsecondary environments. Through such a process, adjudicated youths have been shown to experience success, develop more positive attitudes toward school, and heighten their self-esteem. Program components, such as community-based work experience and apprenticeship, have also been found to facilitate the success of students (Hackett, 1992; Miller, 1989; Pollard & Kaufman, 1994).

Programs that include vocational education as a key intervention strategy have experienced notable success in providing a supportive educational environment and increasing attachment to school. Adjudicated students who perceive that high school is preparing them to perform entry-level tasks in their chosen occupational field exhibit more positive attitudes and show greater improvement in educational performance (Hayward, 1992; Leon et al., 1991). Table 5.1 illustrates Best Educational Practices for serving this targeted group. Moreover, vocational training for juvenile and adult offenders has been shown to be positively correlated to reduced recidivism (Hackett, 1992).

# PERSONS INVOLVED IN THE TRANSITION PROCESS

## Creating the Team

Students with disabilities upon entering school are recipients of an IEP. As has been discussed, the IEP contains the goals and objectives for the students to assist them in acquiring the academic skills necessary for school progression and community participation. During the elementary years a number of educational professionals and support personnel provide the needed educational opportunities. When students enter middle school and/or reach the age of 14, transition planning becomes a key part of the IEP planning process. The introduction of transition components requires that additional educational personnel and adult service providers start to become involved in the process.

The educational personnel may involve practical arts teachers who offer training in the areas of home maintenance, cooking, personal business, woodworking, and other life skills areas. They must be involved in the IEP/transition component development process to ensure that placement in these classes is in the best in-

**TABLE 5.1**

Characteristics of Adjudicated Youth With Disabilities and Implications for Best Educational Practices

| Characteristics | Implications |
|---|---|
| Low self-esteem<br>  Low regard as individuals<br>  Low regard as family members<br>  Low regard as members of society | Need to enhance youths' self-esteem<br>  Provide opportunities for youths to experience<br>  success in and out of the classroom |
| Unfavorable home atmosphere<br>  Lack of familial closeness/cohesiveness<br>  Feeling of parental hostility toward youths<br>  Lack of affection for parent<br>  Intrafamilial conflict and tension<br>  Lax and/or inconsistent discipline | Need to provide a supportive environment<br>  Provide family/parenting education<br>  Provide counseling services<br>  including support in handling<br>  anger and conflict management<br>  Adhere to a consistent discipline plan |
| Detached from school<br>  Significant school problems<br>  School suspensions<br>  School experience perceived as irrelevant<br>  Poor attendance | Need to link youths with school<br>  Establish school as a positive, stable setting—<br>  a "safe haven"<br>  Provide relevant learning experiences<br>  Institute a mentoring program |
| Unfavorable social bonding<br>  Lack of prosocial and interpersonal skills<br>  Delinquent associates<br>  Peer pressure contributing to deviant behavior<br>  Substance abuse | Need to develop social/living skills<br>  Provide comprehensive social/<br>  interpersonal skills training<br>  Provide opportunities for prosocial interaction<br>  Develop linkages with service providers (social<br>  welfare, support groups, etc.) |
| Inadequate educational performance<br>  History of frustrating educational experiences<br>  Deficient academic skills<br>  Insufficient vocational and employable skills<br>  Low occupational expectations | Need to ensure educational success<br>  Identify youths' learning styles and adapt/<br>  individualize instruction<br>  Provide both basic academic skills and vocational<br>  training<br>  Adopt relevant, functional curriculum<br>  Provide individualized career plans and<br>  experiential job opportunities |
| High incidence of disabilities<br>  Mild/moderate mental retardation<br>  Learning disabilities<br>  Behaviorally impaired | Need to determine disabilities and provide<br>  appropriate remediation<br>  Employ quality assessment, resulting in<br>  well-articulated transition components within<br>  the IEP |

terest of the children. In addition, the teachers must have the support necessary to provide safe and experiential opportunities for these students. By knowing the learning styles and needs of these students, the teachers can plan accordingly. They must know what support services they can receive, (i.e., paraprofessionals to assist with note taking or in laboratory settings).

Successful inclusion for students with disabilities in career-based courses depends greatly on the acceptance of the teachers. If they are educated on the needs of the students, have sufficient supports, and can see success on the part of the students, then transition development will be greatly enhanced for all those involved. With teacher support, parents will also feel much better about the educational development of their child. All involved must see a future for the students.

Adult service providers start to enter the transition planning process at the middle school level. They are becoming a part of the team that will help the students as adults to function within the community, live independently to the extent possible, and participate in gainful employment. The adult service providers need to understand the educational process that is occurring so they can fit their services into the continuum. Early transition planning includes preparing students for the provider services that occur in the later stages.

Parents' role in the IEP process is set forth not only by law, but by common sense. It is only logical that parents have input along with their children in the educational planning process. As transition components are introduced, parents start to realize that their children are becoming young adults and that decisions need to be made in preparation for postsecondary opportunities. The processing of this fact can be hard for parents since they want to protect and support their children while knowing that they have to let go and extend some form of independence to the children. In meeting with the IEP team, unrealistic transition and/or career requirements or requests may be put forth by the parents as a result of "leaving the nest" syndrome. Only through careful and concise sharing of information and maximum involvement by the parents can realistic transition planning be achieved.

As with any planning process, communication is the key. All involved stakeholders must understand how their contributions are being integrated into the total process. The outcome desired is maximum participation in the adult setting by the maturing adult. The steps, the years, and the participants required to get there are the keys to successful transition.

## USING THE SAALE MODEL IN TRANSITION

The SAALE model is the systematic approach to adapting to the learning environment. This model is designed for application in many different settings, but the one to which the most salient application can be made is that of transition. Transition is an evolving process that requires change in programs, support services, and instructional settings. These changes are dictated by students' needs, interests, and preferences. As the students mature, new plans need to be made and programs introduced. When preparing students to take their place in adult life, systematic approaches need to be taken in order to adapt the learning and/or career environments to be user friendly.

If school personnel can acquire the skills to use the SAALE model on a regular basis, it is easy to then transfer the model components to the career education arena. It is like a hiker who enjoys looking for wild animal tracks in the forest. At first it is hard to distinguish between the tracks of an opossum and a raccoon. With some instruction and practice, the difference between the two becomes obvious, after which the tracker moves on to other track identifications. The SAALE model works in much the same way. Practice leads to application.

When using the SAALE model for transition, several steps need to be followed to make the process effective and efficient.

## Understanding the Students

Since transition planning is student centered, an understanding of the students' needs, interests, and preferences must be first in the process. Data needs to be collected through formal and informal assessments that will give a picture of each student and the next steps needed to facilitate transition progress. The knowledge needed will include psychological stability, physical endurance, transferable skills, parental desires, and support services needed.

## Understanding the Career Options

Transition planning involves knowing what students want and attempting to match these wants with reality. What can the students realistically do in the work world? Through a series of explorations and assessments, the answers to these questions become much clearer. Career exploration involves such techniques as job shadowing, field trips, guest speakers, and so on, all of which are designed to give exposure to choices.

## Creating a Match

Each workplace has a unique personality. Some are loud, noisy, fast paced, and pressure driven. Others are slower of pace and quiet. Still others require people skills or self-direction and working alone. Workers must be able to adapt to the work settings. Since humans have different personalities, an effort has to be made to match the personality of each student with the personality of the workplace. If a comprehensive career exploration program has been offered then the match will be much easier. Keep in mind the transition coordinator must be knowledgeable about both the students and the workplaces to make sure suitable matches are created. Knowing how adaptable the student can be is the key to success in matching.

## Working with the Employer

The SAALE model can be used here as well. In approaching the employer the transition coordinator needs to be looking for ways the workplace can be adapted to meet the needs of the perspective employee; the student. First would be to identify the expectations of the employer, then addressing the fears the employer has about working with persons with disabilities, answering questions about safety, insurance, and supervision. Once these issues have been discussed, the adaptations needed can be quickly identified. Adaptations are of two types: those related to attitudes toward the disabled and those required of the physical facilities. The physical facilities are the easiest to adapt. Attitudes are always the hardest, although, with systematic steps of knowledge sharing, they can be changed as well.

Two very helpful phrases to use when working with employers, both of which are taken from the Americans with Disabilities Act (ADA), are "essential job functions" and "reasonable accommodations." *Essential job functions* are those tasks directly related to the successful completion of work no matter what the setting, site, or personnel involved. *Reasonable accommodations* are those modifications made in the workplace to assist the disabled employee in the successful completion of the work. Neither of these should present undue hardship on the employer nor disrupt the workplace. By applying these definitions to the previous discussion, adaptation becomes easier to understand and apply.

## Making Sense of the Adaptations

The strength of any model is its ability to change to fit the situation. The SAALE model is a systematic approach to producing a positive outcome. Transition coordinators must keep asking questions to ensure that they are getting the outcomes needed to meet the students' needs. These questions are as follows:

Have I explored all of the options?

Have I used all of the resources?

Are these the opportunities I would want for myself?

Have I kept the students' needs foremost in the planning?

Using the SAALE model for transition application is complementing the adaptability of the model itself. Applying the model transition to transition planning is the logical next step. The user of the model always needs to be aware of the surroundings, both within and outside of the school, that best facilitate success for the student. By adapting the learning environment in a supportive way, the student then can focus on gaining experience in the area of career training, independent living, and community participation. Each of these three areas can benefit from the application of the SAALE model. Collectively they constitute a very complete and comprehensive transition planning model.

A. Career Training

B. Independent Living

C. Community Participation

# TRANSITION ATTITUDE BOUNDARIES

Everyone strives for a feeling of comfort and security. On a chilly fall evening it is great to slip into a favorite sweatsuit, settle into the recliner, remote in hand, and have 150 channels of television to watch. For that moment in time all is well with the world.

Now picture teenagers entering the middle or high school years. As adolescent students enter into new environments, stress follows them due to the new interactions. They have questions about how they look, what others will think of them, how they will fit in, and so on. Issues revolving around clothes, electronic toys, CDs, and social relationships are the core of life. Other factors such as planning for life, career choice, and school achievement are located much lower on their radar. Educators strive to enter the teen world and offer opportunities for students to increase their academic proficiency, plan for the future, and acquire life competencies. History has shown that these educators have had a degree of success, but it is a real challenge.

Compound the stress of being a teenager, raging hormones and all, with having a disability, and the stress level soars. Youths divide themselves into groups based upon both known and unknown reasons. Some divisions are related to gender, others to ethnicity, others to like interests vocationally or avocationally, and others are divided off by other students. Stigmas are attached to certain groups. Students with disabilities, especially those with nonvisible disabilities, are often recipients of this dividing. The stigma of special education is cast on these students and they oftentimes have much difficulty in finding their place in the school's social structure. In order to find their place in the school social structure they act out inappropriately. They then get recognition through disciplinary action by school officials. They gain a form of status. Others gain status in their minds through gang participation, drug use, and dropping out. The extreme cases result in suicide, all of which contributes to a very grim picture.

To help eliminate this grim picture, transition planning must include socioemotional learning environments that are supportive, yet give a sense of independence. During the elementary years students are generally instructed in one room by one teacher, with maybe a paraprofessional and an occasional support person, such as a speech therapist. Entering middle school brings about many dramatic changes. The students are maturing physically, starting to focus on social relationships, changing school sites and rooms, and having a number of different teachers. Their comfort zone has been changed dramatically and they are in need of support. This support must be given in an appropriate way. These students want support, but they want independence; they want freedom of choice, but not the consequence of actions; and the list goes on.

The answer to these emerging student changes and support needs lies with the IEP teams. They know the students and their needs and can be reflective of the changes that are occurring with the students. The introduction of transition components brings new opportunities to the students and the IEP team. Receiving teachers need to have an understanding of the unique learning needs of the students and how they can assist in meeting these needs. Good teaching is good teaching, no matter who the students are. If teachers are given strategies and support for these students, then the environment will be much more supportive.

All people are nervous the first time they go out on an interview for a job. Imagine if you had always been protected from having to face strangers alone, and now you are being asked to face one and ask for employment. It is a scary concept!

There are a number of different ways that students with disabilities can develop confidence in themselves and their abilities during their transition years.

## Volunteer Work

Students should be encouraged to volunteer within their community. Sources could be churches, community centers, and youth groups. The students will meet many new people who will want to help them. The students are being given an opportunity to help others while helping themselves.

An example is a severely physically challenged middle school student who wanted to clean up his neighborhood. He is a chair user with only limited range of motion in one arm, yet with an adaptive device he was able to go out and spend time picking up litter. As people saw him and his efforts they wanted to help as well. He soon had an "army" of helpers. He then started sorting the litter into categories for recycling. With several different adaptive devices he was able to sort aluminum cans from tin and different kinds of plastic. He sold the collected materials for recycling and used the money to build benches in the neighborhood park. For his efforts he was given the national "Yes I Can" award by the Foundation for Exceptional Children. He developed confidence that is impossible to measure. When he started exploring career opportunities he was not afraid to talk with employers about his career plans.

## Job Shadowing

The students are placed for a brief period of time (approximately 20 hours) in a work setting where they follow one employee through the work routine. The stress of having to meet and work with many different individuals is reduced, and the worker and the students get comfortable with each other. In addition, the teacher, transition coordinator, or paraprofessional is always close by, should the students have a need. The students receive two benefits from this experience. One, by getting to meet and follow a worker they have chosen, they are developing social interactions outside of school boundaries. Two, they get to observe and learn about a career area that is of interest to them, and therefore are gaining career experience. After the job shadowing experience is concluded, the students return to the classroom and are debriefed on what they have observed and learned. They are then ready for their next level of exploration.

## Work Experience

Job shadowing is meant to expose the students to general career clusters. Work experience is just what the name implies: giving the students experience performing job-related work. As a result, they are learning two important work skills: (a) employable skills such as being neat, clean, on time, and getting along with others, and (b) specific skills related to the job, such as stocking shelves at the grocery store. Work experience jobs may or may not be directly related to the students' career plans.

The students are gaining work experience in settings other than in school or home and are expanding their social interaction with an ever-growing group of associates. Since transition planning is for life, students with disabilities really need to develop their social skills for community use. Often, it is found that students with disabilities that are not accepted or made fun of in school have status within the employment setting. This is due to their acceptance as workers and contributors.

## Career Employment

Career employment is the last step in the transition sequence prior to leaving secondary school. Students are placed in work settings that are directly related to their career choices. Training plans are developed outlining the training the students will receive and the responsibilities of the students and the employers. Issues of supervision, insurance, and safety are also covered in the plans. Transition coordinators or job coaches directly supervise the students full time at first. The students work no more than 20 hours per week, and they can be brought back to the school at any point if they do not work out on that site. The coordinators or coaches slowly withdraw from the sites as the students progress in confidence, skill, and integration. Full withdrawal from job sites is considered a successful placement. After full withdrawal the students are supervised directly by the employer, and the coordinators or coaches stop by on a weekly basis to review the progress made on the training plan. If the program is successful, the students would then be hired by the employers upon completion of secondary school or would go on to postsecondary training in that career area.

The previously listed programs are intended to develop a sense of confidence within the students that will enable them to be comfortable in a variety of different settings. Social skills will be developed that will enable them to function within their community.

A number of factors contribute to student motivation. Two of these are self esteem and confidence. If the students have a sense of who they are and how they can contribute, they will have a much higher level of motivation to achieve. Through support from teachers, parents, and employers, motivation can be greatly enhanced. Peer relationships are difficult enough without students having to experience a lack of respect from teachers as well.

## ADAPTING THE BEHAVIORAL ENVIRONMENT

Behaviors occur for a number of different reasons, with reasons ranging from simple to complex. No matter what the cause, these behaviors must be formatted and structured in such a manner that they are acceptable to societal norms, or removal from society will follow.

Experience has shown that many nonacceptable behaviors occur due to a lack of understanding or direction on the part of the students. As students mature, a sense of self is being developed, involving such areas as music, dress, and hobbies. During this phase students are striving for identity.

Through comprehensive transition planning, career exploration will be a major part of the students' middle and high school educational process. These students will start to develop an understanding about their career area, and as they job shadow and gain work experience, this understanding becomes even more clear. They start to see the education sequence that is required for entrance into their chosen career area, and they develop life plans around their career choice. Behavior requirements for the community and workplace start to be understood.

When an employer tells a student that not following directions or talking back will not be tolerated in the work setting, it has much more impact than when a teacher explains it. This is because a teacher is *supposed* to reprimand students, while an employer is doing the same thing, but in a *real life* setting. This slow transition of maturing from a school setting to a work setting is a must for students. By being introduced to the community and work at an early age, students can start to see how they need to develop self-control of behaviors that are not acceptable as an adult.

The work experience and career employment programs help to define the parameters for behavior in a clear and realistic manner. The students start to develop the self-control necessary for life success. During the middle and high school years the transition planners need to work with the special and regular teachers to help define the troublesome areas of behavior and work with the students in overcoming them, since this is the only way that students will be able to enter the workforce.

Experience has shown that students reduce their unacceptable behaviors when they are in educational settings that offer practical application of their learning experiences. Courses such as practical arts, career planning, and vocational training offer students the opportunity to practice positive behaviors that are acceptable in the workplace. In addition, many students have never been taught what is acceptable behavior. Many transition/career programs contain sections that work with students on developing acceptable behaviors both in and out of school.

# ADAPTING THE PHYSICAL ENVIRONMENT

## Physical Facilities

Students with disabilities require two types of physical modifications. The first of these are modifications that will enable them to enter into the instructional setting. The requirements for these modifications are set forth in the provisions of the Americans with Disabilities Act. All new construction and any remodeling of existing structures need to be ADA compliant.

The other type of physical modifications are those with equipment, machines, and workstations. The specific modifications will depend upon the nature of the disability and the work that is to be completed by the student. There are many different resources available to assist with these modifications. The most readily accessible is the Job Accommodation Network (JAN). JAN is a resource center that provides free consultation to businesses and educational facilities on how to modify and/or adapt equipment, machines, and workstations for persons with disabilities. Most of the recommendations are simple and inexpensive. JAN has a toll-free number for easy accessibility: JAN-1-800-526-7234.

## Career Preparation

The ultimate goal of transition is for students to enter into some form of postsecondary experience. In order for students to do this, they must have access to classes that will give them this preparation. In planning for the various student outcomes, there often isn't enough room left in the schedule to accommodate career preparation opportunities. The push for academic success is necessary and needed, but application of academic knowledge is just as important.

Many IEP teams, when planning for transition, place students in a traditional laboratory class like home maintenance, thinking this is sufficient for career preparation. Classes of this kind are important for students' general growth, but they are general knowledge courses, not vocational preparation courses. The students need to be scheduled into courses that assist them in acquiring personal skills with employment applications. The home maintenance course will assist them in maintaining their personal dwelling space, as well as help them to perform minor repairs, color applications, etc. A personal business course will assist them in acquiring competencies in the areas of credit buying, budgeting, and personal finance. A computer applications course will give them the skills needed to work in a number of different business settings, such as retailing, warehouse stocking, etc. All of these courses are practical knowledge courses for general application, but they are not vocational preparation courses.

Counselors and IEP team members must advocate for scheduling students into classes where they can acquire the necessary career and vocational technical skills needed to succeed in the world of work. Many school schedulers do not see the importance of vocational technical training, so they do not find time within the students' schedules to enable them to enroll. Whether students are going directly into the workforce or are planning on some form of postsecondary training, they must have some career exploration experiences from which they can draw upon when making decisions.

Programs like job shadowing, work experience, and career employment require at least two hours of block time. There are many different variations within typical school schedules that will enable the students to secure these experiences. Integrated academic programs are moving to block scheduling of 2 to 4 hours. Students with disabilities need to be placed in this type of scheduling. With proper supports (such as the resource teacher going into the vocational technical classroom with the students), special needs students will be able to focus on the training being provided with minimum transition trauma. Also, the students must have course schedules set up toward the completion of high school that will allow the individuals time to be out in the community working, interning, or apprenticing while taking the required academic courses.

# ADAPTING LESSON PLANS

## Real Life Applications

Transition planning is focused upon life after high school for students with disabilities. Since this is the goal of transition, then the goal of instruction has to be the preparation of students for this process to take place. What knowledge do they need to succeed in adult life? Many programs have developed competencies that students need for independent living, community participation, and employment. These competencies need to be integrated into the academic classes with illustrations of their applications. Immediate use of newly acquired knowledge is the basis for much vocational technical training and has a great application for transition students.

In a math class a student learns to measure in units of cups, quarts, and gallons. Of what benefit is this knowledge? By applying this knowledge in a career setting, the student starts to develop a command of the information. The lesson plans need to show application, rather than just testing for the sake of testing. When the student first uses the knowledge of quarts to measure tomato sauce for making a pizza during a job shadowing experience, application starts to come alive, and there is a reason for learning.

Resource teachers need to work with regular teachers, especially those in the vocational technical fields, to show them how modifications can be made that do not alter the training requirements but allow the students to achieve. Regular classroom teachers have the content knowledge; they just need some insight and assistance on how to deliver the content in a way that the special needs learners can understand. As a team these teachers can create learning paths that enable the students to acquire math, English, and employment skills that are school-based and career-applicable. This is transition application in the truest form.

Educators must integrate career applications into their lesson plans on a continual basis. What is done in the seventh grade must be reinforced in the eighth, and so on. When school completion arrives, the student will have learned the skills to the extent that they can easily transition into postsecondary settings.

# ADAPTING THE FORMAT OF CONTENT

In business it is said that success is based upon location, location, and location. In teaching youths with disabilities, it is delivery, delivery, and delivery. Content for secondary youths must be formatted in a manner that captures their attention, inspires motivation, and gives a sense of accomplishment when completed. In career preparation training this can be done in a number of ways that will engage the students in the learning process.

# Career Theme

Instructional content that has a career theme gives students a sense of the world around them. Formats that have students interviewing workers in the community about the skills they need will help to bring classroom requirements into focus. The students then can come back to the classroom and develop a school-based enterprise for their integrated academic study. Since there are many different activities involved in the school-based enterprise, the students get the opportunity to use many different learning formats. Through instructional analysis it can be determined what content must be covered to maintain the integrity of the course, while offering it through a variety of different formats. By using a theme approach, the variety of content and format enables the students to work within their learning styles while gaining the required competencies. An example of this variated format approach is the use of a school-based enterprise theme.

The students can complete an entire unit of study using a school-based enterprise theme. The students:

- Form a company
- Select a product or service
- Research the product or service
- Form a board of directors
- Apply for employment
- Assign work tasks
- Conduct market research
- Do cost analysis
- Deliver product or service
- Handle money
- Assess learning outcomes

As can be seen by these steps, all aspects of education are being covered. The academic skills are being used to progress through all of the developmental steps. The human relations and social skills are being enhanced by working together. By using a team approach, regular and special education teachers are working jointly with the students. The benefits of school-based enterprises are:

- Real-world application of academic skills and concepts
- Learning how to ask questions
- Integration of academic and career education
- Learning how business and industry operates
- Problem solving
- Teamwork

- Social interaction with each other
- Development of employable skills
- Development of specific work skills
- Financial resources for student use
- Wise use of time
- Motivation

The challenge and reward for teachers working with secondary transition students is the opportunity to identify different formats for content delivery. By observing other teachers, adopting a theme approach, and exploring student learning styles, many of the individual student learning challenges can be met. The rewards come as a result of student success not only in performing academically but in successfully making the transition to postsecondary opportunities.

# ADAPTING STUDENT EVALUATION

## A Growing Concern

All fifty states, the District of Columbia, and Puerto Rico have established standards to which local school districts must align their curriculum and instruction. Students, teachers, and administrators will be held accountable for knowledge acquired as measured by standardized assessments or some other form of proficiency demonstration. This movement will cause teachers to view very closely the modifications and applications they make in their lesson plans, content format, and evaluations. Youths with disabilities are being placed in a difficult position between the push for higher standards and graduation tests. Evidence of this is the increased number of dropouts by students with disabilities (Phelps & Hanley-Maxwell, 1997), and with the increased dropout rate comes substantially lower rates of employment, income, and participation in postsecondary education.

IDEA 97 eliminates the previous practices of opting students out of the assessments. The law now requires that schools provide any necessary accommodations to ensure that students with disabilities become fully included in the state and local district measures of accountability. As a result of this requirement, alternative methods of evaluation or modification of the standardized assessments will have to be forthcoming. The key will be to keep the modification and/or accommodations student centered.

Transition planning requires the students to prepare for employment or postsecondary training. They want to complete their high school education, which will result in a high school diploma or equivalency. Thus, the assessments that are to be conducted should be reflective of the competencies possessed that lead to assimilation into the community. The questions that surface revolve around what the realistic competencies for life are. Once these questions are answered, the next questions have to be addressed: What is the best way for these students to demonstrate their life skills? Which evaluation method is the most reasonable?

Clark (1998) proposed the following definition of *transitions assessment*.

Transitions assessment is a planned, continuous process of obtaining, organizing, and using information to assist individuals with disabilities of all ages and their families to make all critical transitions in students' lives both successful and satisfying. (p. 2)

As can be seen by this definition, assessment must be ongoing and is continuum based. As students mature and their choices expand they need assistance in evaluating their skills and accomplishments. These evaluation points will serve to illustrate progress being made and future training needed. If the assessments are not realistic or comprehendible by the students, then they will not contribute to the students' transition process.

There are a number of different assessment methodologies that can be used to collect information about students' transition progress. Collectively these methodologies contribute to an accurate picture of the status of the students.

## Vocational Assessments

Vocational assessments are designed to gain information and data about student interests and abilities. All students should have a vocational assessment during their middle school years. This creates a baseline of information from which career planning can be developed. As the students mature, assessments should be conducted again to identify any changes that have occurred in interest or ability.

## Career Assessments

Career assessments provide information from which decisions relating to all areas of adult life can be made. Career assessments gather information in areas such as roles as family members, citizens, and community participants.

## Academic Assessments

Academic assessments are those conducted by school officials to determine student progress. They may be teacher developed or nationally standardized. Those developed by the teacher are intended to assess student competence at that point in time, whereas standardized tests are intended to assess year-long growth.

## Work Samples

Work samples are used to assess student interests, abilities, work habits, and personal and social skills. Formal work samples are commercially produced and have standardized instructions and scoring. Informal work samples are developed locally. Informal work samples are generally based on local work opportunities. Informal work samples can be developed by career and/or special educators or vocational evaluators. Work samples allow the students to see the direct application of their efforts on the workplace.

## Curriculum-Based Assessment

Curriculum-based assessment is used by educators in academic settings. The assessment instruments are developed by the content teachers in conjunction with support teachers, such as special education or resource teachers. The basis of the assessment is to identify what the student has been taught within a curriculum.

## Situational Assessment

Situational assessment involves observing and assessing individuals in situations close to the settings in which the individuals will find themselves in the future. These include living, working, and community settings. Data collection involves information on how students function in these settings and assists in developing education recommendations on areas needing further instruction or support. Contributors to this assessment may be teachers, job coaches, parents, adult service providers, and community service providers.

All of the previously listed assessment formats contribute information and data, giving a picture of the student. It can be seen that these assessments are not a moment in time, but are on a continuum. All people change with time in relation to needs, interests, and preferences. Continual assessment, no matter the format, enables evaluators to create a profile for students that will be useful for transition planning and ultimately career placement.

## ADAPTING GRADING

Grading has as its intent to notify the learner and teacher of progress being made. American education has assigned letter grades to the grading process so that if a student receives an A on a test and accumulates enough of these As, they will receive an A in the course. By receiving the A it is assumed that the student possesses the competencies of the course. This may or may not be the case; it is only an assumption. It may only mean that the student has performed in such a manner to secure the needed points leading to the A. No evidence of competence is attached to the grade. Educators, employers, parents, and, most importantly, students are looking for further evidence of competence. An effective method of evidencing competence is the use of the career portfolio.

The career portfolio is an ongoing collection of the students' best work, skills and accomplishments, activities and participation, and goals and plans for the future. Portfolio contents may include such minor items as a simple thank you note for helping a teacher, or a major community award for a helping activity. It may also include a listing and documentation of academic and career success. The specific contents do not really matter. What does matter is that the contents reflect the abilities of the students.

Career portfolios come in a number of different formats. They range from simple three-ring notebooks in which students place evidence of successes, to commercial expandable folders with data and table listings of information about the students. No matter what format is used, they must be student-centered. Students decide on what evidence of success they want to include. In some schools, the portfolios are kept in a required academic classroom, such as English. In others, they have a dedicated room where the students come to work with their portfolios. Career portfolios have to have regular maintenance; that is, they must be a source of regular additions. Students cannot let too much time lapse between additions, or something might be left out.

The following are the different steps in putting together a good portfolio.

## Collection

The first step in putting together a portfolio is gathering a variety of student efforts. Examples would be writing samples from the student. These samples might be from things written at home, academic assignments, and/or work composed for outside activities, such as youth group announcements.

## Selection

As new materials are being added to the portfolio, the students need to review the included material and decide whether to add new materials and/or delete previous material. This is a growth process. The students, with guidance, can look at the examples and start to see their path of maturity in the materials. Each selection should include materials that illustrate new competencies the student has acquired.

## Reflection

Self-evaluation is one of the goals of portfolio development. To develop self-directed, internally motivated students, they must be given an opportunity to develop the capacity to self-assess and modify. This effort in the development of the portfolio has to be reinforced and encouraged in all classes across the curriculum. Reflective worksheets, peer-response sheets, and teacher/parent interviews are highly effective tools in this process.

## Connection

The inclusion of certain materials and examples of this work in the portfolio should illustrate a connection between what students are learning and how they will use this newly acquired knowledge after secondary school. As examples of writing have been included and then updated with better examples, the students can see that writing skills are used to communicate concerns, needs, and requests. They begin to see that there is a reason for what is being taught in schools. Also, application is being made to the transitional process of moving to adult life.

Once the portfolio is put together, it can be used by educators and students for a variety of purposes.

## Diagnostic Portfolio

This portfolio is kept by the transition coordinator for the purpose of assisting teachers in assessing the children's growth in specific skills. Documents in this type of portfolio are usually selected by the teacher at various developmental stages or points during the year and then compared to the students' previous work. Progress can then be evaluated and new goals for the students can be determined. This information is shared with parents, other teachers, future teachers, and other involved educational professionals.

## Working Portfolio

This portfolio is a work in progress. The students continue to add current materials and examples to the portfolio as the year progresses. The content of the portfolio will contain examples of many different kinds of efforts by the students as supported by the different teachers. Some materials will be completed; others will be works in progress. All of the materials contribute to creating a snapshot of student progress and are used in developing future goals for and with the student.

## Exhibition Portfolio

This portfolio is a showcase of the students' efforts. This is the end product of what the students have been doing. It is used to show future employers and postsecondary institutions what has been accomplished and is reflective of academic development, career planning, and individual aspirations.

As can be seen, exhibition portfolios are ongoing efforts of assessment that reflect student growth, planning, and competence. The portfolios enable students to show in ways other than just grades that they have acquired certain skills. The advantages of the career portfolios are as follows:

1. Provide an opportunity for self-exploration and self-evaluation
2. Provide a summary of learning
3. Provide a record of academic achievement
4. Provide a pathway for transition planning
5. Organize career goals and prepare for career exploration
6. Provide a record of nonacademic activities
7. Provide examples of community participation
8. Provide a list of references and resources
9. Illustrate alternative assessments
10. Illustrate post–high school career plans

Alternative grading of any type must enable students to show their competence through a method or methods that are consistent with an acceptable evaluation format. There are many different forms of alternative assessment that are available, and educators must select those that will show student progress, while enabling adult service providers to see the status of the students and their future training potential. Career portfolios are a comprehensive method of doing this.

Any form of grading will work if it measures student success. Unfortunately, this is often not the case. In planning for alternative evaluations, educators must be sure that they have explored all of the options available and that these options will give a clear and accurate picture of the student's status.

In transition, the students are in a state of flux from one setting to another. In evaluation, the students are illustrating the reason for being allowed to move from one setting to another, and that is competence. No matter what alternative form of grading is used, students must be provided the opportunity to illustrate their newly acquired skills in a manner that is supportive to them and informative to postsecondary receivers, like employers and technical trainers.

# PART TWO

# Including All Students: The Process and the Content

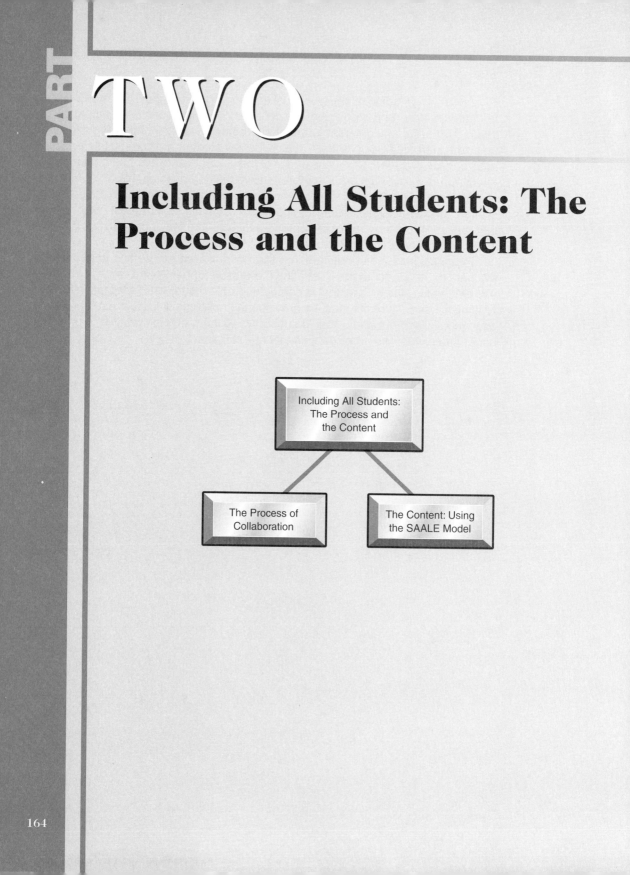

In part 2 we begin our study of inclusion, which, as the flowchart demonstrates, has two parts: process and content. Both parts are essential. *Process* is how we get together to teach, and *content* is what and how we teach.

Chapter 6 examines the process of inclusion, while chapter 7 discusses approaches to content. Chapters 8 through 16 detail that content, offering a multitude of practical ideas that are organized for effective teaching.

# CHAPTER 6

## *The Process of Collaboration*

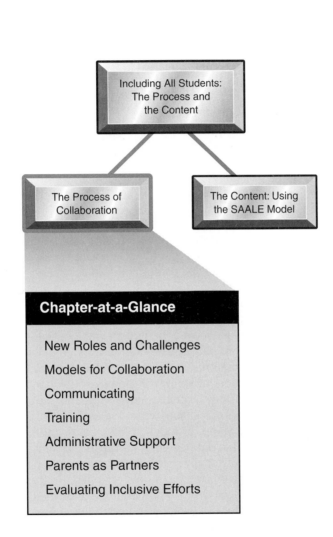

Including All Students:
The Process and
the Content

The Process of
Collaboration

The Content: Using
the SAALE Model

**Chapter-at-a-Glance**

New Roles and Challenges

Models for Collaboration

Communicating

Training

Administrative Support

Parents as Partners

Evaluating Inclusive Efforts

Regular education initiative (REI), shared responsibility, educating all students, full inclusion . . . these catch phrases echo across educational America. The neat compartment of "my students" versus "your students" no longer prevails. "Our students" is the focus. Children as a whole move somewhat freely during the school day, receiving instruction unique to their needs. Teachers seek a quick answer to student educational diversity and look to other colleagues and the community for answers and support. Parents seek a common ground in education for their children with special needs. Children strive to blend in with peers and find acceptance in all school activities.

This chapter presents the issue as well as ongoing discussions about equal opportunities for all and the shared responsibility for the educational outcomes of all students. It examines those implications from a variety of perspectives.

## NEW ROLES, NEW CHALLENGES

The focus on providing equal educational opportunities for students with disabilities and those at risk has helped us realize that traditional roles and responsibilities must be altered. No longer can general educators direct their teaching efforts to the middle level of the class, using standardized teaching techniques, curriculum, testing procedures, and grading systems. Special educators have also needed to modify their views of themselves, particularly their role as entities separate from the rest of the school. New roles and issues have emerged (Bauwens & Hourcade, 1995) that involve consultation with general educators about strategies to use with students with special needs within the context of the general education classroom (Gersten, Darch, Davis, & George, 1991; Idol, 1988). Building administrators can no longer follow traditional grouping, placement, and scheduling practices, nor can they expect to meet students' needs by the lockstep sequence of the traditional curriculum within the structure of a graded system (Stainback, Stainback, Courtnage, & Jaben, 1985). District administrators must realize that maintaining separate budgets for general and special education is not cost efficient and therefore not fiscally defensible. Increasingly, parents are realizing that they can no longer leave their children's education in the hands of the experts; they, too, are now considered expert members of their children's educational teams. Finally, students with disabilities and those at risk must assume some responsibility for their own educational outcomes, as much as their abilities allow. They must let their teachers and parents know when modifications in the general environment are needed, which modifications are successful, and which ones are not. The reality of education is that no individual can or should assume full responsibility for a student's success in inclusive settings. Teachers, parents, administrators, related services personnel, counselors, students, and the general school community must accept and share responsibility to provide equal educational opportunities to all students, regardless of their diversity.

# Role Definition

Role definition is the first step in any successful team effort, especially if team members are assuming new roles or altered ones. A good starting point is to identify all potential team members who will share the responsibility for an individual student's educational program. At the very least, the team consists of the general and special education teachers, the parents, the principal, and, when appropriate, the student. It is important, however, to consider all members of the school community who may be involved in a student's educational program. Other team members could include paraprofessionals; speech-language, occupational, or physical therapists; guidance counselors; administrators other than the principal; specialists in vision, sign language, interpretation, orientation and mobility, or adaptive physical education; other school-based staff such as band directors, media specialists, and coordinators of talented and gifted programs; vocational education coordinators; and community-based employment supervisors.

A common pitfall of team development is to place students in supplementary classes such as music, art, or physical education without giving those staff members an opportunity to learn about the students' special needs and to participate in problem solving (Kjerland, Neiss, Franke, Verdon, & Westman, 1988). Thus, it is important to view each individual in the school building who has contact with the student as a potential team member. Use these three important questions to consider potential members: Is this individual a teacher who would need to provide interventions in the curriculum to accommodate the special learning needs of the student? Does this person offer services and expertise needed to help support the student in another teacher's classroom or during certain school activities? Is this individual involved, or should he or she be involved, in the student's life?

Once team members have been identified, it is helpful to delineate the basic contributions or expectations of each individual (Figure 6.1). Because members' roles can be expected to change as the students' needs change, role definition should be an ongoing process. Team membership also may change as the student progresses and no longer needs the support of certain members or moves from one grade or level to the next.

## Role Expectations and the Special Education Process

Another helpful practice is to identify the role expectations of each team member according to the sequence of the special education process. At different stages of the process, team membership may shift temporarily. As Figure 6.2 shows, the general education teacher, the parents, and the special education teacher play key roles at the prereferral stage, functioning as co-consultants in the development of strategies to meet the needs of students at risk in the general education setting. A support staff member or paraprofessional also may help by gathering information about the students and implementing intervention strategies. Ideally, the process ends here when interventions in the general education setting are successfully implemented and monitored.

**The special educator should strive to**
- Recognize that the techniques of instructional and behavioral management used by regular educators can be effective means of working with students with special needs
- Understand that teachers in regular classrooms must respond to the needs of many students rapidly
- Acknowledge that placing a student with special needs in a general classroom does not relieve that teacher of any responsibilities to the other students
- Realize that no classroom teacher can devote the majority of time to any one student for any length of time
- Recognize that teaching techniques or programs that may be a success in a separate special education class may not be appropriate for the general classroom environment

**The general educator should strive to**
- Understand that the special education consultants may be responsible for a large number of students in a variety of settings and therefore have a limited amount of time to devote to each student
- Realize that it is unlikely that a new intervention strategy or instructional approach will have an immediate effect and that a fair trial must be given before a technique is judged ineffective
- Acknowledge that all students differ in the extent of instructional accommodations they need; many recommended techniques by the consultant may be extensions of techniques from regular education
- Maintain a familiarity with each student's IEP, sharing responsibility with the consultant for determining how goals and objects can be reinforced during the course of general classroom activities

**Both special and regular educators should strive to**
- Acknowledge that both teachers have specialized skills but that their experience, values, and knowledge bases may differ
- Acknowledge that both special and general educators are stakeholders in a child's educational process

**FIGURE 6.1**
Facilitating collaborative consultation: Goals for special and general educators.

If the student continues to have difficulty after a variety of preventive or prereferral strategies have been tried, the general education teacher, in consultation with the parents, may decide to refer the student to the principal, or another designee, as the first step in the special education process. Depending on district or state policy, an intermediate step may occur between referral and assessment. This step involves presenting the student to a school-based screening committee, which may be known as a child study committee (CSC), pupil personnel team (PPT), or educational management team (EMT). The committee may either recommend alternative strategies to try in the general classroom or, with informed parental consent, refer the student for assessment.

A variety of multidisciplinary team members must participate in the assessment process, as specified in IDEA regulations. The general education teacher and the parents are not required to participate as team members, but they can provide valuable information about the students' current performance levels in a variety of

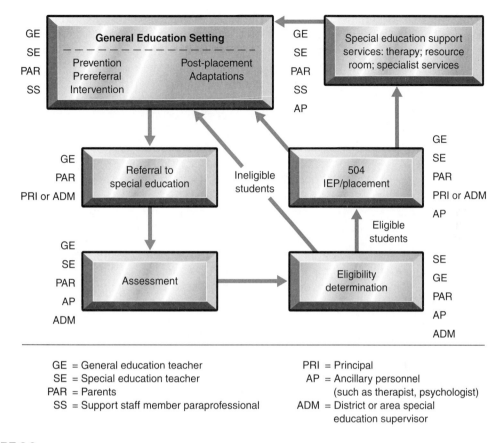

**FIGURE 6.2**
Team involvement in prereferral (level of participation may vary by state or locality).

settings. Thus, they act as advisors to the multidisciplinary team. (See chapter 2 for an overview of the entire prereferral to placement process.)

An important feature of the assessment process is that it is a closed-loop system. Students found eligible for special education services, as well as those referred for assessment but found ineligible, continue in their general education placements both during and after the assessment and eligibility process. This enables students to maintain their home base in general education as the process unfolds, while continuing to receive the benefit of educational interventions planned and implemented by the collaborative efforts of the general and special education teachers.

## MODELS FOR COLLABORATION

Collaboration is the key to successful integration of students at risk and those with disabilities into the general education environment. In the past, collaboration between special and general educators occurred on a limited basis outside of the required team meetings during the steps of the special education identification and placement process. Consultation has most often been linked to existing special education resource programs, whereby the resource room teacher fulfills a limited consultative function to general education teachers (Kauffman & Pullen, 1989). In many school districts, resource room teachers by definition are allowed to serve only those students with valid IEPs. In practice, consultative services under this model are typically delivered in the resource room as opposed to the general education classroom. In many instances, resource room teachers are unable to carry out their responsibilities as consultants because their activities are limited to assessment and instruction in the resource room (Wiederholt & Chamberlain, 1990). Over the years consultation has evolved as a major classroom role.

## Collaborative Consultation

A more responsive approach to collaboration between general and special educators emerged during the 1990s. *Collaborative consultation* is "an interactive process that enables people with diverse expertise to generate creative solutions to mutually defined problems" (Idol, Paolucci-Whitcomb, & Nevin, 1987, p. 1). West and Idol (1990) have identified three major purposes of collaborative consultation: (a) to prevent learning and behavioral problems, (b) to remediate learning and behavioral problems, and (c) to coordinate instructional programs. Using a collaborative approach greatly enhances the likelihood of success because the proposed solutions or strategies are generated from a wider knowledge base than that of any individual team member. Burdette & Crocket (1999) state that collaborative consultation is an integral part of supplementary aids and services as defined in IDEA 1997. Three questions arise:

(a)  How can teachers effectively provide an appropriate education to students with disabilities in heterogeneous classrooms and feel competent in the process?
(b)  Does teacher consultation provide support to teachers responsible for effective instruction?
(c)  What barriers and facilitators exist for the implementation of school-based consultative services? (pp. 432–433)

It is helpful to understand three terms commonly used during the inclusive process: *consultation, collaboration,* and *teaming. Interactions: Collaboration Skills for School Professionals* (Friend & Cook, 1992) is an excellent resource for learning more about the process of inclusion, and it defines the terms this way:

> *Consultation:* A voluntary process in which one professional assists another to address a problem concerning a third party. (p. 17)
> *Collaboration:* Interpersonal collaboration is a style for direct interaction between at least two coequal parties voluntarily engaged in shared decision making as they work toward a common goal. (p. 5)

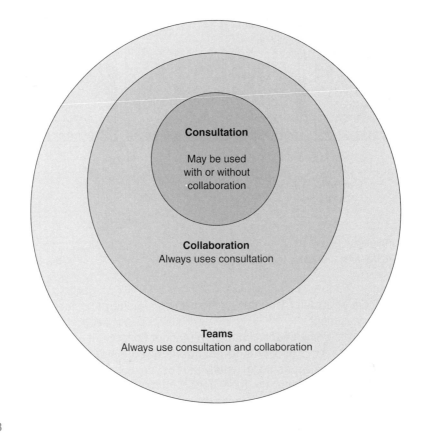

**FIGURE 6.3**
Interaction of consultation, collaboration, and teams.
*Source:* A special thanks to Marilyn Friend for her assistance with this figure.

> *Team:* A relatively small set of interdependent individuals who work and interact directly in a coordinated manner to achieve a common purpose. (p. 24)

Figure 6.3 shows how these three terms interact. Consultation may be conducted without collaboration and teams. However, whenever collaboration and teams are involved, consultation is activated. In other words, a teacher may come to your classroom to share an idea and thus act as a consultant. But collaboration and teaming cannot occur unless you become involved. Figure 6.4 presents a model of consultation, collaboration, and teams (Friend & Cook, 1996).

The special education teacher consultant model was developed to address the learning difficulties of students with disabilities through support and consultation provided to their general classroom teachers (Greenburg, 1987). In contrast to traditional consultative services that typically involve calling in an outside expert for a one-time look at a program, classroom, or student, the teacher consultant model is built on the collaboration of school-based staff. Thus, ongoing consultation is available as staff

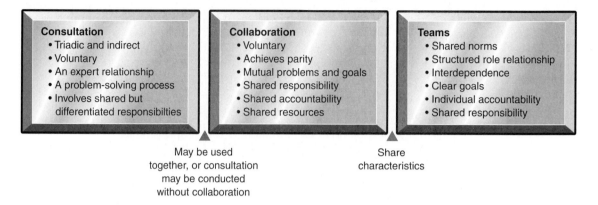

**FIGURE 6.4**
Consultation/collaboration/teams model.
*Source:* A special thanks to Marilyn Friend for her help with this figure.

members pool their resources and expertise to generate solutions to in-house problems and issues.

The role of the special education teacher consultant encompasses several basic functions. One aspect is to help general educators understand that students with special needs can successfully participate in inclusive settings (Lewis & Doorlag, 1987). Beyond this, the most important component of the role is to facilitate instructional or curricular decision making by the general classroom teacher or among team members regarding an individual student's educational needs. Key to the teacher consultant's success is establishing an atmosphere that encourages the exchange of ideas and advice rather than following a more traditional practice of giving advice to those seeking guidance.

If you look back at Figure 6.1, you will see some goals for general and special educators that support the reciprocal nature of the collaborative relationship. Much of the decision making carried out by team members will concern adapting the general classroom environment to accommodate the needs of inclusive students. Among the main functions of the special education consultant are gathering information, making observations, and facilitating discussion among team members that will result in instructional modification at the appropriate level of the hierarchy.

Other duties of the special education consultant will depend in part on the type of consultation program in effect. Teacher consultative services usually take one of two forms: indirect or direct (Schulte, Osborne, & McKinney, 1990). Each form is used with approximately equal frequency (West & Brown, 1987).

In *indirect consultation,* the special educator provides technical assistance to the general class teacher. The consultant helps the general education teacher assess needs, arrange the physical environment, plan for instruction, prepare or adapt lesson plans and materials, and develop student evaluation and grading procedures for the students with disabilities. The consultant does not, however, deliver any direct instruction to students, a role that is maintained by the general education teacher. The main advantage is that the indirect approach allows the consultant to serve many students in a limited amount of time. A primary disadvantage is that it may be difficult to determine conclusively whether improved student performance is directly related to the intervention efforts of the consultant via the teacher (Heron & Harris, 1987). Another drawback is that the consultant may not have an adequate amount of time to spend addressing any one student's needs.

In *direct consultation,* the special education teacher carries out some direct instruction within the general classroom setting in addition to providing the technical assistance of indirect consultation. The main disadvantage of providing direct consultative services to individual students is the added demand on the consultant's time, a factor that can be directly translated into increased costs (Heron & Harris, 1987). An obvious advantage is direct service to the student, which provides more opportunities for one-to-one instruction. The direct model also benefits the general classroom teacher by freeing more time for other students and the consultant by enabling more direct and consistent monitoring of the effects of the interventions.

Both direct and indirect consultation benefit students and teachers in many ways. Although there is limited research conclusively demonstrating the effectiveness of the consultative model (Schulte et al., 1990), a substantial amount of professional literature addresses the practical benefits of collaborative consultation (Idol & West, 1987; Lewis & Doorlag, 1987; Reynolds, Wang, & Walberg, 1987; Thousand & Villa, 1990). These benefits include the following:

- Reduced referrals to special education
- Maintenance of general education placements for students with disabilities, promoting inclusion with peers and reducing stigmatization
- Ongoing feedback and professional growth opportunities for teachers
- Increase in direct contact time between student and teacher
- Provision of needed resources that can be used with all students in the classroom
- Increased likelihood that all students' instruction will match the general education curriculum
- Potential for increasing teachers' accountability
- Potential for maximizing instructional outcomes
- Professional and personal satisfaction for teachers
- Improvement of staff morale
- Consistent availability of the consultant, which is not the case with outside consultants
- Availability of an effective vehicle for instructional decision making for all students with and without disabilities

When we consider the many advantages of the consultative approach, we may wonder why its use is not more extensive (i.e., used for all students with special needs in all school districts). There are some perceived disadvantages to this approach that have interfered with its widespread implementation. One commonly cited drawback, especially by those not experienced in its use, is that it seems to eliminate or reduce a teacher's freedom and autonomy (Thousand & Villa, 1990). General education teachers may fear having another educator in their classrooms on a general basis, assuming that it will interfere with their individual teaching styles and force them to modify the tried-and-true instructional approaches they have developed and refined during their professional careers. They may be concerned that having another adult in the classroom will prove disruptive to the students. In addition, while general education teachers may welcome assistance for their students with special needs, they may have concerns about the performance and behavior of those students when the special education consultant is not physically present to provide individual support and instruction.

Special educators also have concerns about implementing the consultative model. Perhaps their greatest concern relates to schedule and caseload—whether they will have sufficient time to meet the needs of all students and their teachers or to carry out all the duties of the consultative role (Idol-Maestas & Ritter, 1985). Lack of administrative support is another factor that inhibits success in school consultant programs (Idol-Maestas & Ritter, 1985; Nelson & Stevens, 1981). Another concern relates to providing feedback to general educators. Observing on-the-job teaching performance can threaten even close relationships among colleagues (Rocha, Wiley, & Watson, 1982). It can be an uncomfortable task for the untrained consultant, especially if the general education teacher resists the consultant's role or does not enthusiastically endorse the inclusion of children with disabilities. A less obvious concern may involve the security of the consultant's role. Special education consultants may fear that they will no longer be needed if they do an outstanding job of helping general educators become skilled in meeting the needs of mainstreamed students.

## Cooperative Teaching

Also known as co-teaching, *cooperative teaching* is another model for integrating students with special needs into the general education classroom. As in direct consultation, the special educator participates in instruction in the general classroom. In cooperative teaching, however, the special educator has increased responsibility for classroom instruction. In most co-teaching situations, special educators continue to take the lead in activities such as child study, consulting with parents, and offering individual, intense instruction to students in need (Reynolds, 1989). Unlike a strict consultation model, co-teaching means that both teachers share equal responsibility for planning, instructing, evaluating, and monitoring all members of the class. A distinct advantage is the opportunity for co-teachers to combine their individual strengths and expertise to address particular student needs (Relic, Cavallaro, Borrelli, & Currie, 1986).

Typically, minimal standards are set for co-taught programs, which limit the number of students in a class and prescribe an allowable ratio among teachers, general education students, and special education students. For example, a program might designate that two full-time teachers will be assigned to the class and that no more than one-quarter of the class may be comprised of students with IEPs or identified high-risk students. Students also may need to meet certain standards, such as the ability to read content-area materials, before being placed in co-taught classes. Co-taught classes offer the obvious advantage of enabling students to receive instruction in inclusive environments with necessary support without being singled out as the targets of special instruction (Relic et al., 1986).

Friend (1995) presents several co-teaching models to help us see that, when two teachers are in one room, many choices of interaction are available. Table 6.1 presents co-teaching options. Here are some additional tips:

1. You should develop a master list with the categories *do list, your list, my list, our list,* and a *gray list* when you sit down with your co-teacher and list all the tasks to be implemented during the teaming process. Table 6.2 presents a working model.

   Gray-list tasks are those that teachers cannot immediately agree on but will come back to and discuss later. You will quickly see that there are more points of agreement than disagreement.

**TABLE 6.1**
Co-teaching options.

| Option | Definition/Characteristic |
| --- | --- |
| One teach, one observe | One teacher has the primary instructional responsibility while the other gathers observational information on students in the class. It is important to remember that either teacher can take on either role. |
| One teach, one drift | This approach is an extension of the previous one. One teacher has the primary instructional responsibility while the other assists students with their work, monitors behavior, corrects assignments, and so on. |
| Station teaching | Teachers divide instructional content into two parts (such as vocabulary and content, new concepts and review). Each teacher instructs half the class in one of the areas; they then switch student groups so that all students receive the same instruction. |
| Parallel teaching | Each teacher instructs half the student group. The two teachers address the same instructional material. |
| Remedial teaching | One teacher instructs students who have mastered the material to be learned while the other takes students who have not mastered the material and reteaches it. |
| Supplemental teaching | One teacher presents the lesson in standard format. The other works with students who cannot master the material, simplifying it and otherwise adapting it to meet their needs. |
| Team teaching | Both teachers present the lesson to all students. This may include shared lecturing, dividing responsibilities for presenting the instruction, or what one teacher has affectionately called "tag team teaching" in which one teacher begins the lesson and the other takes over when it seems appropriate. |

**TABLE 6.2**
Judy's List

| Do List | My List | Your List | Our List | Gray List |
| --- | --- | --- | --- | --- |
| List all tasks to be completed.<br>• lunch money<br>• direct instruction<br>• grading papers, etc. | We *both* agree that these are your tasks. | We *both* agree that these are my tasks. | These are the tasks we can share. | Tasks we cannot agree on immediately. List and act on these last. |

2. During inclusionary procedures, one teacher can position him- or herself in the corner of the room. If that teacher cannot hear a question or an answer, he or she may raise a hand for a repeat. It is quite possible that students also did not hear.

3. Let students provide the strategies that work best for them. Sometimes we forget the most important player in the IEP: the student.

4. Support personnel can provide a one-page handout listing their students' strengths, needs, successful techniques, and so on. This will be extremely helpful for the general classroom teacher.

5. When students are auditorially distracted in a large classroom, purchase earplugs for them to wear when they do their work. Older students like the smaller earplugs; younger students like the big ones.

6. Assign teachers for parallel programming who are particularly good at this type of assignment. A peer helper also may be assigned to the student receiving the parallel lesson. (*Parallel programming* means teaching a subject on different levels.)

7. A major step toward a successful co-teaching program is the ability of team teachers to work together.

In many areas of our country, the concept of "push-in" is applied to the co-teaching model. This is when the student at-risk or with special needs is "pushed into" the general education classroom. Most frequently, a co-teaching model will be used.

Gerber and Popp (1999) found a high level of satisfaction among students, parents, and the co-teaching model. However, parents were concerned with the lack of communication between parents and the school and with the loss of continuity among grade levels.

The following responses were collected from observing (Wood, 2000) and requesting information from students in a co-taught class:

• When I attend this class I feel like a "someone." The class is small and the teachers know my name.

- There is always an extra teacher to answer a question when I am confused.
- Last year I was suspended ten times—this year only twice.
(A smile came over the teacher's face since she realized that this *was* quite an improvement.)
- If one teacher turns her back, you better watch out. There is always another teacher on the "loose."
- I receive more help in this class. Last year the teacher was too busy with other students to help me.
- We have a phone in the room. Last year when it rang, I would get into trouble. This year when it rings, I know that one teacher answers and one watches me.

## Peer Collaboration Process

Pugach and Johnson (1995) conducted a study on the benefits of the *peer collaboration process,* a four-step problem-solving process. The "purpose of the process is to enable classroom teachers to develop a clearer understanding of problems they encounter in the classroom and potential solutions to those problems" (p. 103). The steps include (a) clarifying questions, (b) summarizing the information generated in the first step, (c) generating at least three interventions for the problem and predictions of possible results, and (d) developing an evaluation plan to measure the accuracy of the intervention plan and the outcome of the implementation. Pugach and Johnson found that the teachers in the intervention group, compared to a control group, became more confident in intervention planning and showed a higher degree of affect. A structured approach to problem solving in the classroom assists in developing successful solutions.

## Teacher Support Teams

A third school-based approach to meeting the needs of all students in inclusive settings is teacher support teams. Several types of team arrangements have proven successful in promoting collaborative consultation between special and general educators. Perhaps the most broad-based type of support is provided by *teacher coaching teams.* In general, the purpose of coaching teams is "to build communities of teachers who continuously engage in the study of their craft" (Showers, 1985, p. 63). These teams are often organized during training activities designed to promote the use of a certain instructional strategy or curriculum approach. Teachers then have the support of their peers as they try to implement new strategies in their classrooms after the training.

Intervention assistance teams and school-based resource teams are similar in that both are formed to address a particular type of problem. *Intervention assistance teams* are formed as needed, and members may come from within or outside of the school building. Each member will have expertise in a particular intervention strategy. In contrast, *school-based resource teams* are always formed by personnel within the building. A variety of professionals, including teachers, administrators, and support staff, may serve as members (West & Idol, 1990).

*Teacher assistance teams* (TAT) are the most strictly defined type of teacher support team. Like the models just described, TAT promotes the use of a school-based problem-solving team to generate intervention strategies for individual students or groups. A team is usually comprised of a core of three members representing various grade levels or disciplines, with the classroom teacher who has requested assistance serving as the fourth member. The team may address a wide variety of issues, including intervention strategies for a particular student, modification of the curriculum, or communication with parents. A distinguishing characteristic of a TAT is that it is teacher-oriented rather than child-oriented because its main purpose is to support teachers. Another distinctive aspect is the importance that training plays in the ultimate effectiveness of team members (Chalfant & Pysh, 1989). Figure 6.5 shows the roles of sample TAT members.

# COMMUNICATION AMONG TEAM MEMBERS

Establishing clear channels of communication among team members can address and possibly prevent many of the concerns surrounding the collaborative consultation and co-teaching models. As we have discussed, there are predetermined occasions in the special education process when team members need to communicate (such as CSC, PPT, or EMT meetings and during IEP development). However, the less formal, daily communication may be of greater concern to educators and parents, who are assuming a wide variety of duties in a limited amount of time.

Safran and Safran (1985) have developed a practical model of communication between general and special educators that can be effectively used in collaborative consultation. Their flexible model includes both personal meetings and written communication and enables teachers to systematize and streamline communication. One useful component is a three-way meeting early in the student's placement between the general education teacher, the special education teacher consultant, and the student to discuss goals, expectations, and scheduling. At this meeting, the teachers and the student may clarify important issues about the role of each teacher, such as who will grade the student's work and assign the final class grade or who will be primarily responsible for communicating with the parents. Another issue is deciding which teacher the student should approach to discuss the ongoing appropriateness of adaptations and identify any unmet needs. Even the youngest students should have the benefit of this type of meeting, for it encourages them at an early age to assume some responsibility for their own educational outcomes.

Group conferences can be an effective means of sharing information among time-limited professionals (Safran & Safran, 1985). Meetings can be arranged for teachers and others who share a particular grade level, subject, or student. For example, teachers of one student could periodically meet as a group with the consultant to discuss the student's common needs across classes and successful adaptations that individual teachers may have tried. This will not only save the con-

**Regular education teachers**
- View the student as a regular member of the class, not a visitor
- Modify teaching techniques, course content, evaluation, and grading procedures to accommodate the student's special learning needs
- See and use the expertise of others in making necessary adaptations
- Incorporate IEP goals into typical activities and interactions according to the team's instructional plan

**Parents**
- Present family values and priorities for the student's educational program
- Provide insight into the student's functioning in a variety of environments
- Provide a vision of the student's future

**Special education teachers**
- Provide consultation and collaboration
- Suggest or make adaptations in curriculum, materials, or equipment
- Incorporate IEP goals into typical activities and interactions

**Administrators**
- Draw together regular and special education resources
- Ensure staff training and team consultative support
- Help solve logistical and programmatic issues

**Therapists**
- Ensure functional approaches to addressing therapy needs in typical activities and interactions (such as self-care, getting onto the bus or swing, using equipment during shop or home economics)

**FIGURE 6.5**

Sample roles and responsibilities of TAT members.

*Source:* Kjerland, L., Neiss, J., Franke, B., Verdon, C., & Westman, E. (1988, Winter). Team membership: Who's on first? *Impact: Feature Issue on Integrated Education, 1*(2). Minneapolis: University of Minnesota, Institute on Community Integration. Adapted by permission.

sultant time in meeting individually with the teachers but will enable the teachers to draw on one another's expertise. Grade-level meetings may be helpful in an instance where a standardized test will be given to all students. The consultant could meet with all teachers in advance to discuss allowable accommodations in administering the test to students with disabilities. In subject-centered meetings, teachers might confer with the consultant as a group when revising curriculum, developing study guides, or selecting texts or materials to be sure that they are appropriate for special students or can be adapted without too much difficulty.

While special educators may have cornered the market on excessive paperwork, written communication can nonetheless be effective in supplementing face-to-face contact among busy educators. The weekly report form in Figure 6.6 is

---

*WEEKLY REPORT*                                              *DATE* _____

*STUDENT'S NAME* _____        *TEACHER'S NAME* _____

CLASSROOM BEHAVIOR:  GOOD              AVERAGE              WEAK              YIKES!—S.O.S.
                                          ☐                    ☐                  ☐                      ☐

Description of behavior (e.g., J. J. shouts out during whole-group instruction—OR—J. J. is a very polite child.)

_____

_____

_____

_____


ACADEMIC:                    GOOD              AVERAGE              WEAK              YIKES!—S.O.S.
                                 ☐                    ☐                  ☐                      ☐

Subject _____        Special Skill: _____
            (e.g.: Math)                              (e.g.: 2-digit addition with carrying)


Comments/Other: _____

_____

_____

_____

_____

---

**FIGURE 6.6**
Weekly Report.

*Source:* Developed by Diane Pichelmann-Sutherland and Judy W. Wood, copyright 2000.

useful in helping the special educator keep track of the included student's progress. Figure 6.7, Red Alert, may be used when immediate help is needed by the general education teacher.

# TRAINING IN CONSULTATION AND TEAMWORK

Another front-line attack strategy in overcoming the perceived disadvantages of collaborative consultation is teacher training. Through systematic, ongoing training ef-

---

**RED ALERT!**  DATE _____

STUDENT'S NAME _____   TEACHER'S NAME _____

CLASSROOM BEHAVIOR:

Description of behavior: _____

_____

_____

_____

_____

ACADEMIC:

Subject _____   Special Skill: _____
          (e.g.: Math)                              (e.g.: 2-digit addition with carrying)

Comments/Other: _____

_____

_____

_____

_____

---

**FIGURE 6.7**
Red Alert.
*Source:* Developed by Diane Pichelmann-Sutherland and Judy W. Wood, copyright 2000.

forts, teachers, administrators, and others can learn to become both effective providers and consumers of consultative services as well as valuable team members.

A look at the status of training efforts at the preservice level underscores the discrepancy between training and practice. In a national survey to obtain information about the status of preservice team training, Courtnage and Smith-Davis (1987) found that 48 percent of the 360 responding special education preservice training programs did not offer interdisciplinary team training. Courtnage and Healy (1984) were able to locate only eight special education teacher training institutions that offered distinct team training programs outside of the context of other course offerings.

The status of preservice training in consultation appears to be equally limited. The lack of adequately defined and implemented training programs has been cited as a major obstacle in consultant training (Kurpius, 1978). West and Brown (1987) found that the majority of states surveyed (23 of 35 respondents) reported no certification requirements for competency in consultation, indicating that there appears to be little incentive for institutions to develop programs to prepare teacher consultants.

Because of the limited availability of preservice training programs in team building and consultation, much of the training that does take place occurs at the inservice level through state-, university-, or locally sponsored inservice offerings. Inservice training is by nature more limited in scope and sequence than preservice training. Therefore, it is important to identify skills and knowledge critical to the successful functioning of teams and teacher consultants when developing inservice training or seeking out training opportunities to develop one's own skills.

One skill area common to training programs in consultation and team building is interpersonal communication and interactive skills (Idol & West, 1987; Safran & Safran, 1985). These skills include observations, interviewing, and negotiations. Aside from their obvious application to group interaction, these skills also help providers and consumers of consultation as they negotiate the ups and downs of shared responsibility for students in inclusive settings.

A second objective of many training programs is to develop a strong underlying knowledge base for problem solving. Common targets for training in this area include (a) techniques for individualization of instruction, (b) characteristics of students with disabilities and awareness of factors that place a student at risk, (c) identification of resource personnel and awareness of their roles, (d) knowledge of adaptive evaluation techniques, (e) knowledge of educational materials and how to adapt them, (f) knowledge of positive behavior intervention techniques, and (g) understanding of the learning process (Courtnage & Smith-Davis, 1987; Idol & West, 1987).

Building on this foundation, the special education teacher consultant also needs to develop an in-depth knowledge of the general education environment throughout the school building. It is this type of on-the-job training that can make the difference in the teacher consultant's effectiveness and acceptance by other staff members. The teacher consultant should strive to do the following (McKenzie et al., 1970; Rocha et al., 1982; Salend & Salend, 1986; Spodek, 1982):

1. Acquire a working knowledge of special subject areas, including curriculum content and sequence, materials, and teaching strategies used in the general classroom.
2. Develop and use a shared vocabulary with general educators.
3. Learn what nonacademic skills are deemed important by inclusion teachers and what social skills are needed for the student to be accepted by peers in the general education setting.
4. Learn a variety of monitoring techniques to ensure that instruction is effective.
5. Recognize and reinforce strategies of general educators that are effective with *all* learners and acknowledge the relevancy of general classroom activities to the student with special needs.

1. Are the approaches I have recommended feasible for use in the regular education environment, or are they more appropriate for use in a separate special education class?

2. Do the adaptations enable the student to participate in cooperative learning activities with peers, or do they isolate the student with a disability within the classroom?

3. If I have recommended an adaptation requiring new materials or supplies, have I helped the regular education teacher obtain them?

4. Am I recommending adaptations for the regular educator to carry out that I would be able to implement under similar conditions without undue stress?

5. Do I continually update my understanding of what occurs in regular classes and what regular educators realistically can and cannot accomplish within the confines of a typical school day?

6. If there are unresolved issues or questions regarding any aspect of the consultative relationship, do I share them with the regular education teacher before discussing them with other teachers or administrators?

**FIGURE 6.8**
Self-evaluation questions for the special education teacher consultant.

The teacher consultant who has acquired these skills and knowledge and continues to update them will more likely be perceived as one of the general grade- or subject-level staff members rather than an outsider straying in from special education to offer advice to general educators on "their" students.

Teacher consultants may periodically assess their own performance using the self-evaluation questions shown in Figure 6.8.

General educators also must strive to develop certain competencies that will enable them to be better consumers of consultative services and, in many instances, function in a co-consultant capacity. A key role for the general educator is to ask the right questions and relay critical information to the special education teacher consultant, especially if the consultant has a limited amount of time to spend in the classroom. Figure 6.9 offers some self-evaluation questions to help general education teachers periodically assess their contributions to the consultative relationship.

## THE IMPORTANCE OF ADMINISTRATIVE SUPPORT

Administrators are in a unique position to promote successful collaboration between special and general educators. Because of their dual roles of instructional leader and building administrator, principals are central to the implementation and maintenance of effective collaborative arrangements. Not only can they affect the necessary administrative procedures to accommodate students with special needs in inclusive settings, but they can also provide access to necessary training opportunities for staff members who are implementing classroom adaptations. District-level administrators, who play more central roles in the allocation of resources and development of districtwide policies, can also have a direct influence on the implementation of integrated programming at the building level.

1. Do I give the suggested adaptations a fair trial before concluding that they are inappropriate or ineffective?

2. In the consultant's absence, do I keep a running log of questions, observations, and comments regarding mainstreamed students to share with the consultant at a later time?

3. If a recommended approach is not feasible for use in my classroom or conflicts with my professional values, do I clearly make the consultant aware of this instead of carrying it out inconsistently or not at all?

4. Do I make a conscientious effort not to treat the students with disabilities as too "special," particularly during activities when adaptations are not necessary?

5. Do I and other staff members under my supervision maintain confidentiality pertaining to the identification of, and issues related to, the individual needs of mainstreamed students in our classroom?

6. If there are unresolved issues or questions regarding any aspect of the consultative relationship, do I share them with the special education teacher consultant before discussing them with other teachers or administrators?

**FIGURE 6.9**
Self-evaluation questions for the regular educator.

## Student-Related Administrative Issues

Careful scheduling may enhance a student's chance of success in inclusive environments (see chapter 10). Building administrators usually maintain a good awareness of an individual teacher's strengths and preferences and should be able to make a good match for most students and teachers. Ideally, if training opportunities in collaboration and teaming are made available to all teachers, the choice of teacher will no longer be a prime consideration when scheduling students with disabilities or those at risk.

A second student-related issue is grade-level expectations. In the past, some administrators have held to rigid, standardized, grade-level expectations when determining placement, tracking or grouping, promotion, and graduation. As the student body changes to include more students at risk and those with disabilities, such rigid standards must be abandoned in favor of more practical, student-oriented procedures (Stainback et al., 1985). In some instances, building administrators may have to negotiate with district administrators for permission to deviate from district-mandated procedures.

## Faculty-Related Administrative Issues

One of the most critical factors in the continued success of any collaborative model is the availability of adequate support systems to assist the general educator in developing and implementing alternate instructional strategies (Greenburg, 1987). While staff training is the key, access to ongoing support by and for general education teachers is also necessary. In addition to making funds available for teachers and other school-based staff to receive initial training to accommodate students with special needs in general education environments, administrators must be aware of the need for continued training to keep staff abreast of current developments in assessment, curriculum, adaptive approaches, and application of technology.

Administrators must also address the issue of building time into teachers' schedules to allow for collaborative problem solving, team meetings, peer coaching sessions, documentation of student progress, and development and adaptation of materials (Idol & West, 1987; Spodek, 1982). Administrators can also work to balance a teacher's share of the responsibility for inclusion by making adjustments in schedules. For example, by decreasing class size, administrators can adjust the schedules of general classroom teachers who have several students with disabilities included in their classrooms without the support of a direct teacher consultant. If this is not possible, a paraprofessional can be made available to decrease the student-teacher ratio for at least part of the day. At the same time, administrators should make sure that an overload in the teacher's schedule does not, by default, leave too much responsibility for adapting curriculum and delivering individualized instruction to paraprofessionals unless they have received special training (Kjerland et al., 1988).

Administrators should also be careful about trying to foster collaboration among faculty members by placing the special education teacher consultant in a supervisory role over general education teachers with inclusive students. Doing so jeopardizes the give-and-take nature of the collaborative relationship and can have negative consequences for the students if problems arise.

A final consideration for administrators is the allocation of resources. If district- and building-level administrators continue to allocate funds separately for special and general education, they send a clear message to personnel that collaboration is not required or even supported. By pooling resources, duplicative spending can be reduced while providing visible evidence of administrative support for collaborative activities (Greenburg, 1987).

## PARENTS AS PARTNERS

### Parental Involvement During Prereferral

While some parents may be reluctant to become members of a team comprised mainly of professionals, all parents possess a wealth of information that can be extremely helpful in promoting the success of their children in inclusive classrooms. As we discussed in chapter 1, parents can observe their children in a variety of settings and have the unique advantage of being able to assess a child's performance over time. Thus, parents may be the first to notice that a child is having difficulty in the general classroom environment. This may be especially true for children with mild disabilities or those at risk, whose problems in the classroom may be initially manifested as emotional or behavioral difficulties at home. In these instances, parents may request a conference with the teacher to discuss proactive classroom adaptations, and can be very helpful in providing information about the child's learning style and suggesting how past educational experiences may be influencing his or her present level of performance. Figure 6.10 (p. 188) lists some questions that parents may ask the classroom teacher before a referral is initiated.

**Academic classroom**
- In which subject is my child having particular difficulty?
- Is my child having difficulty in all or most subject areas or only in certain subjects?
- Are there any medical concerns (such as seizures, hearing loss, visual impairments) that should be looked into as a possible cause for my child's difficulties?
- Does my child's performance vary significantly between the morning and afternoon or on certain days of the week?
- What is my child's current level of performance in this skill area in comparison to the performance of others at this age level and in the class?
- What modifications in course content, pacing, and materials have been tried with my child? Which ones have proven successful? Which of these modifications should I carry out at home?
- How will I know when homework has been assigned? Is my child aware of the penalty for late or incomplete work?
- What appear to be my child's favorite subjects in school?

**Nonacademic classroom**
- Does my child stay in his or her seat?
- Does my child raise his or her hand and wait to be acknowledged?
- Does my child walk quietly in line and follow other school rules in the cafeteria, library, gym, and so on?
- Is my child's behavior significantly different from that of other children in the class? If so, exactly what does my child do or not do that is considered inappropriate?
- What do you do when my child behaves inappropriately?
- Does my child understand the classroom rules? Are they posted in a place where students can refer to them as needed?
- Does my child's behavior vary significantly between the morning and afternoon or on certain days of the week?
- What can I do to provide a consistent approach to behavior management between school and home?
- How many times a day is my child leaving the classroom for support services?
- Does he or she have difficulty reorienting to the classroom upon return?
- Is my child able to keep track of his or her belongings? Is there a system in place in the classroom for storing belongings?
- What leadership responsibilities does my child have? Are they carried out successfully?

**Nonacademic social**
- Does my child have friends in the classroom?
- Does my child initiate contact with other students? Does he or she respond appropriately when others initiate contact?
- Does my child interact appropriately with other students on the playground, in the cafeteria, on the bus, and during other free times?
- Is my child being teased or ridiculed by other students? If so, are there any adjustments we can encourage in behavior, appearance, or manner to improve this situation?
- What are my child's favorite activities during the school day?
- Does my child appear to be happy at school most of the time?

FIGURE 6.10
Questions from parents.

## Parental Involvement During Assessment and Placement

As we have discussed, parents are notified of key steps in the special education placement process (such as parental permission for initial assessment or writing the IEP) and are encouraged to participate. In addition to providing consent, parents may contribute valuable information to the assessment process. Their involvement and consent must be obtained before a student transfers from special education services to full-time general education without benefit of an IEP. Requirements for participation in other phases of the process, such as the school-based screening committee or eligibility determination, vary from one state to another and may vary among school districts within states. In most instances, however, schools are agreeable to a parent's request to participate in all phases of the process (Anderson, Chitwood, & Hayden, 1990).

## Parental Involvement After Placement

The questions in Figure 6.10 can also help parents obtain information about post-placement adaptations to the general education curriculum that have been made or need to be developed. Some of the necessary adaptations may be apparent when the IEP is written, but the need for others may not become obvious until the student has spent time in the general education environment. For this reason, parents as well as other team members must remain aware of the student's status in the mainstream setting. They should keep in mind that the IEP is not meant to be a static document but may be changed as often as necessary to represent the student's current educational status and needs.

## Parental Support Needs

It is unlikely that the effects of a child's disability or at-risk condition will be noticeable only at school. Parents will usually be the first to suspect that their child has special learning needs or notice that their child is frustrated, discouraged, and unhappy in the general class environment. As the child's level of frustration and anxiety grows, so does the parents'. For parents of children at-risk and others at the prereferral stage, each school week may be a roller coaster of good and bad days, with no apparent pattern of, or explanation for, the child's successes and failures. Parents may try techniques for support and encouragement that were successful with their other children but feel helpless or inadequate when these same approaches meet with limited success. As a child with special needs enters the formal referral and assessment process, parents may feel ambivalent. Typically, they hope their child will not be identified as having a disability, yet they hope to find a reasonable explanation for his or her difficulties and gain some relief through effective intervention.

Once children have been referred for an evaluation, their parents can be put in touch with a parent resource center or parent-to-parent program, if such resources exist in their state or locality. Thus, they can become informed of the special education process and of their rights and responsibilities and also contact other parents of children with similar disabilities and resulting needs. However, such resources are not usually available during the prereferral process, and the child's general education teacher may be the parents' main source of information and support. Therefore, an important responsibility of the special education consultant or resource teacher is to make all team members, particularly general educators who have primary contact with parents during prereferral, aware of sources of support within the school system and the community.

## Levels of Parental Involvement

Parental awareness of a child's educational program and the level of coordination between home and school can make an important difference for many students in inclusive settings (Lewis & Doorlag, 1987). However, professionals must keep in mind that parents may or may not choose to become involved at various levels in their childrens' educational programs. Some may elect to take part in each step of the process, while others may choose or be able to participate only in those events they view as critical, such as IEP development. The level of parental involvement varies not only from one student to another but also between two parents of the same child and for an individual parent over time.

Differences also exist in parents' preference for the level of integration into inclusive settings that they feel is appropriate for their children. Some parents want their children to receive services only in general education settings without the stigma of special labels or services. The collaborative consultation or co-teaching models may be particularly appealing to these parents. Other parents may prefer a self-contained or separate setting, believing that their child can receive a more appropriate and individualized education in a special program. In any case, parents' preferences and the personal values, experiences, and beliefs that support their decisions must be respected. As Turnbull and Turnbull (1986) advise, "Professionals should be particularly sensitive and tactful when they discuss special educational placement with parents, remembering that values, competing interests, and service availability are three important components of parental decisions" (p. 185).

Although parents may prefer placement in an integrated setting, they may continue to have mixed feelings about the benefits gained from inclusion. On one hand, they may feel that an integrated setting has many advantages to offer their child, including the reduction of labels and the positive academic and social influence of peers (Heron & Harris, 1987). In addition, parents may view the general education setting as one that can more adequately prepare their child for the demands of the regular work environment and the inclusion of adult life after leaving school.

However, some parents may fear that students in the general education setting will not accept their child as an equal and may not make the inclusive student feel welcome. If their child has been in a self-contained setting, parents may worry that he or she has not acquired the appropriate social skills to be readily accepted in inclusive settings and therefore may be the target of teasing or ridicule. Of greater concern to some parents is the increased student-teacher ratio in inclusive settings, which they fear may prevent their child from receiving necessary individual-ization of instruction or special programming. They may be unsure of their child's ability to conform to certain teacher expectations and perform successfully in the competitive climate of many general education classrooms (Heron & Harris, 1987).

## Paraprofessional and Collaboration

Another vast growing professional field which relates to collaboration is the para-professional. Many areas around the country are training "paras" to assist within the general education classroom. This extra help is of great value to the general and special educator. The responsibilities are now shared with a third party. However, many paraprofessionals receive mixed messages: "I need help" but "watch your boundaries." The roles for the paraprofessionals must be clearly defined and must meet their comfort level. Find out the paras' interest levels and ability levels. Use their strengths. Remember, many paras have been doing this "teaching thing" longer than many educators. Respect is of great importance. Use these helping hands and minds wisely, and you will be surprised how the workload lightens.

# EVALUATION OF INCLUSIVE EFFORTS

The saying goes, "The best offense is a good defense." The checklist in Figure 6.11 is an excellent tool for the evaluation of inclusive efforts. At the beginning of the school year, complete half of the appropriate box. At the end of the school year, re-turn to the checklist and check blocks actually addressed—Example: Attend inclu-sion inservice

## Evaluation of Individual Student Outcomes

Once students with special needs have been placed in a general education setting, they must be monitored constantly and closely to ensure that the instruction is ef-fective and continues to meet their needs (Rocha et al., 1982). Such monitoring is necessary for students who have been found eligible for special services as well as for those who were found ineligible or whose needs were addressed by prereferral strategies.

Responsibility for student evaluation should be shared among all team mem-bers, with the general educator and the special education teacher consultant tak-ing primary responsibility for the task. Student evaluation data should be gath-ered by direct observation of the student in the inclusive setting as well as by review of the student's work and tests. The overall goal of student evaluation should be to determine if instructional accommodations are working or if reeval-uation is needed so that further adaptations can be made. While the collaborat-ing professionals should be able to answer questions concerning the effective-ness of educational methods or content, they also need to address other less technical yet equally important questions regarding the student's functioning in

| Responsibilities | General Education Teacher | Special Education Teacher | Principal | Support Services | Parents & Community | School District |
|---|---|---|---|---|---|---|
| **General Responsibilities** | | | | | | |
| Describe the school's position on inclusion | | | | | | |
| Prepare the teaching staff for inclusion | | | | | | |
| Offer teachers a choice of inclusion teaching | | | | | | |
| Describe the inclusion program to parents | | | | | | |
| Provide full support services in the general class | | | | | | |
| Establish an inclusion support group | | | | | | |
| Explain the inclusion program to school personnel | | | | | | |
| | | | | | | |
| **Specific Professional Responsibilities** | | | | | | |
| Ensure compliance with state and federal guidelines | | | | | | |
| Provide student information to the inclusion team | | | | | | |
| Supervise the teaching assistant(s) | | | | | | |
| Serve as the student case manager | | | | | | |
| Monitor individualized education program (IEP) standards | | | | | | |
| Maintain cumulative folders | | | | | | |
| Participate in parent conferences | | | | | | |
| Assign grades on report cards each semester | | | | | | |
| | | | | | | |
| **Learning to Be an Inclusion Team Teacher** | | | | | | |
| Attend inclusion inservice | | | | | | |
| Function as part of the inclusion team | | | | | | |
| Respect the role of each school inclusion team member | | | | | | |
| | | | | | | |

**FIGURE 6.11**

Checklist for Successful Inclusion.

*Source:* Federico, M. A., Herrold, W. G. Jr., & Venn, J. C. (1999). *Helpful tips for successful inclusion: A checklist for educators.* Reston, VA: The council for exceptional children: Teaching exceptional children. p. 80.

| Responsibilities | General Education Teacher | Special Education Teacher | Principal | Support Services | Parents & Community | School District |
|---|---|---|---|---|---|---|
| **Teacher-Student Interaction** | | | | | | |
| Adapt curricular activities for students with disabilities | | | | | | |
| Teach student peers to assist students with disabilities | | | | | | |
| Use adaptations in classroom activities | | | | | | |
| Develop daily lesson plans | | | | | | |
| Work one-on-one with students as needed | | | | | | |
| Design interaction activities for students | | | | | | |
| Assign "buddies" to students with disabilities | | | | | | |
| | | | | | | |
| **Beliefs About Teaching Inclusion** | | | | | | |
| Maintain a sense of humor | | | | | | |
| Treat the inclusion class as "Our Class," not "My Class" | | | | | | |
| Become a community of inclusion learners | | | | | | |
| Avoid labeling children in the inclusion program | | | | | | |
| Treat all students as equals | | | | | | |
| Use appropriate behavior management | | | | | | |
| | | | | | | |
| **End-of-Year Responsibilities** | | | | | | |
| Administer end-of-year standardized testing | | | | | | |
| Assign final grades on report cards | | | | | | |
| Determine student promotions | | | | | | |
| Determine inclusion program successes | | | | | | |
| Identify inclusion program failures | | | | | | |
| Invite others to join the inclusion team | | | | | | |
| Select teachers for the next year's inclusion classroom(s) | | | | | | |
| | | | | | | |

1. Is the student involved whenever feasible as a decision maker regarding the educational program?

2. Does the student's schedule permit grouping with same-grade peers across a range of academic and nonacademic subjects?

3. Do the instructional adaptations tend to draw undue attention to the student in the classroom? If so, how can they be made less obtrusive?

4. Is adequate support provided for the student when reentering the classroom after receiving a support service in another setting?

5. Does participation in support services or resource room activities cause the student to miss nonacademic activities such as assemblies, free time, and enrichment classes?

**FIGURE 6.12**
Sample evaluation questions for nonacademic student outcomes.

inclusive environments. Figure 6.12 displays some sample evaluation questions related to nonacademic areas of a student's inclusive program. Similar questions reflecting each student's needs and educational environment should be presented periodically to team members, parents, and the student to evaluate the continued appropriateness of the nonacademic aspects of the student's program.

## Evaluation of General Program Outcomes

The adequacy of the total inclusive effort should be evaluated periodically to determine the positive effects of the program and to identify needed areas for program modification. Ferrara (1984) targeted four areas of focus for evaluation of inclusive efforts:

1. Determine the impact of implementation of inclusive efforts on the achievement and social adjustment of students with mild disabilities and on teachers and other students. How have teachers modified instruction, materials, and assessment procedures, and how have these modifications been implemented and supported and by whom?

2. Examine the number and types of contact between special and general educators. Are contacts student-related? Do they address all inclusive students? Do most of the contacts concern discipline or instruction or both?

3. Examine inservice training provided to team members on the topic of inclusion. How many teachers participated in the training, did they find it valuable, and was the information specific enough to be of use?

4. Determine the degree and appropriateness of inclusion practices. Do students attend all periods in which a course is taught, are they integrated with same-age or same-grade students, and are some students attending only nonacademic classes?

In addition, inclusive program evaluation efforts should address team effectiveness and participation. Questions could pinpoint the composition of the team, the coequal nature of the team relationships, the frequency and length of team meetings, and the relationship of team activities to student outcomes.

When planning evaluation of a school's inclusive program, evaluators should remember that the most useful evaluation techniques are responsive to the persons who receive or benefit from the services being offered (Idol, Paolucci-Whitcomb, & Nevin, 1987). A responsive evaluation must address the interests of stakeholders—those individuals whose lives are affected by the program or whose decisions will influence the program's future (Bryk, 1983). Stakeholders in inclusive intervention programs include teachers, support and ancillary staff members, administrators, parents, and students. Because each of these individuals has a slightly different perspective on inclusive efforts and outcomes, soliciting their input through either formal or informal evaluation techniques will result in data that can have a noticeable impact on the school's inclusive program and promote the success of every student in the general education environment.

## CONCLUSION

While collaborative consultation may not provide an easy answer to every issue or problem that has surfaced in response to the inclusive movement, effective consultative services for students with mild disabilities, students at risk, and their general education teachers can make a difference in the educational outcomes for individual students as well as for the success of general inclusion efforts in a school building. As the line of demarcation between special and general education becomes less rigid and is eventually erased, general educators, special educators, support and ancillary staff, administrators, and parents will continue to be faced with the challenge of working collaboratively to extend the benefits of inclusion efforts to all students in the building and the community.

# CHAPTER 7

# The Content: Using the SAALE Model

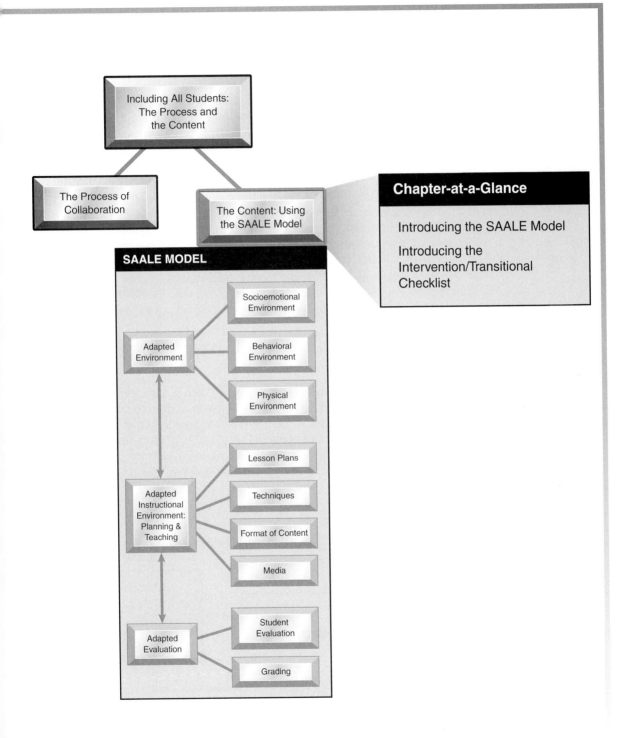

The second part of inclusion, content, is as significant as the process component. The SAALE model (or *S*ystematic *A*pproach for *A*dapting the *L*earning *E*nvironment), a three-part paradigm, is one way to select the content or accommodate it for inclusion. The paradigm is actually broken into three steps: the model itself, the intervention/transition checklist, and the strategies (Figure 7.1).

A *paradigm* is a large concept that remains constant, and all information (model, checklist, and strategies) has a place in the concept. Thus, SAALE is practical and effective when the user can mentally see all three steps as part of a larger whole. Your professor has a video to help you see the cohesiveness of the SAALE model. But remember, it only works when the three parts stay together.

This chapter introduces and defines steps 1 and 2 of the SAALE model. Step 1 is the model itself. Here I discuss each block, explain how everything you know and will know works as part of the model, and help you develop a logical understanding of how the model fits into the school day. Step 2 is the intervention/transition checklist, which I will define and then show you how to use.

To standardize educational vocabulary (such as the terms *modify, adapt, accommodate, intervene*), we will also discuss ways to think along the same "vocabulary lines."

## THE SAALE MODEL

IDEA (Reauthorization of the Individuals with Disabilities Education Act, 1997) places a call to general education to provide even greater access to students with disabilities. In meeting the goal of IDEA, "teachers must provide useful alternatives in both curricular materials and instructional delivery" (1999). Nancy Safer, executive director of the Council for Exceptional Children, states that "one size does not fit all." Teaching students with special needs requires that the "design" of the cur-

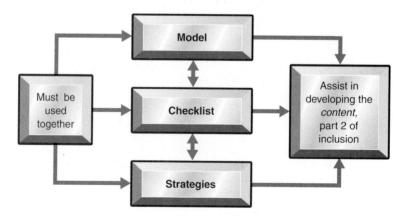

**FIGURE 7.1**
The three steps of SAALE.

ricular content may require a change in order for the students to access regular education curriculum. This goes back to "it is not only *what* we teach but how we teach" that opens doors for students who learn differently.

Lou Danielson (1999), states that the concept of "universal design" is one practice which helps students reach educational goals.

> In terms of learning universal design means the design of instructional materials and activities that makes the learning goals achievable by individuals with wide differences in their abilities to see, hear, speak, move, read, write, understand English, attend, organize, engage, and remember. Universal design for learning is achieved by means of flexible curricular materials and activities that provide alternatives for students with differing abilities. These alternatives are built into the instructional design and operating systems—they are not added on after-the-fact. (p. 2)

Why the fuss about universal design? Answer: The SAALE model and discussion to follow is truly universal design in motion. The SAALE Model has been around since the late 1970s and universal design is presently emerging as a best practice.

Research on the SAALE model (Wood, 1987) has repeatedly shown that the use of the model provides significant educational gains in diverse populations. This model is a growing concept and any best practice fits somewhere within the model's pattern. Now let's take a look at the SAALE model, prepare a foundation for effective teaching, and get ready for the remainder of the text.

Visualize the school day not as a whole but as several environments that continuously interact. That is how the SAALE model divides the school day. The model provides a framework to help educators decide where in the instructional day a student is having or will have a mismatch with his or her immediate environment. Figure 7.2 demonstrates the components of the model.

The school day can be divided into three major parts: (a) the socioemotional/behavioral environments, (b) the physical environment, and (c) the instructional environment. The instructional environment may be further divided into six sections: lesson plans, techniques, content, media, technology, and evaluation. In any one of these major areas, the educator can make a simple accommodation or modification that will make education more appropriate for a special-needs or at-risk student, thereby providing the least restrictive environment. Accommodations are simple adjustments to teaching, testing, or other areas within the environment. For example, if a student cannot read the textbook, the teacher can make several adjustments to the text to accommodate the lower reading level of the student, thus enabling the student to learn the material.

The socioemotional/behavioral environments involve numerous aspects of school. Issues include the attitudes of educators and students and ways of improving these attitudes. In addition, we spend a great deal of time helping students develop appropriate social skills so that they will be more effective within the environment.

In the physical environment, we are concerned with scheduling and grouping students as well as providing an environment that is free of physical barriers.

**FIGURE 7.2**
Components of the SAALE model.

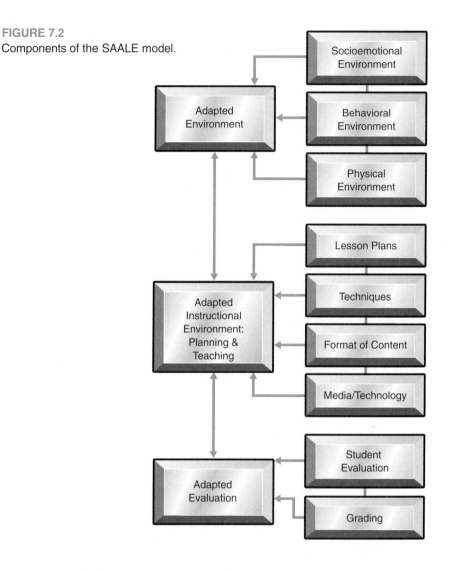

The instructional environment involves the academic work of learning. Specific accommodations can be made at any point when a student has difficulty with teaching technique or content. For example, imagine a math teacher who cannot deliver math content to a particular student. A mismatch of some kind has occurred within the instructional environment. However, by providing a simple intervention—perhaps adding a visual aid to accommodate a lecture—the teacher can correct the mismatch.

The concept of *mismatch* is the real trick in teaching. It is important to understand that mismatches are not *caused* by a child or teacher. A mismatch is simply a point where the child cannot succeed because the teacher has expectations which are not compatible with the student's abilities. For example, if a student cannot copy from the chalkboard and the teacher requires copying from the chalkboard, then you have a mismatch. Now, there is nothing wrong with requiring copying from the blackboard or not being able to copy; the point is we have a mismatch. No one is at fault. We simply have a point (mismatch) of intervention. I have changed my stand on who has the mismatch from the view expressed in the previous edition. With maturity I have grown to understand that what happens happens. No one is ever too old to learn. Teachers do the best they can; even if they are not doing their best for a student, I am convinced that they simply do not know what to do. If they did, they would do it. However, because we are professionals, we must (a) find the mismatch and (b) develop and implement the appropriate intervention. Children are not going to adjust to the environment; the environment must be adjusted to the student. For too long we have tried to make students fit our molds, but we can no longer follow this reasoning.

Let me go one step further in explaining what I mean about mismatch. Let's pretend that I've cut my finger. The doctor says, "I think a Band-Aid will be an appropriate intervention." Then the doctor puts the Band-Aid on my knee. My knee may feel better, but my problem is a cut finger. The intervention must match the problem.

The next day I cut my finger again and return to the same doctor. The doctor says, "This time I will pour a Coke over your finger." I appreciate the intervention, but Coke has nothing to do with the problem (Figure 7.3). I am trying to demonstrate that the intervention must fit the mismatch. I call this *intervention mismatch specific.*

**FIGURE 7.3**
The wrong interventions.

## Logical Connections: Putting What You Know Into the SAALE Model

To demonstrate how to place and use everything you know into the visual SAALE model, I would like to teach you the concept of *logical connections.* Let's pretend that I'm giving you one of my business cards. Now, what might be the purpose of your having one of my cards? Well, you can write to me, call me, fax me, or perhaps e-mail me. But if I return in three months and ask if you still have my card, odds are that you will have lost it or at least left it at home.

Now let's pretend that I'm giving you one of my business cards and telling you that I'll return in three months. If you can produce my card at that time, you'll receive $10,000. Will you have the card when I return? You bet! You now have a logical connection between my card and a special meaning.

When you are given something with no meaning (or logical connection), it has no value. However, if you have something and someone teaches you *why* it is important to learn, keep, or know, it has value. We often forget to provide logical connections for our students. For example, we issue textbooks and assume that the student realizes that the text has a connection with a specific course. But we must teach students what the text is for and how to use it. Throughout the year we constantly make those logical connections for the student.

Now that you understand what a logical connection is, let me use the term in reference to you. Figure 7.4 presents the SAALE model (see also Figure 7.2) in a file

**FIGURE 7.4**
How the SAALE model is like a filing cabinet.

drawer format. Visualize the model as a large filing cabinet with nine drawers. Each drawer represents one of the blocks in the model. Everything you know and everything you will know can be filed away in a drawer. Can you remember some of the college courses you took and simply did not understand why? Now you have a place (a mental drawer) to file away the information learned. For example, did you take a course about teaching reading? Well, what you learned fits neatly into the content drawer.

As you study part 2, you will begin to see how all the information you learn can be filed away. When a student has a mismatch, you can identify where within the model the mismatch is occurring, mentally pull out the drawer, and select an intervention for the mismatch. You see, an intervention is simply doing something that you have not tried. If one idea does not work, then try another. The remaining chapters in this book correspond with each block in the model. In this way, I will help you fill up the file drawers.

Now let's draw some logical connections between the SAALE model and your own knowledge.

*Where the SAALE model fits into the school day.* There are many things going on during a school day. For our purposes, however, we are going to simplify the school day into three blocks: student outcomes (what we want students to learn), curriculum (what we will teach the students, based on student outcomes), and the students themselves (Figure 7.5).

For students to reach selected or established outcomes, they must learn the curriculum. Therefore, your curriculum (which will be based on student outcomes and *should* be student appropriate) must be taught effectively to the student. The model provides a framework that helps teachers continually watch for mismatches so that they can more effectively get the curriculum to the students and thus reach the established outcomes. We are aligning the curriculum to the students.

Figure 7.6 expands on Figure 7.5: Where the SAALE model fits into the school day. And it visually explains where interventions come into play and where in this whole process state assessments fit.

The curriculum has been thought of as what we teach and interventions were those "things which are too much trouble to do." The curriculum takes so much time that no time is left for preparing and implementing interventions.

**FIGURE 7.5**
Where the SAALE model fits into the school day.

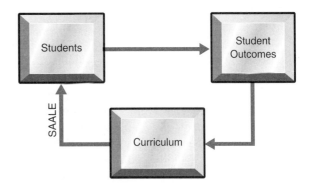

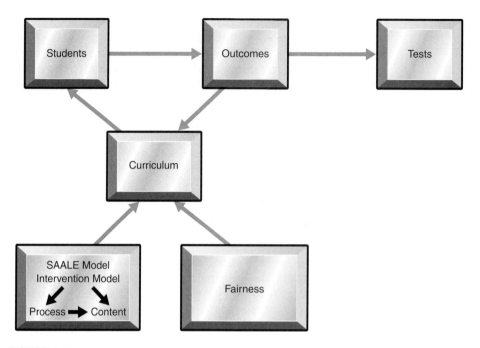

**FIGURE 7.6**
Intervention model (SAALE Model) and curriculum.

Let's regroup how we think and make the intervention process an integral part of the curriculum. One does not function without the other. Figure 7.7 shows you what I mean. From now on let's become a new generation of teachers—ones who see curriculum and interventions as equal. However, remember that the interventions *must be applied* in an organized manner. The SAALE model provides the organization of identifying the mismatch, finding the correct intervention, and applying it as we teach the curriculum. Figure 7.7 visually displays this thought process.

Briefly, I would like to show you why and how this model fits into history (Figure 7.8). In the early years of education, only privileged males received an education. Women cooked, spun yarn, sewed, and did other household tasks. But as time passed, our country began to develop a two-track educational system: general education and special education. The systems were extremely separate, including facilities and curriculum. By the 1970s, special education slowly began to move into general education buildings. However, the curriculum remained separate.

In the late 1970s I taught a special education class that met in the basement of the school, even though there were empty rooms on the first and second floors. My class was as far removed from the other children as possible. We had to eat lunch and go out to recess at times separate from the general education students. We have really come a long way since then.

In the 1980s students with special needs were gradually moved or integrated into general education classes. Mostly you would see these students in art, music,

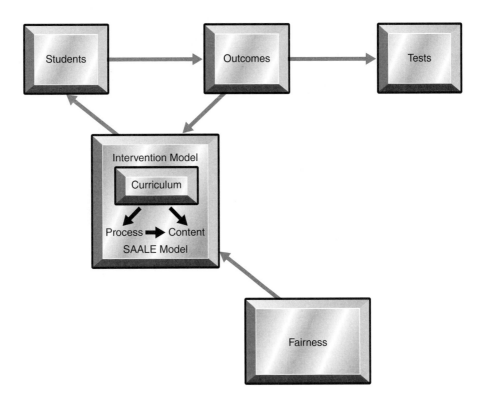

**FIGURE 7.7**
Intervention model (SAALE Model) assists in delivery of curriculum to students.

and physical education classes. Resource or self-contained classes for students with disabilities were still major models for placement. Nonetheless, interventions for general class curriculum were slowly surfacing. In the 1990s, we moved toward an inclusive environment within our schools. As we discussed in chapter 1, inclusion is our goal. But for our students to become included with general education, four doors need to open and stay open: the socioemotional, behavioral, physical, and academic doors.

*How the SAALE model helps you open doors.* Our students need to fit in socially, behaviorally, physically, and academically in order to be successful in general education classes. Imagine coming home late one evening and discovering you have the wrong door key in your hand. Will you remain outside all night or try another key? The logical answer is to try another key. This is exactly what we must do for students: try another key or intervention to unlock the door and keep it open (Figure 7.9). If you look at Figure 7.9, you will see the socioemotional, behavioral, physical, and academic doors on the SAALE model.

I want you to think *SAALE model* when you see that a student is having difficulty with instruction. In other words, I want you to think about where the mismatch might be occurring. Then you will be on the right path toward identifying the problem.

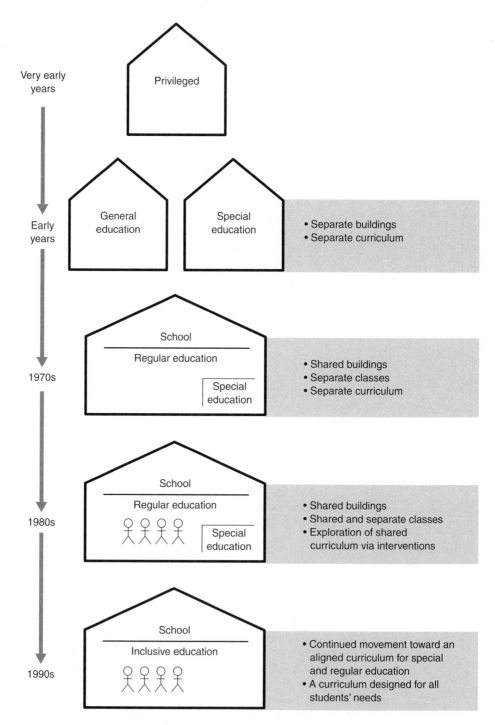

**FIGURE 7.8**
How the SAALE model fits into history.

**FIGURE 7.9**
The four doors to general
education classrooms.

# THE INTERVENTION/TRANSITION CHECKLIST

The key to success in any inclusive placement is the appropriate intervention to the learning environment. A major function of the school-based team guiding the student's learning outcomes is the identification of needed areas of interventions in the inclusive environment. The intervention/transition checklist is a helpful and practical method of identifying where adaptations in the learning environment may be needed (Wood, 2000). This simple device enables teachers and other team members to compare characteristics of the general class setting with the performance levels of the student in that setting. The entire checklist appears in Appendix A at the end of this book. However, the checklist will be discussed here; specifically, how it is to be used.

The intervention/transition checklist is divided into three sections. Section 1 assesses the three major components of the SAALE model: (a) the socioemotional/behavioral environments, (b) the physical environment, and (c) the instructional environment. Identifying possible mismatches between a student's performance and any of these aspects of the learning environment is the first step to developing prereferral or postplacement interventions. For example, if the checklist reveals that a history teacher requires students to copy extensive notes from the board, and the student has difficulty copying, then a mismatch has been identified. The general and special education teachers work cooperatively to develop necessary accommodations for the student, perhaps by providing a graphic organizer for note taking. The remaining chapters in this book provide numerous suggestions for ways to adapt each of these learning environments.

Section 2 of the checklist assesses related environments. Completing this section helps team members assess the student's performance during other academic portions of the school day.

Many times the high-risk student has difficulty within one or more of the related environments, resulting in his or her removal from the regular class. Although learning is going on in the classroom, the high-risk student is no longer participating. Therefore, the area of *related environments* becomes extremely important.

Figure 7.10 displays the part of section 1 that assesses the skill of note taking. In this classroom, students are expected to copy notes from the board, copy notes prepared by the teacher, take notes from a lecture, and copy notes from a textbook. Lecture outlines or photocopies of other students' notes are not available. According to the notations reflecting present performance level, this student is able to copy notes from the chalkboard and can read teacher-written notes. However, he or she is unable to take organized lecture notes, take notes from a textbook without assistance, or take notes using an outline as a guide. For these skill areas, there is a mismatch between the inclusive environment and the student's present skill level. The special and general educators and the student can now work together to develop accommodations that will enable the student to be successful in completing assignments that require note taking.

Beyond identifying needed areas for accommodations, the checklist can be used in several other ways. For students receiving instruction in a variety of classrooms, the checklist or appropriate subsections can be used to compare students' performances across educational settings. Each of the student's teachers may complete a copy of the checklist, or the special education teacher consultant may complete copies of the checklist while observing each classroom. This enables team members to compare observations about the student's learning environments and needs throughout the school day and develop consistent interventions.

The checklist can also be effective for students who are making a transition into the general education setting from a self-contained or resource placement. The special education teacher fills out the "student's present performance level" column and reviews the checklist with the general education teacher before the student joins the general classroom. This gives the general education teacher insight into

| Characteristics of Mainstream Setting | Check if it Applies | Student's Present Performance Level | Has Mastered Skills | Is Working on Skills | Is Unable to Perform Skills |
|---|---|---|---|---|---|
| IV—MEDIA | | | | | |
| A. Note-taking Technique Used | | | | | |
| 1. Copied from board | ✓ | Can copy notes from chalkboard | ✓ | | |
| 2. Prepared by teacher | ✓ | Can read teacher-written notes | ✓ | | |
| 3. From lecture | ✓ | Can take organized lecture notes | | | ✓ |
| 4. From textbook | ✓ | Can take notes from textbook | | | ✓ |
| 5. Lecture outline provided by teacher | | Takes notes with outline as guide | | | ✓ |
| 6. Carbon copy of notes available | | Reads notes taken by another student | | ✓ | |

**FIGURE 7.10**

Sample from section 1 of the intervention/transition checklist.

*Source:* Wood, J. W. (2000). *Intervention/transition checklist.*

the student's learning characteristics and special needs, enabling him or her to make accommodations in the learning environment to facilitate a smoother transition. For transitioning students who continue to be identified as students with special needs, the checklist can be used to generate objectives for the IEP.

Teachers can also make valuable use of the checklist in conferences with the parents. Too often, teachers present the parents with test scores or grade reports that provide information about achievement and failure but offer no reasons for them. Using the checklist as a before-and-after comparison of the student's current level of performance (for example, at the beginning and midpoint of the school year), teachers can give parents concrete information about how the educational environment may be contributing to performance and which interventions have proven successful. Parents, in turn, can use the information to help structure an appropriate learning environment for the student at home. This will help prevent the frustration that often results when parents attempt to help students with homework but use inappropriate pacing, methods, or materials.

The following list summarizes eight ways to use the checklist:

1.   A special education teacher who is considering placing a student in an inclusive environment sends copies of the checklist to several general teachers and asks them to fill out the "characteristics of setting" column. The special education teacher fills out the "student's present performance level" column. The results of the checklist are used to make the best possible match between the general classroom and the student to be included. For example, if the science teacher uses small-group instruction almost exclusively in her class, and the student works best in a small-group setting, a possible match has been made. On the other hand, if assessment reveals that the history teacher requires students to copy extensive notes from the chalkboard, and the student has difficulty copying, educators will question the wisdom of placing the student in that class or consider interventions for copying. Remember, the history teacher is still doing an excellent job; teachers are simply matching the student to an inappropriate environment.

2.   The special education teacher fills out the "student's present performance level" column and sends it to the general teacher either before or after a child has been placed into the general classroom. This gives the general classroom teacher information about the student's learning characteristics and facilitates a closer match between teaching procedures and student learning style. For example, if the teacher uses the lecture approach, and the included student has listening problems, a good match has not been made. However, if the teacher makes some simple adaptations to the lectures (such as using the overhead projector as a visual aid or providing the students with a printed lecture outline), then the student's placement in the class may be appropriate.

3.   The special education teacher observes the inclusive setting and fills out the checklist independently or together with the general teacher. Results are then compiled by the special education teacher and shared with the general education teacher, helping to determine the appropriateness of the mainstream placement.

4.   The special education teacher uses the checklist to identify skills that the student needs to master before entering an inclusive setting and includes these skills in the student's IEP. For example, if the teacher discovers that a student cannot accurately copy notes from the chalkboard, the IEP should include note-taking skills as an objective.

5.   The checklist can assist multidisciplinary teams in determining a student's readiness for inclusion.

6.   The child study committee, teacher assistance team, and others use the checklist to assess a student before deciding on a special education evaluation or planning an IEP.

7.   The "student's present performance level" column can be completed by the classroom teacher and placed in the student's folder for next year's teacher to review.

8.   The checklist can be used to document appropriate prereferral interventions.

# ESTABLISHING A COMMON VOCABULARY

Now that we have studied the SAALE model and the checklist, we will begin discussing different strategies that may be stored in your mental filing cabinet. First, however, we need to establish a common vocabulary. We casually throw out the words *adapt, modify, intervene, accommodate,* and so on; yet we may not be thinking along the same lines.

As you can see from Figure 7.11, I call this my "rubber band theory" (Thanks to Jerry Fouchey, who originally introduced me to the idea). But before discussing the rubber band theory, we should define three terms:

- *Interventions.* This means anything we do that we have not tried yet. It includes the following two terms:
  - *Accommodate.* This is a simple stretch of the rubber band that provides a strategy to help a student reach an objective or a benchmark. Accommodations are no big deal.
  - *Modify.* In this case, the whole rubber band must be moved down to reach a child. It includes working on the child's grade level, helping the child, and hoping that the child will eventually reach the benchmark. Modifications may also include a totally different curriculum for the student. We are not expecting the child to reach standard grade-level objectives but may focus instead on life skills, functional academics, and so on.

Figure 7.11 demonstrates the rubber band theory. As you can see, schools establish objectives or benchmarks (what they want the child to accomplish). However, students come with different abilities, which the figure shows as different shapes. Many students (represented by the square) can reach a benchmark after

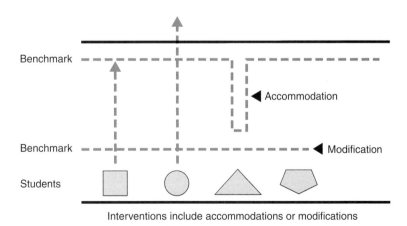

Interventions include accommodations or modifications

**FIGURE 7.11**
Rubber band theory.

direct instruction. Some students (represented by the circle) not only reach the benchmark but can bounce above it. Many students (represented by the triangle) need only a stretch of the rubber band (an accommodation) to reach the benchmark. Some students (represented by the pentagon) need the benchmark moved in order to learn (modification).

## CONCLUSION

Making the transition from one educational setting to another can be either a positive experience or a frustrating one for a student with special needs or one who is at-risk for school failure. By assessing the setting and determining whether the student has the skills needed to enter the environment, educators can enhance the chances for successful learning.

Now that we have learned about two parts of the three-step process (the model and the checklist) and are using the same vocabulary, we will move ahead to step 3: strategies or interventions. Remember that everything you already know, and will learn, can be placed into your filing cabinet (our model). The rest of this book will suggest hundreds of ideas for you to consider.

Your professor has computer software that completes these three steps and develops a mismatch plan for students. However, reading and understanding the remaining chapters will help you help the computer. That is, the computer will develop a program, but you may wish to add to the possible intervention list.

At this point, you may also want to look back at the flowchart at the beginning of part 2 to review where we have been and where we are going on our journey to inclusion. Each part and chapter has been carefully designed to give you a sequential plan for the book. The chapters build on each other.

# CHAPTER 8

## Adapting the Socioemotional Environment

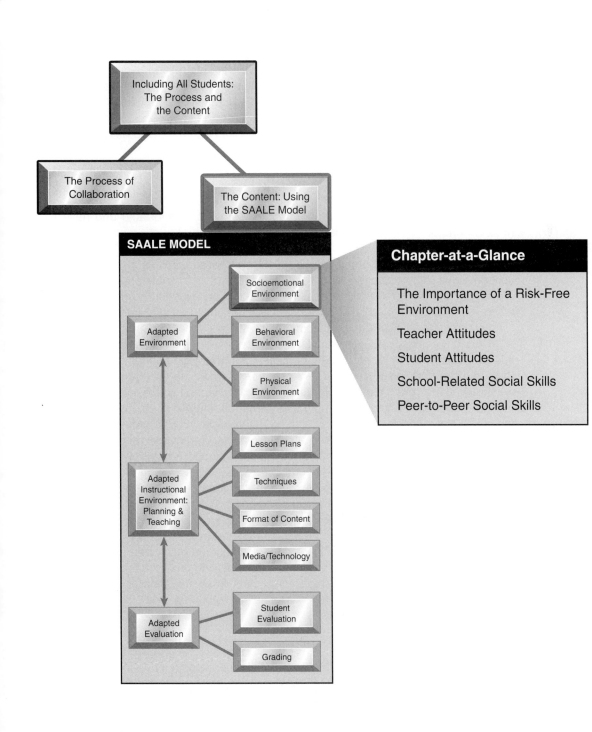

Including All Students:
The Process and
the Content

The Process of
Collaboration

The Content: Using
the SAALE Model

**SAALE MODEL**

Adapted
Environment

Socioemotional
Environment

Behavioral
Environment

Physical
Environment

Adapted
Instructional
Environment:
Planning &
Teaching

Lesson Plans

Techniques

Format of Content

Media/Technology

Adapted
Evaluation

Student
Evaluation

Grading

**Chapter-at-a-Glance**

The Importance of a Risk-Free
Environment

Teacher Attitudes

Student Attitudes

School-Related Social Skills

Peer-to-Peer Social Skills

The *socioemotional environment,* or the affective climate and the social interactions that occur there, is the foundation of an effective classroom. It has a significant effect on a student's success or failure. Before instruction begins, this environment sets the stage for a successful learner. Often when a student is experiencing difficulty at school, teachers immediately focus on what the learner cannot do instructionally. But the true mismatch may lie in the socioemotional aspects of the school or class. In this chapter we focus on areas where mismatches can occur in socioemotional environments.

## SOCIOEMOTIONAL ADAPTATIONS FOR THE CLASSROOM

In a warm, positive environment, all children feel more comfortable and have a greater opportunity to learn. What is a risk-free environment? Let's think first about *risk-filled* environments.

Recall a teacher you had in high school or perhaps a professor you've had in college. Have you ever waited with breathless anticipation for that person to ask you a question, not knowing which question you would be expected to respond to or when you would be called on? Perhaps the teacher called on students randomly to read aloud. In such cases, your anticipation may have become almost too great.

During my undergraduate studies I had a professor who was unpredictable in this way. I never knew when I would be called on, what types of items were going to be on the tests, or how my papers or projects would be graded. I also had a teacher who took great pleasure in pointing out how wrong I was when I answered. In elementary school my class would take turns reading aloud. Because I was an extremely poor reader, I almost had a nervous breakdown before my turn arrived.

These were certainly not risk-free environments. An environment that is risk-free is one in which students are not afraid to take chances. A risk-free environment is a safe place for students where mistakes are seen as "stepping stones" to success. Before everyone runs to the playground, the teams are established. No one must stand anxiously waiting to be picked. When an answer is incorrect, the student is praised for trying. Everyone's efforts are appreciated. A risk-free environment is safe, relaxed, and nonthreatening to students.

There are many components involved in establishing a risk-free environment. They include teachers' attitudes, students' attitudes, and the social preparation of students. The remainder of this chapter discusses ways of creating a risk-free environment by modifying these attitudes and helping students grow socially.

## TEACHER ATTITUDES

The classroom teacher plays an important role in the success of an included child. Establishing a warm socioemotional climate helps teachers to maximize student achievement (Rosenthal, 1974). The teacher's attitude toward students is the major catalyst that affects interaction and achievement. "Whether in special or general education, there is growing evidence that the single most important school influence in a student's education is a well-prepared, caring, and qualified teacher" (Council for Exceptional Children, "Bright Futures for Exceptional Learners," www.cec.sped.org).

According to research, teachers' attitudes about inclusion are becoming more positive (Wood, 1989). When inclusion first became a reality, teachers generally expressed reservations about accepting special-education students into the general classroom setting. Teachers were concerned about what may have been perceived as dumping students with special needs back into regular classrooms. Teachers felt unprepared to work with diverse special populations and feared these students would demand too much of their time in classes that were already full. Teachers were also concerned about their roles, increased paperwork, and possible conflict with special education teachers, related service providers, and fulfilling parents' expectations. In a study by Michele Wood, University of California, Santa Barbara, results indicated that "in the initial stages of inclusion, teachers maintained discreet role boundaries through a relatively clear, albeit division of labor. As the school year progressed, role perceptions became less rigid as the teaming became more cooperative" (Wood, 1998).

Therefore, many teachers who once felt isolated and alone in their classroom now see a network of resources if they are willing to be open to suggestions and to risk changing their presentation of material or how they might review or design a test. Many of the suggestions help not only the special student in the classroom, but the slow learner or at-risk student as well.

For inclusion to be successful, positive teacher attitudes are essential. Equally important, general educators believe that teachers need appropriate support and training (Knoff, 1985; Myles & Simpson, 1989). Meyen, Vergason, and Whelan (1993) suggest that teacher attitudes should be continually reassessed. Areas of assessment may include "opinions of perceived success or failure in providing curriculum content, increased learning for all students involved, student discipline, team efforts, and grading procedures" (p. 101).

More needs to be done to provide training for teachers and school staff on attitudes and acceptance, not only for students with special needs but for the increasing number of students from cultural, racial, and ethnic diverse populations. Training needs to provide information on supports for maximizing student success and providing appropriate interventions and accommodations when necessary.

Meyen et al. (1993) also believe that acquiring knowledge about specific student behaviors may help the teacher understand students. For example, "because of their impulsiveness, loud presence in the classroom, and persistence of their questions, comments, and demands, ADD [attention deficit disorder] children try teachers' patience and tend to become unpopular members of the classroom group. Teachers have to understand that much of this behavior is not intentional, not a part of a ploy to defy educational authority" (p. 256).

## Teacher Expectations and At-Risk Students

According to Good (1987), the issue of teacher expectations drew wide attention when Rosenthal and Jacobson (1968) released their research on the self-fulfilling prophecies within the class. The researchers gave false data to teachers regarding student achievement and discovered that student learning outcomes increased when the teacher *expected* students to achieve. Even though the work received wide acclaim, it was also attacked by professionals. Nevertheless, most people now agree that teacher expectations do affect learning outcomes.

Studies show that a teacher's expectations are often an accurate assessment of student ability. Hence, teacher expectations for student behavior are not necessarily inappropriate. The problem of teacher expectations may not be one of simple identification or labeling of students (i.e., recognition that one student is relatively less able than another) but rather of *inappropriate knowledge* of how to respond to students who have difficulty learning (Good, 1987, p. 33).

Drawing on the research of Good and Brophy (1987), Good (1987) lists 17 teacher behaviors that communicate particular expectations toward low achievers (pp. 34–35):

1. Waiting less time for "lows" to answer
2. Giving low achievers answers or calling on someone else rather than trying to improve their responses by giving clues or repeating or rephrasing questions
3. Rewarding inappropriate behavior or incorrect answers by low achievers
4. Criticizing low achievers more often for failure
5. Praising low achievers less frequently than "highs" for success
6. Failing to give feedback to the public responses of low achievers
7. Paying less attention to low achievers or interacting with them less frequently
8. Calling on low achievers less often to respond to questions
9. Seating low achievers farther away from the teacher
10. Demanding less from low achievers
11. Interacting with low achievers more privately than publicly, and monitoring and structuring their activities more closely
12. Grading tests or assignments in a differential manner, in which high achievers but not low achievers are given the benefit of the doubt in borderline cases
13. Having less-friendly interaction with low achievers, including less smiling and fewer other nonverbal indicators of support and less-warm or more-anxious voice tones
14. Providing briefer and less-informative feedback to the questions of low achievers
15. Providing less eye contact and less other nonverbal communication of attention and responsiveness in interaction with low achievers
16. Evidencing less use of effective but time-consuming instructional methods with low achievers when time is limited
17. Evidencing less acceptance and use of low achievers' ideas

# The Special Education Teacher's Role in Preparing the General Class Teacher

Special educators are in a unique position to promote positive inclusive experiences as well as to offer support and expertise to their general education peers. Special personnel and general teachers of special students need to work together to plan and implement inclusion.

The special education teacher may employ several methods for providing support for general teachers who serve special education students in their classrooms. Dardig (1981) shares eight tips:

1. Reassure colleagues that their fears are unfounded and that inclusion can be a beneficial experience.
2. Help the general teacher identify general classrooms that appear to be appropriate for the student with a disability.
3. Arrange for selected special students to visit the general classroom before placement to become acquainted with the teacher and class members.
4. Seek inservice training about the characteristics of various disabling conditions and the methods of working with these children.
5. Provide instructional materials and resources. General educators may reciprocate and share materials that might be useful in the special classroom.
6. Arrange for support services as needed for consultation or delivery of services, such as school psychology and physical therapy.
7. Teach special skills through modeling or demonstration to help the teacher learn to help the child function well.
8. Explain the benefits of inclusion for all children.

## Communication

Communication—the exchange of ideas, information, and suggestions—is crucial to establishing a good working relationship between special and general education teachers. Because the general educator faces the task of accommodating instruction in inclusive classrooms, the special educator bears more, although not all, of the responsibility for making the communication process easier. To communicate better, special education teachers must understand themselves, realize that others see and respond to them as they project themselves, be able to listen, demonstrate an understanding of others' concerns by acting in positive ways, respect the problems and concerns of their colleagues, and respond quickly to the needs of others.

Understanding oneself leads to good communication. In addition, knowing and internalizing the role of special educator and then projecting that role in a positive way gives others guidelines for communication. If special educators project confidence in their abilities, others trust that competence. However, the reverse is also true. If special educators project a lack of confidence in their abilities, others may view them as incompetent.

Listening is the basis of all communication. Often we listen to what is being said without actually hearing it. Special educators must not only listen but also hear the concerns of general educators. Then they can show evidence of hearing those concerns by reacting to their colleague's needs in a positive manner. For example, special education teachers who quickly provide the appropriate instructional material, suggest an alternative teaching technique, or assist in designing a behavior management plan for an inclusive student show that the problems of others are important. Once general educators believe that the door of communication is open, effective inclusion becomes a reality. (See chapter 6 for information on collaborative consultation models.)

The development of a positive working relationship between general and special educators has a significant effect on the child with special needs. To promote effective communication, special and general educators should do the following:

1. Establish a communication system.
2. Discuss each placement together.
3. Help each other individualize instruction.
4. Work together to adapt subject matter.
5. Share materials.
6. Help each other adapt evaluation procedures.
7. Take the initiative; be flexible, dedicated, reliable, organized, imaginative, and enthusiastic.
8. Involve others by sharing plans and ideas.
9. Seek support and suggestions from others.
10. Set realistic goals.
11. Work to improve interpersonal relations.
12. Remember that presenting a positive attitude will change attitudes about inclusion both inside and outside the school.

## STUDENT ATTITUDES

Like adults, students develop a set of attitudes about themselves and their peers. Students who have been found eligible for special education services or are at risk for school failure usually have experienced learning difficulty for a long time. Often educators wonder why students have low self-esteem or why they seem unmotivated. Failure is a cumulative process. It does not occur overnight, and the damage it causes cannot be repaired overnight. Students with disabilities traditionally have lower positions of status than their nondisabled peers do, and this pattern of rejection holds true in both general and special classes (Simpson, 1980).

Simpson (1980) noted four factors that are crucial in understanding the attitudes of general education students toward students with disabilities. First, patterns of discriminatory behavior may actually be relatively normal. In other words, discrimination may be a subtle human characteristic. Infants discriminate among people based on differences in voice sound or physical appearance. Attitudes can be modified, but they may be a natural response to developmental or perceptual characteristics.

Second, attitudes toward students with disabilities may exist with or without labels. Some students with disabilities are discriminated against because of their social skills or lack thereof. Even though a label identifies a student as obviously different, the actual identification probably occurred before the label.

Third, the attitudes of students toward disabilities are significantly influenced by the people around them, a finding that holds true for our attitudes in general. This factor places great importance on the positive attitudes of the teacher and other important people in the children's lives.

Fourth, the attitudes of students toward persons with disabilities are greatly influenced by numerous social, physical, and experiential factors.

## Preparation for Inclusion

Even though we consider the general classroom to be the home base for the student with a disability, we need to make preparations to provide a smooth transition for all concerned. Some special students may spend a large portion of their day receiving services in alternative settings. Students with mild disabilities will spend most of their day within the general classroom in multiage or multiability groupings. In either case, students as well as teachers need support.

*Preparing general education students.* Wood and Reeves (1989) have three suggestions for preparing general students for inclusion: (a) help them understand the nature of disabling conditions, (b) offer instructional units, and (c) use simulation activities.

Helping students understand the nature of disabling conditions is crucial to peer acceptance. When we understand that everyone has strengths and weaknesses, it becomes OK to be different. A student once wrote, "If everyone in the world were just alike, we wouldn't miss anyone when they died" (Scott F. Wood, personal communication). This student was expressing his belief that to be different is really to be special.

A simple activity for teachers to use is to have students sit in a group and list ways in which they are alike and ways in which they are different. When group members discuss their responses, the teacher can help them see that being different is really being special. From the list, their various interests and strengths will surface. Let the students share these interests and strengths and decide how they can use them to help others in the class. For example, a student who is good in math can volunteer to be a math tutor. Another student who excels on the playground can offer to help others with games. Find ways for each student to share with the class.

Teachers can also use instructional units to help general education students develop more positive attitudes toward students with disabilities. These units may be either infused into the curriculum or taught with separate programming. Infusion involves teaching within the daily topic. For example, a teacher may be teaching a civics unit on citizen rights and, along with this topic, may address the rights of persons with disabilities. Separate programming refers to teaching as a separate unit. A unit on the rights of persons with disabilities could be taught as a single subject. Other suggestions include researching persons with disabilities, leading a class discussion about barrier-free environments, learning the causes of various disabilities, surveying students about attitudes toward persons with disabilities, and learning about the many outstanding contributions of persons with disabilities.

Simulation activities are also helpful in teaching students about disabilities. Simulations should not be used as introductory activities; rather, they can be applied successfully after students learn about the coping skills of people with various disabilities. Many state departments and local agencies will provide speakers and equipment for class simulations.

Here's an idea for younger students, which the teacher can use before a student with an obvious disability joins the class. Let students make hand puppets and decorate the puppets to look like themselves. The teacher makes a hand puppet that portrays the disability of the new student. A student's puppet may ask the teacher's puppet, "How did you get this way?" "How can I help you?" "Can you play with the rest of the class?" This activity allows students to ask questions openly and helps them develop a better understanding of persons with disabilities.

Table 8.1 offers additional suggestions for increasing student knowledge and information about disabilities.

*Preparing students with special needs.* There are many skills that special students need to function within the general class environment. Whether a student is new to the general class or has previously spent a large portion of time there, he or she needs skills to help make the transition smoother.

The structure of the class can present major problems for students with special needs, who must be taught the rules and routines. In most classes, rules address seating arrangements, how to enter and leave the class, the required format for heading papers, the proper procedure for turning in completed work, the grading policy, how to request a drink of water or permission to go to the restroom, the proper procedure for sharpening pencils and requesting supplies, what to do when tardy to class, the teacher's policy for making up work, the penalty for late work, the testing schedule, the structure of class procedures, and procedures for class participation. Even if teachers post and review rules, the students may not truly understand them. After reviewing the rules and routines, teachers should encourage students to discuss them and ask questions if a rule is unclear. To avoid embarrassment, older students can ask such questions after school or during a study break.

Figure 8.1 presents a checklist of rules and routines. The teacher may complete the checklist and give it to the students, who can keep it in a notebook for reference. This checklist is also excellent for substitute teachers because it helps them clearly understand classroom expectations.

TABLE 8.1
Increasing student knowledge about disabilities.

| | Suggestions |
|---|---|
| Understanding the nature of disabilities | Discussion to increase knowledge about disabilities<br>Discussion about the feelings and activities of students<br>Videos explaining various disability areas<br>Guest speakers who have disabilities<br>Pictures on the wall of persons with disabilities<br>Information about disabilities in specific academic areas |
| Instructional units | Suggestions for projects or book reports to help students gain insights about disabilities: for example, research new technologies for persons with disabilities or review how the media has portrayed persons with disabilities<br>Reports on the life of persons with disabilities who have excelled in their careers: (1) nature and cause of disability, (2) how the disability affected the person's life, (3) the person's accomplishments, and (4) emotions of the person and his or her family<br>*Artists:* Ludwig von Beethoven, deaf; Elizabeth Barrett Browning, spinal injury and bedridden; Ray Charles, blind; José Feliciano, blind; Aldous Huxley, blind; James Stacy, amputee (arm/leg); Stevie Wonder, blind; Al Capp, amputee (leg); Miss America 1995 Heather Whitestone, hearing impaired<br>*Athletes:* Dave Bing, blind (one eye); Tom Dempsey, birth defect (stump foot and arm); Carlos May, minus a thumb; Roy Campanella, paralyzed (neck down); Wilma Rudolph, childhood polio; Jim Abbott, birth defect (arm)<br>*Politicians:* Winston Churchill, speech impairment; Robert Dole, withered arm; Daniel Inouye, amputee (arm) |
| Learning centers | Newspaper articles about individuals with disabilities in the workforce; comprehensive questions that students answer after reading the articles; related vocabulary terms that students can define in their own words; blank paper on which students can write short essays describing their reactions to the articles |
| Simulation activities (not for use as introductory activities) | Teaching coping strategies<br>Experiencing a disability through the use of special equipment and specific instructions<br>Involving students with disabilities in the simulation<br>Training school peer teams to conduct the activities<br>Allowing students to share reactions and feelings |
| Structured interaction strategies | Opportunities for students without disabilities to work or interact socially with students with disabilities. Resource: Anderson & Millreis. (1983). *Structured Experiences for Integrated Handicapped Children.* Rockville, MD: Aspen. Provides more than 100 field test activities, exercises, and experiences for interpretation<br>Collaborative skill instruction, in which teachers identify skills (sharing materials and ideas, checking to see if everyone understands) to be practiced by students during academic activities<br>Peer tutor system |

Class _____     Teacher _____     Period ____

1. Seating arrangement:

    _____Open          _____Assigned

2. Behavior for entering class:

    _____Visiting with friends allowed

    _____Visiting with friends not allowed

    _____Place personal belongings in desk, locker, or bookshelf, etc.

    _____Place class materials on desk

    _____Copy classwork from board

    _____Copy homework assignment from board

    _____Other _____

3. Behavior when leaving class:

    _____Leave when the bell sounds

    _____Leave only when dismissed by the teacher

4. Format for heading papers:

    Model of format _____

    [ ]      [ ]

    _____Location on paper

5. Procedure for turning in completed work:

    _____Will be discussed with each assignment

    _____At beginning of each class

    _____At end of each class

    _____Only when requested by teacher

    _____

6. How to request a drink of water:

    _____

7. Procedure for going to the restroom:

    _____

8. Procedure for going to the clinic:

    _____

9. Procedure for going to the office:

    _____

10. Procedure for sharpening pencils and requesting supplies:

    _____

11. What to do when tardy to class:

    _____

12. Procedure for going to the locker:

    _____

13. Policy regarding book covers and jackets:

    _____

14. Policy on care of texts:

    _____

15. Materials needed for class:

    _____

16. Procedure if you do not have class materials:

    _____

17. What to do when you need to leave the class or cannot cope:

    _____

18. Class policy for making up work:

    _____

19. Penalty for late work:

    _____

20. Grading policy:

    _____

FIGURE 8.1
Checklist of rules and routines.

21. Testing schedule:

_____

22. Structure of class procedures:

_____

23. Where to put trash:

_____

24. Can I chew gum or have snacks?

_____

25. How to ask for assistance:

_____

26. When talking is allowed:

_____

27. Procedure for asking questions:

_____

28. Procedure for responding to questions:

_____

29. Procedure if you are unsure about asking a question in front of peers:

_____

30. Rules of attire:

_____

31. Rules for clothes that advertise:

_____

32. Rules about cigarettes and alcohol:

_____

33. Rules about inappropriate language:

_____

34. Procedures for cleaning up work area:

_____

35. Procedures for going from general education classroom to special education, Chapter I, physical therapy, occupational therapy, speech, etc.:

_____

36. Procedure for returning to general education classroom from services listed in number 35:

_____

37. What do I do when a substitute is in the classroom?

_____

38. Procedures for entering when a co-teaching model is in progress:

_____

For younger children you may want to videotape last year's students modeling the rules. When fall arrives, and as you discuss each rule, you can show the rule modeled on the videotape. Tell the children that if they work very hard, they will be the movie stars for next year's children. However, be sure that you have administrative permission to videotape students. You may need written permission. Also, remember to show the modeled rules one at a time with practice sessions. Showing all the rules at one sitting may overwhelm young children.

# SOCIAL ADJUSTMENTS

## School-Related Social Skills

In addition to specific rules and class outlines, the special student often displays a mismatch in the area of social skill development. Frequently, a student may fall behind academically, and the teacher will become concerned. When the student's social behavior is inappropriate, the concern increases. School-related social skills can and should be taught to students because many special-needs and at-risk children do not have a repertoire of appropriate skills to respond to school-related events. Table 8.2 presents selected school-related social skills with accompanying teaching suggestions. For older students, the teacher may wish to discuss these skills, add appropriate ones to the rules and routines checklist (Figure 8.1), and use the list as a student handout. For younger students, educators may prefer to use the suggestions in Table 8.2 as classroom activities.

## Peer-Related Social Skills

Peer-to-peer skills contribute to social competence and peer acceptance. These skills fall into three categories: communication (Table 8.3), social interaction (Table 8.4), and self-control (Table 8.5). Each table includes selected social skills (left column), words to be defined (middle column), and suggested activities for teaching the social skills (column on right). A note to remember . . . in the "words-to-be-defined" column, I have listed *suggested* words for defining. The exact words must be selected for defining based on the developmental level of the student being taught. Defining words becomes a teaching prerequisite to teaching the social skill. For example, the skill of "understanding student/teacher roles" may need the word *role* defined when teaching young children. Some children may think that a role is something to eat (roll) or perhaps everyone is going to "roll" around on the floor. Therefore, the word *role* must be defined. A role is a duty or job. Helping students understand selected words provides a baseline for teaching a social skill.

## Sample Social Skill Lesson

Tables 8.2 through 8.5 provide selected teaching ideas for numerous social skills. Appendix C provides a complete lesson for grades 1–8 for teaching the social skill, personal development: self-control. This format will be useful for developing each skill in the tables provided.

# CONCLUSION

Set the stage for a risk-free environment so that students can maximize learning. They need a class setting built on trust, respect, and goodwill. Teachers who reflect positive attitudes toward *all* students help them to begin to build stronger self-esteem and develop school- and peer-related social skills, which are necessary to function in both the general class setting and their adult lives.

**TABLE 8.2**

School-related social skills.

| Skill | Vocabulary to Introduce | Activities for Teaching Skill |
|---|---|---|
| Understanding student/teacher roles | student<br>teacher<br>responsibility<br>authority<br>inappropriate | 1. Discuss responsibilities of the teacher and the student.<br><br>Teacher:<br>• Takes roll.<br>• Writes lesson plans.<br>• Keeps things in order.<br><br>Student:<br>• Listens carefully.<br>• Follows directions.<br>• Cooperates.<br><br>2. Have class add rules to each of the lists in number 1.<br><br>3. Role-play the following situations:<br><br>Adult as authority:<br>• Get in line.<br>• Be quiet in the hall.<br>• Put equipment away.<br>• It's time to clean up.<br><br>Student as authority:<br>• Close the door.<br>• Work quietly.<br>• Collect papers.<br><br>4. Have class add rules to each of the lists in number 3.<br><br>5. Write the following list on the board and ask the students to put an *S* next to things that are the students' responsibilities and a *T* next to those that belong to the teacher:<br>• Plan lessons.<br>• Develop tests.<br>• Grade papers.<br>• Do homework.<br>• Give homework assignments.<br>• Take lunch count/money.<br>• Write assignments on board.<br>• Complete all assignments.<br>• Play during recess.<br>• Pass out papers.<br>• Write notes to parents.<br>• Correct inappropriate behavior.<br>• Work quietly.<br>• Follow directions.<br>• Make sure everyone does his or her homework.<br>• Give out report cards. |

*(continued)*

TABLE 8.2
Continued.

| Skill | Vocabulary to Introduce | Activities for Teaching Skill |
|-------|-------------------------|------------------------------|
| | | • Go on errands. |
| | | • Raise hand to ask for help. |
| | | • Stay in seat unless told otherwise. |
| | | 6. Make a list of classroom situations and allow students to take turns role playing: <br> • Taking roll/lunch count <br> • Cleanup time <br> • Time to go to P.E. <br> • Dismissal <br> • Giving a lesson |
| Respecting others' space | space <br> invade <br> touch <br> grab <br> share <br> cooperate <br> nervous <br> threatened | 1. Have a discussion about space and what space belongs to the students: <br> • Desk <br> • Chairs <br> • Closet <br> • Bedroom <br> • Work stations <br> • Lockers/cubbies |
| | | 2. Discuss what it means to respect each other's space. |
| | | 3. Discuss the importance of maintaining appropriate personal distance in a conversation. Let students demonstrate comfortable and uncomfortable distances. |
| | | 4. Play "what if." Provide a list of experiences/situations for students to discuss: <br> • What if someone sits too close? <br> • What if someone tugs at your clothes? <br> • What if someone takes something off your desk? |
| Ignoring distractions | | 1. Have the students make a list of distractions in the classroom that slow them down or prevent them from completing their work. |
| | | 2. Brainstorm ways for coping with the distractions listed in number 1. |
| | | 3. Develop a signal for students to use when they become distracted. |
| Listening | listening <br> attending <br> hear <br> look <br> eye contact | 1. Have a class discussion about the importance of being a good listener. |
| | | 2. List situations at home when one must listen. |
| | | 3. List situations at school when one must listen. |
| | | 4. Role-play the situations in groups of twos and threes. |

| Skill | Vocabulary to Introduce | Activities for Teaching Skill |
|---|---|---|
| | | 5. Develop a listening cue for the class. This could be a big ear for the younger children and a hand signal for the older students. |
| | | 6. When a student has a problem with listening, have him or her repeat the directions, instructions, etc. |
| | | 7. Develop a listening checklist for older students. |
| | | 8. Play "Simon says" and let students carefully listen to directions. |
| | | 9. Teach students to maintain eye contact while listening. |
| | | 10. Discuss the importance of careful listening for specific information. |
| Following directions | directions listen follow understand | 1. Have a class discussion about the importance of following directions. |
| | | 2. Review behaviors necessary for following directions:<br>• Look at the speaker.<br>• Listen.<br>• Repeat directions to yourself.<br>• Ask for clarification if needed.<br>• Perform directions. |
| | | 3. Develop simple worksheets with pictures of trees, stars, balls, etc. Give the student directions to follow. Draw circle around the tree, connect the stars to the balls with a red crayon, etc. |
| Requesting permission | permission polite information emergency asking | 1. Conduct a class discussion about reasons for requesting permission in different settings:<br>• At home.<br>• With friends.<br>• At school.<br>• On the bus. |
| | | 2. For each situation listed under the four settings in number 1, have students answer the following questions:<br>• What types of things would you request permission for?<br>• Whom would you request the permission from?<br>• How do you request the permission?<br>• When would you request the permission? |
| | | 3. Discuss the steps for requesting permission in each of the settings in number 1. |
| Requesting assistance | help ask | 1. Discuss the correct procedures for asking assistance:<br>• Have you clearly thought through the problem? |

*(continued)*

TABLE 8.2
Continued.

| Skill | Vocabulary to Introduce | Activities for Teaching Skill |
|-------|-------------------------|------------------------------|
| | assistance<br>thank you<br>please<br>procedures | • How will you make the request?<br>• How will you indicate to another person that you need assistance?<br>• Did you wait for your turn to be assisted?<br>• Did you thank the person assisting you?<br><br>2. Make a list of times students need assistance at home:<br>• When doing homework.<br>• When doing chores.<br>• When they do not understand a request.<br><br>3. List persons at home whom they may request assistance from:<br>• Mother<br>• Brother<br>• Grandparents<br>• Father<br>• Sister<br>• Aunts/uncles<br>• Baby-sitter<br><br>4. Model the appropriate way for making a request at home.<br><br>5. List situations when students may need assistance at school:<br>• When they do not understand directions.<br>• When they cannot find materials, etc.<br>• When they have made a mistake.<br>• When they do not understand a lesson.<br><br>6. List school personnel whom they may request assistance from:<br>• Teachers<br>• Clinic aide<br>• Principal<br>• Custodian<br>• Classroom aide<br>• Librarian<br>• Secretary<br>• Cafeteria worker<br><br>7. Model the appropriate way for requesting assistance at school.<br><br>8. Role-play the request for assistance at home and at school. |
| Requesting clarification | clarify<br>information | 1. Discuss the necessity for asking for clarification so that we can follow directions or act on information. |

| Skill | Vocabulary to Introduce | Activities for Teaching Skill |
|---|---|---|
| | directions<br>understand | 2. Discuss the consequences of not requesting clarification. |
| | | 3. Make a list of situations where clarification might be needed. |
| | | 4. Discuss the steps one takes when requesting clarification:<br>• Think carefully about what was said.<br>• Think about your request.<br>• Raise your hand.<br>• Look at the person and speak clearly.<br>• Ask for more specific information if you do not understand.<br>• If still confused, ask the person if he or she will meet with you later.<br>• Thank the person for his or her assistance. |
| | | 5. Practice requesting clarification for the situations in number 3. |
| Participating in class | participate<br>volunteer<br>join<br>cooperation<br>appropriate | 1. Discuss what participation means and the importance of voluntary participation. |
| | | 2. Establish guidelines for class participation:<br>• Be a good listener.<br>• Ask appropriate questions.<br>• Volunteer answers.<br>• Don't interrupt. |
| | | 3. List situations when students participate in a class discussion:<br>• When the teacher asks for a response.<br>• Volunteering a response. |
| | | 4. Role-play the situations listed in number 3. |
| | | 5. Discuss road blocks and keys to participating in class:<br>• Road blocks (lack of interest, fear of looking foolish, not understanding, not knowing the answer, fear of giving the wrong response).<br>• Keys (listen to activity, look at speaker, realize that many students are afraid of looking foolish). |
| | | 6. List on the board ways in which students can participate in the class or group:<br>• Giving ideas.<br>• Offering and accepting help.<br>• Agreeing or disagreeing.<br>• Listening to others. |

*(continued)*

231

TABLE 8.2
Continued.

| Skill | Vocabulary to Introduce | Activities for Teaching Skill |
|---|---|---|
| | | • Following directions.<br>• Following rules.<br>• Encouraging others. |
| Solving problems | problem<br>solution<br>choose<br>options<br>cooperation<br>situation | 1. Discuss a problem-solving/choice-making process:<br>• Identify the problem/options.<br>• Consider all possible solutions.<br>• Discuss the pros/cons of each listed solution.<br>• Develop a plan of action.<br>• Put the plan in action.<br>• Evaluate the success of the plan. |
| | | 2. Have students make a list of problems they have encountered. |
| | | 3. Role-play solving the problems listed in number 2 using the procedures in number 1. |
| | | 4. Help the student understand choice making and its role in solving problems. |
| | | 5. Provide situations where choices must be made. Let the student select a choice in each situation. |
| | | 6. Discuss the ramifications for each choice. |
| | | 7. Present the class with a problem scenario and have them solve each problem using the steps in number 1:<br>• A fight begins in the hall, and no teacher is present.<br>• Someone pushes you in the hall.<br>• A member of the class is acting up, and the whole class is going to lose a privilege if the student does not stop.<br>• Someone teases you at school.<br>• You are told to do tomorrow's homework for reading, and you need to do today's math homework. |
| Accepting responsibility | responsibility<br>accept<br>fulfill<br>contribute in<br>charge of | 1. Discuss the concept of accepting responsibility. |
| | | 2. Review the responsibilities you have as the teacher:<br>• Arrive at school on time.<br>• Grade papers.<br>• Prepare lesson plans in advance.<br>• Take care of students in your class, etc. |
| | | 3. List on the board the responsibilities of the student at school:<br>• Be on time to class.<br>• Prepare homework on time.<br>• Study for class. |

| Skill | Vocabulary to Introduce | Activities for Teaching Skill |
|---|---|---|
| | | • Exhibit appropriate conduct.<br>• Respect others' space and property.<br>4. List on the board the responsibilities of the student at home:<br>  • Be on time for meals.<br>  • Do chores.<br>  • Take care of possessions.<br>  • Watch over younger brothers/sisters. |
| Changing activities | transition<br>change<br>order<br>quiet<br>smooth | 1. Make a list on the board of school-related transition times:<br>  • From home to bus/ride.<br>  • From bus to school.<br>  • From school to classroom.<br>  • Changing activities.<br>  • Changing periods/classes.<br>  • From classroom to bus/ride.<br>2. Discuss ways of making transitions smoother:<br>  • Stop what you are doing.<br>  • Look at the teacher/driver/aide.<br>  • Listen to any directions or explanations.<br>  • Remain quiet.<br>  • Ask questions if you do not understand.<br>  • Discuss any problems with a teacher/driver, etc.<br>3. Role-play transitioning for various situations.<br>  • Snack time.<br>  • Lunch time.<br>  • Change in activities.<br>  • Going to bus.<br>  • Change in classrooms.<br>  • End-of-day activities.<br>  • Recess/physical education. |
| Using free time wisely | free time<br>choose<br>busy<br>productive<br>wise<br>play<br>break | 1. Lead a class discussion about the meaning of free time.<br>2. Make a list of free-time situations at home.<br>3. Make a list of free-time situations at school.<br>4. List positive consequences of the wise use of free time:<br>  • Finishing homework.<br>  • Getting extra help.<br>  • Extra after-school time.<br>5. Set up a free-time center in the classroom. Provide a selection of activities that promotes the wise use of free time.<br>6. Have students keep a list of how they use their free time. |

*(continued)*

**TABLE 8.2**
Continued.

| Skill | Vocabulary to Introduce | Activities for Teaching Skill |
|---|---|---|
| Working cooperatively in a group | cooperate<br>give and take<br>work together<br>compromise<br>negotiate<br>bossy<br>know-it-all<br>flexible | 1. On the board list students' situations where cooperation is needed.<br>2. Make a list of ways to cooperate in a group:<br>• Sharing materials.<br>• Sharing responsibilities.<br>• Compromising/negotiating.<br>• Participating.<br>• Dividing up tasks.<br>• Exchanging information.<br>• Asking for information.<br>• Helping other group members.<br>3. Role-play the situations in number 2.<br>4. Make a list of consequences of not cooperating.<br>5. Choose a project in which the class can practice cooperation. Let the students evaluate their efforts. |
| Following rules | rules | 1. Discuss why rules are important.<br>2. Make a list of various situations and the rules necessary for each:<br>School bus rules:<br>• Sit in seat.<br>• Talk quietly.<br>• Listen to the bus driver.<br>• Follow directions.<br>• Keep hands inside the bus.<br>• Use safety belts.<br>• Enter and exit bus safely.<br>Hall rules:<br>• Keep hands and body to self.<br>• Be quiet.<br>• Walk instead of run.<br>Library rules:<br>• Speak quietly.<br>• Look at books on the shelf.<br>• Select one to three books from the shelf.<br>• Sit with books at table.<br>• Select one book to check out.<br>Cafeteria rules:<br>• Wait your turn in the lunch line.<br>• Take appropriate utensils, napkin, etc.<br>• Make choices for food items and drink. |

| Skill | Vocabulary to Introduce | Activities for Teaching Skill |
|---|---|---|
| | | • Pay cafeteria clerk. |
| | | • Seek place to sit (Look for a friend to sit near). |
| | | • Stay in seat. |
| | | • Use good manners. |
| | | • Throw away trash. |
| | | • Talk quietly. |
| | | • Return tray. |
| | | • Wait to be dismissed and leave quietly. |

Playground rules:
• Play within designated areas.
• Play alone or with friends.
• Share playground equipment and take turns.
• Cooperate with others' ideas.
• Stop playing immediately when called.
• Tell teacher if ball goes over the fence.

Assembly rules:
• Enter quietly and be seated.
• Listen for other instructions.
• Speak softly if you must speak at all.
• Keep hands to self.
• Watch performance by keeping eye on performer.
• Clap after the performance.
• Wait to be dismissed.
• Leave quietly.

Office rules:
• Look to see if the person is busy before speaking.
• Use nonverbal messages to signal if you need help.
• Use polite language.
• Close door quietly.

3. Make a list of coping skills needed when you are told that you have broken a rule and you do not understand:
• Be polite.
• Keep calm.
• Ask for the rule to be stated.
• Ask for the rule to be clarified.
• Repeat the rule back to another person.
• Ask for another opportunity to show that you know the rule.

*Source:* Department of Student Services and Special Education. (1990). *Social services competency curriculum. Communication: School-related* (vol. 3). Fairfax, VA: Fairfax County Public Schools. Adapted with permission.

**TABLE 8.3**
Peer-to-peer social skills: Communication.

| Skill | Vocabulary to Introduce | Activities for Teaching Skill |
|---|---|---|
| Interpreting facial cues and body language | communication nonverbal verbal interaction proximity expressions emotional states such as: nervous, worried, angry, exhausted, upset | 1. Explain to students how their own and others' facial expressions, body postures, and hand gestures convey meaning. Refer to the concept of body language. Discuss nonverbal components, including eye contact, posture, proximity, signals, and expressions.<br><br>2. Discuss the importance of attending to nonverbal communication:<br>• The need to check out the situation before "moving in"<br>• The need to consider how the other person is feeling<br>• The need to consider the message we send to others<br><br>3. Demonstrate various facial expressions, body postures, and hand gestures. As a group, decide what each movement or expression could mean. List examples of both positive and negative messages your body can convey.<br><br>4. Take turns transmitting an emotional feeling, using only an isolated body part. Try to guess what is being communicated. Do this for the whole group, or break up into teams.<br>• Only the mouth.<br>• Only the smallest finger.<br>• Only the shoulders.<br>• Only the eyebrows.<br><br>5. Show conflicting nonverbal cues by giving two different cues with two different parts of the body. |
| Making eye contact | eye contact message convey expressive eyes feelings | 1. Discuss feelings associated with the use of eye contact:<br>• Feeling important because others are listening to you and paying attention.<br>• Feeling unimportant because others are not listening or paying attention.<br>• Feeling embarrassment or discomfort because others are looking at you closely or for a long time.<br><br>2. Demonstrate the use of proper eye contact with a student or an aide. Maintain eye contact while involved in a verbal exchange, pointing out the value of using proper eye contact.<br><br>3. Have students pair up and practice sending messages with their eyes. Messages could include the following:<br>• Kindness and understanding<br>• Anger<br>• Confusion<br>• Disappointment |

| Skill | Vocabulary to Introduce | Activities for Teaching Skill |
|---|---|---|
| Adjusting language to situational demands | adjust<br>appropriate<br>inappropriate<br>casual<br>formal<br>respect<br>softly<br>excited<br>offensive | 1. Discuss the idea of using correct language in various situations. This comparison can be done graphically by showing pictures of different people wearing different clothing in various situations.<br>2. Discuss with the students why some people traditionally are addressed in a more formal way or receive more respect than others. Give an example: talking to the principal versus talking to a friend.<br>3. Talk about how we can tell which people we can be more casual with compared to those with whom we may want to be more formal.<br>4. Discuss with students the elements that could make a statement inappropriate or offensive to certain people:<br>• Specific words used<br>• Tone of voice<br>• Volume<br>• Topic chosen<br>5. Identify some reactions to offensive language. |
| Using greetings and farewells | polite<br>pleasant<br>greet | 1. Explain why it's important to greet others:<br>• To acknowledge their presence.<br>• To express friendliness or friendship.<br>• To be polite.<br>2. Talk about how a person might feel if he or she were intentionally ignored.<br>• Embarrassed<br>• Hurt<br>• Humiliated<br>• Concerned |
| Interrupting appropriately | interrupt<br>polite<br>rule<br>excuse me<br>emergency<br>courteous<br>necessary<br>conversation<br>pardon me<br>pleasant | 1. Introduce lesson by explaining that even though we often hear, "Don't interrupt," there are times when interrupting is necessary.<br>2. Have the class list times when they think interrupting is OK:<br>• Students are fighting in the hall.<br>• An adult has asked you to get your teacher right away.<br>• Someone is starting to faint.<br>• The student thinks the teacher has made a mistake, as in giving instructions, etc. |

*(continued)*

TABLE 8.3
Continued.

| Skill | Vocabulary to Introduce | Activities for Teaching Skill |
|---|---|---|
| | appropriate/ right inappropriate/ wrong body language nonverbal cue | 3. Emphasize the importance of reading the situation before interrupting:<br>• Relaxed conversational situation as opposed to serious conversation.<br>• Pauses in discussion when participants are glancing around. |
| | | 4. List words that could be used in interrupting:<br>• Excuse me.<br>• I'm sorry to interrupt, but. . . .<br>• Pardon me. |
| Expressing needs and wants | important vital personal need want necessity physical psychological hunger love affection | 1. Discuss what personal needs and wants are and explain that everyone has needs or wants. Examples:<br>• Need for shelter.<br>• Need for dressing assistance.<br>• Need for water.<br>• Need to go to the bathroom.<br>• Need to eat.<br>• Need to be warmer or cooler.<br>• Need to go to the clinic.<br>• Need to feel safe.<br>• Need to feel loved.<br>• Want to play a game.<br>• Want a cookie, candy, etc.<br>• Want to go outside. |
| | | 2. If appropriate, differentiate between physical and psychological needs and wants. |
| | | 3. List ways in which people attempt to satisfy their needs:<br>• Eating<br>• Hugging and showing affection<br>• Drinking<br>• Asking for help |
| | | 4. Encourage students to think of those times or situations when they've needed or wanted something. |
| Initiating conversations | appropriate topic situation interesting conversation inappropriate initiate respond | 1. Discuss the concept of conversation, revising vocabulary as necessary. Address students' feelings about conversation (Is it enjoyable, difficult, etc.?).<br>2. Discuss the importance of choosing an appropriate topic for conversation. This can ensure a greater chance for success in the conversation. If the topic is one that does not interest the listeners, attention will be quickly lost. When choosing a topic you must consider the following: |

| Skill | Vocabulary to Introduce | Activities for Teaching Skill |
|---|---|---|
| | | • Whom are you talking to (older, younger; friend, stranger; etc.)? <br> • Where are you (school, home, church, sports field)? <br> • How much time do you have? <br> • How can you tell if someone is interested? <br> • What have you and this person talked about before? <br> • Will the person want to respond to you? <br><br> 3. Review ways of initiating a conversation with peers: <br> • Hello, how are you? <br> • Hi, what are you doing? <br> • Where are you going? <br> • Can you believe this weather? <br><br> 4. Emphasize the expectation of a response from the other person. This provides for the beginning of a conversation. Model or role-play for students. <br><br> 5. List clues for determining the appropriate time to initiate a conversation: <br> • Watch for facial expressions and body language to use as cues for initiating conversation. Is the person available? <br> • Is the person unoccupied and available, or does he or she seem to be working on something and possibly not want to be interrupted? <br> • Is what you have to say important enough to interrupt, or do you want to have pleasant conversation to pass the time? <br> • Remain sensitive to the person's availability. Does he or she seem to be in a rush? Then cut your comments short, etc. |
| Maintaining conversations | maintain <br> relevant <br> mutual <br> interest <br> observe <br> remark <br> comment <br> subject <br> topic <br> listening | 1. Model an effective conversation with the assistance of an aide or volunteer student. Talk about what helped keep the conversation going. <br><br> 2. Emphasize the following points, which are essential for maintaining a conversation: <br> • Keep to the topic. <br> • Talk about things that will interest the other person. <br> • Ask questions to include the other person. <br> • Keep body posture upright to appear interested. <br> • Maintain eye contact. |

*(continued)*

239

TABLE 8.3
Continued.

| Skill | Vocabulary to Introduce | Activities for Teaching Skill |
|---|---|---|
| | | 3. Demonstrate the difference between relevant and irrelevant remarks. Role-play a conversation and insert irrelevant remarks. Help the students pick up inconsistencies. |
| | | 4. Discuss the steps we use in order to make sure we are making relevant remarks in conversations:<br>• Listen to people who are talking.<br>• Notice the subject matter.<br>• Wait for the right time to make a comment.<br>• Comment on the subject matter.<br>• Listen to responses. |
| Joining ongoing conversations | cues<br>proximity<br>low key | 1. List and explain steps for joining in:<br>• Decide if you want to join in the conversation.<br>• Stand next to the group.<br>• Think of ways to join in (ask a question, introduce yourself, make a relevant comment).<br>• Choose the best way for you to join in.<br>• Choose the best time (watch those facial expressions and body language).<br>• Relax! Join in. |
| | | 2. List and model appropriate phrases that could be used when joining in:<br>• Hey, how are you doing?<br>• Are you talking about the movie?<br>• That happened to me once. |
| Ending conversations | conversation<br>ending<br>situation | 1. Introduce conversation enders. Ending or closing a conversation requires the use of a word or phrase that will convey to the listener that the speaker must leave for whatever reason and that the conversation needs to be over. Review vocabulary words as necessary. |
| | | 2. List various situations in which a person might need to end a conversation:<br>• You are late for class.<br>• You have an appointment.<br>• You have run out of things to say.<br>• Someone else needs to speak to you.<br>• Something is said that disturbs you.<br>• The other person doesn't seem to want to talk. |

| Skill | Vocabulary to Introduce | Activities for Teaching Skill |
|-------|-------------------------|-------------------------------|
| | | 3. List various options for ending a conversation:<br>• Wait for an end to the other person's comment and excuse yourself.<br>• Politely interrupt (when in a hurry) and explain briefly why you have to leave.<br>• When there is a lull or pause in a conversation because it is exhausted, politely excuse yourself and leave. |
| Talking on telephone | message<br>answering<br>   machine<br>recording<br>emergency<br>dial<br>information<br>911<br>phone number<br>assistance<br>nonemergency<br>address<br>operator<br>receiver<br>wrong number<br>volume | 1. Bring in a variety of real telephones (touch tone, dial, different styles). The phone company may be able to assist you with this. Set up stations using a different type of phone at each station. Allow children to practice using the various types of phones. Practice dialing.<br><br>2. Label each part of the phone, using the correct vocabulary words. |

*Source:* Department of Student Services and Special Education. (1990). *Social services competency curriculum. Communication: School-related* (vol. 3). Fairfax, VA: Fairfax County Public Schools. Adapted with permission.

**TABLE 8.4**

Peer-to-peer social skills: Interaction.

| Skill | Vocabulary to Introduce | Activities for Teaching Skill |
|---|---|---|
| Making new friends | acquaintance<br>friend<br>introduce | 1. Introduce the topic of making new friends (emphasizing the difference between friends and acquaintances). Review vocabulary when necessary.<br>2. List situations where you might have the opportunity to make new friends:<br>  • Starting a new school year.<br>  • Beginning a new dance class.<br>  • Moving to a new neighborhood.<br>  • Working on a project with a new person.<br>3. Discuss feelings one might experience when meeting new people. |
| Sharing and taking turns | share<br>polite<br>generous<br>sincere<br>turn<br>change<br>patience<br>equal<br>cooperation | 1. Discuss why it is important to share. What are you telling the person when you share?<br>2. List things that a person can share:<br>  • Toys<br>  • Books<br>  • Snacks<br>  • Work materials<br>  • His or her seat<br>  • Time<br>  • Information<br>  • Feelings<br>3. List times when taking turns is particularly necessary:<br>  • Playing a game.<br>  • Talking in a group.<br>  • Using the pencil sharpener.<br>  • Getting a drink from the water fountain.<br>4. Model sharing each of the things in numbers 2 and 3. |
| Expressing appreciation | appreciate<br>thoughtful<br>thank you | 1. Discuss when to let someone know that you appreciate them for what they have done.<br>  • Thank-you notes.<br>  • Words.<br>  • Small gifts.<br>  • Smiles.<br>  • Hugs.<br>  • Letting others know that their kindness was helpful.<br>  • Returning a favor.<br>  • Giving a compliment as a way of thanking.<br>  • Return the kindness by doing something helpful. |

| Skill | Vocabulary to Introduce | Activities for Teaching Skill |
|---|---|---|
| | | 2. Demonstrate with an instructional assistant, or a student, various ways of showing appreciation:<br>• Thank someone for being thoughtful.<br>• Thank a parent for lending you the car.<br>• Thank a relative for a gift. |
| Apologizing | apology<br>fault<br>blame<br>accidental<br>intentional<br>sincere<br>sorry | 1. Discuss the importance of apologizing appropriately:<br>• Positive regard.<br>• Reducing tension.<br>• Showing respect for yourself.<br>• Maintaining good working relations.<br>2. Discuss these points for giving an apology:<br>• Know that accidents do happen.<br>• Know that apologizing will show people it was an accident.<br>• Apologizing will help stop the other person's anger.<br>• Sometimes if there is real damage, it may be necessary to do more than just apologize. |
| Helping others | assist<br>emergency<br>helpful<br>considerate<br>give a hand | 1. Talk about times when you see that another person could use some help, and discuss with the class why we offer to help others. Review vocabulary as necessary.<br>2. Ask students to share experiences in which they have been helpful to others.<br>3. Identify and discuss some things we all consider when offering or accepting help:<br>• Do I need help?<br>• Am I afraid that my pride or the other person's pride will be hurt?<br>• Can I help this person or should I help him or her find help?<br>• How can I ask for help?<br>• It's good to give and get help<br>• Should I help or get help from people I don't like? |
| Showing respect for others | respect<br>disrespect<br>courteous<br>polite<br>negative<br>necessary<br>honor<br>consideration | 1. Introduce the topic of respect. Review vocabulary, starting with the dictionary definition of *respect*.<br>2. Cite several situations or examples where we should show respect. List specific people for whom, and situations in which, respect is required. |

*(continued)*

243

TABLE 8.4
Continued.

| Skill | Vocabulary to Introduce | Activities for Teaching Skill |
|---|---|---|
| Respecting cultural differences | beliefs<br>customs<br>neighborhood<br>race<br>language<br>religions<br>holidays<br>countries<br>clothing<br>unique<br>different<br>culture | 1. Explain that culture is the typical behavior and social characteristics of a specific group of people. Discuss respect for another person's culture and how our world is unique because of diversity.<br>2. Give examples of cultural differences in various parts of the world:<br>• Clothing<br>• Language<br>• Holidays<br>• Dating and marriage<br>• Family<br>• Food<br>3. Demonstrate how you can show respect for another person's culture (interest, tolerance, accommodation):<br>• It's really interesting that your family celebrated your 13th birthday.<br>• I brought something special for you to eat because I know you don't eat this.<br>4. Ask students to role-play showing respect for cultural differences. |
| Joining in | join<br>sharing<br>participate | 1. Introduce the topic of joining in, reviewing vocabulary as necessary.<br>2. Have students share situations where they have wanted to join but didn't:<br>• Wanted to join a game, but the teams were already picked.<br>• Wanted to join a club but didn't know anyone in it.<br>3. Establish guidelines for joining in:<br>• Check out the situation.<br>• Use the right procedure (outline step-by-step procedure).<br>• Ask for help if needed. |
| Disagreeing | disagree<br>opinion<br>argue<br>negotiate<br>respect<br>polite | 1. List several situations where people may disagree or have a difference of opinion:<br>• Disagree with a grade the teacher has given you.<br>• Disagree with something your parents say about you.<br>• Disagree with a team member.<br>• Disagree about what to do with a friend in your spare time. |

| Skill | Vocabulary to Introduce | Activities for Teaching Skill |
|-------|------------------------|-------------------------------|
| | | 2. Have students talk about personal situations where they have had to disagree. How did they start their disagreement? What did they say? How did they feel? What was the reaction? |
| | | 3. Talk about how to express your disagreement. Emphasize that people don't always agree even after they talk about the difference. They might need to negotiate. |
| Reading social environments | verbal<br>nonverbal<br>interactions<br>feelings<br>interpret<br>facial<br>    expressions<br>body<br>    language<br>environment<br>situation | 1. Discuss what social situations are, and make a list of various social situations. Examples: restaurant, picnic, theater, dinner at a friend's house. |
| | | 2. Emphasize the need to change behaviors depending on the situation. |
| | | 3. Have students draw pictures or take pictures from magazines that depict social situations. Discuss appropriate behavior for each social situation pictured. |
| | | 4. Help students identify the following:<br>  • Nonverbal elements of interaction.<br>  • Verbal expressions that correspond to feelings.<br>  • Verbal expressions that are inconsistent with feelings. |
| | | 5. As social situations arise, use each situation to identify appropriate behaviors. Before field trips (walking trips, plays, etc.) discuss various aspects of the situation:<br>  • How to dress.<br>  • How to behave.<br>  • How to prepare. |

*Source:* Department of Student Services and Special Education. (1990). *Social services competency curriculum. Communication: School-related* (vol. 3). Fairfax, VA: Fairfax County Public Schools. Adapted with permission.

**TABLE 8.5**
Peer-to-peer social skills: Self-control.

| Skill | Vocabulary to Introduce | Activities for Teaching Skill |
|---|---|---|
| Adapting to changes | routine<br>unexpected<br>unavoidable<br>flexible<br>postponed<br>canceled<br>schedule<br>alternative | 1. Discuss with students all of the routines that they can think of:<br>• Getting dressed<br>• Getting to school<br>• Class routine<br>• Family routines (chores, meals)<br>• Holiday routines, visits, trips<br><br>2. Explain that routines bring order to our lives and that we feel comfortable when we know what to expect. Explain that feeling in control of our day is a good experience. When plans change or we can't do things in our usual ways, we may have negative feelings. However, we may feel excitement or fun instead.<br><br>3. Role-play the following situations:<br>• Someone else sits in the chair where you always sit.<br>• A field trip to the zoo was canceled due to rain.<br>• The third-period assembly speaker doesn't show up, so you have geometry instead.<br>• Your teacher is sick, so you have a substitute.<br><br>4. Introduce gradual planned changes in the students' schedules. Have students help plan changes and monitor their own behavior. |
| Controlling anger | emotional states such as nervous, worried, angry, exhausted, upset communication nonverbal verbal interaction impulsive expressions aggression | 1. Ask students to list situations that can make people angry:<br>• Being teased or embarrassed<br>• Being hit, kicked, etc.<br>• Being told you can't do something<br>• Being ignored<br><br>2. Ask students to list some common reactions to anger. What do people do when they are angry? What are the consequences?<br>• Cry<br>• Scream or yell<br>• Hurt someone back<br>• Withdraw to your room<br><br>3. Discuss the importance of thinking before you act. Impulsive behavior may hurt others, make others mad, make you feel bad later, hurt you, or destroy your chance to do what you decide is best.<br><br>4. Outline steps for dealing with anger:<br>• Stop and think. |

| Skill | Vocabulary to Introduce | Activities for Teaching Skill |
|---|---|---|
| | | • Decide why you are angry. |
| | | • Are there other things that also are making you angry? |
| | | • Tell the person making you angry to stop it. |
| | | • Discuss your feelings with the person who is making you angry. |
| | | • Walk away. |
| | | • Talk to an adult. |
| | | • Ignore the person and do something else. |
| Accepting disappointments | disappointed sad angry frustrated resume express alternative expectation | 1. Explain that disappointment means the feeling of not having your expectations or hopes met. |
| | | 2. Give students examples of situations when a person might feel disappointed. |
| | | 3. Ask students to give examples of times when they have felt disappointed. |
| | | 4. Outline positive ways to react to disappointment: |
| | | • Know that it's O.K. to feel sad or disappointed. |
| | | • Verbalize feelings to a friend or interested adult. |
| | | • Resume your activity and try to think of other things. |
| Accepting criticism | criticism opinion fact negative positive constructive mistake accept error | 1. Discuss the difference between constructive and destructive criticism. Give examples of each. |
| | | 2. Discuss why one might be criticized. One might receive criticism for accidentally making a mistake, for doing something wrong, or sometimes for doing something very well. This might happen when others do not know the details of a situation, or it may happen when others in control are having a bad day. |
| | | 3. Discuss the feelings that accompany being criticized (angry, hurt, defeated, embarrassed) and the negative ways we sometimes react: |
| | | • Stop doing the activity that was criticized. |
| | | • Continue doing the activity in the same way. |
| | | • Show verbal anger. |
| | | • Show physical anger. |
| | | 4. Model appropriate responses when a student points out the error: |
| | | • Oops. |
| | | • Thank you for catching that. |
| | | • Even teachers make mistakes. |
| | | • I'll change that. |

(continued)

TABLE 8.5
Continued.

| Skill | Vocabulary to Introduce | Activities for Teaching Skill |
|---|---|---|
| | | 5. Discuss appropriate responses to criticism of schoolwork errors. List key steps for ways to respond to criticism:<br>• Listen.<br>• Ask questions if needed.<br>• Acknowledge with "thanks" or "oops."<br>6. Hand out 3" × 5" cards to the class. Ask students to write on the cards those things they would like to change about themselves. Encourage students to use positive terms rather than putdowns. (Put a few examples on the blackboard.) |
| Accepting praise | praise<br>compliment<br>attitude<br>proud<br>comment | 1. List situations where one can expect to receive praise.<br>2. Ask students to give examples of times that they receive praise:<br>• How did you feel?<br>• How did you respond?<br>3. Explain that a polite response is expected when they get a compliment or praise. Ignoring or denying praise may be seen as impolite.<br>4. Outline steps for responding to praise:<br>• Listen to the compliment.<br>• Show pleasure through facial expression and body language.<br>• Thank the person for giving praise.<br>• Try not to deny praise.<br>• Offer praise when appropriate.<br>5. Role-play situations where students compliment each other:<br>• Someone praises you for a nice job that you've done on a school project.<br>• Someone praises you for being helpful.<br>• Someone praises you for having a good attitude. |
| Coping with rejection | excluded<br>rejected<br>ignored<br>needed<br>popular<br>isolated<br>left out<br>lonely<br>confused<br>hurt<br>turned down | 1. Explain that rejection means being left out of an activity or turned down by someone.<br>2. Talk about the feelings that go with rejection (anger, hurt, frustration, loneliness, embarrassment).<br>3. Outline steps that may be used to react to being rejected:<br>• Observe body language and interpret the social situation to determine the appropriateness of joining.<br>• Attempt to join the group by approaching the activity.<br>• Ask if you can join in. |

| Skill | Vocabulary to Introduce | Activities for Teaching Skill |
|---|---|---|
| | | • Determine why you were rejected. Was it because of your behavior or some other reason?<br>• Leave the general area if not able to join the activity.<br>• Begin an independent activity or seek others to talk to or spend time with.<br>• Seek adult assistance if the problem continues. |
| Responding to threats | threats<br>impulsive<br>consequence<br>negative<br>responsibility<br>owning the<br> problem<br>option<br>intimidated | 1. Explain the meaning of a threat (someone stating that they will do harm).<br>2. Discuss types of threats:<br>• Saying they will do something that you won't like.<br>• Saying they will hurt someone.<br>• Saying they will damage someone's property.<br>3. Discuss appropriate responses to a threat. Discuss the importance of thinking before you act. Impulsive behavior may make others mad and make matters worse, may make you feel bad later, may hurt you, or may destroy your chance to do what you decide is best.<br>4. Outline positive ways to deal with threats:<br>• Listen carefully.<br>• Stop and consider your options.<br>• Move away from the person making the threat.<br>• Tell an adult about the threat. |
| Responding to embarrassment | embarrassed<br>uncomfortable<br>self-<br> confidence<br>coping<br>responding<br>blush | 1. Identify situations in the classroom where a student might feel embarrassed:<br>• You forgot your homework.<br>• Your shirt is ripped.<br>• You have to read in front of the class.<br>2. Discuss what embarrassing situations have in common:<br>• Happen in public.<br>• Bodily reactions—blush, sweat, voice problems.<br>• Blow to self-esteem.<br>• Others laughing at you or teasing you.<br>3. List the common feelings that embarrassment brings out:<br>• Feeling stupid.<br>• Feeling isolated or alone.<br>• Feeling as if you want to hide or run away.<br>4. List some ways that people show their embarrassment:<br>• Looking at the floor.<br>• Looking away.<br>• Blushing. |

*(continued)*

**TABLE 8.5**
Continued.

| Skill | Vocabulary to Introduce | Activities for Teaching Skill |
|---|---|---|
| | | • Laughing or making jokes.<br>• Running away.<br>• Crying.<br>• Getting angry.<br><br>5. Outline positive options for responding to an embarrassing situation:<br>• Tell yourself, "It's OK Everybody makes mistakes."<br>• Remain quiet throughout the situation.<br>• If you are speaking, keep your mind on what you're saying.<br>• Accept advice and information intended to prevent you from further embarrassment.<br>• Leave the situation as soon as possible.<br>• Attempt to regain your self-confidence with humor.<br>• Say politely, "Excuse me," "Oops," "I'm sorry."<br>• Make changes if possible.<br>• Continue the original activity with changes. |

*Source:* Department of Student Services and Special Education. (1990). *Social services competency curriculum. Communication: School-related* (vol. 3). Fairfax, VA: Fairfax County Public Schools. Adapted with permission.

# CHAPTER 9

## Adapting the Behavioral Environment

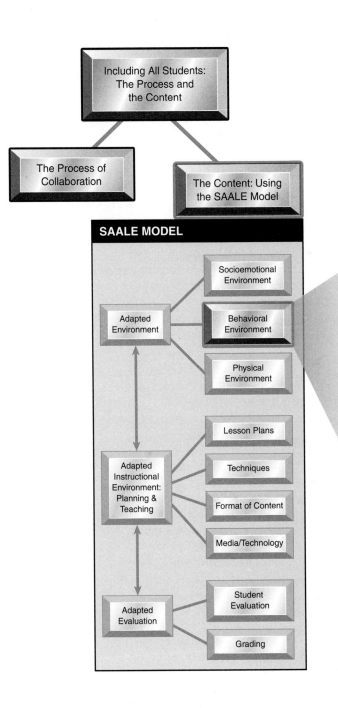

**SAALE MODEL**

Including All Students: The Process and the Content

The Process of Collaboration

The Content: Using the SAALE Model

Adapted Environment
- Socioemotional Environment
- Behavioral Environment
- Physical Environment

Adapted Instructional Environment: Planning & Teaching
- Lesson Plans
- Techniques
- Format of Content
- Media/Technology

Adapted Evaluation
- Student Evaluation
- Grading

**Chapter-at-a-Glance**

Setting the Tone

Providing Class Structure

Techniques for Surface Behavior

Techniques for Behavior Management

Motivating Students

Managing student behaviors is an ongoing process that occurs simultaneously with teaching. When teachers have assessed their students properly, have carefully adapted the physical environment, and have appropriately planned instruction to fit students' needs, most management problems will disappear. But no system is foolproof; sometimes problem behaviors distract from the positive instructional atmosphere that teachers have so carefully built.

This chapter addresses teacher behavior, providing structure, surface behavior techniques, and behavior management techniques.

## THE TEACHER SETS THE TONE

The teacher sets the tone in the classroom. He or she adjusts the lighting, controls the temperature, arranges the seating, decides how to present lessons, elects when to give tests, and chooses what types of tests to administer. The teacher sets the affective atmosphere of the classroom and the stage for learning. According to Purkey (1978), the teacher alone has the power to invite or not invite each student to learn. The teacher's attentiveness, expectations, encouragement, attitudes, and evaluations strongly influence students' perceptions of themselves as learners. Thus, the teacher's behavior influences the students' behavior. To assess their potential influence on student behavior, teachers should ask themselves the following questions:

- Do I leave my personal problems at home?
- Am I in good physical and emotional health?
- Am I happy with my role in life?
- Does my voice convey confidence?
- Does my walk convey confidence?
- Do I have a positive self-concept?
- What is my attitude toward my peer group?
- What is my attitude toward children?
- Do I accept the responsibility of students at risk?
- Do I feel comfortable about admitting mistakes?
- Will I change my opinion when someone presents a valid reason for doing so?
- Do I have a sense of humor?
- Can I laugh at myself?
- Am I an attentive listener?
- Do I teach subjects or children?

Figure 9.1 asks several questions about teacher behavior that can help teachers evaluate whether they are contributing to misbehaviors. Figure 9.2 offers eight behavior suggestions for the teacher.

### Am I consistent in responding to children's behavior?

If your response to children's conduct—good or bad—is unpredictable, children will have difficulty learning how to behave. Your students should know the consequences of appropriate behavior and misbehavior. Give clear directions, hold firm to your expectations, and be consistent in following through with rewards and punishment.

### Am I rewarding the right behavior?

Children who present difficult management problems often are ignored when they are behaving appropriately. Often, the only time they receive attention is when they are criticized or reprimanded for misbehavior. Sometimes teachers make the mistake of praising them for something else or making physical contact with them in attempts to offer loving correction when they misbehave. Make sure that children are receiving your attention primarily when they are behaving appropriately. Make certain that desirable conduct receives a hefty amount of recognition and that misbehavior does not.

### Are my expectations and demands appropriate for children's abilities?

When expectations are too high, children feel too much pressure and experience too much failure. When expectations are too low, children become bored and may feel resentful. Make certain that your expectations fit each child's ability level so that the children are challenged while their progress is obvious.

### Am I tolerant enough of children's individuality?

Children have as much right as adults to express their individuality. Many children rebel against teachers who demand strict uniformity and regimentation or are unwilling to encourage appropriate individuality. Make certain that your rules and expectations allow sufficient room for harmless preferences and idiosyncracies.

### Am I providing instruction that is useful to children?

People do not learn quickly or happily when they see no point in what they are doing. First, make sure that you have chosen the most important things to teach.

Then, if children do not see the importance of what you are teaching, point out the value of what they are learning. If they still do not understand, find a way to make the material interesting or worth their while, perhaps by offering meaningful rewards of privileges for learning.

### Are children seeing desirable models?

Children are great imitators of their teachers and their high-status peers. Make certain that if children are imitating you, they are behaving appropriately. Monitor your own behavior, and change it if necessary. Call attention to the desirable conduct of children's peers. Point out the kind of behavior you want to see.

### Do I avoid being generally irritable and overreliant on punishment as a control technique?

Teachers set a tone in their classrooms by their general attitudes toward persons and events. A teacher who is easily upset, frequently short-tempered, quick to punish minor misbehavior, and hesitant in expressing approval is virtually certain to foster irritability and defiance in students. General irritability and a focus on punishment suggest depression, and a teacher's depression may contribute to children's depressive behavior.

### Am I willing to try a different approach to the problem or to seek the help of colleagues or consultants?

A teacher who resists the suggestions of others, insists on "going it alone," or discards any different approach as useless or doomed to failure is not likely to be successful for long. Teaching presents complex behavior management problems for which even the most competent teacher needs consultation. An attitude of openness and a willingness to look outside oneself are essential for success.

**FIGURE 9.1**

Questions about teacher behavior.

*Source:* Kauffman, J. M., Pullen, P. L., & Akers, E. (1986). Classroom management: Teacher-child-peer relationships. *Focus on Exceptional Children, 19,* 3. Copyright 1986 by *Focus on Exceptional Children.* Adapted by permission.

| | |
|---|---|
| Fairness: | Teachers must demonstrate fairness in assignments, giving help, etc., or they cannot expect students to begin to like them. |
| Appearance: | Appearance is often mentioned by students when they describe teachers for whom they have high regard. Good grooming and a pleasant appearance are interpreted as a sign of respect. |
| Humor: | William Glasser says humor is a form of caring. Teachers need not be joke tellers, but those who respond openly to humorous moments or who can kid lightheartedly with students seem to strike particularly responsive chords. |
| Courtesy: | Courtesy in the classroom helps build personal relationships and is frequently responded to in kind. |
| Respect: | Teachers show respect by encouraging students to express ideas without criticism, by valuing student products or by not "putting down" a student. When respect is extended it is usually returned. |
| Realness: | Students see teachers as "real" only when the teacher allows them to do so. Teachers share anecdotes with students from their own lives, integrating personal experiences into explanation and presentations. |
| Re-establishing Contact: | After a student has been reprimanded, re-establishing contact by showing that a grudge is not held helps the student re-enter the emotional flow of the classroom. |
| Active Listening: | Teachers listen carefully to the content, reflect back the message, and do so with feeling. |

**FIGURE 9.2**
Behavior suggestions for the teacher.

*Source:* Saphier, J., & Gower, R. (1997). *The skillful teacher: Building your teaching skills,* 5th ed. Carlisle, MA: Research for Better Teaching. Adapted with permission.

Many years ago I had a student who was trying to tell me something. Finally, he said, "Mrs. Wood, you are not listening to me!" I replied, "Of course I am." The student replied, "No, you are not because your eyes are not looking at me!" I learned a valuable lesson. Listening must be done with both your ears and your eyes.

## Preventive Planning

Another way to manage behavior is to prevent a misbehavior before it begins. The Utah State Board of Education (1992) has 12 tips for preventive planning:

1. Appropriate and motivating curriculum
2. Positive teacher response
3. A structured daily schedule
4. Staff training

5. Environmental engineering

6. Instructional pacing

7. Notes to home

8. Precise commands

9. Data collection

10. Parent conferences

11. Special equipment

12. Supervision

I will discuss each topic briefly and follow the discussion with a cartoon that pictures the planning approach.

*Appropriate and motivating curriculum* (Figure 9.3). Curriculum must be appropriate for the functional level of each child. Work that is too difficult or too easy is likely to increase inappropriate behavior. Testing and evaluation skills are important tools that help teachers discover these functional levels.

*Positive teacher response* (Figure 9.4). A high rate of positive teacher responses will reinforce students for appropriate and correct behavior. Teachers who provide more positive than negative responses have students who want to remain in the classroom rather than be removed to another environment.

*A structured daily schedule* (Figure 9.5) . A structured daily schedule helps students to remain on task—that is, be engaged in academic or other activities that

**FIGURE 9.3**
Appropriate and motivating curriculum.

**FIGURE 9.4**
High rate of positive teacher response.

**FIGURE 9.5**
A structured daily schedule.

**FIGURE 9.6**
Staff training.

demand the students' time and attention. This eliminates many behavior problems because unengaged time is likely to accelerate students' inappropriate behaviors. A daily schedule must maximize on-task behavior, and the schedule must be followed. A sufficient number of staff members must be present to make high rates of on-task behavior feasible.

*Staff training* (Figure 9.6). Staff training is essential. Formal and informal inservice classes must be conducted in order for all staff members to become and remain competent in the use of behavioral interventions.

*Environmental engineering* (Figure 9.7). Environmental engineering is the arrangement or manipulation of the physical environment and stimuli to facilitate appropriate responses and avoid disruption that can adversely affect students. Here are several examples:

- Divide the classroom into one area for quiet reading, another for seat work, and another for small-group work.
- Create rules that state how loud or quiet students must be.
- Arrange the room so that students cannot easily look out windows or doorways into halls.
- Keep a teacher between the students and open areas if there are runners in the class.

**FIGURE 9.7**
Environmental engineering.

**FIGURE 9.8**
Instructional pacing.

*Instructional pacing.* (Figure 9.8). Instructional pacing refers to the rate at which the teacher presents instructional material to the learner. Proper instructional pacing is not too fast, which can frustrate students. Nor is it too slow, which can bore them or make them vulnerable to distractions.

*Notes to home* (Figure 9.9). Notes to home can provide clear, precise communication between school and home. In order to work, they must be sent on a regular basis. Also, the majority of feedback to parents must be positive.

*Precise commands* (Figure 9.10). A teacher's precise verbal statements can enhance student compliance with appropriate behavior. For example, if a student will not sit down, the instructor says, "Bill, please sit down!" (five-second delay); "Bill, you *need* to sit down *now!*" (five-second delay). The behavior should have appropriate consequences for both compliance and noncompliance.

*Data collection* (Figure 9.11). Teachers should collect information about how well a child is doing in academic or behavior programs. Collecting information can help the teacher determine if the program is effective. By evaluating the data, the teacher knows when to make changes.

*Parent conferences* (Figure 9.12). Parent conferences should be arranged so that parents may be notified of the student's difficulties. Teachers should also attempt to involve them in problem resolution. Parents may be involved through ongoing phone calls or school visits.

*Special equipment* (Figure 9.13). Adaptive equipment that students require to be successful is available and being used throughout the country. Equipment may

**FIGURE 9.9**
Notes to home.

**FIGURE 9.10**
Precise commands.

involve items such as large-print materials, typewriters, computers, or augmentative communication devices.

*Supervision* (Figure 9.14). Schools provide adequate and appropriate supervision as needed for students to succeed or to prevent problems.

# PROVIDING CLASS STRUCTURE

When trouble occurs in the classroom, teachers should first assess themselves and the environment. If they are still having difficulty managing student behaviors, they should look at class structure.

Frequently, mild misbehaviors will disappear when the student is given structure within the class environment. Providing boundaries for students facilitates a risk-free environment and allows students the freedom to relax within the class, knowing what is and is not expected. Not knowing how to behave or being unclear about the teacher's expectations creates a confusing situation for many students.

**FIGURE 9.11**
Data collection.

**FIGURE 9.12**
Parent conferences.

**FIGURE 9.13**
Special equipment.

**FIGURE 9.14**
Supervision.

By effectively introducing structured rules, teachers can control the environment of the class and prevent inappropriate behaviors. For example, the teacher should let all students, especially those with special needs, know what behaviors are permitted. Inappropriate behavior will often disappear when students know their limits. For teachers, setting rules for behavior establishes a structure for managing the classroom environment. For students, working within the boundaries of the rules establishes a structure for being responsible. Teachers can use the following guidelines when setting rules:

1. Involve students in formulating the rules.
2. Keep the list of rules short.
3. Keep the rules short and to the point.
4. Phrase the rules positively.
5. Don't just mention the rules when someone misbehaves; remind students about them at other times.
6. Post rules in a conspicuous place and review them regularly.
7. Record the number of times that rules have been reviewed with the class.
8. Make different sets of rules for different activities. Let students know when those different rules apply.
9. Only make rules that can be enforced.
10. When a student first breaks a rule, review the rule together one on one. Explain that he or she should now be familiar with the rule because the two of you have just reviewed it. Therefore, the next infraction of the same rule will result in a consequence. Explain exactly what the consequence will be.

Setting boundaries by clearly establishing, defining, and explaining rules creates an environment conducive to learning. You can use the rules and procedures checklist in chapter 8 to help provide class structure.

## SURFACE BEHAVIOR TECHNIQUES

When problems occur with students with mild disabilities, teachers often anticipate and fear long, involved management strategies, which can be both time consuming during the instructional period and last for a period of months. However, not all behavior problems are that serious. Long and Newman (1980) have developed techniques for what they call *surface behaviors*—behaviors that merit attention but do not demand total management programs.

Teachers should think of surface behaviors as minor infractions. Many teachers already have techniques for handling surface behaviors in their repertoires and merely need to remember a few tricks for coping with certain minor behavior problems.

## Tolerating Certain Behaviors

Before considering intervention, teachers should realize that some behaviors deviating from the norm should simply be tolerated. Long and Newman (1980) identified three situations in which teachers should tolerate some behaviors that they would otherwise not tolerate. These include learner's leeway, behavior symptomatic of a disability, and behavior reflecting a developmental stage.

*Learner's leeway.* This is the stage during which a student tries to master a new academic skill or learn or practice a new social skill. Teachers cannot expect perfection the first, second, or even third time the student attempts to master the skill. At this stage, teachers tolerate mistakes, and students understand that mistakes are normal and permitted.

Providing such leeway often eliminates the frustration of the mainstreamed student. Students with mild disabilities typically need many trials before they acquire skills. Often they simply do not pick up on social cues and, as a result, do not behave acceptably. For example, when a teacher corrects a student for interrupting, other students may learn not to interrupt from that example. However, the student with a mild disability may or may not learn through this indirect and incidental experience and thus may continue to interrupt.

*Behaviors symptomatic of a disability.* Many teachers do not tolerate specific behaviors because they lack knowledge about disabilities. Thus, school systems need to provide ongoing training for teachers to recognize and identify disabilities and the behaviors associated with them. Some of these behaviors are obvious: For example, a student with asthma certainly should be exempted from strenuous physical exercise on days when the asthma is active. However, children with learning disabilities, who may behave impulsively, might have their behavior misread as disruptive and therefore suffer unwarranted consequences. Children with emotional problems often display symptomatic behaviors that are generally considered inappropriate within the regular class environment.

Although these behaviors must at times be tolerated, they should not be overlooked. The special class teacher, in conjunction with the regular class teacher, should address these overt behaviors using the objectives of the student's IEP.

*Behavior reflecting a developmental stage.* This refers to behavior typical of a certain developmental or age level. For example, all teachers expect second-grade students to behave impulsively at times; however, they may become upset when sixth graders act the same way. Knowing what behaviors are usual for a certain developmental level helps teachers overlook them.

In addition, teachers need to know that some students with disabilities develop at a slower rate than nondisabled students do, and developmental norms may vary among students with disabilities. For example, a student with mild retardation will develop mentally at one-half to three-fourths the rate of a student with normal intellectual capabilities. Developmentally, the student with retardation at age 10 would not function in the same ways as an average student at the same age. A nondisabled child usually will pass through the impulsive developmental level by fifth grade, but the student with a disability in sixth grade may not have left it behind.

Once teachers understand developmental differences, they can more easily tolerate a variety of behaviors.

## Interventions for Surface Behaviors

In some situations, the teacher cannot permit or overlook certain behaviors in the classroom. At these times, the teacher needs a systematic plan for intervention. Long and Newman (1980) discuss techniques they have found to be successful in interventions with surface behaviors. These techniques can be used on a daily basis. The trick is to match the correct technique with the surface behavior and use it immediately when the behavior occurs.

*Planned ignoring.* This simple technique requires little training but a great deal of patience (Figure 9.15). Research psychologists refer to this technique as extinction—that is, eliminating a behavior by ignoring it. Planned ignoring means that the teacher immediately rewards students when they act appropriately and totally ignores students as long as they behave inappropriately. But the teacher must be patient. When a behavior that was previously rewarded with attention is suddenly ignored, the inappropriate behavior usually increases before it decreases. The student cannot understand why the teacher is not paying attention to a behavior that has always elicited a response, albeit a negative one. Teachers should keep calm, grit their teeth (if necessary) and wait for the appropriate behavior.

Here is an example: A student pulls on the teacher's clothing for attention. The teacher ignores the student, which eventually causes the student to stop.

**FIGURE 9.15**
Planned ignoring.

*Signal interference.* Teachers use a nonverbal signal to let a student know that they see the inappropriate behavior occurring or about to occur (Figure 9.16). For example, a teacher may use hand gestures to say, "Be quiet," "Sit down," "Come here," or "Give it to me." Teachers may also snap their fingers, use eye gestures, flick the light switch, or turn their backs to the group. Frequently, by using signal interference, teachers can stop the inappropriate behavior or, better yet, never let it start.

*Proximity control.* Proximity control means moving close to the student who is exhibiting inappropriate behavior (Figure 9.17). Often a teacher only needs to stand near the student or place a hand on the student's shoulder. This technique has a calming effect on some students and helps maintain control without interrupting the current activity.

*Defusing tension through humor.* This technique uses humor to defuse a potentially explosive situation. For example, imagine that a teacher is reading a book about witches to a class of kindergarten students on Halloween (Figure 9.18). One bright young boy looks up at her and says, "You're a witch, aren't you?" The teacher immediately slams down the book and tells all the students to return to their seats and put their heads on the desk for 15 minutes.

Now imagine that the teacher laughs and replies, "And you should see how fast I can ride my broom!" She has eliminated the problem, and the story continues uninterrupted.

**FIGURE 9.16**
Signal interference.

**FIGURE 9.17**
Proximity control.

**FIGURE 9.18**
Diffusing tension through humor.

**FIGURE 9.19**
Support for routine.

*Support for routine.* A simple but effective technique for young children and students with mild disabilities involves providing support for the student's routine (Figure 9.19). Displaying a chart in a special place on the board to show the week's or day's schedule provides security for the student. Then the teacher can announce in advance whenever schedules need to change and what the new schedules will be. Such preparation gives the student consistency and avoids problems.

Here's an example: The school nurse appears at the door of a first-grade class and tells all the children to line up. A little boy begins to cry, and nothing can calm him. At last the nurse says, "I'm only going to check your eyes." The boy replies, "But I thought you were going to give me a shot!" Advance preparation for the change in the routine can prevent anxiety and save the class from disruption.

*Interest boosting.* This technique involves taking an interest in the student who may be off task or on the verge of acting out. Walk up to the student and mention one of his or her hobbies or interests. After a brief conversation, walk away. Often the student will go back to work, and the inappropriate behavior will not recur. Sometimes a student may become interested in only one aspect of a lesson or in a topic unrelated to the lesson. The teacher can use interest boosting to channel interest and get the student back to work.

For example, a fourth-grade class is studying prehistoric animals, but one student, who is fascinated with dinosaurs, cannot attend to any other class assign-

**FIGURE 9.20**
Interest boosting.

ments. The teacher, realizing the problem, suddenly becomes greatly interested in dinosaurs and decides to do a unit on them, putting the fascinated student in charge of the unit. The student can work on the dinosaur topic only during a selected period of the day and after other work is completed. Thus, interest boosting encourages the distracted student to learn more but allows the teacher to maintain the day's structure (Figure 9.20).

*Removing distracting objects.* Many well-planned and well-intentioned lessons have gone astray because the teacher failed to remove distracting objects from the classroom (Figure 9.21). To solve this problem, simply walk up to the student and remove the object from the desk or the student's hand. Or begin the lesson by saying, "I see some very tempting objects on some desks. I don't want to be tempted to stop our lesson to play with them, so please remove the objects by the time I have counted to 3."

## BEHAVIOR MANAGEMENT TECHNIQUES

Sometimes teachers need to know about more complex behavior management processes. According to Sulzer-Azaroff and Mayer (1977), teachers should implement a behavior management process when the student makes several independent requests for assistance, behaves differently from the comparison group, or dramatically changes his or her behavior.

**FIGURE 9.21**
Removing distracting
objects.

## Identifying Target Behaviors

The teacher should first identify the target behavior—the behavior that clearly needs to be changed. However, such behaviors must be explicitly defined, observed, and measured so that everyone involved in the student's program can agree that the behaviors are detrimental to the student's social or academic development.

When defining a target behavior, the teacher must refer to observable, unambiguous characteristics. For example, stating that Bobby misbehaves in class or that Joy is not doing well in science provides neither measurable data nor defines a specific behavior. In contrast, stating that Bobby hits the other students in class, grabs their papers and pencils, and throws spitballs across the room lets everyone know exactly what behaviors need modifying. Similarly, saying that Joy is failing science, has difficulty grasping fifth-grade concepts, cannot take class notes, and cannot focus on the important points of the lesson pinpoints Joy's specific behavior weaknesses.

After clearly defining the target behavior, the teacher must record or count how often the behavior occurs. Recording target behaviors is necessary to determine

| Daily Schedule | Time | Day 1 | Day 2 | Day 3 | Day 4 | Day 5 | Day 6 | Day 7 | Day 8 | Day 9 | Day 10 | Day 11 | Day 12 | Day 13 | Day 14 |
|---|---|---|---|---|---|---|---|---|---|---|---|---|---|---|---|
| Opening exercises | 8:30–9:00 | 1 | 1 | 1 | 1 | 1 | 1 | 1 | | | | | | | |
| Reading circle | 9:00–10:30 | | | | 2 | 3 | 2 | 5 | | | | | | | |
| Snack time | 10:30–11:00 | | | | | | | | | | | | | | |
| Math | 11:00–12:00 | | | | | | | | | | | | | | |
| Lunch | 12:00–12:30 | | | | | | | | | | | | | | |
| P.E. | 12:30–1:15 | | | | | | | | | | | | | | |
| Global studies | 1:15–2:30 | | | | | | 1 | 1 | 1 | | | | | | |
| Prepare for bus | 2:30–2:45 | | 2 | 4 | 1 | 3 | 2 | 1 | | | | | | | |
| School dismissed | 2:45 | | | | | | | | | | | | | | |

FIGURE 9.22
Record of when Bobby hits other students.

the extent to which the target behavior occurs, but it also helps the teacher evaluate the effectiveness of the technique used to change the target behavior. Once teachers establish that a student's behavior needs to be changed or modified, they can implement a behavior management program.

Figure 9.22 presents a 14-day schedule for recording Bobby's hitting behavior. If we look at the first seven days, we can see a pattern developing. Bobby hits at a low rate during the morning's opening exercises (8:30–9:00), but the hitting intensity increases during reading circle (9:00–10:30). After snack time, Bobby refrains from hitting and does fairly well until it is time to prepare for the bus ride home. Thus, we see that Bobby does rather well after snack time and after P.E. A morning snack before 8:30 might be helpful because Bobby may not eat breakfast. And Bobby could be selected as a bus helper during the 2:30–2:45 time period. This would keep him busy in a positive way.

The teacher should become familiar with several behavior management techniques and select the one best suited for the student. Many articles in the education field describe various behavior management techniques. A few of the more common techniques are positive reinforcement, token economy, contingency contracting, and free time.

*Positive reinforcement.* Most people feel good when someone says, "Gee, you look nice today," or when they get paid, or when they overhear a compliment. Educators call this *positive reinforcement.* Positive reinforcement means giving a reward to increase or maintain a behavior. In the classroom, for example, a teacher smiles at the student who has satisfactorily completed an assignment or compliments a student for sharing nicely with a neighbor. When using positive reinforcement, teachers must be sure they have chosen the appropriate reinforcer because what reinforces one student may not reinforce another.

One way to find out what reinforces a student is to ask. In fact, some teachers develop a reinforcement menu for every student in their class. The teacher has a card indicating all the items that each student finds reinforcing. When it becomes obvious that a student has tired of a specific reinforcer, the teacher replaces it with another one. Students can even complete an interest inventory so that the teacher knows what reinforces the student (Figure 9.23). Teachers can also observe students closely to find out what to use.

Reinforcers fall into three major categories: social, tangible, and activity. Because society basically functions on social reinforcement, such as praise for a job well done or a smile of acknowledgment, students need to learn to perform tasks related to their jobs or behave in a socially acceptable manner without tangible or activity reinforcements. However, teachers should use tangible or activity rewards

My favorite school subject is _____

Three of my favorite things are

   1. _____

   2. _____

   3. _____

My favorite TV show is _____

I do not like to do _____

Three things I would like to have are

   1. _____

   2. _____

   3. _____

Three places I would go to are

   1. _____

   2. _____

   3. _____

**FIGURE 9.23**
Student interest inventory.

when beginning a behavior management program. Here are some examples of reinforcers and suggestions for rewards:

- *Social:* verbal, physical, or gestured stimuli to increase or maintain behavior.

Praise from the teacher, a smile, personal time with the teacher, playing with a classmate of choice, a pat on the back, sitting next to the teacher at lunch.

- *Tangible (token):* item given for performance of a specified target behavior.

Checkmarks, points, happy faces, stars, stickers, rubber stamps, balloons, award buttons, award slips, magazines.

- *Activity:* activities earned for appropriate behavior.

Dot-to-dot pictures, word games, crossword puzzles, coloring books, free time, bingo, art activities, field trips, Frisbees, reading with a friend, watching a film, watching TV, time in the library, playing teacher, extra time to complete homework, extra computer time.

Figures 9.24 through 9.35 show a number of art projects that can be used as tangible reinforcers.

After target behaviors have been identified and measured and the appropriate type of reinforcer selected, the teacher can begin implementing a positive program, following these guidelines:

- Select appropriate reinforcements for the student.
- Reinforce only those behaviors that need changing, modifying, or increasing.
- Reinforce the appropriate behavior *immediately.*
- At first, reinforce the desired behavior each time it occurs.
- Once the student has learned, changed, or modified a behavior, reinforce only intermittently (that is, on an alternating basis).
- If using a tangible or activity reinforcement, apply a social reinforcer simultaneously.
- Later, withdraw the tangible or activity reward slowly and keep reinforcing the student's behavior with social rewards.

It is important to use immediate, continuous, and consistent reinforcement when a behavior is being learned.

*Token economy.* A token is a tangible item given to the student for performing a specified target behavior. It has no intrinsic value but acquires value when exchanged for a material reinforcer or reinforcing event. For example, a paycheck has no intrinsic value until a person cashes it in for money. After the person receives the cash, he or she often exchanges it for material items or reinforcing events.

| | |
|---|---|
| Tangible Reinforcement: | "Pencil Mate" |
| Materials: | Pencil |
| | 5-inch pom-pom made from yarn or purchased felt (for hands, feet, nose, and mouth) |
| | Glue |
| | Movable eyes |
| | Scissors |
| Instructions: | 1. Make a hole through center of pom-pom. |
| | 2. Cut felt to make hands, feet, nose, and mouth. |
| | 3. Glue appendages to the pom-pom. |
| | 4. On back of pom-pom, attach a note about the student. |
| | 5. Mount figure on the pencil. |
| Use of Reinforcement: | Tell students they will receive a "Pencil Mate" after they complete a specific assignment. If their progress continues, they may take the pom-pom home to show their family. |

**FIGURE 9.24**
Art project.

| Tangible Reinforcement: | "The Key to Success" |
| Materials: | Poster board of different colors |
| | Yarn or string |
| | Markers |
| Instructions: | 1. Draw various sizes and shapes of keys on the poster board. |
| | 2. Write each child's name on a key. On other keys, write phrases such as " _____ minutes of free time," "This can be traded for _____," or "You are the owner of _____ ." |
| | 3. Give each child a key. |
| | 4. From yarn or string, let them make key rings. |
| Use of Reinforcement: | During the day children can earn keys for appropriate academic or social behavior. They may collect their free time at the end of each day by turning in their keys. |

**FIGURE 9.25**
Art project.

| Tangible Reinforcement: | "Leader of the Pack Bookmark" |
| Materials: | Poster board paper |
| | Scissors |
| | Glitter, sequins, etc. |
| Instructions: | Design different bookmarks for the students to use or keep. |
| Use of Reinforcement: | Give a bookmark to a student for reading when not required to do so or use it for a student who returns a library book and can answer questions about the book. |

**FIGURE 9.26**
Art project.

| | |
|---|---|
| Tangible Reinforcement: | "Shining Star" |
| Materials: | Poster board<br>Brightly colored felt<br>Glitter |
| Instructions: | 1. Cut out stars from poster board (3 or 4 inches wide).<br>2. Cut felt using the poster board for a pattern.<br>3. Glue together.<br>4. If desired, put glue around edges and sprinkle with glitter. |
| Use of Reinforcement: | The stars can be given or pinned to children who are exhibiting behaviors that earn them the titles of "Star Pupil," "Top Dog," or "Excellent Work." These can be taken home or worn as a necklace. |

**FIGURE 9.27**
Art project.

| | |
|---|---|
| Tangible Reinforcement: | "Pencil Warmer" |
| Materials: | Styrofoam cone (3-inch diameter) |
| | Felt (for arms, feet, buttons, and hat) |
| | Cardboard |
| | Pom-pom made from yarn or purchased |
| | Scissors |
| | Glue |
| | Aluminum Foil |
| | Two-sided tape |
| | Hole puncher |
| | Thread and needle |
| Instructions: | 1. Press a pencil into cone to form a pencil holder |
| | 2. Fit a piece of foil into the hole to secure. |
| | 3. Cover entire cone with felt. |
| | 4. Cut feet, arms, and buttons out of remaining felt. |
| | 5. Attach pom-pom to cone with needle and thread. |
| | 6. Make hat out of cardboard. |
| | 7. Cover hat with felt. |
| | 8. Glue arms, feet, buttons, and hat to cone. |
| Use of Reinforcement: | This pencil warmer is attached to a child's pencil at the beginning of the day. It may be taken away for a short period of time for inappropriate behavior. |

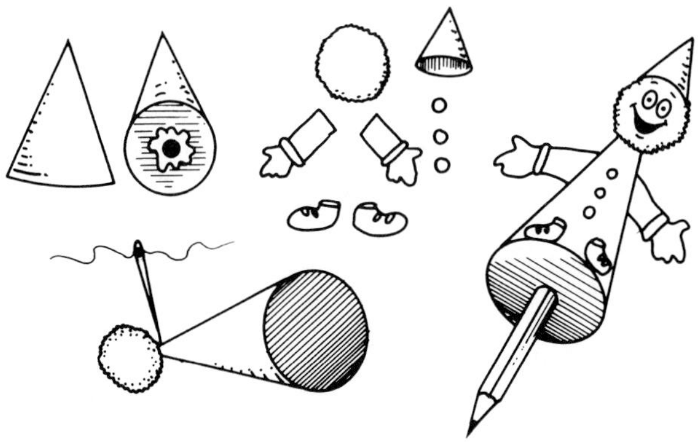

**FIGURE 9.28**
Art project.

| Tangible Reinforcement: | "Finger Puppet" |
|---|---|
| Materials: | Heavy felt |
| | Scissors |
| | Needle and thread or yarn |
| | Movable eyes |
| Instructions: | 1. Cut two pieces of felt in the shape of a finger (about 3 inches by 1½ inches). |
| | 2. Stitch together with thread of the same color. |
| | 3. Glue on two eyes and draw a face with a permanent marker. Add hair made of yarn if you wish. |
| Use of Reinforcement: | Each child gets a puppet in the morning. A student may lose the puppet for 5 minutes for inappropriate or disruptive behavior. |

**FIGURE 9.29**
Art project.

FIGURE 9.30
Art project.

| | |
|---|---|
| Tangible Reinforcement: | "Squiggly" |
| Materials: | Yarn |
| | Movable eyes |
| Instructions: | 1. Crochet or chain-stitch a small circle and a long chain for a tail. |
| | 2. Glue on eyes. |
| Use of Reinforcement: | Squiggly can keep children company at their desks if they are in their seats. It can be tied to a pencil or put around a wrist and then taken home at the end of the week. |

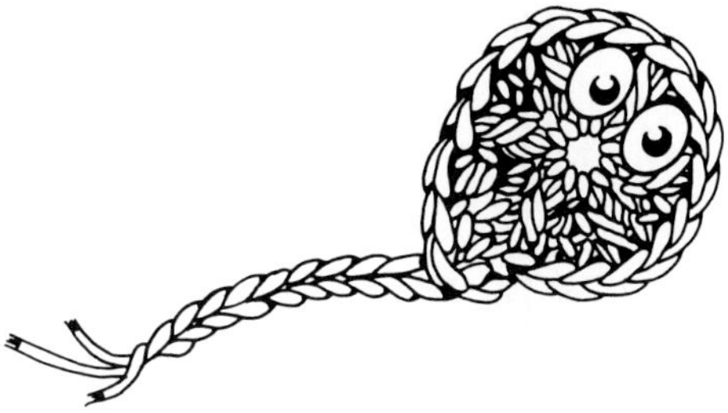

FIGURE 9.31
Art project.

| | |
|---|---|
| Tangible Reinforcement: | "Everybody Loves a Clown" |
| Materials: | Popsicle sticks |
| | White construction paper |
| | Markers |
| Instructions: | 1. Cut out patterns of clown on construction paper and decorate. |
| | 2. Glue to Popsicle stick with child's name or behavior written on it. |
| Use of Reinforcement: | Display the clown in the room and let children take it home at the end of the day to share with the family. |

FIGURE 9.32
Art project.

FIGURE 9.33
Art project.

**FIGURE 9.34**
Art project.

**FIGURE 9.35**
Art project.

8. Teacher evaluates token system.

7. Teacher initiates token system.

6. Teacher asks student to explain system.

5. Teacher explains rules of token system to student.

4. Teacher and student select reinforcers to exchange for tokens. Reinforcers must appeal to student.

3. Teacher posts appropriate behavior on chart or on student's desk.

2. Teacher clearly identifies target behavior that will earn tokens for the student.

1. Teacher identifies target behavior.

**FIGURE 9.36**
Steps for implementing a token economy.

Figure 9.36 shows the eight steps necessary for implementing a token economy system within the classroom. As in any behavior management program, the first step involves identifying the target behavior. Once the behavior is identified, the student must understand what behavior must be exhibited to receive the tokens. Additionally, the teacher must clearly explain the tokens and what they may be exchanged for. The student should be capable of performing the desired behavior; otherwise, the token system will be doomed to fail before it even starts. The teacher can record the desired behavior on a wall chart or on a small chart on the student's desk. For younger students, draw pictures of the desired behavior on the charts. For secondary-level students, who may resent having their behaviors recorded on a wall chart, the teacher can respect their privacy by listing behaviors in a small reward book.

The teacher must then select the backup reinforcers for which the tokens will be exchanged. Backup reinforcers may be small toys, candy, privileges, or special activities. The reinforcer must appeal to the student. Teacher and student may choose an appropriate backup reinforcer together. When the token system involves more than one student, the teacher should have a variety of backup reinforcers. The student needs to clearly understand what a token is, how many tokens have to be earned before receiving the backup reinforcer, when the reinforcer will be received, and how the number of tokens will be recorded. The teacher should explain the rules of the system and ask the students to explain them back to ensure their understanding.

A well-designed token system will allow the teacher to gradually withdraw material reinforcers and replace them with social reinforcement. An effective token system should be implemented simply, function well, and not distract from the instructional process. The teacher should evaluate the token system's effectiveness and, as with any technique, change it when it loses its effectiveness.

*Contingency contracts.* With a contingency contract, a student and teacher agree to accomplish a specific objective. Contracts formally apply "Grandma's Law": "You get to do what you want to do after you do what I want you to do." To set up a contract, the teacher and student choose the behavior, task, or skill to work on; agree on how many times the behavior should occur or how long the student should spend on the task; determine how long the contract should be in effect; decide what the reinforcer should be if the student successfully completes the task; and sign the contract. Consequences of the contract should be realistic and understood: Students should know what to expect if they meet the criteria of the contract and what to expect if they do not. Regardless of whether students meet the contract's criteria, they and the teacher should eventually evaluate the contract and decide if a new one is needed.

Contracts are fun to develop and design, and students should help the teacher create them. Contracting works well in mainstreamed classes because it provides structure for students with mild disabilities; they know what is expected of them socially and academically. The contract also provides a visual and ongoing progress report for the mainstreamed student. Most important, regular and special education teachers can develop the contract together, providing a bridge between two classrooms for the mainstreamed student.

*Free time.* Free time can be given to students as a reward for successfully completing their assignments or for doing something special. The student may use free time to work on an art project, listen to a record, go to the library, or simply sit at a desk and choose an activity. But students must earn free time.

Here are some tips for teachers who use free time in their classrooms:

1. Designate special areas in the room for free time.
2. Offer varied activities on different instructional levels in the free-time areas.
3. Remember that activities that are too difficult for students are not rewards.
4. Make sure that you explain to students how they can earn free-time privileges.

You may also want to try the following ideas for free time:

- Use movable screens to divide the areas, making special places for the students.
- Place an old-fashioned bathtub filled with pillows, books, and magazines in the back of the classroom.
- Take the door off a closet and place a large bean bag in it for free-time reading.
- Use pieces of carpet for magic rides to free time.
- Have areas for boys only and for girls only.
- Provide free-time art areas.
- Provide free-time game areas.
- Select one of the student's friends to share the free-time area.
- Provide free-time library passes.
- Allow 10 minutes at the end of each period for free-time winners.

# FUNCTIONAL BEHAVIORAL ASSESSMENT

Foster-Johnson and Dunlap (1993) provide a method for functional assessment and developing intervention plans. *Functional assessment* is "a process whereby informed hypotheses statements are developed about relationships between events in the environment and the occurrence of a student's challenging behavior. The results of this process are then used to develop a behavior management plan that will reduce the problem behavior" (p. 46). Figure 9.37 shows the components of the behavior management plan, and Table 9.1 lists sample hypotheses statements and possible interventions.

Functional assessment as required by IDEA is discussed in chapter 2. A sample functional behavioral assessment plan is presented in Figure 9.38.

# MOTIVATING STUDENTS

Students are motivated when they "buy" into what is being presented. This is intertwined with who you are as a teacher. If you're fair, empathetic, and willing to modify when appropriate, you will gain an incredible edge with your students. They will respect you and want to do well. Moreover, they will be more receptive to redirection or private discussions about problems when such becomes necessary. The foremost characteristic they intuit is, are you *really* interested in them? Treating them with respect lays the foundation for motivation. As with all students, respecting the dignity of "reluctant learners" and students with behavioral challenges is still the cornerstone for developing rapport and the effective use of most strategies.

Everything that we do as adults or children, we do for a reason. Sometimes the reason is not a good one, but there is still a reason for what we do. You must give students a *reason* to do well. For some, intrinsic satisfaction for a good grade is enough, but for many, more external forms of motivation are necessary. Tangible

Conduct a Functional Assessment

1. Collect information
   - Identify and define the target behavior.
   - Identify events/circumstances associated with the problem behavior.
   - Determine potential function(s) of the problem behavior.
2. Develop Hypotheses Statements About the Behavior
   - Write statements about events/circumstances associated with the problem behavior.
   - Write statements about the function/purpose of the behavior.

Develop an Intervention
(Based on hypotheses statements)

1. Teach alternative behavior.
2. Modify events/circumstances associated with the problem behavior.

**FIGURE 9.37**
Components of a behavior management plan.
*Source:* Foster-Johnson, L., & Dunlap, G. (1993). Using functional assessment to develop effective, individualized interventions for challenging behaviors. *Teaching Exceptional Children, 25*(3), 44–55.

and intangible rewards help to motivate where other techniques fail (techniques such as threats, calling parents, discipline referrals, shouting/yelling at them, and so forth). This does not imply that you should never call a parent or send students to the office when they prevent you from teaching, but to do these things as a first option should be avoided. Usually the only change you can elicit when continuing to use strategies that have no positive effect on student behavior is an elevation in your blood pressure.

Motivational strategies are limitless. A teacher of senior English has on her desk a bag of various snack-sized candies, and she invites each student to take one before class begins. This strategy sets the tone for a positive, upbeat lesson. If this works with seniors, it will also work with students in any grade. A middle school teacher stands in his doorway and shakes hands with students as they enter his class, welcoming each one by name. This teacher has virtually no problems with his students. No tangible reward is given. He just acknowledges that they are worth

TABLE 9.1
Sample hypotheses statements and possible interventions.

| | Intervention | |
| Hypotheses Statements | Modify Antecedents | Teach Alternative Behavior |
| --- | --- | --- |
| Suzy starts pinching herself and others around 11:00 A.M. every day because she gets hungry. | Make sure Suzy gets breakfast. Provide a snack at about 9:30. | Teach Suzy to ask for something to eat. |
| Jack gets into arguments with the teacher every day during reading class when she asks him to correct his mistakes on the daily reading work sheet. | Get Jack to correct his own paper. Give Jack an easier assignment. | Teach Jack strategies to manage his frustration in a more appropriate manner. Teach Jack to ask for teacher assistance with the incorrect problem. |
| Tara starts pouting and refuses to work when she has to sort a box of washers because she doesn't want to do the activity. | Give Tara half the box of washers to sort. Give Tara clear directions about how much she has to do or how long she must work. | Teach Tara to ask for a break from the activity. |
| Frank kicks other children in morning circle time and usually gets to sit right by the teacher. | Give each child a clearly designated section of the floor that is his or hers. | Teach Frank how to ask the children to move over. Teach Frank how to ask the teacher to intervene with his classmates. |
| Harry is off task for most of math class when he is supposed to be adding two-digit numbers. | Ask Harry to add the prices of actual food items. Intersperse an easy activity with the more difficult math addition so Harry can experience some success. | Teach Harry how to ask for help. Teach Harry how to monitor his rate of problem completion, and provide reinforcement for a certain number of problems. |

greeting, therefore establishing an inviting atmosphere. Another teacher uses a variety of modification techniques depending upon the student and the situation. These techniques include waiving a low grade, allowing a student to retake a quiz or test, reducing or modifying assignments to permit a student who is hopelessly behind to "catch up," contracting with a student (in writing) to improve work output or behavior in return for a guaranteed grade, positive notes or phone calls home to parents for a particularly good effort, specific praise, use of individualized checklists, and other techniques that imaginative and innovative teachers use with success. It is important to remember that a teacher may never do *less* than the modifications called for in an IEP, but he/she may always *do more* than what is called for. With that as a guide, there is no limit to what you can do to motivate your students and lay the foundation for success.

**King William County Public Schools**
**Functional Behavior Assessment:**
**Summary Sheet**

**How do the following items affect the student's behavior?**

Physical characteristics
Cognitive limitations/abilities
Communication limitations
Motor/perceptual abilities
Social skills
Physiological issues

_____

_____

_____

**How do the characteristics of the student's disability affect behavior and learning?**

_____

_____

_____

_____

**Are these lifestyle factors that affect behavior and learning?**

_____

_____

**Describe the behavior (both primary and secondary) and its current rate/strength.**

_____

_____

_____

**How do you know the behavior is about to occur?**

_____

_____

**Brainstorm, then discuss, possible functions of the behavior.**

_____

_____

_____

_____

_____

*(continued)*

FIGURE 9.38

Functional behavioral assessment plan and behavior intervention plan.

**KING WILLIAM COUNTY PUBLIC SCHOOLS**

What is the function(s) of the behavior?

_____
_____
_____
_____

Given the function of the behavior, what things need to be rearranged in the environment?

_____
_____
_____
_____
_____

What skills does the student lack and where/by whom/when will these skills be taught?

_____
_____
_____
_____
_____

How can we provide extra motivation to the student for skills he currently has?

_____
_____
_____

How should staff react when the behavior occurs?

_____
_____
_____
_____
_____

FIGURE 9.38
Continued.

**King William County Public Schools**
**Behavior Intervention Plan**

Date: _____   School: _____

Student's Name: _____

**Behavior Requiring Intervention (justification of need for service)**

_____

_____

_____

**Prevention**

**How will the school staff help to change the situations (who, what, where, when) that were associated with the behavior of concern?**

_____

_____

_____

**Intervention**

**Identify the behaviors or coping skills that the student now displays that will be reinforced.**

_____

_____

_____

**Identify the positive consequences for displaying appropriate or replacement behaviors.**

_____

_____

_____

**Identify the negative reinforcements for continuing the behavior of concern.**

_____

_____

_____

**How will the behavior be measured to document improvement? (Attach example of behavior contract, as appropriate.)**

_____

_____

_____

*(continued)*

**KING WILLIAM COUNTY PUBLIC SCHOOLS**

**Teaching**

**Identify the behaviors or coping skills that will be taught to replace the problem behavior.**

_____

_____

_____

**How and when will these behaviors be taught?**

_____

_____

_____

**Parent Participation**

**What type of specific assistance will the student's parents provide to help the student modify this behavior? What community agencies can the parents contact to obtain assistance?**

_____

_____

_____

This behavior intervention plan will be reviewed on _____ by the student's IEP team.
                                                   Date

| Date | Signature of Persons Present | Relationship to Student |
|------|------------------------------|-------------------------|
| _____ | _____ | _____ |
| _____ | _____ | _____ |
| _____ | _____ | _____ |
| _____ | _____ | _____ |

I did participate in the development of this plan, and I do approve of the plan
YES ___ NO ___

I did not participate in the development of the plan, and I do approve of the plan
YES ___ NO ___

Signature of Parent/Guardian/Surrogate: _____ Date: _____

Case Manager: _____

FIGURE 9.38
Continued.

## CHECKLIST

A tool that teachers can use in providing structure and organization for those students who need such modifications is the use of a comprehensive, individualized checklist. When the checklist is constructed *properly,* when it is personalized to the student and his/her specific needs, and when it includes a system of reinforcers, it can become the most powerful modification technique and communication tool you can use.

## CONCLUSION

By setting the tone for a positive behavioral environment and using simple surface management techniques, teachers can establish an environment that is risk free for students. Teachers should look at classroom management as a total process, not just a way of handling students' behavioral problems. This will help them cope with any problems that do occur.

# CHAPTER 10

## Adapting the Physical Environment

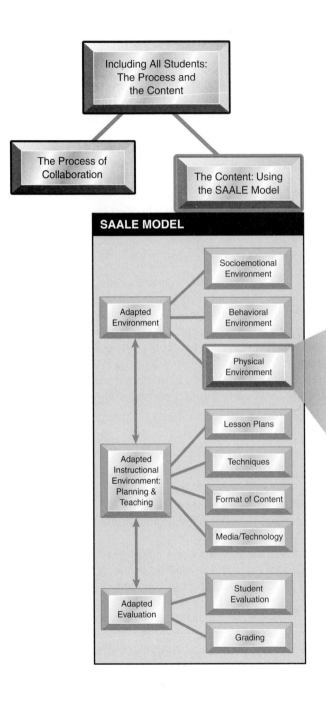

Including All Students:
The Process and
the Content

The Process of
Collaboration

The Content: Using
the SAALE Model

**SAALE MODEL**

Adapted
Environment

Socioemotional
Environment

Behavioral
Environment

Physical
Environment

Adapted
Instructional
Environment:
Planning &
Teaching

Lesson Plans

Techniques

Format of Content

Media/Technology

Adapted
Evaluation

Student
Evaluation

Grading

**Chapter-at-a-Glance**

Accessibility Standards

Preparing the Master Schedule

Grouping for Instruction

Designing the Classroom

F or those of you who have followed the more than 20 years of development of the SAALE model, you are in for a structure change. As introduced in part 2, the block of the model introduced a pattern change. Continuing with this chapter, this "change" will be developed.

Now, why the change? Because all of the sudden the writer decided to reverse the order of the physical environment and the socioemotional environment. Well, one of my reviewers made this suggestion and it made me think. (Yes, writers do that occasionally.) After all these years with the old model's structure, *change* of the placement of the physical environment to the top of the model made sense. The physical environment should be first, closely followed by the behavioral, then socioemotional environments.

Now, why all this rambling? I think that it is important to realize that as professionals, we *must* be constantly open to change. I feel that it is good for you to know that your author changes. . . .

The only thing that never changes is that everything is *always* changing.

Teachers change constantly and teachers also instruct students within the tightly woven framework of the school day. For harmonious and structured management, schools design the day around various schedules and physical arrangements. This framework affects students and teachers because it affects the types of subjects, class size, resources, students' choice of subjects, and educational philosophy. Schedules and physical environments vary in different schools, districts, and states. Regardless of the framework used, however, educators want to be able to adapt it to make instruction easier and more productive. This chapter considers accessibility standards, scheduling, grouping for instruction, and classroom design.

## ACCESSIBILITY STANDARDS

Chapter 1 discusses the major legislation that established a foundation of services for students with special needs and those at risk. These mandates also set standards for *accessibility,* which means that the environment must be free from obstacles that prevent a student with disabilities from having the same convenience as individuals without disabilities.

Many years ago, when I was in Mississippi working on my undergraduate degree, a young man in a wheelchair attended the university. In the school of business he had a class on the third floor. Naturally, the building was not accessible. (*Barrier free* was the term used then.) The man would wait at the entrance steps until two other men lifted his chair to the first floor. If they were going no further, they placed his chair at the bottom of the steps to the second floor. This process continued until the man finally made it to the third floor. When class was over, fellow classmates assisted him back to the sidewalk. Even though the young man's peers were helpful and he himself was brave and persistent, such a situation would not repeat itself today. Accessibility is mandated by law.

Figure 10.1 summarizes accessibility standards in the Americans with Disabilities Act (ADA).

**Parking**

Accessible

Shortest route to entrance

96″ wide with 60″ access aisles

Alternatives: van-accessible parking spaces

Universal parking space design

**Parking signs**

Each space with unobscured sign

Each space with universal symbol of accessibility

**Accessible exterior routes**

At least one accessible route within the site from public transportation stops and all other means of entrance to the site

Walkways at least 36″ wide

Curb ramps

**Exits**

Accessible routes also serve as emergency exits

**Doors**

Minimum clearance width 32″; maneuvering clearance between doors

Thresholds not to exceed ½″ in height; ¾″ at exterior sliding doors

**Elevators**

Accessible elevators on accessible routes; call buttons in lobbies and cars 42″ above floor

Visual signal for sending and answering each call

Braille characters

**Stairs**

Handrails on both sides

**Ramps**

Slope of ramps 112° or less

Minimum width 36″

Clearance areas at top and bottom of ramps

**Alarms**

Signal devices in all common areas

**Telephones**

Accessible to wheelchair users

Hearing aid and TDD compatible; adjustable volume controls

Cords at least 29″ long

**Drinking fountains**

Accessible to wheelchair users

Controls operable with one hand; easy to operate

**Restrooms**

Height of toilets 17″ to 19″ from ground

Grab bars 33″ to 36″ from floor

Toilet stalls: minimum depth 56″

Urinals: maximum height 17″ from floor

Sinks: maximum height 34″ from floor

Controls operable with one hand; easy to operate

Clear floor space in front of sink

Mirrors; maximum height 40″ from floor

**Operating mechanisms**

All operable equipment, dispensers, receptacles, electrical outlets, etc., between 15″ and 54″ side reach, 48″ forward reach

FIGURE 10.1

Summary of accessibility standards in the ADA.

# PREPARING THE MASTER SCHEDULE

Schools organize the parts of a school day according to a master schedule. The soundness of this schedule determines the effectiveness of administrative detail, plant facilities, instruction, and overall school organization.

Both special and general educators need a working knowledge of the school's master schedule. Special teachers need to understand the administrative framework of the school's schedule to place the included student appropriately. General classroom teachers need input into selecting the types and degrees of disabilities for which they will need to prepare. Both teachers can suggest minor changes that will prevent major problems in inclusion.

Because elementary schools have self-contained grade units (multilevel and multigrade) with only occasional class changes for specific academic subjects such as reading or math, their master schedules are less complex than those of secondary schools. Many elementary schools function with heterogeneous grouping within each class, while some use homogeneous grouping methods, such as having classes within one grade level grouped around students of similar ability and achievement. Elementary schools usually schedule art, music, and other such subjects on a weekly revolving basis.

Many elementary schools schedule the language arts and math blocks in the morning. Allowing students with mild disabilities to float in and out of the block provides appropriate instruction and allows more time for other subjects. For example, a language arts block running for 2 1/2 hours may contain reading, spelling, and grammar skills sections.

In such a case, the student with special needs should be able to attend the spelling and grammar skills sections in the general classroom and attend reading in the resource room (depending on school philosophy). Planning these blocks of time with the resource teacher before designing the elementary master schedule helps keep the daily schedule running smoothly.

At the secondary level, planning the master schedule becomes more difficult; as a result, placing students with mild disabilities and students at risk appropriately presents greater problems. The principal usually has the ultimate responsibility of preparing the master schedule; however, the guidance counselor or other individuals may do much of the actual planning. Whoever schedules students with special needs should consult the special education teacher and the inclusion teacher before the master schedule is finished.

Professionals and parents have considered many factors in the attempt to improve the success rate of public schools. One factor often considered is the master schedule. Three critical aspects of the daily routine dictated by the master schedule are grouping the students, effective use of space, and the role of staff in the learning process (Kruse & Kruse, 1995).

Master schedules can be classified into two basic types: traditional (or conventional) and block (or flexible). There are various block scheduling designs. We will look at the history of the traditional schedule and the types of flexible scheduling models that are emerging today. Examples, advantages, and disadvantages will be presented, as well as sample schedules representing different block formats.

# Traditional Scheduling

Traditional schedules include five to seven 50-minute classes each day. Classes last either one semester or the entire school year. This typical school day is based on the Carnegie Standard Unit (CSU), which was created as a result of studies completed at the turn of the 20th century by the Carnegie Commission. The commission copied studies of factory sites and employee production to determine and improve efficiency. Thus, education evolved into an environment where teachers were expected to produce results in a given amount of time. Quantity of time was correlated with efficient production. This system has remained unchanged in American schools for most of the century.

The CSU refers to the time that a student spends in class for each subject, which is seen as a correlation among completion, passing, and mastery of each academic subject. This unit is applied toward credit hours that a student must earn to graduate. For each class students pass per semester or year, they receive credit toward the total number of credits they need to graduate and enter trade schools and colleges.

In the traditional schedule, the teacher remains stationary while students rotate from classroom to classroom. Each significant subject, such as math or English, is given equal time during the school-year calendar. Nonbasic subjects are given less time. Thus, traditional secondary schools resemble factories in both structure and mood. The difference is that in the work world, employees do not move from station to station every hour, using different materials, following a different set of rules, and having a different boss.

Because students have five to seven classes every day, they consistently have a great deal of homework. The most significant classes, such as English, meet for the entire school year. Therefore, students who fail classes have only an intensive summer class in which to make up the failed classes. Consequently, they often lag behind their peers and never truly catch up.

The traditional schedule determines the structure of the school year for both students and teachers. It affects the use of space and has led to tracking and rigidity in structure, grouping, and teaching (Buckman, King, & Ryan, 1995; Kruse & Kruse, 1995).

# Intensified Block Scheduling

This approach was first introduced in the 1960s and is now making a comeback (Buckman et al., 1995). *Block scheduling* or *intensified block scheduling* is a blanket term used to describe schedules where time is arranged differently from the traditional method. Like traditional scheduling, it depends on the use of the CSU (in other words, time equals success). However, time increments are altered. Students attend fewer classes per day and spend a greater length of time in each class. Because class time is intensified, students can complete a year of course work in either one semester or one quarter. This schedule still meets the credit time allotments of the traditional schedule but in an intensified time period.

Like traditional scheduling, intensified block scheduling incorporates a one-dimensional approach to learning in which students are taught one subject at a time. It also maintains the traditional routine: The teacher actively supplies information, and students passively take it in. Students with experience in both traditional and block scheduling often have a difficult time coping.

Nevertheless, many teachers like intensified block scheduling because it allows room for additional classroom activities, such as varied student grouping, cooperative learning, and lab time. Many say there is an overall decrease in the teacher workload, which theoretically leads to better planning and better teaching. With fewer students, teachers say they can get to know their students better (Buckman et al., 1995).

A reported concern of the intensified block scheduling is how to cope with extended periods. Because tradition has ingrained the 45- to 50-minute class period, changing our mind-set to comply with an extended block is difficult. A good rule-of-thumb is to "change not what you are teaching but how you teach what you teach" every 15 to 20 minutes. Consider the following to help with this new mind-set:

1. Provide an agenda for the class just as if you are attending a meeting. List how much time each activity will require.
2. Discuss the agenda provided with the class and ask if anyone will need extended time for any item on the agenda.
3. Post the agenda or prepare a large chart to put in student view, which can be adjusted each day.
4. Always have consistency in your agenda (class opening, homework review, new homework assignments, projects due, questions from yesterday, today's objective, procedures, etc.). Figure 10.2 presents a sample agenda board.

Suggestions for the 15- to 20-minute periods of activities include:

- Total group instruction
- Small-group instruction
- Using varied grouping activities, such as jigsaw, the shield (chapter 10), and the editing clock (chapter 13)
- Peer tutoring
- Lab activities
- Allowing stretch time every 15 minutes
- Quick snack
- Asking students what will help with on-task behavior

## Flexible Block Scheduling

This system is usually implemented in middle schools, which are not as tightly bound to the CSU as high schools are. In flexible block scheduling, large blocks of time are inserted into the typical structure of the day. Classes last 90 to 112 minutes and generally meet every other day. The key difference in this type of sched-

```
┌─────────────────────────────────────────────────────────────────────┐
│                              Day's Agenda                             │
│   Date: _____        Class: _____         │
│                                                                       │
│   Class Opening                                                       │
│   Homework review                                                     │
│   Homework for next class                                             │
│   Questions from yesterday                                            │
│   Today's objective:                                                  │
│   Procedures to meet objectives                                       │
│     1.  Computer lab                                                  │
│     2.  Seat work                                                     │
│     3.  Small group work                                              │
│     4.  Total class review                                            │
│     5.  Questions                                                     │
│   Future Events                                                       │
│     1.  Projects due _____ │
│     2.  Family night _____ │
│                                                                       │
└─────────────────────────────────────────────────────────────────────┘
```

**FIGURE 10.2**
Day's Agenda.

uling is the use of interdisciplinary, crosscurricular teacher teams and more flexible grouping and regrouping of students.

In the nine-block flexible scheduling model, students have four 94-minute classes each day, which alternate according to a daily schedule of A/B days. The schedule also has three 112-minute blocks, meeting every other day on an alternating daily or weekly schedule with A/B/A days or weeks (Huff, 1995).

## Hybrid Scheduling

Hybrid scheduling combines traditional master scheduling with block scheduling. Classes are offered in block form in all of those academic areas, levels, and grades where there are not set levels to be achieved. Introductory courses are offered in the traditional manner, as are AP and other courses designed to prepare students to pass specific examinations. If students are not comfortable with the block classes or are not doing well in them, they have the option to continue with classes offered in the traditional manner. Classes are offered in both single and double modules for students who do not feel comfortable with the double system or for those courses that do not fit into a student's schedule. Some courses are offered on a semester-long basis, while others are yearlong.

All class assignments are based on students' choices. Schedules are not assigned; rather, students select what they want to take in double and single modules. Students take required courses on an intensive schedule, which leaves them more time to take electives. Thus, they can take a greater variety of classes and get a jump-start on introductory university classes. At a time when society increasingly expects young people to understand a wide variety of information, hybrid scheduling enables students to choose courses that coincide with their interests as well as prepare them for future college and trade school experiences (Boarman & Kirkpatrick, 1995).

## 4 × 4 Scheduling

This scheduling model is based around a 4-period day. Classes are 1 semester long, with 2 semesters per year for 4 years. Thus, it is sometimes referred to as 4 × 2 × 4 scheduling.

Students have a daily schedule of four 90-minute classes each day. This makes the daily school schedule more manageable for both teachers and students. Students can take more classes during a 4-year period than they can with traditional scheduling. However, they have fewer changes among teachers, rules, homework, and peer groups. Grades are distributed during three-quarters of each semester (every 30, 45, and 90 days), and students take a final exam every 90 days. Exams are strictly coordinated so that students have no more than two exams per day during exam weeks (Edwards, 1993, 1995).

## Academic Teams

This model is used by Stinson Middle School in San Antonio, Texas. The school is divided into eight academic teams. Each team has the autonomy to adjust the schedule: five 45-minute classes, one 25-minute advisory time, and two P.E./elective times.

## The British Columbian Model

Schools in British Columbia, Canada, use an amazing schedule format. Students study two subjects intensely for 10 weeks. Each subject is allotted 2½ hours each day (L. V. Rogers, personal communication). The format has several benefits: (a) students have the afternoon hours for work; (b) teachers try alternate instructional strategies because "chalk and talk" does not work for a 2½ hour block; (c) there are fewer transition times each day; (d) longer block periods are better for subjects such as home economics and industrial arts; and (e) longer periods allow room for project work and cooperative learning time. Table 10.1 presents the advantages and disadvantages of each scheduling pattern. Figures 10.3 and 10.4 offer two different examples of how a weekly block schedule may look.

**TABLE 10.1**
Advantages and disadvantages of scheduling options.

| Schedule Format | Advantages | Disadvantages |
|---|---|---|
| Carnegie Standard Unit | • Significant subjects such as math and English are given equal time during a calendar school year. | • Secondary schools resemble factories, both in structure and mood.<br>• Five to seven classes a day create more homework each evening.<br>• Students who fail a course have only an intensive summer class to make up the failed class. |
| Intensified block scheduling | • Schedule allows for additional classroom activities such as varied grouping of students, cooperative learning, and lab time.<br>• There is an overall decrease in the teaching workload.<br>• Teachers have more time for planning and better teaching.<br>• Teachers have fewer classes to prepare and fewer students to work with on both an hourly and a daily basis.<br>• Teachers have an opportunity to get to know students better.<br>• More time is allowed for teaming and crosscurricular teaching.<br>• There are longer lunch periods. | • A teacher who continues to lecture for an extended period will lose class attention.<br>• Students who need a great deal of attention and reinforcement may have trouble.<br>• Some teachers feel that planning is more difficult and requires more time.<br>• Students have fewer opportunities to go on field trips because a day out of school means that students will miss a lot of material. |
| Flexible block scheduling | • Teachers work in teams, some following blocks, others following the traditional schedule.<br>• Practice for longer periods of time is helpful for some students.<br>• Practice can receive more/longer supervision.<br>• Students can put into immediate practice what they have learned. | • Scheduling is difficult for students with short attention spans unless the block is carefully designed.<br>• Overload of information may become a problem.<br>• Once assigned to a team, switching teams is next to impossible. |

*(continued)*

TABLE 10.1
Continued.

| Schedule Format | Advantages | Disadvantages |
|---|---|---|
| Hybrid scheduling | • Intensive schedule allows more time for electives.<br>• Longer periods allow time for students to take college preparatory classes.<br>• This type of scheduling allows an avenue for students who have trouble adjusting to the extended class periods. | • Scheduling may be stigmatizing for the student who takes the traditional schedule and has trouble adjusting to extended periods. |
| 4 × 4 scheduling | • The daily school schedule is more manageable for both teachers and students.<br>• Students can take more classes over a four-year period than they can under a traditional system.<br>• There are fewer changes in teachers, rules, homework, and peer groups.<br>• Scheduling reduces the risk of failure among the average population because students are less likely to fall behind. | • When one class is missed, it is much harder to catch up.<br>• Struggling students may be overloaded with work and concepts. |

FIGURE 10.3
Orange day/blue day.

*Source:* Liz Graf, West Springfield, VA.

| Orange Day | Blue Day |
|---|---|
| 1st period | 2nd period |
| 3rd period | 4th period |
| 5th period* | 5th period* |
| 6th period | 7th period |

Every other day, the schedule alternates: orange/blue/orange/blue, in 1½-hour blocks.

*5th period meets every day for 47 minutes.

| Monday | | Tuesday | | Wednesday | | Thursday | | Friday | |
|---|---|---|---|---|---|---|---|---|---|
| 1st | 50 | 1st | 100 | 2nd | 100 | 1st | 50 | 1st | 50 |
| 2nd | 50 | | | | | 2nd | 50 | 2nd | 50 |
| Homeroom | 25 | Homeroom | 25 | Homeroom | 25 | Homeroom | 25 | Homeroom | 25 |
| 3rd | 50 | Break | 25 | Break | 25 | 3rd | 50 | 3rd | 50 |
| 4th | 50 | 3rd | 100 | 4th | 100 | 4th | 50 | 4th | 50 |
| Lunch | 35 | | | | | Lunch | 35 | Lunch | 35 |
| 5th | 50 | Lunch | 35 | Lunch | 35 | 5th | 50 | 5th | 50 |
| 6th | 50 | 5th | 100 | 6th | 100 | 6th | 50 | 6th | 50 |

**FIGURE 10.4**
Sample schedule (in minutes).
*Source:* Shelly Leiterman, Muskegon, MI.

**TABLE 10.2**
Course offerings by grade.

| Sixth Grade | Seventh Grade | Eighth Grade |
|---|---|---|
| English | English | English |
| Math | Math | Math |
| Science | Science | Science |
| History | History | History |
| Reading | Reading | Reading |
| P.E. | P.E. | P.E. |
| Fine arts | Health/comparative lit (one semester each) | Elective |
| *Elective (computer keyboard; 12 weeks each) | Elective | Elective |

The schedule at Sul Ross Middle School in Northside Independent School District, San Antonio, Texas, provides a total picture of blocking in progress. Table 10.2 lists course offerings by grade, Figure 10.4 demonstrates a sample schedule, Table 10.3 shows sample block lesson plans, and Figure 10.5 displays a monthly calendar.

## Looping

Looping provides students with the same teacher or set of teachers for a 2-year period. Looping could be implemented within or without a block type schedule. Examples of the loop would be when one teacher has a class for 4th and 5th grades,

**TABLE 10.3**
Sample block lesson plans.

| Plans | Minutes |
|---|---|
| **Beginning of the year:** | |
| D.R.S.—2 | 10 |
| Novel study—read chapter<br>1. Teacher read (or group/paired/individual)<br>2. Discussion | 30 |
| Minilesson (How to choose a book) | 10 |
| Book talk | 5 |
| Choose books/read silently | 20 |
| Group share topic: Why I picked out this book (give three reasons) | 10 |
| Collect materials | 5 |
| Total | 90 |
| **Later:** | |
| D.R.S.—2 | 10 |
| Read aloud | 10 |
| Book talk | 5 |
| Minilesson | 15 |
| S.S.R. with self-selected novels | 20 |
| Response to what was read today | 5 |
| Cooperative learning reinforcing minilesson | 20 |
| Collect materials | 5 |
| Total | 90 |
| **R. W. with writing:** | |
| D.R.S.—2 | 10 |
| Read aloud | 10 |
| Book talk | 5 |
| S.S.R. with self-selected novels | 20 |
| Writing—if using prompt, discuss prompt/model; exchange letters if student/student | 40 |
| Collect materials | 5 |
| Total | 90 |

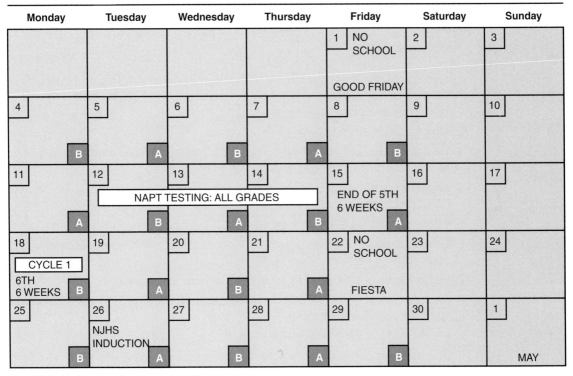

**A** and **B** indicate alternating day schedules.

FIGURE 10.5
Monthly calendar.

or, at the secondary level, when the English teacher has the same group of students for 9th- and 10th-grade English.

I have seen secondary schools who "loop" with the guidance counselors. One counselor has Q through Z students each year. This allows for the counselor to become acquainted with a family of children, learn about the family, and keep that "family" throughout the secondary years.

As in any situation when everything is working well, everyone is pleased. If all are not pleased, the "marriage" could be long.

However, in looping with teachers, skill building (scope and sequence) would not be interrupted. Just like life, a good match is super for both teacher and student, and the reverse is also true.

# Starting a Flexible Blocking Schedule

Here are a few suggestions to consider when moving from a traditional schedule to a flexible one:

1. Get full support from the faculty. Invite teacher administrators and counselors from other flex schools to talk to faculty and parents before the change. Hold inservices and observation periods.
2. Give faculty members an element of choice.
3. Be patient, positive, and honest. Prepare students and staff members for stress as the scheduling changes.
4. Begin with a trial period to see if the school really wants to implement the new scheduling style.
5. Administrators must be very supportive of the block scheduling model.
6. School should provide departmental workshops so that time is used wisely and creatively.
7. Include special educators in schedule planning and decisions.
8. Be sure that A/B days are always consecutive. Don't have a flex scheduling holiday between them.
9. Allow more planning time for teachers.
10. Plan courses for students wisely and offer enough classes so that students don't take courses just to fill time gaps.
11. Include the whole school in the new schedule, not just selected classes.
12. Be aware of problems concerning special education students and teachers.
13. Change back to traditional scheduling if block scheduling does not work.
14. Break the blocks into small teachable chunks.
15. Have alternative plans. Be flexible and organized. Vary your activities.
16. Listen to the opinions of students, parents, and other staff members.
17. Know the parameters of your school's curriculum. Try to anticipate how things will turn out. Ask for help.

# Block Scheduling and Special Education

General educators consistently mention the positive aspects of block scheduling, such as more time to address themes or topics, better teaching, more cooperative learning, and more time for hands-on classroom projects. Negative issues concern additional planning time, inconsistency due to chunks of time between classes, and difficulties for students who need to make up classes and homework.

However, research hardly addresses the effects of block scheduling on students in special education. One issue that concerns many teachers is the amount of time students spend in each class. This can mean a flood of new materials and new activities, which may be too much for some students. In addition, they can be confused about which classes meet each day. Special education teachers report that they require a greater variety of planning than general education teachers do. In short, many special education teachers feel that block scheduling is great for general education students but not recommended for special education students.

A *curriculum matrix* is a visual of classes offered. It can be one way for teachers to help students with disabilities cope with block scheduling, although it is also suitable for traditional scheduling. Figure 10.6 illustrates a unit or theme curriculum matrix.

## Methods of Scheduling within the Master Schedule

Once a school decides on a master schedule, it must place students within it. Schools usually use one of three approaches: computer scheduling, self-scheduling, or hand scheduling. No matter what kind of schedule administrators choose, special and general educators should provide input about class selection for students with disabilities. Hand scheduling is the most common approach, and 91 percent of general educators and 93 percent of special education teachers report that they assist in the scheduling process for special students.

*Computer scheduling.* Because a computer can carry the workload of many staff members, numerous schools have changed to computerized master scheduling. A computer's memory can store a large number of parameters, so this approach helps administrators process and rapidly print individual student schedules.

In spite of these advantages, most available programs present problems for students. For example, computerized scheduling prohibits the school from selecting particular general education teachers to work with an included student. It also makes grouping students with mild disabilities into particular resource classes or general classes virtually impossible. In addition, the computer makes it especially difficult to meet the individual needs of special students. For example, it may not be flexible enough to schedule the student into morning rather than afternoon sections, alternate required courses with electives, or provide resources for academic relief.

*Self-scheduling.* A number of schools let students self-schedule all classes within the master schedule. Even though numerous schools succeed using this method, problems do occur. Kelly (1979) surveyed approximately 700 students to determine which variables most influenced them during scheduling. The students named parents, friends, counselors, teachers, and written information as variables, ranking parents as the most influential variable in self-scheduling. Kelly recommended that schools change preregistration advising to coincide with parental and peer advice, change written materials, make self-scheduling procedures more rigid, and consider self-scheduling for juniors and computer scheduling for freshmen and sophomores.

Kelly failed, however, to identify other problems inherent in self-scheduling, such as class overcrowding, popularity differences among teachers, and the

**Adaptations for**  Sally Sample

**Class:**  Sixth-grade science          **Teacher:**  Mr. Demo

**Unit or Theme:**  Energy              **Date:**  January 1997

| **Topics** | **Class Activities** | **Sally's Participation** |
|---|---|---|
| 1. Static electricity | 1. Group work | Yes for most group activities |
| 2. Current electricity | 2. Book work | Look at pictures in text |
| 3. Circuits | • Read text | Have other related books read |
| 4. Home uses (home meter, etc.) | • Answer questions | to her |
| 5. Energy conversion | 3. Experiments | Yes for all experiments |
|  | 4. Project on circuits | Adapted project |
|  | • Orally present project |  |
|  | 5. Quizzes and tests | Adapted test on key concepts |

**Key Concepts**

1. Be careful with electricity (around plugs and outlets).

2. Vocabulary/sight words:

   caution
   danger
   electricity
   outlet
   plug
   shock
   on/off
   power

3. Appliances use electricity. Learn how to use some simple appliances to turn on and off (lights, radio, tape recorder, VCR, computer, etc.).

4. Save energy by turning off appliances when done.

**Adaptations**

1. Make a scrapbook of electrical appliances (from a catalog).

2. Sort pictures (electrical and nonelectrical).

3. Sight word activities:

   • Listen to sight words on language master.

   • Match sight words.

   • Match pictures depicting sight words.

   • Match sight words to picture.

   • Read sight words to a peer.

4. Operate appliances. Locate on/off or power control buttons, plug, outlet, etc.

5. Listen to books read about this topic. Get them from elementary school library or REMC.

6. Assist in making a simple light circuit board.

7. Demonstrate the use of circuit board for presentation with guided questions from paraprofessional.

8. Take an activity test based on key concepts.

**FIGURE 10.6**

Unit or theme curriculum matrix.

*Source:* Developed by Bonnie Jackson.

percentage of students selecting inappropriate classes. Most important, he omitted the self-scheduling of special education students from the survey.

If a school uses self-scheduling, teachers must carefully consider the placement of the student with mild disabilities and use the following suggestions to make the process go more smoothly:

1. A resource teacher should be familiar with the overall master plan and the scheduling of all classes.
2. Each student with mild disabilities should be assigned to a resource teacher during the self-scheduling process. The school might impose some limitations on special students. For example, the school might designate the resource period or choose specific general teachers to teach such students, leaving the students with only the option of period selection.
3. The school should give students with mild disabilities a checklist of required courses before registration.

*Hand scheduling.* Many American schools design the master schedule by having an administrator handwrite the components of the school's day into the master plan. Even though hand scheduling is frustrating, tedious, and time consuming, it is the most efficient way to schedule the student with special needs. Whatever scheduling method a school uses, it should hand-schedule all special-needs students into the master plan.

Students with disabilities need a great deal of individual attention, much of which is mandated by the IEP. Selecting appropriate classes for the student with mild disabilities requires much attention. Whoever schedules the special student must consider the personality of the student, the personality of the teacher, and existing conflicts between students. Potential problems can be avoided through hand scheduling.

Hand scheduling also allows administrators to select one or two teachers to serve as the home base for the student with special needs. Such an arrangement allows the general and special class teachers more time together to prepare instruction. If a school has selected a team-teaching model, hand scheduling also allows for closer grouping of students for whom special education teachers need to provide consultation or teaming with general teachers. At the same time, hand scheduling allows the scheduler to select teachers who understand that students learn through different modes, at different rates, and with different strategies. On the other hand, hand scheduling allows general classroom teachers to say which types of students with special needs they feel they can adequately teach. By carefully selecting a common core of teachers to serve all students, the scheduler reduces the number of teachers with whom a resource teacher has to communicate. Also, when a common core of general teachers serves one grade level of inclusive students, the scheduler can plan common off-periods to allow for greater collaboration among teachers. Finally, hand scheduling can reduce the number of resource teachers with whom the general teacher must communicate and thus reduce the general teacher's paperwork.

Some disadvantages exist with hand scheduling for inclusive students even though these are outweighed by the advantages. For example, hand scheduling costs more time, money, and staff effort. The students' schedules and class rolls for the teachers must be typed, and both the scheduling and the typing must be done in the summer. Also, staff members should complete the hand scheduling of inclusive students before they schedule general students.

## Specific Considerations in Scheduling

After a school decides which type of master schedule to use for adapting the inclusive student's learning environment, it must try to avoid specific scheduling problems. Table 10.4 provides a checklist for avoiding such problems. Teachers and administrators should note that most planning problems can be avoided if all groups keep the lines of communication open.

The following suggestions, although not appropriate for every school's situation, give schools and teachers specific guidelines that will improve the outcome from preparing the master schedule.

1. Maintain manageable class size in resource class.
2. Place resource students taking the same course with the same general education teacher.

**TABLE 10.4**
Checklist for scheduling students with mild disabilities.

|  | Yes | No |
|---|---|---|
| 1. Include resource classes on the master schedule as a regular class offering. | _____ | _____ |
| 2. Obtain input from resource teacher about |  |  |
| • Student groupings desired (ability and personality) | _____ | _____ |
| • Selection of regular teachers, especially teachers to be avoided |  |  |
| • Other individual needs of mildly disabled students | _____ | _____ |
| 3. Obtain input from general education teachers about categories of students desired. | _____ | _____ |
| 4. Obtain input from counselors or teachers about peers who need to be separated from one another because of discipline problems. | _____ | _____ |
| 5. Obtain input from counselors or teachers about peers who need to be scheduled together for tutoring or assistance. | _____ | _____ |
| 6. Obtain input from resource teacher about possible conflicts between student's request and IEP. | _____ | _____ |

3. Group students in each resource class by grade or ability levels. For example, four students who read poorly and need extra help but are scattered among three ninth-grade classes should be in the same resource class.

4. Include special education teachers in the preparation of the school's master schedule so that they can prevent scheduling problems and represent special students' needs.

5. Schedule off-periods for special education teachers around the resource schedules of students with special needs.

6. Schedule one-period elective offerings concurrently.

7. Select effective general education teachers who are successful in working with special-needs and at-risk children to serve as home-base teachers.

8. Notify general education teachers when schedules are complete so that they have time to select materials and prepare individual assignments.

9. Balance sections throughout the day. If courses are taught on different levels, sections should be available in both the morning and the afternoon.

10. Plan morning sections for vocational students, co-op students, and athletes.

11. Alternate academic courses with basic and college preparatory sections.

12. Match student's learning style and teacher's teaching style.

13. Schedule common planning periods for general education teachers and resource teachers.

14. Provide a balance in class size in home-base classes.

15. Provide basic instruction for primary-level students in the morning.

16. Use hand scheduling for resource students.

17. Allow all teachers who will serve as home-base teachers or special education teachers to help plan the schedule collectively to encourage their feeling of ownership.

18. Consider the needs of general education teachers.

No matter what type of master schedule a school chooses, it must build some flexibility into that schedule for the benefit of students with mild disabilities and the teachers who work with them.

## Scheduling Problems and Suggested Solutions

More than 50 percent of educators feel that problems are created when students with disabilities move back and forth between the general class setting and the resource setting. We can divide these problems into three groups: (a) transition concerns after the initial identification of a disabling condition, (b) transition concerns as students move back and forth between the resource class and the general class (home base), and (c) instructional or class-transitional problems related to transition within the general education class.

The physical environment for a student can be disrupted if transitions are not smooth. Tables 10.5 through 10.7 give examples and solutions for each concern.

**TABLE 10.5**
Transition concerns after disabling condition is identified.

| Problem | Suggested Solutions |
|---|---|
| Student does not want to go to a resource setting. | • Talk with the student about focus, questions, needs.<br>• Explain why the student is going to the resource class.<br>• Slowly phase the student into the new setting.<br>• Assign a student peer to answer questions.<br>• Review concerns after first visit.<br>• If the student does not respond positively, evaluate the situation and consider consultation services. |
| Student does not want to leave a self-contained or partial resource setting to go to the regular class setting. | • Talk with the student concerning fears, questions, needs.<br>• Discuss the new classroom before placement.<br>• Explain why the student is going to the regular class.<br>• Slowly phase the student into the new setting.<br>• Complete the checklist for rules and routines with the student (Figure 8.1)<br>• Stay in close contact with the student after placement.<br>• Assign a regular class buddy. |
| Initial transition from resource to regular setting is difficult. | • Talk with the student to develop a clearer understanding of the problem.<br>• Talk to the teacher to obtain a different or second view of the problem.<br>• Go over the rules and routines checklist with the student (Figure 8.1).<br>• Assign a buddy. |
| Student feels lack of support during the initial change. | • Always have a scheduled time to visit with the student.<br>• Provide a bonding teacher for the student.<br>• Have regular and special education teachers work closely together to discuss progress or problems.<br>• Develop a mainstreaming checklist to be used periodically. |

*Source:* Adapted from Wood, J. W. (1991). *Project SHARE*. Richmond, VA: Author.

**TABLE 10.6**

Transition concerns as students move between the resource class and the regular education class.

| Problem | Suggested Solutions |
|---|---|
| Student takes too much time traveling to room assignments. | • Check to see if sufficient time is allotted.<br>• Provide a core of teachers in one area of building to cut traveling to a minimum.<br>• Assign resource teacher to a certain number of grades and locate the resource class within that grade cluster.<br>• Talk to students to see if they have an answer to the problem.<br>• Assign a buddy if the student approves. |
| Student is always late to resource/regular class. | • Check to see if the student is embarrassed about going into the special education class.<br>• Provide an alternate plan that alleviates the embarrassment.<br>• Allow the student to return to the locker with a pass after checking into the class. |
| Student cannot cope with activity in the hallways. | • Allow the student to travel between bells/periods.<br>• Allow the student to go to next class a minute or so before the bell. |
| The special and regular classes are too far apart. | • Do not isolate special education classes.<br>• Allow extra time for the student to reduce the stress of rushing. |
| Movement of children during classes disrupts the regular class. | • Movement should be made between periods/bells.<br>• Have the student collect materials for the move before the beginning of class.<br>• Before movement, seat the special education student close to the class door. |
| Teachers cannot keep track of individual students. | • Provide a seating chart of the class.<br>• Write into the lesson plan who will leave and when they will leave. |

*Source:* Adapted from Wood, J. W. (1991). *Project SHARE.* Richmond, VA: Author.

**TABLE 10.7**
Transition concerns within the regular education class.

| Problem | Suggested Solutions |
|---|---|
| Student is unable to cope with changes when entering the room after returning from resource class. | • Have an assigned seat so the student will know immediately where to go.<br>• Have an assignment on the desk for the student.<br>• Assign a buddy to work with the student.<br>• Move close to the student to signal reassurance.<br>• Have a specific schedule for the student. |
| Teacher has difficulty integrating students back into the curriculum when they reenter the room. | • As soon as the student enters the class, review for the whole class what you are doing and where you are—a checkpoint for the lesson.<br>• If taking notes, provide a copy for the student.<br>• Use a buddy.<br>• Have a consistent class structure. |
| Student forgets to bring the proper textbooks, homework, or materials to class. | • Provide folders for each student in which to keep papers that are often lost.<br>• Provide a checklist for the student for materials needed.<br>• Place this checklist on the locker door or in front of the text notebook. |
| Special-needs student has difficulty functioning in groups. | • Assign a peer buddy.<br>• Keep groups small.<br>• Assign a specific task that is appropriate academically and socially for the student.<br>• Provide a checklist of activities or expectations. |
| Student needs to be excused from certain class projects, assignments. | • Be clear with the regular teacher about what the student should be excused from. For example, do not count off for spelling for student who has difficulty with or a disability in spelling.<br>• Provide alternative or more appropriate assignments for the student. |
| There is a lack of communication between regular and special education teachers or lack of time for communication. | • Use a mainstreaming checklist to communicate student progress.<br>• Keep lines of communication open.<br>• Have resource teachers touch base with one another on a r egular basis.<br>• Schedule common planning periods. |

| Problem | Suggested Solutions |
|---|---|
| Students become frustrated by the regular class subject matter. | • Check about the appropriateness of the subject matter.<br>• Explain to the teacher that the student may not be on grade level.<br>• Work closely to provide appropriate instructional adaptations.<br>• Be sure that the student experiences success. |
| Regular teacher expresses concern about a different standard and expectation for the special education student. | • Realize that all students should have individualized expectations.<br>• Help teachers to see that expectations that are too high do not best serve the student.<br>• Provide support for the teacher in helping him or her with the how-to's of working with the special education student. |
| Special education students cannot complete assigned work in the time allotted. | • Check to see if the work is appropriate for the student's functional level.<br>• Provide additional time.<br>• Reduce the amount of work.<br>• Realize that all students cannot do the same amount of work. |
| Different teacher expectations pose a problem for the special education student. | • Make a list of each period with each teacher's expectations for the student.<br>• Help students understand expectations.<br>• Help teachers coordinate expectations.<br>• Check to see that expectations are reasonable. |
| Student has difficulty performing on grade level. | • Realize that in reality many students do not perform on the grade level where they are placed.<br>• Individualize for each student.<br>• Provide appropriate adaptations for each student. |
| Regular class teacher feels overworked because of the range of functional levels within the class. | • Provide the teacher with adaptations for group instruction, such as graphic organizers.<br>• Team teach or coteach with the regular teacher.<br>• Help develop adaptations for the teacher. |

*(continued)*

## TABLE 10.7
Continued.

| Problem | Suggested Solutions |
|---|---|
| Special education student is unable to get along with regular students. | • Develop school-related social skills for the student.<br>• Evaluate the problem to find the true source.<br>• Work with the regular student if necessary.<br>• Teach coping skills to the special student.<br>• Work out a coping plan. |
| Groups/class lesson is already in session when the special education student arrives. | • Have a consistent class structure so the student, upon reentry, will know what to expect.<br>• Do a lesson checkup and review what you have covered and where you are.<br>• Use a lecture outline and refer to the outline to orientate the student.<br>• Provide a buddy. |
| Student misses work from the regular class when attending the resource class. | • Do not hold the student accountable for work missed, especially if it is for a whole period, such as a science class.<br>• Provide a set of class notes.<br>• Tape-record the section that was missed.<br>• Remember that the student cannot function like the average student. Consequently, the student will have great difficulty with the class work when present and even more difficulty when not present.<br>• Try not to doubly punish the student for having special learning needs. |
| Student/teacher has difficulty remembering when it is time to go to resource class. | • Never embarrass the student in front of peers by announcing it is time to go to special education.<br>• Remember that the secondary-level student is extremely sensitive about going to a resource setting.<br>• Write on your lesson plan book and on the seating chart the day and time when a student should go to a resource class.<br>• If you realize that it is time for a resource class, quietly remind the student.<br>• Respect a student's need for confidentiality.<br>• Remember that this issue may seem small to an adult and large to a child. |

| Problem | Suggested Solutions |
|---|---|
| Special education student is embarrassed when entering the regular education class. | • Try to have entry times between bells/periods.<br>• Have a specific task or assignment for the student.<br>• Do not call attention to the student entering the class.<br>• Provide a seat assignment that allows the student to enter the classroom discreetly. |
| Regular education teachers display negative attitudes regarding special-needs students. | • Try to schedule students into classes where they are wanted.<br>• Provide strong support for the teacher.<br>• Remember that when you see anger, the hidden emotion is fear.<br>• Remember the fear may indicate a feeling of not knowing what to do. |
| The class pace is too fast for the special-needs student. | • Check the class level to see if it is appropriate.<br>• Develop adaptations for the student.<br>• Above all else, work to help the student not be frustrated.<br>• Remember that setting up a student for failure serves no one. |
| Special education student feels unwelcome in regular education class. | • Talk to students about their feelings.<br>• Develop an action plan with the teacher, child, and parent.<br>• Assign a peer buddy. |
| Proliferation of specialists serving the student results in splintered services and greater scheduling difficulties. | • Carefully plan schedules with children in mind.<br>• Assign specialists by age groups or IEP objectives.<br>• Closely monitor the number of times a student is removed.<br>• Refer to the IEP committee if the success of the student is in jeopardy because of our zealousness to serve the child. |
| Special education students must leave subjects they enjoy or where they experience success (such as art, music, physical education, assembly) to go to resource class. | • Allow special students to attend special subject areas.<br>• Remember that these areas are frequently stress-free and offer opportunities for success.<br>• Arrange resource for a different period on days when special subjects are offered.<br>• Remember that the student who is pulled from a special subject or class is being punished for needing special services.<br>• Develop the student's schedule for the student's convenience, not the teacher's. |

*Source:* Adapted from Wood, J. W. (1991). *Project SHARE*. Richmond, VA: Author.

# Scheduling within the Resource Setting

Although the general class setting is the placement choice for most students with disabilities, numerous special education students must, for instructional purposes, go to the resource setting. The resource room has become a viable alternative to self-contained placements for educating the student with disabilities in the least restrictive environment. D'Alonzo, D'Alonzo, and Mauser (1979) describe the five basic types of resource rooms typically found in schools. As of 2000, these selections are still being used:

1. The *categorical* resource room focuses on one primary type of disability.
2. The *cross-categorical* resource room groups clusters of two or more categories of children.
3. The *noncategorical* resource room serves students with mild or severe learning and behavior disabilities with the possible inclusion of nondisabled students.
4. The *specific-skills* resource room targets a specific curriculum area or deficit (such as reading or mathematics).
5. The *itinerant* resource room is a mobile nonstationary resource environment that travels to the geographic area when and where the specialized education services are needed.

Resource rooms have distinct advantages for students with mild disabilities. Assuming that the teachers have a positive attitude toward inclusive students, resource rooms will enhance each student's sense of self-worth. Resource rooms also make it possible for students to build and maintain relationships with nondisabled peers and have nondisabled role and age models. The resource room gives students more opportunities for intentional learning, more provisions for incidental learning (media, field trips, guest speakers, and group interaction), and more occasions for the resource teacher to reinforce general class work. In fact, the resource room model is designed around constant and positive reinforcement and feedback. It also provides the inclusive student with additional time for completing classwork, homework, or tests; an environment free of anxiety; alternative materials, learning stations, and equipment not available in the general classroom; and an environment more easily adaptable to special behaviors such as short attention spans and hyperactivity.

According to Hart (1981), scheduling within the resource room, or intraresource scheduling, requires close attention to structure. Children who have limited attention spans, perseverate in their activities, or have difficulty transferring learning from one activity to another can all benefit from a carefully developed schedule. Hart lists three major factors for teachers to consider when developing the resource room schedule:

1. Present the most difficult subject early in the day while students are fresh. For example, elementary schools commonly schedule reading and language arts

during the first time blocks of the day. Secondary schools should also consider placing subjects requiring the most concentration during the morning periods.

2. Make schedules consistent so that students can become familiar with the day's events. Teachers should discuss schedule changes, such as a field trip or a guest speaker, before they occur.

3. After students become thoroughly comfortable with the schedule, teachers should deliberately alter it once in a while. In this way, they can help their students become more comfortable with change.

These considerations apply primarily to students who spend a large percentage of the school day in the resource room. Nevertheless, structure in the resource room is also important for those who attend class there only occasionally and spend the remainder of their day in the general academic setting. Such students also need an established routine. For example, a teacher might require students to check their assignment box for the day's activities when they enter the classroom rather than wait for the resource teacher to tell them what to do. Also, students need to keep materials and books in a definite place and maintain separate notebooks for each subject. In addition, they should follow set procedures when completing homework, studying for tests, and taking tests within the resource room. Following a daily routine helps the student, who often feels anxious and frustrated, to develop good work habits and a sense of stability and security. Figure 10.7 gives two examples of student schedules in the resource room.

---

**Student A: Second-Period Resource**

| | |
|---|---|
| 9:00–9:10: | Teacher reviews spelling words. |
| 9:10–9:20: | Student studies words. |
| 9:20–9:30: | Teacher calls out words. |
| 9:30–9:50: | Student defines words and writes sentence for each word. |
| 9:50–9:55: | Teacher reviews assignments for next period and homework assignments with student. |

**Student B: Third-Period Resource**

| | |
|---|---|
| 10:00–10:15: | Teacher explains English homework. |
| 10:15–10:40: | Student works in group with other students on English homework and assignment. |
| 10:40–10:55: | Student works independently at computer station on English exercise. |

---

FIGURE 10.7
Sample resource room schedules.

# Scheduling within Inclusive Environments

As resource students move into general classes, teachers must make numerous adjustments in their teaching and adapt the learning environment for those students. A little preparation will make scheduling flow smoothly.

1. Before beginning a new task, give the students a warning; simply announce to the class that in 5 minutes the old assignment will end and a new task will begin.
2. Give instructions in short, direct sentences.
3. List the instructions sequentially on the board.
4. Give a short handout to students so that they will know the expectations for the period.
5. At the end of the period, hand out written assignments with the expected date of completion noted.
6. Be sure that each student understands all assignments.
7. Give a copy of the day's schedule and assignments to the resource teacher so that they may be reinforced.

# GROUPING FOR INSTRUCTION

Grouping procedures vary from school to school and from teacher to teacher. Many teachers feel that grouping within the classroom creates an even heavier workload. However, children do learn at different rates and therefore do not always learn best in one large group. According to Affleck, Lowenbraun, and Archer (1980), because of "the diversity of academic skills found within any general classroom, small-group instruction is more appropriate than whole-group instruction for basic academic subjects" (p. 152). Suydam (1985) found that, in teaching mathematics, achievement is significantly higher for students taught in individual and team modes as compared to whole-group instruction. Key variables were the ability to self- or partner-check and frequent mastery checks.

The issue of class size is much discussed within education today. This has been a continuing issue. According to the National Association of Elementary School Principals, a teacher should be assigned no more than 15 students per class up to the third grade. However, the U.S. Department of Education reports that the average teaching load is approximately 21 to 1 (26 to 1, factoring in all professional staff positions). The state of California reports a 33 to 1 ratio, and in some cases 39 to 1 or 40 to 1 (Kelly, 1990).

These increases in class size usually dictate whole-group instruction. But whole-group instruction does not provide the best benefits to students academically: questions go unattended, easily distracted students remain off task, and students become lost in the masses. Instruction continues to move along, leaving students with special needs and those at risk lost and confused, which in turn means that many of these students drop out of school.

Fortunately, there are a variety of ways to group students that will help teachers individualize within whole-group situations. Here are some examples.

## Creative Grouping

When teachers group students, students become labeled. This can present a problem: No matter what the teacher calls the group, all children know which ones are bright, average, and slow. Creative grouping, however, allows for a diversity of academic skills, thus eliminating labels and giving students the freedom to move among groups.

Creative grouping may be used at either the secondary or elementary level. Teachers set up the groups according to academic subject and then break the subject into specific objectives or skills. They assign a student to a creative group based on the specific skill that the student needs to work on. No one is locked into a group because each student moves into another group after mastering the skill. Figure 10.8 shows a chart for a creative mathematics group that allows a student to complete a skill, keep a personal record, and then move on.

Creative grouping may include at least three variations, all of them working simultaneously: a learning station, a seatwork station, and a small-group instructional station. When class begins, the teacher color codes or numbers the stations and gives each student a direction card or uses a list on the board to indicate the station the student should use first. Remember, a student who masters a given skill can enter a new creative group.

| | Jason | Anna | Scott | Valerie | Eddie |
|---|---|---|---|---|---|
| Identifies penny, nickel, and dime by name | | | | | |
| Identifies penny, nickel, and dime by value | | | | | |
| Identifies quarter, half-dollar, and dollar by name | | | | | |
| Identifies quarter, half-dollar, and dollar by value | | | | | |

FIGURE 10.8
Chart for a creative mathematics group.

## Interest Grouping

Interest grouping is a method of grouping students based on their specific interests. For example, in reading, students may select the same types of books to read. In social studies, students may be interested in the same period of history. These students may be grouped by interest and develop a series of questions, review a specific book, or research a certain period.

## Research Grouping

Research groups can be established by giving each group a specific problem to research. Each group then reports back to the class with the results of the research. A checklist may list specific research questions to be answered and possible sources to investigate.

## Cooperative Learning

*Cooperative learning,* a worthwhile grouping strategy for heterogeneous student populations, is a method of structuring the class where students work together to achieve a shared academic goal (Schniedewind & Salend, 1987). Students become accountable for their own academic behaviors as well as those of their peers. Although structured procedures for implementing cooperative learning within a class are reported in the literature, teachers may choose to develop the type of structure that best suits their teaching styles and the group's learning style.

*The teacher's role in cooperative learning.* The teacher's role in developing a cooperative learning environment includes making decisions, monitoring and intervening, setting tasks and positive interdependence, and evaluating and processing (Johnson, Johnson, & Holubec, 1987).

First, teachers decide what size of group will be most appropriate for the class and which students will be assigned to each group. The room must be arranged to facilitate group interactions, and all material must be organized and developed. The roles for each group member must be assigned. These roles include a summarizer, who restates the major conclusions or answers that the group has arrived at; a checker, who ensures that all members can explain an answer or a conclusion; an accuracy coach, who corrects any mistakes in another member's explanations or summaries; and an elaboration seeker, who asks other members to relate material they previously learned (Johnson & Johnson, 1986).

Second, teachers monitor and intervene during the cooperative learning lesson. During this stage, teachers monitor the students' behavior, observing each group member to see what problems are developing. Teachers also provide task assistance, clarify instruction, review important aspects of the lesson, and answer questions. Intervention may become necessary if a teacher sees that a student does not have the collaborative skills needed for working in a group. The teacher also provides closure for the lesson, summarizing the major points covered (Johnson & Johnson, 1986).

Third, teachers set tasks and foster positive interdependence. They should clearly explain the academic task and the lesson's objectives. They then structure positive goal interdependence, explaining the group goal and the importance of working collaboratively. The accountability of each individual must be structured, maximizing the learning of each group member. Group tasks must be structured. The criteria for success must be clearly stated and the desired behavior for each group member clearly defined (Johnson & Johnson, 1986).

Fourth, teachers evaluate the learning outcomes for each student as well as how the group functioned as a whole (Johnson & Johnson, 1986). Teachers must be clear about individual and group expectations at the beginning of the activity so that each student will understand the goal.

*Tips for implementing cooperative learning.* Cooperative learning is a carefully planned process. Before implementing it, teachers should consider the tips in Figure 10.9.

*Formats for implementing cooperative learning.* The beginning teacher can use four basic formats to implement cooperative learning: peer teaching, group projects, the jigsaw, and the shield.

Teachers should not overlook one of a school's most valuable resources—its students. Within class groups, teachers can assign peer tutors to assist students who are having difficulty with the content of a lesson. For example, peer tutors may record assignments so that the student with mild disabilities can listen to the tape for extra reinforcement. Peer tutors can also work one-on-one using a flannel board, manipulating real or paper money, and helping a student with special needs at the computer. At the secondary level, peer tutors can help small groups of students with disabilities look up their chapter study questions, work on class work or homework assignments, and participate in study or review sessions. A peer can also call out words during group or individual spelling tests. Because students with disabilities often need to have their words called out more slowly, using peers and grouping for spelling tests makes such an adaptation possible.

Peer tutoring has numerous advantages: facilitating the interaction between nondisabled students and students with disabilities; making use of children's insights about how to teach recently learned or newly presented content to another student; making learning more cooperative and less competitive; and providing experiences related to living in a democracy, to caring, and to being cared for (Cartwright, Cartwright, Ward, & Willoughby-Herb, 1981).

In a project group, "Students pool their knowledge and skills to create a project or complete an assignment" (Schniedewind & Salend, 1987, p. 22). All students are included in the process, and motivation is heightened. Each student contributes to the group project based on his or her skill level. But if the group project is not structured, the burden of task completion may be shouldered by only one or a few students.

The jigsaw format is an adaptation of the project group format in which "each group member is assigned a task that must be completed for the group to reach its goal" (Schniedewind & Salend, 1987, p. 22). The teacher has more specific task input, and more individual accountability is established. Here are the steps for structuring a jigsaw lesson (Johnson et al., 1987, p. 57):

**Some Ways to Ensure Positive Interdependence**

1. One pencil, paper, or book given to a group.
2. One paper written from a group.
3. Task divided into jobs; it can't be finished unless all help.
4. Pass one paper around the group; each member must do a part.
5. Jigsaw materials; each person learns a part and then teaches it to the group.
6. A reward (like bonus points) if everyone in the group succeeds.

**Some Ways to Ensure Individual Accountability**

1. Students do the work first to bring to the group.
2. Pick one student at random to orally answer questions studied by the group.
3. Everyone writes, then certifies correctness of all papers; you pick one to grade.
4. Listen and watch as students take turns orally rehearsing information.
5. Assign jobs or roles to each student.
6. Students get bonus points if all group members do well individually.

**Some Expected Behaviors to Tell Students (Pick four or five that fit)**

1. Everyone contributes and helps.
2. Everyone listens to others with care.
3. Encourage everyone in your group to participate.
4. Praise helpful actions or good ideas.
5. Ask for help if you need it.
6. Check to make sure everyone understands.
7. Stay with your group.
8. Use quiet voices.

**Some Things to Do When Monitoring**

1. Give immediate feedback and reinforcement for learning.
2. Encourage oral elaboration and explanation.
3. Reteach or add to teaching.
4. Determine what group skills students have mastered.
5. Encourage and praise use of good group skills.
6. Determine what group skills to teach students next.
7. Find out interesting things about your students.

FIGURE 10.9

Tips for implementing cooperative learning.

*Source:* Johnson, R. T., Johnson, D. W., & Holubec, E. J. (Eds.). (1987). *Structuring cooperative learning: Lesson plans for teachers* (pp. 55–56). Edina, MN: Interaction. Copyright 1987 by Interaction Book Company. Reprinted by permission.

**Some Ways to Process Group Interactions**

**Small Groups**

1. What did your group do well in working together today?
2. What could your group do even better tomorrow?

**Whole Class**

1. What skills did we do well in working together today?
2. What skills could we do even better tomorrow?

**Individual (Self)**

1. What did you do well in helping your group today?
2. What could you do even better tomorrow?

**Individual (Other)**

1. Name one thing a group member did which helped your group.
2. Tell your group members that you appreciated their help.

FIGURE 10.9
Continued.

1. Distribute a set of materials to each group. The set needs to be divisible into the number of members of the group (2, 3, or 4 parts). Give each member one part of the set of materials.

2. Assign students the individualistic tasks of (a) learning and becoming an expert on their material and (b) planning how to teach the material to the other members of the group.

3. Assign each student the cooperative task of meeting and sharing ideas about how best to teach the material with someone who is a member of another learning group and has learned the same material. This is known as an "expert pair" or "expert group."

4. Assign students the cooperative tasks of (a) teaching their area of expertise to the other group members and (b) learning the material being taught by the other members.

5. Assess students' degree of mastery of all the material. Reward the groups whose members all reach the present criteria of excellence.

The jigsaw and the shield are further developed for the reader in Figures 10.10 and 10.11 (Laham, 2000).

# The Jigsaw

**Step # 1: Personal Reflections**

Individually        Write        _____ Minutes

**Step # 2: Sharing Ideas—Small Groups**

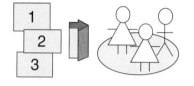  

Same Color        Record on your number        _____ Minutes/Questions

**Step # 3: Combining Ideas**

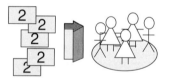   

Same Number        Review & Clarify        _____ Minutes        Charts

**Step # 4: Reporting Out—Whole Group**

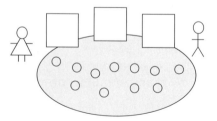

FIGURE 10.10

The jigsaw.

*Source:* Laham, S. L. (2000). *Working together: A practical guide for facilitators.* Reprinted with permission.

| | |
|---|---|
| Title: | **The Jigsaw** |
| Process Step: | Individual and group listening |
| Use: | Processing of information and issues presented to group |
| Time: | Process description      5 minutes |
| | Group formation      2–3 minutes |
| | Each Question      4–6 minutes |
| | Compiling      10–20 minutes |
| | Reporting Out/Processing      20 minutes + |

Preparation:

I. Identify intent for jigsaw processing.
    A. Processing of information (what we heard individually and as a group).
    B. Implication/application of information (what this information means, how it applies to our situation).

II. Develop questions for jigsaw.

    A. Use three or five questions.
        1. Avoid fours in groups of questions.
        2. Discourage polarity.
    B. When processing information:
        1. The first two (or three) questions sample the same information.
            a. Allows for more discussion within the groups.
            b. Supports dialogue within the groups.
            c. Supports learning of listening skills.
        2. Focus final question(s) on missing items or areas.
            a. Allows the groups to capture concerns.
            b. May provide amplification of high interest or concern.
            c. When processing for implications/application, develop questions that sample for that area.

III. Determine the method to assign persons to small discussion groups.
    A. Random assignment.
        1. Count off by numbers.
        2. Use an energizer such as data processing to arrange members into a new sequence and break into groups.
    B. Card assignment.
        1. Distribute cards with number and color randomly.
        2. Arrange cards in categorical groups (e.g., grade level position).
            a. Arrange groups so all categories are represented in all groups.
            b. Self-selection.
            c. Assignment by facilitator.

*(continued)*

|  |  |
|---|---|
|  | C. Announce them by: |
|  |    1. Posting on board. |
|  |    2. Pre-coding materials. |
|  |    NOTE: Do not reveal assignments prior to small groups. |
|  | IV. Prepare charts with: |
|  |   A. Overall charge to the group. |
|  |   B. Purpose of the discussion. |
|  |   C. Questions for the jigsaw process. |
|  |   D. Directions to the jigsaw process. |
|  |     1. See Figure 10.10 for the jigsaw process template. |
|  |     2. You may wish to distribute the process directions. |
|  | V. Duplicate questions for group use. |
|  |   A. Copy of all questions to all members. |
|  |   B. Recording sheet with one question on a sheet for small group work. |
| Operation: | I. Introduce activity by reviewing the purpose of the discussion. |
|  | II. Describe the process in general. |
|  |   A. Use small groups to discuss. |
|  |   B. Will allow everyone to discuss all questions. |
|  |   C. Will provide time to report to the whole group on the results of discussion. |
|  | III. Review questions with the group as a whole. |
|  |   A. Ask for questions about the questions. |
|  |   B. You may choose to have participants individually reflect on the questions and make notes for the discussion at this point. |
|  | IV. Assign participants to small groups. |
|  |   A. Have participants move to new locations. |
|  |   B. Distribute questions, if not distributed in step III, once all are seated. |
|  | V. Review the process and time frame: |
|  |   A. The process. |
|  |     1. Each person will record the groups' comments on one question. |
|  |     2. At the end of discussing all questions, new groups will be formed with like-items. |

**FIGURE 10.10**
Continued.

B. The time frame.
   1. Give them a fixed time for each question.
   2. Adjust time frame based on discussion.

VI. Monitor group discussion:
  A. Move from group to group, answering questions regarding the focusing questions.
  B. Prompt discussion within small groups.
  C. Call "time" between questions.

VII. Reform groups into like-item groups:
  A. Review directions for the like-item small groups.
   1. The purpose is to compile and clarify responses.
   2. Give total time for like-item small groups.
   3. Prior to compiling them, suggest that they review responses from all groups for the item.
   4. Ask questions within the small group for clarification.
  B. May want to ask the group to review responses and prioritize them based on the similarities found.
  C. Distribute chart paper with question on top to each group.
   1. Give each group two markers for writing.
   2. Tell them whoever writes does not have to report.

VIII. Reporting Out.
  A. Have groups report out on the questions in order.
  B. Check for understanding of items as they are recorded.
   1. Ask: "Does this capture your discussion?".
   2. Prove for clarification on items.
    a. Want to clarify group ideas.
    b. Encourage discussion through the facilitator to clarify ideas.
    c. At the end of the processing, check for understanding.
     1. Ask: "How well does this capture the sense of the group?".
    d. Processing for patterns or trends in the responses *after* all groups have reported out can support the group in moving forward.

# The Group Shield

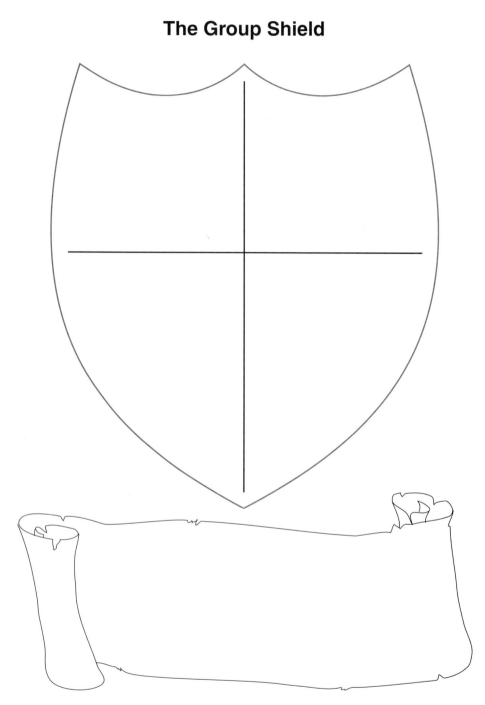

## Our Motto

FIGURE 10.11
The shield.

*Source:* Laham, S. L. (2000). *Working together: A practical guide for facilitators.* Reprinted with permission.

| | |
|---|---|
| Title: | **Group Shield** |
| Process Step: | Agreement |
| Use: | Summarize progress thus far<br>Summarize learning thus far<br>Feedback to group |
| Time: | Development of shield  10–5 minutes<br>Presentation of shield  5–10 minutes<br>Processing of activity  15 minutes + |
| Preparation: | I.  Identify four summarization categories.<br>  A. To summarize progress thus far, consider:<br>    1. What we have accomplished thus far?<br>    2. What we have left to do?<br>    3. How we are working to accomplish our task?<br>    4. What is getting in the way of our work?<br>  B. To summarize learning, consider:<br>    1. What we have learned thus far.<br>    2. What we wish we had learned.<br>    3. Feedback to the instructor.<br>    4. Feedback to our fellow learners.<br>  C. To provide feedback to the group, consider:<br>    1. What the group has learned to do.<br>    2. What the group is working on.<br>    3. How we are doing as individuals.<br>    4. How we are doing as a group.<br>II.  Prepare individual shields to distribute to all.<br>III. Prepare on chart paper.<br>  A. Group shields.<br>  B. Questions for four quadrants of the shield.<br>    1. Use a symbol to represent the question.<br>IV. Have plenty of multicolor chart markers. |
| Operation: | I.  Introduce the activity by reviewing its purpose.<br>II.  Break participants into groups of five to eight people.<br>III. Present the shield and the quadrant questions.<br>IV. Review the task.<br>  A. Develop a group shield and a one-word motto for our efforts.<br>  B. Represent the responses to the question in pictures.<br>  C. Ask for clarification. |

*(continued)*

V.   Give the groups the time frame for the development of the shield and begin.
     A. Distribute chart paper, shield, and markers.
     B. Monitor discussion and probe for clarity.

VI.  Have groups individually present shield to the group as a whole.
     A. Ask them to explain the symbols and motto.
     B. Ask questions for clarification only.
     C. Prompt applause at the end of each presentation.

VII. Process the shields as a group of the whole.
     A. Ask for trends observed.
     B. Ask for patterns observed.
     C. Ask for inconsistencies/consistencies.
     D. Ask for discoveries or insights after seeing all shields.

VIII. Summarize across comments.

**FIGURE 10.11**
Continued.

# CLASSROOM DESIGN

The physical environment of a classroom should stimulate students if effective learning is to occur. Before developing a classroom design, teachers may use the checklist in Table 10.8 to evaluate the effectiveness of the classroom's physical environment. The physical environment includes all physical aspects of the room: wall areas, lighting, floors, and room area. Being aware of the classroom's physical organization can help teachers prevent classroom problems.

Class designs should be developed around the type of grouping strategies selected by the teachers. At both the secondary and elementary levels, classroom designs are important because they dictate whether a teacher uses small-group instruction, one-on-one instruction, or whole-class instruction. Once teachers decide which type of instructional design to use during a lesson, they can alter room arrangements to meet their needs. Because no one design works best for every student, teachers need to change from time to time. Students can often help to choose a viable design for the day's lesson.

## Learning Centers

A *learning station* or *learning center* is a selected space in the classroom where students may go to work on a new assignment or on a skill or concept previously taught. The learning station approach to teaching or reinforcing skills saves the classroom teacher's time and energy. At the same time, it allows the mainstreamed student freedom of choice in activities, successful completion of tasks, and imme-

**TABLE 10.8**
Checklist for creating an effective classroom environment.

|  | Yes | No |
|---|---|---|
| **Wall areas** | | |
| Walls clean to prevent distractions. | _____ | _____ |
| Bulletin boards neatly designed and seasonally up-to-date. | _____ | _____ |
| Bulletin boards available for students' use and display. | _____ | _____ |
| Windows clean or neatly covered. | _____ | _____ |
| Blackboards in view of all students, clean and undamaged. | _____ | _____ |
| **Lighting** | | |
| Proper window lighting. | _____ | _____ |
| Ceiling lighting sufficient. | _____ | _____ |
| **Floors** | | |
| Clean | _____ | _____ |
| Obstructive objects removed. | _____ | _____ |
| Barrier-free for wheelchairs, etc. | _____ | _____ |
| **Room Area** | | |
| Appropriate chair sizes for age level. | _____ | _____ |
| Arrangements for left- as well as right-handed students. | _____ | _____ |
| Areas provided for small-group instruction. | _____ | _____ |
| Areas provided for independent instruction. | _____ | _____ |
| Areas in room designated for specific behaviors, such as quiet time, reading in twos, game areas, motor areas, art areas. | _____ | _____ |
| Learning centers provided. | _____ | _____ |
| Study carrels provided. | _____ | _____ |
| Areas designated for listening to tapes, such as recordings of lessons or chapters in books. | _____ | _____ |

diate feedback for correct or incorrect responses. The learning station gives the teacher a way to individualize instruction and work with specific educational objectives. Common in elementary schools, learning stations are rarely used in secondary classrooms. Nevertheless, they can give the secondary teacher a desirable instructional alternative.

*Setting up a learning center.* For a teacher who has never used the learning station approach or has used only commercial learning stations, I will review the criteria for establishing a good station. Voight (1973) lists six criteria to consider in establishing such centers (pp. 2–3):

1. Each learning center should contribute to the achievement of the individual's purposes. Each child should confront basic skills, facts, concepts, and large ideas.
2. The learning center should deal with a significant area of study that the student finds interesting. It should be open-ended to foster individual creativity. It should provide opportunities to develop problem solving, critical thinking, and creative thinking. It should challenge an individual to strive toward higher levels of learning.
3. Learning experiences at the center should be related to past personal experiences and should lead to broader and deeper new experiences.
4. Learning center activities should have practical time limits related to the child's developmental level so that the child can complete tasks.
5. Directions at each learning center should help students quickly gain an overview of the task. Directions need to be clearly stated so that students understand where to begin each task and when they have completed a task successfully.
6. The design of a learning center should depend on the subject matter presented to the student.

Next, the teacher must decide what subject to emphasize at the station. For example, should it be a reading station, a math station, a just-for-fun station, a social studies station, a vocational interest station, or a things-to-make station? The creative teacher can think of many more possibilities. Kaplan, Kaplan, Madsen, and Taylor (1973) suggest that teachers seriously consider the reasons for student and teacher use. They believe that the learning station can serve the student as a self-selected activity for independent study, a lesson follow-up, an activity in place of a general assignment, or an enrichment activity. For the teacher, the learning station can become a place for lesson follow-up or small-group instruction and an excellent resource for individualized activities. But a learning station should never be a place for busy work or for getting students out of the way for a few minutes.

After teachers establish standards for the learning center and decide on subject areas, they must locate resources. Piechowiak and Cook (1976) suggest that teachers should begin by going through the enrichment materials that have probably been stored away. Also, teachers should notify other teachers about items needed in the center. Supplies will multiply rapidly. Here are some other suggestions (Piechowiak & Cook, 1976, pp. 20–21):

1. Break language arts material into short lessons and write them on individual task cards.
2. Group math sheets into skill areas, and combine them in a box with plastic overlays and grease pencils, thus making programmed learning kits.
3. Gather good art projects, divide them into step-by-step procedures, and write the directions on cards for independent use at the make-it table.

4. Crossindex the basal science and social studies texts. Make them available for student research.

5. Accumulate odds and ends of everything to use as valuable materials for the art center, the make-it table, or experimentation.

6. Record some of your favorite children's stories for the listening center. Devise follow-up activities to check comprehension.

7. Make some blank books for creative writing. Gather pictures for writing and thinking exercises.

8. Use old basal readers and workbooks; they may supply a wealth of material for activity cards. Cut them apart and make books of individual stories. Rip up pages to use for word-study activities. Cut pictures to use for phonic task cards or sequential development exercises.

9. Do the same thing with old math texts. Turn the supplemental exercises in the back into math games.

10. Spend allotted school funds for a variety of materials. Instead of buying 30 copies of the same reading text, buy five different series in groups of six. When teachers use learning stations, they no longer need to place large group orders for texts.

11. Collect tables, chairs, boards, and other items that other teachers discard—they may be just the thing you need later.

12. Haunt the media center. Most directors are delighted to have someone show interest in audiovisual aids. When they know the type of material teachers are looking for, directors will do all they can to locate them.

13. Rediscover the school building. Some valuable resources may be hiding in the back of a storage closet.

*Advantages of learning stations for inclusion.* Learning stations serve multiple purposes in instructing students. For one thing, the teacher saves time during the day because a group or an individual can work alone at the station. In addition, learning stations in inclusive classrooms have the following specific advantages:

• Many students prefer to work alone, and the learning station gives them this option.

• Self-correcting learning stations provide immediate feedback about correct or incorrect responses without embarrassment.

• Special-needs students can work at their own pace without pressure.

• From a variety of activities, students can select the most appropriate.

• Because students in inclusive environments may work below the level of other students in the general classroom, learning stations provide them with appropriate activities at their own levels.

• Activities at the learning station can reinforce the objectives specified on the student's IEP.

- Learning centers reinforce the mode of learning best suited to the mildly disabled student. For example, if the student learns better visually, the teacher can present more activities in a visual manner. If the student learns better auditorially, the teacher can put activities on tape recorders.

## Bulletin Boards for Incidental and Intentional Learning

Most classrooms have at least one bulletin board. Teachers usually design bulletin boards as seasonal decorations or as special places to display work. However, bulletin boards can also reflect a specific learning purpose. Bulletin boards designed for incidental learning are simply placed around the room with the hope that students will pick up a little extra learning. For example, in one school, the halls are painted to look like highways, street signs hang over classroom doors, and the ABCs run around the walls. It is hard to get a drink of water without learning a little multiplication. As children line the halls, incidental learning takes place in every direction they look. Many books have ideas that teachers can use to design bulletin boards for incidental learning.

In contrast, intentional learning is planned learning. Teachers can design bulletin boards based on a lesson or current events. One school has a "good morning news" bulletin board for the class. The teacher broadcasts the news, and each student brings an item for the bulletin board or the announcements. This method uses intentional learning effectively.

*Types of bulletin boards.* Figure 10.12 presents different types of bulletin boards with a brief description of each. Teachers may adapt the content format to match the individual needs of students.

*Bulletin board planning.* Greer, Friedman, and Laycock (1978) list eight steps to use when planning bulletin boards:

1. Decide early on a theme or key idea to be expressed by the bulletin board. Seek a new, fresh approach to content. Think of putting the title in an eye-catching location; consider the expected size and location of the audience; plan for lettering and arrangement that can be seen at the normal viewing distance.

2. Start early to determine exactly what the display should communicate and have students participate. Determine specific student goals, which may include, for example, giving at least eight students responsibility for planning and making a bulletin board display and providing the opportunity for them to develop headings, captions, and other written materials.

3. Plan the display on paper well ahead of time.

4. Keep in mind who will see the bulletin board or display.

5. Consider where the bulletin board could best be exhibited to achieve instructional purposes. Placing it in the classroom is not always necessary; it might be best in a corridor as a special display or in another location.

6. Think of attention-getting devices. Use push buttons, strings to be pulled, items to be touched, or any technique to invite viewers to react to or study the dis-

| | |
|---|---|
| **Language involvement bulletin board** | This bulletin board is designed with round rotating disks that are used interchangeably for any subject or content. |
| **Slide-study bulletin board** | This bulletin board can be used for any subject area. Slides are taken related to the desired subject matter and stored in compartments attached to the bulletin board. |
| **Auditory-action bulletin board** | This bulletin board contains an activity mounted beneath the display on the bulletin board. A cassette is prepared by the teacher, which guides the students through the required lessons. |
| **Lift panel bulletin board** | These bulletin boards are made with pieces of construction paper folded in half. The outer flap of the panel contains a question or idea. The inner flap is secured to the bulletin board and contains the answer or solution. |
| **Sentence strips bulletin board** | Strips are attached to the bulletin board and may convey relevant printed information or questions. They may be changed frequently to maintain interest. |

**FIGURE 10.12**
Types of bulletin boards.

*Source:* Greer, J. G., Friedman, I., & Laycock, V. (1978). Instructional games. In R. M. Anderson, J. G. Greer, & S. Odle (Eds.), *Individualizing educational materials for special children in the mainstream* (pp. 267–293). Baltimore: University Park Press. Copyright 1978 by Pro-Ed, Inc. Adapted by permission.

play. Give viewers choices, ask them to make decisions, and challenge them to avoid making mistakes in responding.

7. Use color. Tastefully used, color can contribute to attractiveness. Color can make important content stand out.

8. Incorporate audiovisual devices. Many slide projectors have an automatic slide-changing feature. Have students develop photographic or hand-drawn slides or titles.

Teachers must adapt the learning environment before adapting instruction. But once they have prepared the master schedule, planned scheduling with the best interest of the child in mind, and designed the actual physical environment of the room, they can take a close look at how to teach.

# CONCLUSION

This chapter focuses on adapting the physical environment for students with special needs and those at risk. Preparing the physical environment helps build a framework for learning. After the master schedule has been carefully planned, scheduling or transitional concerns addressed, and grouping techniques established, the teacher can begin the instructional process.

# CHAPTER 11

## Adapting Lesson Plans

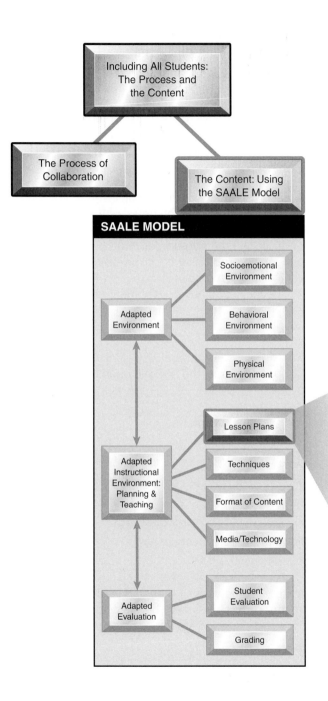

## Chapter-at-a-Glance

The Process of Lesson Planning

Components of a Lesson Plan

Presenting a Lesson

Adapting a Lesson Plan

When we begin a vacation or a trip, we decide where to go, make a list of items needed, develop a plan of action, a guide or map, and decide on a timetable for travel. When we arrive at our destination, we implement our planned activities. After our journey is completed, everyone sits around and relives the good times, perhaps laughs at the bad, and decides what we would or would not change. Then we begin to plan for a new experience.

Lesson plans are no different from our journeys. Lesson plans serve as blueprints for the school day and the year's activities. They dictate student-teacher interactions and instructional outcomes. Planning helps our vacations to be a success. Effective teaching springs from well-planned, well-organized, well-presented lesson plans.

In a special education class, "A lesson plan focuses directly on the teaching objectives that should derive from the student's goals and objectives on his/her IEP" (Payne, Polloway, Smith, & Payne, 1981, p. 119). The IEP is a link between the student's needs and the appropriate education that is to be delivered. However, the IEP does not indicate the specific planning process to be followed in developing lessons. In a general classroom setting, the lesson plan focuses on the teaching objective not only for a student with special needs but also for the total group. The general educator uses the same lesson plan for many students. However, the student with special needs or the student at risk often cannot follow the activities as presented in the lesson plan and may fall behind.

This chapter offers suggestions to help both general and special education teachers adapt general class lesson plans to meet the specific needs of students who are having difficulty within the class. We will discuss the following topics:

- The process of lesson planning and collaboration during the process
- A model for lesson planning
- The relationship between the three principles of learning and the lesson plan
- The components of a lesson plan and teacher intervention for each component
- Techniques for delivering the lesson plan
- A format for adapting the lesson plan in collaborative planning
- A model for teaching with multiability students in one class
- A taxonomy model for interventions

This chapter also introduces a broad framework for managing transitions during the instructional process. Thus, it directly influences the specific issues discussed in chapters 12 through 15. Try to keep this chapter in mind as you continue reading the rest of this book.

# THE PROCESS OF LESSON PLANNING

The planning process actually begins when the school system selects the curriculum to be implemented within its schools. At this point, texts are adapted to teach skill scope and sequence. Frequently, state departments of education dictate the skill scope and sequence for their school systems, which must then be translated into curriculum components and lesson plans at the local level. Only after these initial plans are made do educators sit down to work out weekly lesson plans.

## The Benefits of Lesson Planning

Formats and ways of presenting lessons vary from teacher to teacher. Hoover and Hollingsworth (1975) believe that lesson planning has several benefits. For example, plans can serve as "useful guidelines or blueprints" for the teacher. They must, however, remain flexible enough to allow the teacher to adapt to whatever situation may arise. In fact, if the prepared teacher has set up "general goals, some definite activities, and some specific sources of materials," then students can play a part in planning. Planning also allows the teacher to direct attention to the "important problems of motivation and individual differences." Indeed, planning often increases the teacher's understanding of the problems students have with learning. Planning lessons can help a teacher both focus and balance "goals, subject matter, activities, and evaluation." The teacher can even use the lesson plan as a "reference to important statistics, illustration, difficult words, special procedures." Teachers who make notes on their plans after lessons are finished can use their plans to see patterns in successful approaches and outcomes to improve their teaching in later years. Finally, because every teacher plans lessons in a different way, planning allows a teacher to put a personal stamp on the lesson and the classroom (pp. 159–160).

During the planning process, educators work toward the goal of developing an appropriate lesson plan for all students. A major factor to consider before and during the planning process is the relationship between the curriculum and the student's IEP. Many students with special needs respond to the general curriculum just like all other students. Some need differing levels of interventions. Others use a completely different curriculum. Thus, educators must carefully match the IEP objectives for each student to the instructional process for that child.

## Collaboration in Lesson Planning

Most often, the special education teacher becomes actively involved in the lesson planning process only when the general education teacher is in the last stage of planning: developing a daily lesson plan. However, it is more beneficial to the student with special needs if the special education teacher becomes involved in the first phase of planning: the yearly lesson plan. A year's worth of learning outcomes as set forth in daily plans might be attainable for students without disabilities but difficult for a special-needs student. It's a losing battle to try to keep a student in a general class where the skills being taught are instructionally too advanced. A balance must be maintained between skills taught and those that are reasonably attainable.

Many special-needs and at-risk students can achieve success during general lesson plan activities when intervention points are identified and appropriate accommodations or modifications are provided. This process depends on careful, well-planned collaboration between the general and special education teachers. As teachers work together, they should follow several guidelines:

1. Realize that modifications to the general class lesson plan may be necessary.
2. Be specific in listing what will occur during each component of the lesson plan. Include an objective, strategies, resources, and evaluation.
3. Allow time for both teachers to review the lesson plan and develop appropriate modifications.
4. Be flexible when an adaptation or modification does not work.
5. Be prepared to develop an alternate modification.
6. Realize that when a modification is made to the lesson plan, the plan is still valid and not watered down.
7. Be as flexible in modifying the students' assignments or evaluations as you are in modifying the objectives and strategies.
8. Realize that you are always modifying the lesson plan to achieve student success and the attainment of objectives.

## Lesson Plan Model

Figure 11.1 is a lesson plan model and shows how the remaining chapters in this book fit into the planning process.

As you can see, a lesson plan has four major parts: an objective, strategies, resources, and evaluation. During the strategies section, the educator introduces, develops, and summarizes. During development, educators teach using three principles of learning: acquisition, retention, and generalization. At any point during the strategies section, educators may adapt technique or content. Modifications may also be made in resources and evaluation.

## General Principles of Learning and the Lesson Plan

If teaching is the interaction between teacher and learner, then effective teaching is planning that interaction based on the principles of learning. The three principles of learning are acquisition, retention, and generalization. Acquisition (original learning, learning a new idea, skill, or concept) can be taught by using one of a few strategies (Table 11.1). In Table 11.1 you will also see that retention, remembering over an extended period of time, can be taught with any of four strategies. Generalization or transfer, taking what is learned in one situation and using it in a second situation, can be reinforced through the strategies of intertask similarity, instructions to transfer, and overlearning. Tables 11.2, 11.3, and 11.4 discuss each principle individually and list corresponding strategies with definitions. Teaching suggestions for each strategy are also presented.

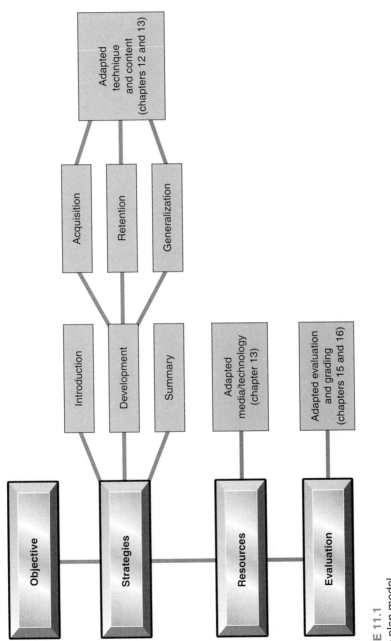

**FIGURE 11.1**
Lesson plan model.

**TABLE 11.1**

General principles of learning and strategies for teaching each principle.

| Principle of Learning | Definition | Strategies for Teaching |
|---|---|---|
| Acquisition | Original learning; the learning of a new skill. | -Instruction and intent<br>-Whole and parts methods<br>-Distribution of practice<br>-Amount of material<br>-Recitation<br>-Knowledge of results<br>-Amount of practice<br>-Oral and visual presentations<br>-Orientation and attention<br>-Structure |
| Retention | Remembering over an extended period of time. | -Overlearning<br>-Type of retention measure<br>-Instructions to recall<br>-Reminiscence |
| Generalization | Taking what is learned in one situation and using it in a second situation. | -Intertask similarity<br>-Instructions to transfer<br>-Overlearning |

*Source:* © Judy Wood

**TABLE 11.2**

Acquisition: Learning a new skill.

| Strategy | Teaching Suggestions |
|---|---|
| **Instruction and intent:** focusing student's attention on the task | • Use colors, bold print, etc.<br>• Provide step-by-step directions, placing each direction on one 3-by-5-inch index card.<br>• For younger children use picture cards.<br>• Use tape recorders to give directions plus a written checklist to watch as directions are presented orally.<br>• Use wall charts with pictures and word clues.<br>• Review class outlines before class discussion.<br>• Provide study guides before test.<br>• Be clear about class objectives and structure.<br>• Use a rule list.<br>• Use technology. |
| **Whole and part methods:** whole method presents tasks as a whole; part method presents tasks in parts | **Whole methods**<br>• Present a word as a whole; then break it down into specific sounds or parts.<br>• Review the outline for the lesson as a whole.<br>• Begin a chapter with a brief summary. |

TABLE 11.2
Continued.

| Strategy | Teaching Suggestions |
|---|---|
| **Whole and part methods:** *continued* | • Show the completed product before the student begins to work on the exercise. <br> • Show the video of a novel before the students read the novel. <br><br> **Part methods** <br> • Break skills down into small steps, teaching from lowest to highest skill. <br> • Place each step of an exercise on a checklist so student can clearly see parts in progressing order. <br> • Number directions in order. <br> • Tape short segments of a literary work so that the student may listen in parts. <br> • Give tests in small sections. <br> • Focus on parts of the outline or organizer that make the whole. <br> • Focus on specific steps or segments in video. <br> • Use organizers. <br> • Use computer graphics to emphasize wholes and parts. |
| **Distribution of practice:** the amount of practice required | • The amount of distribution of practice depends on the attention span of the student. <br> • Practice may be mass practice (long periods of practice on a task) or distributed practice (practice in small segments). <br> • Practice vocabulary or spelling words in sets of five. <br> • Practice a rest-and-return approach to practice. <br> • Practice with a friend. <br> • Change the way information is presented but not the information. <br> • Change from large groups, small groups, computer, etc. |
| **Amount of material:** the size of the task and the number of items in it | • The amount of material may vary depending on the student's ability to handle specific amounts. <br> • Worksheets may contain the same information, but quantity should be monitored. <br> • Spelling test may be split in half. <br> • If the educator feels that the student needs more material to learn the task, then the distribution of material should be monitored. |
| **Recitation:** practicing a new task after the teacher has removed the original material | • Have students review a new list of vocabulary words with definitions. Have the students use the words without viewing the list. <br> • Present a new word orally and have the students repeat the word within a sentence into a recorder. <br> • Let the students play games that use material previously presented by the teacher. <br> • Use the computer lab. |

*(continued)*

TABLE 11.2
Continued.

| Strategy | Teaching Suggestions |
|---|---|
| **Knowledge of results:** providing immediate feedback on answers | • Instant feedback is necessary for students to know whether their responses are correct or incorrect.<br>• It has been said that if a student learns the answer incorrectly it will take 250 times hearing the correct answer to correct the error.<br>• Use computers or self-correcting materials.<br>• Provide math problems in puzzle format so that only the correct answer completes the puzzle.<br>• Place the correct response on the reverse side of activity cards.<br>• Develop overlays for tests, such as fill-in-the-blank, multiple choice, or true-false.<br>• Develop overlays for activities so that correct answers appear either beside the answer given by the student or on top of the student's answer.<br>• Let peers provide answer feedback. |
| **Amount of practice:** the total number of practice sessions students need to learn a task | • Use games to teach a concept. Change to another activity teaching the same concept.<br>• Point out practical uses of the concept. |
| **Oral and visual presentations:** presenting material both orally and visually | • Use brightly decorated bulletin boards.<br>• Use large print on all transparencies.<br>• Use flashcards, TV, video, filmstrips, games, and pictures.<br>• Use tape recorders, radios, and recorders with earphones.<br>• Provide recorded books.<br>• Hang mobiles from the ceiling with new information to be learned.<br>• Place information around drinking fountains. |
| **Orientation and attention:** pointing out details and focusing on material | • Use videos and computers.<br>• Review the objective.<br>• Point out details of lesson outline.<br>• Provide an organizer.<br>• Use bright colors.<br>• Use PowerPoint to present lesson. |
| **Structure:** organizing the material to be learned in a manner that the student understands the task at hand | • Use acquisition outlines.<br>• Provide organizers.<br>• Review the daily class procedure.<br>• Provide logical connections for students, showing where this information fits into material already learned.<br>• Remember that just because you understand the material's structure does not mean that the student understands. |

TABLE 11.3
Retention: Remembering over time what has been taught.

| Strategy | Teaching Suggestions |
|---|---|
| **Overlearning:** practicing a skill beyond the point of acquisition | • Provide learning stations or centers with numerous activities designed to teach the newly acquired skill.<br>• Overlearning does not mean boredom.<br>• Let students create ways to practice new skills.<br>• Develop games that reinforce the new skills.<br>• Continue teaching concepts via the computer. |
| **Type of retention measure:** the retention measure a teacher uses to teach test material | • The three types of retention measures are:<br>　Recognition: the selecting of previously learned items from unlearned or false items (a multiple-choice test);<br>　Structured recall: supplying items within a specific context (essay tests or fill-in-the-blank items); and<br>　Relearning: the time or effort required to relearn previously learned material.<br>• Match how you teach with how you test.<br>• Provide study guides that clearly specify the type of items on the test.<br>• Teach students how to study for different test types.<br>• Provide students with types of items on test. |
| **Instructions to recall:** directing the student to learn with the specific idea of recalling the material later | • Use color-coded notes.<br>• Use note-taking techniques emphasizing specific details.<br>• Provide study guides.<br>• Use highlighter type.<br>• Use outlines and highlight specific details.<br>• Highlight material as discussed. |
| **Reminiscence:** after a long practice session and rest, the student should have an increase in performance | • Design short checkup tests for students to complete after rest and extended practice.<br>• The practice-rest cycle may have to be repeated several times for some of the students.<br>• Reward students for information learned, even if it is only a small amount.<br>• Help students to keep a personal chart of progress.<br>• Provide snacks after long practice sessions.<br>• Allow a "physical movement" period after a long practice session. |

**TABLE 11.4**
Generalization: Transferring what is learned from one situation to a second situation.

| Strategy | Teaching Suggestions |
|---|---|
| **Intertask similarity:** showing the student the similarity between two different tasks | • Emphasize the similarity between manuscript writing and cursive writing.<br>• Point out how addition and multiplication relate.<br>• Show students how pasting leaves into a book is similar to keeping a notebook in the upper grades.<br>• Explain how rules in the first or second grade may differ from those in the upper grades. However, rules are rules.<br>• Use highlighters to point out details. |
| **Instructions to generalize:** showing the student how learning in one situation will be useful in another | • Show how basic math facts will help the student keep a checkbook.<br>• Point out how reading will help you fill out job forms.<br>• Emphasize how learning to read relates to passing the driver's education class, leading to a driver's license. |
| **Overlearning:** practice beyond the point of mastery | • Remember that overlearning is not the same as boredom.<br>• Return to skills taught to reinforce the skill.<br>• Use new and creative ways to teach the same skill.<br>• Allow mental/physical rest periods. |

After looking at Tables 11.1 through 11.3, you can see that modifications and adaptations are simply good teaching. For example, if you use an outline while teaching, you are not watering down. You are simply using a teaching tip for putting into practice 1 of the 10 strategies for teaching acquisition (structure).

Table 11.5 provides an example of acquisition, retention, and generalization and how a teacher would carry these principles throughout the teaching process. Table 11.6 is blank. Try your hand at implementing each of the three principles in a teaching situation.

## COMPONENTS OF A LESSON PLAN

All lesson plans have several essential parts, although various authors may give these parts different names. Jarolimek and Foster (1981) provide a simple and useful description of four major lesson plan parts:

1. The *purpose* states instructional objectives, including what students should learn from the lesson.

2. The *learning process* lists learning materials or media needed to teach the lesson.

3. The *sequence of lesson* describes the work-study activities that will occur during the lesson.

4. The *evaluation* describes the activities designed to close the lesson.

**TABLE 11.5**
Principles of learning application.

| Skill Taught: *Book Reports* <br> Principle | Teaching Strategy | Class Activity |
|---|---|---|
| Acquisition | Oral/Visual Presentation | • Develop mobiles. <br> • Use an outline. <br> • Use organizers. <br> • Tape-record major points. |
| Retention | Instructions to Recall | • Review details developed in mobile. |
| Generalization | Instructions to Transfer | • Relate story details to real-life situations. <br> • Use organizer. |

**TABLE 11.6**
Principles of learning application.

| Principle | Teaching Strategy <br> (Tables 11.2, 11.3, 11.4) | Class Activity <br> (Tables 11.2, 11.3, 11.4) |
|---|---|---|
| Acquisition | | |
| Retention | | |
| Generalization/transfer | | |

Certain components such as objectives, strategies, resources, and evaluation always appear in a well-constructed lesson plan, no matter what names or formats are used. Table 11.7 depicts the four main components and subcomponents necessary for intervention planning.

**TABLE 11.7**
Lesson plan components.

| Component | Suggested Adaptations/Modifications |
|---|---|
| **Objective:** a statement of the specific learner outcomes that should result from the lesson | • Clearly state the objective to reflect the behavior outcome and how the behavior will be measured.<br>• Check to see that the objective is student oriented.<br>• Select instructional objectives that are in the appropriate domain for the learner.<br>• Graphically show the learner how today's objective fits into yesterday's lesson and will tie into tomorrow's lesson.<br>• Make a list of all possible subobjectives for the main objective.<br>• Put all subobjectives into the logical sequential order for teaching.<br>• Make a list of all prerequisite skills needed before the student can master the stated objective.<br>• Be prepared to alter any objective if it is not meeting the needs of the learner. |
| **Strategies:** the work-study activities that occur during the lesson<br><br>*Introduction:* setting the stage for the work-study activities that will occur during the lesson<br><br>• Review what is to be learned.<br><br><br><br><br>• Demonstrate what student should learn.<br><br><br>• Use mind capturer or activator.<br><br>• Consider past lessons or students' experiences. | <br><br><br><br><br><br><br><br>• Review the instructional objective before developing the lesson's activities.<br>• Modify the objective if necessary for student success.<br>• Reassess students' prerequisite skill level.<br>• Explain how today's lesson is related to yesterday's lesson.<br>• Provide a model of a completed assignment on task to be completed.<br>• Using the whole-part-whole method, review the assignment/task.<br>• Provide directions that are sequential, written, and reviewed orally.<br>• Use manipulative or hands-on activity to boost interest.<br>• Note whether students have prerequisite skills for mastering objective.<br>• Ask questions on students' taxonomy levels about past lessons.<br>• Provide example from own experience and relate to lesson (modeling technique).<br>• Ask students to share similar experiences; relate student comments to present lesson. |

| Component | Suggested Adaptations/Modifications |
|---|---|
| • Relate lesson to a future life event or purpose for learning the lesson. | • Show students how today's lesson will have meaning in their future.<br>• Let students provide examples of how what they learn today will be helpful tomorrow. |
| *Development:* the sequence of work-study activities that will occur during the lesson |  |
| • Select strategies for teaching for acquisition. | • *Acquisition:* learning a new skill<br>Get the student's attention and explain the intent of the lesson.<br>Use whole-part-whole activities (provide a lecture outline).<br>Plan for practice and distribute the practice throughout the lesson.<br>Cover only small segments of material if the lesson is long.<br>Provide students with immediate feedback on their progress.<br>Use multisensory approaches while teaching the activities.<br>Point out specific details that you want the student to learn.<br>Plan for appropriate note-taking procedures.<br>Plan for adaptation for note taking if needed.<br>Provide structure during the lesson by explaining how the activities relate and how the lesson will be evaluated. |
| • Select strategies for teaching for retention. | • *Retention:* remembering over an extended period of time<br>Provide for overlearning by developing extended activities that teach the lesson.<br>Help students see that how you teach relates to how you will test.<br>Teach students the different types of retention measures.<br>Point out specific information you will want students to recall at a later date.<br>After a short rest from the material, check for recall and retention.<br>Reteach if the student has not retained the skills. |
| • Select strategies for teaching for generalization. | • *Generalization:* transferring what is learned from one situation to a second situation<br>Point out the similarities between the tasks learned.<br>Show how the information learned will be useful in another situation. |
| • Select the appropriate activities for teaching each part of the model. | • Assist in overlearning by letting students participate in independent practice. Overlearning does not mean boredom. |

*(continued)*

353

**TABLE 11.7**
Continued.

| Component | Suggested Adaptations/Modifications |
|---|---|
| | • Carefully select appropriate activities for teaching for acquisition, retention, and generalization. |
| • Select the appropriate activities for teaching each part of the model. | • Remember that each part of the three-part model must be mastered before the student begins the next step. |
| • Be sure that all activities are based on the appropriate objective level. | • Check each activity to be sure that you are teaching the objective, and that you are teaching on the appropriate instructional level. |
| • Sequence all activities. | • Organize all activities from lowest to highest level of difficulty. |
| | • Sequence the activities within each segment of the model. |
| • Identify any necessary intervention points during the lesson for students experiencing difficulty. | • Using the intervention checklist (appendix A), identify any intervention point within the lesson for a student who is experiencing difficulty. |
| | • Remember that to continue with the lesson when a student is lost defeats the lesson's purpose. |
| • Identify the necessary areas of modification or adaptation: technique, content, media. | • Identify the necessary areas of mismatch for the student (teaching technique, content, media). |
| • Develop the appropriate modification for the areas identified above. | • Select the appropriate adaptation or modification adaptation for the identified area. |
| • Plan for an adapted learning environment. | • Assign peer tutors to students with disabilities if needed. |
| | • Organize creative groups for instruction. |
| | • Select grouping arrangements. |
| *Summary:* tying together the lesson's events | |
| • Conclude lesson. | • Select closing activities on an instructional level of mainstreamed students. |
| | • Assess students' mastery of concepts. |
| • Students describe what they have learned. | • Assist mainstreamed students in selecting what to share. |
| | • Ask students to tell about what they have learned. |
| | • Have students draw pictures of what they have learned. |
| | • Invite students to present projects. |
| **Resources:** a list of the learning materials and media needed to teach the lesson | |
| • Compile all materials to be used in presenting the lesson. | • Assess materials as to instructional level. |
| | • Select a variety of materials which address different perceptual learning styles, (i.e., visual, auditory). |

| Component | Suggested Adaptations/Modifications |
|---|---|
| • Select appropriate media/technology to be used with the lesson.<br><br>• Prepare resources for adapting the learning environment. | • Adapt media/technology.<br>• Select a variety of media and uses for lesson plan implementation.<br>• Match media/technology to perceptual learning styles of student.<br>• Select bulletin boards for incidental and intentional learning.<br>• Design learning centers to enhance the instructional activities. |
| **Evaluation:** checking for mastery and areas for reteaching<br><br>• Teacher assesses student learning.<br><br><br><br><br><br><br>• Student assesses self.<br><br>• Students assess each other.<br><br><br><br><br>• Teacher assesses self.<br><br><br><br><br><br>• Student assignments. | <br><br><br>• Check to see that the way you test reflects the way you taught for retention during the strategies component of the lesson plan.<br>• Provide the student with information regarding test type before testing.<br>• Teach the student how to study for the test based on test type.<br>• Assess effectiveness of instructional objective.<br>• Assess instructional level of activities.<br>• Assess activities not mastered and consider further adaptations of the plan.<br>• Give student self-correcting materials for immediate reinforcement.<br>• Provide models with which students can compare their work.<br>• Provide one-on-one peer tutor to give feedback.<br>• Oversee student assessment of peers. (Peers' criticism can harm self-concepts.)<br>• Were all students included in lesson plan's activities?<br>• Did each student experience success?<br>• Was I aware of the instructional level of each student?<br>• Did each student reach expected learning outcome?<br>• Did I effectively manage student behaviors?<br>• Was the learning environment adapted to meet students' learning needs?<br>• What changes should I make the next time I present the lesson?<br>• Be sure that assignments are on the appropriate instructional level for students.<br>• Do not overwhelm students with too large an assignment.<br>• Design assignments so that students will experience success.<br>• Relate all assignments to the lesson.<br>• Give assignments for a specific reason, not just to give an assignment.<br>• Inform students of the purpose of the assignment. |

# Objective

The objective of the lesson is a statement of specific learner outcomes that should result from the lesson. Objectives should be clearly stated, express the intended outcome behavior, and identify how the outcome behavior will be measured and focused on the student. Objectives should be carefully written in the domain level appropriate for the student. These levels include knowledge, comprehension, application, analysis, synthesis, and evaluation (see chapter 12). Objectives should be shared with learners so that they will be aware of the purpose of the lesson at all times. For younger students, the teacher may need to paraphrase the objective or provide a visual representation of the desired outcome to help them understand the objective. It may be helpful to show graphically how today's objective continues yesterday's objective and will tie into tomorrow's objectives. This provides a connection for students, who may not readily see the logical sequence of the skills being taught.

After a teacher selects and approves of an objective, he or she moves ahead to the next steps: (a) making a list of all subobjectives (breaking down the class objective), (b) analyzing the subobjectives by task (putting them into sequential order from simple to complex), (c) listing the necessary prerequisite skills students must have before they can master the objective, and (d) deciding where the point of entry for a special-needs or at-risk student occurs.

*Functions of instructional objectives.* Educators report four major objections to the use of instructional objectives (Tenbrink, 1977):

1. Writing good instructional objectives requires a lot of work and expertise.
2. Using instructional objectives hampers the process of individualizing and humanizing education.
3. The use of instructional objectives curtails spontaneity and decreases the teacher's flexibility.
4. Using instructional objectives leads to trivial learning outcomes.

Although these points may be valid, the benefits of objective planning and writing far outweigh such objections. For example, instructional objectives are useful in the following situations (Tenbrink, 1977):

- Planning lessons
- Selecting learning aids such as textbooks and films
- Determining appropriate assignments for individual students
- Selecting and constructing classroom tests
- Determining when to gather evaluation data
- Summarizing and reporting evaluation results
- Helping learners determine where they are and where they need to go as they strive toward becoming independent learners

Refer to Table 11.7 for suggestions about adapting the objective component of lesson plans.

# Strategies

After the objectives have carefully been selected, written, displayed, and explained, the educator begins the second phase of lesson planning—developing strategies. Here the teacher must determine the instructional makeup of the lesson as well as the sequence the lesson should follow. While developing this section, the teacher should remember the stated objectives and build strategies carefully around them. Unfortunately, it is common to find excellent objectives and excellent strategies that do not match. Such an instructional mismatch can mean that a student will not be able to attain the objectives.

The strategies section of the lesson plan is developed around three major parts: the introduction, the development, and the summary.

*Lesson introduction.* In the lesson plan introduction, the teacher should state and/or demonstrate what students should learn; use a provocative question, artifact, or hands-on activity to stimulate student interest in the lesson; or link the present lesson to past lessons or student experiences.

The teacher should make sure that he or she follows these five steps during the introduction:

1. Review what is to be learned, including the major instructional objective and all subobjectives. Think in terms of preparing the student for the lesson itself, and make sure that instructional objectives are on the student's level and in sequential order. Also include an assessment of the students' prerequisite skills.

2. Demonstrate what the student should learn. This might include a whole-part-whole method using a lecture outline and providing sequential written directions.

3. Use a mind capturer or activator such as a manipulative or hands-on activity to boost interest.

4. Link past lessons or students' current or past experiences, which makes the lesson more meaningful for students.

5. Relate the lesson to a future event. Students can see purpose in learning a lesson if it relates to their functional future.

Refer to Table 11.7 to learn more about the introduction to a lesson.

*Lesson development.* Here the teacher selects activities to achieve the lesson's purpose, describes these activities, and chooses an instructional model around which to organize the lesson. As you saw in Figure 11.1, the development stage should be built around three aspects of the learning model: acquisition, retention, and generalization. For each of the model's parts, the educator should plan the appropriate adaptation or modification if needed. Frequently, by the time he or she is developing a lesson, the teacher may be aware of intervention points for specific students.

For other students, however, the need for identifying an intervention point may emerge as the lesson progresses. The intervention/transition checklist is a useful tool for intervention point identification (see chapter 7 and appendix A).

As the lesson develops, the teacher should keep several major points in mind:

1. Select strategies for teaching for acquisition, retention, and generalization.
2. Select the appropriate activities for teaching for each part of the model.
3. Be sure that all activities are based on the appropriate objective level.
4. Sequence all activities.
5. Identify any necessary intervention points during the lesson for students experiencing difficulty.
6. Identify the areas that need modification or adaptation: technique, content, or media.
7. Develop the appropriate modification for the areas identified in item 6. (Each area will be discussed later in this book.)
8. Plan for an adapted learning environment.

Refer back to Table 11.7 for suggested adaptations or modifications in lesson development.

*Lesson summary.* Here the major points of the lesson are summarized and the lesson's events tied together. The teacher may choose to have students describe what they have learned by performing one of several activities, such as question/discussion, demonstration, or presentation of a project. Table 11.7 presents the components of the lesson summary with considerations for adapting or modifying it.

## Resources

In the resources section of the lesson plan, the teacher identifies any materials and media to use to achieve the lesson's purpose. Such resources may include pages or chapters in a pamphlet, text, or workbook; filmstrips or films; guest experts; field experience; special settings; art or cooking supplies; or audiovisual equipment. Assessing the instructional level of materials, matching perceptual learning styles with media, using a variety of materials or media, and adapting the learning environment are all part of developing resources. Refer back to Table 11.7 for more information about resource selection.

## Evaluation

Evaluation, the final component of the lesson plan, is designed to measure student outcomes, identify a teacher's need to reorganize lesson plans, and target areas for reteaching. Evaluation may appear to be the last component in the lesson plan format, but actually it should be an ongoing process.

During evaluation, the teacher notes ways to assess student learning or the success of the lesson. Teachers can assess students by checking behavioral objectives, using informal questions, or administering formal pre- and posttests. Or a teacher may choose to have students check their own work by providing them with feedback, a model of a completed activity, or an illustration of the lesson's concept or process. Another method is to have students assess one another's work. To determine the lesson's degree of success, a teacher may analyze students' reactions during the lesson, the value of the lesson as a learning experience, or the teacher's own teaching performance.

Student assignments are also a major component of evaluation. Assignments are part of the evaluation process as well as an extension of content mastery. They give the teacher an opportunity to see if the student has mastered the skill and if reteaching will be necessary. Refer back to Table 11.7 for suggestions about student evaluation and assignments. We will return to the subject of evaluation later in this book.

## PRESENTING THE LESSON

Intervention can be as simple as presenting the lesson effectively. Therefore, while planning lessons, teachers should also think about how they will present those lessons to students. Cooper and colleagues (1977) suggest five stimulus variation techniques that teachers can use to deliver the lesson effectively: kinetic variation, focusing, shifting interaction, pausing, and shifting the senses.

*Kinetic variation* refers to changes in the teacher's position in the classroom. It assumes that a teacher will move from place to place within the room to improve communication rather than sit behind a desk for the whole period. The teacher's movements should be smooth and natural, neither distracting from the lesson nor disturbing the student.

Kinetic variation includes one or a combination of the following motions: (a) moving freely from right to left and then from left to right in front of the classroom; (b) moving freely from front to back and then from back to front; and (c) moving freely among or behind students (Cooper et al., 1977). This technique also enables the teacher to use proximity control to intervene with problem behaviors (see chapter 9).

*Focusing* is the "teacher's way of intentionally controlling the direction of student attention" (Cooper et al., 1977, p. 136). Focusing can be verbal, behavioral, or both. Teachers can focus students' attention verbally by asking specific questions or using accent words such as "for example," "look," "how," or "find." Behavioral focusing may involve using body language: for example, facial expressions, eye contact, or pointing or other hand gestures to attract or direct attention.

*Shifting interaction* refers to the teacher's use of any one of the following interaction styles: teacher-group, teacher-student, or student-student. Teacher-group interaction puts the teacher in control, lecturing and directing discussion as needed. Teacher-student interaction is also teacher-directed, but the teacher becomes more of a facilitator, asking questions to clarify a story or answering questions raised by students after they have completed a lab assignment. Student-student interaction centers around students, with the teacher "redirecting student questions to other students for comment or clarification" (Cooper et al., 1977, p. 138). When planning a lesson, teachers should strive to include a variety of interaction styles.

Teachers can also use *pauses* or moments of silence effectively during a lesson. For example, a teacher can completely regain students' attention by becoming silent. Cooper et al. (1977) list 10 effective uses of pausing (p. 139):

1. It can break informational segments into smaller pieces for better understanding. Reading oral problems or dictating material for transcription requires careful attention to the effective use of pausing.
2. It can capture attention by contrasting sound with silence (alternating two distinctly different stimuli). Remember that attention is maintained at a high level when stimuli are varied, not when one increases the intensity of a single stimulus.
3. It can be a signal for students to prepare for the next teacher action.
4. It can be used to emphasize or underscore an important point.
5. It can provide time for thinking about a question or formulating an answer.
6. It can prevent teachers from unconsciously dominating discussion.
7. It encourages teachers to listen to individual student responses. People do not listen well when they are talking.
8. It can create suspense or expectation. For all types of literature, the effective reader uses the pause to stir emotion and heighten anticipation in the listener.
9. It can help provide a model of listening behavior for other students.
10. It can be used to show disapproval of undesired student behavior.

*Shifting the senses* means presenting information through more than one of the five senses—seeing, touching, hearing, smelling, and tasting. The importance of shifting senses for mainstreamed students cannot be overemphasized. Assimilating information through various perceptual modalities helps those students learn the information in as many ways as possible.

Teachers who use these stimulus variation techniques enhance their teaching. When teachers plan the lesson carefully, adapt it when necessary for mainstreamed students, and include techniques for adding variety to the presentation, they increase their chances of stimulating all students to learn.

## Intervention Taxonomy

A taxonomy is a classification method to orderly arrange items in related groups. Specific relationships among and within the groups are identifiable. A taxonomy or some other theory model should show a clear correspondence to life in the real world.

Over the years I have often heard general education teachers say, "I simply do not have the time to prepare and implement all of the interventions that are required for my class of students." From special education teachers I have repeatedly heard, "I cannot be in so many places at one time" and "There just is not enough of me to go around." Both sets of educators are correct. There is not enough time to accomplish what teachers are asked to do.

Wood, Womack, and Feola (1996) conducted a national survey of 2,500 educators, both general and special, to see if a taxonomy for interventions existed. Results of the survey indicated that indeed it did. General and special educators who worked closely together saw the taxonomy. However, educators who "did their own thing" or did not collaborate saw no correlation between interventions and levels.

To explain this idea further, I am going to give you my famous "potato lecture." Imagine that I have nine bags of potatoes: the first bag weighs 1 pound, the second 2 pounds, the third 3 pounds, and so on (Figure 11.2). I can peel, cook, and serve bags 1, 2, and 3 without assistance. If you peel and cook the potatoes in the 4-pound bag, I can serve. However, as the bags of potatoes become heavier (requiring more time to peel, cook, and serve), I need more and more help.

In other words, the heavier the bag (or higher the intervention type), the more support the educator needs. The general educator can handle types 1, 2, and 3 without assistance. But when they begin to move into type 4 and higher, they need more time and support.

Figure 11.3 describes the nine intervention taxonomy levels. This taxonomy will be useful in teacher-training programs and the allocation of resources and support. It may also assist in solving the dilemma of grading within inclusive environments.

**FIGURE 11.2**
Potato bags.

**Type 1:** interventions made to lesson plan format that are useful to all students

**Type 2:** interventions made to lesson plan format for student choice

**Type 3:** interventions specific to student mismatch that general education teacher can make independently

**Type 4:** interventions specific to student mismatch developed by team effort or support personnel and implemented by general education teacher

**Type 5:** interventions specific to student mismatch developed by both general teacher's team or support personnel and implemented by general or special education teacher or support staff (instructional aide or paraprofessional) in a regular class setting

**Type 6:** interventions specific to student mismatch developed by team or support personnel and implemented by special education teachers or support staff in a general class setting

**Type 7:** interventions specific to student mismatch developed by team or support personnel and implemented by special education teacher or support staff in alternative environments (outside the general class setting)

**Type 8:** parallel lesson developed by general or team support personnel and implemented in a general education or alternative environment

**Type 9:** alternative lesson developed by general or team support personnel and implemented in a general education or alternative environment

**FIGURE 11.3**

Intervention taxonomy levels.

*Source:* With permission from Judy W. Wood © (1996).

The present taxonomy illustrates ways of accomplishing lesson planning in inclusive settings through collaboration. Instructional intervention is needed for students in inclusive as well as alternative environments. The greater the student's need for alternative learning methods, the more intense a level of planning is required. Today's emphasis is on inclusion and helping all students achieve successfully. A need to describe the interactions among general educators, special educators' building/center and central office administration, students, parents, and other members of the student's intervention planning team became noticeable.

The intervention intensity taxonomy serves many purposes and seeks to provide objectives which facilitate decision making for professionals. Types of intervention intensity taxonomy actions which may be used in the decision-making process are listed below.

- Is a vehicle to help educators analyze how inclusive practices and modifications will be developed and delivered.

- Provides a framework which illustrates the process of collaboration among special and general educators as they provide appropriate instruction in the least restrictive environments.

- Provides educators with the ability to clearly define roles and responsibilities for all service providers as they cooperatively decide who will develop and deliver instructional modification.

- Is useful to campus and district administrators in assessing program needs, determining staff allocation, and identifying staff development needs.

- Is available to educators in moving forward from the theory of inclusion to the successful practice of inclusion.

Through frequent usage of the taxonomy, other specific options may become evident and could be added to the above purposes and objectives. Using the taxonomy will help to increase one's circle of knowledge and networking opportunities with colleagues, agencies, and this author to share service findings.

## How the Intervention Intensity Taxonomy Fits Into the SAALE Model

Many of the taxonomy users have been trained in the use of the SAALE model. In review, this model is visualized as a "container for organizing all that one knows and will know in his/her professional future." The model divides the school day into eight manageable environments and proceeds to find where a student has a "mismatch" in one or more of these environments (remember, the checklists help to find the mismatch). When a mismatch is identified, an intervention is selected and the intervention is *typed* from 1–9 (Figure 11.4).

Figure 11.4 graphically presents how the intervention taxonomy fits into the SAALE model. The example shown is taken from the organization of the instruction block of the model. The *skill* is note taking, the *mismatch* is the student *cannot* copy from the board, the selected intervention is to use a carbon set of notes, and *intervention type* is a type 3.

Table 11.8 presents a work plan for the intervention steps. Using the plan requires six simple steps:

1. *Identify* the mismatch between the student and classroom setting;
2. Decide on which *type* from the nine taxonomy levels (1–9) of intervention to select and use. Refer to Table 11.8 for assistance.
3. As a team, decide in which *setting,* regular class or alternative environment, the intervention will be implemented;
4. As a team, select which educator will *develop* the intervention;
5. As a team, decide who will implement the intervention; and
6. Lastly, record the timelines for development and implementation for accountability purposes. See Table 11.9.

As mismatches are identified, specific pragmatic needs for each student or perhaps an entire class will begin to surface. Educators will begin to see interventions or strategies as simply "doing that which you have not tried." Students may benefit

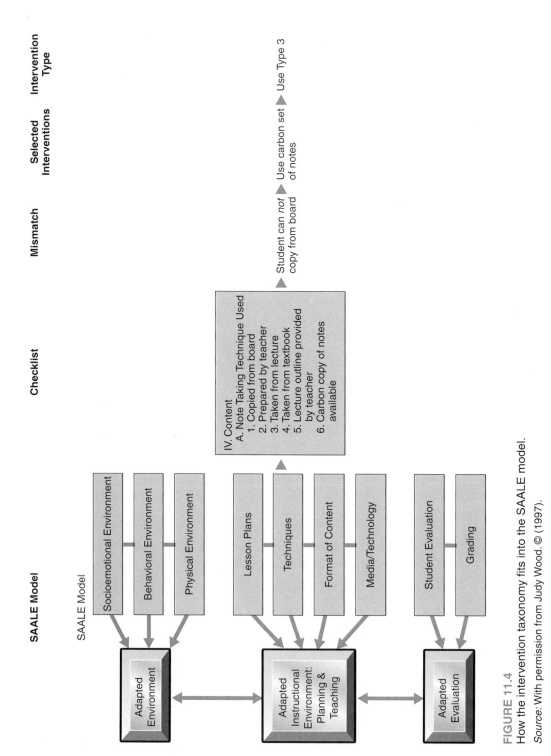

**FIGURE 11.4**

How the intervention taxonomy fits into the SAALE model.

*Source:* With permission from Judy Wood. © (1997).

**TABLE 11.8**
Intervention intensity taxonomy for lesson planning.

| Type | Intervention Intensity | Setting | Developed By | Implemented By |
|---|---|---|---|---|
| 1 | Interventions which may be made to lesson format that are useful to all students | regular class | general education teacher | general education teacher |
| 2 | Interventions made to lesson plan format for student choice | regular class | general education teacher | general education teacher |
| 3 | Interventions specific to student mismatch that general education teacher can make independently | regular class | general education teacher | general education teacher |
| 4 | Interventions specific to student mismatch that are developed by special education teacher and implemented by general education teacher | regular class | special education teacher | general education teacher |
| 5 | Interventions specific to student mismatch that are developed by both general and special education teachers and implemented by general and/or special education teacher and/or support staff (i.e. instructional assistant or paraprofessional) in a regular class setting | regular class | general & special education teacher | general & special education teachers and/or support staff |
| 6 | Interventions specific to student mismatch that are developed by special education teachers and implemented by special education teachers and/or support staff in a regular class setting | regular class | special education teacher | special education teachers and/or staff |
| 7 | Interventions specific to student mismatch that are developed by special education teacher and implemented by special education teacher and/or support staff in alternative environments (outside the regular class setting) | alternative environment | special education teacher | special education teachers and/or staff |
| 8 | Parallel lesson that is developed by general and/or special education teacher and implemented in a regular education and/or alternative environment | regular class and/or alternative environment | general & special education teacher | general &/or special education staff |
| 9 | Alternative lesson that is developed by general and/or special education teacher and implemented in a regular education and/or alternative environment | regular class and/or alternative environment | general & special education teacher | general &/or special education staff |

*Source:* With permission from Judy Wood. (1997).

**TABLE 11.9**

| Sample Staff Development Need for Interaction Assessment Form | | | |
|---|---|---|---|
| **IDENTIFIED BEHAVIOR** | **IDENTIFIED INTERVENTION AND TYPE** | **RESOURCES NEEDED** | **UNSURE OF HELP NEEDED** |
|  |  |  |  |

*Source:* Wood, J.W. (2001). With permission.

from similar or the same intervention. The *classroom* will emerge as *many clear needs* and not as *a total* to be taught. Educators will begin to see that interventions serve *all* students and not just those in instructional need.

## ADAPTING A LESSON PLAN

Developing and adapting the lesson plan is a shared responsibility for general and special education teachers. There are numerous ways in which this process can be completed. For educators working side by side within the general class, the task of adapting for a specific child is easy. For general educators who do not have a special education teacher in the room or who have numerous at-risk students in the class, the lesson plan format in Figure 11.5 can be a helpful tool. It can be (a) completed by the general education teacher for each day's lesson, with adaptations made by the special education teacher for a specific student, or (b) completed in total by the general education teacher. Suggestions from an intervention plan help educators complete the form.

Figure 11.5 presents a four-column format for one day's lesson plans. Under the date, the teacher indicates the taxonomy level of the objective. This checklist helps the general education teacher remain aware of the taxonomy level and be consistent in following through with the level across the objective, strategies, and

| Objective | Strategies | Resources | Evaluation |
|---|---|---|---|
| The student will be able to list and define the parts of the ear and the steps for the travel of sound in the ear. | Lecture on the parts of the ear and how sound travels | • Display of ear<br>• Filmstrip<br>• Chapter in text<br>• Handout about parts of ear | Fill-in-the-blank test |

Date:

Taxonomy level

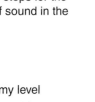

   ✓  Knowledge

   ✓  Comprehension

_____ Application

_____ Analysis

_____ Synthesis

_____ Evaluation

**Teaching techniques**

• Use acquisition outline.

• Use structured organizer to show relationship of parts of ear.

• Use visual of ear with lecture.

**Format of content:**

• Develop a task analysis listing steps of how sound travels in the ear.

• Color-code each step in each ear part.

**Adapted media**

• Label each ear part on the display.

• Use a checklist for viewing filmstrip.

• Record reading materials.

• Put ear parts and definitions on 3″ × 5″ cards.

• Use overlay transparency for practicing ear parts.

• Project ear on chalkboard and practice drawing sound track.

• Provide study guide.

**Evaluation:**

• Provide word bank.

• Tell students what type of test items will be used on the test.

**Student assignment:**

• Be sure that the assignment is on the appropriate cognitive levels.

• Modify assignment based on each student's ability.

**FIGURE 11.5**
Lesson plan intervention format.

evaluation sections. It also reminds the special education teacher of the objective level. If the level is inappropriate, the special education teacher can make a note on the plan for the general class teacher.

In the first column, the teacher lists the lesson objective; in the second column, the strategies used; in the third column, the lesson's materials and resources; and in the fourth column, plans for evaluation. The lower section of each column provides space for the special education teacher to note adaptations. Under adaptations, in the first column, the special education teacher may list specific names of students who will use the adaptation and note if they will be working at a different taxonomy level. Space is also provided for notes about the objective. The second column is divided into two sections: teaching techniques and format of content. The special education teacher can provide specific suggestions for each area as they relate to the strategies in the lesson. In the third column, space is provided for resource suggestions. In the fourth column, space is provided for the special education teacher to comment on the lesson evaluation and student assignment sections of the general class plan. This simple format encourages ongoing suggestions for the teacher during the lesson process.

## Instructional Flow Chart

Figure 11.6 presents an instructional flow chart for assisting educators teaching multigrade or multilevel classes. Everyone can't be at the same place at the same time. With many different abilities within one class, oneness is not possible or effective.

The chart is divided into the express route and the scenic route. Starting with the first block, students read the upcoming chapters. A pretest is given. Those students who show mastery of the chapter move to the express route, where they plan a research project and produce a product that must be shared with the class. Stu-

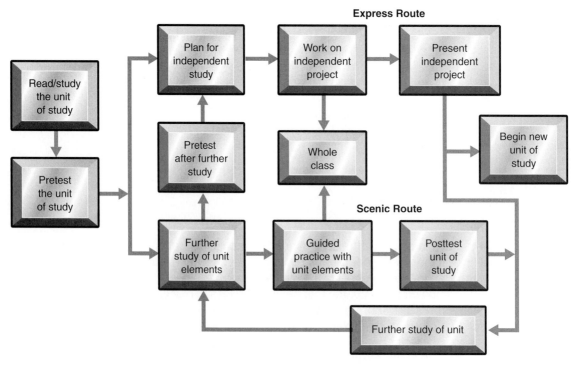

**FIGURE 11.6**
Unit of study cycle.

dents experiencing difficulty with the pretest move to the scenic route, where a class is designed to teach content.

This procedure may be modified into many different formats. For example, perhaps for one unit all students can travel the express route. It is extremely important that students may be tracked or realize that a pattern exists.

Figures 11.7, 11.8, and 11.9 illustrate possible project ideas. (Thanks to Pat Hamilton for her help on both the chart and the projects.)

---

**Topic:** Diorama

1. Select a person, place, or thing from the period we are studying.
2. Research it carefully.
3. Prepare a three-dimensional presentation using box.
   a. Color background.
   b. Put figures of different sizes in front.

**Evaluation:** Display your work for evaluation.

**Time limit:** 3 days

**You may do a topic only once per semester. You must choose a different topic for each project.**

Write a plan for your project.

The title of my project is _____

The references that I **think** I will need for my project are

1.
2.
3.

The supplies that I **think** I will need for my project are

1.
2.
3.

I will need to work in the following locations to complete my project:

1.
2.
3.

---

FIGURE 11.7
Diorama project.

---

**Topic:** Timeline

1. Select a topic from the period we are studying
2. Place significant dates about your topic on the timeline.
3. Make the timeline large enough to be seen when displayed on the wall.


**Evaluation:** Display your work for evaluation.

**Time limit:** 3 days

**You may do a topic only once per semester. You must choose a different topic for each project.**


Write a plan for your project.

The title of my project is _____


The references that I **think** I will need for my project are

1.
2.
3.

The supplies that I **think** I will need for my project are

1.
2.
3.

I will need to work in the following locations to complete my project:

1.
2.
3.

---

**FIGURE 11.8**
Timeline project.

# CONCLUSION

As teachers prepare lesson plans, they should take time to make adaptations for special-needs and at-risk students. By working collaboratively in the development and implementation of lesson plans, general and special education teachers can provide appropriate instruction for all students. Teachers will discover that when they adapt their lesson plans to the specific needs of learners, students *can* learn the lessons.

**Topic:** Read a historical novel

1. Select a novel based in the period we are studying.
2. Make a journal entry about your reading each day.
3. Your journal will be discussed at the end of the project.
4. Be prepared to answer questions.

**Evaluation:**  Turn in journal for evaluation.

**Time limit:**  5 days

**You may do a topic only once per semester. You must choose a different topic for each project.**

Write a plan for your project.

The title of my project is _____

The references that I **think** I will need for my project are

1.
2.
3.

The supplies that I **think** I will need for my project are

1.
2.
3.

I will need to work in the following locations to complete my project:

1.
2.
3.

**FIGURE 11.9**
Reading project.

To summarize this chapter, I have prepared a simple flow chart or organizer which shows us where we started—the three prerequisites of learning—and where each section of this chapter fits. It is important to use the resources from all sections of this chapter in order to make information accessible and to help students feel supported. Lesson planning and implementing is a *must* first-step process for teaching. The remaining chapters further develop the planning process.

# CHAPTER 12

# Adapting Teaching Techniques

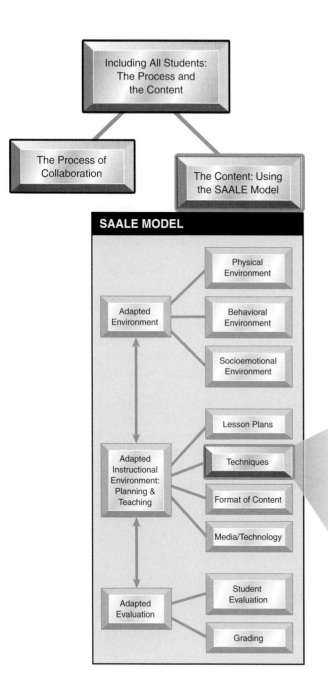

SAALE MODEL

Including All Students:
The Process and
the Content

The Process of
Collaboration

The Content: Using
the SAALE Model

Adapted
Environment

Physical
Environment

Behavioral
Environment

Socioemotional
Environment

Adapted
Instructional
Environment:
Planning &
Teaching

Lesson Plans

Techniques

Format of Content

Media/Technology

Adapted
Evaluation

Student
Evaluation

Grading

**Chapter-at-a-Glance**

Structuring for Student
Success

How Students Learn

Adapting Teaching Techniques

Instruction is a teacher's major responsibility to children, school, and community. Good instructional planning paves the way for an organized school day and for the smooth delivery of information vital to children's academic development. But instead of defining instruction as simply imparting specific content, teachers should think of instruction as an ongoing process; the teacher delivers information to children who receive and assimilate it. Teachers who adapt instruction to meet the needs of all students, especially those with mild disabilities, discover that they deliver information more effectively and students learn it more easily. Instruction becomes a continuous process of presenting information, adapting information, representing information, and testing for concept mastery. Making adaptation a natural component of this continuum helps students succeed.

The teaching technique is the delivery system that transmits content from teacher to students. If the technique is not appropriate for a student, then the content will most likely never be delivered. This chapter examines the importance of structure in student's lives, learning styles, and teaching and adaptations for specific modes of teaching.

## STRUCTURING FOR STUDENT SUCCESS

"Many at-risk youngsters thrive in well-structured learning situations . . . " (Carbo & Hughes, 1988, p. 57). A structured environment provides predictability, and predictability reduces anxiety. Students who have difficulty imposing structure on the learning process benefit greatly from the efforts of educators to incorporate structure within the instructional process.

Students who naturally do well in school appear to have the ability to reduce the chaos of disorganized information and impose their own structure on material to be learned. The second type of learner is the random learner. And there is a natural tendency within our system to *avoid* imposing structure on the random learner because "no one will do this when the student leaves school and moves into adult life." In reality, however, if we help disorganized or random learners impose structure, then they will transfer those skills into adult life.

Lessons in which the pattern of organization reflects structure are effective for all learners.

1. Structure provides a pathway for organizing information.
2. The work effort is reduced for learners because they do not have to process the information first and then establish order or a connection to understand the information.
3. The patterns of thought in a structured lesson or class can be generalized into other learning situations.

Providing structure instructionally is imperative for many learners. We cannot wait for learners to figure out how to structure or organize information to be learned. Structuring must become a natural part of instruction. George Frowert, a successful young adult, defines structure as "the ability to organize oneself efficiently enough in order for one to remain self-sufficient." Perhaps by imposing instructional structure we can assist children and young adults such as George with this process.

# HOW STUDENTS LEARN

Students want to learn to acquire knowledge or skills. Designing and implementing effective instruction so that students learn to their fullest capacity challenges us all. If learning means the acquisition of knowledge or skills, and the teacher wants to help students with that acquisition, then the teacher needs to understand the process of learning in general.

This brings us back to the beginning—learning or the capacity to learn is based on intellectual ability. The theories of intellect are numerous. Costa & Kallick (2000) present several influential theories of intelligence:

*Intelligence can be taught.* Arthur Whimbley (Whimbley, Whimbley, & Shaw, 1975) opened the discussion that intelligence could be taught and therefore not exclusively genetically inherited (p. 4).

*Structure of the intellect.* Guildford and Hoeptner (1971) reported 120 factors of intellect. The 120 abilities could produce combinations of factors. Twenty-six factors related to school success, and interventions could amplify intelligence (pp. 4–5).

During one of my postgraduate classes, I had the wonderful opportunity to study under psychologist Dr. Raymond Muskgrove. Dr. Muskgrove taught a complete course on theories of intelligence, with the Guilford model being his favorite. It is a fascinating theory/model that I encourage readers to investigate further. I was impressed that Guilford identified early on how important interventions and their relationship to learning are.

(Another note regarding my professor, Dr. Muskgrove. He was a colleague of B.F. Skinner and worked beside Skinner in the lab watching the rats scurry about. I was always fascinated with the old pictures of Dr. Skinner (who passed away in the 1980s) and Dr. Muskgrove standing in the lab. Both were so young, and history was written all over those pictures. I salute both great men and will forever be grateful for having the great opportunity to study with the late Dr. Raymond Muskgrove.)

*Theory of cognitive modifiability.* Feuerstin believed that intelligence is not fixed, but instead is a function of experience. This theory is the underlying thread of modern theory which states that intelligence can be taught and that everyone is gifted to a degree and retarded to a degree (p. 5).

*Multiple forms of intelligence.* Howard Garner (1983, 1999) reports many ways for learning to be expressed. The popular model lists the following intelligences: verbal, logical/mathematical, kinesthetic, musical, spatial, naturalistic, interpersonal, and intrapersonal. These intelligences may be developed throughout our lifetime.

*Intelligence as success in life.* Sternberg, Torff, and Grigorenko (1998) report three intelligences, which grow throughout life: analytical, creative, and practical (p. 6).

*Learned intelligence.* David Perkins (1995) "further supports the theory that intelligence can be taught and learned." He believes that three important mechanisms underlie intelligence:

- *Neural intelligence* is "genetically determined, hard-wired original equipment" that one has inherited and that determines the speed and efficiency of one's brain. Neural intelligence cannot be altered much.

- *Experiential intelligence* is context-specific knowledge that is accumulated through experience. It means knowing one's way around the various settings and contexts in which one functions. A person's reservoir of experiential intelligence can be expanded.

- *Reflective intelligence* is the "good use of the mind; the artful deployment of our facilities of thinking." It includes self-managing, self-monitoring, and self-modifying. Perkins (1995, p. 264) refers to this capacity as "mind-ware," which can and should be cultivated (p. 6).

*Emotional intelligence.* Daniel Coleman (1995) simply states that intelligence and emotions are intertwined. One develops with the other.

*Moral intelligence.* Robert Coles (1997) believes that inner character development through interactions with environment and persons within one's environment produce a "moral archeology," a moral code of ethics (pp. 6–7).

## Learning and Cognitive Styles

*Learning styles* are students' individual approaches to learning. Knowledge of the different ways that students may approach a learning situation and awareness of the influences on these approaches pave the way for successful teaching. Some students with mild disabilities may use one learning style or another, but many reflect a composite of different styles, showing that children learn in many different ways.

In addition to having a distinctive approach to a learning situation, a student has a *cognitive style.* According to Fuhrmann (1980), "The cognitive components create learning . . . . Each of us develops a typical approach in our use of our cognitive characteristics to perceive, to think, and to remember. This approach constitutes our cognitive learning style" (p. 2).

Keefe (1979) places the many cognitive styles into two major categories: reception styles, which involve perceiving and analyzing functions; and concept formation and retention styles, which pertain to generating hypotheses, solving problems, and remembering. According to Fuhrmann (1980), these two cognitive categories "can be described by a series of continua, with an individual style being found at any point" (p. 2). Table 12.1 shows individual differences in reception, concept formation, and retention styles.

**TABLE 12.1**
Cognitive styles: Learner and teacher descriptions.

| Learner Style | Learner Needs | Teacher Role | Teacher Behavior |
|---|---|---|---|
| *Dependent:* may occur in introductory courses, languages, some sciences when learners have little or no information upon entering course | • Structure<br>• Direction<br>• External reinforcement<br>• Encouragement<br>• Esteem from authority | • Expert<br>• Authority | • Lecturing<br>• Demonstrating<br>• Assigning<br>• Checking<br>• Encouragement<br>• Testing<br>• Reinforcing content<br>• Transmitting<br>• Grading<br>• Designing materials |
| *Independent:* may occur when learners have much more knowledge or skill upon entering the course and want to continue to search on their own; may feel instructor cannot offer as much as they would like | • Internal awareness<br>• Experimentation<br>• Time<br>• Nonjudgmental support | • Facilitator | • Allowing<br>• Providing requested feedback<br>• Consulting<br>• Listening<br>• Negotiating<br>• Evaluating |
| *Collabortive:* may occur when learners have knowledge, information, ideas, and would like to share them or try them out | • Interaction<br>• Practice<br>• Probing self and others<br>• Observation<br>• Participation<br>• Peer challenge<br>• Peer esteem<br>• Experimentation | • Colearner<br>• Environment setter | • Interacting<br>• Questioning<br>• Providing resources<br>• Modeling to share<br>• Providing feedback<br>• Coordinating<br>• Evaluating<br>• Managing<br>• Processing observer<br>• Grading |

*Source:* Fuhrmann, B. S., & Grasha, A. F. (1983). *A practical handbook for college teachers* (p. 115). Boston: Little, Brown. Adapted by permission.

# Conditions Affecting Learning Styles

In addition to an awareness of learning and cognitive styles, teachers should understand the many other conditions affecting the way children learn. The relationships among teaching and learning styles, students' perceptual styles, time, sound, seating arrangements and place, class procedures, group size, and students' attention spans all influence the learning process.

*Interaction between teaching and learning styles.* How students respond, how well they respond, or why they do not respond at all often depends on the interaction between teaching and learning styles. Johnson (1976) describes two student learning styles: the dependent prone and the independent prone. The Fuhrmann-Jacobs model of social interaction (Fuhrmann, 1980) adds a third: the collaborative prone. A student may be learning in all three styles but prefer a certain style in a certain situation. Thus, if some students prefer the dependent style for learning new information, but the teacher presents the material in the independent style, the students may not learn as quickly or as well as they could otherwise. Teachers should try to match their teaching styles to their students' learning styles as often as possible or vary their teaching styles so that, in any given situation, each student can use the learning style he or she prefers.

Students in an inclusive classroom usually prefer the dependent learner style. However, when students with special needs have some information about the subject, they tend to use the collaborative style.

*Perceptual styles.* A student's perceptual style refers to the sense through which the student best receives information: visual (seeing), auditory (hearing), or kinesthetic (touching). Most children tend to use one perceptual style more than the others. For example, 80 to 85 percent of all people are visual learners and learn best when they can see the information presented (for example, on the chalkboard, through overhead projectors, or with filmstrips).

Auditory learners learn best when they can hear the information presented (for example, in a lecture). A classroom teacher who uses the lecture method can help auditory learners by recording the lecture for students to play back later.

Some students need kinesthetic feedback to learn; for example, the teacher can provide sandboxes so that students draw or trace the letters of the alphabet in the sand and get kinesthetic feedback. Teachers need to plan instruction so that it addresses the student's dominant perceptual mode.

*Perception, processing, and retention.* Figure 12.1 shows the impact of perception, processing, and retention on the learner. First, information enters the student through any one of three areas of perception: visual, auditory, or kinesthetic. Modifications in those areas help educators effectively impart information.

Next, information is processed and retained (which is the subject of this entire book). Students must organize information and impose some sort of structure or associate strategies. Long- and short-term memory are extremely important in the processing/retention component.

Finally, students express the information they have processed and retained, using any of three output components: fine-motor expression, written/motor ex-

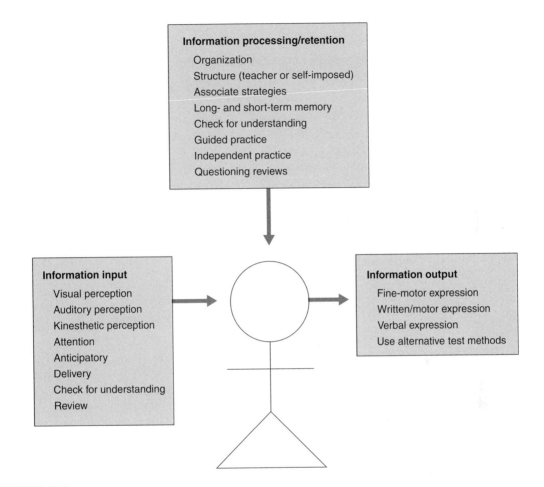

**FIGURE 12.1**
Perception, processing, and retention.

pression, or verbal expression. Information output can be measured using numerous models. Modifications during the output stage help teachers get the most from the student.

Figures 12.2 through 12.7 and Table 12.2 suggest appropriate accommodations for each perceptual area.

*Seating arrangements.* When students first come into class, where do they sit? Do they return to the same places the next day? Teachers attending a class or a meeting prefer certain places—by the window, next to the door, in the front row, or in the back of the room—and children also have such seating preferences. Teachers should try to provide students with a seating arrangement flexible enough for variety but structured enough for consistency.

**Characteristics**

- Frequently loses place when reading or copying
- Has trouble discriminating among similar shapes, letters, and words
- Does not enjoy pictures, slides, or books
- Has difficulty reading and copying accurately from chalkboard
- Shows signs of eye strain such as squinting, blinking, and holding head close to page
- Has trouble following written directions from board or printed page
- Works slowly on printed assignments or tests
- Displays poor sight vocabulary
- May use fingers to keep place while reading
- Skips words or reverses words when reading aloud
- Cannot visualize things in mind
- Demonstrates erratic spelling or incorrect letter sequences
- Does not notice details on pictures, maps, and photographs
- Confused by work sheets containing a great deal of visual stimuli
- Has difficulty remembering what is seen
- May whisper to self while working with visual material

**Accommodations for all subject areas**

- Give the child the clearest copy of the photocopied work sheets.
- Make sure students are seated close to the teacher, board, or work area.
- Make an effort to write clearly and neatly on the board and on work sheets.
- Try always to give verbal information or an explanation along with a visual presentation.

FIGURE 12.2

Visual perception problems and accommodations.

*Source:* Fugen, S. A., Graves, D. L., & Tessier-Smith, P., *Promoting successful mainstreaming: Reasonable classroom accommodations for learning disabled students.* Rockville, MD: Montgomery County Public Schools. Adapted with permission.

**Accommodations for reading/literature**

- Use color highlighting on work sheets to cue the student to important words and concepts.
- Introduce new vocabulary in context before a reading assignment.
- Allow students to use index cards to keep their place while reading.
- Pair students for reading assignments.

**Accommodations for math**

- Encourage students to verbalize the steps involved in solving a problem as they work through it on paper.
- Give practice in reading word problems just to identify the key words and determine the operation needed to solve the problem.
- Alert students to the importance of paying close attention to the signs of operation on randomly mixed problem work sheets; for example, in the written directions, write WATCH THE SIGNS!
- Exchange practice work sheets with another teacher, which gives each double materials without double work.

**Accommodations for social studies/science**

- Pause periodically during an oral presentation to ask for questions and give students a chance to add notes to their papers.
- Summarize at the end of the lecture and encourage students to ask questions about what they may have missed in their notes.
- Review the notes from the previous lesson before beginning a new presentation.
- Assign the student with learning disabilities to a reliable work group in lab situations.

**Characteristics**

- Has trouble distinguishing fine differences between sounds and words (such as *d-t* and *pin-pen*)
- Loses interest or concentration during lectures
- Has difficulty following a series of oral directions
- Cannot accurately record notes from oral presentations
- Displays poor receptive vocabulary
- Repeats what is told before acting or responding
- Often repeats the same question
- Asks questions about oral directions and facts previously given
- May watch the speaker's face intently or lean forward toward the speaker
- Does not enjoy listening to records or rhythmic activities
- Becomes irritated by extraneous noise
- Has difficulty learning and applying phonetic rules
- May have difficulty remembering what is heard

**Accommodations for all subject areas**

- Seat students in a location where sound is clear; avoid seating near distracting sounds or noises.
- Keep oral directions short and simple. Give one-step directions at first. Gradually increase to two-step directions and so on.
- Accompany oral directions with written directions. List them sequentially, using vocabulary appropriate for the students.
- Ask students to paraphrase your oral directions. Call upon different group members to do this.
- Alert the students when you are giving directions by setting the stage. ("This is important. I'll give you the directions now.") Alert an individual student through eye contact, teacher positioning, or a gentle touch.
- Be conscious of your rate of speech. Talk slower if students indicate they are having difficulty staying with you.
- Assist students to stay with you during instruction by using gestures and changes in the tone and pitch of your voice.
- Allow the students to move to a quiet place in the classroom to do their independent work.
- Write key points on the board for students to copy for studying during a lecture or oral presentation.
- Allow a classmate to use carbon paper to take notes for a student with learning disabilities during a lecture. This allows the student to concentrate on listening. After the lecture, the student can add to the notes his or her classmate took.
- Summarize the key points of your lesson with a visual prop. For instance, after a lesson, use the overhead projector to do a simple work sheet together. This work sheet may use a fill-in-the-blank, true-false, or multiple-choice format. Individual work sheets may or may not accompany the overhead.

**FIGURE 12.3**

Auditory perception problems and accommodations.

*Source:* Fugen, S. A., Graves, D. L., & Tessier-Smith, P. *Promoting successful mainstreaming: Reasonable classroom accommodations for learning disabled students.* Rockville, MD: Montgomery County Public Schools. Adapted with permission.

## Accomodations for all subject areas — *continued*

- Try to use visual support (pictures, photographs, charts, maps, films, filmstrips, overheads) with auditory presentations. Many audiovisual materials are available upon request from the school media center.
- Circulate about the room, inconspicuously repeating directions to those who need them. Assign a buddy to repeat directions.
- Take notes yourself or assign a student to take notes on the board, chart paper, overhead, or ditto master during class discussions. This frees the students with learning disabilities to concentrate on listening. Allow the class to copy the notes at the end of the period, or run copies from the ditto master for students who need them.
- Teach students how to listen. Emphasize the importance of correct listening posture, eye contact with the speaker, removal of distracters, and the intent to remember.

## Accommodations for reading/literature

- Prepare students for listening by giving them an outline to follow and fill in during class presentations. The outline can be presented on the board or overhead or as an individual handout.
- Set up an audiovisual center with headsets to reinforce listening skills through high-interest visual materials—for example, cassette/book or filmstrip/cassette kits. Stories with repetitious words or phrases may be used.
- Break up oral presentations with visual or motor activities. It is difficult for a student with auditory problems to sit passively while listening for an entire period.

## Accommodations for math

- When reading word problems aloud to students, give them a visual clue. Chart or graph the problem on the board, rewrite it simply, use manipulatives, or allow students to draw a picture.
- Show an example of how the problems are to be solved at the top of work sheets. Another option is to complete the first problem or two with the students before they complete the page independently.
- Make a basic problem-solving sequence chart to post in the room. Here is an example:

  1. Read the problem.
  2. Identify key words.
  3. Identify the operation.
  4. Write the number sentence.
  5. Solve the problem.

## Accommodations for social studies/science

- Provide ample wait time for students who are having difficulty answering questions. Give a partial sentence, gesture, or visual aid as a clue, if necessary.
- Give students work sheets to follow along with a filmstrip or a film. Stop the film at appropriate points to allow students to fill in the work sheet. This will break up the listening activity into shorter segments. Summarize the film at its conclusion so that students do not lose sense of the whole.
- Use a film or a filmstrip to provide an overview when introducing new material. It can be shown again at the end of the unit to summarize.

**Characteristics**

- Tries things out; touches, feels, manipulates
- Expresses things physically; jumps for joy, pushes, tugs, stomps, pounds
- Gestures when speaking; is a poor listener; stands very close when speaking or listening; quickly loses interest in long verbal discourse
- Starts the day looking neat and tidy but soon becomes disheveled through physical activity
- Seems impulsive
- Prefers to attack problems physically; seeks solutions that involve the greatest activity
- Handwriting that appears good initially but deteriorates as space runs out on the paper and the student exerts more and more pressure on the writing instrument
- Prefers stories with lots of action, especially in the beginning; rarely an avid reader
- Fidgets a lot while handling books
- Often a poor speller; needs to write words to see if they look correct

**Accommodations for all subject areas**

- Provide opportunities for direct concrete physical involvement in activities.
- Allow opportunities for materials manipulation.
- Allow opportunities for writing on paper and the chalkboard, drawing, and hands-on activities with real objects that can be touched.
- Use hand signals, small-group discussions, and activities that involve emotions and feelings or enable students to move around.
- Play music as a good method of involving movement; sculpture and clay molding are preferable to painting.
- Plan field trips that enable students to dance or play percussion instruments or to touch items.
- Try activities that allow for gross-motor movement reinforced by visual stimulation.
- Avoid verbal lectures and sedentary classroom activities as much as possible.

FIGURE 12.4

Kinesthetic perception problems and accommodations.

*Source:* Fugen, S. A., Graves, D. L., & Tessier-Smith, P. *Promoting successful mainstreaming: Reasonable classroom accommodations for learning disabled students.* Rockville, MD: Montgomery County Public Schools. Adapted with permission.

**Characteristics**

- Displays poor handwriting and has difficulty forming letters and numbers
- Has difficulty in activities requiring cutting or pasting
- Finds it hard to trace or color within given borders
- Has trouble with speed and neatness in taking notes
- Shows fatigue and restlessness during writing or drawing tasks
- Handwritten work often appears sloppy and disorganized
- Has difficulty manipulating or using small objects and tools
- Usually works slowly in completing written work
- Has trouble making straight lines for connecting points, matching answers, or labeling maps
- Displays poor copying skills

**Accommodations for all subject areas**

- Set a good handwriting example. A teacher's own handwriting serves as a model for students' writing.
- Place the paper to be copied directly at the top of students' papers rather than to one side or the other when copying is necessary.
- Teach students how to erase and make corrections without beginning over each time. This is a minor matter that can make a big difference in the appearance of students' papers. Students may be able to eliminate unclear, distracting erasures by using erasable pens.
- Minimize copying activities by providing the information or activities on work sheets or handouts. Introduce copying exercises slowly, gradually lengthening the amount of material to be copied.
- Assign follow-up activities that reduce students' writing requirement. Paired talking activities, cooperative small-group assignments, short-answer activity sheets, and instructional games all provide students with opportunities to review skills and knowledge without requiring lengthy written answers.
- Allow a peer with good note-taking skills to use carbon paper to make an extra set of notes for students with learning disabilities.
- Encourage students to acquire typing skills and to type homework assignments.
- Sometimes breaking crayons or pencils forces the child to grip the writing utensil in a more controlled and appropriate manner.

*(continued)*

**FIGURE 12.5**

Fine motor problems and accommodations.

*Source:* Fugen, S. A., Graves, D. L., & Tessier-Smith, P. *Promoting successful mainstreaming: Reasonable classroom accommodations for learning disabled students.* Rockville, MD: Montgomery County Public Schools. Adapted with permission.

### Accommodations for reading/literature

- Establish a routine for having students enter new vocabulary into a "word bank" on index cards. Cards can be color-coded for different subjects. Give students opportunities to use these cards to complete skills activities. (For example, ask students to use the cards for classifying activities, matching antonyms or synonyms, or identifying parts of speech.)

- Occasionally allow students to use manipulatives for composing words or sentences. You may use letter puzzle pieces or cubes from commercial materials.

### Accommodations for spelling/writing

- Help students understand the importance of good handwriting. Show how correct answers may be marked as incorrect because of poor letter formation. Help students understand that good hand-writing is a communication skill that allows others to understand their written ideas and thoughts.

### Accommodations for math

- Begin with the easiest problems and add the harder problems in a progressive order on work sheets.

- Fold or divide math paper into fourths, sixths, eighths, and so on. Place one problem per box.

### Accommodations for social studies/science

- Give students study guide questions or other advanced organizers for reading assignments.

- Teach students how to use the divided page method of note taking. To begin, students divide a sheet of dated notebook paper lengthwise into thirds by folding. On the left-hand side of the paper, students write key concepts in a word or short phrase. The center section is used to record important subpoints or supporting details relating to each key concept. The right-hand side is used to write a brief summary of the notes on the page. When studying, students refold the paper on the fold line so that their notes are on the outside. The student reads the key point and then tries to recall the important supporting data. To check, he or she turns to the other side of the notes.

- Help students to understand that their notes should serve as a study guide. It is important that they write down the key points, not every word in a lecture.

- Teach students to use abbreviations for note taking. It may be helpful to post abbreviations for specific subject matter vocabulary.

- Ask students to preview the text pages pertinent to your next lecture the night before. The preview may be accomplished by the SQ3R method or simply by skimming the material. This way the student will be ready for the lecture and more apt to recognize important points when mentioned.

- Give students plenty of opportunity to recall new information. Learning is promoted when students do more than just reread.

**FIGURE 12.5**
Continued.

**Characteristics**

- Has difficulty writing answers on paper but may be able to give correct answers orally
- Written vocabulary much weaker than spoken vocabulary
- Handwritten work sloppy and disorganized
- Written ideas and concepts usually stronger than writing mechanics (for example, spelling, syntax, vocabulary level)
- Has trouble writing a sentence with a complete thought
- Demonstrates poor spelling skills
- Tests better on objective tests than on tests that require writing (essays and definitions)
- Frequently does not complete written assignments

**Accommodations for all subject areas**

- Allow students more time to complete written assignments.
- Allow students to give all short answers to questions (single word or phrase).
- Allow students to complete an assignment that calls for written sentences by doing half in sentences and half in short phrases. Gradually students can move toward writing sentences for each question.
- Stress accuracy, not speed. Emphasize the importance of content and legibility.
- Give students some class time to work on written reports. This will enable the teacher to lend needed assistance.
- Be specific in your comments about written work. For example, instead of writing "poor grammar," write "use *doesn't* instead of *don't*." Whenever possible, also give individual feedback.
- Avoid comments that reflect value judgments. Instead of "messy," write "erase mistakes fully before rewriting."
- Allow students to check and correct their own work sheets against a model (individually or in a group). This gives students accurate and complete written information needed for improvement.
- Permit students to use pictures, drawings, and diagrams as part of their written products.
- Post a proofreading checklist in class for students.
- Ask students to skip every other line when writing a rough draft.
- Allow students to do taped or live oral reports instead of written reports. An outline or short written summary may still be required.
- Allow students to answer fewer questions or problems on work sheets requiring written statements—for example, every other problem or asterisked questions.

*(continued)*

**FIGURE 12.6**

Written/motor problems and accommodations.

*Source:* Fugen, S. A., Graves, D. L., & Tessier-Smith, P. *Promoting successful mainstreaming: Reasonable classroom accommodations for learning disabled students.* Rockville, MD: Montgomery County Public Schools. Adapted with permission.

**Accommodations for all subject areas — *continued***

- Consider making work sheets that reduce writing requirements—for example, multiple choice, short answer, matching, or fill-in-the-blank.
- Allow students to check math problems on calculators after working a set number of problems rather than having all problems completed before checking. This reduces writing fatigue while providing more immediate feedback.
- Permit students to work independently in an area free of distractions (away from windows, doors, or traffic areas). Intense concentration is often necessary for students with learning disabilities to write their best.
- Try assigning a different type of task or a modification of the original task as an alternative to asking students to do a poorly completed assignment over again. For example, instead of insisting that sentences be written within the lines, provide wide-lined paper or a typewriter.
- Encourage students to revise, edit, and proofread drafts before making final copies of their reports. Feedback will help students write better final copies. It also gives students the chance to do their own proofing.
- Use journals and diaries as an informal means for encouraging interest and fluency in writing.
- Try using all-student response cards in small-group settings. All students would have the same set of index cards, with each card containing a specific answer. In response to a question posed by the teacher, each student finds the card with the answer he or she believes is correct and holds up the card to the teacher. The teacher gives the correct answer and an explanation to the group if anyone has responded incorrectly. This type of activity could be used for math drills (cards would have numbers on them) or a homonym lesson (cards would have words on them, such as *pare, pair, pear*). Another use of response cards is for multiple-choice questions. Different-colored response cards can represent answer choices, such as blue = A, orange = B.
- Allow students to audiotape answers or work with peers, tutors, or volunteers who perform the writing tasks.

**Accommodations for reading/literature**

- Provide students with study guides for novels and units.
- Teach students to outline.
- Provide students with a purpose for reading. It is helpful for students to understand that we read differently for different purposes (to answer a specific question, to locate information, or for pleasure).

**Accommodations for spelling/writing**

- Provide a picture, title, topic sentence, or other prewriting activity to help students begin a creative story. Give students the opportunity to talk about their ideas and jot down key words before writing.
- Cut comic strips to help students organize ideas for writing. Students may be given the strips to sequence in the proper story order. These can serve as guides for writing.

FIGURE 12.6
Continued.

**Accommodations for spelling/writing — *continued***

- Give students guides for structuring creative writing stories by providing an organizational format.
- Give older students story starters (the first part of a story) to read before they are asked to write the story conclusion.
- Group students together to write round robin stories. Each student is responsible for an assigned portion of the whole story. One student may act as the recorder.
- Guide students' writing by giving them specifications or criteria sheets for the content and mechanics of written assignments. These can be valuable proofreading tools for students.
- Emphasize the importance of developing a topic sentence and then sentences of supporting detail when writing paragraphs.
- Provide a structure for writing reports or research papers by giving the class an outline of headings and subheadings to guide their paragraph development.
- Ask students to include the initial wording of the question that their sentence answers.

  *Sample question:*　　Why did Mrs. Smith lie to the police?

  *Sample answer:*　　Mrs. Smith lied to the police because she thought her brother was guilty.

- Ask older students to use the beginning margin line printed on notebook filler paper as a guide. If necessary, ask them to draw their own ending margin line on the right-hand side of the paper. Younger elementary students may need to draw, or have drawn for them, similar margin lines on both sides of the paper.
- Have students prenumber their answer sheets to ensure accurate matching of answers to question numbers.

**Accommodations for math**

- Turn lined paper vertically to help students organize math problems. This will help keep the ones, tens, and hundreds places lined up correctly.
- Use large graph paper if turning the paper vertically does not correct the problem. One numeral can be written in each square. Gradually make the transition to regular paper.

**Accommodations for social studies/science**

- Modify instructional materials that involve fine-motor skills (such as filling in charts, maps, diagrams) by
  1. Using sharp-colored pencils instead of crayons or wide markers
  2. Providing more space for color labeling
  3. Allowing extra time for completion
  4. Setting an index card at borders to prevent going out of bounds

**Characteristics**

- Does not enjoy discussions, oral presentations, or reading aloud
- Has difficulty explaining himself or herself clearly and coherently
- Displays poor speech—articulation, fluency, expressiveness
- Unable to vocalize thoughts rapidly
- Uses slang or colloquial terms instead of more precise words
- Spoken vocabulary that is much weaker than written vocabulary
- Reluctant to volunteer ideas or respond verbally to questions
- Remarks that are often irrelevant, confusing, or inaccurate
- Uncomfortable speaking in a group
- Has difficulty recalling a word he or she wants to use
- Uses grammatically incorrect sentences

**Accommodations for all subject areas**

- Give students a little extra time to respond. Many students have to struggle inwardly before being able to complete their thoughts verbally.
- If students are having difficulty, give them a hint to help them along.
- Urge students to use outlines or notes when presenting oral reports.
- Encourage students to use visual aids or handouts in conjunction with oral reports.
- Give students the opportunity to read silently before asking them to read orally.
- Structure opportunities for student verbal expression on a one-on-one basis and in small groups. Avoid calling on students to answer aloud in a group as punishment for inattentiveness during discussions.

**FIGURE 12.7**

Verbal problems and accommodations.

*Source:* Fugen, S. A., Graves, D. L., & Tessier-Smith, P. *Promoting successful mainstreaming: Reasonable classroom accommodations for learning disabled students.* Rockville, MD: Montgomery County Public Schools. Adapted with permission.

Some students lose interest in assigned tasks when they sit in the same seats day after day. Possible variations include having students sit on small mats on the floor, taking students to the library for class, or going outside for the lecture. One secondary school, for example, provides learning stations under the trees and uses logs for seating. Teachers then register for outside stations at the times they want.

When adapting classroom seating arrangements for students with mild disabilities, the teacher must consider any special needs the children may have. Also,

**Accommodations for all subject areas— *continued***

- Limit the length of students' oral presentations. Gradually the length can be increased as students feel more comfortable in front of their peers.

- Actively involve students in listening during other students' presentations. This can be accomplished by deciding, as a group, on the important points of oral presentations. A rating sheet can be made. Students can then rate each other. This method also guides students as they do their own presentations and may avoid misunderstandings about grades.

- Sometimes permit students to use all-student response cards in small groups instead of giving verbal responses (see Figure 12.).

- Ask specific, structured questions. This will permit the students to use the elements of the question to organize their answers. For example, "Can you tell me one way that comets and meteors are alike?" instead of "compare comets and meteors."

- Arrange small discussion groups and paired talking activities that permit students to practice verbal skills in a smaller, more comfortable setting.

- Permit students to tape their oral presentations instead of doing them live in class.

- Allow students to do projects in lieu of oral reports occasionally, such as demonstrations or displays that demonstrate their understanding of new skills or knowledge.

- Encourage the use of notes, letters, messages, and journals as an alternative to verbal expression.

- Pass the microphone to each reader so that everyone can hear.

- Younger classes can post what day of the week they will be called on to read orally.

- Tell students a day ahead what they will be asked to read tomorrow.

many students with disabilities are easily distracted and need to be placed close to the teacher.

*Class procedures.* Class procedures are more effective when based on the teacher's awareness of students' various learning styles. It is important to match assignments with learning styles when assigning students to projects, library work, reports, seat work, or learning centers, especially because the average class assignment is usually too difficult for the student with mild disabilities. The teacher can divide the same assignment into several short segments and use a variety of techniques for presenting the information. Class evaluation procedures also should vary according to learning styles. For example, a teacher can evaluate the work of a student with mild disabilities by simply observing, collecting work samples, or

**TABLE 12.2**
Perceptual areas: Behaviors and techniques.

| | | The Visual Modality | | |
|---|---|---|---|---|
| **Pupil Who Is Strong Visually May** | | | **The Teacher May Use** | |
| Show the following strengths: | Show the following weaknesses: | Formal assessment techniques: | Informal assessment techniques: | Instructional techniques |
| • Possess good sight vocabulary<br><br>• Demonstrate rapid reading skills<br><br>• Skim reading material<br><br>• Read well from picture clues<br><br>• Follow visual diagrams and other visual instruction well<br><br>• Score well on group tests<br><br>• Perform nonverbal tasks well | • Have difficulty remembering a sequence of oral directions; may ask, "What are we supposed to do?" immediately after oral instructions are given<br><br>• Appear confused by great amounts of auditory stimuli<br><br>• Have difficulty discriminating between words with similar sounds | • Give lists of words that sound alike. Ask pupil to indicate if they are the same or different.<br><br>• Ask pupil to follow specific instructions. Begin with one direction and continue with multiple instructions.<br><br>• Show pupil visually similar pictures. Ask him or her to indicate whether they are the same or different.<br><br>• Show pupil a visual pattern, such as a block design or Peg-Board design. Ask pupil to duplicate. | • Observe pupil in tasks requiring sound discrimination, such as rhyming, sound blending.<br><br>• Observe pupil's sight vocabulary skills. These skills should be strong in visual learners.<br><br>• Observe to determine if the pupil performs better when he or she can see the stimulus. | • *Reading:* Stress sight vocabulary, configuration clues, context clues.<br><br>• *Mathematics:* Show examples' functions.<br><br>• *Spelling:* Avoid phonetic analysis, stress structural clues, configuration clues.<br><br>• *Generally:* Allow a pupil with strong auditory skills to act as another child's partner. Allow for written rather than verbal responses. |

*Source:* Maryland State Department of Education, Division of Instructional Television. *Teaching children with special needs: Elementary level.* Owings Mills: Author. Copyright by Maryland State Department of Education, Division of Instructional Television. Adapted by permission.

## The Auditory Modality

| Pupil Who Is Strong Auditorially May | | The Teacher May Use | | Instructional techniques |
| --- | --- | --- | --- | --- |
| Show the following strengths: | Show the following weaknesses: | Formal assessment techniques: | Informal assessment techniques: | |
| • Follow oral instructions very easily | • Lose place in visual activities | • Present statement verbally; ask pupil to repeat. | • Observe whether pupil reads using a finger or pencil as a marker. | • *Reading:* Stress phonetic analysis, sight vocabulary, or fast reading. Allow pupils to use marker, fingers, and so on, to keep their place. |
| • Do well in tasks requiring phonetic analysis | • Read word by word | • Tap auditory pattern beyond pupil's point of vision. Ask pupil to repeat patterns or indicate if they are the same or different. | • Observe whether pupil whispers or barely produces sounds to correspond to reading task. | • *Mathematics:* Provide audiotapes of story problems. Verbally explain processes as well as demonstrate. |
| • Appear brighter than tests show him or her to be | • Reverse words when reading | | • Observe if pupil has difficulty following purely visual directions. | • *Spelling:* Build on syllabication skills; use sound clues. |
| • Appear very articulate | • Make visual discrimination errors | • Provide pupil with several words in a rhyming family. Ask pupil to add more. | | • *Generally:* Use work sheets with large unhampered areas. Use graph paper to align problems. Allow for verbal rather than written responses. |
| • Perform well verbally | • Have difficulty with written work; have poor motor skills | | | |
| | • Have difficulty copying from the chalkboard | | | |

*(continued)*

TABLE 12.2
Continued.

## The Kinesthetic Modality

| Pupil Who Is Strong Kinesthetically May | | The Teacher May Use | | |
|---|---|---|---|---|
| **Show the following strengths:** | **Show the following weaknesses:** | **Formal assessment techniques:** | **Informal assessment techniques:** | **Instructional techniques** |
| • Exhibit good fine- and gross-motor skills and balance<br><br>• Exhibit good rhythmic movements<br><br>• Demonstrate good cutting skills<br><br>• Manipulate puzzles and other materials well<br><br>• Identify and match objects easily<br><br>• Demonstrate neat handwriting skills | • Depend on the guiding modality of the visual or auditory mode because kinesthetic is usually a secondary modality. | • Ask pupil to walk on a balance beam or along a painted line.<br><br>• Set up an obstacle course involving gross-motor manipulation.<br><br>• Have pupil cut along straight, angled, and curved lines. | • Observe pupil in athletic tasks.<br><br>• Observe pupil maneuvering in classroom space.<br><br>• Observe pupil's spacing of written work on a paper.<br><br>• Observe pupil's selection of activities during free play. For example, does he or she select puzzles or blocks as opposed to records or books? | • *Reading:* Stress the shape and structure of a word; use configuration clues.<br><br>• *Mathematics:* Use objects in performing the arithmetic functions; provide calculators.<br><br>• *Spelling:* Allow students to practice writing new words before a test. |

using formative evaluation procedures. Matching the evaluation procedure to the student's learning style helps the teacher evaluate instructional objectives as well as appropriately evaluate the student.

Class procedures must also take into account the emotional aspects of learning styles. Fuhrmann (1980) eloquently summarizes the work of Dunn, Dunn, and Price (1979) on these emotional elements: motivation, persistence, responsibility, and structure.

For highly motivated students, a teacher needs only to give requirements and resources, but poorly motivated students require special attention to bring out their interest and desire to learn. For example, a student who is poorly motivated by a traditional lecture class may be highly motivated by a programmed text or a small discussion group.

The same length and type of assignment is probably not appropriate for all students because both attention span and persistence vary greatly. Furthermore, persistence is related to motivation; the greater the motivation to achieve in a particular learning experience, the more persistent a student is likely to be in completing the task. Sequenced learning tasks, with clearly defined steps and a final goal, offer the teacher some flexibility in meeting the needs of students with differing degrees of persistence.

Like motivated students, responsible students require only clear assignments and resources to succeed. Irresponsible students, however, often experience failure and discouragement in such an environment. Usually, students lacking responsibility have historically failed to achieve in school and therefore lack the confidence to assume responsibility. Teachers must attend first to their lack of confidence by offering opportunities for them to experience small successes. Individualizing assignments, breaking objectives into smaller components, trying experimental assignments, and using all types of learning aids and resources may encourage such students.

Students also differ in their response to structure—to the specific rules and directions they must follow to achieve certain objectives. More creative students often like a wide variety of options from which to choose, while those who are less creative may respond better to a single, well-defined method. Again, the emotional elements are related to one another because the more motivated, persistent, and responsible students require less structure than do the less motivated, less persistent, and less responsible ones (Fuhrmann, 1980).

Teachers, therefore, should make assignments, instruct, evaluate students, and carry out other class procedures on the basis of what they can determine about their students' learning styles and the emotional factors contributing to those styles.

*Group size.* The group size most effective for instruction varies according to the different learning styles of students and the content and purpose of the instruction. Some students learn better in small groups, some in large groups, and others one to one. Careful analysis of student performance helps the teacher select the most appropriate method. Most students with disabilities do not function well in large groups; instead, very small groups and one-to-one instruction are usually more effective.

*Attention span.* Although each student has a different attention span, many students with mild disabilities have short ones. Thus, teachers in inclusive settings should vary teaching techniques and activities accordingly. In fact, teachers who match task to attention span find that students master tasks at a faster rate.

For example, a teacher can divide a math lesson for a student with a short attention span into (a) working problems at the desk, (b) completing additional problems at the board, and (c) going to the learning center to continue with the same math skill but in a different setting. Teachers should first evaluate tasks according to the type of attention span required to complete them. Then they should adapt both their method of delivery and the tasks themselves to the variations of attention spans within the classroom.

*Domains of learning.* After teachers understand students' various learning styles and how certain conditions affect those styles, they need to know about the three domains or taxonomies of learning: cognitive, affective, and psychomotor. Instruction falls into one of these three domains and then into one of several levels within each domain. To learn your instructional domain and level, consult Table 12.3, which presents the major levels of the three taxonomies as constructed by Bloom (1956); Krathwohl, Bloom, and Masia (1964); and Dave (1970).

A teacher's instructional objectives fall into a specific level of one of the taxonomy structures. Usually, teachers teach in the cognitive domain. They should determine the student's present level within the cognitive domain and begin teaching at that level. For example, if an English teacher is presenting a unit on sentence writing (synthesis) and has a student with mild disabilities in the class who is learning the parts of speech (knowledge), the teacher must switch to the knowledge level for that student. The student's present level determines where the teacher should begin teaching. Table 12.4 explains how each level of the cognitive domain relates to students with mild disabilities.

## Learning Styles and Instruction

After assessing the learning styles of thousands of at-risk students, Carbo and Hodges (1988) concluded:

> The majority of these youngsters learn best in an informal, highly structured environment that contains soft light and has headsets available for those who learn best with quiet or music—such environments that seldom are provided in our schools.

Compared to achievers, at-risk youngsters also tend to be significantly less visual and auditory and have higher preferences for tactile/kinesthetic stimuli and greater needs for mobility and intake (food or drink). They tend to be unmotivated or strongly adult motivated, can concentrate and learn best with an adult or with peers, are most alert during the late morning or early afternoon hours, and most important, are global learners (p. 55).

Figure 12.8 presents analytical and global student characteristics.

TABLE 12.3
Major levels of cognitive, affective, and psychomotor domains.

| Level | Objective | Description |
|---|---|---|
| | | **Cognitive** |
| Basic | Knowledge | • The learner can recall information (i.e., bring to mind the |
| (low) | | appropriate material). |
| | Comprehension | • The learner understands what is being communicated by making use of the communication. |
| | Application | • The learner uses abstractions (e.g., ideas) in particular and concrete situations. |
| | Analysis | • The learner can break down a communication into its constituent elements or parts. |
| | Synthesis | • The learner puts together elements or parts to form a whole. |
| Advanced | Evaluation | • The learner makes judgments about the value of material or |
| (high) | | methods for a given purpose. |
| | | **Affective** |
| Basic | Receiving | • The learner is sensitized to the existence of certain phenomena |
| (low) | | (or attending) or stimuli. |
| | Responding | • The learner does something with or about the phenomenon beyond merely perceiving it. |
| | Valuing | • The learner believes that a thing, behavior, or phenomenon has worth. |
| | Organization | • The learner arranges internalized values into a system of priorities. |
| Advanced | Characterization | • The learner organizes the value hierarchy into an internally |
| (high) | | (or value complex) consistent system. |
| | | **Psychomotor** |
| Basic | Imitation | • The learner begins to make an imitation (i.e., copy) when exposed |
| (low) | | to a behavior. |
| | Manipulation | • The learner performs an act according to instructions. |
| | Precision | • The learner performs an act independent of a model or instructions. |
| | Articulation | • The learner coordinates a series of acts by establishing appropriate sequences and harmony. |
| Advanced | Naturalization | • The learner acts automatically and spontaneously with the least |
| (high) | | amount of energy. |

*Source:* Rich, H. C. (1992). *Disturbed students: Characteristics and educational strategies.* Baltimore: University Park Press. Copyright 1982 by Pro-Ed, Inc. Reprinted with permission.

**TABLE 12.4**
Cognitive domain and students with disabilities.

| Level | Consideration for the Student |
|---|---|
| Knowledge | If the teacher uses a variety of teaching methods and adapts content, students with mild disabilities can succeed at this level. Long-term retention may be difficult. |
| Comprehension | Most students with mild disabilities can comprehend information. Repetition may be necessary. Concrete rather than abstract information is easier to comprehend. Children with comprehension problems need special assistance. |
| Application | Applying concrete rather than abstract information is easier for students. Hands-on teaching and functional uses of information make application easier for students. |
| Analysis | Use whole-part-whole teaching method. Make analysis concrete by letting students with mild disabilities see or touch the division of the whole into parts. |
| Synthesis | Use whole-part-whole teaching method. Make synthesis concrete by letting students with mild disabilities see or touch the combining of parts into a whole. |
| Evaluation | This is the most difficult level for many students with mild disabilities. Evaluation in life situations is a natural teaching approach here. |

Carbo and Hodges (1988) have identified successful strategies used by teachers for at-risk students:

1. Identify and match student's learning style strengths, especially perceptual and global/analytic abilities.
2. Share information about learning styles with students.
3. De-emphasize skill work requiring a strong analytic learning style.
4. Begin lessons globally.
5. Use a variety of methods in reading.
6. Provide appropriate amounts of structure.
7. Allow youngsters to work with a peer, friend, teacher, or alone depending on their sociological preferences.
8. Establish quiet working sections sufficiently distant from noisy areas.
9. Create at least one special work area in the classroom by placing file cabinets or bookcases perpendicular to a wall.
10. Experiment with scheduling the most difficult subjects during the late morning and early afternoon hours.

## Gardner's Frames of Minds

Let's review what we have studied so far in this chapter, and why. First, we looked at instructional structure, which is necessary for a random learner who does not

**Analytic students often:**

1. Process information sequentially and logically
2. Solve problems systematically
3. Concentrate and learn when information is presented in small logical steps
4. Enjoy doing puzzles (crossword, jigsaw)
5. Like to follow step-by-step directions
6. Can understand a rule without examples
7. Enjoy learning facts such as dates and names
8. Enjoy learning rules and using them
9. Enjoy learning phonics
10. Understand and apply phonic rules
11. Recall letter names and sounds easily
12. Can decode words out of context
13. Recall low-interest words (*what, fan*) almost as easily as high-interest words (*elephant, monster*)
14. Are critical and analytic when reading
15. Can identify the details in a story
16. Recall many facts after listening to or reading a story
17. Easily list story events in logical, sequential order
18. Like to do reading skill exercises

**Global students often:**

1. Concentrate and learn what information is presented as a gestalt or whole
2. Respond to emotional appeals
3. Tend to like fantasy and humor
4. Get wrapped up in a story and do not concentrate on the facts
5. Process information subjectively and in patterns
6. Need to know the essence of a story before reading/hearing it
7. Need examples of a rule to understand the rule itself
8. Understand concrete examples better than those that are abstract
9. Easily can identify the main ideas in a story
10. Are unconcerned about dates, names, or specifics
11. Recall information easily when it is presented in the form of an anecdote
12. Will concentrate and pay attention better if the goal of the lesson is clearly stated at the beginning
13. Need to learn with high-interest, meaningful materials
14. Do not enjoy doing isolated skill exercises
15. Are able to learn a reading skill if the lesson is drawn from a story already read
16. Understand better if a story is enhanced by visuals (drawings, cartoons, photographs)
17. Recall high-interest words (*elephant, circus, dinosaur*) much more easily than low-interest words (*met, bet*)
18. Use story context to figure out unknown words

**FIGURE 12.8**

Analytical and global student characteristics.

*Source:* Carbo, M. (1982). *Reading style inventory.* Roslyn Heights, NY: Learning Research Associates. Copyright 1982 by M. Carbo. Adapted by permission.

have the natural tendency to impose structure or see logical connections. Second, we looked at learning styles and their importance to learning. The more we know about a student's learning style, the better match we can make between the child's style and the delivery system used to relay the content or subject matter. Now I would like to share Howard Gardner's theory of multiple intelligences (Gardner, 1999).

Understanding the nature of intelligence is just as important as understanding learning styles. Gardner has written numerous books about his philosophy of intelligence, the mind, and so on. His definition of intelligence "is the ability to solve problems, or to create products, that are valued within one or more cultural settings" (Gardner, 1993). It is important not to measure intelligence through paper and pencil tests. Instead, we should introduce someone to a task and see how well that person can progress beyond the novice stage with or without support. Gardner's multiple intelligence theory focuses on the "distinction among *intelligences, domains,* and *fields.* . . . At the level of the individual, it is proper to speak about one or more human intelligences, or human intellectual proclivities, that are part of our birthright" (1993, pp. xvi). He continues:

> Domains, of course, involve human beings, [and] they can be thought of in an impersonal way—because the expertise in a domain can in principle be captured in a book, a computer program, or other kind or artifice. . . . The field—a sociological construct—includes the people, institutions, award mechanisms, and so forth that render judgments about the qualities of individuals' performances. . . . The trio of intelligence, domain, and field has proved not only useful for unraveling a host of issues raised by MI theory, but also particularly fruitful for studies of creativity. . . . The answer is that creativity should not be thought of as inhering principally in the brain, the mind, or the personality of a single individual. Rather, creativity should be thought of as emerging from the interactions of three nodes: the individual with his or her own profile of competencies and values; the domains available for study and mastery within a culture; and the judgments rendered by the field that is deemed competent within a culture. . . . The creative individual is one who regularly solves problems or fashions products in a domain, and whose work is considered both novel and acceptable by knowledgeable members of a field. (Gardner, 1993, pp. xvi–xvii)

Gardner separates intelligence from single IQ scores into eight areas: linguistic, musical, logical-mathematical, spatial, bodily-kinesthetic, interpersonal, intrapersonal, and naturalist intelligence. Just as it is important to understand that students learn in different ways, it is important to know if a student excels in one of Gardner's intelligences. For example, I worked with a student who was extremely low linguistically yet excelled in logical-mathematical intelligence. The reading text was rewritten into a form of math logic, and we progressively moved the student into a standard reading book. Math remained the student's strength, however, and became the delivery system that encouraged the student to read.

Figure 12.9 presents Gardners' eight levels of intelligence with information related to teaching and learning. This figure helps link the intelligence level, sensitivity, inclination, and ability (Silver, Strong, & Perini, 2000).

| Disposition/ Intelligence | Sensitivity to: | Inclination for: | Ability to: |
|---|---|---|---|
| **Verbal-Linguistic Intelligence** | the sounds, meanings, structures, and styles of language | speaking, writing, listening, reading | speak effectively (teacher, religious leader, politician) or write effectively (poet, journalist, novelist, copywriter, editor) |
| **Logical-Mathematical Intelligence** | patterns, numbers and numerical data, causes and effects, objective and quantitative reasoning | finding patterns, making calculations, forming and testing hypotheses, using the scientific method, deductive and inductive reasoning | work effectively with numbers (accountant, statistician, economist) and reason effectively (engineer, scientist, computer programmer) |
| **Spatial Intelligence** | colors, shapes, visual puzzles, symmetry, lines, images | representing ideas visually, creating mental images, noticing visual details, drawing and sketching | create visually (artist, photographer, engineer, decorator) and visualize accurately (tour guide, scout, ranger) |
| **Bodily-Kinesthetic Intelligence** | touch, movement, physical self, athleticism | activities requiring strength, speed, flexibility, hand-eye coordination, and balance | use the hands to fix or create (mechanic, surgeon, carpenter, sculptor, mason) and use the body expressively (dancer, athlete, actor) |
| **Musical Intelligence** | tone, beat, tempo, melody, pitch, sound | listening, singing, playing an instrument | create music (songwriter, composer, musician, conductor) and analyze music (music critic) |
| **Interpersonal Intelligence** | body language, moods, voice, feelings | noticing and responding to other people's feelings and personalities | work with people (administrators, managers, consultants, teachers) and help people identify and overcome problems (therapists, psychologists) |
| **Intrapersonal Intelligence** | one's own strengths, weaknesses, goals, and desires | setting goals, assessing personal abilities and liabilities, monitoring one's own thinking | meditate, reflect, exhibit self-discipline, maintain composure, and get the most out of oneself |
| **Naturalist Intelligence** | natural objects, plants, animals, naturally occurring patterns, ecological issues | identifying and classifying living things and natural objects | analyze ecological and natural situations and data (ecologists and rangers), learn from living things (zoologist, botanist, veterinarian) and work in natural settings (hunter, scout) |

**FIGURE 12.9**

Intelligences as Dispositions.

From *So Each May Learn: Integrating Learning Styles and Multiple Intelligences* (p. 11), by H. F. Silver, R. W. Strong, and M. J. Perini, 2000, Alexandria, VA: Association for Supervision and Curriculum Development. © 2000 by Silver Strong & Associates, L.L.C. Reprinted with permission.

*To purchase this title, please call 800-962-4432 or visit www.silverstrong.com online.

# ADAPTING TEACHING TECHNIQUES

A teaching technique or strategy is a method of imparting knowledge, skills, or concepts to a learner. Historically, colleges and universities have recommended various teaching techniques to educators, who in turn have used those techniques in public and private schools. How teachers teach and what types of strategies they employ depend greatly on previous training, models observed, areas of interest, value judgments, and common sense. According to Jarolimek and Foster (1981), "There is a great deal of disagreement, even among well-informed persons, about what constitutes good teaching and how teaching should take place" (p. 109).

This section, then, does not try to teach teachers how to teach but simply presents a variety of techniques that teachers can use in different situations or modify for particular students. Specifically, the section concerns ways of adapting instruction within two major teaching techniques: mastery learning and teaching modes (which includes Bloom's taxonomy).

## Mastery Learning

*Mastery learning,* a term first used by Bloom (1968), provides the learner with immediate feedback from the teacher and a process for making corrections when necessary. IDEA emphasizes individualizing instruction for students with disabilities. The move to individualize, however, can increase managerial problems within the classroom. The diversity of students' abilities, demands placed on teachers for learner outcomes, increased class sizes due to economic constraints, and demands for new instructional skills are all pressures that can be eased by using one instructional strategy: mastery learning.

Bloom says that the teaching and evaluation process needs "some sort of 'feedback and corrective' procedure," a way of monitoring student progress so that teachers can "certify competent learners . . . , diagnose individual learning difficulties (feedback) . . . , [and] prescribe specific remediation procedures (correctives). . . . When the student does not understand a concept or makes an error, the ideal tutor first identifies the error, then reexplains the concept from a different perspective or in a different manner, and finally checks the student again before moving on" (Guskey, 1981, p. 12).

According to Guskey, mastery learning has three major steps. First, the teacher divides the material for a year or a semester into small segments or units. Pacing of the units is left up to the teacher. Second, instruction begins, and an evaluation is conducted. Third, test questions are carefully designed to test only the units taught. A student who answers any questions incorrectly consults the key. Alternative sources for further instruction and finding the correct answer accompany each test question.

Through this systematic correction of missed questions, students master more of the material. Mastery learning works well with students who have mild disabilities because it allows the teacher to individualize instruction within the group setting of the regular classroom. Table 12.5 presents the three steps of mastery learning and suggests ways to adapt or apply each step in the mainstreamed classroom.

**TABLE 12.5**
Adapting master learning for the mainstream.

| Steps in Mastery Learning | Possible Adaptations for the Regular Classroom Teacher |
|---|---|
| *Step 1.* Divide material into units or objectives for teaching. | • Select teaching objectives on instructional level of student.<br>• Select units on student's interest level.<br>• Consult with special education teacher about units or objectives the student with disabilities may be unable to complete. |
| *Step 2.* Begin instruction. Conduct evaluation. | • Determine prerequisite skills needed before teaching objective.<br>• Use task analysis to break down objectives.<br>• Note student's learning style.<br>• Assign tutors to assist student in learning objectives.<br>• Use alternative grouping procedures (see chapter 10).<br>• Adapt evaluation process (see chapter 15). |
| *Step 3.* Students check test questions missed and go to key to find additional resources for relearning missed items. | • Be sure students were able to answer test questions. Could they read the test? Did they understand the directions? Did the test questions need modification?<br>• Assist students in finding supplementary resources for missed test questions.<br>• Before student begins remedial work, assess material. Is it on student's instructional level?<br>• Be sure student understands what to do.<br>• Assign peer tutor to special-needs student for reading material and answering questions. |

## Teaching Modes

Jarolimek and Foster (1981) have identified four major teaching modes: expository, inquiry, demonstration, and activity (Figure 12.10). Each mode has specific teaching techniques common to it, and teachers can adapt or modify all these techniques for students in inclusive settings.

*Expository mode.* Teaching in the expository mode centers around the "concept exposition, which means most simply to provide an explanation" (Jarolimek & Foster, 1981, p. 110). This mode, probably the most popular among educators, requires extensive directive teaching. The class focuses on the teacher, who explains or disseminates the information; students are involved only minimally. General education teachers report using this mode 53 percent of the time during instruction, while special education teachers use the expository mode only 24 percent of the time. Table 12.6 presents the specific teaching techniques used in the expository mode, with suggested adaptations for each. In four of these techniques—lecture, telling, explanation, and discussion—the teacher orally delivers information. These four techniques account for 93 percent of the time that regular education teachers teach in the expository mode and 87 percent for special education teachers (Wood, 1993).

| Expository | Inquiry | Demonstration | Activity |
|---|---|---|---|
| Lecture | Asking questions | Experiments | Role playing |
| Telling | Stating hypotheses | Exhibits | Constructing |
| Sound filmstrip | Coming to conclusions | Simulations | Preparing exhibits |
| Explanation | Interpreting | Games | Dramatizing |
| Panels | Classifying | Modeling | Processing |
| Recitation | Self-directed study | Field trips | Group work |
| Audio recording | Testing hypotheses | | |
| Motion pictures | Observing | | |
| Discussion | Synthesizing | | |

**FIGURE 12.10**
Specific techniques used in various teaching modes.

*Source:* Jarolimek, J., & Foster, C. D. (1981). *Teaching and learning in the elementary school* (pp. 131–132). New York: Macmillan. Copyright 1981 by Macmillan. Adapted by permission.

Presenting new skills or concepts orally (lecturing, explaining, discussing, telling) can make learning extremely difficult for the student who cannot impose structure on learning. Educators can use the following suggestions for adapting these types of techniques.

1.  *Multisensory input.* Visual-aid materials that address a variety of learning styles should be an important instructional consideration. Because students learn through many sensory systems, educators need to use numerous modes to enhance oral presentations and provide multisensory input for students. Students need to be taught in the different perceptual styles—visually, auditorially, and tactually. Using the overhead projector to present main points or underline or circle main ideas is an excellent technique for orientation to material. Videotapes provide instant playback of information for reinforcement. Students who miss a portion of the class will also benefit from a videotape. Audiotape recorders are excellent audiovisual aids for reinforcement of oral materials. Graphic materials such as globes and maps reinforce both visually and tactually the material to be learned. Bulletin boards assist the teacher in presenting new information or providing reinforcement. Presenting information for multisensory input not only enhances classroom instruction but also provides for and addresses the perceptual learning styles of students.

2.  *Acquisition outlines.* Acquisition outlines present students with a graphic whole-part-whole method of learning. This method of adapting assists students in seeing the whole of the presentation and then hearing a discussion of the parts. The acquisition outline serves as a formative study guide. The teacher should provide an acquisition outline when presenting new information, concepts, or skills to be learned. Before the test, a summative study guide is provided, which sets the

**TABLE 12.6**
Expository mode: Alternative teaching techniques.

| Teaching Techniques | Alterations or Modifications for Mainstreamed Students |
|---|---|
| Lecture | • Provide lecture outlines.<br>• Provide copy of lecture notes.<br>• Use transparencies to provide visual presentation simultaneously with lecture. |
| Telling | • Keep lecture short.<br>• Be specific about information given.<br>• Be sure you have students' attention.<br>• For students with short attention spans, give information in small segments. |
| Sound filmstrip | • Provide visuals when possible.<br>• Give earphones to students easily distracted by sounds. |
| Explanation | • Keep explanations simple and direct.<br>• Give them in simple declarative sentences.<br>• Provide outline of explanation. |
| Audio recording | • Present recordings with visuals.<br>• Give earphones to students easily distracted by sounds. |
| Motion pictures | • Orient students to movie before showing.<br>• Be sure length is appropriate.<br>• Place students with auditory problems close to sound.<br>• Review main points of film.<br>• Provide brief outline of main points. |
| Discussion | • Ask questions you know students can answer.<br>• Keep discussion short.<br>• As points are made, list them on board or transparency.<br>• Divide class into groups for brief discussions.<br>• Keep students on topic.<br>• Involve everyone on appropriate levels.<br>• Use organizer to group ideas and show conclusion drawn. |

stage for studying (see chapter 13). The teacher can place the acquisition outline on the overhead projector or give each student a copy to be completed. When introducing the outline, the teacher should follow these steps:

    a.  Introduce the topic.

    b.  Explain how the topic for today continues yesterday's lesson and will extend into tomorrow's lesson.

   c. Introduce each of the major topics (points 1, 2, 3, and so on).
   d. Point out that related topics are listed beneath each major point.
   e. Return to point 1.
   f. Review the topics listed under point 1.
   g. Begin the discussion of point 1.
   h. When the lesson is over, return to the whole outline and review the topics.
   i. Have the student file the outline in the appropriate notebook section.
   j. Save a copy for the teacher's note-taking file.

Acquisition outlines keep students from guessing what will be coming next, help them perceive the organization of the presentation, and serve as a formative study guide for test review. Here are some general tips for using acquisition outlines:

   a. The acquisition outline can be developed into one of three formats: blank, partial, or completed. The more difficulty a student has in organizing and absorbing orally presented information, the more information should be provided on the outline.
   b. When covering a point that is further explained within a text or a handout, tell the students to write the page number from the text or the name of the handout in the left margin.
   c. If some points on the outline require extensive note taking, the teacher may provide a handout to promote accurate reception of information and save instructional time.

Examples of acquisition outlines appear in Figures 12.11 and 12.12.

**FIGURE 12.11**
Acquisition outline: Top-down, bottom-up format.

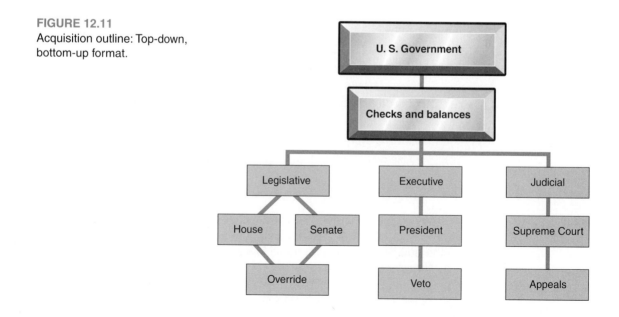

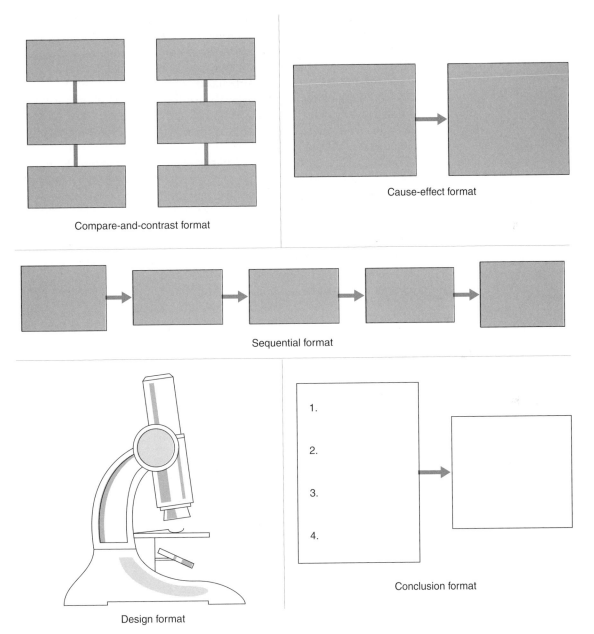

Compare-and-contrast format

Cause-effect format

Sequential format

Design format

1.

2.

3.

4.

Conclusion format

**FIGURE 12.12**
Acquisition outlines.

**3.** *Structured organizers.* A structured organizer is a visual aid used to present graphically the major and minor topics of a presentation. As with acquisition outlines, structured organizers may be developed into transparencies or handouts or displayed on a flip chart or chalkboard. The organizers may be blank, partial, or complete.

Lovitt (1989) reports six benefits of structured organizers:

    a. Students are better able to follow the teacher's presentation, helping to keep them actively involved.

    b. New information can be related to previous learning, allowing teachers to build cumulative review.

    c. Charts, tables, and graphs can stimulate student interest, making lessons more appealing.

    d. Teachers are more systematic and thorough in their presentations. By preparing graphic organizers ahead of time, teachers are more likely to present material in a step-by-step manner.

    e. Students learn organizational skills through example and use. They may generalize and transfer these skills to other areas, which in turn increase student achievement.

    f. Graphic organizers can be used to promote higher-level thinking skills.

Figures 12.13 and 12.14 illustrate types of structured organizers and offer tips for using them. (Thanks to C. J. Galante, Judith Stone, Rocky Gallards, Linda Heierman, and Julie McKelvey for their suggestions.)

**4.** *Audiotaping presentations.* Frequently students are unable to write down all the important information provided. The student who is a strong visual learner may miss important facts. Letting students tape-record the presentations provides for additional reinforcement at a later time.

| Word | Definition | Sketch | Explanation |
|------|-----------|--------|-------------|
| Teacher gives this from the story. | Teacher gives this. | Student sketches the word. | Student explains the sketch. |

| Concepts Covered | | | |
|------|-----------|--------|-------------|
| **Books/Stories Read** | **Facts Unique to Each Story** | | |
| | | | |

**FIGURE 12.13**
Structured organizer for vocabulary development: Mind sketching.

1. In teaching works like *Brian's Song*, by William Blinn, and *The Old Man and the Sea*, by Ernest Hemingway, this approach could be helpful. The exercise was to look at the qualities that one finds in a hero. The students were asked to define what a hero was and to select three characteristics (qualities) that one finds in most heroes. These qualities may include: determination, perseverance, patience, skill, love for the game (job), and so on. Students were then asked to compare the two characters using these characteristics (qualities).

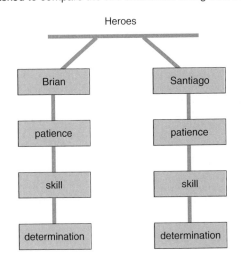

2. This is a structure that works for building a paragraph.

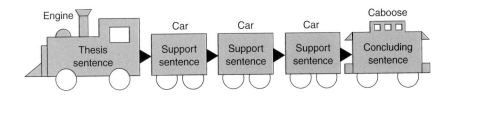

3. Have students (or with help from teacher) write main idea, details, and so on, on individual index cards. Cards can then be manipulated into organizers, outlines, or paragraphs.

4. Enlarge design organizers on copier to allow students to write on parts in class or at home.

(*continued*)

FIGURE 12.14
Tips for using structured organizers.

5. Use a house design for comparison.

Example: This structured organizer can be used as an outline or a comparison by putting each main heading in the chapter at the top and supporting information in the windows. This may be adapted for primary grades.

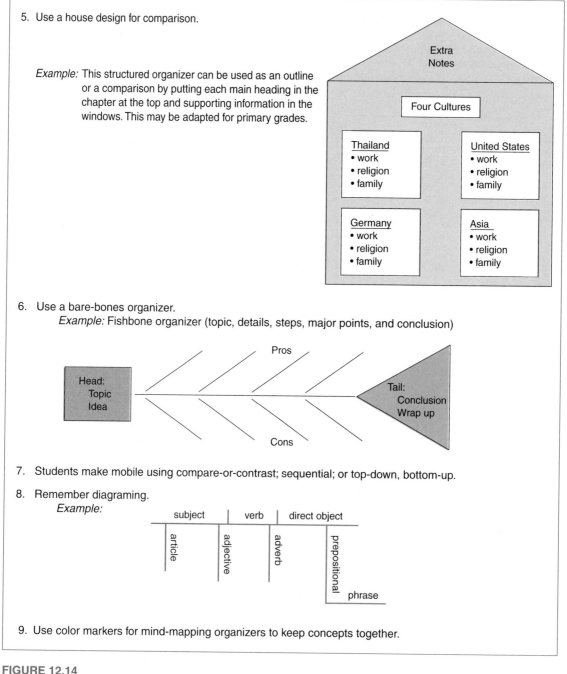

Extra
Notes

Four Cultures

Thailand
• work
• religion
• family

United States
• work
• religion
• family

Germany
• work
• religion
• family

Asia
• work
• religion
• family

6. Use a bare-bones organizer.
   Example: Fishbone organizer (topic, details, steps, major points, and conclusion)

Pros

Head:
Topic
Idea

Tail:
Conclusion
Wrap up

Cons

7. Students make mobile using compare-or-contrast; sequential; or top-down, bottom-up.

8. Remember diagraming.
   Example:

subject | verb | direct object

article | adjective | adverb | prepositional

phrase

9. Use color markers for mind-mapping organizers to keep concepts together.

**FIGURE 12.14**
Continued.

10. Use static cling vinyl (sold in several colors). Cut into strips, write labels for organizers, peel backing off, and stick to laminated poster of design organizer.

11. Organizer for comparing and contrasting of essay:
    - Pass out colored index cards. Each student receives several blue and several pink cards.
    - Teacher reads story with compare-and-contrast points.
    - Students write likenesses on the blue cards.
    - Students write differences on the pink cards.
    - Move to graphic organizers by having students staple all of their pink note cards to pink sheets of paper and blue note cards to blue sheets of paper.
    - Use the chalkboard for organizing the cards into a blocking format.
    - Introduction and concluding paragraph ideas are written on white paper.
    - Students now have manipulatives, color, and patterns to follow as they develop their ideas into sentences for each paragraph.

12. Organizers for persuasive paragraph:
    - Students receive two sets of cards, some green and some pink.
    - Discuss an issue (for example, requiring all students to wear uniforms).
    - Students list reasons for and against the position on their note cards. Green cards are used for pro arguments; pink for con arguments.
    - After writing their reasons, one per card, students count the pros and cons. If they have more pros, their essay will support the pro position and vice versa.
    - Organize their arguments into some type of order.
    - Staple cards to green and pink paper.
    - Begin blocking procedure.

13. For first graders, use different-colored markers on the dry-eraser board. For example, when contrasting two stories, *The Little Red Hen* and *The Little Yellow Chicken,* put Red Hen's comments in *red* markers and Yellow Chicken's in *yellow.* This helps students differentiate between the two.

*Inquiry mode.* The inquiry mode involves "asking questions, seeking information, and carrying on an investigation" (Jarolimek & Foster, 1981, p. 116). This mode of teaching follows five basic steps: "(a) defining a problem, (b) proposing hypotheses, (c) collecting data, (d) evaluating evidence, and (e) making a conclusion" (p. 116). The teacher's guidance is still important, but the inquiry mode allows for more teacher-pupil interaction and encourages a team approach to teaching. For many students, however, the teacher often needs to provide some additional structure. Table 12.7 suggests teaching techniques for the inquiry mode.

The inquiry mode is used 23 percent of the time by regular educators and 35 percent by special educators. Of the techniques listed (see Table 12.7), regular

**TABLE 12.7**
Inquiry mode: Alternative teaching techniques.

| Teaching Techniques | Alterations or Modifications for Mainstreamed Students |
|---|---|
| Asking questions | • Use appropriate wait time. |
| | • Ask questions on appropriate level of taxonomy scale; vary questions to meet different taxonomy levels of students. |
| | • Call student's name before directing a question to him or her. |
| | • Do not embarrass students by asking questions they cannot answer. |
| Stating hypotheses | • Have students choose from two or three hypotheses instead of having to formulate their own. |
| | • Provide model for writing hypotheses. |
| Coming to conclusions | • Present alternative conclusions. |
| | • List information needed for conclusions. |
| Interpreting | • Assign peer tutor to help. |
| | • Present alternative interpretations. |
| Classifying | • Use concrete instead of abstract concepts. |
| | • Provide a visual display with models. |
| Self-directed study | • Give specific directions about what to do. |
| | • Make directions short, simple, and few. |
| | • Collect and place resources for study in one area. |
| Testing hypotheses | • Assign peer tutor. |
| Observing | • Give explicit directions about how and what to observe. |
| | • Provide sequential checklist of what will happen so that student sees steps. |
| | • Have student check off each step observed. |
| Synthesizing | • Assign peer tutor to help. |
| | • Provide model of whole. |

education teachers report asking questions 66 percent of the time, while special education teachers ask them 59 percent of the time. Asking questions of students with disabilities and those at risk can accomplish many things during the lesson. According to Davies (1981), questions help motivate students by getting their attention or gaining their interest, encourage students to think, involve more than one student in the instructional process, and provide feedback for the teacher on students' progress.

Raphael (1982) suggests four types of questions, which can be placed into either of two categories: in-the-book questions and in-the-head questions. Helping students understand question types or marking the question type for them helps when they are attempting to answer questions orally or are looking in a text to find answers to written questions. Table 12.8 lists the four types of questions and their characteristics.

As teachers teach, they deliver information, require students to learn the information, and ask questions from one of the six levels of Bloom's cognitive taxonomy to see if students have retained the information. Asking questions is a natural part of instruction. Teachers ask questions to assess student attention and comprehension, but they need to realize that questions also reflect taxonomy levels. Adapting instruction for students in inclusive settings involves knowing the level of one's questions and changing that level if necessary. Questions directed at special-needs students should relate to their specific levels of learning. (Look back at Table 12.3 to see the six levels of Bloom's taxonomy for the cognitive domain.)

Particular word choice can help teachers relate instruction to specific levels on Bloom's taxonomy. Figure 12.15 lists verbs to use for stating behavioral objectives. Table 12.9 offers examples of questions by taxonomy level.

**TABLE 12.8**
Question types.

| Broad Categories | Question Type | Characteristics |
|---|---|---|
| In-the-book questions | 1. Right-there questions | • Literal questions |
| | | • Detailed in nature |
| | | • Found *right* in text |
| | | • *Example:* "What color are the girl's eyes?" |
| | 2. Think-and-search questions | • Answer in text but not in one place. |
| | | • *Example:* Putting events into sequence |
| In-the-head questions | 3. Author-and-you questions | • Inferences/conclusions required |
| | | • Involve learner's prior knowledge |
| | | • *Example:* "Why did the man decide to wear black?" |
| | 4. On-your-own-questions | • Cannot be answered from the text |
| | | • Learner must use own experience |
| | | • Questions asked before reading |
| | | • Extensive questions |
| | | • *Example:* "How are modern cars and the cars of the 1920s different?" |

*Source:* Raphael, T. E. (1986). Teaching question and answer relationships. *Reading Teacher, 39,* 516–523. Adapted with permission.

1. *Knowledge:* remembering previously learned material

| | | | |
|---|---|---|---|
| cite | know | pick | state |
| define | label | pronounce | underline |
| fill in | list | quote | write |
| find | match | recall | |
| group | memorize | recite | |
| identify | name | reproduce | |

Answer who? what? when? where?

2. *Comprehension:* ability to grasp the meaning of material

| | | | |
|---|---|---|---|
| account for | discover | manage | re-word |
| alter | expand | paraphrase | show |
| change | explain | relate | substitute |
| convert | extend | reorganize | summarize |
| define | give examples | rephrase | translate |
| demonstrate | group | represent | vary |
| depict | illustrate | restate | |
| describe | interpret | reward | |

3. *Application:* ability to use learned materials in new and concrete situations

| | | | |
|---|---|---|---|
| apply | employ | predict | select |
| choose | evidence | prepare | show |
| classify | experiement | present | solve |
| compute | interview | put into action | use |
| construct using | manage | put together | utilize |
| demonstrate | manifest | put to use | |
| direct | model | record | |
| discover | organize | relate | |

Answer how many? what? what is? Write an example.

**FIGURE 12.15**
Verbs for stating behavioral objectives.

4. *Analysis:* ability to break down material into its component parts so that its organizational structure may be understood

| | | | |
|---|---|---|---|
| analyze | determine | divide | search |
| ascertain | diagnose | examine | separate |
| associate | diagram | find | simplify |
| break down | difference | infer | sort |
| classify | discover | inspect | survey |
| compare | discriminate | outline | take apart |
| contrast | dissect | put into categories | uncover |
| designate | distinguish | reduce | |

5. *Synthesis:* ability to put parts together to form a new whole

| | | | |
|---|---|---|---|
| blend | develop | makeup | rearrange |
| build | devise | modify | revise |
| combine | expand | originate | rewrite |
| compile | extend | plan | suppose |
| compose | form | pose | synthesize |
| conceive | generalize | predict | theorize |
| construct | imagine | produce | write |
| create | integrate | propose | |
| design | invent | project | |

Answer how can we improve? what would happen if? how can we solve?

6. *Evaluation:* ability to judge the value of material for a given purpose

| | | | |
|---|---|---|---|
| appraise | criticize | evaluate | rate |
| assess | critique | grade | recommend |
| award | decide | judge | weigh |
| compare | deduce | justify | |
| conclude | defend | measure | |
| contrast | determine | rank | |

TABLE 12.9
Examples of questions by taxonomy level.

| Taxonomy Level | Sample Questions |
| --- | --- |
| Knowledge | 1. *What* is the capital of the United States?<br>2. *Where* was the first Civil War battle fought?<br>3. *What* country produces the most oil?<br>4. *Identify* the main idea of the paragraph. |
| Comprehension | 1. What is the *main idea* of the poem?<br>2. *Explain* what communism means.<br>3. *Describe* a democracy.<br>4. *Summarize* the story in your own words. |
| Application | 1. *Predict* what would happen if the restrictions on immigration from Mexico were lifted.<br>2. You have been given a problem in plane geometry. Which of these answers is correct? (*solve*)<br>3. *Classify* the three poems below as sonnets, odes, or ballads.<br>4. *Which* of the following animals are mollusks? |
| Analysis | 1. *Why* did Mark Twain write about the Mississippi River?<br>2. *Analyze* Poe's short story "The Tell-Tale Heart." Indicate his uses of imagery and cite examples from the story.<br>3. Now that we have studied Mendel's theory, what can we *conclude* about the children of parents who both have blue eyes?<br>4. *Outline* chapter 8 of your test. |
| Synthesis | 1. Imagine you are president of the United States. How would you handle the situation in Libya? (solve problems)<br>2. *Design* an exhibit for the science fair called "The Underwater World." |

The following general suggestions will help teachers determine how to ask questions of students with disabilities and those at risk:

1. Ask questions at the taxonomy level where the student is functioning.
2. Provide wait time for responses. Extra time is necessary for responses to divergent questions (Kindsvatter, Wilen, & Ishler, 1988). Research shows that teachers usually allow about 1 sec for a response, but students typically need 3 to 5 sec (Rowe, 1974).
3. Allow wait time for all students to think about an answer given by one student before proceeding to the next question.

4. Ask questions in a planned and patterned order or sequence. Factors that influence the choice of sequence include the lesson's objective, student's ability level, and student's understanding of the content covered (Kindsvatter et al., 1988).

5. Remember that some sequencing begins with lower-level questions and progresses to higher-level thinking. Some students will start with higher-level questions and remain there (Kindsvatter et al. 1988).

6. Because responses to lower-level questions determine student understanding of content, use those responses as an indication of starting points for reteaching.

7. Allow student to formulate questions to ensure active participation in the questioning process (Kindsvatter et al., 1988).

8. State questions clearly and specifically.

9. When asking a question, state the question, call the student's name, and repeat the question.

10. Encourage all students to participate in the questioning process by responding in a positive way to all student responses.

11. Avoid sarcasm, reprimand, personal attack, accusation, or no response at all as teacher responses to student answers (West, 1975).

12. If students hesitate to raise their hands to ask questions in class, tape pockets to their desks containing cards (any color will do). Have students take out the cards and put them on the corner of their desks if they have questions or do not understand. Check for these cards as you walk around the room.

13. Have a question box on the teacher's desk for students who are hesitant to answer questions.

14. Use color responses. All students will have three cards for responding. When a question is asked, each student will put a card at chest level. For example:

    Green: Ask me; I know.

    Yellow: Maybe I know; I'll try.

    Red: Don't call on me; I don't know.

15. Have students respond to questions as follows:

    Four fingers: I know the answer.

    Three fingers: I know the answer, but I don't want to answer.

    Two fingers: I don't know the answer.

    One finger: Please rephrase the question.

16. Have a "ponder period" where students sit in groups to ponder questions and answers before the question activity.

17. Give each student two chips. This gives a child the opportunity to answer a question or contribute information. When chips are used, the person has made his or her contribution. This helps the teacher give many children the opportunity to contribute.

18. Tell a student who may not know answers to raise one hand and place the other hand on the desk. Skip that student. When one hand is up and the other hand is not on the desk, the student is signaling that he or she knows the answer to the question.

*Demonstration mode.* Essential components of the demonstration mode are "showing, doing, and telling" (Jarolimek & Foster, 1981, p. 120). Like the expository mode, the demonstration mode depends on directive teaching. Because it presents information in a concrete way, this method is essential for teachers to use when instructing students with disabilities.

Table 12.10 presents techniques used in the demonstration mode, with suggested alterations for included students. The demonstration mode is used only 3 percent of the time by general educators and 6 percent by special educators. Of the techniques listed in Table 12.10, general educators use experiments 34 percent of the time, while special educators use modeling 36 percent of the time.

Modeling is an excellent technique to use for students who are having difficulty understanding the information presented. Models may be visual (such as a map, chart, or globe) or verbal (such as a language mode). Models may also be participatory, where the teacher demonstrates a skill and the students become actively involved. Here are some suggestions for modeling:

1. Exaggerate the modeling presentation.
2. If the steps in the model are lengthy or difficult, use several short time spans rather than one long demonstration.
3. Videotape the modeling demonstration for students to replay and replicate.
4. When repeating the steps in a model, use the same sequence you used in the original presentation.
5. Provide a checklist of the steps in the model for students to follow as the teacher demonstrates.
6. Provide auditory clues along with visual cues.
7. When a student is implementing a model, reward the student's behavior.
8. Use modeling for social, technical, or academic skills.
9. As a student models a desired skill, use the situation to point out the behavior to other students.

*Activity mode.* The activity mode of teaching is "a set of strategies that involve pupils in learning by doing things that are, for the pupils, meaningfully related to the topic under study" (Jarolimek & Foster, 1981, p. 127). This method of teaching is best described by an old Native American proverb: "I hear and I forget, I see and I remember, I do and I understand." By using the activity mode, teachers provide students with actual experience and thus a clearer understanding of concepts. The activity mode is used 21 percent of the time by general educators and 35 percent of the time by special educators. Table 12.11 suggests activities to accompany the techniques in the activity mode.

The technique of group work is used 66 percent of the time by general educators and 72 percent of the time by special educators. Group work is a method of structuring a class so that students work together to achieve a shared academic

**TABLE 12.10**
Demonstration mode: Alternative teaching techniques.

| Teaching Techniques | Alterations of Modifications for Mainstreamed Students |
|---|---|
| Experiments | • Provide sequential directions.<br>• Have student check off each completed step.<br>If teacher demonstrates, let student assist.<br>• Be sure student fully understands purpose, procedures, and expected outcome of experiment.<br>• Set up incidental learning experiences.<br>• Display materials.<br>• Model the activity.<br>• Provide an outline and a handout/checklist.<br>• Make a list of lab procedures and assign a lab procedure.<br>• Tape instructions and videotape demonstrations. |
| Exhibits | • Assign projects according to student's instructional level.<br>• Have student select project topic from a short list.<br>• Provide directions and list of materials needed.<br>• Be sure project does not require skills student lacks.<br>• Have student display his or her exhibits. |
| Simulations | • Do not embarrass the student by requiring him or her to do something that the student cannot do.<br>• Make sure the student understands directions, terms used, and expected outcome. |
| Games | • Design games making skills, not winning, the priority.<br>• Make directions simple.<br>• Highlight important directions with color codes.<br>• With peer tutor, let student prepare own game.<br>• Design games; emphasize skills needed by student. |
| Modeling | • Model only one step at a time.<br>• Use task analysis on steps.<br>• Use visual models when possible.<br>• Exaggerate the presentation to make the concept being modeled clear.<br>• Use several short time spans rather than one long demonstration.<br>• Model in hierarchical sequence.<br>• Use video modeling for student to replay.<br>Perform in same manner as the first presentation.<br>• Provide a lecture outline on which the student may take notes. |
| Field trips | • Prepare students by explaining destination, purpose, expected behavior, and schedule.<br>• Provide a checklist of expectations. |

**TABLE 12.11**
Activity mode: Alternative teaching techniques

| Teaching Techniques | Alterations or Modifications for Mainstreamed Students |
|---|---|
| Role playing | • Be sure student understands role.<br>• Short lines or no lines at all may be best.<br>• Respect privacy of student who does not want role.<br>• Let such a student assist another role player. |
| Constructing | • Select project for students or have them select from a short list.<br>• Try to use projects that include special education objectives.<br>• Provide sequential checklist. |
| Preparing exhibits | • Assign peer tutor to help.<br>• Use alterations suggested for "constructing." |
| Dramatizing | • Respect privacy of those who do not want parts.<br>• Let such students help others prepare sets, and so on. |
| Processing | • Clearly state steps.<br>• Make steps sequential and short.<br>• List steps on board. |
| Group work | • Assign peer tutor.<br>• Select activity in which students can succeed.<br>• Use variety of grouping procedures (see chapter 10). |
| Game/contest | • Be sure game matches lesson objective.<br>• Check game to see if required decision-making skills match students' ability level.<br>• List rules for engaging clearly on board.<br>• Keep pace appropriate.<br>• Assign a buddy.<br>• Provide feedback for game skill as well as for social skills used. |

goal. As you have learned, there are three kinds of group work: peer tutoring, group projects, and jigsaw. For details about each one, refer back to chapter 10.

Group work has several advantages:

1. Students are responsible for other group members, which encourages liking and learning among students.
2. Assignments can be individualized without working one to one.
3. Teachers can structure students' assignments so that each group member can succeed.
4. Mainstreamed students can be given a short, simple part of the assignment.

5. Group work reduces the time a teacher must spend in preparation.
6. It improves behavior control by minimizing the time focused on one student.
7. It motivates reluctant students through social interaction.
8. It prevents boredom through a variety of group assignments.
9. Students can contribute something from their area of expertise. For example, if they are good in art, they can volunteer (or be assigned) to do the art for the group.
10. Because all students are equally involved in the group's decision, mainstreamed students feel highly motivated.

Role playing is another useful technique in the activity mode. Here are several suggestions for incorporating it into your teaching:

1. Select the role-playing situation.
2. Warm up with some simple charades or another similar exercise.
3. Explain the general situation to participants and observers.
4. State the problem to be worked on, including the setting.
5. Explain the roles that participants will be playing.
6. Explain the roles that the audience will be expected to perform.
7. Start the role playing with a discussion.
8. Follow the role playing with a discussion.
9. Evaluate the exercise.

Role playing has several advantages:

1. Students can express their true feelings without risk.
2. Students can discuss private issues without embarrassment.
3. Students learn to empathize with others by taking on another identity.
4. Students practice alternative behaviors and attitudes.
5. Role playing brings academic subjects to life and thus makes them more meaningful.
6. Motivation and interest increase because they are based on an activity.

## Womack's Teaching Modes

Dr. Sid Womack of Arkansas Technical University has divided instruction into four modes: expository, demonstration, inquiry, and individualized instruction. (His fourth mode closely parallels my fourth mode, activity.) Within each mode Womack defines eight areas: comment, assumptions, role of teacher, role of learner, instructional resources, methods of evaluation, weaknesses and likely problem areas, and summary.

Figures 12.16 through 12.19 present an overview of Womack's modes. For each of Womack's four modes, the four figures provide a comment regarding the mode; assumptions; the role of the teacher and learner; instructional resources needed; how to evaluate, possible weaknesses and problem areas; and a summary. (I want to thank Dr. Womack for giving me permission to use his work.)

## Comment

This descriptor includes several categories of instruction, including formal lecture, informal lecture, teacher-led discussions, parables, anecdotes, and several types of audiovisual presentations.

## Assumptions

1. There is an essential body of knowledge that all learners should know.
2. Learners are relatively homogeneous with regard to the content variable at hand. They all know approximately the same information, or at least all the learners have a minimal and common level of knowledge.

## Role of teacher

The teacher directs the learning program. The teacher arbitrarily selects the modality of the presentation, the pace at which new ideas are approached, the amount of supervised practice that will be given, at what point formative evaluation will be done, which criteria will indicate a need for reteaching or repetition, what kinds of questions will be used, and when and how summative evaluation will be done.

## Role of learner

Learner is expected to meet requirements established by teacher: reading, answering questions, and so on. Learner is expected to "follow the leader" (that is, the teacher).

## Instructional resources

Learner receives certain prescribed information, looking for and learning the interpretations and summaries of others. Resources are best used to summarize. Expository mode relies heavily on verbal learning. Filmstrips, slides, films, and videotapes can help create a learning-rich classroom. Guest speakers can also be invited as well (although this may create a demonstration lesson or an integrated format).

## Methods of evaluation

Methods include conventional standardized tests or teacher-made criterion-referenced tests.

## Weaknesses and likely problem areas

1. The teacher is very vulnerable in classrooms where the discipline traffic is high. If the teacher has to take a student out of the classroom for any reason, learning totally stops for all of the (presumed) innocent students who had nothing to do with the incident. In secondary school environments it is common practice for troublemaking students to act in rotation from day to day to "spare" the class from learning.

**FIGURE 12.16**
Womack's expository mode.

**Weaknesses and likely problem areas—*continued***

2. If the expository mode is virtually the only mode used, assumption 2 is rarely met, in spite of the fact that most teachers teach this way. When diagnostic teaching is done, it reveals a striking heterogeneity among learners with regard to any content field. The learners are not level regardless of any leveling system that a district might attempt to impose. More enlightened programs in the 1970s learned to work with this characteristic of students instead of trying to ignore or combat it. With the political pressures on education today, recognition of individual differences is mostly ignored and will be until the pendulum swings the other way.

3. Higher dropout rates have become more common in secondary programs where expository modes are used. (See the December 1987 *Phi Delta Kappan* about America's dropouts.) This may be because, with whole-group approaches, individual differences are more likely to be ignored. When we ignore individual differences we subject many students to unfair competition.

## Summary

Expository lessons are not all bad; they are the primary means of imparting information at the college level, for instance. However, the overall maturity level of college students helps overcome the occasional mismatches between teacher and learner pace, teacher modality and learner-preferred modality, need for more repetition, and so on. Assumption 2 is frequently violated in other school environments because there is less overall maturity of learners and less uniformity of minimum levels of academic competency. Well-done expository lessons can be informative, enlightening, and effective if the teacher takes account of these things:

1. Teacher or administrator needs to take account of assumption 2 by some formal means.

2. Lesson planning demands will be higher for this type of lesson than any other. Content outline becomes essential for teacher and substitute.

3. Lesson needs an anticipatory set that clearly and behaviorally states what the observable outcomes of the lesson will be. The objectives should in most instances be shared with the class.

4. Teacher should anticipate which parts of the lesson will probably have to be repeated for all learners. This is difficult for less experienced teachers.

5. Formative evaluation should be systematically planned for and used to avoid losing the class in the content. Today's children are not likely to tell the teacher at the precise moment when they did not understand something because of peer pressure.

6. Teacher should make plain when he or she is changing topics or categories. Teacher might even say, "This is where you make a new Roman numeral or paragraph in your notes."

**Comment**

This category includes other categories such as laboratory, some types of field trips, dramatizations, construction, recitals, and exhibitions.

**Assumptions**

1. Learning will occur if learner is exposed to a functioning model or guide.

2. The models are true and accurate models of what the finished products or behaviors should be.

3. Learners' learning hierarchies and maturities are sufficiently developed so that they are capable of perceiving the salient characteristics portrayed by the demonstration.

**Role of teacher**

Plan, organize, and execute a demonstration that presents key ideas to be learned clearly. Demonstration should be factually correct. Teacher should clarify which parts of the demonstration are relevant to the desired learning and which "just come with the package."

**Role of learner**

Learner observes, listens, and follows the presentation carefully. Some participation may be required. Bruner, Gagné, Piaget, and others of the same period tell us that long-term retention will be much more likely if students do more than just observe the demonstration but get to touch, smell, do, and so on whatever is relevant and safe in the demonstration.

**Instructional resources**

Use whatever materials and equipment are needed to conduct the demonstration. In most elementary and many secondary science programs, resources are in pitifully short supply. This will have a bearing upon teachers' reasonable expectations.

**Method of evaluation**

Use a written test or discussion to detect understanding or misconceptions. Use a student demonstration to see if the student can do the steps or processes that are modeled.

**FIGURE 12.17**
Womack's demonstration mode.

# CONCLUSION

Providing structure, understanding learning and learning styles, and incorporating alternative modes of instructional delivery help students receive information in an organized manner. Imposing structure to the delivery process and to infor-

**Weaknesses and likely problem areas**

1. Demonstrations, to be meaningfully perceived, need to be preceded by some exposition. A brilliant demonstration can be lost on students if they have not been told what to look for in it. They may focus on the demonstrator's English, clothing, or mannerisms instead of relevant aspects of the demonstration.

2. The demonstrator needs to be capable of executing a good model of whatever is to be learned. If he or she is demonstrating how to play a piece of music, the demonstration needs to be note-perfect. If he or she is modeling the pronunciation of French words, the model needs to be one that students can imitate.

3. Ensure that demonstration equipment and personnel will be safe. There should be precautions taken to make sure that disinterested others (for example, students in other classes) will not be adversely affected by the demonstration, as in the hydrogen sulfide demonstrations in some chemistry classes.

4. Demonstrations, while more open-ended than expositions, still need to be tied to specific objectives. Demonstrations without this element tend to degenerate into theatrics.

**Summary**

An evaluation of a demonstration lesson should contain, at a minimum, these elements:

1. Is the lesson located in sequence after sufficient exposition to direct students to the demonstration's relevant attributes?

2. Does the demonstration serve its intended function as an active device?

3. Is this demonstration appropriate to learners' overall level of maturity?

4. Where does this demonstration fit into a task analysis? Does it have a place at this juncture, or is this just theatrics?

5. Was the model factually correct in its relevant attributes?

6. Were the relevant attributes pointed out before the demonstration?

7. Was the demonstration followed with an opportunity for students to show that they had grasped the relevant details of the experience?

mation helps the learner to assimilate and retain information. "Telling is not teaching and told is not taught." How we *deliver* instruction becomes a carefully planned exercise.

### Comment

Included in this category are field trips, student reports, written reports or term papers, and problem solving (not calculations).

### Assumptions

1. School serves children best by teaching them to be self-directed critical thinkers and problem solvers.
2. Students in an inquiry/discovery lesson have enough maturity in tool subjects such as reading to be able to follow the directions given to complete an inquiry lesson successfully.
3. Students are self-directed enough to enjoy and benefit from a learner-centered rather than a teacher-centered lesson.
4. There has been sufficient completion of students' learning hierarchies for them to make the inductive leap to the next level of the hierarchy.

### Role of teacher

Teacher is a guide-stimulator, a facilitator who challenges the learner. The teacher sets goals for learners but allows students to reach goals at different paces or possibly by different paths. The teacher may play the role of classroom librarian when he or she helps students locate and make the best use of reference and other materials. The teacher may serve as coordinator or assistant principal in the sense of interfacing with other teachers, resource persons, or the school librarian. This teacher needs to have a broader understanding of curriculum and the operations of the school than does a mere expositor who comes to class and gives notes to students. The ability to do discovery/inquiry represents a mark of maturity for a teacher.

### Role of learner

Learners take the initiative to find things out for themselves. They ask questions. They are free to explore. Instead of responding to teacher questions, they discover answers. Learner's role should be clarified so that he or she knows when to report in (conference) with the teacher before going on to the next step in the investigation.

### Instructional resources

This mode does not require specific instructional materials. Any conventional resources (such as textbooks, resource people, library) can be used. Learner is encouraged to use a broad range of data sources. It is not important *what* resources are used, but *how* the learner uses them.

### Method of evaluation

Evaluation is based on the extent to which knowledge has been transmitted. Standardized tests that focus on assessment of critical-thinking/problem-solving skills are sometimes used, as are criterion-referenced tests. Special opportunities exist for the use of open-ended and higher-order questions.

**FIGURE 12.18**
Womack's inquiry mode.

### Weaknesses and likely problem areas

The weaknesses of this mode of instruction lie primarily with our own histories as students. Research tells us that, for better or worse, we are likely to teach as we were taught rather than as we were taught to teach. The vast majority of us were taught by expository means when we were students. Thus, we are breaking new ground when we attempt to use inquiry/discovery strategies. The mode takes a special teacher who is willing to try something new.

Most of us in teacher education arrived after surviving three degrees of expository teaching. We were probably exposed to inquiry methods by the lecture method. If inquiry is so great, then why isn't it used more in college teaching?

In isolated instances it is—more likely where faculty members have had some opportunity (or compelling reason) to try these ideas out in the real world, preferably in a public school setting. After trying innovations such as inquiry or individualized teaching, and wearing off the rough edges, the teacher educator is ready to help another teacher through this process.

Thus, the teacher who wants to incorporate inquiry teaching needs an appropriate model. As more college faculty and supervisory personnel have experience with this mode and individualized instruction, both forms of instruction will become more common.

### Summary

A plan to evaluate inquiry teaching would most likely include these elements:

1. Did the teacher build the knowledge pyramid enough so that the students will be able to progress to the next step of content with a minimum of teacher assistance?

2. Evaluate the degree and nature of individual conferences with students. Is there always a crowd around the teacher's desk? This usually means that the students were dismissed to individual work without knowing enough about the subject to be able to go on unassisted.

3. Did the teacher anticipate which resources would be needed and make those readily available? Does the teacher have to leave the class or classroom frequently to place students one at a time in the library, lab, and so on?

4. Are students checking in with the teacher at regular and prescribed intervals? Are stalemates and blind alleys being nipped in the bud?

5. Does the teacher allow a sufficient amount of freedom for students to move about and get materials?

6. What about the evaluations for students at the end of their projects or units? Are students being directed toward higher-order thinking, or are they just on a paper chase to collect trivia?

7. In the midst of all of this inquiry activity, are state-required minimum essentials or standards being met or surpassed?

8. Does the teacher allow large blocks of time for this type of activity? Or is he or she always trying to call the group back together? Homogeneity is not the goal of inquiry teaching.

9. Are students off task? How does the teacher redirect stragglers?

### Comment

Other titles for this category include programmed instruction, self-paced instruction, learning packets, contract learning, performanced-based instruction, alternative learning paths, and mastery learning.

### Assumptions

1. Students may accept a portion of, or all of, the other three modes of instruction.
2. Students are not homogeneous with regard to relevant or other variables.
3. Heterogeneity between students will increase, not decrease, as they mature and become more sophisticated in their learning.
4. Most students will learn if given a chance to do so at their own pace within their modality preferences (visual, auditory, kinesthetic).

### Role of teacher

Teachers set the stage for instruction. The teacher provides an environment for activities based on learner needs. The intent is a worry- and stress-free environment. The teacher is a learning facilitator with a very broad understanding of curriculum (almost jack-of-all-trades). If the teacher doesn't know the answer to something, he or she will know where to look it up. The teacher's classroom looks like a mini-library, with learning centers, working bulletin boards, computers and software, encyclopedias, possibly out-of-adoption textbooks, and other learning resources stored semi-neatly.

The teacher still sets goals and cooperatively sets criteria and means for evaluation of student learning. The teacher diagnoses and sets means of learning based upon learner's modality preferences, learning histories, self-direction, and interests.

Instruction is individualized in one or more of three ways: by pace, by modality preference, or by interest. In the present era of legislated learning, unfortunately, there is little room for individualizing by interest.

### Role of Learner

Learner is centrally involved in the learning process. Exercise of initiative and responsibility is the basic role. Learners are supposed to report in to the teacher at prescribed and regular intervals. They may learn at their own rates, but a rate cannot be zero.

### Instructional resources

Projects should unify the student's school experience. They should take place in a highly individualized, loosely structured environment with a problem-solving orientation. A recommended resource to use is a token economy. This is useful for motivation, feedback, and discipline. Formal training in behavior modification is necessary if this mode is to be used with moderately or severely handicapped students.

### Methods of evaluation

Evaluation bears little resemblance to traditional forms. Students should show how well they use tools of learning such as reading, writing, spelling, and speaking in solving problems and meeting their needs. Progress is thought of in terms of prior status, not comparison with peers or nationally derived norms.

However, progress *can* be compared to national norms, usually with little fear of embarrassment. In a classroom in Oklahoma where I taught seriously emotionally disturbed high school students, the average gain in one year was 3.07 grade levels. This compared with an average yearly gain of 0.52 years in traditional, expository classrooms.

**FIGURE 12.19**
Womack's individualized instruction mode.

## Weaknesses and likely problem areas

Right now this mode of teaching is largely in the province of selected master teachers and Ph.D.s who find themselves back in public school. Yet it is virtually unknown for teachers who develop a system like this to try it, drop it, and go back to one of the first three modes of instruction already mentioned.

Assuming that the teacher is capable of organizing $N$ number of lessons for $N$ students in a given day, the biggest potential flaw of individual teaching is the capacity to get behind the teacher's desk and stay there. The system runs so smoothly that it appears to run itself. You have to make yourself get out there and read with the students, probe them for what they are doing, make suggestions, and stay on their backs to keep busy and keep reporting in systematically.

This kind of teacher can be unjustly evaluated by administrators whose own teaching maturity stops at one of the lower levels. If the evaluating administrator is expecting to observe a teacher-centered lesson where all students experience a set or closure at the same moment, this teacher may be in trouble. Such decision points occur in an individualized classroom but at different times. Sometimes there is no overt teacher behavior to suggest that monitoring and adjusting might be occurring; rather, it is built into the materials that the teacher made available to the student. This does not mean that the teacher is not providing instruction ("teaching"). It is by his or her hand that these good things are happening. Anyone who has ever had an individualized classroom knows that none of it "just happens."

One peril of the system is that there is a noticeable shortfall of failures. Parents who like to see (academic) blood will protest a system where some students are not made to fail. The goal of individualized instruction is not the certification of masters and nonmasters (failures, as some would love to call them) but the education of all. (For more on mastery learning, read previous sections of this chapter.)

## Summary

To evaluate the individualizing teacher, pick two or three individual students and see what they do for a period. Trying to follow the operations of an entire class under these conditions will be confusing at the least and wrongfully incriminating at the worst. At the minimum, look for these things:

1. No student stays totally off task for more than two minutes.

2. Every student has study materials of some kind in front of him or her and is actively engaged in learning within 120 sec of the tardy bell.

3. Learning materials still reflect the curriculum that the rest of the school is following. There are no tangents.

4. There is differentiation of modalities; for some students most of the material is visual, for some auditory, and for some multimedia.

5. Students practice school courtesies much as they would in any other classroom.

6. Other facets of school life continue as they would in other classrooms: lunch, grade reporting, attendance, and so on.

7. At different and separate points, each student participates in unfamiliar, enactive, and symbolic phases of instruction; it is not unfamiliar followed by more of the same.

8. Evaluation of student learning takes place (tests, reports, and so on).

9. The teacher still shows the professional attention and respect that students in another kind of classroom should receive.

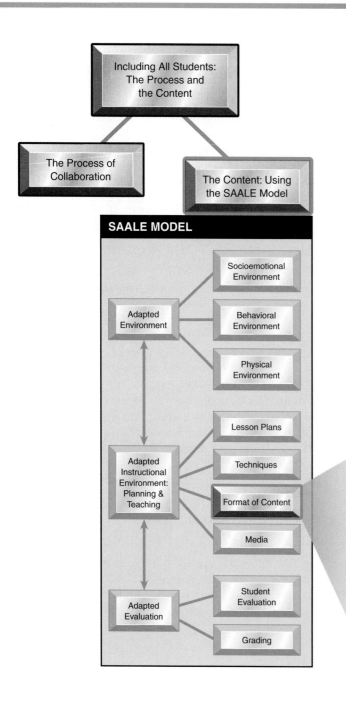

**SAALE MODEL**

Adapted Environment
- Socioemotional Environment
- Behavioral Environment
- Physical Environment

Adapted Instructional Environment: Planning & Teaching
- Lesson Plans
- Techniques
- Format of Content
- Media

Adapted Evaluation
- Student Evaluation
- Grading

Including All Students: The Process and the Content

The Process of Collaboration

The Content: Using the SAALE Model

**Chapter-at-a-Glance**

Organizing Content

Adapting the Presentation of Content

Using Whole Language

Using Task Analysis

Adapting Assignments

After teachers select the appropriate teaching technique to deliver the lesson, they may have to consider alternative ways of presenting the academic content. For example, teachers usually teach the subject of reading from a basal textbook and teach math using exercises and examples in a textbook. Assignments to prepare for tomorrow's class may be given at the end of today's class. Work sheets traditionally are used in classrooms across the country.

But what happens to the student who simply cannot achieve success with the strategies and formats used for teaching the content? Sometimes, even if techniques have been adapted, the student still may not understand the material. In such cases, the regular class teacher should ask the following questions:

1. Does the student have the skills to complete the required task?
2. If not, does the student have the prerequisite skills for beginning the required task?
3. Does instruction begin at the student's functioning level?
4. Was the teaching technique appropriate for delivering the instruction to the student?

After answering these questions, the teacher may see a need to modify the strategies and formats used for reorganizing instruction.

This chapter discusses and presents ideas for providing a more clear understanding of the content for students. The content is the subjects being taught: reading, math, social studies, science, art, physical education, etc. There are three major areas of focus when we are analyzing our content or subject: What are the organizational skills needed to help the student understand the subject being taught and be in a constant state of learning for test and review? What are some strategies educators can use to bring life (understanding) to the content of a subject as it is being taught? When the class is over and assignments are presented, our job is only beginning. How can educators adapt assignments to meet individual students' needs?

## ORGANIZING CONTENT

Structure is an important component of content or subject matter, as it is for other blocks of the SAALE model. Remember, when educators provide structure, students will eventually, and naturally, learn to impose their own. Organizing content has six important parts: directions, work sheets, note taking, notebooks, study guides, and taped texts.

### Directions

Giving directions is one of the first things done in class and also one of the tasks done most frequently. If students have not heard, listened to, or understood the directions, they are lost from the start. There are three aspects of directions: before giving directions, giving oral directions, and providing written directions. Each part is crucial to the process.

*Before giving directions.* Think about the following suggestions before you give directions:

1. Be sure you have all students' attention. You can get their attention in many ways—wearing a funny hat, holding up a small directions flag, and so on.
2. Allow the class to select the direction clue to be used each month. This gives them ownership in the process.
3. Check to see that everyone has the necessary materials for recording directions (such as paper, pencils, and highlighters).
4. Try not to scold anyone before giving directions. Embarrassment may prevent students from paying attention.
5. Offer small prizes to sections of the class that focus on the direction clue first.
6. Number each direction if more than one is to be used.

*Giving oral directions.* Here are some tips for giving oral directions:

1. Get students' attention.
2. Eliminate unnecessary words.
3. Speak in short, simple sentences.
4. Give only one direction if possible.
5. Use a visual backup and speak slowly, stopping after each direction if more than one is given.
6. Remember, no matter how slowly you speak or how long you pause, some students can only process one direction and not a series of directions.
7. Ask for volunteers to repeat the directions.
8. Keep visual support present during the activity. In other words, do not erase the visual backup before the activity/assignment has been completed.
9. Have a system in place for students who do not understand directions. In other words, they should know what to do to find out. Do not tell them to raise their hands because some students are embarrassed about doing this. Develop a discreet way for them to get clarity.
10. If repeating directions, restate them exactly the same way (for auditory processing difficulties).

*Providing written directions.* I have several suggestions for providing written directions:

1. Use few words.
2. Provide an example.
3. Read the directions orally as the students highlight the written directions.

4. Keep directions on the page that a student is working on. If the assignment is on more than one page, the directions should appear on a card, the chalkboard, or another easily accessible place.

5. Be sure that the students understand all parts of, and all words in, the directions.

6. Have a backup system for students who do not understand the directions. Remember that students who do not understand the directions are usually those who do not want to raise their hands in front of their peers. Find a discreet way for them to get information.

## Work Sheet Modifications

I have never been a big fan of work sheets. However, the reality is that work sheets are used frequently in schools. A work sheet should have a definite purpose related to the task at hand and should not be used as busy work.

One of my favorite stories regarding work sheets occurred several years ago. I frequently visit schools and observe many wonderful, talented, creative educators. I also like to drop into the teacher's lounge, where you can truly feel the pulse of a school. This particular day I was having a Coke and visiting with the teachers. I noticed that one teacher was running off a stencil on a mimeograph machine. (Most of you probably have never seen a mimeograph machine. In the past, this was how teachers did their copying. Ask your professors. I bet they remember!) The teacher's stack of work sheets grew higher and higher. Curious (as usual!), I walked over to look at the stack of papers, wondering what was so important. When I found out, I'm sure the look on my face showed everyone my shock. All those papers were the same. Each sheet was filled with an enormous letter *C,* which students were supposed to trace with a crayon.

Observing my look of bewilderment, the teacher said, "These boys and girls certainly need lots of work on the letter *C.*"

All I could think was "It looks like they're going to get more than they want." But naturally, I remained professional, smiled politely, and returned to my chair.

My point is that work sheets must have a purpose. You should think about that purpose when constructing, implementing, and evaluating them.

*Construction.* Here are some tips for constructing work sheets:

1. Limit the amount of material on each page.

2. Focus on only one concept at a time.

3. Provide large, readable print or type.

4. Make sure the work sheet teaches what you intend it to teach.

5. Do not use work sheets for busy work.

6. Keep directions simple.

7. Do not hand out numerous work sheets at one time.

8. When a student finishes one work sheet, do not just hand out another.

*Implementation.* Think about these ideas before implementing work sheets.

1. Provide short, clear directions.
2. Present all directions both orally and visually.
3. Be sure students clearly understand directions.
4. Have students color code or highlight directions.
5. Present only one work sheet at a time.
6. Allow students to work with a buddy when completing the work sheet.
7. Allow students to complete part of the work sheet or odd/even sections.

*Evaluation.* Here are three tips for evaluating work sheets:

1. Provide self-correcting work sheets. Answer cards may be used for checking answers, or a completed work sheet may be used.
2. Permit students to correct their own work sheets.
3. If work sheets are turned in, be sure they are graded and returned.

## The Note-Taking Process

Note taking is a skill that requires instruction, structure, and practice, although teachers often assume that it is an easy task for students. Many students in inclusive settings have difficulty taking notes because of their inability to organize ideas or concepts, distinguish main points or ideas, or transfer information from written or oral formats. Some students also have deficits in processing or in motor skills.

Students must have the correct information in a format useful for study if we expect them to learn class information and pass class tests. The note-taking process serves as a study process for many students, especially if the class is organized and systematic. Learning how to take notes in difficult situations is a skill that may be carried not only into other classes but into adult life as well. Learning note taking, learning the method of adaptation that is required, and getting a complete set of notes provide instructional security for students. Their anxiety is reduced when they know that they have the proper information from which to organize their study.

Many students fail tests because of incomplete notes, not because they do not know the material. Test success is extremely dependent on having good notes. Thus, the point of intervention could be working on students' note-taking abilities.

Before providing adaptations for the note-taking process, educators need to consider the sources from which the notes will be given. Will the information be orally presented through lectures, movies, videotapes, or filmstrips? Or will it be in written format, using the chalkboard, an overhead projector, a textbook, newspapers, magazines, or PowerPoint? Students should also develop an awareness of the source of the notes and specific adaptations they need for each source.

Second, teachers should tell students about the type of test to expect from the notes, such as multiple choice, essay, or short answer. This helps the student focus on how the material will be presented in the testing situation.

We often think of note taking as a single large skill that students use in the classroom. Actually, there are two distinct types of note taking, and each requires different skills. Figure 13.1 shows the process of note taking.

**FIGURE 13.1**
The note-taking process: Oral material and printed material.

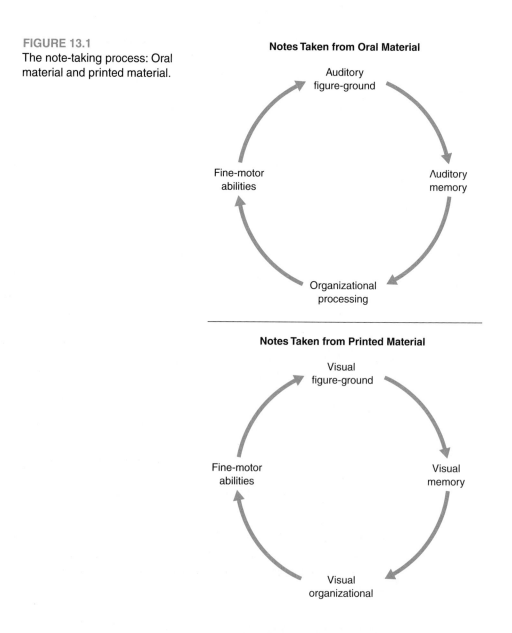

*Taking notes from oral material.* Material given orally includes lecture, video, filmstrips, and so on. Think of this type of note taking as a four-step process. First, the student must auditorily pick up the information (figure-ground). (In this case, *figure-ground* means hearing a word and selecting it from a background of other words.) Second, the student must remember what was just said (auditory memory). Third, some sort of organizational processing takes place. What is the topic? What are the major and minor parts? All information is not equal. Fourth, the material heard must be transferred into written format. Five motor abilities come into play here. The process is continuous, not as jerky as it seems in this discussion.

What kinds of trouble do special-needs students have with this kind of note taking? Imagine that you are a student with poor auditory memory. By the time you write down part of what you heard and return your attention to the speaker, pockets of information are missing from your notes. I call this "Swiss cheese" note taking.

The lecture is one of the most common situations in which students take notes from oral information. Students have difficulty taking notes from a lecture for a number of reasons. These include an inability to impose structure, visual-processing problems, deficient motor skills, and auditory processing problems. Many students are unable to listen to the teacher, extrapolate the major and minor concepts, and put this information on their paper. For them, everything that the teacher says appears equally important. Students with visual-processing deficits may not be able to move their eyes from one focus point (the teacher) to a new focus point (the paper) smoothly enough to take notes quickly. Deficient fine-motor control may cause handwriting problems so that students cannot read their own notes. Auditory-processing problems may cause students to be unable to hear the lecture clearly and accurately, resulting in incomplete or incorrect notes.

One suggestion for adapting the note-taking process is to provide a lecture outline. An outline gives the student the major and minor parts of the coming lecture, either on a single page or on one or more pages, with space allotted for filling in notes. Chapter 12 offered suggestions for structured organizers, which can also help students who have trouble taking notes on oral material.

Before beginning the lecture, the teacher should follow these steps:

1. Present the topic or objective of the material to be covered.
2. Relate the material to the sequence of material taught yesterday and to the total course sequence.
3. Introduce the lecture outline by pointing out the major points (points 1, 2, 3, and so on).
4. Remind students that minor or supporting information will be listed under each major topic.
5. Give the page numbers where students can find the information in the text.
6. Begin the lecture and indicate noteworthy information.
7. Throughout the lecture or discussion, refer to the outline number to keep students on track.

8. If paper shortage is a concern, present the outline on the chalkboard or use an overhead projector.

9. At the conclusion of the lecture, briefly summarize the information covered.

Use tape recorders for recording lectures or discussions. Students may bring their own recorders, or the teacher can record the lecture and allow students to check out tapes at a later date.

As a class lecture progresses, use the chalkboard to help organize the information. Develop a chart format with headings. During the lecture, fill in key information for students to copy. When the class is completed, students will have a set of notes organized by categories to make studying and review easier.

Good listening is essential for taking notes from lectures, class discussions, reviews, or other oral presentations. Students should be trained to listen. Teachers should remember that, after a while, everything begins to sound the same. Therefore, it is important to take an occasional "listening break." Pause for a stretch, tell a story that is related to the topic, or insert a joke. Breaking the constant flow of the lecture helps the listener attend to noteworthy information.

Give signals to let students know what is important to write down. Students who have difficulty with structure may also have difficulty distinguishing major and minor details. When you come to part of the lecture that you know students must remember for a test or other reason, give a clue: for example, say, "This is noteworthy." Be sure that students know what the clue words are. Tell students they should either underline the noteworthy information or put a star in the margin. By giving clues, you are (a) keeping the students on track, (b) helping students attend to the important information, and (c) teaching the difference between major and minor information.

*Taking notes from printed material.* Taking notes from printed matter can also be difficult for students. This kind of note taking falls into two areas: far-point copy and near-point copy. Far-point copy is required when you are copying from the overhead projector, chalkboard, flip chart, and so on. Near-point copy is required when, for example, you are copying math problems from a textbook onto paper or copying from one paper to another.

Figure 13.1 displays the four skills required for a student to be able to copy from printed matter. As you look at the figure, visualize students who have a difficult time finding their place in printed material when they move their eyes from book to paper (visual figure-ground). With such a problem, taking notes can take forever. Because note taking requires many skills, just one breakdown point can throw the student significantly behind.

Taking notes from the chalkboard relies heavily on good skills in visual tracking, handwriting, and organization. If the skills are not fully developed, the mainstreamed student may have great difficulty getting the notes. The arrangement of class seating is essential. The teacher should be sure that students are seated so they can see the chalkboard easily as well as avoid distractions. If you are going to provide a complete set of notes for students who are unable to copy from the board, you may have them copy only certain sections. This will keep students working with the class but take away the stress of trying to get all of the notes. Students can then focus on the discussion, knowing that a complete set of notes will follow.

When giving notes from the overhead projector, you may make the same adaptations described for the chalkboard. In addition, keep covered any information you have not yet discussed so that students cannot see it until you are ready to present it. When you are ready to discuss the information, allow time for students to copy it before you begin. If you are talking as the students write, many will miss your discussion.

Often you may ask students to take notes from preprinted material such as textbooks, magazines, and newspapers. If the notes are being written for future study and review, students may wish to use the format presented in Figure 13.2: If a student is copying material onto a note card, similar information may be placed on the card. The teacher should make sure to put the page number of the material on the card and number the cards when finished.

| Name: _____ | |
|---|---|
| Topic: _____ | Class: _____ |
| Source of material: _____ | Period: _____ |
| Page numbers: _____ | Date: _____ |

| As you develop the outline, put important facts, vocabulary, and dates in this column. The specific page number may also be listed. | Outline material in this section<br><br>I.<br>   A.<br>   B.<br>   C.<br>II.<br>   A.<br>   B.<br>   C.<br>III.<br>   A.<br>   B.<br>   C. |

**FIGURE 13.2**
Format for taking notes from printed matter.

*General note-taking tips.* The information in this section applies to note taking from any material, whether presented orally or in written form. Figure 13.3 offers a number of note-taking suggestions. (I'd like to thank the following educators for their contributions: Cathy Wobser, Sandra Gilbert, Maureen Thomas, Cathy Perini-Korreck, Marshall Welch, and Ida Crandall.)

To help students improve their approach to note taking, show them how to format the paper they plan to take notes on. Here are some suggestions about formatting:

1. Teach students to use only two-thirds of their paper for note taking and one-third for study and review:
   a.  Have students take notes in the right-hand column.
   b.  As the notes are being given, point out important dates, facts, vocabulary, and so on; have the student put facts into the left-hand column.
   c.  When you have completed a section of notes, stop and ask the class to review its notes and list in the left-hand column possible text questions.
   d.  Review the questions presented and have the class complete missing information.
2. After note taking, students can work with a buddy to study and review notes.
3. Have students develop a format for their notepapers. This will help them to organize, file, and retrieve for later review.
4. Loose-leaf paper means easier filing. However, commercial notebooks can be purchased if you prefer students to keep notes in a spiral-bound book.

You can also help students after the note-taking process:

1. Teach students how to use the notes for study and review.
2. Assign buddies or study-and-review teams to work together using the notes.
3. Buddies can color code notes. Use three colors: one for vocabulary, one for facts to remember, and one for concepts to study. The teachers can quickly check to see if important information is highlighted.
4. Buddies can check one set of notes with another and, in the left-hand column, write missing information.
5. Teach students to file their notes in an organized manner. Work on this process for an extended period until students develop the structure themselves.
6. Before the test, refer to notes by dates/topics that should be reviewed. Tell the students the test type for specific notes.
7. It is good practice to keep an extra set of class notes on file in the class. Students who are absent or who have missed sections of notes can refer to this set for assistance. File the notes by class date for easy retrieval.

1. Save a set of notes from another class to give to the student.
2. Give the student a copy of the teacher's notes (see Figure 13.4).
3. Let one student copy his or her notes to give to the student who has difficulty taking notes.
4. Use an organizer for taking notes on poems. For example:

| Title | Author | Type | Poetic Devices Used |
|---|---|---|---|
| Summary of Poem:<br><br>Class Discussion:<br>    What I learned from the discussion:<br>    Questions I have about the poem: | | | |

5. Seat the student appropriately to avoid auditory or visual distractions.
6. Provide structured organizers for note taking.
7. Provide a lecture outline for note taking.
8. Develop a who, what, when, where, how, and why outline for note taking.

Who ———— [        ]

What ———— [        ]

When ———— [        ]

Where ———— [        ]

How ———— [        ]

Why ———— [        ]

| Who | What | When | Where | How | Why |
|---|---|---|---|---|---|
|  |  |  |  |  |  |
|  |  |  |  |  |  |
|  |  |  |  |  |  |
|  |  |  |  |  |  |
|  |  |  |  |  |  |
|  |  |  |  |  |  |

9. When having students copy from the chalkboard or overhead projector, use various colors of chalk or pens. Each sentence should be written in a different color (blue, pink, green). This method is very useful for all students in finding information in a visual field. But be careful: too many colors overwhelm and distract.

*(continued)*

**FIGURE 13.3**
Note-taking suggestions for oral or written materials.

10. After a film, divide the chalkboard into four sections and use words or pictures to review. This is an easy note-taking idea for young children.

11. When handing out study work sheets to be kept in a student folder, have students highlight the important information. Many students can never read all of the material, but will or can read the highlighted information.

12. Be sure all notes to be copied are typed or printed. Cursive writing is extremely hard to read.

13. Use the 1/3–2/3 folding method for note taking. This may be used for lecture notes or chapter notes. Put main idea or question on left side and answer or detail on right side. For example:

| Felony | Crime for which the punishment is one year or longer. |
|--------|-------------------------------------------------------|

14. Provide a classroom set of clipboards as an incentive for children to get physically involved in note taking from the chalkboard.

15. Provide a binder available to all students in one place in the room. Have two volunteers/secretaries copy their notes and place them in the binder at the end of each class. The teacher makes 6 to 8 copies of the better set and places them back into the binder. The next day students with note-taking difficulties may get a complete set of notes from the day before.

16. Use a *KIM* sheet for note taking. It looks like this:

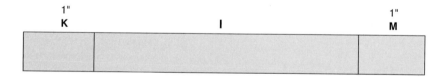

   a. Students make their chart using any type of paper.

   b. **K** is for key words. **I** is for information about the key word, which can be numbered or lettered. **M** is for a memo to help students remember the information, page, and so on.

   c. This method is generic for any class. Students always have the outline when needed. When using the **KIM** sheet to study for a test, you can cover the **K** column and read clues from the **I** column and check answers, or cover the **I** column and use **K** as clues. If writing a report, **K** is your topic, and **I** is the information for each paragraph or sentence.

**FIGURE 13.3**
Continued.

17. Use the *T* note method. Divide your paper into a simple *T*. For example:

| Main idea | 1. detail 1<br>2. detail 2<br>3. detail 3 |
|---|---|

a. Take all main ideas down on the left side of the paper.

b. All details that go with the main ideas are placed on the right side of the *T* and are numbered.

c. Vocabulary words go to the left and definitions on the right.

d. *T* notes are easy to study by either folding the paper or overlapping papers as shown below.

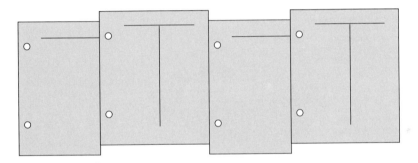

18. Use the note-taking–note-making method. For example:

| **Note taking**<br><br>Notes that the teacher gives in about 8-minute increments.<br>    Stop! | **Note taking**<br><br>What the students make out of the notes given:<br>  • Rephrasing<br>  • Questions<br>  • Any type of response |
|---|---|
| **Drawing**<br><br>On the back of another sheet students draw their understanding of concepts from the lecture. | **Relating**<br><br>Students make associations and explain them in a paragraph.<br>Share in class the next day. |

## Basic Water Conservation and Management Principles

1. Intercept the force of the running water
2. Slow it down
3. Control it
4. Reduce the amount of water leaving the land source
   - Sheet erosion moves the soil surface in a large usually unseen thin sheet
   - Erosion takes place anywhere there is bare soil
   - Water beats away at the soil, loosening soil particles and moving them short distances or even far away
   - Erosion causes sediment to fill reservoirs, lakes, and streams that kills aquatic life
   - Erosion can clog water delivery systems that bring water to cities
   - In cities where there is more pavement than soil, water runs off quicker and fills storm drains and sewer systems. This is what causes flooding.

## Water and Conservation

Water can generally be managed and conserved as it becomes available through precipitation.
   - Water management begins with soil management
   - Soil erosion begins with a drop of water blasting soil particles, like a bomb

**FIGURE 13.4**

Student notes given by teacher prior to class.

*Source*: Science, Spring Oaks Middle School, 2000.
A special thanks to Ashly Tardif, Houston, TX.

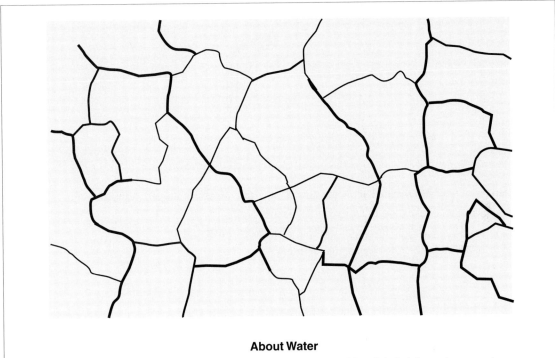

**About Water**

Water surrounds us. It is in the air as rain, ice, snow, steam, and fog. It is in lakes, streams, rivers, oceans, and glaciers.

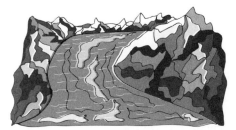

*(continued)*

Humans are about 65% water

    Blood = 80–90%

    Muscles = 75%

Water isn't ever new, it is recycled time and time again. No new water is being manufactured.

Water is 2 hydrogen molecules and 1 oxygen molecule. $H_2O$.

The Earth's surface is about 75% water but only 3% is fresh water.

Precipitation falls to Earth from clouds, rain or snow.

The process then starts over again

### Key Processes of Hydrological Cycle

1. Evaporation: water goes from liquid to gas stage
2. Transpiration: water given off through leaves

**FIGURE 13.4**
Continued.

3. Precipitation: raining or snowing
4. Infiltration: fill the pore spaces between individual soil particles
5. Respiration: breathing
6. Combustion: burning

## The Water Cycle—Nature's Recycling System

Recycling: to pass through a cycle or a part of cycle again

Hydrological cycle: a natural process of water molecules recycling from the land, to the air, and back to the land

Sun's energy warms the water and the vapor goes into the atmosphere

In the atmosphere the vapor is formed into clouds

Clouds are carried by weather patterns

Providing adaptations for notes is a crucial support for students. If students are unable to get a complete set of notes, how can we expect them to be successful on tests? The ideas I have presented help bridge the gap between notes and students.

Let's look at a few tips which help students help themselves. Figure 13.5 presents note-taking tips which students can incorporate into their own skill base. These are also good ideas for the college student.

Before closing this section, I want to leave you with one thought:

It is not important that students *take* the notes. It is important that they *get* the notes.

## Notebooks

At the beginning of each school year, teachers across the United States announce, "In this class, you will keep a notebook." Some teachers provide the format for the notebooks, while others leave the format open. Here are suggestions for helping students organize and keep notes, for notebook checkups, and for test review from notes.

*Organizing the notebook.* Before organizing the notebook, the teacher should examine the structure of the class. For example, how does the structure relate to the types of tests given? Does the class follow a certain structure each day? Notebook organization should reflect that structure.

Table 13.1 shows the notebook organization for a class in geography.

By making students aware of the match between class structure and notebook format, and including the test item type for each section, teachers help students think of the class from beginning to end. Other tips for organizing notebooks include using dividers for each subject and section and keeping separate notebooks in a loose-leaf binder for each subject. Figure 13.6 offers additional notebook organization ideas. (I'd like to thank Betty Powell and L. Wakefield for their contributions.)

TABLE 13.1
Sample notebook organization.

| Class Structure | Notebook Format | Reorganized Notebook Format | Test Item |
|---|---|---|---|
| Class opening | Class notes | Atlas notes/maps | Listing questions |
| Atlas questions from the overhead projector | Maps | Study questions/notes | Short-answer |
| Study questions from homework | Quizzes | Lecture outline/notes | Multiple choice, |
| Class lecture | | Quizzes | true-false |
| | Exams | Exams | |
| Tomorrow's assignment | | | |
| Class closing | | | |

Prepare for the class by completing background reading prior to the class.

Get to class on time so that you don't miss the teacher's opening statements which are often a statement of the purpose of the lecture.

Don't try to write down every word the teacher says. Focus instead on key phrases, important points, new terms, summary statements, names, dates, etc. Choose one example of a point to record rather than trying to write down each one in detail. Do record all the points in a list.

Keep your mind focused on what the teacher is saying. Try not to look around or think of other things.

Taking notes in outline form will help you focus on main ideas.

Develop your own short-hand system for commonly used words and phrases, for example: b/c for because, w/o for without, $\cong$ for approximately, $\uparrow$ for increased, $\therefore$ for therefore, vs. for versus, $\neq$ for does not equal. Also create a course-specific set of abbreviations, such as: cong. for congressional, adm. for administration, gov't for government, dem/rep for democrats and republicans, etc.

Don't write down small words such as *a, the, is* that are not needed to understand the information.

Remember that your notes are for your own use. Don't be overly concerned about neatness or correct spelling.

If a word is used that you don't know or can't quite understand, write it down phonetically, circle it, and ask a classmate about it or look it up later.

When the teacher uses phrases such as, "This is important," "The main point . . . ," or "An important finding . . . ," prior to presenting the information, mark this information by putting a star in the margin of your notes.

When the teacher uses phrases such as "First . . . second . . . third . . . ," "At this stage . . . ," " Finally . . .," recognize these as transitional words that signal a sequence of steps or events.

Notice when the teacher raises the volume of her voice or repeats a word or phrase. This probably signals important information.

Leave plenty of white space in your notes and wide margins for expanding your notes later.

Use a pen rather than a pencil for taking notes. A pen will slide across the paper more quickly and your notes won't smudge and fade like those taken in pencil.

Put the date and day on each set of notes. Draw a line after the last sentence you write and indicate "end."

If you have a question about what the teacher is saying or missed some information, wait until she has completed her thought before interrupting to request repetition or clarification.

If you consistently have difficulty copying lengthy information from overhead transparencies, ask if you can get copies of the transparencies or if you can look at them during a break or after class to fill in information you missed.

If you are going to tape-record a lecture let the teacher know that you plan on doing this. Always try to back up the tape with notes.

Review your notes as soon as possible after class, filling in information you missed.

Rewriting your notes right after you take them may help you learn the information and also gives you a chance to organize your notes for future study.

Arrange for another student to use carbon paper for a second set of notes. This is most helpful if you need to focus on the lecture and not split attention between listening and taking notes.

**FIGURE 13.5**

Note-taking tips for students.

*Note:* For practice on note taking, see Flemming, L., & Leet, J. (1994). *Becoming A Successful Student.* Harper Collins College Publishers.

1. Organize a "desk elf" for younger students. Use one basket per child for glue, scissors, crayons, books, pencils, and so on. Maintain a desk folder for papers to keep or work on and a home folder for things to go home. Keep desk elves on a shelf.

2. "Tub teaching" for young students helps keep students organized who change classes. Each student is given a Rubbermaid tub with built-in handles to transport books and materials. The tub slides easily under desks and can travel with the students as they move from room to room.

3. Students may keep a table of contents and a point sheet in their notebooks. For example:

| | Table of Contents | |
|---|---|---|
| Date | Page number | Topic |
| | | |

| | Point Sheet | | |
|---|---|---|---|
| Date | Grade | Page | Test/quiz |
| | | | |

4. Give student an activity sheet for keeping a record of activities.

5. Of greatest importance, organize the notebooks with the class. Divide the notebook sections based on your class structure.

6. Be sure each student has a buddy who cross-checks to see if the notebook is being set up properly.

7. Notebooks can be obtained through local businesses or organizations.

8. Put boxes in the halls at each year's end and have students put all items they don't want into the box. You will be surprised at the materials you will get.

9. Last, but certainly not least, organizing notebooks is part of instruction and not just a task assigned for an out-of-class activity.

**FIGURE 13.6**
Suggestions for organizing notebooks.

*Keeping the notebook.* Keeping notebooks can become a major problem for many students. So during the first day or two of class, work with students as they build their notebooks. Explain the overall format; provide an example of a completed notebook; and show students the relationship among class, notebook, and tests. Have each student compile their notebooks in class. Review the final product. This may seem like wasted time, but you will find that it is time well spent. For many students, directions are not sufficient because students cannot follow through with structure without support. For the first two or three weeks, continue to work with the class each day on keeping the notebook in order. Eventually, you can reduce the number of prompts. Remember, the student who would never get a notebook together alone is the one who benefits most from notebook building in class.

Figure 13.7 suggests more notebook-keeping tips. (Thanks to Suzi Lockamy, Gloria Robin, and Alice Jane Rouse for their contributions.)

---

1. To help students keep study outlines in their notebooks, color code the outlines or other materials. Each chapter outline is printed on green paper. If students lose the outline (or other handout), they get another one (no questions asked). But the new handout will be yellow. If they lose the yellow one, they get another one, but it will be red. This helps the teacher eyeball organizational skills, and students truly don't want any yellow or red papers in their notebooks.

2. Periodically during the grading period, have a notebook cleaning party. Save materials that will be needed later in folders, which the teacher keeps. Tell students what may be thrown out or taken home for kitchen art.

3. Keep a monthly organizational chart at the front of the student's notebook. At the beginning of each month replace the old chart with a new one, with the student's record and significant events/tasks to remember. For example:

|  | Monday | Tuesday | Wednesday | Thursday | Friday |
|---|---|---|---|---|---|
| Week of May 1–5 | Quiz in math |  | Science project due | Map quiz | English vocabulary test |
| Week of May 8–12 |  | Social studies report: Mexico |  | Test on short story unit |  |
| Week of May 15–19 |  | Social studies test chapters 5–7 | Science lab due |  |  |
| Week of May 22–26 |  | Math quiz | English paper due | P.E. test: tennis |  |
| Week of May 29– April 3 |  | Oral report P.E. |  |  | Math test |

*(continued)*

**FIGURE 13.7**
Keeping a notebook.

4. A subject time-organization chart also may be used weekly. For example:

| Subject | | Monday | Tuesday | Wednesday | Thursday | Friday | Saturday | Sunday |
|---|---|---|---|---|---|---|---|---|
| Social studies | Time | | | | | | | |
| | Task | | | | | | | |
| Science | Time | | | | | | | |
| | Task | | | | | | | |
| Language arts | Time | | | | | | | |
| | Task | | | | | | | |
| Math | Time | | | | | | | |
| | Task | | | | | | | |
| P.E./health | Time | | | | | | | |
| | Task | | | | | | | |

5. When you are finished with a set of materials or an activity, put the materials into the appropriate section of the notebook and have a buddy cross-check. This process takes only seconds and saves great confusion down the line.

**FIGURE 13.7**
Continued.

*Notebook checkup.* A checkup is an easy way to help students continue to keep their notebooks organized. Inform the class that you will have a notebook quiz from time to time. The quiz will consist of asking questions from different sections of the notebook by date of notes. This type of quiz will be an easy way to get an *A*. On the first quiz, record only the *A*s and remind the rest of the class that simple organization guarantees an *A*. The second quiz will count for all students. Personally, however, I like positive grades for good notebooks and am opposed to marking students down for not having their notebooks.

The notebook is also used for test review. Before a test, distribute a study guide and review it for the test. The notes become a vital part of the study process. Tie together the study guide and the notes taken during this study period. Help students see that studying and reviewing notes will improve their test scores significantly. Teach students to distribute their studying over shorter periods of time.

Here is a notebook-checking tip: Instead of grading notebooks, have a notebook test at the end of a grading period or term. For example, ask, "Quiz number 2 (March 3) was about _____?" If the student has the quiz paper, he or she can easily make a perfect grade. If the student has lost the paper, he or she is free to make copies of another student's quiz before the notebook test. However, other simple notebook tests can involve checking to see if everyone has his or her notebook in class or having two students (or more) work together to catch up on missing papers.

# Study Guides

A study guide helps students develop a focus plan for study and review. As teachers teach, study guides become instruments for improving structure both as the lesson develops and when the lesson is over and test review begins. Study guides benefit students in numerous ways:

1. Study guides provide organization of information for studying purposes.
2. Study guides help students develop a whole-part-whole concept for the material being presented.
3. Study guides present information in a sequential, logical manner.
4. Study guides tie together the information from yesterday to today and tomorrow.
5. Study guides impose structure on information to be learned.
6. Study guides impose a point of focus for the teacher.
7. Study guides facilitate collaboration between special and general education teachers.
8. Study guides help parents assist their children in study and review.
9. Study guides aid students in preparing for specific test types.
10. Study guides help students to impose structure in other classes without guides.

*Types of study guides.* There are two types of study guides: formative and summative. Each serves a specific function for imposing structure and organizing material.

A formative study guide organizes information in short, distributive segments. The guide focuses on specific details of the information covered. An example is the acquisition outline or lesson frame discussed in chapter 12. As a new concept or section of information is presented, students follow the class discussion and record important details in an organized manner. As we discussed in chapter 12, this outline may be on one page or on several pages, and it should have space for notes. The teacher may provide an incomplete outline for students to complete or an outline that has the details already completed. A second option is helpful for students who have difficulty taking notes. Each outline should list the page numbers for the specific information, the title or objective for the lesson, and the lesson date. After the class, students should be instructed to place the outline in the appropriate notebook section. Figure 13.8 presents a sample formative study guide for grade 5.

Study Guide (Formative)

Subject:  Science

Student Name:

Grade level:  5

Activity:  Develop one acquisition outline and one organizer for the subject and
grade level listed above.

Subject:  Science

Topic:  Parts of a Seed

I. Embryo (page 10)

    A. Monocot

    B. Dicot

II. Food storage tissue (pages 11–12)

III. Seed coat (page 15)

    A. Function

    B. Appearance

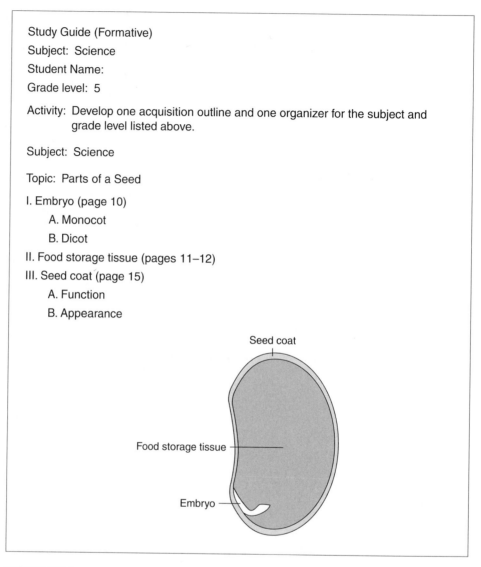

**FIGURE 13.8**
Sample formative study guide.
Thanks to Luanne Berry.

Summative study guides help students prepare for a quiz or test on information learned. They are designed to provide general information about the notes to be quizzed, which lays the foundation for organizing the study effort. The teacher may direct the student to put all formative study guides in sequential order by date and place the summative study guide first. The summative study guide will provide structure for the student's study effort.

Figures 13.9 and 13.10 present sample summative study guides for secondary and elementary levels. The guides can be completed by the teacher or with the class. Figures 13.11 through 13.13 present study guides for grades 1 and 5. These examples should give you an idea how the formative and summary study guide may be developed for multilevel abilities and subjects.

Students are directed to the guide in order to review the lesson or test objective, the textbook, workbook, or handouts to be covered, and key words or vocabulary to be learned. If the test includes short-answer or essay items, review questions are a must. These questions will help the student organize study and review essay questions. The type of test and number of items and point value are also a necessity. The type of test reflects the type of retention measure the teacher used while teaching the lesson. In other words, if the lesson focused on specific dates, people, and facts, then the test is a recognition measure. If the lesson focused on general concepts such as "How did the invention of irrigation affect the lives of the people?" then the test is a subjective measure. Just remember this advice:

*Study guides need to be given out to students before a unit of study or at the beginning of a new chapter.*

*Organizing for study.* After the student has completed the formative and summative study guides, organizing for study becomes the next focus. Many students still need the guided practice of planning for the study process. Using the monthly organization chart and the subject time-organization chart facilitates this process. The teacher may provide a chart form for students to complete by themselves or with the class.

The monthly organization chart can be placed at the beginning of the notebook and completed daily. As tests, quizzes, projects, and papers are assigned, the student records each in the appropriate daily box for the month. To see a sample monthly organization chart, look back at Figure 13.7.

The subject time-organization chart provides structure for organizing the study time needed for each subject on a weekly basis. In planning the subject time-organization chart, the student refers to the monthly organization chart to be sure to include any important study items. These charts can be kept in the notebook or some other convenient place. Look back at Figure 13.7 to see a sample subject time organizer.

*General study tips.* Here are some general study tips:

- Keep notes and guides organized.
- Plan study time for each task.
- Review all class notes nightly.
- Develop flash cards for recognition of information.
- Plan a specific time and place for study.
- Develop a plan for reinforcement of study.
- Help students see the value of planned, organized study.

Student: _____     Date of test: _____

Subject: _____     Date guide issued: _____

Teacher: _____

**Study Guide**

1. Lesson/test objective:

2. Textbook/workbook/manual pages to be covered:

3. Handouts/lectures/films/speakers/demonstrations/labs/maps/charts to be covered:

4. Key words/vocabulary to be learned/location:

5. Review questions for organizing study:

6. Type of test to be given:

|  | Number of items | Point value |
|---|---|---|
| _____ Multiple choice | _____ | _____ |
| _____ Matching | _____ | _____ |
| _____ True-false | _____ | _____ |
| _____ Fill-in-the-blank | _____ | _____ |
| _____ Word bank included? | _____ | _____ |
| _____ Short answer | _____ | _____ |
| _____ Essay | _____ | _____ |
| _____ Diagrams/charts | _____ | _____ |
| _____ Maps | _____ | _____ |
| _____ Word bank for map? | _____ | _____ |
| _____ List of maps to review | _____ | _____ |
| _____ Practical tests | _____ | _____ |

Math items:

|  | Number of items | Point value |
|---|---|---|
| _____ Computation/equations | _____ | _____ |
| _____ Word problems | _____ | _____ |
| _____ Formulas | _____ | _____ |
| _____ Graphing | _____ | _____ |
| _____ Proofs | _____ | _____ |
| _____ Other; please describe | _____ | _____ |

7. Other suggestions for study and review:

Thank you for your help!          Student signature:_____

                                  Parent signature: _____

**FIGURE 13.9**
Summative study guide: Secondary level.

*Source:* Wood, J. W. (2001). Summative study guide. *Reaching the hard to teach.* With permission.

Important vocabulary:

_____

Review questions:

_____

Possible short-answer questions:

_____

Important topics:

_____

Parent signature: _____

FIGURE 13.10
Summative study guide: Elementary level.

Study Guide (Formative)

Subject:        Science

Student Name:  Betty Barger

Grade level:     1st

**Important Vocabulary:**

1. Eggs (page 2)

2. Larva (caterpillar) (page 3)

3. Pupa (chrysalis) (page 3)

4. Adult (butterfly) (page 4)

**Review Questions:**

1. Can you show the sequence of the life cycle of a butterfly? (Use prepared pictures)

2. Can you label the stages in the life cycle of a butterfly? (Prepared cards with words are used)

3. Label the prepared sheet showing the stages in the life cycle of a butterfly with a number 1, 2, 3, 4 showing the sequence in the stages.

**FIGURE 13.11**

Sample Formative Study Guide for Science.

*Source*: Wood, J. W. (2001). Sample formative study guide for science. *Reaching the hard to teach.* With permission.

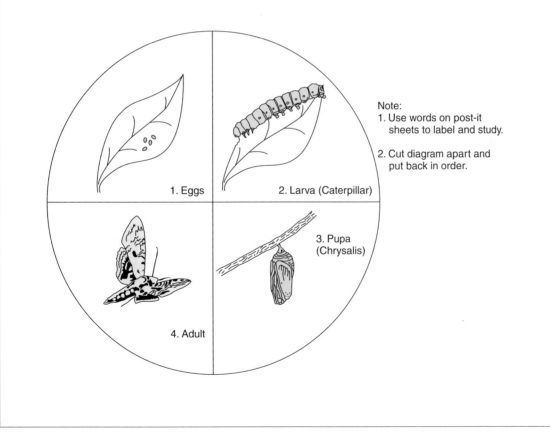

Study Guide (Summary)

Subject:　　　　Science

Student Name:　Betty Barger

Grade level:　　1st

Topic: Life Cycle of the Butterfly

Four Stages

A. Egg

B. Larva (caterpillar)　　　　Show pictures of each and label

C. Pupa (chrysalis)

D. Adult (butterfly)

**Organizer: Design Format**

1. Eggs

2. Larva (Caterpillar)

3. Pupa (Chrysalis)

4. Adult

Note:
1. Use words on post-it sheets to label and study.

2. Cut diagram apart and put back in order.

FIGURE 13.12

*Test Review:* Student will label each stage of the butterfly.

*Source:* Wood, J. W. (2001). Sample summary study guide for science. *Reaching the hard to teach.* Adapted with permission.

# Study Guide

Student: _____    Date of test: _____

Subject: Reading _____    Date of study guide: _____

Teacher: _____

## Study Guide
### (Summary)

| Needed study materials/pages: | Key points addressed: | | |
|---|---|---|---|
| | **Test** | | |
| Key vocabulary words: | Type | Number of items | Point value |
| | | | |
| | Suggestions/Comments for study: | | |

Student signature: _____

Parent signature: _____

**FIGURE 13.13**
Sample Study Guide for Reading

*Source*: Wood, J. W. (2001). Sample summary study guide for reading. *Reaching the hard to teach.*

## General Study Tips for Older Students

Try the following ideas to help you begin your study and make the best use of your time.

- Develop a study schedule for one week to one month in advance.
- Always cross off an assignment when completed. This is an excellent self-motivator.
- Always use an assignment notebook.
- Plan to break up long assignments with a brief rest period, or work on a different subject.
- Schedule rewards for finishing your assignments.
- Sit close to the front of class.
- Make sure your have a complete set of notes.

## Taped Books

All subject areas have texts which support the course. A major issue in our country is that students do not read "on grade level." This is the reality. Another reality is that students are presented or issued texts for subjects and the texts are on a subject-specific grade level. We expect students to read the texts (which are above their grade level) and pass the class. Although all of this does not make reasonable sense, it is a reality. We can teach students subject content *even* when they cannot read. If we are going to issue textbooks, all along knowing the student cannot read the material, then it is our professional responsibility to see that students receive the subject content in a manner in which they can learn.

I know that in the best of worlds everyone will be on grade level. However, this just is not the case in America's schools. The dilemma worsens as students move into higher grades. The gap between the reading and math levels of the student widens. So we *must* begin to tackle this issue. Yes, we keep working on the skills, but learning content is a major focus.

Figures 13.14 and 13.15 present ideas for recording texts and tips for using taped texts.

## Adapting the Presentation of Content

Student success may sometimes depend on the teacher's ability or willingness to adapt the presentation of content. The following activities provide a starting point for developing your own ideas. Many creative educators use inventive adaptations in the class, and the ideas in this chapter represent only a small number of the many possibilities. As much as possible, Activities are organized into similar

| Tip sheet for recording taped texts. |
| --- |

1. Get the course syllabus from the student so that you will know when specific sections of the text are needed.

2. Ask the student to clarify which sections and pages are needed.

3. Be sure you have written permission from the publisher to record the text (the student or the taping service should supply this).

4. Secure an extra copy of the text. Sometimes complementary copies for the purpose of recording can be obtained from the publisher, instructor, or campus bookstore.

5. Allow 30 seconds of empty brown tape at the beginning.

6. Then announce cassette number and leave 15 seconds of tape silent (to go back later and add chapter and page numbers).

7. State title, author, publisher, copyright information, and your name.

8. At the beginning of each chapter, state the page number, chapter number, and name of the chapter.

9. Indicate "heading" or "subheading" as you read each one.

10. Read and spell out each name the first time it appears in a chapter. Do the same for foreign names or technical terms.

11. For long quotes, read as "quote . . . end quote."

12. For material in parentheses, read as "parenthesis . . . end parenthesis."

13. For graphs, tables, figures, and pictures, read the caption only. Read as "caption . . . end caption."

14. Read footnotes immediately following the sentence in which the footnote number appears. Read as "note (number) . . . end note" and then return to the text.

15. At the end of each side, state "End of cassette number (I, etc.) on page number _____."

16. Go back to the beginning of the tape and add the page numbers.

17. Label the tape. Include the title, author, edition, cassette number, side number, chapters, and pages.

**FIGURE 13.14**

Tip sheet for recording taped texts.

*Source:* Lendman, C. (1995). *Volunteer reader/taping service handbook.* Columbus, OH: Association on Higher Education and Disability.

**Tips for students using taped texts.**

- Listen for short periods of time, stopping periodically to review and summarize what was said.

- Use the text as additional stimulus, to keep focused and to assist with pronunciation.

- Use headphone sets to eliminate outside noises and distractions, if necessary.

- Some students may need to close the text and their eyes in order to cut down on the amount of stimuli being received.

- Delineate the cassette's side and page changes using the printed cards enclosed with the tapes.

- Mark side and page changes with colored pens in order to clarify the text information.

- Find a quiet, distraction-free environment.

- Concentrate on listening and integrating the material. Auditory learning demands "active listening."

- Take notes while listening. Highlight the text and use the pause button when necessary.

- Adjust the tape recorder's speed control buttons to slow down or speed up the reading.

- Allow enough time to listen and relisten to the text. Listening to tapes takes time.

- Use the tape counter to mark important text information.

Note: Because of the time involved in ordering, taping, and receiving taped texts, students may need to preregister for courses and begin getting the needed texts

**FIGURE 13.15**

Tips for students using taped texts.

*Source:* Lendman, C. (1995). *Volunteer/reader/taping service handbook.* Columbus, OH: Association on Higher Education and Disability.

categories. In addition, they are coded *E* (elementary), *S* (secondary), or *E/S* (either elementary or secondary). Here is an example.

Activity (E/S):   Alternatives to writing book reports

Adaptation:
1. *Book jacket or bookmark:* Illustrate a cover for the book, or design a bookmark with characters or a setting from the book.
2. *News report:* Summarize the book by writing a news report as if the events in the story actually took place. Pretend to be a TV anchorperson and give the report.
3. *Ending rewrite:* Give the book a new ending. Pursue different ways the story could have ended.
4. *Advertisement:* Dress and act like a character from the book and "sell" the book to the class.
5. *Write the author:* The student can write to the book's author in care of the publisher. Students should make comments about books they have read.
6. *Poetry:* Summarize a book by retelling it in poetry form.
7. *Character journal:* Write a journal portraying a character from the book. The journal should be written in first person and describe the character's thoughts, feelings, and ideas.
8. *Plays:* Rewrite the book in play form. For longer stories, take a chapter or chapters and write an act or scene of the play.
9. *Models:* Make a model of the setting or characters from the book.
10. *Bulletin board:* Use a classroom bulletin board to describe and display the setting, characters, and theme of the book.
11. *Map:* Draw a map of the story setting to show the story action. Use the map as a prop when discussing the book.
12. *Life-sized posters:* Make life-size characters to use as props when presenting an oral book report.
13. *Letter:* Write a letter telling a friend about the book. Describe setting, characters, and plot.
14. *Comic book:* Summarize the book in the form of a comic book. This would be a good idea for unmotivated readers who are very interested in drawing and art.
15. *Oral and taped presentation:* This is an easy alternative to written reports. With taped reports, sound effects can be added to interest the audience.

16. *Condensed book:* Write and illustrate a short synopsis of the book. This is similar to what certain magazines do to advertise a book.

17. *Illustrations:* Draw main characters, setting, or a climactic scene from the book.

18. *Panel discussion:* For students who are reporting on the same book, form a panel and have a question-and-answer period.

19. *Demonstration:* For how-to books, students can demonstrate what was learned. For example, for a book about cake decorating, a student could bring in a cake and show the steps in decorating.

20. *Timeline:* Draw a timeline of events as they happened in the story. Illustrations may be added to explain events.

21. *Popular music:* Have students write and perform (or record) rap songs about the book.

22. *Shoe box filmstrips.* Have students illustrate and summarize the books on cards and then put the cards into a shoe box. When a reader flips the cards, they look like a filmstrip. These filmstrips are kept in the class, and other students look at them and decide whether to read the books.

23. *Tape-recording stories.* Let students tape-record their short stories. You will be surprised how much students know orally that they can't express in a written format.

Frequently, students in inclusive settings can master the academic content presented in general education classes. However, learning will be easier when alternative ways of presenting content become standard procedure in general classrooms. For example, in a class on English grammar, success may depend on the teacher's ability to adapt or modify the presentation of content.

A wonderful experience happened in one of my workshops, which clearly explains what I am saying by "adapting the presentation of content." This story was related to me by teacher A.

One day teacher B came into teacher A's room, complaining that a young girl in the class simply could not learn how to do a certain skill. Teacher B said, "I have shown that student how to do the skill *seven* times, and she still cannot get it."

Teacher A asked, "Did you show the student the same way each of the seven times?"

"Why, yes," replied teacher B.

Teacher A said, "The problem is that *you* don't get it!"

When a student cannot learn a skill one way, we need to adapt our teaching. This is adapting the format of content.

## General Class Assignments

| | |
|---|---|
| Activity (E/S): | Participating in oral classroom discussion |
| Adaptation: | To help a student listen to questions and give appropriate answers, allow him or her to use a tape recorder. Tape questions with pauses for the student to respond. This gives the student a chance to play back the question and organize the answer. As the student becomes more comfortable with oral discussions, taping can be reduced. |
| Activity (E/S): | Giving oral reports |
| Adaptation: | Allow students who are giving oral reports or speeches to use prompts, such as cards, posters, or visual models. Reports can also be presented using puppets or costumes. |
| Activity (E): | Storytelling |
| Adaptation: | Provide story starters for students who have trouble with original ideas. Allow students to tape-record stories to help them formulate ideas or make presentations. |
| Activity (E/S): | Plays |
| Adaptation: | Allow students with visual tracking difficulties to code or highlight their lines. |
| Activity (E/S): | Comprehension |
| Adaptation: | Highlight *who, what, where* questions in different colors. For example, highlight *where* questions in yellow, *who* questions in blue, and so on. |
| Activity (S): | Understanding idioms |
| Adaptation: | Ask students to demonstrate using concrete illustrations. |
| Activity (E/S): | Understanding compound words |
| Adaptation: | Provide cards with individual words on them and have the student select two. Put these two words together or exchange with a friend. Nonsense words can be created and drawings or magazine pictures used to illustrate the new compound word. |
| Activity (E/S): | Motivating readers |
| Adaptation: | After years of reading failure, students become turned off to reading. Therefore, it is up to the teacher to find reading material that interests these individuals enough to find reading acceptable and enjoyable. Figure 13.16 offers a list of motivators for reluctant readers. |
| Activity (E/S): | Organizing and critical thinking |
| Adaptation: | Figure 13.17 offers five tips. (Thanks to Froma Foner and Joan Sanders for their contributions.) |

FIGURE 13.16
Motivation
materials for
reluctant readers.

| | |
|---|---|
| Joke and riddle books | Greeting cards |
| Album jackets | Comic books |
| Comic strips | Tongue twisters |
| Travel brochures | Transportation schedules |
| TV schedules | Catalogues |
| Advertisements | Classified ads |
| Telephone book, Yellow Pages | Cookbooks |
| Society columns, *Dear Abby* | Biographies |
| Sports page | How-to books |
| First-aid books | Driver's education manual |
| Magazines | The Internet |

| | |
|---|---|
| Activity (S): | Figurative language/learning parts of speech |
| Adaptation: | Table 13.2 offers a suggestion. |
| Activity (S): | Antonyms and analogies |
| Adaptation: | Figure 13.18 demonstrates a three-step process for prompting students' selection of antonyms and analogies. (I'd like to thank the LO Department, G. C. Marshall High School, Fairfax County (VA) Public Schools.) |
| Activity (E/S): | Making predictions and drawing conclusions |
| Adaptation: | This skill may be modified by (a) reading the passage to the students and (b) presenting several choices of outcomes from which the student selects the correct answer. |
| Activity (E/S): | Reading graphs and maps |
| Adaptation: | Use high-interest information on the graph or map: for example, favorite TV shows. |
| Activity (E/S): | Draw a chapter |
| Adaptation: | As children read a novel, have them draw pictures of each chapter to help them remember events in the story. Drawings are kept in students' journals as a ready reference for sequence and events. |
| Activity (E/S): | Understanding the four kinds of sentences |
| Adaptation: | Provide a basic sentence key: four cards with the type of sentence on one side and an example on the back. |

1. Most needlework stores carry plastic sheets or strips that are easy on your eyes when working on a pattern (such as counted-cross stitch). The usual colors are yellow and blue. These strips or sheets may be placed on the reading material.

2. The gels (colored plastic sheets that are placed over theater lights) may be placed over reading material. Let the student select the color of choice and place over the page to be read. This helps for focus.

3. Place a Yellow Pages information guide in your classroom. Use a wide three-ring binder with tabs. After students have read a book they must complete an activity: sociogram, diorama, opinion/proof, cartoon, report, and so on. When each of the activities is explained, make an example and place it in the Yellow Pages behind the activity-labeled tab. You may place a student example behind your example with detailed requirements and directions. Thus, the teacher only has to explain once, and students have an ongoing prompt.

4. Here is a way to organize story elements:

S + Ch + Co + Pl + Cl + Th

| **S**etting | **Ch**aracters | **Co**nflict | **Pl**ot | **Cl**imax | **Th**eme (lesson learned) |
|---|---|---|---|---|---|
| Time | People | Self | | | |
| Place | Animals | Others | | | |
| Mood | Others | Nature | | | |
| | (aliens, etc.) | | | | |

5. Here is a critical thinking tip:

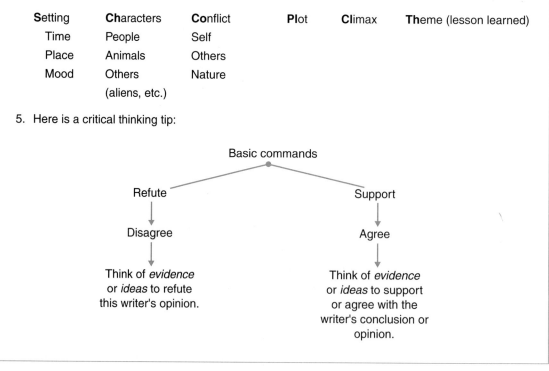

FIGURE 13.17
Reading tips.

TABLE 13.2
Figurative language prompt for short stories.

| | Page Number | Column | Top 1/3 of Page<br>*Middle 1/3 of page*<br>Bottom 1/3 of Page |
|---|---|---|---|
| Alliteration | 27 | 1 | T |
| | 27 | 2 | B |
| | 28 | 2 | M |
| | 31 | 1 | M |
| Metaphor | 27 | 2 | M |
| Simile | 30 | 1 | B |
| Personification | 28 | 2 | T |
| Hyperbole | 31 | 1 | T |
| | 32 | 2 | M |

1. What you know
2. What you are reasonably sure of (an educated guess) through
   a. Association
   b. Prefixes
   c. Base words
   d. Personal creation within sentence
3. What you don't know
   Strategy for SWAG (*Scientific Wild-Donkey Guess*)
   a. If you know the prompt:
      • Pick answer you don't know.
         i. If more than one, choose B, C, or D.
         ii. If more than one in B, C, and D, pick longest.
   b. If you don't know the prompt, and don't know some choices
      • Pick as above or what you didn't know.
   c. If you don't know the prompt but know all choices, take the longest answer from B, C, and D. If longest is tied, then select least familiar.

   If in doubt, guess the longest of B, C, and D. This has 33–40 percent accuracy.

**FIGURE 13.18**
Antonyms and analogy prompts.

Activity (E/S):    Sentence writing

Adaptation:       Prepare substitution tables for teaching sentence structure (Anderson, Greer, & Odle, 1978). Begin with a simple sentence substitution table using the subject-predicate pattern.

| 1 | 2 |
|---|---|
| Girls | play. |
| Boys | run. |
| Children | sing. |

This activity can be extended from teaching simple agreement between subject and predicate to more complicated sentences.

| 1 | 2 | 3 |
|---|---|---|
| I'm | going | to the White House. |
| You're | going | home. |
| He's | going | to school. |
| She's | going | to Frayser. |
| It's | going | to Dixiemart. |
| We're | going | to the grocery. |
| You're | going | downtown. |
| They're | going | to the post office. |

Activity (E):     Punctuation

Adaptation:       Using newspaper cartoons, replace the cartoon bubbles with assigned sentences and allow the student to punctuate them. You may want to provide a choice of punctuation marks.

Activity (E/S):   Punctuation

Adaptation 1:     Tape-record sentences. Provide a work sheet that has the same sentences with punctuation marks omitted. As students listen to each sentence, they follow along on the work sheet and add the correct punctuation. The teacher may want to include two or three choices of punctuation marks at the end of each sentence so students can circle correct responses. For example, "Is your house on fire (.! ?)"

Adaptation 2:     Give students a punctuation key to use when punctuating sentences. The key consists of four cards, each containing a punctuation mark and sample key words or sentences.

Adaptation 3:     In preparing work sheets or listing sentences on the board, group sentences by punctuation types. For example, list all sentences requiring question marks or periods together. After students have acquired the skill, begin to mix the sentences, first using only two types of punctuation marks and then adding a third.

Activity (E/S):    Compound words

Adaptation:        Give students a work list with three columns. Tell students to select the first words from columns 1 and 2 and combine them in column 3. After students have learned the concept, mix the words in columns 1 and 2. Then have students select the appropriate word from column 1 and match with a word from column 2 to make a compound word in column 3.

| 1 | 2 | 3 |
|---|---|---|
| after | noon | afternoon |
| some | one | someone |
| with | out | without |
| any | body | anybody |

Activity (E/S):    Spelling

Adaptation 1:      Divide the spelling list into halves or fourths for students with mild disabilities. Often they can learn how to spell the words, but not as quickly as other students.

Adaptation 2:      Provide "structure spellers" for students who have trouble remembering all of the words on the spelling list.

interesting i__ t __ __ e __ __ __ __ g

America __ m e __ i __ __

Activity (S):      Pluralizing irregulars

Adaptation:        Develop a format for making plurals on transparencies. Students can use the format over again for each new word. Figure 13.19 suggests one possible approach.

Activity (E/S):    Creative writing

Adaptation:        Don't be overly critical of grammatical errors in creative writing activities. Be concerned about the creativity, praise the efforts, and provide assistance with rewriting.

Activity (E/S):    Finding reference materials

Adaptation:        Teach students to use a variety of reference materials. Provide a list and map that shows the location of these items in the library.

Activity (E/S):    Collecting reference information

Adaptation:        Give students a reference check work sheet to help keep track of reference information.

Activity (S):      Writing a business letter

Adaptation:        Give students a visual model with lines to be filled in at appropriate parts of the letter. This prompt can be reduced by using dotted lines in place of solid lines.

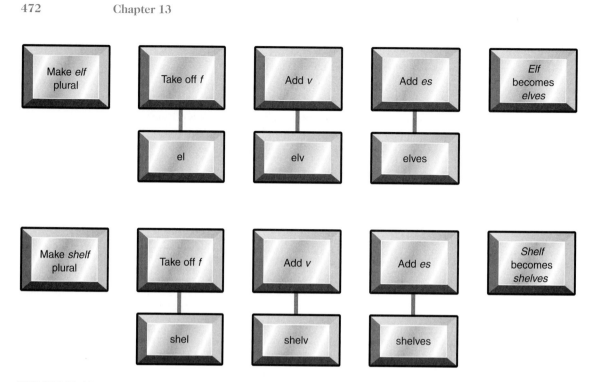

**FIGURE 13.19**
Pluralizing irregulars.

| | |
|---|---|
| Activity (E/S): | Writing multiparagraph papers |
| Adaptation: | Figure 13.20 presents an organizational format for helping students develop a framework for writing multiparagraph papers. (Thanks to Tonya Evers for her contributions.) |
| Activity (E/S): | Proofreading checklists |
| Adaptation: | Figures 13.21 and 13.22 suggest two types of checklists. |
| Activity (S): | Organizing research material |
| Adaptation: | Use a graphic organizer: |

1. List the topic to be researched on the first line.
2. After reading or taking notes on the topic, divide information into major headings.
3. On index cards, list all words that represent the major headings.
4. Organize words into major areas.
5. Place words under appropriate subheading.
6. Place the words into the organizer format.

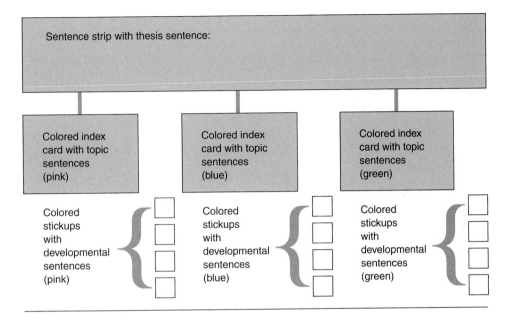

Directions:
1. Put up the organizer on the class wall as it is developing.
2. Before writing or organizing let students ask questions regarding topic or objective.
3. Students can move cards and stickups around to develop or change sequence of material.

**FIGURE 13.20**
Group activity for writing a multiparagraph paper.

Figure 13.23 illustrates a graphic organizer.

| | |
|---|---|
| Activity (E/S): | Vocabulary |
| Adaptation: | Figure 13.24 presents seventeen ways for modifying the teaching of vocabulary. (Thanks to the following educators for their contributions: Alyce Goolsby Kennard, Midway (TX) Independent School District, Saharli Cartwright, Andie Brown, Rodney Conrad, John W. Wilkie, Jr., and Lisa Pharr.) Figures 13.25 through 13.27 suggest other ideas for vocabulary practice. |
| Activity (E/S): | Understanding rules and laws |
| Adaptation: | Students can role-play selected rules or law-breaking vignettes and then discuss what consequences are suitable for certain crimes. This is a good opportunity to discuss why certain rules and laws exist and look at their positive aspects. |
| Activity (E/S): | Understanding different cultures |

FIGURE 13.21
Proofreading checklist.

**Form**

____ 1. I have a title page with centered title, subject, class, name, and date.

____ 2. I have a thesis statement telling the main idea of my paper.

____ 3. I have an outline that structures the major topics and minor subheadings.

____ 4. I have footnoted direct quotations and paraphrased material.

____ 5. I have made a footnote page using correct form.

____ 6. I have made a bibliography, using correct form, of all reference materials.

**Grammar**

____ 1. I have begun all sentences with capital letters.

____ 2. I have put a period at the end of each sentence and a question mark at the end of each question.

____ 3. I have used other punctuation marks correctly.

____ 4. I have checked words for misspelling.

____ 5. I have reread sentences for correct noun-verb agreement and awkward phrasing.

____ 6. I have checked all sentences to be sure each is complete.

**Content**

____ 1. I have followed my outline.

____ 2. I have covered each topic from my outline thoroughly and in order.

____ 3. Each paragraph has a topic sentence.

____ 4. The paper has an introduction.

When you've finished writing, you should read your essay to make sure it's complete.
Use the checklist below to edit your work.

**Check one**

**Yes**     **No**

_____   _____   I began with a topic sentence.

_____   _____   I provided details to support the topic sentence.

_____   _____   I finished with a summary statement.

_____   _____   All my sentences are complete.

_____   _____   My handwriting is legible.

_____   _____   My spelling is correct.

If you checked yes for all of the statements, you've mastered the steps in writing a good essay response!

**FIGURE 13.22**
Essay checklist.

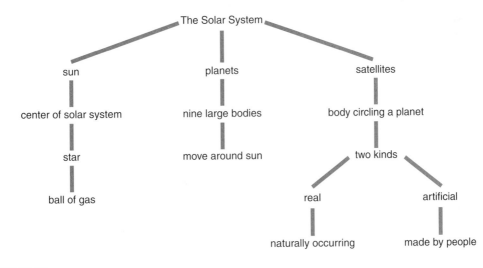

**FIGURE 13.23**
Graphic organizer.

1. Enlarge the diagram of a plant, or perhaps an animal cell. Place the correct vocabulary word on a sentence strip backed with tacky paper. Let the student place the correct word on the correct diagram part.

2. The same technique may be used in social studies. The correct CONTENT may be stuck on the correct place on the map: OCEAN, STATES, and so on.

3. Have students place a vocabulary word on one side of the page and the definitions on the other. The paper may be copied by the teacher and placed in the student's notebook or in a class notebook. The original paper can be cut into flash cards. For example:

| Vocabulary Word | Definition |
|---|---|
| Vocabulary Word | Definition |
| Vocabulary Word | Definition |
| Vocabulary Word | Definition |

4. Have students draw a picture to go with the vocabulary word as a clue. For example:

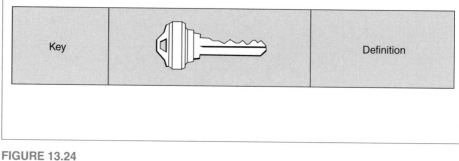

| Key | | Definition |
|---|---|---|

FIGURE 13.24
Teaching vocabulary.

5. A wonderful and fun way to teach vocabulary and to keep all of those words and definitions in one place is to make a vocabulary booklet. For example:

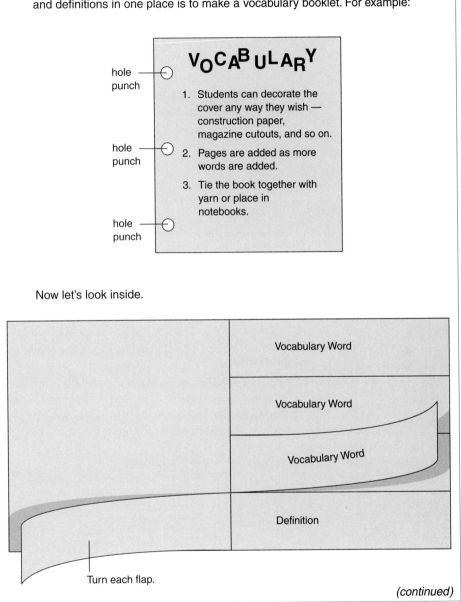

Now let's look inside.

Turn each flap.

(continued)

6. Use color coding to keep track of vocabulary cards. The different colors represent different subjects: blue for history, pink for reading, and so on. Because the white cards are less expensive, use highlighter pens to color code or use small stick-on dots. In the corner of the card, write the chapter, number, and/or period.

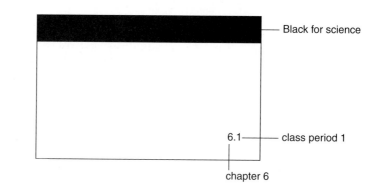

Black for science

6.1 — class period 1

chapter 6

7. For storing vocabulary cards, use sports card holders. Punch holes and put into folders or notebooks. The cost is approximately $3.99 for 25 sheets. The 3″ × 5″ cards will have to be cut to the size of baseball cards.

8. Vocabulary cards may also be stored in baggies. Place tape on the baggie to label each set of cards.

9. In preparing vocabulary cards, write the word on the blank side and the definition and a sentence using the word in context on the lined side.

10. Tape-record words, definitions, and sentences. Listen while getting ready for school, before going to bed, while waiting for the school bus, or when riding in the car.

**FIGURE 13.24**
Continued.

11. Vocabulary cards can be typed and printed on construction paper, cut with a paper cutter, and made ready for students, with or without a buddy, to complete. For example:

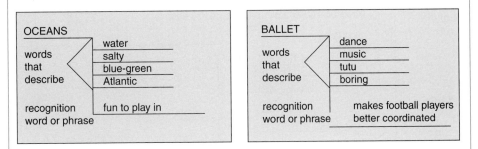

12. When flash cards (vocabulary or informational) go home, have the parents sign a note saying that the child has answered all cards correctly and give five bonus points to be added to the test score. Students with no parent in the home, or one who is having difficulty, may ask someone else to sign his note. The student still gets the five points and you have a measure of the student's ability level.

13. For flash cards, put the word on one card and the definition on a separate card (not on the back of the word card). This makes it easy to match the word to the definition. Also, put little numbers on the back of each card so that the student will get immediate feedback of response.

14. Make sure that you teach all vocabulary that is interchangeable and explain why it is interchangeable or use only one set of vocabulary and test it. For example:

> War between the States:
>
> North = Union = Yankees = Blue
>
> South = Rebels = Confederate = Gray

15. Watch the vocabulary tests that come with teacher guides. Frequently, the definitions we discuss in class look nothing like the definition in the test guide.

16. Some students do not know how to decode the words in the definition and thus do not understand the words even after looking up the definition. Go over the definition and decode all words.

17. Let students design Trivial Pursuit questions to share with each other and with their parents.

Write clear directions.

Have students use sentences in a meaningful context.

Reinforce and provide practice of new concepts by drawing pictures.

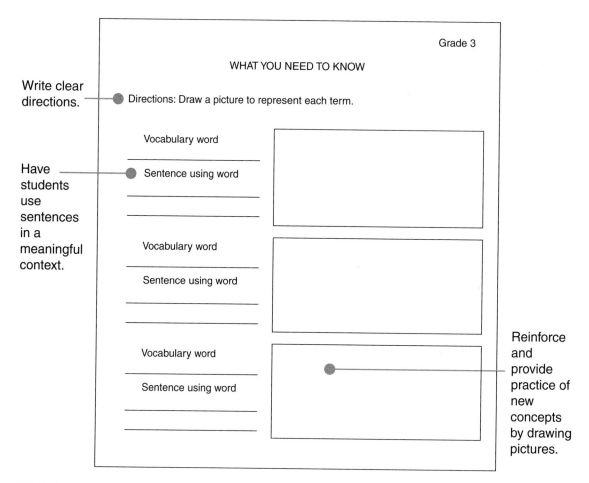

**FIGURE 13.25**
Vocabulary: Sentence and picture.

Adaptation:  Students with disabilities often have trouble visualizing life in other countries. When studying different cultures, allow students to "live" in that culture. Encourage them to dress, act, speak, eat, work, and play in the culture. Class periods could be devoted to experiences such as cooking and eating authentic meals, making costumes, or learning the languages. Discuss what is important to the culture and how it would feel to be a person from that setting.

Activity (E/S):  Using maps

Write clear directions.

Provide category words to help students organize information and remember it.

Provide page clues to help students locate information.

Allow sufficient space for writing meaning.

WHAT YOU NEED TO KNOW
Social Studies

Chapter 11: "Jacksonian Democracy" (pp. 200–204)

Directions: Read the pages in your text and write the meaning of each word in the space provided.

| Vocabulary | Page | Write the meaning of each word below |
|---|---|---|
| CONCEPTS | | |
| Utopian Movement | 200 | |
| Reform | 200 | |
| PUBLICATIONS | | |
| Liberator | 201 | |
| PEOPLE | | |
| Mary Lyon | 202 | |
| Horace Mann | 202 | |
| Dorthea Dix | 204 | |
| SYSTEMS | | |
| Underground Railroad Spoils System | 200 | |

**FIGURE 13.26**
Vocabulary: Word and meaning.

Adaptation: Begin with something familiar to the students. Make a map of the school and have students label specific points. Then have them map out their neighborhoods. Eventually progress to states, sections of a country, and finally whole countries.

Activity (E/S): Reviewing maps

Adaptation: Make an overhead transparency of a blank map. Project the map onto the chalkboard and have students write in specific information being reviewed, such as states, capitals, and rivers. Students can erase and repeat until they've learned the material.

Activity (E/S): Understanding graphs and charts

Write clear
directions.

Have
students
draw
pictures as
a way to
illustrate
the concept
in a semi-
concrete
way.

Give an
example
that will
serve as a
model for
students.

Allow
sufficient
space for
drawing
picture.

WHAT YOU NEED TO KNOW
Math

Geometry Terms

Directions: Draw a picture to represent each term. Number 1 is done for you.

| Term | Picture |
|---|---|
| 1.  Angle | |
| 2.  Midpoint | |
| 3.  Point | |
| 4.  Parallel lines | |
| 5.  Plane | |
| 6.  Ray | |
| 7.  Congruent segments | |
| 8.  Line segment | |
| 9.  Line | |
| 10.  Intersecting lines | |

**FIGURE 13.27**
Vocabulary: Word and picture.

| | |
|---|---|
| Adaptation: | Use high-interest information such as favorite TV shows, foods, and sports. Figure 13.28 gives an example. |
| Activity (S): | Understanding sequence of events on a timeline |
| Adaptation: | First, have students list important events in their lives and the approximate date when each occurred. Provide a timeline and have students transfer the information onto it. Figure 13.29 gives an example. |
| Activity (E): | Studying products made in different sections of the United States |
| Adaptation: | On the bulletin board, draw an outline of the United States. Develop a series of transparencies with shading for different areas of the country. Pose a question such as "What are the major corn-producing states?" A student will select the correctly shaded transparency to project onto the U.S. outline on the bulletin board. |

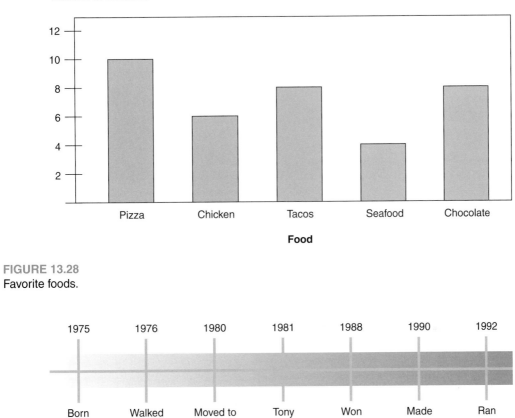

**FIGURE 13.28**
Favorite foods.

**FIGURE 13.29**
Timeline.

| Activity (E/S): | Solving word problems using structured organizers |
|---|---|
| Adaptation: | Figure 13.30A offers two suggestions. (Thanks to Diane Damback for her contributions.) |
| Activity (E/S): | Solving word problems |
| Adaptation: | Use Figure 13.30B. |
| Activity (E/S): | Steps in problem solving |
| Adaptation: | See Figure 13.30C. (Special thanks to Helen Giestie.) |
| Activity (E): | Money |
| Adaptation: | Make the concept meaningful by using paper money. Begin by using several paper one-dollar bills. To show that two half-dollars |

**Suggestion:** Dr. Jones bought a dress on sale for 20 percent off. The original price of the dress was $80.00. She had a coupon for $5.00 off any purchase. After paying with a $100.00 bill, how much change did she get?

Find out the 20 percent discount.

$$\frac{20}{100} = \frac{x}{80} \qquad 100x = 1600$$

Subtract discount from original price.

```
  80
- 16
  64
```

Subtract $5.00 for coupon.

```
  64
-  5
  59
```

Subtract final price of dress from $100.00 bill.

```
  100
- 59
  41
```

**Suggestion:**

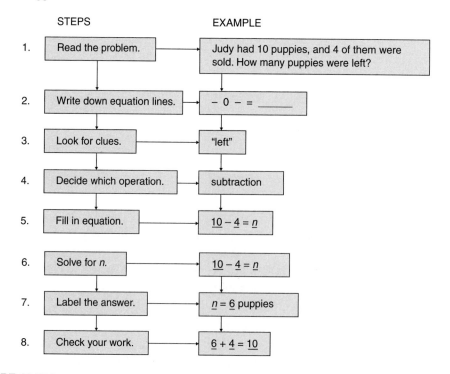

FIGURE 13.30A
Solving word problems using structured organizers.

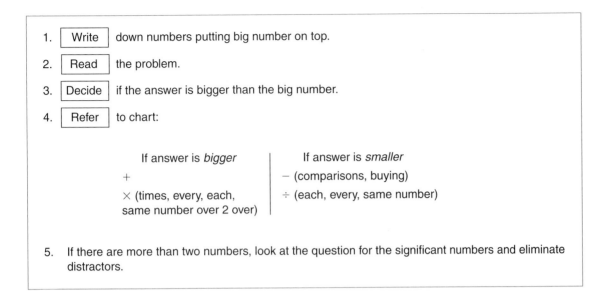

1. [ Write ] down numbers putting big number on top.

2. [ Read ] the problem.

3. [ Decide ] if the answer is bigger than the big number.

4. [ Refer ] to chart:

| If answer is *bigger* | If answer is *smaller* |
|---|---|
| + | − (comparisons, buying) |
| × (times, every, each, same number over 2 over) | ÷ (each, every, same number) |

5. If there are more than two numbers, look at the question for the significant numbers and eliminate distractors.

**FIGURE 13.30B**
Solving word problems.

constitute one dollar, cut one paper dollar in half. Then place the two halves on the whole paper dollar and ask the student to put the cut paper dollar together. This activity functions just like putting parts of a puzzle together. The activity may be extended to other fractions of a dollar such as fourths or tenths.

Activity (E):    Addition and subtraction

Adaptation:    Block off each column of numbers so that students don't get distracted visually. Figure 13.31 gives an example.

Activity (E/S):    Division

Adaptation:    Use a model to teach division. Fade parts of the model as students begin to understand where each number belongs. Figure 13.32 gives an example.

Activity (E/S):    How to study for a math exam

Adaptation:    Give students some advice. (Thanks to Lee Cairel for these suggestions.)

1. Start early. Don't be afraid to ask review questions in class. Probably six more students have the same question.

2. Find out when your teacher is available for extra help out of class. Then go see him or her.

1. Read the question and *circle* what you are trying to find.
2. Determine the unit of measure in which your answer should be expressed.
3. Write down the values you know with the correct units of measure.
4. Choose the correct formula, one which includes what you know and what you are looking for with no other gaps.
5. Fill in the formulas with your values, being sure to include the correct units.
6. Isolate the unknown on one side of the equal sign.
7. Solve for the unknown and follow through with the units.

   Example: What mass of aluminum will have a volume of 15 cm³? Aluminum has a density of 2.7g/cm³.

   density = 2.7 g/cm³          D = m/v

   volume = 15 cm³

   mass = ?                     2.7 g/cm³ = m/15 cm³

   (15 cm³)(2.7g/m³) = m

   40.5g = mass

   Answer Sheet for Prompt

   Looking for _____

   Know _____

   Formula Calculation _____

   Answer _____

FIGURE 13.30C
Steps in problem solving.

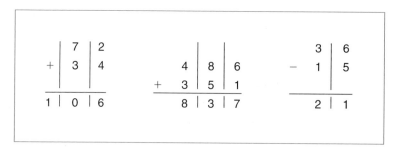

FIGURE 13.31
Blocking columns of numbers.

**FIGURE 13.32**
Division model.

$$8\overline{\smash{)}32} \qquad 8\overline{\smash{)}32} \qquad 8\overline{\smash{)}32}$$

3. Scan the last chapter exam to review skills already learned.

4. Know exactly *what* the exam will cover and *when* it will be. (Chapter exam? definitions? solving problems? must show work? part credit given?)

5. Think about the name and objective of the chapter (what is the chapter talking about?). Draw pictures in your mind and think about them. Draw pictures on paper, too.

6. Review each section and do a few problems in each homework assignment. (Do some odd-numbered problems; they usually have answers in the back of the book.) Also, ask your teacher about problems that you forgot how to do or didn't get the right answers for.

7. Study important properties and vocabulary words and know how to use them.

8. Review any notes you have taken; go over any examples and quizzes from the chapter.

9. Look over the chapter review at the end of the chapter; go back again to sections that are fuzzy. Ask questions.

10. Take the chapter test at the end of the chapter as if it were an exam. For any problems that are difficult, ask your teacher.

11. Finally, look over the chapter test again the night before, and get a good night's sleep.

12. Have a healthy breakfast in the morning, and come ready to do a good job on the exam.

| | |
|---|---|
| Activity (E/S): | Division |
| Adaptation: | Develop a "check-off" chart for helping students divide. |
| Activity (E/S): | Sequential Graphics (Figure 13.33) |
| Adaptation: | Use color coding (Figure 13.34). |
| Activity (E/S): | Division |
| Adaptation: | Use steps of assisting (Figure 13.35). |
| Activity(E/S): | Math Prompts for Math Vocabulary |

**FIGURE 13.33**
Graphics

*Source*: Wood, J. W. (2001). Solving algebra equations. *Reaching the hard to teach*. With permission.

1.  Develop a "check off" chart for helping students divide.

$$
\begin{array}{r}
25 \\
3\,\overline{)\,75} \\
-64 \\
\hline
15 \\
-15 \\
\hline
00
\end{array}
$$

÷ divide
× multiply
− subtract
↓ bring down

**FIGURE 13.34**
Color coding

*Source*: Wood, J. W. (2001). Solving algebra equations. *Reaching the hard to teach*. With permission.

2.  When using sequential graphics, add color. For example, *green* for the beginning step, *yellow* for the middle, and *red* for the end.

Example: Solving algebra equations

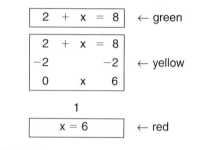

| Adaptation: | Multiplication | Division |
|---|---|---|
| | Cue Words: | Cue Words: |
| | multiply | divide |
| | product | quotient |
| | times | divided by |
| | twice (×2) | halved  (divide by 2) |
| | doubled (×2) | quartered (divided by 4) |
| | tripled (×3) | equal parts |
| | quadrupled (×4) | |

Activity (E/S):  Choosing the correct operation

Adaptation:  Use the 4-step method:

Step 1: Understand the problem

Step 2: Make a plan

Step 3: Carry out the plan

Step 4: Check the answer for reasonableness.

Activity (S):      Lab assignments

Adaptation:      Many schools ask students to complete part of a lab assignment sheet before the teacher's demonstration and to finish the sheet after the demonstration. Table 13.3 shows how to adapt a lab assignment for the mainstreamed student.

Teachers also need to prepare the physical environment for a lab. They should (a) plan ahead to accommodate students with disabilities and (b) interview students concerning their needs, keeping communication open. Student needs may involve the following:

1. Adjustment of table height so that students using a wheelchair can pull up to the table.
2. Accessible sinks for cleanup.
3. Microscope stands at eye level and within arm's reach.
4. Display models or chemistry sets at seat level.

---

Dividing

Steps:

1. Divide the dividend by the divisor in the greatest place value position possible.
2. Multiply.
3. Subtract.
4. Bring down the next digit or digits.

Repeat steps 1 to 4 until the remainder is less than the divisor.

To check, multiply the quotient and the divisor, add the remainder to get the dividend.

Examples

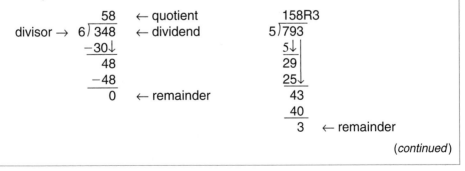

(*continued*)

---

FIGURE 13.35

Steps for Division

Source: Wood, J. W. (2001). Steps for division. *Reaching the hard to teach*. With permission.

Think About It!

Answer the question and solve the equation.

(a) How many fives in 10? $\rightarrow$ 10 $\div$ 5 = a

(b) How many fours in 16? $\rightarrow$ 16 $\div$ 4 = b

(c) 30 students in the class.

    6 students on a team.

How many teams are there?

        30 $\div$ 6 = N

Complete this table

| Since | We know that |
|---|---|
| 6 $\times$ 5 = 30 | 30 $\div$ 5 = <u>6</u> |
| 7 $\times$ 6 = 42 | 42 $\div$ 6 = <u>7</u> |
| 24 $\times$ 17 = 408 | 408 $\div$ 17 = <u>24</u> |
| 52 $\times$ 36 = 1872 | 1872 $\div$ 36 = <u>52</u> |

Mental Math

Try to move across each row without using pencil and paper.

If you do your work correctly, you will end with the starting number.

1. | 24 | $\div$4 | 6 | $\times$2 | 12 | $\div$3 | 4 | $\times$5 | 20 | +8 | 28 | $\div$7 | 4 | $\times$6 | 24 |

2. | 40 | $\div$5 | 8 | +7 | 15 | +5 | 20 | $\div$4 | 5 | $\times$7 | 35 | +7 | 42 | $-$2 | 40 |

**FIGURE 13.35**
Continued.

5. Adequate space around tables and entrances to allow access by wheelchairs, walkers, and so on.

6. Flexible arrangement of lab space to allow changes when needed.

7. Transition time to and from various activities to accommodate students who may take longer to move from one area to another.

When preparing students for a lab, teachers should do the following:

1. Prepare materials being used in advance. (For example, open jars if screw tops are difficult for students with physical impairments.) Waiting for activities to begin can be frustrating for students with AD/HD.

2. Encourage students to speak to you about directions that may be unclear to them, or state instructions several times throughout lab activities.

**TABLE 13.3**
Adapting a lab assignment.

| Lab Assignment Outline | Standard Student Response | Adaptations for Mainstreamed Student |
|---|---|---|
| Title of lab | Student completes | Fill in for student. |
| Materials | Student completes from observing teacher or reading text. | Complete for student or let peer tutor assist. |
| Purpose of lab | Student completes from text or lecture. | Complete for student. |
| Lab procedures | As teacher demonstrates, student records the procedure. | List procedures on the board so student can follow each step. Provide a check sheet and have student check off each step. |
| Observations | Student records the observed experiment. | Let student tape-record the observed demonstration. |
| Conclusion | Student records. | This step requires the evaluation level of Bloom's taxonomy, so the teacher may choose to omit it for a mainstreamed student. |
| Analysis/questions | Student responds. | Provide answers for the mainstreamed student. |

3. Keep lab activities structured and limit directions.
4. Be open to the use of tape recorders or other forms of backup support.
5. Summarize and review information covered at the end of each session.
6. Consider alternative test-taking and grading procedures.
7. Keep overhead transparencies or written materials simple and free of clutter.

Here are some lab tips for students:

1. Speak with your lab instructor concerning your individual needs and concerns.
2. Allow yourself extra time to get prepared and comfortable before lab begins.
3. If you are using a tape recorder or any other device, discuss it with the instructor in advance.
4. Cue yourself using key terms or phrases if you have difficulty maintaining focus.
5. If information is unclear to you, speak with your instructor or ask questions.
6. Review your lab notes immediately after class to help retain information.
7. Limit distractions to help you focus on tasks and schedules in the lab.

8. If you have difficulty following the sequence of steps in a procedure, ask for a printed copy of the procedure prior to class so that you can familiarize yourself with the steps. As you complete each step, mark it off.

9. Supplement your notes with diagrams to illustrate concepts, procedures, etc. Develop and use a shorthand method for noting technical terms that appear often in your notes.

10. If you are aware of physical accommodations or technological adaptations that will enable you to use the lab more fully (e.g., a straight chair fastened to a platform on casters; foot-operated rather than hand-operated equipment), discuss these with your instructor.

Activity (S):     Teaching students with disabilities to drive

Adaptation:      Here are some suggestions:

1. Our attitude toward persons with disabilities is their biggest handicap.

2. Sincerity is sensed easily by a person with a disability.

3. Find something to praise, no matter how small the accomplishment, especially during the early lessons. This builds rapport and relaxes the student.

4. Be honest. For example, if the student needs to stay off the expressway and out of rush-hour traffic, tell him or her to plan driving times during the least busy times of the day.

5. Students do not want sympathy; they want independence. Be objective and positive and expect their best performance.

6. Follow up on students to ensure that the correct vehicle modifications are made.

7. During the final phases of driving, encourage parents and other members of the family to observe the student's driving. Explain the purpose and importance of each piece of equipment.

8. It is very easy for us to help the student in his or her efforts to drive (for example, learning to use the key quad to turn the ignition), but the real reward is seeing the student successfully and independently achieve this goal. Don't rush to help. Be patient and look at the expression on the student's face when he or she finally succeeds. The time is worth it.

9. When you must tell a student you are unable to help him or her at a particular time, never say never. Tell the student, "I am placing your evaluation on file at the present time and will contact you as soon as I am able to help you." Research and modern technology are constantly changing. At the same

time, if you truly sense that the person will never drive, don't give false hope. Be honest and explain in detail. At this time, the person's emotions will surface, so be gentle.

10. Ninety percent of driving depends on vision. If you detect a visual problem during the evaluation, require that a medical evaluation be sent to you to ensure that this can be corrected.

Before completing our section on activities and adaptations for teaching select subject matter, I would like to introduce you to one of seven *Power Prompts* created by Randy Lawson with Judy W. Wood (2000), which is an example of assisting the student in turning an essay into a fun project.

Activity (E/S):    Writing a narrative essay.
Adaptation:       Figure 13.36.

## MODIFICATIONS AND WHOLE LANGUAGE

"Whole language is an attempt to build curriculum based on what we know about natural language learning." It avoids using a skill-sequence approach that seems logical to adults. Breaking language into small parts to be learned in sequence "seems logical only until you watch how little kids are handling language" (Jerome Harste, personal communication).

According to the Association of Supervision and Curriculum Development, components of whole language theory include the following:

**1.** Focus on meaning, not the component parts of language. Children learn language from whole to part. Therefore, instruction in reading and writing should begin by presenting whole texts (engaging poems and stories) rather than zeroing in on the bits and pieces that make up language (words, syllables, and sounds in isolation). By keeping language whole, teachers focus on its purpose—to communicate meaning—rather than reduce language to a set of abstractions that children can't relate to. Teach skills in context, not in isolation. Children learn the subskills of language such as letter-sound relationships, spelling, punctuation, and grammar most readily when these skills are taught in the context of reading and writing activities. Teachers should coach children in skills as the need for skills arises rather than march children in lockstep through a sequenced-skills curriculum.

**2.** Expose children to lots of good literature. High-quality children's literature is the heart and soul of a whole language program. By acquainting children with stories and nonfiction works that capture their interest, teachers motivate children to become adept readers and writers and plant the seeds of a lifelong love for books. Shared literature also provides a meaningful context for teaching skills.

**3.** Get children writing early and often. Teachers should encourage young children to write as soon as they can hold a pencil rather than wait until they have learned to read. Reading and writing develop best in tandem. When children write,

**Power Prompts Narrative**

Taking an essay test is like going to the dentist, except you don't get the lollipop when it's all over. You painfully open a test booklet, and you see long-winded questions requiring long, dreary answers about drippy topics like why rainforests are so rainy.

Created by Randy Larson with Judy W. Wood, Ph.D.

**Boring!**

A ***Power Prompt*** is the part of an essay question that says what you have to do to answer correctly. Some prompts will say to PROVE or EVALUATE or DEFINE or DESCRIBE or ILLUSTRATE something about a topic like "justice" or "freedom."

### Narrative

Narratives (brief stories) can often put some life into your essay answers and make them more to-the-point when writing about hard-to-explain concepts or ideas. For example, if the ***Power Prompt*** says, "*Define 'bravery' and illustrate how this concept relates to freedom,*" you might include in your answer a brief **NARRATIVE** (story) about a time when bravery was important to your own personal freedom; maybe you stood up to a bully or something. Whatever your story is, make sure it's to the point. Don't ramble for six pages. You have only a few moments to answer most essay questions, so if you decide to include a story in your answer, be brief when you respond to ***Power Prompts*** that command you to **Illustrate, Prove, Define, Evaluate**, or **Describe** a concept or an idea.

To respond to ***Power Prompts*** correctly, you need to know what they mean. Any of these ***Power Prompts*** could be answered by using a brief NARRATIVE as part of your written response.

**ILLUSTRATE**: give *examples* to make your point clear and to give a clear picture of the topic. An example could be a STORY.

**PROVE**: give reasons, facts and *examples* to convince your reader that your ideas or viewpoints are true and right and valid.

**DEFINE**: provide the clear meaning of a term or concept. You can show how the term is different from other terms or has ideas that are similar. You could give an *example* of how the term works in real life: use a brief STORY.

**EVALUATE**: decide if an idea or concept or decision is good or bad, useful or useless. You could show how your evaluation of the topic is the best by giving a clear example: a STORY.

**DESCRIBE**: draw a word picture of how something is done, or how it should look. Pretend you are a reporter and tell the facts that you want the reader to SEE.

---

**TEQ: Tricky Essay Question**

Which ***Power Prompt*** above would be most easily answered using a brief, powerful NARRATIVE? WHY?

---

**FIGURE 13.36**
Power prompts: Narrative.

# Get Your NARRATIVE Example Here!

**Question:** *Define* the term "friendship," and *illustrate* (show) the value of true friendship in all areas of human life.

## POWER TIP!!!!

Good things come in three's: **Morning, Noon, and Night – Breakfast, Lunch, and Dinner – Beginning, Middle, and End**, especially the end of school!

When you write an answer to an essay question, use the last good thing listed above; use a three-part structure — have a clear **beginning**, a solid **middle**, and an interesting **ending**.

For example, in the essay answer next door, the beginning is the definition part of the answer. The middle is the story, the narrative, about the two boys who were friends. The end is the summary that wraps up the essay and ties the story into the definition.

**Beginning:** Define the term "friendship"

**Middle:** Story about "friendship"

**End:** Tie the story into the definition of "friendship." Make the ending as interesting as possible.

True friendship is a deal made between people that says, "We will not betray each other. We'll be there when one of us needs the other." This kind of social bargain is at the heart of human life. Without true friendship, life would be like a bird with one wing.

There is a story that illustrates this point. A boy named Manuel caught beautiful birds to sell to tourists who came through his mountain village. Manuel's best friend, Carlos, wanted to go along into the mountains to capture the soft-singing birds, but Carlos was blind and couldn't go.

Over time, Carlos became jealous of Manuel's good fortune, so one night he turned all his friend's birds loose and smashed the little wooden cages. Manuel was enraged and searched the village for the criminal who did this terrible deed.

Carlos hid and did not see Manuel for many days. Finally, Manuel went to Carlos and asked if he knew who did the destruction.

Carlos said, "I did it. I am sorry. I could not control my anger. You have freedom and you have money. You have a fine business. I have nothing."

Manuel said, "You have one thing more than money. You have my friendship, and always will. I am sorry I have left you out of things because of your blindness. From now on, I will go out to catch the birds, but when I return, you will help me build the cages and you will give the birds each of their names. We will split the money down the middle, like a ripe melon."

Friendship is being partners with someone in the deepest sense. It is based on forgiveness and on wanting the best for another person. Without friendship, the best parts of life would be impossible to experience. Like a bird with two wings, only when we are true friends with another person, can we truly "fly."

*(continued)*

**SEQ'S - SAMPLE
ESSAY QUESTIONS**

**An essay is
a long
answer to a
short
question!**

1. *Prove* the importance of music by *illustrating* how life would be without the presence of music in the world.

2. *Evaluate* the actions of Hansel and Gretel toward the witch in the cottage. Was it okay for them to stick her in the oven? Were they just trying to protect themselves, or was there another reason for their actions? Were they right or wrong in doing what they did?

3. *Describe* the effect of an alien from a distant galaxy dropping in on one of your Aunt Tilly's Tupperware parties that she has at her apartment every second Friday after every full moon.

4. *Define* the term "nerd" and *illustrate* how nerds are having a tremendous impact on the world around us, especially in the area of computer science.

5. *Evaluate* the performance of a Salad Shooter as compared to a cleaver-wielding Japanese chef at a high-speed restaurant in San Francisco or New York, then *describe* how the Salad Shooter has changed the way the world relates to vegetables.

6. *Describe* the game of "grammar polo" and *prove* that it is the world's most boring sport.

7. *Illustrate* how the absence of all fast-food restaurants in America would result in widespread starvation for teenagers from coast to coast.

8. *Define* "middle age" and *describe* what life will be like when you are a middle-aged human.

**FIGURE 13.36**
Continued.

they master phonics relationships because they must constantly match letters with sounds to write what they want to say.

    **4.**   Accept invented spelling. Whole language teachers do not expect perfect spelling from the beginning. Instead, they encourage children to make their best efforts. Children's crude approximations reveal to what degree young writers have cracked the phonetic code. Over time, children's spelling becomes more conventional, and teachers gradually insist on more correct spelling.

    **5.**   Allow pupils to make choices. Teachers should let children choose at least some of the books they read and topics they write on. When children have some control over their learning, they are more motivated and retain what they learn longer.

The concept of whole language works from the whole to the parts. This technique for teaching acquisition (whole-part-whole) was discussed in chapter 11. Within the context of teaching whole language, an educator can still make modifications, which fit into the instructional process at any time.

When thinking of ways to adapt the presentation of content, do not overlook teacher manuals. They contain many resources for teachers to use that are excellent for the student.

# TASK ANALYSIS

*Task analysis* is the breakdown of skills within a task into sequential steps. When you are teaching specific content and realize that a student still does not grasp the concept, check to see if the skill could be broken down into smaller steps. Then teach each step separately.

Task analysis can be used for the entire course when you divide all content into specific skills to be taught. As Anderson et al. (1978) point out, "At any point in the learning process, the child may have failed to acquire mastery of any skill or concept necessary for success at subsequent levels" (p. 168). Such gaps in acquiring a skill make it difficult for students to go beyond a certain point in an assignment.

Anderson et al. suggest three steps for teachers to follow in rearranging textbooks. First, the teacher should study the table of contents and identify the skills covered by the book. Second, the teacher divides those skills into major tasks and subtasks and arranges subtasks sequentially in order of planned instruction. Third, the teacher tabulates page numbers for examples of all the subtasks. The teacher can then use these examples in class as exercises, practice assignments, or test examples or questions. Table 13.4 uses task analysis to reorganize the content of a mathematics textbook.

Using task analysis to break down textbooks for students offers them more opportunities for success. They can acquire major skills more easily when the instructional material is organized for quick access to specific and smaller skills.

Teachers can also reorganize language-arts texts so that they can sequentially teach the skills required at a specific level. Many times, the major subjects in a basal language-arts text, as listed in the table of contents, are not in sequential order. To reorganize the table of contents, the teacher must first determine the prerequisite skills for each major area.

Table 13.5 presents excerpts from a basal language-arts text and a sequential reorganization of the table of contents. The teacher does not deviate from the basic topics to be taught but simply redesigns the order of the material. By rearranging texts into small sequential skills, the teacher makes it possible for students to complete assignments.

In applying the task analysis model, the regular classroom teacher uses the principle underlying Bloom's domain of cognitive learning: identifying the specific skill being taught and breaking down the skill into steps, proceeding from the easiest to the most difficult. Figure 13.37 shows how learning to use the dictionary can be broken down into 14 steps.

**TABLE 13.4**
Task analysis of math book content.

| Major Tasks and Subtasks | Instructional Examples on Page: | Text Examples On Page: |
|---|---|---|
| *Addition* | | |
| Addition combinations | 5–7 | 9–13, 462 |
| Tens in addition | 14 | 14–15 |
| Hundreds in addition | 14 | 16 |
| Column addition | 16–17 | 17–27, 56, 454, 458 |
| Regrouping in addition | 28 | 28–29 |
| Estimating sums | 30 | 31–34, 37, 55–56 |
| Mental addition | 35 | 35–36 |
| *Subtraction* | | |
| Subtraction combinations | 7–9 | 9–13, 463 |
| Tens in subtraction | 14 | 15, 38 |
| Hundreds in subtraction | 14 | 15–16, 38 |
| Regrouping in subtraction | 40–41 | 42–47, 56, 455, 459 |
| Expanded notation | 42 | 42 |
| Subtraction of fractions | 48–49 | 49–51 |
| Estimating differences | 51 | 51–52, 53–56 |
| Mental subtraction | 53 | 53–55 |
| *Multiplication* | | |
| Multiplication combinations | 57–59, 60, 62–63 | 59, 61, 464 |
| Properties of multiplication | 66 | 67 |
| Number pairs and graphs | 70–71 | 72–73, 76–77 |
| Multiplying using tens | 72, 74–75 | 72–73, 76–77, 456, 460 |
| Multiplying using a machine | 78–81 | 81 |
| Mental multiplication | 82, 86 | 82–83, 86–88 |
| Estimating products | 84 | 84–85, 88 |
| *Division* | | |
| Division combinations | 65 | 65, 465 |
| Properties of division | 66 | 67 |
| Division involving remainders | 67 | 68–69, 92, 457, 461 |
| Dividing a number by single digit | 69, 92–93 | 68, 93, 103, 457, 461 |
| Dividing using tens | 72, 92 | 78, 89, 94–95, 103, 457, 461 |
| Trial quotients | 95–97 | 97–98 |
| Estimating quotients | 96–99 | 99–100, 102–103 |
| Mental division | 101 | 101–102 |

*Source:* Anderson, R. M., Greer, J. G., & Odle, S. J. (Eds.). (1978). *Individualizing educational materials for special children in the mainstream* (p. 169). Baltimore: University Park Press. Copyright 1978 by Pro-Ed, Inc. Reprinted by permission.

**TABLE 13.5**
Reorganizing a table of contents.

| Original Table of Contents | Sequentially Reorganized Table of Contents |
|---|---|
| Writing sentences | Learning parts of speech |
| Writing letters | Writing sentences |
| Learning parts of speech | Using correct punctuation |
| Writing paragraphs | Writing paragraphs |
| Using correct punctuation | Writing letters |

According to the example in Figure 13.37, students with no dictionary skills would have difficulty beginning with step TA-10. However, because the task has been broken into such small steps, the teacher can begin where the student presently functions, whether it be step TA-1 or a higher level.

When teaching a concept or skill in a specific academic area, the teacher needs to analyze the skill and decide whether or not the student has the prerequisite skills for learning it. A teacher who thinks a student is ready to learn the new skill should then examine the skill further to see if it can be organized into sequential steps. Breaking a new task into small sequential steps makes learning easier for the student who may have learning difficulties.

# ADAPTING ASSIGNMENTS

This section is divided into six parts: tips for assignment books, assignment assumptions, types of assignments, steps for adapting assignments, homework adaptations, and guidelines for implementing homework.

## Tips for Assignment Books

Before any assignment is given, students need to establish an organization process for keeping assignments. Figure 13.38 suggests tips for assignment books.

## Assignment Assumptions

Educators make many assumptions about assignments. While I was visiting a sixth-grade social studies class, the teacher gave the assignment for the next day as the class was coming to a close: "Bring in one article that reflects what we studied in class today."

The bell rang and all the students, except for one young man, hurried out of class to the next one. The young man walked up to the teacher and said, "We don't have a newspaper for an article in my home."

TA-1    Given five books, including a dictionary, the student will point to and state the function of the dictionary.

TA-2    Given directions to say the alphabet, the student will recite it in proper sequence.

TA-3    Given a random selection of 10 letters, the student will arrange them in alphabetical order.

TA-4    Given a list of not more than 10 words, beginning with different letters, the student will write the words in alphabetical order.

TA-5    Given a list of not more than 10 words, beginning with the same first letter, the student will write the words in alphabetical order.

TA-6    Given a list of not more than 10 words beginning with the same first two letters, the student will write the words in alphabetical order.

TA-7    Shown a dictionary page, the student will point to and state the function of the guide words.

TA-8    Shown a dictionary page, the student will point to and state the function of the entry words.

TA-9    Given oral directions to state the meaning of the word *definition,* the student will do so.

TA-10   Given a list of two guide words and a list of entry words, the student will write those entry words that come between the two guide words.

TA-11   Given a list of entry words and a dictionary, the student will write the page number on which the entry word is found.

TA-12   Shown an entry word in a dictionary, the student will state the number of definitions listed for that word.

TA-13   Given a list of entry words and a dictionary, the student will find the words and write definitions for each word.

TA-14   Given a sentence containing a specific word, the student will write the definition of the word as used in that sentence.

**FIGURE 13.37**

Task analysis of dictionary skills.

*Source:* Vermont State Department of Education, Division of Special Education and Pupil Personnel Services. "Reading competency #6a—Gets information from resource material: Dictionary." In *Basic skills sequence in English* (p. 10). Montpelier: Author. Copyright by Vermont State Department of Education, Division of Special Education and Pupil Personnel Services. Reprinted by permission.

**Selecting/organizing assignment books**

1. Many school supply sections in stores sell assignment books. When selecting a book:
   - Be sure the size is appropriate for the student's notebook or book bag.
   - Check the assignment book to see if the sections are appropriate for the student.

2. Many schools have assignment books preprinted for students. Here are some suggestions and a list of advantages:
   - All students will have the same assignment book.
   - Because everyone will be using an assignment book, no student will feel awkward.
   - Let students design the cover for the assignment book. Conduct an election to vote on the class choice. This introduces ownership in the assignment book.
   - The book could include a space for the yearly schedule.
   - Include a letter from the principal, student body president, or another "famous" person.
   - Each year the letter could come from a "mystery writer" to be held in strict confidence until the books are handed out.
   - A guessing contest with prizes could be used to see who this year's mystery writer will be.
   - The book could contain general information, school rules, services, activities, and a monthly calendar listing all important events.
   - The last section could provide weekly divided sections for assignments, due dates, class periods, and a special reminder section.
   - One benefit of a school-provided assignment book is that no one does without because of cost.

3. Use a teacher's plan book as an assignment notebook. Set it up for a student's individual schedule.

**FIGURE 13.38**
Tips for assignment books.

The teacher quickly replied, "Oh, just use a magazine article. Any article will do. Now hurry, or you will be late for your next class."

As I watched the young man walk down the hall, I imagined a 0 for class tomorrow. I wanted to say to the teacher, "Don't you have ears?" That student was trying to tell his teacher that he was willing to complete the assignment but had no materials at home.

The teacher's assumption? Students have at home what they need to complete assignments.

We simply cannot make assumptions about students. Figure 13.39 lists other assignment assumptions.

1. We assume that students can copy the assignment from the board correctly.
2. We assume that students can complete the assignment.
3. We assume that the assignment is not too difficult.
4. We assume that the assignment is not too long.
5. We assume that students understand the assignment because they do not raise their hand when we say, "Are there any questions?"
6. We assume that students have materials needed to complete the assignment.
7. We assume that students have the money necessary to buy the materials to complete the assignment.
8. We assume that the students' parents will help them with the assignment.
9. We assume that the students' parents can do the assignment.
10. We assume that the students have parents.
11. We assume that the parents are home.
12. We assume that the parents care.
13. We assume that students have a home.
14. We assume that students have time to complete the assignment.
15. We assume that the students care if they complete the assignment.
16. We assume that the students or parents have the language skills necessary to complete the assignment.
17. We assume that the students have proper places to complete the assignment.
18. We assume that we are the only teachers giving homework.

**FIGURE 13.39**
Assignment assumptions.

# Types of Assignments

Assignments, the learning tasks that reinforce concepts taught during class instruction, are crucial to skill acquisition. However, for various reasons, some students may not be able to complete an assignment.

There are two types of assignments: control and no control. Control assignments include in-class assignments and other assignments over which the teacher has complete control. These include class discussions; problem solving; group experiments; group projects; and independent seat work assignments such as reading from the text, answering questions, and completing work sheets. When students are working on these assignments, the teacher has the power to make any necessary adjustments for a student. The teacher can answer questions or observe a student's work. If an assignment is too difficult, lengthy, or confusing, the teacher can immediately remedy the situation.

When students take assignments home, the teacher begins to lose control. No-control assignments are those that are no longer under the supervision of the teacher. Homework falls into this category. The teacher has now lost all control or power to provide direct assistance during students' work on the assignment.

Homework is assigned for a number of reasons (Turner, 1984):

1. Homework facilitates learning through practice and application.
2. Homework individualizes learning for all students.
3. Homework is assigned for that work not completed during the school day.
4. Homework teaches independent study skills and helps develop good work habits.
5. Homework communicates to parents which concepts and skills are taught in class.

Figure 13.40 presents a task analysis of in-class/out-of-class assignments. Figure 13.41 suggests tips for adapting assignments. (Thanks to Julie Duff for her contributions.)

For a no-control assignment, the teacher must be absolutely sure that the student has the skills necessary to meet success. Lee and Pruitt (1970) divide homework into four categories: preparation, practice, extension, and creativity. Table 13.6 shows each category and suggests adaptations for teachers to use with students experiencing difficulty with homework.

Salend and Schliff (1988) offer several guidelines for implementing homework. These appear in Table 13.7.

1. Student attends to oral directions.
2. Student processes oral information.
3. Student takes notes from oral directions.
4. Student attends to written directions.
5. Student processes visual information.
6. Student can far-point copy.
7. Student independently works on in-class assignment.
8. Student asks questions when necessary.
9. Student has organizational skills needed for keeping assignments in notebook.
10. Student remembers to place out-of-class assignment in book bag.
11. Student takes books from locker and puts into book bag.
12. Student takes book bag home.
13. Student has necessary materials to do assignment.
14. Student has skills to begin out-of-class assignment independently.
15. Student has skills to complete out-of-class assignment independently.
16. Student places out-of-class assignment into folder in book bag.
17. Student takes book bag to school.
18. Student takes assignment to proper class.
19. Student can ask questions if assignment is not understood.

**FIGURE 13.40**
Task analysis for completing in-class/out-of-class assignments.

# CONCLUSION

This chapter has been developed to help you "uncover subject matter." We are assigned subjects to teach and in conjunction with our teaching we are constantly developing strategies and formats for assisting in teaching the content. If a student cannot divide, find an organizational strategy to help the student understand the skill.

1. Be sure that student has the correct information on the assignment (page numbers, date due, and so on).

2. Review the assignment and check for questions.

3. The assignment should be geared to the level of each student.

4. Structure each assignment so that all students can experience success.

5. Provide immediate feedback on all assignments.

6. If the assignment requires students to look up answers to questions, use an asterisk to distinguish implied fact from literal questions requiring a stated fact.

7. If the assignment is lengthy, provide class time to complete it partially or divide assignment time into two or more days.

8. Identify an assignment buddy for each student. The buddy may be another student within the class, a student in another class, or a friend or parent outside of class. This provides a support system for the student who may not know how to complete the assignment.

9. Assignments may be given to two or more students. It is suggested that class time be given for shared assignments and that split grading be used.

10. Teach students the concept of grade averaging with and without zeros. Many students do not realize the difficulty of trying to raise an average after just one zero on an assignment.

11. Allow students the option of dropping one or more low assignment grades per grading period.

12. Establish assignment passes earned for good work, which can be cashed in when an assignment is forgotten or a low grade is received.

13. Be consistent in placing the assignment for class or homework in the same place each day.

14. Provide written and oral directions for assignments.

15. If an assignment requires several steps or stages (such as projects), provide a checklist for the students.

16. If the assignment is to be copied from the board, provide a copy for the student who may have difficulty copying.

17. If the assignment is to be copied from the text, allow the student who has difficulty copying or who copies slowly to copy only the answers.

18. Work sheets should be clear and uncluttered. Watch for the overuse of work sheets. Don't make the reward for completing one work sheet another work sheet. Also, giving a stack of work sheets can be overwhelming.

19. Tell students to put books they need to take home in the locker with the spine to the back of the locker and on the right side of the locker. At the end of the day, the student reaches into the locker and retrieves all spine-back books to take home.

20. Require a method of recording assignments.

21. Make copies of the assignments for a week and give the student and the resource teacher a copy.

22. After the class assignment is completed, tell the student where to put the assignment and what to do next.

23. Do not punish the student by making him or her finish assignments during free time, recess, or after school.

24. For in-class assignments, give a warning when it is almost time to turn in the assignment.

*(continued)*

**FIGURE 13.41**
Tips for adapting assignments.

25. Orient students to the major points of the assignment.

26. Begin all assignments with a planned opening and a purpose.

27. Practice for assignments should be distributed instead of given in a mass.

28. Relate all activities within an assignment directly to the objective of the assignment.

29. Assess the assignment for the appropriate instruction level.

30. Use feedback from previously completed assignments to indicate the quality of the next assignment.

31. To assist students with organizing assignments, have every content area on a different color of paper. Each assignment will get placed in the appropriate section.

32. At the end of each class let students have 15 minutes to start on their homework. Circulate around the class to see who needs help. Just before the bell rings, ask each student to circle the last problem they completed. Assign everyone to do five more problems for homework. This allows for differences in the number of problems students can complete in a given period of time. Everyone doesn't have to do 1 through 30, but everyone gets independent practice.

33. Do you have trouble with students not being responsible for homework? Try giving them a clipboard with the assignment sheet and all homework sheets attached. It must be returned the next day and signed by a parent.

34. To make sure that students clearly understand assignments in class or out of class, have each student turn to a buddy and repeat what he or she thinks the assignment is and how to respond.

35. Allow students to do auditory homework.

36. Let students turn in homework early, then grade homework early, and return to student for correction before final grading.

37. Have one night during the school week for "no homework" night (K–12). This gives families a break or provides a catch-up time for students.

38. Have all major tests, projects, spelling tests, book reports, and so on due on Wednesday. This gives the weekend for catchup.

39. Start spelling units on Wednesday and test on the unit the following Wednesday. This really helps the child and parent. Weekends can be used for studying.

40. Each Monday provide an assignment grid with all assignments/tests indicated. Place on bulletin board. This helps organize study time. For example:

| | Monday | Tuesday | Wednesday | Thursday | Friday |
| --- | --- | --- | --- | --- | --- |
| Social studies | | | | | |
| Science | | | | | |
| Reading | | | | | |
| Spelling | | | | | |
| Math | | | | | |

41. Assign projects to be completed at school. Teacher may provide display boards, materials, help, and so on. Children have equal opportunity regarding socioemotional level. This also avoids parent project participation stress.

**FIGURE 13.41**
Continued.

**TABLE 13.6**

Types of homework and suggested adaptations.

| Type of Homework | Example | Suggested Adaptations |
|---|---|---|
| *Preparation:* homework assigned to assist students' preparation for the next day's lesson/class | • Reading a chapter<br>• Reviewing a film | 1. Provide recorded materials for materials to be read.<br>2. Review in class before the lesson to assist students who cannot prepare ahead of time.<br>3. Allow students to prepare with a buddy.<br>4. Provide a summary of material to be read.<br>5. Provide a checklist for steps on procedures to be reviewed. |
| *Practice:* homework assigned to reinforce the skills taught during the day's lesson | • Working on math problems<br>• Answering questions about class lecture | 1. Be sure that the student understands the assignment.<br>2. Review assignment directions.<br>3. Review the assignment.<br>4. Provide a model.<br>5. Provide guided practice before independent practice.<br>6. Check for student functional level and match assignment.<br>7. Provide alternative amounts of assignments to students who cannot complete the same quantity as others. |
| *Extension:* homework assigned to extend or transfer skills taught | • Book reports<br>• Practicing computer skills | 1. Provide models for required reports.<br>2. Provide a checklist of procedures.<br>3. Allow buddies to work together on a shared assignment.<br>4. Be sure that students have been taught for acquisition and retention before requiring transfer. |
| *Creativity:* homework that requires synthesis of skills and concepts previously taught | • Term papers<br>• Research assignments | 1. Allow partners on projects.<br>2. Provide a clearly explained checklist with examples for all projects.<br>3. Do class projects that model each step of an independent project before assigning the latter.<br>4. Remember that students who have difficulty with structure need guidance with assigned projects, papers, and research projects.<br>5. Consider alternative assignments for students who may not be at this level. |

**TABLE 13.7**
Guidelines for implementing homework.

| Homework Practice | Guidelines |
|---|---|
| 1. Selecting the type of homework | • Consider the instructional purpose of the assignment as it relates to the type of homework.<br>• Practicing material learned in class may require drill-oriented assignments.<br>• Preparing students for future lessons should be structured to provide prerequisite information that will be necessary for a successful class lesson.<br>• Extending or transferring types of homework takes what a student may have learned and applies it to a more complex situation.<br>• Creating new ideas requires that students synthesize learned skills. |
| 2. Deciding on the content of homework | • Consider the type of homework (preparation, practice, extension, creativity) in deciding on the content.<br>• Have individual content for each student.<br>• Parallel IEP objective and content of homework.<br>• Realize that preparation of homework may be difficult for a student who cannot read or who traditionally has difficulty with assignments.<br>• Relate practice homework directly to skills taught in class.<br>• Evaluate the understanding level of concepts and skills taught before assigning practice homework. |
| 3. Determining the amount of homework | • This depends on the student's age and educational placement.<br>• Use homework sparingly in the early grades.<br>• Avoid weekend homework.<br>• Consider level of understanding and completion of class assignments to indicate the amount of homework that can be completed.<br>• Consider the specific disability of a student.<br>• Consider the amount of homework in other subjects.<br>• Consider homework already given in subject for the week. |
| 4. Explaining homework to students | • Inform students of<br>    the purpose of the assignment<br>    the directions necessary for completion<br>    the date due<br>    the required format<br>    the necessary materials needed for completion<br>    the source for assistance if needed<br>• Repeat all assignments orally and visually. |

TABLE 13.7
Continued.

| Homework Practice | Guidelines |
|---|---|
| | • Provide a model of a completed assignment.<br>• Provide examples that will be duplicated.<br>• Check to see that students fully understand the assignment. |
| 5. Assisting students with their assignments | • Teach the value of having a selected time and place for homework.<br>• Review the materials that the students will need to complete the assignment.<br>• Provide homework folders.<br>• Establish a homework hotline or class network system for answering questions when a student is in trouble and at home.<br>• Help students to remember books needed for homework. |
| 6. Motivating students to complete homework | • Make homework assignments as interesting as possible.<br>• Prevent homework from being punishment.<br>• Help students to see the effects of zeros on grades by teaching the principle of averaging.<br>• Praise students for completed homework.<br>• Try to understand why a student does not do homework. Many times it may be related to home situations or lack of understanding.<br>• Consider alternatives for students who do not complete homework. |
| 7. Evaluating homework | • Evaluate daily and provide immediate feedback.<br>• Allow students to provide corrections for a grade change.<br>• Let students have homework pass grades to be used to drop low homework grades.<br>• Provide grade averaging based on correctness as well as for attempting assignment. |
| 8. Involving parents in homework | • Keep communication open between teacher and parents.<br>• Remember that many parents may not understand the homework well enough to assist their child.<br>• Consider the fact that after a long day's work and extended family responsibilities, parents may be too tired to monitor homework.<br>• Consider family-oriented activities that can serve as homework. |

*Source:* From Salend, S. J., & Schliff, J. (1988). The many dimensions of homework. *Academic Therapy, 23*(4), 397–403. Copyright 1988 by Pro-Ed, Inc. Adapted and reprinted with permission.

# CHAPTER 14

## Adapting Multimedia Approaches: Assistive Technology and Technology Applications in the Information Age Classroom

*with Dr. Rachel Wise*

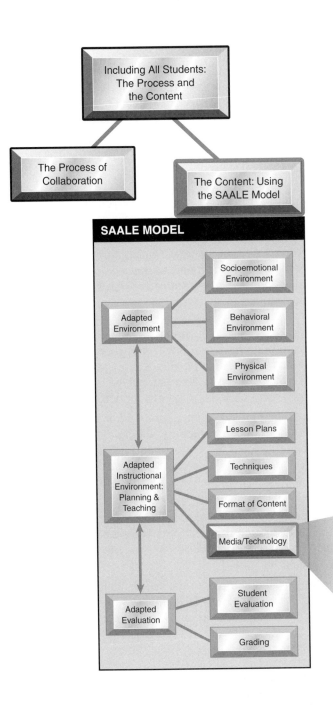

Including All Students:
The Process and
the Content

The Process of
Collaboration

The Content: Using
the SAALE Model

**SAALE MODEL**

Adapted
Environment

Socioemotional
Environment

Behavioral
Environment

Physical
Environment

Adapted
Instructional
Environment:
Planning &
Teaching

Lesson Plans

Techniques

Format of Content

Media/Technology

Adapted
Evaluation

Student
Evaluation

Grading

**Chapter-at-a-Glance**

Using Visual Media

Using Audio Media

Today's learning environment must reflect the society in which our students live; a world enriched by the multimedia experiences of the information age. This chapter will review the concepts of media presented in the previous editions of this text, but will assist the reader in finding the direction for meeting the unique needs of all students through the ever expanding world of information and multimedia. In previous editions, this chapter has been divided into visual and auditory media. For the purposes of today's integrated, multimedia world, the benefits to an auditory learner and visual learner will be integrated throughout the discussion of multimedia tools and strategies.

## BULLETIN BOARDS

As discussed in chapter 10, "Adapting the Physical Environment," using the bulletin board is an effective way to deliver information visually. As with many of the topics discussed in chapter 10, there is a strong relationship between adapting multimedia approaches and adapting the physical environment. Creating a stronger visual or auditory presence in the classroom through multimedia and technology strengthens the learning experiences for all students. Some strategies involving the power of bulletin boards for enhancing learning are as follows:

- A bulletin board shows a surfer on a wave. The wave was extended into the room. The surfer could be moved onto the wave, under the wave, around the wave, and so on. Can you guess what the teacher was teaching with this bulletin board? Prepositions! Prepositions are very abstract, but the surfer bulletin board turned this abstraction into a concrete learning experience.

- A bulletin board is an excellent place for exhibiting student work. While focusing on the ability to communicate a concept, students' writing samples about the concept or pictures that communicate the concept can be placed on the bulletin board. To provide an opportunity for all student work to be displayed, vary the topics or concepts and include a rotation list to ensure no student has been overlooked when posting class work.

- A bulletin board makes an excellent student assignment. Create teams of students in the class that have the rotational responsibility of developing a bulletin board. This strategy can also be used to create a little healthy competition and creativity between teams of students.

- A bulletin board can "come alive" with the incorporation of a small portable CD or tape player. A bulletin board on the life of Dr. Martin Luther King can include a tape clip of one of his speeches. Review chapter 10 for additional suggestions about planning bulletin boards.

## CHALKBOARD/DRY ERASE BOARD

The chalkboard/dry erase board is a common support item found in almost every classroom. When using the chalkboard/dry erase board, be sure that it is clean and that the color of chalk/marker shows up from all angles of the classroom. Strategies for using the chalkboard/dry erase board for enhancing learning include:

- Organize your ideas and keep writing to a minimum. For example, if you are discussing explorers, what they discovered, and important dates, develop a table with three headings (explorers, what was discovered, important dates) and write it on the chalkboard/dry erase board. After the class discussion, each student will have a clear, organized picture of the day's lesson.
- Use one section of the board on a daily basis to identify the day's schedule, homework assignments, special events, etc.
- A calendar of upcoming assignments and checkpoints for those assignments can help students start to plan and organize their time effectively. For example, if a term paper is due in 30 days, the weekly reminder could state the component of the paper that should be completed by the end of the week in order to complete the entire paper within the 30 days.
- Use color to differentiate between key points of a lesson.
- Use free hand drawing to assist students in understanding key points or concepts through the use of vocabulary and illustrations.
- Have students work in pairs or small groups at the board on some problem-solving type of activity.
- Use the chalkboard/dry erase board in conjunction with additional media in the environment to strengthen all classroom activities. This is especially valuable when planning the use of bulletin boards and transparencies/presentation software.

## ADAPTING TEXTBOOKS AND SUPPLEMENTAL PRINT RESOURCES

In yesterday's classrooms, textbooks were among the most common materials in a classroom. In the classroom of today, textbooks are only one of the media of focus, and in many secondary-level classrooms, class instruction is moving away from one single textbook to the use of multiple computer-generated information resources.

Teachers issue a class textbook or written resource materials for that specific grade level and require students to read the text and complete the appropriate activities. Many students never complete this task, and teachers wonder why they are not trying. However, reading becomes increasingly difficult for many students with disabilities as they grow older. Specifically, in the upper grades reading the textbook is an impossible task for many at-risk youth and for students with mild disabilities. Of course, we want all students to develop as many skills for reading as possible, but we expect students with disabilities and those at risk to maintain the general classroom pace. When this is our expectation, then educators must begin to implement modifications for the material to be read. Reading instruction should continue, but student support must be implemented as well.

Several years ago, a secondary-level teacher was approached about modifying the text for an 11th-grade student. The teacher replied, "Oh, he reads on the second-grade level and must continue to learn to read. Modifying the text would provide a crutch for the student, and he would not learn to read." At a certain time in the education sequence, we must begin to introduce students to ways in which to open doors to printed materials. When using textbooks as a tool for teaching, we must provide structure to this material, just as we have provided structure to instruction. It was time to teach this 11th-grade student how to survive with printed materials beyond his reading level.

The following suggestions for adapting textbooks or printed matter apply to all students. Some ideas should be used regularly to introduce new text and all new chapters. Many ideas may be necessary only in an extreme case, such as an inability to read. The ideas follow the sequence that a teacher would use to present the text and each chapter.

Figure 14.1 graphically presents the model for presenting and adapting textbooks.

| Teacher presents organization/structure of textbook | Teacher presents organization/structure of each chapter as assigned | Teacher assigns chapter to be read | Supplementary materials/modification for texts |
|---|---|---|---|
| ↓ | ↓ | ↓ | ↓ |
| Explains purpose of text | Purpose of chapter | Assigns small sections | Color coding |
| ↓ | ↓ | ↓ | ↓ |
| Introduces all sections of reading materials | Graphic organizer of textbooks | Tape-records chapters | Teach with pictures |
| ↓ | ↓ | ↓ | ↓ |
| Reviews the table of contents | Outline of chapter | Lowers reading levels | Maps and charts |
| ↓ | ↓ | | ↓ |
| Prepares a visual (graphic organizer) for the text, showing the placement for each chapter | Chapter vocabulary | | Movies, videotapes, filmstrips |
| | ↓ | | ↓ |
| | Chapter questions | | Work sheets |
| | ↓ | | ↓ |
| | Checklist of things to attend to in text | | Software/CDs |
| | | | ↓ |
| | | | Internet sites |

**FIGURE 14.1**
Adapting textbooks.

As illustrated in Figure 14.1, *teachers should first review the organization and structure of the textbook. Tell the students the purpose or objective of the text, and how this text and the course relate to the sequence of courses.* For example, if the social studies text covers a specific period in history, explain this to the class. Relate how this section in history begins with the time period where last year's course ended. Present a visual of the sequence of social studies texts for several grades. This process helps students to begin to tie together their educational sequence. *All sections of the text should be introduced at this time.* Many students do not realize that their text contains a glossary of terms or an index, which they can use to trace subjects within the text. *After the section review, focus on the table of contents, pointing out the parts of the texts. Provide a graphic organizer for the table of contents.* An example is the graphic organizer that appears at the beginning of each part of this text, giving the reader an overview of how all the parts fit together to work as a whole. This organizer is repeated at the beginning of each part and each chapter. When students have a mental picture of the structure of the text, it is time to move to the chapters.

*The organization of each chapter should be explained before teaching the content.* Several suggestions for providing structure within the chapters include stating the purpose and using graphic organizers, chapter outlines vocabulary, chapter questions, and focus checklists. *Present the purpose or objective of the chapter, just as with the overall text.* What will this chapter cover? *Develop a graphic organizer* that shows the chapter within the total picture of the text by simply revising the organizer for the total text. A graphic organizer can be developed to display each major and minor part of the chapter. *Provide an outline of the chapter* that includes and extends the parts of the graphic organizer. The chapter outline could serve as a lecture outline (formative study guide) as discussed in chapter 12. Allow space for note taking and place the page numbers for each text part in the left margin by each section. For each major part of the chapter, provide a brief summary outline to give a short overview of the section. These steps will help when the sentences in a text are too long and make reading difficult. The next step in the model in Figure 14.1 is *to introduce chapter vocabulary.* Helping students with disabilities learn vocabulary means better acquisition of learning as well as retention of new words. Figure 14.2 presents suggestions for adapting vocabulary.

The next step in the model for adapting textbooks (Figure 14.2) is *making adaptations for chapter questions.* The process of completing answers to chapter questions poses a major difficulty in working with reading material in many subjects. You may want to try one or more of the options in Figure 14.3.

*A checklist* for following the sequence of events in a story or chapter is especially helpful for students who have difficulty reading for specific details. The checklist will also provide an outline of events. You may write page numbers beside each step on the checklist. You also may provide study questions for each step. Students may check off each step as they read the section. This will help students focus on what they are reading.

The third phase of the model in Figure 14.1 includes adaptations to make when *assigning the chapter to be read.* Review the chapter graphic organizer to

1. Make a list of all boldfaced and italicized words and those presenting new concepts from the chapter. List the words in the order they occur within the chapter. Record the corresponding page number to the left of each word.

2. Beside each vocabulary word, provide a synonym or simplified definition.

3. Provide all students with the list of new vocabulary words before introducing the content of the chapter.

4. If students have difficulty looking up definitions or key words, provide the definition. This will cut down on their amount of work so they can spend time learning the definition of the word that is the task we are asking them to do.

5. Instead of having the student copy vocabulary words and their definitions on notebook paper, have them write each word separately on the front of a 3″ × 5″ card and the corresponding definition on the back. These steps save time and will produce a set of flash cards for reinforcement activities. The cards can be filed in a box in order by chapter number.

6. When working with the flash cards, follow these steps:
   - The student holds the flash card and looks at the word.
   - Another student, a teacher, or a parent holds a list of the words and their definitions.
   - The student looks at the word and supplies the definition.
   - The student immediately flips the card over, checking the definition on the card against his or her response.
   - Only work on 5 words at a time, adding another 5 after the first 5 are mastered. After learning the second 5 words, review all 10 words. Now add 5 more words. Then review all 15. This type of distributed practice is much better for memory load.

7. Be sure that the student knows what type of test you will use for vocabulary. For example, if the test will be a fill-in-the-blank without a word bank, the study process will be different from studying for a test with a word bank.

8. Tape-record the words for each chapter with each definition. This process will help students who cannot read the words initially to learn the words and their definitions. Be sure to number the words and read the number on the test.

**FIGURE 14.2**
Adapting vocabulary.

show students how the chapter fits into the whole. *Assign only small sections to be read at a time.* If you assign too much to students who have difficulty reading or who track slowly, some will choose to not even attempt the assignment. Some may begin but find the assignment too laborious to continue. The teacher may *tape-record the text or sections of the text.* When students follow in the text while listening to the same material recorded, they are using both the visual and auditory channels, thereby increasing their chances of retention.

1. Do not require that all questions be answered.

2. Reword questions to simplify vocabulary or sentence structure.

3. Avoid questions that require lengthy responses.

4. Allow students to answer questions without writing down the questions.

5. For students who have difficulty reading, make a study list of all questions as they occur, either within the context of the chapter or at the end of the chapter. Provide the correct answer and the page number where the answer can be found within the chapter.

6. Some students may need the questions and answers recorded on tape, allowing them to read along with the tape. With the recording, they would learn some information rather than no information, as in the case of a poor reader.

7. Some students will benefit from having the page number where the answer can be found. This step will reduce busy work for the student and will help the slow reader focus on the question.

8. Remember to teach all students that the answers to questions usually occur sequentially within the text. For example, the answer to question 1 will appear in the text before the answer to question 2.

9. Allow students to copy each chapter question on a 3″ × 5″ or 5″ × 8″ card and number each question. As the students read the chapter, place the card with question 1 on the table beside the text. Tell them to read, looking for the answer to question 1. When they find the answer, they flip the card over and write the answer on the card, along with the page number in the text where the answer is found. They return to the text with the flash card for question 2 in front, again looking for the answer. This process assists slow readers by allowing them to read the text one time and finish with the answers to all the chapter questions. The set of cards can be used individually or with a buddy for review. This is a timesaving idea resulting in a set of flash cards. If you want to grade the questions, have the students turn in the cards.

**FIGURE 14.3**
Adapting chapter questions.

When tape recording, be sure to follow these suggestions:

- Put each chapter on a separate tape.

- Label each tape with the chapter and page numbers.

- When recording, read the page number first; then read the text on the page. Tell the listener about any figures or tables by stating the page number and the table or figure number.

- After referring to a table or figure, say "return to text."

- When moving to a new page, state the page number.

- When the selection is complete, state "end of selection."
- Read the table of contents for each chapter along with the chapter title and page numbers.
- File all tapes in large boxes. Label each row of tapes by text title. These file boxes may be purchased at most record or videotape stores.

Companies that prepare commercially recorded texts are excellent resources (see Table 14.1), and they usually carry large inventories. For example, Recordings for the Blind (609-452-0606) carries an inventory of 90,000 recorded texts. If a text is not in stock, they will record it free of charge. This service is available to students who are visually impaired, blind, physically disabled, or learning disabled; and it continues for life. College texts and work materials may also be recorded. A student must apply to receive the service.

*Lowering reading levels (3.3)* is another step in the model. Common sense tells us that a large percentage of students in classes will not read on grade level. Three factors to consider when reducing the reading level of printed material are vocabulary, sentence and paragraph construction, and physical format. Figures 14.4 and 14.5 present suggestions for each of these areas.

The fourth phase in the model in Figure 14.1 involves *supplementary materials and modification for texts. Color-coding* helps students organize what they are about to learn and helps them prioritize the learning. Using three different colors, mark key words and concepts with one color, important facts and information with another, and definitions with a third. Colors should be standardized throughout the school to avoid confusion, and a color-code key should be posted at the front of the coded text. *Teaching with pictures* is an excellent way to help poor readers or nonreaders follow a lesson or discuss ideas for a project. Many libraries contain books of pictures about history, science, and other subjects. Have students look through a sequence of pictures to focus on the clothes of different periods. Specific details in old pictures can show the way people's lives change over time and give students a look at specific events during the period. Students could focus on a sequence of events or on cultural changes. *Maps and charts* are useful in teaching students who cannot read at all or who are on their grade level. Maps may be enlarged, with picture clues posted on them. For example, when studying Mexico, picture clues might include posting pictures of crops in the appropriate areas on a map, illustrating types of clothing or demonstrating transportation on the map visually. *Movies, videotapes/digital videodiscs, and filmstrips* may be used for reinforcement activities or supplementary assignments. Students who have difficulty reading can get vital details of an assignment through these media. For example, before assigning a novel to be read, the class may watch a movie that gives an overview of the book. *Work sheets* are frequently used in classes for assignments and practice. When students have difficulty reading the text, they will also have difficulty reading the work sheets. Chapter 13 presents suggestions for modifying work sheets. *Software/CDs* are often found as companion materials with textbooks and textbook adoptions. It is

**TABLE 14.1**
Mail order sources.

Although many companies publish and sell abridged audio books, only a few offer unabridged books on a rental basis. Tapes that are shipped in postage-paid mailers may be kept for 30 days. Broken cassettes are replaced for free.

### Book/Tape Companies

- Audio Book Company, P. O. Box 7111, Pasadena, CA 91109; (818) 799-4139. More than 100 titles available at an average cost of $8 per title.
- Audio Book Contractors/Classic Books on Cassettes, P. O. Box 40115, Washington, DC 20016; (202) 363-3429. Approximately 110 cassettes of children's and adult classics for sale or rent for one-third the purchase price.
- Books for Listening, 289 Country Way, Scituate, MA 02066; (617) 545-6959. Classics and popular literature, approximately 75 titles, at $6.50 to $14.00.
- Books on Tape, Box 7900, Newport Beach, CA 92658; (800) 626-3333. Publishes an annual catalogue and monthly updates. Rentals from $9.50 to $17.50 per box. Discount plans include 10 percent off for ordering three books at one time, 10 percent off plus a free selection for ordering 10 books. Interval shipment available. Gift certificates for $15.00 or more available. A current promotion allows a customer to order a book as a gift for a new customer for $5.00. If the recipient places an order, the giver receives a free rental.
- Cheshire Cat Children's Bookstore, 5512 Connecticut Ave NW, Washington, DC 20015; (202) 244-3956. Classic books for children and teenagers available for rent at $5 per week.
- Politics and Prose Bookstore, 5010 Connecticut Ave. NW, Washington, DC 20008; (202) 364-1919. They have about 50 books on tape, mostly of 19th-century classic novels, available for rent at $5 per week.
- Recorded Books, P. O. Box 409, Charlotte Hall, MD 20622; (800) 638-1304. Publishes a bimonthly catalogue. Rentals range from $7.50 to $20.50. Discount plans include 10 percent off for ordering three books at one time; free postage for ordering 10 books.
- Tape Rental Library, P. O. Box 107, Covesville, VA 22931; (804) 292-3705. Subscribers pay a $120 annual rental fee and may exchange cassettes as often as desired. Classics as well as management and personal-development tapes are available.

### Public Libraries
Libraries in the Washington, DC, area find it hard to keep shelves stocked for walk-in patrons, but are building their collections.

- Library of Congress Talking Books Program, National Library Service for the Blind and Physically Handicapped, Washington, DC 20542, or contact your local library for information. Tapes and equipment lent free to people with handicaps who can't read conventional print materials. Eligibility must be certified by a physician. More than 40,000 recorded books available through the mail.
- "On cassette 1987–1988," an annotated guide to audiocassettes, available in library reference sections.

Prefixes and suffixes add to complexity. Latin roots increase abstraction. To increase readability:

1. Introduce new terms and concepts slowly and allow lots of practice before introducing the next new term.
   - ✓ *Example:* An atom contains particles of matter called *electrons, protons, and neutrons.*
   - ✓ *Modification:* An atom is often described as "the smallest particle of an element." You know that an atom is matter. It has mass and takes up space.

2. Use synonyms of a lower order in place of complex words. Care should be taken to avoid losing the writer's intent.
   - ✓ *Example:* We should not adjudicate the theological praxis of aught categorizations of homo sapiens to be factious.
   - ✓ *Modification:* We should not judge the religious customs of any group of humans to be silly.

3. Make a slight revision, add an insertion, or completely rewrite. Again, care should be taken to avoid losing the writer's intent. It may be necessary to add an extra phrase, sentence, or even a paragraph in order to make an abstract concept more clear.
   - ✓ *Example:* Milk that has been pasteurized is considered safer for you.
   - ✓ *Modification:* Milk that has been pasteurized (heated to 140–155 degrees) is considered safer for you. (Heating kills the bacteria in the milk.)

4. Nominalization should be avoided. Nominalizations transform verbs and modifiers into nouns, usually resulting in abstract meanings.
   - ✓ *Example:* The praising of his song made him happy.
   - ✓ *Modification:* He was happy that they praised his song.

5. Avoid overdirecting.
   - ✓ *Example:* When you see an asterisk (*), stop the tape, for this is going to act as a stop sign for you, and you know that a stop sign or a red light means you have to stop.
   - ✓ *Modification:* Stop the tape when you see an asterisk (*).

FIGURE 14.4
Reducing reading levels through vocabulary.

Excess punctuation (commas, semicolons, and slashes) indicates complexity in sentences and paragraphs. To increase readability:

1. Break sentences into smaller units of thought.
   - ✓ *Example:* In ancient Egypt, similar tests for cool beverages developed, but a different solution was forthcoming since a more temperate climate kept Egypt ice free even in winter.
   - ✓ *Modification:* The people of ancient Egypt also liked cool beverages. However, the warmer climate kept Egypt ice free even in winter. A different solution was needed.

2. Use conversational narrative.
   - ✓ *Example:* The death of leadership exhibited in this project was reflected in the tendency of the managers to address implementation problems in an ad hoc manner.
   - ✓ *Modifications:* The lack of leadership in this project was shown by the way the managers did not plan for possible problems.

3. Avoid irrelevant words, phrases, and sentences.
   - ✓ *Example:* Lincoln was shot in the head at the Ford Theater in Washington, DC, by John Wilkes Booth, an out-of-work actor.
   - ✓ *Modification:* Lincoln was shot at the Ford Theater by John Wilkes Booth.

4. A slight revision may lead to clarity.
   - ✓ *Example:* In the upper atmosphere, great number of ions are present hence the name ionosphere.
   - ✓ *Modification:* The name *ionosphere* comes from the presence of great numbers of ions in the upper atmosphere.

5. Retain grammatical markers. Words such as *because, if, before,* and *after* imply a cause-and-effect relationship and should not be deleted.
   - ✓ *Example:* The engine failed. The plane crashed.
   - ✓ *Modification:* Because the engine failed, the plane crashed.

6. Readability is increased if the topic sentence is the initial sentence in a paragraph.
   - ✓ *Example:* The issue of slavery was important to the South, but there were other factors involved, including states' rights versus federal rights, the commercial interests of the plantation versus manufacturing concerns, and international versus intranational trade. All contributed to the friction between the North and South. The Civil War was brought about by many factors.
   - ✓ *Modifications:* There were many reasons for the Civil War. The issue of slavery was important to the South, but there were other factors involved, including states' rights versus federal rights, the commercial interests of the plantations versus manufacturing concerns, and international versus intranational trade. All contributed to the friction between the North and South.

FIGURE 14.5
Reducing reading levels through sentence and paragraph construction.

important to review these resources and incorporate the appropriate supplemental materials or activities into the instructional lessons. These materials often contain audio and graphical information, which enhances the lesson for students with disabilities. *Internet sites* should not be overlooked, especially when recommended or referenced within the textbook. These sites may also provide audio and graphical resources for the lesson, but also may contain resources that provide suggestions for adapting materials for the lesson or concepts being presented.

Locating resources for implementing textbook adaptations can be a difficult and time-consuming process. The following resources may help you prepare and implement textbook adaptations (Wood & Wooley, 1986):

- Check to see if any of your school's clubs will take on textbook adaptations as a yearly project.
- If several teachers are using the same textbook, divide up the techniques so that each will have to prepare only a small portion. For example, one teacher may adapt a vocabulary, another the questions.
- After students complete the answers to chapter questions, use their papers to prepare study guides.

## AUDIOVISUAL MEDIA: ADAPTING AND PREPARING FOR THE USE OF TELEVISION/VIDEOCASSETTE RECORDERS (VCRs) OR DIGITAL VIDEODISCS (DVDs)

The use of television, VCRs, and DVDs has virtually replaced the use of the filmstrip or 16mm film in most of today's classrooms, although the recommendations discussed in this section can apply to the 16mm movie or to filmstrips. None of the audiovisual technology can be overlooked when discussing the needs for accommodating students with disabilities. Television, VCRs, and DVDs are used daily in many classes to support class instruction. When using any of these types of visual presentations, teachers should give students a checklist with points to focus on, which should be reviewed before the presentation, followed during it, and used as a summary afterwards. At the end of this chapter are three samples of audiovisual checklists, all suitable for videos, movies, filmstrips, speakers, field trips, and so on (see Samples 14.1 through 14.2).

In each of these sample formats, the teacher supplies the title, length, and purpose of any AV equipment. The teacher lists the major points before the presentation and reviews them with the class. During the presentation, students take notes under each point. After the presentation, the teacher reviews each point listed on the left and the students take additional notes while working with a buddy and complete the class follow-up notes section on the right. The students and the teacher then summarize the presentation. A point to remember is that even adults have difficulty sitting in workshops and viewing videotapes, movies, and filmstrips. Keep

Title (completed by teacher):

Length (completed by teacher):

Purpose (completed by teacher):

**Major Points Covered**

Notes before/during AV presentation:                Class follow-up notes:

Look for the following:

1. _____        _____

   _____        _____

2. _____        _____

   _____        _____

3. _____        _____

   _____        _____

4. _____        _____

   _____        _____

Summary/discussion:

Sample individualized student computer checklist.

---

Computer Experience

Computer lab _____ Classroom _____ Home _____ Apple _____ Mac _____ Other _____

Access method _____

Able to independently activate computer _____ Able to word process _____ Save data _____ Print _____

Current rate _____wpm copying from paper with _____ errors for _____words

_____wpm creative writing from prompt with _____ errors for _____ words

**Career Focus for Future (if applicable, consider job/task analysis)**

**Technical Resources**

Location of lab _____ Availability of lab _____

Computer type(s) and numbers accessible:

Windows _____ Describe _____

Macintosh _____ Describe _____

Other _____ Describe _____

Available peripherals _____

Availability of adaptive access devices _____ Describe _____

Availability of other hardware: Large-screen TV _____ CD-ROM _____ Videodisc _____ VCR _____

Computer screen projection _____ Describe _____

Software availability _____

_____

**Human Resources**

Classroom assistant _____ Team teacher _____ Parent volunteer _____ School technical teacher _____

Curriculum area

Goal _____

**Category (check all that apply)**

Drill and practice _____ Tutorial _____ Simulation _____ Utility _____ Problem solving _____ Interactive game _____

**Comments**

_____

this in mind when asking children to do the same. The following suggestions apply to the passive use of audiovisual materials (student is observing/listening to pre-developed audiovisual resources).

### Videos/Movies

- Preview all videos or movies before using in the classroom, especially if it is a new release. Changes may have been made that you were not anticipating. Also, be sure the video or movie is approved for use in your school/district. If it is not, you may need to get approval from a school administrator if the subject or content could be controversial.
- Be sure that the video or movie is not too long. If the video or movie is more than 30 min in length, divide it between classes. Or plan to have short stopping points (ideally every 15–20 minutes) to involve the class in a discussion of key points.
- Use videos or movies to reinforce lectures or present additional information.
- Use videos or movies to present problems or situations that can serve as a basis for class discussions.

### Filmstrips

- Though seldom used anymore, filmstrips can still reinforce key concepts.
- Students can view filmstrips on individual viewers.
- If there is no audio with the filmstrip, be sure to read to the class.

Most audiovisual resources are considered a passive tool for learning, allowing little participation by the student. It is essential for teachers to develop strategies for creating active learning environments through the use of audiovisual materials. Some suggestions for including the student as an active participant include:

### Videotaping

- Videotape class demonstrations to be played back at a later date.
- Videotape the visual explanations of math problems for review.
- Allow students to develop their own videotapes.
- Let students videotape their explanations of class lessons for use with peers.

### Digitizing Video or Photography

- Students can blend the skills of developing presentations, lessons, assessments, etc., by blending the technologies of digital video or photography with today's computer technology.

# OVERHEAD PROJECTORS/COMPUTER PROJECTION SYSTEMS

The overhead projector is still a very common piece of equipment used by teachers, especially at the secondary content level. The principles that are a foundation for the use of the overhead projector can be carried over to the use of computer-generated presentations. This section suggests ways of making and using adaptations for presentations that may involve the use of overhead projectors or computer-projection systems, ideas for making transparencies or presentations more effective, tips for teaching with transparencies or computer-projection systems, and ideas for using the overhead or computer-projection system according to subject area.

## Uses and Adaptations for Overhead Projectors and Computer-Projection Systems

There are numerous ways in which teachers can effectively use the overhead projector or a computer-projection system. Here are a few examples:

- Provide a visualization to support the main points in a lecture. This visualization can be created through the development of a series of notes or drawings on transparencies or in a computer-generated presentation such as Power-Point or Claris Works.
- Introduce new concepts or new material by creating a "set" that highlights new terms or vocabulary through use of a drawing or picture that represents the concept.
- Encourage class discussions or full class participation by identifying key questions, drawings, or pictures that will stimulate discussion on the topics related to the instructional lesson. This strategy is particularly effective for presenting math concepts in a problem-solving scenario.
- Visually reinforce directions by displaying them on the overhead projector or the computer-projection system.

## Ideas for Making Transparencies or Presentations More Effective

Participating in a class on how to prepare computer-based presentations will help you make effective use of computer-projection systems and overhead projectors in the classroom. Some general tips on presentations include:

- Use a font size and type that can be read by anyone in the room. Generally a 24 pt standard font will accomplish this goal.
- Use colors that provide a distinct contrast for easier viewing throughout the classroom.
- Be familiar with the type of lighting in the classroom. If the room maintains a high source of light, use a darker contrast in the background and in the print on the presentation/transparency.

# Tips for Teaching with Transparencies or Computer-Projection Systems*

- To orient students before your lecture, prepare a lecture outline on the overhead projector/computer presentation.

- Permit students to use these technologies for their presentations. This will help them organize their thoughts and ideas.

- Use a variety of colors to generate interest and emphasize or differentiate areas, content, and certain categories.

- Use only a few points or items per transparency/slide. Too much information on a transparency/slide lessens its impact.

- Prepare student handouts that provide information about materials shown on the overhead. This is an easy process when preparing presentations using a presentation software application.

- Use only boldface or a primary type when generating transparencies/slides/presentations.

# Ideas for Using the Overhead or Computer-Projection System According to Subject Area**

### Art Evaluation

1. Use cutout designs to demonstrate shapes or the basic principles of formal and informal balance.

2. Cut headlines from newspapers and catalogs to demonstrate the difference among Roman, Gothic, and text lettering styles.

3. Create a color-lift transparency/slide of a face. By using overlays and water-soluble pens, facial structures can be discussed.

### English

1. Use a transparency/slide to demonstrate the use of library card catalogs, or make excerpts from a reader's guide to explain research guidelines.

2. Use transparencies/slides to construct different paragraphs to explain structure, grammar, spelling, and clarity. (Students could write paragraphs as well.)

*Sources: Brown, J., Lewis, R., & Harcleroad, F. (1977). AV instruction: *Technology, media, and methods* (5th ed.). New York: Macmillan. Copyright 1977 by Macmillan. Adapted with permission, and Fuhrmann, B. S., & Grasha, A. F. (1983). *A practical handbook for college teachers.* Boston: Little Brown. Adapted with permission.
**Source: Green. L. (1982). *501 ways to use the overhead projector.* Colorado: Libraries Unlimited.

3. Transparencies/slides can be used to demonstrate the conjugation of verbs, sentence structure, speech, and the relationship of words.
4. Different styles of letters could be demonstrated on the transparency/slide.
5. Make a transparency/slide of excerpts from good papers you have collected to demonstrate the technique of good writing.

**Math**

1. Use geometric shapes to teach fractions.
2. Make a transparency/slide of a graph grid. If the overhead is being projected onto the chalkboard, use chalk to plot the lines on the graph.
3. Use newspaper clippings to present math work problems or exercises in probability.

**Social Studies**

1. To discuss the function of our voting system, make transparencies/slides like sample ballots. Use to discuss candidates, issues in policy, and amendments.
2. Outlines of maps can be generated to teach the concepts of latitude and longitude. Maps can be generated to teach the recognition of states.

**Science**

1. Before conduction experiments, the teacher can prepare transparencies/slides that list the materials to be used.
2. List the steps of an experiment on a transparency/slide. Demonstrate each step.

**Career and Technical Education**

1. Use drawings to help students identify tools and their functions.
2. Use the overhead to visualize the correct technique for sharpening tools.
3. Use transparencies/slides and overlays to explain the parts and the function of a machine and machine safety devices.

## Teaching with Transparencies/Presentation Slides

As you prepare to teach with transparencies or using a computer-generated presentation, you must plan for the use of these tools. Before you teach, during teaching, and after teaching are all times to use these tools. If your lesson plan involves a class discussion, develop a transparency/slide that presents the major points of the lesson. If you have a transparency/slide that contains detailed information, such as a diagram, a map, or parts of the digestive system, give the students a matching copy on which to record notes. Most of the computer-generated presentation applications include steps for printing handouts that can be used by students. Keep a file for transparencies/slides, and organize and label them under subject headings, titles, or lesson topics. Use a database to describe the transparency/slide contents and any accompanying activities. To learn more about how to appropriately use presentation tools in a classroom, classes or an online tutorial is the best way to get started.

# COMPUTER TECHNOLOGY IN TODAY'S CLASSROOM

Education is a responsibility and reflection of society. Education today is quickly reflecting the changes of the information age or our emerging "e-world." To better prepare all students, especially those students with disabilities, understanding the impact technology is having best prepares the teacher to teach students how to be successful in this new age. The information age creates a framework for change in how we learn, what we learn, how we apply what we know to society, and how we prepare for post–high school success. In this information age, students with disabilities can have unlimited opportunities, but if not prepared for this new technological/electronic global world and economy, these same students will face even greater challenges in accessing opportunities.

## School Improvement and Technology

*"It is the ability of all students—no matter whether rich or poor, or whether they are from a small town, a city, a rural area, or a suburb—to learn at the highest levels with the greatest resources and have the promise of a future of real opportunity. This is the potential of technology."*

Richard W. Riley, July 29, 1998
Technology and Education: An Investment in Equity and Excellence

Educators need to be at the forefront of planning for school improvement to meet the needs of all students. School improvement must include a focus on technology planning. This should be a schoolwide inclusive initiative, which should incorporate some of the following characteristics of technology planning:

- Technology skills are defined for all students, and strategies for achieving them are integrated into the curriculum.
- Technology is designed to improve both the quality of curriculum available to students and the instructional methods used to teach them.

- Technology is designed to permit teamwork, allowing students to engage in joint projects with their classmates and with students from other states and regions.
- Technology is used to improve learning by offering more hands-on practice, more time, more content, more problem solving, and more individualized planning.

The handbook, *Technology Connections for School Improvement: Planners' Handbook,* published by the North Central Regional Educational Laboratory and the U.S. Department of Education, is an outstanding tool for incorporating technology planning with local school improvement processes.

### Setting Standards for Students and Teachers

One major component of technology planning is the identification of standards for students and for teachers. Technology can be categorized into *information technology*—the ability to demonstrate a set of skills related to technology literacy for the 21st century, and *instructional technology*—the ability to demonstrate the use of technology tools and applications within a variety of curricular areas. Technology literacy is the foundation of the information age for students and for teachers. Many states have adopted a set of standards reflective of the technology literacy needs of teachers. These standards are being implemented through a variety of preservice and inservice strategies. All teachers should be encouraged to continue to meet and exceed these standards. The standards for students serve as guidelines for the direction of instruction in information technology and for the incorporation of instructional technology within a school and in classrooms. Table 14.2 provides one school district's modification of the National Educational Technology Standards for Students (NETS). An outstanding resource for planning technology standards for students is the *National Educational Technology Standards for Students Connecting Curriculum and Technology,* published by the International Society for Technology in Education (ISTE) NETS Project.

## Models and Approaches to Computer Usage

A 1981 survey conducted by the U.S. Department of Education determined that approximately half of the nation's school districts gave students access to a computer terminal (Coburn, Kelman, Roberts, Snyder, Watt, & Weiner, 1982). However, "the anticipated benefits of the technology are not being realized" (Cosden & Abernathy, 1990, p. 31). Cosden and Abernathy point out further that the future of microcomputers depends greatly on teacher time and assistance, and that these factors must be considered when establishing goals for activities. In their longitudinal investigation of the use of microcomputers among elementary school students, the authors describe the challenges for teachers when integrating computer technology into the curriculum. Two approaches of computer use emerged: classroom based and lab based. Figure 14.6 presents observations from this study regarding the use of each approach.

**TABLE 14.2**
Technology literacy standards.

*It is important that all students be able to demonstrate the following technology literacy skills:*

1. Basic operations and concepts
   - A sound understanding of the nature and operation of technology.
   - The proficient use of technology.
2. Ethical, cultural, and societal issues
   - An understanding of the ethical, cultural, and societal issues related to technology.
   - Responsible use of technology systems, information, and software.
   - A positive attitude toward technology uses that support lifelong learning, collaboration, personal pursuits, and productivity.
3. Technology as a tool for productivity
   - The use of technology tools to enhance learning, increase productivity, and promote creativity.
   - The use of productivity tools to collaborate in constructing technology-enhanced models, preparing publications, and producing other creative works.
4. Technology as a tool for communication
   - The use of telecommunications to collaborate, publish, and interact with peers, experts, and other audiences.
   - The use of a variety of media and formats to communicate information and ideas effectively to multiple audiences.
5. Technology as a tool for research
   - The use of technology to locate, review, and collect information from a variety of sources.
   - The use of technology tools to process data and report results.
   - The ability to evaluate and select new information resources and technological innovations based on the appropriateness of specific tasks.
6. Technology as a tool for problem-solving and decision-making
   - The use of technology resources for solving problems and making informed decisions.
   - The ability to employ technology in the development of strategies for solving problems in the real world.

*Prior to the completion of grade 3 students will:*

- Operate hardware using input and output devices such as the mouse, keyboard, CD-ROM, printer, and VCR. (Standard 1)
- Demonstrate the ability to launch, interact, and exit software packages. (Standard 1)
- Use a variety of developmentally appropriate media and technology for directed and independent learning activities and the creation of products. (Standards 1, 3)
- Communicate about technology using developmentally appropriate and accurate terminology. (Standard 1)
- Demonstrate proper care procedures for hardware and software devices. (Standard 1)
- Work cooperatively and collaboratively with peers, family members, and others when using technology in the classroom. (Standard 2)
- Demonstrate positive social and ethical behaviors when using technology. (Standard 2)
- Practice responsible use of technology systems and software. (Standard 2)
- Create developmentally appropriate multimedia products with support from teachers, family members, or student partners. (Standard 3)
- Use technology resources for problem solving, communication, and illustration of thoughts, ideas, and stories. (Standards 3, 6)
- Gather information and communicate with others using the appropriate technology communication tools, with support from teachers, family members, or student partners. (Standard 4)
- Use technology resources to gather, process, and report information. (Standard 5)

*(continued)*

**TABLE 14.2**
Continued.

*Prior to completion of grade 8, students will:*

- Apply strategies for identifying and solving routine hardware and software problems that occur during everyday use. (Standard 1)
- Demonstrate an understanding of concepts underlying hardware, software, and connectivity, and of practical applications to learning and problem solving. (Standard 1)
- Demonstrate proficiency in the touch method of keyboarding, emphasizing speed, accuracy, and productivity. (Standard 1)
- Exhibit legal and ethical behaviors when using information and technology, and discuss consequences of misuse. (Standard 2)
- Research and evaluate the accuracy, relevance, appropriateness, comprehensiveness, and bias of electronic information sources concerning real-world problems. (Standards 2, 6)
- Use content-specific tools, software, and simulations to support learning and research. (Standards 3, 5)
- Collaborate with peers, experts, and others using telecommunications and collaborative tools to investigate curriculum-related problems and issues. (Standards 4, 5)
- Select and use appropriate tools and technology resources to accomplish a variety of tasks and solve problems. (Standards 5, 6)
- Evaluate electronic information sources concerning real-world problems. (Standard 5)
- Apply productivity/multimedia tools and peripherals to support personal productivity, problem solving, group collaboration, and learning throughout the curriculum. (Standards 3, 6)
- Design, develop, publish, and present products using technology resources that demonstrate and communicate curriculum concepts for audiences inside and outside the classroom. (Standards 4, 6)

*Prior to completion of grade 12, students will:*

- Demonstrate an understanding and explanation of troubleshooting concepts. (Standard 1)
- Make informed choices among technology systems, resources, and services. (Standards 1, 2)
- Identify capabilities and limitations of contemporary and emerging technology resources and assess the potential of these systems and service to address personal, lifelong learning and workplace needs. (Standard 2)
- Analyze advantages and disadvantages of widespread use of and reliance on technology in the workplace and in society as a whole. (Standard 2)
- Demonstrate and advocate for legal and ethical behaviors among peers, family, and community regarding the use of technology information. (Standard 2)
- Use technology tools and resources for managing and communicating personal/professional information. (Standards 3, 4)
- Investigate and apply expert systems, intelligent agents, and simulations in real-world situations. (Standards 3, 6)
- Select and apply technology tools for research, information analysis, problem-solving, and decision making in content learning. (Standards 4, 5)
- Collaborate with peers, experts, and others to contribute to a content-related knowledge base by using technology to compile, synthesize, produce, and disseminate information, models, and other creative works. (Standards 4, 5, 6)
- Evaluate technology-based options for lifelong learning. (Standard 5)
- Routinely and efficiently use online information resources to meet needs for learning and decision making. (Standards 5, 6)

| Classroom based | Lab based |
|---|---|
| • Number of computers available to teachers is limited<br>• Supports education philosophy that equal access to computers must be provided to all students<br>• Must develop computer activities that can be integrated into noncomputer-based activities<br>• Allows computer-based activities to be used that are segregated from ongoing tasks<br>• Teachers usually select the segregated option, so that students find their assigned computer-based activities totally segregated from those of classmates<br>• Students with disabilities may miss vital information in content areas during their computer activities | • Alleviates problems of limited student access<br>• Students may participate in the same activities and in the simultaneous use of the technology<br>• Raises a broader issue about whether lab activities are integrated into the curriculum<br>• Problems may occur because teachers often have a choice in participating in the computer lab<br>• When teachers do not attend labs, they have limited communication with the lab specialist, thus presenting problems for special students who have academic problems and need more instructional precision |

**FIGURE 14.6**

Classroom-based versus lab-based microcomputer use.

*Source:* From Cosden, M. A., & Abernathy, T. V. (1990). Microcomputer use in the schools: Teacher roles and instructional options. *Remedial and Special Education, 11,* 31–38. Copyright 1980 by Pro-Ed, Inc. Adapted and reprinted with permission.

Cosden and Abernathy (1990) identified four roles for teachers in the use of microcomputer technology, each focusing on defining a place for computers within the curriculum. Figure 14.7 describes the four roles and the strengths and weaknesses of each. These approaches provide a foundation for technology planning, as was previously discussed.

## Adapting Technology for Students with Disabilities

As discussed throughout this text, planning and adapting for the unique needs of all students must occur throughout the educational planning process. This is critical for the success of facilitating the use of technology for students with disabilities. Brown (1988) has provided suggestions that are helpful for teachers who are using computers with students with learning disabilities. Those suggestions appear in Figure 14.8.

| Approach | Strengths | Weaknesses |
|---|---|---|
| *Classroom-based computer use:* "computer instruction within class is configured so that one or two students at a time are engaged with the software while the rest of the students are assigned to other activities" (p. 36). | • Allows teacher to select activities he or she thinks are best for students.<br>• Enables teacher to be present if help is needed.<br>• Assists in providing individualization for students. | • Content area integration between computer users and nonusers is low.<br>• Individualized planning is of great importance.<br>• Direct monitoring of student progress is difficult. |
| *Lab-based microcomputer use (teacher-supervised):* "The teacher assumes major responsibility for the microcomputer activities of his or her class during the scheduled lab period" (p. 36). | • Allows for integration of the computer into curriculum, thus eliminating the problem of computer-based activity for some students and not for others.<br>• Allows for direct instruction. | • Teacher must have interest and time for training in computer technology. |
| *Lab-based microcomputer use (computer specialist and teacher cooperation):* "Responsibilities for instruction are shared by the computer specialist and the teacher; the specialist has the major responsibility for implementation of computer instruction, while the teacher maintains responsibility for planning the instruction" (pp. 36–37). | • Allows planning and monitoring time during the computer session.<br>• Allows teacher to rely on the specialist for technology knowledge.<br>• Enables both specialist and teacher to use their individual expertise. | • Problems may arise if communication between computer specialist and teacher does not remain open.<br>• Specialist does not have time to learn specific information about special students. |
| *Lab-based microcomputer instruction (computer specialist-supervised):* "Instructional responsibilities are assigned to the computer specialist" (p. 37). | | • Specialist needs training as an educator but frequently does not have such training.<br>• Computer activities are separated from curriculum. |

**FIGURE 14.7**

Approaches to computer use.

*Source:* From Cosden, M. A., & Abernathy, T. V. (1990). Microcomputer use in the schools: Teacher roles and instructional options. *Remedial and Special Education, 11,* 31–38. Copyright 1990 by Pro-Ed, Inc. Adapted and reprinted with permission.

| Perceptual Problems | Characteristics | Computer Difficulty | General Teaching Suggestions |
|---|---|---|---|
| Visual figure-ground problems | Difficulty seeing visual material from a computer background. | • Reading one line of type in single-spaced copy.<br>• Locating the cursor.<br>• Finding a particular menu command.<br>• Locating a key on the keyboard.<br>• Tracking back and forth between the keyboard and screen. | • Use sense of touch to teach.<br>• Use verbal explanation for commands.<br>• Explain each step and observe as the student practices.<br>• Color code keyboard.<br>• Keep work areas clear.<br>• Tape-record commands to go with written directions. |
| Visual sequencing problems | Difficulty seeing items that occur in sequence. | • Difficulty typing.<br>• Difficulty reading. | • Practice placing pictures in order. |
| Visual discrimination problems | Difficulty seeing distinctive characters and differences. | • Problems distinguishing between letters. | • Practice selecting one color of item from other colors. |
| Auditory figure-ground problems | Difficulty receiving or processing information heard against a competing background. | • May not hear sounds of computer in a noisy area. | • Give directions visually and orally. |
| Auditory sequencing problems | Difficulty hearing sounds that occur in sequence. | • Problem if commands are given orally in sequence. | • Have students repeat directions. |
| Auditory discrimination problems | Difficulty distinguishing differences in sounds. | | • Provide a written sheet of directions or instructions. |

**FIGURE 14.8**
Microcomputer use for specific disabilities.

*Source:* Brown, D. (1988). Be a computer tutor for people with learning disabilities. In H. J. Murphy (Ed.), *Proceedings of the fourth annual conference: Technology and persons with disabilities* (pp. 91–104). Northridge: California State University. Copyright 1988 by H. J. Murphy. Adapted with permission.

The following points are important considerations when planning to use technology in any instructional setting. (Thanks to Dr. Mike Behrmann from George Mason University who originally contributed this information for one of our grant projects.)

### Benefits to Students: Teacher-Directed Activities

- Enables students who are physically unable to generate characters or speech to write, problem-solve, and communicate
- Provides opportunity to learn by doing in a multisensory environment
- Provides material at an individualized pace for initial instruction, review, remediation, and enrichment
- Organizes material in concrete, consistent manner with precise reasonable, attainable goals
- Promotes mastery learning by setting achievable expectations and necessary repetition
- Demonstrates visible proof of progress
- Encourages interactive exploration and use
- Develops studying and self-organizational strategies

### Benefits to Students: User-Driven Activities

- Expands imagination
- Provides intellectual challenge and stimulation by mastering a machine while accomplishing a task
- Encourages independence
- Builds self-esteem
- Provides platform for collaboration with peers for project development
- Creates, edits, and revises original text, graphics, sounds, pictures, and videos
- Makes available materials that are more interactive than textbooks; hypermedia

### Benefits to Educators

- Educators grade book for instant calculation
- Personalized letters are sent to parents containing similar information; mail merges from database into word processing; utilizes mailing labels from databases
- Record management; databases of student information
  Attendance
  Anecdotes
  Student contracts
  Learning style log
  Field trips

- Legible student reports that are easily revisable
- Material generation that is consistent and clear
  Tests and quizzes
  Outlines
  Handouts and displays
  Demonstrations
  Electronic chalkboard
  Discussion prompts
- Readability levels of textbooks and passages used in instruction
- Visual data banks from overheads to handouts to slide shows to multimedia
- Potential for electronic field trips and distance learning with telecommunication facilitation link to other communities, using telephone, fax send/receive capabilities

### Benefits of Using Computers in the Classroom: Types of Computer Applications

*Individual activities*

- Tutorial: Information presented sequentially with demonstration, examples, and practice; may branch to other examples for remediation or enrichment based upon student performance.
- Drill and practice: information presented for practice without guidance. Many math, reading, and spelling programs take this form.
- Simulation: a real-life example of environment reproduced in a computer-based activity to save cost, materials, or exposure to risk. Examples include flight simulation, city management, and the supervisor of a nuclear power plant.
- Tool: user-driven application with open-ended opportunity. Examples include word processing, database, spreadsheet, telecommunications, drawing, painting, and integrated programs.

*Small group (one computer without additional hardware)*

- Writing partners for conferencing, editing, revising
- Teacher-student or student-student conferencing
- Collaborative problem solving based upon software design
- Students teaching others how to use particular programs
- Experimental design software using probes to gather data
- Project development and presentation

*Whole class (usually requires additional hardware for display purposes)*

- Video or laser disc (requires a monitor and sometimes a computer)

- Liquid crystal display (LCD) projection of any program (requires an overhead projector and screen or blank wall)
- Large screen monitor to display any program
- Writing rotation (requires more than one computer as students enter information on one computer, then rotate to another at designated time intervals)
- Class simulation (either software driven or teacher structured, such as creating and managing a business)
- Multimedia projects (linking student-gathered images, text, charts, and graphs, sound animation, and full motion video) to demonstrate particular concepts or skills

*English*

- Writing process (outline, enter, edit-revise, final, share)
- Publishing
- Reading (electronic books on disk)
- Electronic field trips (expand audience for writing, create links with other schools, including taking responsibility for sharing with younger students)
- Vocabulary practice (SAT review)
- Spelling drill and practice, editing using spell checks
- Vocabulary words stored and manipulated as a database
- Auditory word processing, text converted to synthesized speech for additional cues
- Writing with alternative fonts, sizes, styles, and color
- Note taking and outlining
- Word selection using an electronic thesaurus
- Templates for writing to trigger ideas and expression

*Math*

- Drill and practice and tutorial programs
- Supposer software to test geometrical, graphing, algebraic, and trigonometric concepts
- Spreadsheets enabling experimentation with numbers and formulas
- Real-life math experiences: budgetary planning, tax preparation, insurance, and amortization rates
- Writing across the curriculum

*Social studies*

- Simulations enabling "you were there" experiences
- Electronic encyclopedias, atlases

- Mapping skills using demographics and visuals
- Inquiry learning model (ClarisWorks World DB)
  Asking questions
  Stating hypotheses
  Reaching conclusions
  Interpreting
  Classifying
  Self-directed study
  Testing hypotheses
  Observing
  Synthesizing
- Writing across the curriculum

*Science*

- Experimental simulations
- Visual Almanac: Playground Physics
- Problem-solving activities
- Date compilation and manipulation
- Probeware to gather data directly by attaching sensitive probes to a computer
- Image/slide presentation via laser disc, CD-ROM
- Observation of change by entering data linked to graphs and charts that adjust automatically to data
- Writing across the curriculum

*Career and technical education*

- Software tools matched to specific jobs, such as computer-assisted design (CAD) or automotive repair troubleshooting
- Simulated workplace experiences, from interviewing to résumé writing to time card management
- Virtual reality and robotics

*Fine arts*

- Artistic expression and design
- Musical expression and conversion of playing an instrument to musical notation using a MIDI interface

*Foreign language*

- Drill and practice

- HyperGlot: Learn to Speak series (hear, read, write, speak the target language in French, Spanish, and English)
- Laser discs for interactive discussions
- A future for online translation

### Student-Centered Activities: How May They Benefit?

- Organization (file systematic structure: naming, saving, long-term storage)
  *Word processing:* editing, review, text sizing, text to speech capacity, spell checking, grammar checking, outlining, enhanced style, color, alignment, spacing
  *Database:* long- and short-term memory, searching, sorting, presentation of information in different formats, merge for correspondence, mailing labels, pattern searches
  *Spreadsheet:* numeric grid and structured cells containing text, numbers, or formulas
- Time saver (benefits through repeated use)
- Graphic user interface promotes user friendliness (Macintosh or Windows display use icons, pull-down menus, windows, dialogue boxes; therefore, no memorization of commands is necessary)
- Learning by doing in an interactive, multisensory environment
- Learning principles: direct instruction, mastery learning, overlearning, and automatically, built-in performance monitoring, alternative learning styles
- Kinesthetic feedback from moving mouse, using keyboard, coupled with visual feedback
- Writing process assisted at each stage, concluding with legible, customized printouts
- Computer-aided design and drawing
- Cooperative learning: teacher and student focus together on screen. Computer becomes mediator in relationship, place of focus for all involved. The computer can facilitate interaction
- Conversational writing: many dyslexic individuals have strong oral expressive skills. Whole language or language experience activities enable students to write for self and others. The display is always consistent; characters formed exactly the same way
- High-resolution computer screens make material easier to read and comprehend
- Normalization: by using machines that others use in school and in the working world, students experience inclusion rather than exclusion
- Creation of banners, posters, signs, greeting cards, newsletters, art, sound, animation, video stills, and film

- Electronic felt board for designing, cutting, and pasting graphics, text, numeric, chart, sound, animation, and video objects
- Enrichment: access and motivation to higher-order thinking skills
- Outreach via networking or telecommunications

*The future becomes present*

- Access to reference materials (from electronic encyclopedias and atlases to bulletin boards to online services including home shopping, world awareness, travel, connections with other individuals)
- Multimedia
  Original drawings, paintings, music, photography, movie footage, special effects, transitions, "video and audio capture"
  Transfer from teacher centered to user centered
  Project oriented
  Research oriented
  Massive text, sound, and visual databases, archives, such as encyclopedias that include actual video footage and sound from famous people
- Language translation
- Optical character recognition enabling text pages to be scanned into a computer and the text separated into words to be edited, defined, or even spoken
- Voice input to direct the computer without hands
- Connectivity between machines: multimedia entertainment centers, telephone, video searching, selecting, creating
- Extended robotics
- Personal digital assistants and laptops for portable access, including machines that read handwritten input

# CHAPTER 15

## *Adapting Student Evaluation*

*Contributions by Debra Gibson*

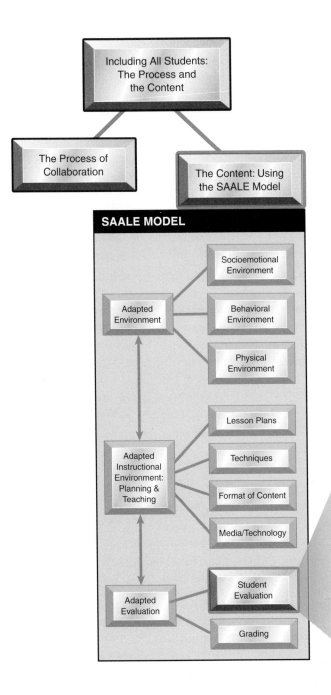

**SAALE MODEL**

Including All Students:
The Process and
the Content

The Process of
Collaboration

The Content: Using
the SAALE Model

Adapted
Environment

Socioemotional
Environment

Behavioral
Environment

Physical
Environment

Adapted
Instructional
Environment:
Planning &
Teaching

Lesson Plans

Techniques

Format of Content

Media/Technology

Adapted
Evaluation

Student
Evaluation

Grading

**Chapter-at-a-Glance**

Problems of Students in
Testing Situations

A Model for Adapting the
Classroom Test

Curriculum-Based Assessment

Student Structure and
Evaluation

Marking or Grading Tests

Since the passage of PL 94-142, general and special educators have been working together to modify curricula, adapt lesson plans, and alter classroom environments to meet the needs of students with mild disabilities. But considerably less attention has been given to the evaluation of such students.

Now, the emphasis in education and educational reform is accountability. "It is not an exaggeration to say that the core component of the educational reform movement of the 1990s is (was) accountability. Education in the United States has been criticized for allowing students to leave school without the skills necessary to compete in a global economy, and increasing pressure is being applied at every level of the system to improve student achievement" (National Association of State Directors of Special Education, Inc., 1997).

As we move into this chapter, it may be helpful to develop an understanding of the most current issues relating to assessment:

- *School Improvement:* Schools strive to improve all aspects of their system.
- *Standards:* Outcomes established by states. All students must achieve.
- *Statewide Assessment:* State tests developed to test if students meet state standards.
- *High Stakes:* The state tests have become high stakes for educators, students, and parents because it affects pass/fail rates, graduation rates, and funding.
- *School Superintendents:* Must have high scores on state tests for their districts. High scores are tied to accreditation, accreditation to funds—and excellent schools to community pride.
- *Alternate Assessment:* State test for students with selected disabilities. An alternate test to the regular state test. The test is established by each state.
- *School Principals:* Are pressured to have school meet the standards to compete within their district.
- *Teachers:* High student scores on state tests reflect good teaching and sometimes job tenure.
- *Students:* Personal high scores on state tests are needed for grade advancement and high school graduation.
- *Parents:* State tests scores for students reflect personal pride.
- *Community:* School districts with excellent state scores draw populations—high real estate—and an overall sense of community pride.

School improvement is tied to accreditation; accreditation is tied directly to funding and community pride. We continually hear about standards. Regardless of whether you are in Virginia, with their "standards of learning," or in another state, there is a state assessment of children and their achievement. Every state is more focused on outcome-based results. In the past, generally, students with special needs were excluded from participation in these assessments, or if students with disabilities were allowed modifications, their scores were not included in the total picture for that district. A publication, *NCEO Policy Directions* (1997), indicated that in 35 states, separate results for students with disabilities were not included in the states' reports. Nine states had separate results for students with disabilities included in general education reports. Two states had results for students with disabilities included, but in a separate report. One state had separate results for students with disabilities included in general and separate reports. Three states had no accountability report at all for students with disabilities.

Why are scores not reported of students with disabilities who indeed take the assessment? In some cases, could it be out of fear that it may lower the districts' scores? More often it is that modifications change the intended purpose of the test. For example, if you read a child a reading test, you are not getting a score of how that child reads and comprehends; instead you are measuring listening comprehension, not reading comprehension, and therefore are getting a score on how the child listens and comprehends. Therefore, the modification alters the purpose of the test.

A common saying heard more recently is that "what gets measured, gets taught." Much of the focus of the national reform movement has been in the area of general education, because there was no systematic collection of data on the achievement results of students with disabilities. Therefore, monies to improve education were intended for general education purposes. With the reauthorization of IDEA, students with disabilities are to be included in the state assessments, with accommodations if appropriate, or an alternate assessment for students who cannot participate in the state assessment. Each state can determine what they consider to be the "high stakes" tests or barrier tests. The National Center on Education Outcomes (1997) found:

- In the states where "high stakes" testing was required, more students were retained;
- Of those students retained, indirect evidence might suggest that more of these students drop out of school. (pp. 9–10)

Standards are a hot topic today and they are important. They have helped unify the curriculum used across a state. In the past when a child transferred within a state, the curriculum in one part of the state could be very different than that in another part of the state. We are becoming a very transient population. If we want to prepare students to be a part of a global society, then truly, curriculums shouldn't be extremely different even from state to state. So we should view standards in a positive light.

A phrase used more consistently now in discussions on standards is that they apply to *all* students. This has and will continue to be a major challenge for education. "All students need to be a part of the accountability system so that they benefit from instructional changes and educational reforms that are implemented in response to information on assessment results. The idea that all students should be included in the accountability process is based on three assumptions:

1. All students can learn.
2. Schools are responsible for measuring the progress of learners.
3. The learning progress of all students should be measured (NCEO, 1996).

**FIGURE 15.1**
Teachers' positions on
big tests.

*Source:* From Henry,
Tamara. (2000, July 13). It's
about helping all children
succeed: Single test score
shouldn't carry most
importance. *USA Today,*
p. 10D. © 2000 *USA Today.*
Reprinted with permission.

## Teachers stake out positions on big tests

High-stakes tests have a place in an overall school reform program.

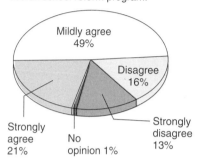

One result of high-stakes tests is that school districts focus more help on low-performing schools and students who need it the most.

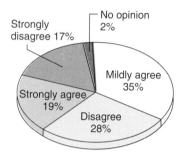

No single test score can be considered a definitive measure of a student's knowledge.

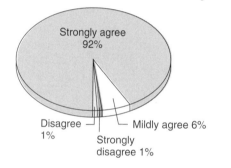

Students take too many tests.

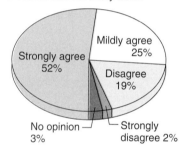

"It is estimated that approximately 85% of students with disabilities, many of whom have been excluded for assessments, are able to participate with or without accommodations" (Ysseldyke, Thurlow, McGrew, & Shriner, 1994). This issue will continue to evolve and change over the course of the next few years. Be involved in the discussions. Parents and politicians need to hear from those "on the frontline" about their perceptions, problems, and successes. In some states it seemed to teachers and administrators that major reform began in the "blink of an eye" (and in some cases, without their input). Their jobs changed rapidly, and their job security felt threatened— all because of emphasis placed on test scores, money, and accreditation.

Stakes are high across the nation. The presidential election of 2000 demonstrated how U.S. educational standards are at the forefront of concern. As always, change is hard and sometimes paced too fast for the public. Even though educators would like standards to improve, their position reflects concern on tests and single test scores. Shown in Figure 15.1, *USA Today* and the American Federation of Teachers (AFT), in an unscientific survey of educators, found that teachers are split on whether high-stakes tests have a place in school reform, agree that high-stakes tests place the focus

**TABLE 15.1**
Percent of accommodations used on basic standard tests.

| Accommodations | Reading | Math |
|---|---|---|
| **Timing/Scheduling** | | |
| Extend the time allotted to complete the test | 128 (49%) | 117 (45%) |
| Allow frequent breaks during testing | 92 (36%) | 78 (30%) |
| Administer test in several sessions over course of day | 54 (21%) | 46 (18%) |
| Alter time of day that test is administered | 38 (15%) | 32 (12%) |
| **Setting** | | |
| Small group administration | 117 (45%) | 109 (42%) |
| Separate room administration | 106 (41%) | 99 (38%) |
| Administration using study carrel | 35 (14%) | 34 (13%) |
| Alternate site administration (e.g., hospital) | 27 (10%) | 24 (9%) |
| **Presentation** | | |
| Repeated directions | 70 (27%) | 60 (23%) |
| Short segment books | 38 (15%) | 34 (13%) |
| Large print | 37 (14%) | 32 (12%) |
| Audiocassettes | 29 (11%) | 40 (15%) |
| Sign language assistance | 28 (11%) | 26 (10%) |
| Braille versions | 22 (8%) | 20 (8%) |
| Magnification devices | 22 (8%) | 20 (8%) |
| **Response** | | |
| Answers in test booklet | 66 (25%) | 68 (26%) |
| Answers recorded | 37 (14%) | 31 (12%) |
| Dictate to scribe | 29 (11%) | 27 (10%) |
| Sign language assistance | 25 (10%) | 23 (9%) |
| Braille writer | 21 (8%) | 18 (7%) |
| Tape-record responses | 21 (8%) | 20 (8%) |
| Word processor | 20 (8%) | 19 (7%) |

*Note:* Frequencies and percentages are based on the 259 returned surveys.
*Source:* Special Education Teacher Responses to the 1997 Basic Standards Testing. (1997). Minneapolis, MN: NCEO, p. 5.

on low-performing students, agree that no single test score can be considered a definitive measure of a student's knowledge, and agree that students take too many tests.

The issue of what accommodations are used and should be allowed on Basic Standard Tests is relevant. The Minnesota Department of Children, Families, and Learning and the University of Minnesota (1997) conducted a statewide survey to find what teachers thought regarding accommodations and state tests. Tables 15.1

**TABLE 15.2**
Common classroom instructional strategies teachers would like to include on basic standard tests.

| Common Instructional Supports | |
| --- | --- |
| **Adapt Instructional Materials** | **Frequency (Percent)** |
| Reduce the number of items | 186 (72%) |
| Give child models of correctly completed work | 176 (68%) |
| Other | 62 (24%) |
| **Adapt Instructional Methods** | |
| Highlight key points | 186 (72%) |
| Use checklists to guide student | 111 (42%) |
| Use self-monitoring sheet | 100 (39%) |
| Other | 51 (20%) |

| Possible Testing Supports Not Currently Allowed in Guidelines | |
| --- | --- |
| **Presentational Format** | **Frequency (Percent)** |
| Interpretation of directions | 180 (69%) |
| Highlight key words or phrases in directions | 174 (67%) |
| Clarify directions beyond script | 162 (63%) |
| Provide additional examples | 135 (52%) |
| Increase spacing between items | 131 (51%) |
| Increase size of answer bubbles | 91 (35%) |
| Use computer-administered test | 82 (32%) |
| Other | 47 (18%) |
| **Response Format** | |
| Point to response | 90 (35%) |
| Use sign language | 59 (23%) |
| Other | 37 (14%) |
| **Timing and Scheduling** | |
| Extend sessions over several days | 161 (63%) |
| More frequent breaks | 148 (57%) |

*Note:* Frequencies and percentages are based on the 259 returned surveys.
*Source:* Special Education Teacher Responses to the 1997 Basic Standards Testing. (1997). Minneapolis, MN: NCEO. p. 6.

and 15.2 present accommodations used on state tests and strategies teachers would like to include on Basic Standard Tests. Accommodation strategies most commonly are decided by states and not teachers.

Finding accommodations for students with disabilities to use when taking state tests is one way of leveling the playing field. However, many students with disabilities cannot take tests designed for most students, and nationally on July 1, 2000, *all* students had to be included within the state assessment process.

# ALTERNATE ASSESSMENT

States are now in the process of developing an alternate assessment for those students who do not participate in the state-required assessment as required in the recently reauthorized IDEA. Each state's alternate assessment will look different; therefore, there may be little consistency from state to state.

> There is confusion about eligibility for alternate assessments. In general, it is agreed that alternate assessments are an option to be made available only to students with the most significant support needs. Both the Assistant Secretary of the Office of Special Education and Rehabilitative Services and the Assistant Secretary of the Office of Civil Rights have indicated in a public letter (September 29, 1997) that the alternate assessment is for "small numbers of students whose IEPs specify that they should be excluded from regular assessments, including some students with significant cognitive abilities." (NCEO, 1998, p. 4)

Alternate assessments were required to be in place by July 1, 2000. States have developed, field-tested, and are still refining this assessment. Training is taking place nationwide. Most will look like a "collection" of student achievements or a portfolio. The students involved in these assessments, again, are your most involved students. The assessments will document their progress in areas similar to the state assessment, and the scores will be reported in the state's report for accreditation. Kentucky was one of the first states to develop an alternate assessment. This is a process (and product) that will continue to develop and change.

## Classroom Evaluation Issues

The term *evaluation* can cover test questions, grading systems, graduation requirements, and competency testing. Special education aims to foster student achievement and potential by individualizing educational programming. As a result, both general and special educators need to recognize the impact that testing, grading, and graduation have on the achievement and self-concept of students. Students need rewards for effort and for attaining goals; therefore, teachers must use evaluation methods that enable students to demonstrate mastery. Mastery must be based on individual student ability or potential, not on the norm. If a student with disabilities could achieve at standard levels, educators would not be providing special services.

Robbins and Harway (1977) point out that "the school-age period is crucial in the development of a child's view of himself" (p. 356). They further explain that the student with disabilities experiences a wide variety of successes and failures that tend to interfere with the development of a sense of identity. In particular, Robbins and Harway demonstrate that, if teachers give students with learning disabilities positive feedback, those students gradually set more realistic goals for themselves.

But because they have encountered a great many failures in school, students with learning disabilities may need constant reinforcement before they become convinced that they can achieve.

Therefore, as teachers evaluate the progress of the student with mild disabilities in the general classroom, they need to consider the student's cognitive and affective development. To ensure student progress, teachers should select the most appropriate and nondiscriminatory method of evaluation. Educators can meet the needs of students by using alternative evaluation techniques. This chapter looks at ways of adapting tests for students, and chapter 16 ends the book with a discussion of alternative grading procedures.

If the primary goal for most students is mastery of concepts, teachers must find ways to give students with mild disabilities opportunities to demonstrate proficiency to general classroom teachers, doubting and unaccepting peers, and themselves. If teachers persist in using traditional testing techniques, they further disable the students that the law attempts to protect. While modifications in curricula and instructional procedures are more prevalent today in general elementary and secondary classrooms, many teachers still resist changing the construction, administration, or site of a test. Many teachers consider the traditional test sacred and thus the only appropriate instrument of evaluation. These same teachers often believe that if the student with mild disabilities cannot demonstrate mastery via this one instrument under the same conditions as everyone else in the classroom, then that student has not achieved and does not deserve a passing grade.

However, such teachers do not realize that frequently the student may indeed have mastered the concept but is simply unable to demonstrate that mastery unless certain modifications are made in the test. What the student lacks are the skills necessary to succeed in a traditional setting. Although some students with disabilities may not reach the same goals as their nondisabled peers, others will surpass their peers through hard work, determination, and perseverance. As John Dewey commented in 1937, each child is "equally an individual and entitled to equal opportunities of development of his own capacity, be they large or small in range" (Dewey, 1937, pp. 458–459).

Before adapting a test, the teacher should evaluate test objectives to see if the test is appropriate. To evaluate test objectives, the teacher should ask the following questions:

- Is content validity present in the test?
- Does the test measure what it is intended to measure?
- Does the test evaluate the skills taught rather than more complex skills or concepts that were not?
- Is the test designed to reflect student knowledge rather than speed, ability to follow complicated directions, or vocabulary?
- Does the test tap knowledge in the same way retention was taught?

# PROBLEMS OF STUDENTS IN TESTING SITUATIONS

Before they have even put pen to paper, many students have encountered problems that could result in test failure. The teacher needs to understand the problems that can arise before and during a testing situation. Then the teacher can move equitably to evaluate students and assist them with solutions.

## Poor Comprehension

*Comprehension* means the ability to understand clearly what is said or explained. Students with mild disabilities often do not understand verbal directions. When the teacher gives a series of directions, they cannot recall each step correctly. Without a clear understanding of what to do or how to proceed, they might either proceed incorrectly or turn in papers with only their names on the page. Certainly, such responses do not accurately indicate the full extent of the student's knowledge. Similarly, written directions are often too lengthy or complicated for the student with mild disabilities. The reading level alone may be above the student's instructional level. Directions may contain words or phrases that the student does not know, may instruct the student to perform several operations, or may ask the student to follow more than one procedure. For example, a student with poor comprehension would have difficulty following and understanding these directions:

1. Write a sentence containing a gerund.
2. Draw a circle around the gerund.
3. Indicate whether the gerund is the subject, direct object, predicate nominative, or object of the preposition by writing S., D.O., P.N., or O.P. above the gerund.

A related difficulty involves abstractions. Some students with mild disabilities can recall facts and deal with concrete ideas but do not respond well to evaluative questions or those requiring inferences or deductive reasoning. For example, the student may understand how to write a paragraph but have trouble writing several paragraphs on an abstract topic such as "Ecology in Action in Our Community."

## Auditory Perceptual Problems: Teacher Variables

Students with auditory perceptual problems cannot process auditory information quickly and easily. The students can hear, but problems in learning occur when they try to process what is heard. However, auditory problems associated with teacher variables can be avoided. The teacher who administers tests orally, for example, greatly penalizes students with auditory deficits. Even simple spelling tests pose problems. Some teachers proceed too fast, not allowing the student enough time to sound out the words and transfer the sounds into their written forms. Some teachers simply call out the words without clearly delineating each syllable or sound.

Some students may experience only minor difficulty with spelling tests but have major problems when the teacher administers quizzes or chapter tests orally. The student must not only process the question through the auditory system—a giant undertaking—but also transfer the information to paper. Sometimes this task is virtually impossible. In addition, the student with auditory disabilities simply cannot recall previously asked questions. Thus, a traditional technique prevents the student from demonstrating concept mastery.

## Auditory Perceptual Problems: Environmental Variables

While teachers can adjust the amount of information they present verbally or the number of tests they administer orally, they may have little control over certain environmental auditory distractions both inside and outside the classroom. Frequently, teachers grow accustomed to a reasonable amount of background noise or sounds and become oblivious to these distractions. Students with auditory problems, however, are not as fortunate. A variety of environmental variables may distract these students from their class work or from verbal information the teacher is presenting. These distractions include noise outside a window; conversations in an adjoining classroom; learning module distractions; announcements on the P.A. system; and incidental noise arising from peers, such as students asking questions, students whispering among themselves, and teachers reprimanding students for talking at unauthorized times.

Because many of these auditory distractions cannot be eliminated or modified, the teacher should realize that, even for a few seconds, these conditions create an environment hostile to learning and one not ideal for testing. The teacher must guard against assuming that, if students would just pay attention, they would be able to understand or, if they would just concentrate more, they could complete the assigned task or test. Students with auditory perceptual problems often find it difficult to discriminate between the sounds coming from the front of the classroom (such as instructions from the teacher) and the sounds filtering into the room from elsewhere. For some, concentrating and remaining focused on the task become virtually impossible in a classroom with normal environmental sounds. For students experiencing auditory difficulties, alternative instructional methods may be needed or alternative testing sites may prove helpful.

## Visual-Perceptual Problems: Teacher Variables

Many students experience problems when they receive information visually. Again, the problem for the student is not an inability to see but an inability to process information received visually. Teacher variables often contribute to the student's visual problem.

For example, most teachers use the chalkboard as an instructional tool. They post spelling words, homework assignments, and other reminders on the board for students to copy into their notebooks. A number of teachers even write tests on the board, while others require students to work math problems, diagram sentences, or complete other tasks at the chalkboard. Many teachers assume that information they write correctly on the board will be copied correctly into notebooks.

The majority of students in the class succeed with ease, but any students with visual-perceptual difficulties experience a variety of problems. Primarily, they have trouble transferring information from the board to their paper or notebook. They may transpose numbers, such as page numbers assigned for homework, or interchange letters, such as spelling words or key terms for a new unit. Students then memorize the information they copied incorrectly, leading to a misrepresentation of their abilities and poor test scores. Copying homework assignments incorrectly leads to additional confusion. At night, students open their books to unfamiliar pages and problems they may not know how to solve; the following day, the teacher may be suspicious of the student's explanation for not completing the assignment. The student with visual-perceptual problems encounters some of the same difficulties when attempting to take a test written on the board, such as trouble transferring information to paper, understanding written directions or questions, and copying correctly. As if these problems were not enough, visual distractions on or near the chalkboard clutter the student's field of vision—for example, homework assignments on the same board as the test, spelling words in another corner, and bulletin boards adjacent to the chalkboard. The majority of teachers keep a clean chalkboard, but not all of them do.

The teacher's handwriting also affects how a student responds to any test. Although most teachers' printing or cursive handwriting ranges from average to excellent, not all teachers can claim such a distinction. Of course, typed tests are better than handwritten ones, but teachers cannot always have their tests typed. A good test does not require typing, but legibility is a must. Teachers with unusual cursive styles should print. If printing also presents problems, the teacher should ask someone else to write the test. The teacher also must ensure that all copies are legible. Not all schools possess the newest or most efficient duplicating equipment, but unreadable copies are inexcusable. Students must be able to decipher the questions to pass the test.

Most teachers use written tests in one form or another—multiple choice, true-false, matching, fill in the blank or completion, essay, and others. The student with visual-perceptual problems will encounter many obstacles with such tests. For example, a teacher may give students a matching test with a long column of descriptive statements and an equally lengthy column of answer choices. Although students may know the answer to the first descriptive statement, they must peruse the entire column of answer choices, from top to bottom, to locate the correct answer. Students spend unnecessary time searching for letter equivalents to answers, sometimes to the extent that they are unable to complete the test. Even more common, some students may be oblivious to time and consequently spend the allotted period on just the matching section, not even attempting the remaining sections.

Length can also become a psychological barrier to success on written tests. At-risk students usually have failed repeatedly. The majority of such students equate tests with unpleasantness. If these students were asked about previous tests or their ability to pass tests, their responses probably would be negative. A lengthy test of three or more pages may discourage students, especially those with visual problems. They may attempt the first page and stop when they realize they cannot finish, or they may feel defeated upon first examining the test. Teachers may overhear remarks such as "I know I don't know the answers to that many questions" or "I know I'll never finish, so why should I even begin?" The number of questions or problems per page may visually overwhelm other students. Their eyes may busily scan and rescan the page; as a result, they cannot focus on individual questions or problems and thus cannot proceed.

Some students with visual problems have difficulty identifying, recognizing, or decoding symbols and abbreviations. Simple mathematical symbols such as $+$, $-$, $>$, $<$, and $=$ may cause visual turmoil for students with visual-perceptual problems. They may confuse one symbol with another, or they may have trouble associating the symbol with its written equivalent—for example, $+$ with *plus.* Students with pronounced visual difficulties usually experience extreme anxiety when attempting to solve algebraic equations like this one:

$$\frac{(2x + 4)}{2} - 4 = (2x + 6) + 3(2x + 3x)$$

Of course, not all students with disabilities will take algebra, but some will need to complete the course if their goal includes a college degree. Others may not take algebra but will encounter basic mathematical symbols throughout their academic and postacademic years.

## Visual Perceptual Problems: Environmental Variables

Visual distractions and stimuli abound, both inside and outside the classroom. The degree of distraction varies from student to student. For some students, most visual distractions are momentary. For others, a single distraction can completely disrupt their present visual field, their ability to concentrate, and their ability to keep working. The distraction may originate outside a classroom window or inside the room, as a result of students moving at their desks or turning in their papers, from peers making motions or gestures, or from visitors entering the classroom. Whatever the source, these disruptions cause students with minor visual problems to become temporarily nonfunctional and those with more serious visual problems to remain nonfunctional indefinitely.

## Time Constraints

Teachers generally strive to develop a test to fit the time frame available for giving it. Most teachers attempt to allow extra time for students who work more slowly than others. For students with disabilities, time often plays a major role in taking a test. Within the group of students with disabilities, individuals may have auditory or visual-perceptual problems, motor coordination difficulties, and, frequently, reading problems. Generally, these students are not intentionally slow or lazy, and they do not mean to aggravate the teacher or disrupt the test. Rather, they have real problems caused by identified learning modality deficits. The teacher needs to remember that students with auditory problems may not be able to answer oral questions in the same time frame as students without such a disability. Similarly, students with visual perceptual, motor coordination, or reading problems probably will not be able to complete most tests designed for the general education student. Teachers must try to avoid penalizing students with recognized exceptionalities and give them an opportunity to demonstrate their proficiency.

## Anxiety

Most teachers have experienced test anxiety at least once during their academic lives. Most admit that test anxiety exists and is very real to the individual experiencing it. Teachers need to understand further that the degree of test anxiety varies considerably from student to student. When anxiety makes a student nonfunctional, the teacher should recognize it as a disability similar to disabilities in comprehension, visual and auditory perception, and motor coordination. Anxiety differs from other disabilities, however, because it is usually temporary. Years of failure and negative responses from teachers, peers, and parents result in measurably lower self-concepts for students with mild disabilities. Because many students automatically associate taking a test with failure, they become fearful and anxiety-ridden even at the thought. Fear and anxiety, along with a history of previous failures, may even cause test phobias for a few students. For all practical purposes, these students simply cannot function in a traditional test setting. Others feel anxiety but not to the same extent. For example, they may be extremely hesitant at the beginning of a test because they lack self-confidence, or they may stop midway through the test because they encounter one or two questions they do not know. Others stop working when they realize that their peers have finished and are turning in their papers. Such students want to at least appear normal. They do not want to be the last ones working or be called "dummies." Still other students allow their initial impression of the length or scope of the test to overwhelm them and, like students with test phobias, become nonfunctional for a while. Anxiety, although difficult to measure, influences a student's ability to take and pass a test. Teachers should consider the anxiety level when evaluating a student's performance and attempt to reduce that level as much as possible by adapting the test.

## Embarrassment

Perhaps what most students with disabilities want is to be like everyone else. Identifying with and being accepted by peers is important to any student, but it becomes essential for the student with mild disabilities.

As students mature into adolescence and young adulthood, a desire for peer acceptance and approval becomes even more pronounced. Students with disabilities, who are acutely aware of their academic inabilities, will sometimes sacrifice a passing grade rather than ask the teacher a question and risk embarrassment in front of their peers. Over the years, students learn to hide or disguise their disabilities. They become specialists in looking busy or presenting an attitude that says, "I don't care," rather than admitting they do not understand how to do the work. In addition, a high percentage of students with disabilities will turn in their test papers simply because nearly everyone else in the class has done so; they cannot risk the embarrassment of being the last ones working. When teachers grade their papers and see very few questions answered, they often incorrectly assume that the student did not study.

Students in inclusive settings are also sensitive about taking tests that differ from those of their peers. They may realize that they are receiving individualized programming, but they understandably want to maintain the appearance of doing the same work as their peers. Some high school students with mild disabilities insist on taking the general test along with their friends, although they know it will not be scored and an individualized test will be administered in their resource class. Other students willingly take a modified test in the general classroom as long as it closely resembles the one being taken by everyone else. The general teacher must remember that, even though students with mild disabilities need to receive praise from parents and special education teachers, they also need to maintain their pride and self-esteem in the presence of peers.

## A MODEL FOR ADAPTING THE CLASSROOM TEST

Adapting classroom tests for students in the mainstream requires following the three-part model shown in Figure 15.2. Adaptations can be made during test construction or test administration or by providing an alternative test site.

### Adaptations During Test Construction

Test construction may be divided into three separate components: test directions, test items, and test design. This section shows adaptations for each of these components.

*Test directions.* Directions are a critical aspect of test construction. Test directions that are not clear and understandable may cause failure for students before they even try to complete the test. Consider the following suggestions for making test directions clearer for all students.

1. Keep directions short.
2. Keep directions simple; avoid unnecessary words.
3. Type directions.
4. If directions are not typed, print neatly.
5. Place all directions at the beginning of each separate test section.
6. When giving more than one direction, list them vertically.
7. List only one direction in each sentence.
8. Underline the word *directions* to focus the student's attention.

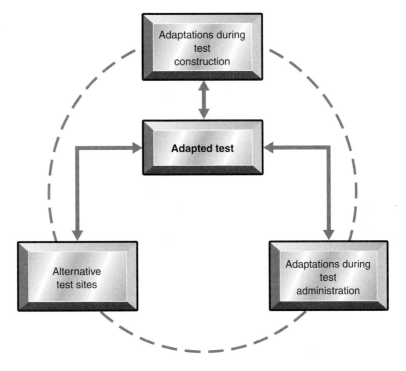

**FIGURE 15.2**
Model for adapting the classroom test.

9. Avoid using words such as *never, not, always,* and *except.* If you must use these words, underline and capitalize them.

10. Define any unfamiliar or abstract words.

11. Color code directions.

12. Avoid making oral directions the only means of communicating the purpose of the test to students. Read directions orally and clearly write them on the test.

13. Tell students the reason or purpose of the test.

14. Go over each direction before the test. Be sure that students understand what they should do.

15. Remember that students who do not clearly understand the directions will be the last to raise their hands and ask for clarification.

16. While the test is in progress, walk around the room and check to see that students are following directions.

17. Teach students that if points are to be lost, they may lose them for not knowing items on the test. They should avoid losing additional points for not following or understanding the test directions.

18. Teach students how to approach tests in a systematic manner. Look over the total test.

19. Read directions to the class at least twice.

*Adapting test items.* The second part of the test construction model is adapting test items. These adaptations do not invalidate or water down the test but simply make test items more appropriate for students experiencing difficulty with the test process. The following suggestions are divided into two types: test items that require simple recognition and those that require structured recall. Remember that a mismatch in testing can occur when we use a type of item that is inappropriate for a student. For example, if a student has difficulty remembering information from recall, a recognition test may be more appropriate.

The five types of test items to be discussed are multiple choice, matching, true-false, fill in the blank, and short answer or essay. Multiple choice, matching, and fill in the blank with a word bank require simple recognition; fill in the blank without a word bank, true-false, and short answer require structured recall.

Multiple-choice items are some of the most useful types of objective test questions. The following suggestions may prove helpful for teachers who are constructing them:

1. Avoid frequent use of fillers. For example:
   a. Either . . . or
   b. All of the above
   c. None of the above

2. Let the student circle the correct answer rather than place answer on an answer sheet or blank form. This reduces the possibility of copying errors when transferring letters to the blanks.

3. Arrange the correct answer and the distractors (incorrect answers) vertically on the page.

   Example: You have a board *48 inches long.* If you cut off a *6-inch piece,* how much is left?
   a. 38 inches
   b. 42 inches
   c. 48 inches

4. Be sure all choices are grammatically consistent.

   Example: Because of poor land and a short growing season, the New England colonies were forced into the economic choice of:
   a. Exporting food
   b. Trading and ship building
   c. Growing and exporting cotton

5. Avoid using more than 10 multiple-choice questions per test.

6. State question and answer choices clearly.

7. Avoid using unnecessary words.

8. Allow and give credit to students if they mark out the choices they know are incorrect answers, even if they did not mark the correct answer. This is an alternative for multiple-choice items that involve thought. Perhaps students cannot determine what is correct, but they can process what's not possible. Both require knowledge of the question.

9. Mark out one or two choices (of four choices) with a black marker for some lower-level students before handing out the test. Usually the choice eliminated is very close to the correct answer and involves thinking.

The matching exercise is designed to measure factual information based on simple association. It is a compact and efficient method of measuring simple relationships. The following suggestions may be helpful when selecting matching items for tests:

1. Place all matching items and choice selections on the same page.

2. Leave extra space between items in columns to be matched.

3. Use homogeneous material for each matching exercise.

4. Use small groups of matching questions. Avoid long matching lists.

5. Have one extra response in one of the columns. For example, if you have 10 items in column A, place 11 choices in column B. This statistically puts the question in the student's favor.

6. Have only one correct answer for each item.

7. Avoid having students draw lines to the correct answer. This may be visually confusing.

8. Keep all matching items brief. The student who has comprehension and reading problems may not be able to process long, wordy items.

9. Place the responses, such as names of explorers, on 3″ × 5″ cards. These become a manipulative exercise. Students can match items to the correct answer by placing the card next to the item. (Thanks to Janice Mael for her suggestion.)

10. Place the list with more lengthy items, usually the descriptive items, in the left-hand column. This makes for less reading and will assist the slow reader.

11. Make a mini–letter bank under the blank to reduce the number of choices.

12. Place the blank for the response after each item in column A.

13. For tests with columns that are reversed, teach students to begin the test working from column B to column A.

14. Teach students to answer questions in reverse.

15. Place the blank before the number in column B.

16. Put responses to matching test items in alphabetical order on the left-hand side to facilitate location of the answer.

Here is an example of a matching test:

| Column A | Column B |
|---|---|
| 1. The island continent | a. North America |
| 2. Bordered by the Atlantic | b. Pacific Ocean |
| 3. Located north of the Mediterranean Sea | c. Africa |
| 4. Bordered by Africa and Asia | d. Indian Ocean |
| 5. The largest ocean | e. Asia |
| 6. Bordered by the Atlantic and Pacific, north of the equator | f. Europe |
| 7. The largest continent | g. Atlantic Ocean |
| 8. Bordered by the Atlantic and Pacific, south of the equator | h. Australia |

The most common use of the true-false test is to measure the student's ability to identify the correctness of statements of fact or definition. The following suggestions for modifications may help teachers construct these items:

1. Avoid stating questions negatively.
2. Avoid long, wordy sentences.
3. Avoid statements that are trivial or do not assess student knowledge.
4. Allow students to circle the correct answer.
5. Avoid using too many true-false questions at one time, preferably no more than 10 items per test.
6. Avoid using *never, not, always,* and *except.* If you must use these words, underline and capitalize them.
7. Avoid having students change false statements to true statements unless you have taught this skill.
8. Place the words *true* and *false* at the end of the sentence.

Example: Imperialism was a cause of World War I. True False

Fill-in-the-blank or completion questions are suitable for measuring knowledge of items, specific facts, methods or procedures, and simple interpretation of data. Because this type of test requires structured recall, it is difficult for many mainstreamed students and should be used sparingly, if at all. In many cases, multiple-choice items may be more appropriate.

If teachers still want to use fill-in-the-blank items, they can attempt to reduce their complexity by using the following suggestions:

1. Write simple and clear test items.
2. Avoid using statements directly from the textbook. Taken out of context, they are frequently too general and ambiguous to be used as test questions.

3. Provide large blanks for students with poor handwriting or motor control problems.

4. Be sure that the blank size matches the response. If the blank is too long or too short, students may think that their response is incorrect.

5. Place the blank at the end of the sentence.

6. Provide word banks for the test.

7. Provide a mini–word bank immediately under the response blank. This reduces memory load and can be implemented on a test that is already constructed.

8. Allow students to circle the correct choice in the mini–word bank.

9. Before the test, tell students whether they will have a word bank on the test.

10. Use a floating word bank that is detached from the test. The student can move the word bank up and down the right side of the page to check for the correct word, placing the words close to the blanks.

11. Have another teacher read your test to check for clear understanding of each item.

12. Place one extra word in the word bank, which statistically puts the test in the student's favor.

13. If a word will be used as a response more than once, list it the appropriate number of times in the word bank.

14. Break the test section into parts: five questions and a six-word word bank. Repeat for each section. For example:

| (1) | (2) | (3) |
|-----|-----|-----|
| jump | stomp | throw |
| run | stop | catch |
| hop | | |

(3) 1. Johnny will _____ the ball to Jim.

(1) 2. After Jim hits the ball he will _____ from base to base.

Teachers use short-answer or essay items to measure learning that cannot be evaluated by objective test items. Most essay or short-answer questions require the student to recall relevant factual information, mentally organize ideas, and write an extensive response. These responses may require skills that are extremely difficult for students with poor organizational abilities or deficient writing skills. Therefore, essay questions should be used sparingly or, with some students, not at all.

Here are some suggestions for using essay questions more effectively with mainstreamed students:

1. Use items that can be answered briefly.

2. Be sure that students know the meaning of clue words, such as *discuss, describe,* and *list.*

3. Underline clue words.

4. Write questions using clue words that correspond to the domain level of the student. For example, *define* is on the knowledge level; *predict* is on the application level.

5. Allow students to outline answers or provide an outline for them.

6. Use structured organizers to organize answers.

7. Make sure that the question is written on the student's independent reading level.

8. Define any unclear items.

9. Word your questions so that the student's task is clearly stated.

10. Use a limited number of essay questions on the test.

11. Always list the point value of each question.

12. Provide space for the response immediately under the question.

13. Allow the student to record the answers rather than write them.

14. Allow extra time to write answers. Remember that some students do not write as quickly as others.

15. Always allow the student to omit one or two essay questions. This reduces anxiety.

16. Provide an answer check sheet that lists the components requested in the response.

17. Indicate on the test whether you expect students' responses to include factual information, inferences, or applications.

18. Always provide study questions for the essay items on the test study guide.

Example: *Compare* and *contrast* life in Germany and the United States. Use this outline to help organize your answer.

   I. Similarities (compare how they are alike)
      A. How is daily life the same in the United States and Germany?
      B. Give two examples
  II. Differences (contrast how they are different)
      A. How is daily life different in the United States and Germany?
      B. Give two examples

*Other test-item adaptations.* In some academic areas, the test item may vary according to subject. For example, in math, computational problems and word problems occur on tests. In science, lab practicals may be used. This section offers suggestions for making adaptations to these approaches.

1. Provide manipulative objects that make the problems more concrete.

2. Avoid mixing different problem formats in the same section. For example, a student with organizational or visual tracking difficulties may be able to solve problem A but may not be able to align the numbers in problem B.

**Problem A**

```
   468
    83
+ 1894
```

**Problem B**

$670 + 40 + 2861 =$

3. Avoid mixing vertical and horizontal problems in the same section. For example, for the student with visual tracking problems or one who has difficulty changing gears from one process to another, the shift in presentation from problem C to problem D may be confusing. It would be better to test the student's knowledge of the two processes in two separate sections of the test.

**Problem C**

```
  8
× 5
```

**Problem D**

$5 \times 6 = $ _____

4. Give formulas and meanings of symbols.

    $<$ means *less than*

5. Give a set of written steps for applying algorithms.

    **Long Division**

    1. Divide
    2. Multiply
    3. Subtract
    4. Check
    5. Bring down

**FIGURE 15.3**

Adaptations for computation problems.

*Source:* Adapted with permission from "Adapting Test Construction for Mainstreamed Mathematics Students" (*Mathematics Teacher*), copyright May 1988 by the National Council of Teachers of Mathematics. All rights reserved.

Computation problems usually require the student to apply an algorithm or a formula to find a numerical answer. Consider the suggestions in Figure 15.3.

Word problems can be very difficult for students with disabilities. The suggestions in Figure 15.4 are helpful during evaluation.

Lab practicals can be used to assess students with mild disabilities. If you've been teaching your students how to operate Bunsen burners, for example, test the

**Adapting Student Evaluation**

1. Use simple sentences. Avoid unnecessary words that may cause confusion.
2. Use a problem context that is relevant to the student's personal experience.
3. Underline or circle key words—for example, *less, more.*
4. Use no more than five word problems per test because they require greater effort to read and understand.
5. Give formulas as reminders of operations to be used.
6. Be sure that the reasoning skills being tested are appropriate to the student's comprehension level. Avoid the use of word problems (with some students) because this use may be testing language and measuring skills above the student's level. For example, a student with a mild disability who has poor reading and comprehension skills may not be able to understand a complex word problem without assistance.

The following example incorporates many of these suggestions:

John lives 3 and 7/10 miles from Fair Oaks Elementary School.

Trish lives 2 and 3/4 miles from school.

Which one lives farther from school? _____

How much farther? _____

**FIGURE 15.4**
Adaptations for word problems.

students by giving them a checklist to work on throughout the lab (Figure 15.5). Let students who need individual help work with a lab partner or in a small group. Follow up with more specific questions, which students should complete with the burner turned off. Teachers can write similar checklist tests for the use of other lab equipment, such as balances, graduated cylinders, and microscopes.

Many students can answer questions better orally than in writing. To test students' safety knowledge, you can make slides of people using improper safety procedures. You can then show these slides and ask students to describe orally which rules are being broken. Another adaptation is to read tests aloud to students with reading disabilities.

For students who learn best through hands-on experiences, you can design tests that evaluate students in a hands-on manner. For example, instead of asking students to label a diagram of an atom on a test, allow them to construct a three-dimensional model of an atom using plastic foam balls. The students can indicate on the model the location and charge of neutrons, protons, and electrons.

*Test design.* Test design is the third aspect of test construction that easily can be adapted. Adaptations in test design include the following:

1. Use test items that reflect techniques you used in teaching. For example, if the students were taught only to recall facts, avoid essay questions.

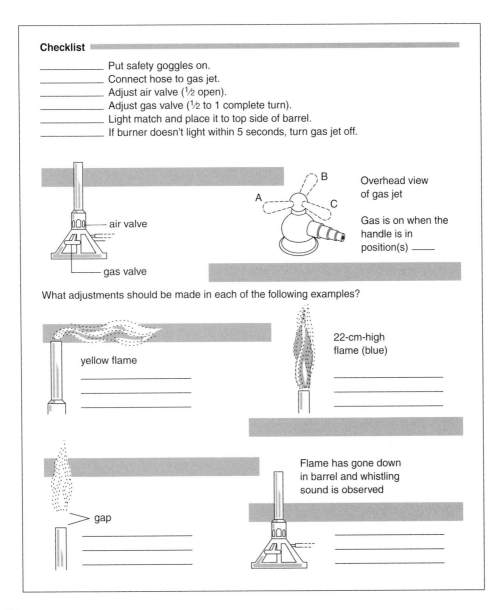

**Checklist**

_____ Put safety goggles on.
_____ Connect hose to gas jet.
_____ Adjust air valve (½ open).
_____ Adjust gas valve (½ to 1 complete turn).
_____ Light match and place it to top side of barrel.
_____ If burner doesn't light within 5 seconds, turn gas jet off.

air valve

gas valve

Overhead view
of gas jet

Gas is on when the
handle is in
position(s) _____

What adjustments should be made in each of the following examples?

yellow flame
_____
_____
_____

22-cm-high
flame (blue)
_____
_____
_____

gap
_____
_____
_____

Flame has gone down
in barrel and whistling
sound is observed
_____
_____
_____

**FIGURE 15.5**

Lab practical for the Bunsen burner.

*Source:* Adapted with permission of NSTA publications from "Stress the Knowledge, Not the Student," by Wood, et al., from *The Science Teacher,* November 1988, published by the National Science Teachers Association, Arlington, Virginia.

2. Type or print legibly. Use large type when available. If you prepare the test in longhand, be sure to list items clearly, concisely, and neatly.

3. Prepare a study guide that matches the design of the test.

4. Adjust readability level of the test to meet the students' needs.

5. Prepare the test in short sections that you can administer individually if necessary.

6. Place one type of question on each page. For example, use one page for multiple-choice questions and another for essay questions.

7. After consulting students privately about personal testing needs, adapt the test to meet those needs.

8. If you use the chalkboard for a test, clear other material from the board, then print or write in large, legible letters. Avoid lengthy tests for students with copying difficulties.

9. Avoid using only oral tests and quizzes.

10. Plan to allow students with disabilities to take tests in the special classroom to overcome problems with time, reading ability, or embarrassment.

11. Clearly duplicate the test using black ink, if available. Avoid using faded purple copies from a duplicating machine for any students, especially those with visual acuity and visual perception difficulties.

12. Use a large sheet of dark construction paper under the test to act as a border. Provide a sheet of paper with a "window frame" cut into it to help in reading the test. This helps students with visual acuity and visual perception problems.

13. If a student has difficulty finishing on time, administer an adapted, shortened version of the test. Another option is split-halves testing, where half the test is administered on one day and the other half on the next day.

14. If a modified test is necessary for an included student, design it to resemble the general test to avoid embarrassment.

15. Arrange tests so that questions that count the most come first. Some students generally work in order and may not finish the test.

16. If possible, use canary yellow paper with black print for the test.

17. Write the point value for each section on the test.

18. Draw a line between math problem rows to help a student finish each row and not get mixed up while moving through the problems.

19. Place a heading for each test section with directions if the directions have changed.

20. Handwriting should be neat and legible.

21. If typing is not possible, print the test.

22. All pages of the test should be numbered.

23. Use a felt marker to divide sections of the test so that the student knows when to move to another set of directions.

24. Watch complexity of sentences so that the test does not become a language test and content is lost.

25. For reading sections, put the reading selection on one page and the questions on a second page. The student can then place reading section and questions side by side.

## Adaptations During Test Administration

The second component of the model for adapting classroom tests (Figure 15.2) involves the administration of the test. Many students with disabilities may need alternative modes of administration when taking the test. Adapting during administration of tests relates directly to the problems that students encounter in the test situation as discussed at the beginning of this chapter. Each problem is listed in Table 15.3 along with suggestions for test administration. General suggestions for

**TABLE 15.3**
Adaptations during test administration.

| Problem | Adaptations |
|---|---|
| Poor comprehension | 1. Give test directions both orally and in written form. Make sure all students clearly understand. |
| | 2. Avoid long talks before the test. |
| | 3. Allow students to tape-record responses to essay questions or entire test. |
| | 4. Allow students to take the test in an alternate test site, usually the resource classroom. |
| | 5. Correct for content only, not for spelling or grammar. |
| | 6. Provide an example of the expected correct response. |
| | 7. Remind students to check tests for unanswered questions. |
| | 8. When the test deals with problem-solving skills, allow use of multiplication tables or calculators during math tests. |
| | 9. Read test aloud for students who have difficulty reading. |
| | 10. Give a written outline for essay questions. |
| | 11. Tape-record instructions and questions for a test. |
| | 12. Use objective rather than essay tests. |
| Poor auditory perception | 1. For oral spelling tests, go slowly, enunciating each syllable and sound distinctly. |
| | 2. Avoid oral tests. |
| | 3. Seat student in a quiet place for testing. |
| | 4. Allow students to take tests in an alternate test site, such as the resource classroom. |
| | 5. Place a TESTING sign on the classroom door to discourage interruptions. |

*(continued)*

TABLE 15.3
Continued.

| Problem | Adaptations |
|---|---|
| Poor visual perception | 1. Give directions orally as well as in written form. |
| | 2. Check students discreetly to see if they are on track. |
| | 3. Give exam orally or tape-record it. |
| | 4. Allow students to take entire test orally in class or the resource room. |
| | 5. Seat students away from distractions (such as windows, door). Use a carrel or put desk facing wall. |
| | 6. Avoid having other students turn in papers during test. |
| | 7. Meet visitors at door and talk in hallway. |
| | 8. Hand a "DO NOT DISTURB—TESTING" sign on the door. |
| | 9. Use alternate test site if student requests it. |
| Student works poorly with time constraints | 1. Allow enough time for students to complete the test. Mainstreamed students may require longer periods of time. |
| | 2. Provide breaks during lengthy tests. |
| | 3. Allow split-halves testing. Give half the test on one day and the remaining half on the second day. |
| | 4. Allow student to take the test in the resource room if necessary. |
| | 5. Allow students to complete only the odd- or even-numbered questions. Circle the appropriate questions for students who may not understand the concept of odd and even. |
| | 6. Use untimed tests. |
| | 7. Give oral or tape-recorded tests. Students with slow writing skills can answer orally to the teacher or on tape. |
| Anxiety/embarrassment | 1. Avoid adding pressure to the test setting by admonishing students to "hurry and get finished" or "do your best; this counts for half of your six-weeks' grade." |
| | 2. Avoid threatening to use a test to punish students for poor behavior. |
| | 3. Give a practice test. |
| | 4. Give a retest if needed. |
| | 5. Don't threaten dire consequences for failure. |
| | 6. Grade on percentage of items completed. |
| | 7. Have students take regular test with class and adapted test in resource room. |
| | 8. Make modified test closely resemble regular test to avoid embarrassing self-conscious students. |
| | 9. Avoid calling attention to mainstreamed students as you help them. |
| | 10. Confer with students privately to work out accommodations for testing. |

1. Students with language or memory deficits often have difficulty with recall of specific information or understanding questions posed in multiple-choice, true-false, or even fill-in-the-blank format. These students often can convey what knowledge they have in a format involving longer answers. (For example, "tell me what you know about the pilgrims, homes, jobs, foods, daily life" or "explain what happens to air when heated."

2. Include a prompt—visual or mnemonic—to remind students of an activity.

3. Include an open-ended question. For example, "What did you learn in this chapter?" "Tell me what you know about magnets."

4. Allow students to take test with three colors of pens to indicate support used (black = took test without any assistance; red = took test with notes; blue = took test with book and notes).

5. Hand out colored stickers to students to place by test section they are choosing not to answer. The stickers may be earned.

6. Children take learning style test (computer disc) and are told of their style preference. Before a test the students gather in common groups based on style strength (visual, auditory, kinesthetic) for study purposes.

   Kinesthetic—Twister, darts, flash cards

   Visual—chalkboard, magazines, flash cards

   Auditory—tape recordings, quizzing orally

7. At the end of each class write down four or five questions about material just covered. This way you will have a study guide, and you will be sure that you have covered the material appearing on the test.

**FIGURE 15.7**
General suggestions for giving tests.

giving tests appear in Figure 15.7. (Thanks to Becky Rhodes and Claire Middleton for their suggestions.)

*Alternative test sites.* Allowing students with disabilities to take their tests in an alternate environment, such as the resource room, is a viable option during the testing situation. Table 15.4 presents some advantages of testing in the resource room.

Modifying tests for resource students is primarily the responsibility of general classroom teachers because they are more familiar with the material presented to the student. However, because the special education teacher knows the individual student's unique strengths and weaknesses, it is best if the general and special education teachers combine their efforts.

To work together to modify any test, general and special education teachers must find opportunities to meet, either during the day or after school. Elementary teachers generally do not have planning periods, so their only option is usually after school. However well intentioned the general and special education teachers

**TABLE 15.4**
Advantages of testing in resource room.

| Specific Problem | Potential Solution |
|---|---|
| Reading difficulties | Oral tests |
| Slow reader | More time |
| Low vocabulary | Questions can be clarified |
| Low comprehension | New vocabulary can be explained |
| | Less pressure |
| | Record test on tape recorder |
| Student embarrassed by taking a test different from one given to peers in regular class | Student has acceptable setting for completing test |
| Student easily confused by verbal or written directions | Student has more opportunity to ask questions and may feel less frustrated |
| Student distracted by activity within regular classroom | Student has a more structured setting that contains fewer distractions |
| Student experiencing test anxiety, frustration | Anxiety reduced |
| | No longer competing with peers |
| | Can work at own pace |
| | Has support of resource teacher |

*Source:* Wood, J., & Englebert, B. (1982). Mainstreaming minimanual. *Instructor, 91*(7), 63–66. Copyright 1982 by Instructor Publications. Reprinted by permission.

may be, faculty meetings, school activities, family commitments, and parent conferences frequently prevent such joint work sessions. Similarly, general and special education teachers on the secondary level rarely share identical planning periods. In addition, planning periods and after-school hours often fill up with conferences and other school and family responsibilities. Alternatives to meeting after school might include the following:

1. General and special education teachers work together to familiarize the general teacher with each student's needs, with the ultimate goal of having the general teacher assume major responsibility for intervention.
2. General and special education teachers work together to familiarize the general teacher with ways in which the special education teacher modifies tests.
3. General and special education teachers work together for a longer period of time, with the ultimate goal of creating a bank of tests from which both can draw throughout the year and then make minor modifications depending on the amount of material covered.

General teachers often fear that general students may resent mainstreamed students for making better grades when they take tests in the resource room. This fear is based on the false assumption that students with mild disabilities will always make better grades because their tests are "easier." In fact, although some students with disabilities may score significantly higher, many are fortunate if they pass. General students usually do not resent their peers who take their tests in a resource setting. Instead, they exhibit compassion: They are pleased when their friends can pass and do well; realize that their friends have problems in school; and often understand that their peers function below grade level, take different tests, and have reasons for being tested in the resource setting. Usually, when teachers handle resource programming and testing appropriately, both general and special education students view the program positively. Even average and above-average students sometimes ask to attend resource classes for temporary assistance or to complete a test, and the majority of slow learners not eligible for special education services would gladly attend resource classes.

The dilemma revolves around equality of evaluation. Just as teachers evaluate by traditional testing methods, they express the results of their evaluation via the use of traditional letter grades (*A, B, C, D, F*) or numerical ones (95, 90, 85, 80). To teachers, students, parents, and the general public, these symbols generally represent a certain standard. When students take different tests but still receive traditional grades, some teachers believe a standard has been violated. This issue has not been resolved; however, the following points should be noted:

1. Students with mild disabilities have definite learning problems, as their placement in special education attests.
2. Authorities recommend alternate site testing.
3. School systems across the nation use alternate grading systems.

For the present, general and special education educators should strive to develop equitable grading policies that will reward students with disabilities for their efforts and encourage all students to work toward their potential.

## Student Preferences for Test Adaptations

Nelson, Jayanthi, Epstein, & Bursuck conducted a study reported in *Remedial and Special Education* (2000, pp. 41–52) attempting to discover the specific testing adaptations of seventh- and eighth-grade students with high-incidence disabilities (like learning disabilities) and general education students with low, average, high, and very high achievement. They found that adaptations most preferred by the entire sample were as follows:

- Open-note tests
- Open-book tests
- Practice questions for study

- Multiple choice instead of short answer/essay
- Use of dictionary/calculator
- Provision of a copy of the test to study
- Provision of extra answer space

Testing adaptations that were least preferred by students in the sample included:

- Teacher reading questions to students
- Tests with fewer questions than given other students
- Tests covering less material than tests given other students
- Tests written in larger print
- Oral responses instead of written ones
- Use of computer to write answers
- Individual help with directions during the test
- Teaching test-taking skills

The study looked further into whether the student's academic status related to preference for testing adaptations. Two other of the most liked adaptations were take-home tests and working in a small group. This study deserves more explanation than space allows here. However, it appears that some of the most preferred adaptations required the least amount of extra teacher time and that all groups of students acknowledged that adaptations are of benefit. Students do not want to be singled out, or made to feel "stupid" or "different" in front of their peers. Teachers need to be sensitive to this as they make adaptations.

## CURRICULUM-BASED ASSESSMENT

Teachers are discovering that the most useful way to assess students' needs and progress is to measure their performance in the context of the curriculum requirements of their classroom setting (Durkin, 1984; Samuels, 1984; Thompson, 1981). Because curriculum requirements vary from school to school, it is not feasible to compare a student's progress to the performance of students everywhere on standardized tests (Jenkins & Pany, 1978; Ysseldyke & Algozzine, 1982). A more general type of assessment, referred to as *curriculum-based assessment* (CBA), has emerged to fill the need for an assessment process based on the student's progress through an individual curriculum.

A major goal of CBA is to eliminate the mismatch that exists between low-achieving students and the sometimes unreasonable demands of the curriculum. For example, a student who is unable to master the second-grade math curriculum may advance to third grade with an incomplete set of skills, facing an even more difficult set of requirements (Bloom, 1976). Such students can succeed if the curriculum is adjusted. CBA allows teachers to determine what skills have been mastered, what skills need to be retaught or reviewed, and what adjustments need to be made in the curriculum.

CBA is "the practice of obtaining direct and frequent measures of a student's performance on a series of sequentially arranged objectives derived from the curriculum used in the classroom" (Blankenship & Lilly, 1981, p. 81). The essential quality of this assessment approach is the coupling of assessment with the curriculum and instruction of the classroom. The term *CBA* is also used to refer to the assessment instrument itself. Using CBA provides an objective measurement of a student's achievement based on specific classroom objectives. The teacher then uses the results to make instructional decisions (Blankenship, 1985).

According to Blankenship (1985), CBA can be given at various times during the school year. At the year's beginning, teachers may use CBA to place students into the appropriate level of curriculum materials, form instructional groups, and identify specific skills that students need to master. They may also use CBA immediately following instruction on a specific topic or skill to assess skill mastery and determine if reteaching is necessary. Following skill mastery, CBA can be used to measure long-term retention.

When developing and using CBA, the goal is to make an instrument to measure the student's present performance and develop a plan to interpret and use the results in educational decision making. Steps for using CBA are listed in Figure 15.8.

CBA has several benefits when compared with other types of assessment (Blankenship, 1985):

1. It is useful for planning instruction.
2. It focuses attention on the relevant skills students need to learn.
3. Teachers become the primary assessors rather than receiving secondhand test results.
4. Students are not retaught material they have mastered.
5. Data can be used at IEP meetings to
   a. Summarize present levels of performance
   b. Suggest appropriate goals and objectives
   c. Document student progress

Teachers are urged to start slowly by developing a CBA on one topic or unit. After becoming familiar with the process, they can develop CBAs for other topics and exchange CBAs with other teachers (Blankenship, 1985).

## Portfolio Assessment

Many schools are implementing portfolio assessment as an alternative to traditional grading or in combination with traditional grading. Figure 15.9 lists eight guidelines for putting power into portfolios. Figure 15.10 provides examples of assessment portfolios by subject area.

Curriculum-based assessment is based on criteria-referenced tests whose content reflects the general education curriculum.

1. List the skills presented in the material selected.
2. Make sure all important skills are presented.
3. Decide if the skills are in logical order.
4. Write an objective for each skill on the list.
5. Prepare items to test each objective.
6. Prepare the test.
7. Plan how the CBA will be given.
8. Give the CBA immediately before instruction on a topic.
9. Study the results to determine the following:
    a. Which students have already mastered the skills
    b. Which students have the prerequisite skills to begin instruction
    c. Which students don't have prerequisite skills
10. Readminister the CBA after instruction to determine the following:
    a. Which students have mastered the skills and are ready to move to a new topic
    b. Which students need more practice
    c. Which students need additional instruction
    d. Which students need modifications in the curriculum
11. Readminister the CBA throughout the year to test for long-term mastery.

**FIGURE 15.8**
Curriculum-based assessment.

*Source:* Blankenship. C. S. (1985). Using curriculum-based assessment data to make instructional decisions. *Exceptional Children, 52*(3), 234. Adapted with permission.

## Authentic Assessment

Authentic assessment requires realistic demands in a real-life setting. It is sometimes used interchangeably with performance assessment, which requires a student to use knowledge learned. Figure 15.11 provides numerous ideas for authentic assessment measurement. Special educators using authentic assessment are able to provide:

multiple opportunities to perform;

more instruction time;

curriculum directly related to assessment;

self-assessment; and

consideration of related variables. (Schelble, 1994)

1. Developing a portfolio offers the student an opportunity to learn about learning. Therefore, the end product must contain information that shows that a student has engaged in self-reflection.

2. The portfolio is something that is done *by* the student, not *to* the student. Portfolio assessment offers a concrete way for students to learn to value their own work and, by extension, to value themselves as learners. Therefore, the student must be involved in selecting the pieces to be included.

3. The portfolio is separate and different from the student's cumulative folder. Scores and other cumulative folder information that are held in central depositories should be included in a portfolio only if they take on new meaning within the context of the other exhibits found there.

4. The portfolio must convey explicitly the student's activities: for example, the rationale (purpose for forming the portfolio), intents (its goals), contents (the actual displays), standards (what is good and not-so-good performance), and judgments (what the contents tell us).

5. The portfolio may serve a different purpose during the year from the purpose it serves at the end. Some material may be kept because it is instructional: for example, partially finished work on problem areas. At the end of the year, however, the portfolio may contain only material that the student is willing to make public.

6. A portfolio may have multiple purposes, but these must not conflict. A student's personal goals and interests are reflected in his or her selection of materials, but information included may also reflect the interests of teachers, parents, or the district. One purpose that is almost universal in student portfolios is showing progress on the goals represented in the instructional program.

7. The portfolio should contain information that illustrates growth. There are many ways to demonstrate growth. The most obvious is by including a series of examples of actual school performance that shows how the student's skills have improved. Changes observed on interest inventories, records of outside activities such as reading, or on attitude measures are other ways to illustrate a student's growth.

8. Finally, many of the skills and techniques that are involved in producing effective portfolios do not happen by themselves. By way of support, students need models of portfolios as well as examples of how others develop and reflect upon portfolios.

**FIGURE 15.9**
Putting power into portfolios.

*Source:* Paulson, F. L., Paulson, P. R., & Meyer, C. A. (1991, February). What makes a portfolio a portfolio? *Educational Leadership,* pp. 61–63. Adapted by permission of the Association for Supervision and Curriculum Development. Copyright 1985 by ASCD. All rights reserved.

### Reading

- Audiotape or oral reading of selected passages
- Original story grammar map
- Transcript of story retelling
- Log of books read with personal reactions, summaries, vocabulary
- Representative assignments; responses to pre-/post-reading questions
- Favorite performance
- Journal entries, including self-evaluation

### Science

- Representative work samples
- Student-selected best performance
- Report from hands-on investigation
- Notes on science fair project
- Journal entries, including self-evaluation

### Writing

- Scrapbook of representative writing samples
- Selected prewriting activities
- Illustrations/diagrams for one piece
- Log/journal of writing ideas, vocabulary, semantic maps, compositions, evaluations
- Conference notes, observation narratives
- Student-selected best performance
- Self-evaluation checklists and teacher checklists

### Social studies

- Representative work samples
- Student-selected best performance
- Design of travel brochure, packet, or itinerary of trip
- Notes on history fair project
- Journal entries, including self-evaluation

### Mathematics

- Reports of mathematical investigations
- Representative assignments
- Teacher conference notes
- Descriptions and diagrams of problem-solving processes
- Video, audio, or computer-generated examples of work
- Best performance
- Journal entries including self-evaluation

### Arts

- Best performance
- Favorite performance
- First, middle, and final renderings of projects
- Tape of performance
- Journal entries, including self-evaluation

### Generic

- Learning progress record
- Report cards
- Personal journal
- Tests
- Significant daily assignments
- Anecdotal observations
- Photographs
- Awards
- Personal goals

**FIGURE 15.10**

Examples of assessment portfolios.

*Source:* Paulson, F. L., Paulson, P. R., & Meyer, C. A. (1991, February). What makes a portfolio a portfolio? *Educational Leadership,* pp. 61–63. Adapted by permission of the Association for Supervision and Curriculum Development. Copyright 1985 by ASCD. All rights reserved.

**Reading**
- Actual or audio-/videotape of reading to peer
- Log and critiques of books read
- Book review
- Book jacket design

**Science**
- Scientific experiment to prove theory
- Original investigation and report of findings
- Journal of observations of moon, stars
- Solutions to local environment problems

**Oral expression**
- Transmission of message to several classes
- Phone call to request information
- Debate about current issues
- Persuasive speech

**Social studies**
- Map of school or community
- Design of museum exhibit on topic of interest
- Advertising campaign for political candidate
- Identification of social problem for co-op group

**Written expression**
- Student interviews
- Article for school paper
- Written resume and job application
- Invitation to party
- Letter to editor

**Arts**
- Design and decoration of bulletin board
- Submission of art to contest
- Artwork design for public building
- Performance in a play

**Mathematics**
- Solving real-life problems using math knowledge
- Solving a puzzle using logic and reasoning
- Monitoring a savings account
- Personal budget

**Generic**
- Reflective journal of learning progress
- Competition for "grant" money
- Planning and teaching a lesson to peer
- Laser disc storage of assessment information

**FIGURE 15.11**
Examples of authentic assessment.

*Source:* Poteet, J. A., Choate, J. S., & Stewart, S. C. (1993). Performance assessment and special education: Practices and prospects. *Focus on Exceptional Children, 26*(1), 7. Adapted with permission.

# STUDENT STRUCTURE AND EVALUATION

The previous three chapters ("Adapting Teaching Techniques," "Adapting the Format of Content," and "Adapting Multimedia Approaches") discuss the importance for students of imposing structure. During the evaluation process, students can continue to have structure imposed and learn how to develop structure for themselves. During this phase, students need to know (a) the category of test, (b) the specific test item, and (c) how to study for each.

## Category of Tests

As mentioned previously, tests fall into one of two basic groups: simple recognition or structured recall. Students must first be taught what each group means to their study effort and which of the test item types fall into each category.

*Recognition tests* require students to examine a group of items or choices and select the correct answer. Because the correct answer is presented within a list of distractors, recall can be prodded. The student may recall after seeing the correct choice. Test items within this category include fill in the blank with a word bank, multiple choice, and matching. Class instruction should focus on retention of specific information such as facts and data. Study guides should require students to focus on specific ideas and the ability to select a correct choice when presented.

*Structured recall* requires the student to recall the answer to a question without a visual prompt. This type of recall is heavy on memory load. Class instruction should focus on general information such as broad topics or ideas. Study guides should include focus questions designed to help students organize the study process around the general area the questions cover. Test items include fill in the blank without a word bank, or completion; short answer; essay; true-false; and listing.

## Tips for Specific Test Items

Table 15.5 lists test-taking tips for each of the item selections. Learning basic command words in selected categories and how to respond to these words is extremely helpful when taking short-answer or essay tests. Figure 15.12 lists the test categories with words that occur frequently on specific kinds of tests. The boldfaced words are the seven most common command words on tests. Students really need to know these seven words, with definitions, and must learn how to structure the test answers.

## MARKING OR GRADING TESTS

Teachers may use the following suggestions when marking or grading tests for students with disabilities or those at risk:

1. When students make low grades, let them tell you why. Give extra points if they can tell you where they need to improve.
2. Give extra points on tests when students include information that you taught but did not cover in test questions.
3. Be careful about letting students check one another's papers. This procedure can prove to be embarrassing.
4. Let students keep a graph of their grades.
5. Return all graded papers folded to respect privacy.

**TABLE 15.5**
Test-taking tips.

| Type of Test Item | Test-Taking Strategy |
|---|---|
| Test directions | 1. Underline important words in the directions such as *list, discuss, define*. |
| | 2. If there are several directions given, number each direction. |
| | 3. Make a checklist (vertically) of the directions. |
| | 4. Check off each direction as you complete it. |
| | 5. Put the directions on cards so that you can move them from page to page. |
| | 6. If you do not understand the written directions, ask the teacher to repeat. |
| | 7. If directions are given orally, ask for a written copy. |
| | 8. Be sure that you understand the directions. If not, ask for help. |
| | 9. Remember, if you lose points on a test, lose them for not knowing the content, not for missing a direction. |
| | 10. Draw a thin line through anything in the direction that does not relate specifically to the test. |
| Multiple-choice | 1. Learn the two parts of a multiple-choice question: |
| | Stem        1. _____ is the color of the sky. |
| | Choices  a. blue b. green c. yellow d. purple |
| | 2. Read the question and try to answer it before reading the answers. |
| | 3. Draw a line through each answer that could not possibly be correct. |
| | 4. Use other questions on the test as cues. |
| | 5. Use rules of grammar (such as *a/an*) as cues to the possible answer. |
| | 6. Read all choices and see what you think the correct response is for each. This will help you eliminate some answers. |
| | 7. If you know a choice is incorrect, draw a line through it. |
| | 8. Be sure that you have read all choices before making your selection. |
| | 9. If you have two options that you feel are equal, select one and write a brief rationale in the margin. Sometimes extra credit is given for thinking. |
| | 10. Be sure to notice if the question asks for the *correct* answer or *best* answer. |
| | 11. Never leave a multiple-choice question unanswered. |
| Matching | 1. Begin with the first term in the column and scan the other column for the answer. |
| | 2. After doing number 1 above. write the letters of possible answers next to the word to narrow down the choices. |
| | 3. After you choose the answer, cross it off in the answer column. |
| | 4. Skip any questions you aren't sure of and come back to them after all the other questions are answered. |
| | 5. If the columns are not reversed, begin with column B and work to A. |

*(continued)*

TABLE 15.5
Continued.

| Type of Test Item | Test-Taking Strategy |
|---|---|
| True-false | 1. Circle important words such as *never, always,* and *not.* |
| | 2. Look at the entire question; all parts must be true to be marked true. |
| | 3. Don't bother looking for a pattern to the answers (such as two true, one false, two true, one false). There probably is no pattern. |
| | 4. Statements are usually false when they indicate *always* true (all, every, none, never, best, only, always, worst, first, not, exactly, totally, because, or invariably). |
| | 5. Statements usually are true when the clue words modify the absoluteness (many, most, fewer, seldom, sometimes, bad, more, may, most, occasionally, generally, equally, frequently, less, seldom, mainly, often, usually, sometimes, probably, might, good, many, fewer, some). |
| | 6. Do not try to "read into" a true-false item. |
| | 7. Remember that all parts must be true or false to be completely true or false. |
| | 8. When a statement contains double negatives use the following strategy:<br>• Underline both negative words.<br>• Change the negative words to positive words.<br>• Reread the statement.<br>• Choose your answer. |
| | 9. Learn common negative words:<br>is not    will not    could not<br>isn't    won't    couldn't<br>do not    cannot    should not<br>don't    can't    shouldn't |
| Completion/<br>Fill in the blank | 1. Use words from the rest of the test as cues to possible answers. |
| | 2. Jot down possible answers to questions you are not sure of and return to them later. |
| | 3. Before the test, check to see if this type of item will be used. |
| | 4. Ask if a word bank will be provided. |
| | 5. If you have a word bank, mark off answers used. |
| | 6. Check the length of the bank. |
| Essay | 1. Check to see if the teacher has included a suggested outline on how to organize answers. Perhaps an organizer may be used in place of the outline. |
| | 2. Before the test, ask if you can answer essay questions using carbon paper to copy your answers. After the test, you can keep the carbon and find additional information about the question. Turn it in for extra points. |
| Reading/<br>comprehension | 1. Read the story twice. |
| | 2. Underline words that tell *who, what, where,* and *when.* |
| | 3. When reading the passage the second time, circle or underline the names of people, places, times, dates, and numbers in the passage. |
| | 4. Look for the main idea that tells what the story is about. |
| | 5. If you do not know the answer, try to eliminate the choices you know are incorrect. |
| | 6. Double-check your answers. |

*Source:* Lazzari, A. M., & Wood, J. W. (1994). *125 ways to be a better test taker.* East Moline, IL: LinguiSystems. Adapted with permission.

Command words can be divided into four categories that tell their purposes. Here are some commonly used command words with purposes and meanings.

**Describing**

Some command words ask you to describe, list, or name things. Below are examples of describing command words and their meanings.

| | |
|---|---|
| Classify | Group people or things according to category. Then, explain how they go together. |
| **Describe*** | Write detailed information about the topic. Use details to create a picture for the reader. |
| Diagram | Use information from the prompt to make a graph, drawing, chart, or organizer. Label all parts and write a brief description of the information presented in the visual. |
| Identify | Answer *who, what, when, where, why,* and *how* about a topic. Keep your answer organized. |
| Illustrate | Use examples to explain your answer. |
| Name | Provide a list. |

**Outlining or explaining**

Some command words ask you to outline or explain information and give details. The following are examples of outlining or explaining command words and their meanings.

| | |
|---|---|
| Analyze | Tell how the main ideas and details are related and why they're important. |
| Comment on | Explain or discuss a topic. You could also criticize the topic. |
| **Compare*** | Tell or show how things are alike. |
| **Contrast*** | Tell or show how things are different. |
| Explain | Give a step-by-step explanation of how something works. |
| **Define*** | Explain what the subject or topic means. |
| **Discuss*** | Look at an idea or details of an idea. Draw a conclusion based on these details. |
| Enumerate | Select the main ideas in the prompt and list them one at a time. |
| **List*** | Write a specific number of details or reasons. Number them. |
| Outline | Organize facts and details into main points and subpoints. |
| Relate | Show how things are connected or related. Tell how one affects the other. |
| Review | Summarize the important points of a topic. |
| State | Give your ideas about a topic. Keep your ideas short and to the point. |
| Summarize | Restate or explain the main points of an idea or topic. |

(*continued*)

**FIGURE 15.12**
Command word categories.

*These boldface words are the seven most common words found on tests.
*Source:* Lazzari, A. M., & Wood, J. W. (1994). *125 ways to be a better test taker.* East Moline, IL: LinguiSystems. Adapted with permission.

**Persuading**

Some command words ask you to provide information to prove, support, or criticize your answer. Below are examples of persuading command words and their meanings.

| | |
|---|---|
| Criticize* | Provide the strengths or weaknesses of the topic. |
| Evaluate | Use your opinion or an expert's opinion to tell why an idea or subject is important. Be sure to present both the good points and the bad points of the idea. |
| Interpret | Use examples or analogies (related words) to give meaning. |
| Justify | Give reasons explaining why a topic or idea is important. |
| Prove | Use facts and details to show that something is true. |
| Support | State the reasons explaining why you agree with a given statement or position, or argue in favor of your own opinion. |

**Ordering**

Some command words ask you to put events in the order in which they happened. Below are examples of ordering command words and their meanings.

| | |
|---|---|
| Sequence | Put events in the order that they happened. |
| Trace | Show the step-by-step progress or history of an idea or event. |

**FIGURE 15.12**
Continued.

6. Place the grade on the second page of the test or at the bottom of the front page. This also allows for privacy.
7. Write "see me" instead of a grade on papers with low marks.
8. Allow students to turn in projects early for teacher review before the due date. This practice encourages students to complete work early and provides the reward of teacher feedback before final grading.
9. If the grade on a project is low, allow the student to redo it for a higher grade.
10. If the test is a short quiz, let the student retake it for a higher grade. Students who receive a low grade will learn that they still need to learn the material.
11. If students can justify an answer on a test, give full or partial credit.
12. If a test question is worth 3 points and a student misses 1 point, write the score as +2 instead of −1.

## Criterion-Referenced Tests

"Criterion-Referenced Tests, or (CRTs), compare a student's performance to a specified level of mastery or achievement. They are available in most academic areas or can be constructed by a teacher, and they are appropriate for students learning specific skills. CRTs can be group or individually administered." This type of test is particularly helpful in telling what a student can and can't do. This is not always the case with norm-referenced tests that give a grade equivalent or standard score. A popular criterion-referenced test on the market is the *Brigance Diagnostic Inventory of Basic Skills-Revised* (McLouglin & Lewis, 1990, p. 21).

# Standardized Tests

Standardized tests are a big issue everywhere in the country. Schools make major decisions regarding student placements in academic groups and yearly promotions or retentions. Teachers are under tremendous pressure for their classes to score high. Principals are pressured to have building scores in line with or better than those of other schools. School superintendents are pressured when local and state papers publish a district's test scores. Colleges select prospective students from test scores.

Standardized tests have been around for a long time and probably will not quickly disappear. Although we have been looking at more holistic methods of assessing student performance (curriculum-based, portfolio, and authentic assessments), we should also consider a few suggestions for standardized tests.

When selecting standardized tests, consider the following:

- The content and skills tested should be the content and skills taught.
- Classroom teachers at all grade levels should be involved in test selection.
- Test manuals should provide necessary information for decision making.

Here are some suggestions for preparing students to respond:

- Check time allowed for the test.
- Become familiar with the test format before taking the test.
- Be clear with students about the penalty, if any, for guessing or leaving questions unanswered.
- Check materials needed for test.
- If time is left over, students should check their work.
- Before test day, review tips for taking selected test items.

Talk with students about how to mark standardized tests:

- Mark responses in provided circles.
- Erase any unnecessary marks.
- Group questions and items on answer sheet into groups of five by marking a line with a colored pen. Do not use a pencil.
- Use another person to mark answer sheet.

- Use a ruler as a marker to keep the place on the answer sheet.
- If the answer sheet is divided into columns, slide the answer sheet under the test booklet when you finish each column.
- Right-handed students should place the test booklet on the left, answer sheet on the right.
- Left-handed students should place the test booklet on the right, answer sheet on the left.

## Using the Computer/Software for Assessment

Just as the computer can be used for instruction, it can be used for assessment as well. However, computer-assisted testing is rarely used for students with disabilities. The Department of Motor Vehicles is using computers for testing applicants and allows for the test to be read by the computer if requested. Computer programs are now available for teachers to record and calculate grades, absences, and other information.

In the past, school psychologists, diagnosticians, special educators, teachers, etc., had to test students and hand score. Hand scoring in many instances took almost as long, if not longer, than administering the test. This increased the risk of error. Many tests now come with computer scoring capabilities that generate printed reports.

## CONCLUSION

This chapter describes some of the new movements in the field of education—accountability, high-stakes testing, the inclusion of students with disabilities in state testing, and test scores and their relation to funding. It also provides suggestions for adapting tests, emphasizing student structure and testing. Now, Chapter 16 looks in detail at grade-related issues.

# CHAPTER 16

## Adapting Grading

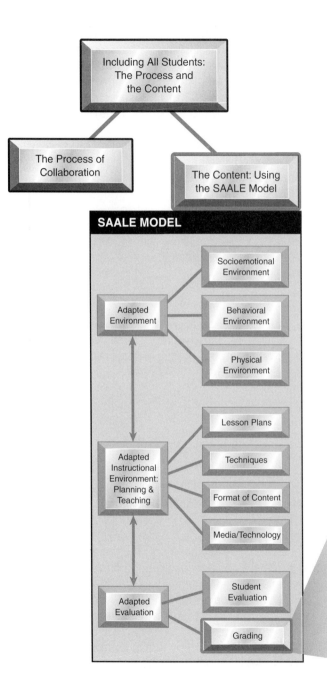

**SAALE MODEL**

Including All Students:
The Process and
the Content

The Process of
Collaboration

The Content: Using
the SAALE Model

Adapted
Environment

Socioemotional
Environment

Behavioral
Environment

Physical
Environment

Adapted
Instructional
Environment:
Planning &
Teaching

Lesson Plans

Techniques

Format of Content

Media/Technology

Adapted
Evaluation

Student
Evaluation

Grading

**Chapter-at-a-Glance**

Purposes of Grading

Grading Students in Inclusive
Settings

Graduation Requirements

Standardized Testing

Teachers are constantly making evaluations of their students' performance. Assigning grades is perhaps the most common and readily observable form of student evaluation, whereby a teacher makes a decision about a student's performance or ability. When assigning a grade, the teacher uses a combination of objective data (such as tests and quizzes, assignments, and class participation) and subjective measures of certain values (such as hard work, perseverance, and creativity) to derive the final grade (Jacobsen, Eggen, & Kauchak, 1989).

It is the subjective aspect of the grading process that causes many teachers to feel uncomfortable with the task. Grades are frequently viewed as a necessary evil imposed on teachers by outside forces, such as district-wide policies and building-level procedures. For many teachers, assigning grades is a job responsibility for which they received little training during teacher preparation programs.

This chapter discusses the purposes of grading, a variety of approaches to grading, issues in assigning grades to students in inclusive settings, the awarding of course credit and diplomas to students who are completing alternative curricula, and student participation in standardized tests such as minimum competency testing.

## PURPOSES OF GRADING

Even though the assignment of grades may not be a favorite task for many teachers, grades can serve several useful functions. Ideally, grades provide feedback to students that will help them achieve their learning objectives. In practice, grades serve several other functions (Jacobsen et al., 1989):

- Providing feedback to parents as an indicator of their children's achievement
- Providing data for grouping students
- Guiding decisions about promotion and graduation
- Providing a basis for making awards and scholarships
- Determining a student's eligibility for extracurricular activities
- Helping determine college eligibility and participation in collegiate athletics

Traditionally, the practice of assigning grades served as an administrative function to differentiate among groups of students rather than as a mechanism to provide useful information to students and parents. Everyone was graded on the same outcomes, and the same measures were used for each student to reach the outcome.

Today, we still have outcomes and measures for reaching. However, education is becoming broader in focus—outcomes may vary for certain individuals and how those outcomes are reached may vary.

Letter grades are still used, but more and more predictors of future success are seen as factors, not just one grade. Students who leave school to enter the workplace need feedback that more closely resembles the type of evaluations they will receive on the job. It is important for educators to continue to strive to develop grading procedures that can more appropriately meet the needs of all students.

# GRADING STUDENTS IN INCLUSIVE SETTINGS

The problems inherent in evaluating students and assigning grades can become even more complex for students in inclusive settings. Here, the integration of students with disabilities into regular education classes has created a dilemma for teachers in terms of assigning grades fairly and objectively (Hess, Miller, Reese, & Robinson, 1987). On the one hand, questions arise about the equity of using different standards to evaluate students in the same classroom. For example, is it fair to the other students in the classroom to award the same letter grades and course credit to an individual who has not met the class performance standards? On the other hand, proponents of individualized grading point out that to do otherwise places an added burden on students already at a disadvantage for competing fairly with their peers and does not provide useful information to students and parents. For example, a grade of "satisfactory" or *C* does not reveal what new knowledge students have gained or how they have performed relative to their individual strengths and weaknesses. Nor does it provide information on the effectiveness of instructional adaptations. Other questions arise concerning who should assume responsibility for grade assignment, which criteria should be used for grading, and what grading process should be used (Cohen, 1983).

A preliminary question to answer when considering the issue of grading a student is whether alternative grading procedures are necessary for that individual. In many cases, making appropriate adaptations of the learning environment, format of content, teaching techniques, and testing procedures will enable the student with special needs to be graded according to the same methods used for other students in the classroom. In instances where accommodations in grading procedures are needed, they should be noted on the student's IEP along with any other adaptations that are necessary. In addition to identifying the grading procedures, the IEP should specify if a grade reporting schedule other than the standard school schedule is to be used and should identify which teacher will be responsible for determining the student's grades.

Figure 16.1 presents a form which may be helpful in assigning or reassigning grades. The skill taught is listed. If modifications are needed, indicate yes, no, or NA, and list modifications. Instructional and testing accommodations are indicated. Lastly, list grade given or grade reassigned. Perhaps an alternative grade is needed. When in debate, complete or discuss this form and insert data. It easily will become evident if an adjusted grade was given or if no effort to average the grades has been tried.

The debate about criteria for assigning grades is not as easily resolved. Hess et al. (1987) have summarized the problems:

> No single best practice has been identified to resolve the problems inherent in assigning grades to students with disabilities who make a sincere effort, but because of their disabilities simply cannot measure up to either the teacher's standard or the school's standard in terms of meeting all the criteria for a given course or class when traditional methods of assessment, instruction, and grading are used. (p. 1)

Skill taught: _____

_____


Skill modification:                    Yes                No              NA
        List: _____

_____


Instructional adaptations used:    Yes                No              NA
        List: _____

_____


Testing accommodations used:    Yes                No              NA
        List: _____

_____


Grade given: _____

Reassigned grade: _____

Grade alternative: _____

Teacher(s) responsible for grade: _____

_____

_____


**FIGURE 16.1**
Grading form.


In general education classes, the most popular way of indicating student performance is still standard letter grades (Munk and Bursuck, 1998). While some teachers may consider grading a student on effort, grading on improvement, or giving two grades (one for effort, one for product), there continues to be debate about the fairness of adapting grading practices.

## Alternative Methods of Grading

Although the development of alternative grading criteria for students with disabilities may not be an easy task, it is an extremely important adaptation that must be made if students with special needs are to have any chance of success in the educational environment. Table 16.1 displays 10 alternative evaluation approaches, which are discussed in detail in this section.

TABLE 16.1
Alternative approaches to evaluation.

| Approach | Example |
|---|---|
| 1. *Traditional grading:* letter grades or percentages are assigned. | Students earning 94 percent or greater of the total points available will earn an *A*. |
| 2. *Pass/fail system:* broad-based criteria are established for passing or failing. | Students who complete all assignments and pass all tests will receive a passing grade for the course. |
| 3. *IEP grading:* competency levels on student's IEP are translated into the school district's performance standards. | If a student's IEP requires a 90 percent accuracy level and the range of 86–93 equals a letter grade of *B* on the local scale, the student receives a *B* if he or she attains target accuracy level. |
| 4. *Mastery- or criterion-level grading:* content is divided into subcomponents. Students earn credit when their mastery of a certain skill reaches an acceptable level. | Students who name 38 of the 50 state capitals will receive a passing grade on that unit of the social studies curriculum. |
| 5. *Multiple grading:* the student is assessed and graded in several areas, such as ability, effort, and achievement. | Student will receive 30 points for completing the project on time, 35 points for including all of the assigned sections, and 35 points for using at least four different resources. |
| 6. *Shared grading:* two or more teachers determine a student's grade. | The regular education teacher will determine 60 percent of the student's grade, and the resource room teacher will determine 40 percent. |
| 7. *Point system:* points are assigned to activities or assignments that add up to the term grade. | The student's science grade will be based on a total of 300 points: 100 from weekly quizzes, 100 from lab work in class, 50 from homework, and 50 from class participation. |
| 8. *Student self-comparison:* students evaluate themselves on an individual basis. | If a student judges that he or she has completed the assignment on time, included the necessary sections, and worked independently, then the student assigns himself or herself a passing grade for this assignment. |
| 9. *Contracting:* the student and teacher agree on specific activities required for a certain grade. | If the student comes to class regularly, volunteers information at least once during each class, and turns in all required work, then he or she will receive a *C*. |
| 10. *Portfolio evaluation:* a cumulative portfolio is maintained of each student's work, demonstrating achievement in key skill areas from kindergarten to 12th grade. | Cumulative samples of the handwriting show progress from rudimentary manuscript to legible cursive style from grades 1 to 4. |

*Pass/fail.* The establishment of general criteria for passing or failing an assignment or a course is a common modification of traditional grade criteria. Because determination of acceptable work is judged by broad-based criteria, the student in the inclusive setting has a greater chance of success in reaching the minimum course competencies. Like any measurement procedure, there are advantages and disadvantages to using a pass/fail system. Vasa (1981) identifies the following advantages:

- Students feel less pressure to compete.
- Students feel less anxiety.
- Students need not cheat or butter up the teacher.
- Students know what the teacher expects of them and work toward a goal.
- The teacher can increase a student's achievement or aspiration level.
- The teacher can carefully examine the student's relative abilities and disabilities.
- The teacher does not have to compare students' work.

However, the pass/fail system does have disadvantages (Vasa, 1981):

- The teacher may not provide corrective feedback in weak areas.
- The passing grade does not distinguish among students of differing abilities.
- Some students do less work when freed of traditional grade pressure.
- Students close to failing feel the same pressures they do with traditional grades.
- Teachers sometimes find minimum standards arbitrary and difficult to define.

*IEP grading.* This approach bases grading on the student's attainment of the goals and objectives specified in the IEP. Because the IEP must specify target accuracy levels or minimally acceptable levels of competence for specific skills or knowledge, built-in criteria for grading exist. Teachers can determine grades by translating the competency levels on a student's IEP into the school district's performance standards. If, for example, the IEP requires 80 percent accuracy, and 80 equals a letter grade of *C* on the local scale, then the student receives a *C*.

*Mastery- or criterion-level grading.* This approach divides content into various subcomponents, with pre- and posttest measures required for each step. Students earn credit only after their proficiency or mastery of a certain skill reaches an acceptable level. One disadvantage of this approach is that students are rewarded or passed for minimum, rather than optimum, performance.

Figure 16.2 displays a sequence of steps leading to the mastery level for the skill of word division. The criterion for each step is used as the pre- and posttest measure. A buddy system with an answer key for checking can help students demonstrate their mastery of each step.

*Multiple grading.* This approach rewards the student in several areas, such as ability, effort, and achievement. The student's final grade usually is determined

**Criteria for word division**

| Step | | Criterion | Date* |
|---|---|---|---|
| 1 | I can separate word list A into two lists: single-syllable words and words with two or more syllables. | 35/40 correct | _____ |
| 2 | I can divide the compound words on list B into syllables. | 35/40 correct | _____ |
| 3 | I can divide the prefix words on list C into syllables. | 35/40 correct | _____ |
| 4 | I can divide the double-consonant words on list D into syllables. | 35/40 correct | _____ |
| 5 | I can divide the suffix words on list E into syllables. | 35/40 correct | _____ |
| 6 | I can divide the words with a single middle consonant on list F into syllables. | 35/40 correct | _____ |
| 7 | I can divide the words with two middle consonants on list G into syllables. | 35/40 correct | _____ |
| 8 | I can list five rules to follow for words that should not be divided. | 5/5 correct | _____ |
| 9 | I can divide the mixed words on list H into syllables and cross out those that should not be divided. | 70/80 correct | _____ |

I mastered the skill of word division on _____
(Date)

Signed, _____    _____
(Student)                                  (Buddy)

*Both student and buddy should initial each date.

**FIGURE 16.2**
Sample mastery- or criterion-level grading system.

by averaging all three grades for each subject area. Some teachers use letter grades with subscript numbers to indicate level (above, on, or below grade level). Carpenter (1985) suggests that the grades assigned should reflect both progress and effort.

Another approach to multiple grading is to separate the process and product when grading students who are working diligently to master a concept or process, such as arithmetic computation, but cannot complete the work accurately (Gloeckler & Simpson, 1988). By assigning a separate grade for each of these "major messages," teachers can maintain school and district standards of grading while acknowledging individual student progress that may not reach mastery level for a particular skill or subject area.

*Shared grading.* Here, two or more teachers determine a grade—for example, when a student in a regular classroom receives assistance from the resource room teacher.

*Point system.* In this approach, teachers assign points to activities or assignments that add up to the term grade. Because teachers can give equal weights to activities other than tests, they are able to individualize their instruction and evaluation much more easily than with traditional grading systems.

*Student self-comparison.* Here, students evaluate themselves on a strictly individual basis about whether they have met the goals and objectives of their instructional program. Many students with disabilities and those at risk have a history of academic failure. This often results in low self-esteem and an inability to recognize their own strengths and achievements. For this reason, it is helpful to give all students opportunities to evaluate their own work, enabling them to recognize their individual progress as well as target areas for improvement. Self-evaluation can help students notice error patterns that they can later strive to avoid, a valuable skill to acquire before leaving school for the workplace. In addition, the technique can free the teacher's time for planning and instruction.

Self-comparison can be used with even the youngest students. Kindergarten and primary-level students can be asked to compare three or four of their own projects or papers done during the school week and then tell which one they like the best and why. In lieu of letter grades, upper elementary students can be asked to apply one of several descriptive statements to their work (such as "terrific," "good try," and "oops!"). More in-depth evaluations, such as the one shown in Figure 16.3, can be used with middle- and secondary-level students, changing the criteria to match the type of assignment.

If a decision is made to let students evaluate their own work, the teacher must be prepared to accept the students' judgments, even if they do not correspond with the teacher's own evaluation of their work. Most often, if a discrepancy exists, it will be in the direction of the students' underestimating their own merits in comparison to the teacher's evaluation.

A number-line or Likert-scale approach can be used to let students compare their evaluation of an assignment to that of the teacher. After the teacher has evaluated the assignment on the graph, students are given a chance to mark their own evaluation on the same graph, or the judgments can be made independently and compared later. The final grade on the assignment is then derived from averaging the two scores. As Figure 16.4 shows, the notations on the graph should be geared to each student's level.

*Contracting.* In this approach, the student and teacher agree on specified activities or assignments required for a certain grade. Contracts allow teachers to individualize both grading requirements and assignments.

**Self-Evaluation**

Assignment: _____     Date: _____

Check *all* that apply:

_____     I completed the assignment on time.

_____     I included all of the required sections.

_____     I met the page limit for this assignment.

*Three* things I did well on this assignment are:

1. _____

2. _____

3. _____

One thing I could do to improve my work on this assignment is:



My overall rating of my work on this assignment is (check *one*):

_____     My best effort          _____     Some room for improvement

_____     A good effort           _____     Needs a lot more work

Signed, _____
                                Student evaluator

**FIGURE 16.3**
Sample form for student self-assessment.

**FIGURE 16.4**
Sample graphs for two levels of student self-evaluation.

Suggested format for primary-level students:

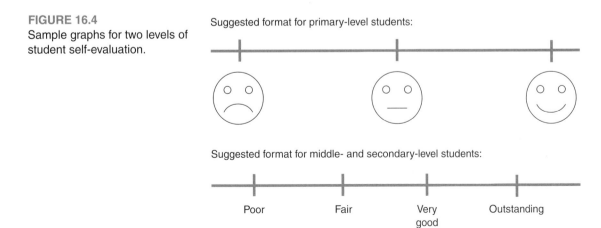

Suggested format for middle- and secondary-level students:

Poor            Fair            Very            Outstanding
                                good

Contracting is a special education technique that has been successfully adopted by many regular educators. A contract is a written agreement between student and teacher about the quantity, quality, and timelines required to earn a specific grade (Hess et al., 1987). A good contract also includes statements about the types of work to be completed and about how the student's grade will be determined. Often, a contract is a direct extension of the IEP, reflecting the performance outcomes for the specific objectives written in the IEP.

One distinct advantage of contracting is that a well-written contract leaves little question about what is expected of the student to earn a passing grade. Another advantage of contracting is that it helps students prepare for the expectations of the workplace: If they perform specified job tasks, meeting a certain standard within a given amount of time, they will receive a reward in the form of wages. A disadvantage is that, if the contract is not carefully written, the quality of students' work can be overshadowed by the quantity.

Contracts should be written in language that is easy for the student to understand. Figure 16.5 displays a hierarchy of contractual conditions that may be agreed upon by student and teacher. Some teachers prefer not to offer the alternative of a *D* or an *F* to students, believing it gives them the opportunity to choose noncompliance. Others feel that if a contractual approach is to be effective, the students should be aware of the consequences of all possible levels of performance. Contracts for younger students should be simpler, with broader-based outcomes, as illustrated in Figure 16.6.

*Portfolio evaluation.* This alternate to traditional grading is now used in many statewide testing programs. Cumulative samples of students' work based on spe-

---

If (student) comes to class regularly, turns in all the required work that is completed with 90 percent or greater accuracy, and does one extra-credit assignment/project, he or she will receive an A.

If (student) comes to class regularly and turns in all the required work with 80 percent or greater accuracy, he or she will receive a B.

If (student) comes to class regularly and turns in all the required work, he or she will receive a C.

If (student) comes to class regularly or turns in 80 percent of the required work, he or she will receive a D.

If (student) does not come to class regularly and turns in less than 80 percent of the required work, he or she will receive an F.

---

**FIGURE 16.5**
Hierarchy of contractual statements.

*Source:* Hess, R., Miller, A., Reese, J., & Robinson, G. A. (1987). *Grading-credit-diploma: Accommodation practices for students with mild disabilities.* Des Moines: Iowa State Department of Education, Bureau of Special Education. Copyright 1987 by the Iowa State Department of Education. Reprinted by permission.

---

**My Contract**

If I . . .

- Take my belongings from my backpack and put them in my desk without being asked
- Come to my reading group the first time it is called
- Clean off my desk after snack and put all the garbage in the trash can
- Raise my hand each time I want to answer
- Put all my finished papers into the "done" basket before lunch

. . . then I will receive a "plus" for the morning's work.

If I . . .

- Line up on the playground the first time the whistle is blown
- Put all the classroom supplies back in the supply boxes after project time
- Put all my finished papers into the "done" basket before I go home
- Put my homework papers into my portfolio to take home
- Put my belongings into my backpack, get my coat from the cubby, and line up before my bus is called

. . . then I will receive a "plus" for the afternoon's work.

| | |
|---|---|
| _____ | _____ |
| Student | Teacher |

_____
Date

---

**FIGURE 16.6**
Sample contract for primary-level students.

cific educational program goals are gathered periodically. At the end of each school year, approximately four pieces of the student's work representing key skills are selected for inclusion in the student's portfolio. The teacher and the student decide which pieces they will put into the portfolio. The remaining pieces could be compiled in booklet form and given to the student's parents as a permanent record. For each key subject area, the portfolio provides evidence of a student's growth and achievement. For example, for the skill area of writing, a student's portfolio might include samples of descriptive, persuasive, and expository writing developed over the course of several years. Because portfolio evaluation compares students' current work with their work in previous years, it eliminates the need to use letter grades in comparing students with others. This makes portfolio evaluation especially useful for those students who have unique talents or strengths in particular skill areas, yet do not perform well on graded tasks (D. Wilkin, personal communication, December 17, 1990).

## Providing Feedback to Students and Parents

Regardless of the criteria or procedure selected for awarding grades, the final step in grading any student's work should be to provide feedback to the student and parents. Many teachers are required to report student progress using traditional report card formats. Report cards are concerned with general expectations for the whole class. For this reason, some schools may recommend or require that a notation be made to indicate those grades for which the program content has been adjusted to meet an individual student's ability. Teachers may choose to supplement report cards with narrative reports or checklists that more accurately reveal information about the student's progress and current status, such as skills that have or have not been mastered, the student's ability to work with others, readiness for future units of instruction, and success of adaptations that have been made in format, content, or classroom environment. This practice may be more widespread at the elementary level, where most report cards continue to be handwritten, as opposed to the middle- and high-school levels, where students usually receive computer-generated report statements that do not provide space for teacher narratives.

A narrative letter is another helpful means of sharing child-specific information with parents. This format enables teachers to communicate more of the qualitative aspects of a student's work than report cards or checklists can do. Used more widely in early childhood and elementary programs, narrative letters can include a description of a student's learning style and pattern of interaction with others as well as lists of books read, projects completed, or materials used. The letter may also include descriptions of specific incidents that reflect an individual student's progress (Spodek et al., 1984).

In addition to report card grades or other standard reporting formats, feedback should be provided to the students in terms that have direct application to their classroom behavior, participation, and study habits. If the only type of feedback given to students is a quantitative reporting of a score or a letter grade, they may not be able to realize the error patterns in their work or generalize a successful approach to a problem from one situation to another. Without understanding what their grade means in terms of the way they approached a problem or assignment, the students may continue to repeat the same erroneous pattern of problem solving in future work. Another disadvantage of presenting only scores or letter grades without constructive or supportive feedback is that it trains students to focus only on the end result of an assignment—the grade—rather than on the learning process.

An issue regarding report cards in many areas is whether to indicate by the grade if the student received interventions during the instruction. This issue runs the continuum across the country. This author thinks that interventions are a natural part of curriculum and instruction, and an indication that an intervention was made is not necessary. Interventions are a natural process. Using outlines for the total class is good practice. Giving a student who cannot use the dictionary the definitions of words is okay. Remember, we must decide what we want students to learn and take the path of least resistance for teaching. *If* the grade given is on work which is not on grade level, this must be indicated to parents and future teachers.

A final consideration for educators when reporting grades is the meaning that grades take on when they are entered in a student's permanent record. Teachers in subsequent years use grades as an indication of a student's ability levels. For this reason, if grades are based on individual ability, a note to this effect should be made on the student's permanent record so that teachers will not hold unrealistic expectations for students. Six other grading alternatives appear in Figure 16.7.

---

Traditional grading poses significant problems when working with learning-disabled students:

- A low grade reinforces failure.
- Grades do not describe strengths and weaknesses.
- Grades do not reflect each student's level of functioning.

Many of these problems may be eliminated by adapting variations of traditional grading and evaluation procedures. The following alternatives suggest a variety of ways that the grading problem may be addressed.

1. Grade by achievement level
   - The student is graded as above average or below average on each level of functioning.
   - A variation may include student self-grading on a daily basis.
2. Grade by progress (the level of performance is not so important as is the rate of learning)
   - Grading is based on how much learning has occurred during a given time limit.
3. Multiple grades (measures achievement, ability, and attitude)
   - A grade of *C* would mean the student has average achievement, has progressed further than expected for his or her ability, and has a good attitude with high interest.
4. Alternative grades
   - The pass-fail and satisfactory-unsatisfactory system may be useful.
   - The teacher may allow for one free grade to be substituted for any one grade during the quarter or semester.
5. Extra credit
   - Allow special projects or assignments for extra credit to improve the grade. For example, if the student makes a poor grade on a test, he or she may be allowed a project on the same course content for credit to supplement the test score.
6. Task mastery grading
   - The student must attain a certain level of mastery in order to receive a grade.
   - A contract may be set between the student and teacher before beginning the course of work.

---

**FIGURE 16.7**
You don't have to give an *F* if you don't want to: Alternative grading techniques.

# GRADUATION REQUIREMENTS

Before the passage of PL 94-142 and section 504 of the Rehabilitation Act of 1973, a limited number of options existed for the education of students with disabilities at the secondary level. Unable to meet the demands of the regular curriculum, many students with disabilities or those at risk dropped out of high school and joined the workforce or, more likely, the ranks of the unemployed. While more secondary-level special education programs began to be developed in response to the mandates of the legislation, many states increased the number of credits required for graduation in an effort to improve the quality of secondary education. Educators faced new dilemmas about awarding diplomas to students with disabilities.

The questions that surround this issue are similar to those surrounding the issue of grading. The basic argument against awarding diplomas to students in special education programs is that a diploma represents a certain level of achievement to the community and to prospective employers, certifying that any student who holds a diploma has met minimum standards in the approved course of study. Opponents view the awarding of diplomas to special education students, who may have completed an adapted or modified version of the approved course of study, as a misrepresentation of a longstanding symbol of accomplishment. Proponents of awarding diplomas to students with disabilities and those at risk point out that participants in a number of different courses of study such as college preparatory, vocational education, and general education traditionally have been awarded the same diplomas and that this practice has been readily accepted by the community and prospective employers alike. Completion of a course of study in special education represents yet another variation in the courses of study represented by the diploma. Another compelling argument in favor of awarding diplomas to all students without regard to the nature of their individual course of study is that to otherwise discriminates against students with disabilities, denying them the same recognition for their efforts that is provided to their nondisabled peers.

## Types of Diplomas

Regardless of the arguments for or against the awarding of uniform diplomas to all students, states have developed a variety of types of diplomas. Depending on state or local policy, one of three types of diplomas may be awarded to special education students. *Regular diplomas* are awarded to students in special education if they have earned the required units of credit, passed a literacy test or minimum competency test, and met other regulations prescribed by the local school board. Typically, participation in a literacy test or minimum competency testing program is an opt-out rather than opt-in program. That is, it is assumed that all students will take the test unless a decision is made to the contrary and is clearly spelled out on the student's IEP. *Special diplomas* or *modified diplomas* are awarded to students in special education who may not have earned the necessary units of credit or passed a literacy test or minimum competency test, but who have satisfactorily met the requirements of their IEPs. *Certificates of attendance* are awarded to students who have not earned units of credit or completed the requirements of their IEPs, but who have completed a prescribed course of study as defined by the local school board. In many districts, the certificate of attendance signifies merely that a student has attended school and does not indicate the level of attendance or amount of participation (Hess et al., 1987; Virginia Department of Education, 1989).

Variations in the requirements for diplomas exist from state to state. In a survey of all 50 states regarding state policies that regulate graduation requirements, Bodner, Clark, and Mellard (1987) found that 17 states require different exit documents for students in special education who do not meet regular graduation requirements, 15 states require the use of the same exit document (a regular diploma) for all students, while 19 states delegate the decision about the type of document to local districts. Regardless of state or local requirements, the IEP should clearly specify the type of diploma the student is working toward, and the implications of the diploma should be discussed with the student and parents as well. This is especially critical if a nonstandard diploma is to be awarded.

## Curricular Approaches to Diplomas

Weintraub and Ross (1980) point out that, unless all students have access to a program of study that leads to a diploma, equal educational access is denied to students in special education. One means of minimizing discrimination against mainstreamed students is the use of a curricular approach to awarding diplomas. In this method, all students are provided with curricula to meet their individual needs. Teachers then can tailor the requirements for graduation to each curriculum, developing minimum competency tests or setting other standards of achievement as needed. One advantage of this approach is that students with disabilities can realistically be expected to earn a diploma upon successful completion of their curriculum. A drawback is that educators have to develop and validate competencies for each curriculum. Another concern is that IEP teams might funnel students into existing curricula, a practice that is contradictory with the PL 94-142 requirement of developing individualized education programs to meet each student's unique needs.

The possible misuse of the curricular approach is cause for concern among some educators. For example, Wimmer (1981) notes that entire portions of some curricula are inappropriate for students with disabilities. She recommends that an alternative curriculum be available for some students with mild disabilities, which should include social and vocational preparation with an emphasis on career development.

Several viable options exist to the broad-scale adoption of standardized curricula for students with disabilities. The majority of these students can participate successfully in the regular education curriculum if the necessary adaptations and accommodations are made. One such option is an approach whereby *special education parallels the general curriculum:* Alternate special education courses are developed that parallel courses in the regular curriculum in terms of course content but have adaptations in the pace of instruction, level of details presented, and materials used. Another option involves using an *alternate special education curriculum:* A special education curriculum is developed that departs from the academic orientation of the regular curriculum, focusing instead on functional life skills. Another approach is the *work-study program,* which allows students to earn credits while they explore various career options. This has been a traditional curricular option for students in general education. It may be an ideal approach for many students with disabilities or those at risk because it enables them to earn credits while focusing on functional skills pertinent to their lives after high school (Hess et al., 1987).

Some professionals advocate a practice of waiving units of credit for some students, favoring the awarding of equivalent high school diplomas for all students (Wimmer, 1981). Many educators do not, however, support waiving credits for any student, instead supporting a policy of "equivalent credit for equivalent time." For example, if a local district policy dictates that 120 hours of instruction generates one credit unit, then students in special education programs should be expected to meet the same standard, with course or curriculum adaptations being made as necessary to enable them to complete the required number of hours (Hess et al., 1987).

The many controversial issues regarding awarding credits and diplomas underscore the need for careful, long-range planning for students with disabilities. Many states require that issues related to a student's graduation be addressed on the student's IEP, which must state the anticipated date of graduation, the criteria that the student must meet to qualify for graduation, and whether the student's right to participate in the minimum competency testing program is to be exercised or waived. The requirement of PL 101-476 that transition services be addressed on each secondary student's IEP also supports the need for advance planning in order to promote a student's movement from school to postschool activities.

# STANDARDIZED TESTING

## Minimum Competency Testing

Minimum competency testing in most cases consists of a standardized test administered in accordance with specific testing protocols. As indicated in the discussion of diplomas, it is widely used as a criterion for awarding diplomas. Minimum competency testing as a requirement for high school graduation is a critical issue for students with disabilities, especially because a student's performance on the test can be the deciding factor in awarding or denying a regular diploma. That decision, in turn, can have a direct influence on the student's future job placement and earning potential.

The relationship between minimum competency testing and employability of adolescents with learning disabilities was explored by Algozzine, Crews, and Stoddard (1986) in a statewide study of the effects of Florida's minimum competency testing program. The results of the study indicate that students with learning disabilities demonstrate competence on fewer communications and mathematics skills than their regular class peers and that, as a group, the students with learning disabilities perform better on certain types of tasks, such as the literal use of words, symbols, and numbers and literal recall of facts and whole number operations. A second area of inquiry was asking whether the test measured skills required by employers. Employers' ratings supported the importance of competence in basic skills and functional literacy, with 92 percent indicating that reading, writing, and solving number problems are important skills for the jobs available for high school graduates within their businesses.

The results of this study support the importance of basic skill instruction for students with disabilities and provide further justification for linking curriculum and course content with employment goals. However, the differential performance of one group of students with disabilities (those with learning disabilities) on this standardized measure once again raises questions about the use of such instruments in graduation decisions. In spite of ongoing concerns about the capacity of minimum competency tests to reflect accurately a student's ability, achievement, or potential for successful vocational performance after completion of high school, many states continue to rely on such tests as a criterion for graduation. In a survey of state directors of special education, 21 of 50 states reported requiring a minimum competency test for graduation (Bodner et al., 1987). Other states reported requiring the test but used it for other purposes. Of the 21 states requiring a minimum competency test, 15 determined the student's exit document or type of diploma on the basis of the test scores.

An encouraging finding of the survey by Bodner et al. (1987) was that 22 states reported specific policies permitting modification in administration of the tests for students in special education. Modifications such as allowing the test to be administered individually, in small groups, or by the special education teacher or permitting extended time limits ensure that the results of the testing accurately reflect a student's level of competency rather than the effect of the student's disability.

## Scholastic Aptitude Test

The Scholastic Aptitude Test (SAT) is another standardized test that may be of concern to some students at the secondary level. Students, educators, and parents should be aware that students with documented disabilities (that is, visual, hearing, physical, or learning disabilities) may register for special versions of the SAT (for example, in large type, in Braille, or on cassette tape). For some students, the use of certain aids such as a reader, a recorder, or a magnifying glass is allowed. Extended testing time is another available option. Eligible students also may choose to take the test at their home schools instead of a central testing site. A more limited option is available for students with documented learning disabilities: an additional 90 minutes of testing time using the regular SAT test booklet and a machine-scored answer form. Score reports for any students who test using one of these two options will indicate that a nonstandard administration was used. Students in need of these options should contact their counselor or write to the Services for Students with Disabilities, P.O. Box 6226, Princeton, NJ 08541-6226 (College Entrance Examination Board).

# CONCLUSION

Questions surrounding the awarding of grades, course credit, and high school diplomas are emotionally charged and continue to be issues of concern with respect to students with disabilities and those at risk for school failure. While questions will continue to surface, one overriding conclusion is clear: If fair and equitable outcomes in grading, minimum competency testing, and awarding of course credit and diplomas are desired, parents, teachers, and administrators at the state and local levels must continue to work cooperatively to develop policies and procedures that provide equal educational opportunities for all students. In addition, both special and general educators must develop or upgrade the skills necessary for not only accommodating students with special needs in inclusive settings but also providing them with equal opportunities for success during their school years and thereafter.

# EPILOGUE

Thank you for making this journey with me. Indeed, the pleasure has been mine. As you continue your personal journey into the exciting world of education, I wish you well. You will take the torch of learning and walk into the future. You are our children's hopes. Carry the torch proudly, remembering the seriousness of your charge.

# APPENDIX A

## *Intervention Checklist*

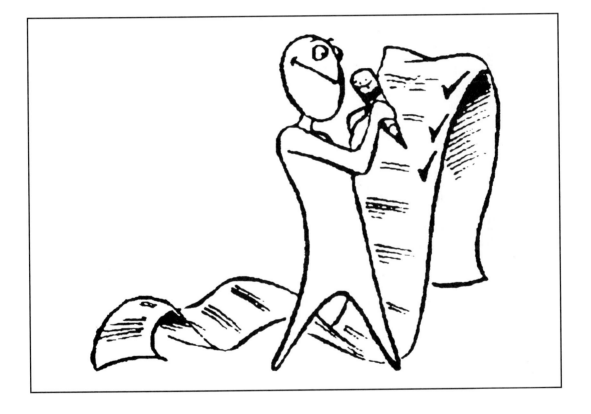

# INTERVENTION CHECKLIST FOR CONTENT AREA CLASSROOM

Student being evaluated: _____

Teacher: _____Subject: _____

Grade or type of class: _____ Date: _____

Educator completing the observation: _____

*Directions:* The following sources may be used to complete this form:

1. Student Interview

2. Teacher Interview

3. Parent Interview

4. Information from Records

5. Other Appropriate Sources

| Characteristics of Setting | Check if It Applies | Student's Present Performance Level | Has Mastered Skills | Is Working on Skills | Is Unable to Perform Skills |
|---|---|---|---|---|---|
| I. SOCIO-EMOTIONAL/ BEHAVIORAL/ENVIRONMENT | | | | | |
| A. Regular Students Have Positive Attitudes Toward Students with Disabilities | | Has positive attitude toward self | | | |
| | | Has positive attitude toward regular students | | | |
| B. Student Interaction | | Interacts appropriately in the following ways: | | | |
| 1. Individual | | Individual | | | |
| 2. Cooperative | | Cooperative | | | |
| 3. Competitive | | Competitive | | | |
| C. Counseling | | | | | |
| 1. Teacher frequently counsels students | | Seeks guidance as needed | | | |
| 2. Little time provided for student counseling | | Expresses personal and/or academic problems appropriately | | | |

| Characteristics of Setting | Check if It Applies | Student's Present Performance Level | Has Mastered Skills | Is Working on Skills | Is Unable to Perform Skills |
|---|---|---|---|---|---|
| D. Classroom Management System | | Works best under the following management system: | | | |
| 1. Teacher's management style | | | | | |
| a) Behavior modification | | Behavior modification | | | |
| b) Authoritarian | | Authoritarian | | | |
| c) Laissez-faire | | Laissez-faire | | | |
| d) Democratic | | Democratic | | | |
| e) Other (list) | | Other (list) | | | |
| 2. Classroom Rules | | Adapts to any management system | | | |
| a) Rules explained/posted | | Understands orally presented rules | | | |
| b) Adherence to unstated rules required | | Understands written rules | | | |
| c) Student involved in rule making | | Follows unstated rules | | | |
| d) Reinforcement provided for rule following | | Participates in rule-making process | | | |
| | | Requires external reinforcement to follow rules | | | |
| E. Dress/Appearance | | Dresses appropriately | | | |
| 1. Dress code enforced | | Follows dress code | | | |
| 2. Concern given to appearance by most students | | Presents neat appearance | | | |
| | | Requests help from regular teacher as needed | | | |
| F. Student Requests Help Within the Regular Classroom | | Requests help from teacher's aide as needed | | | |
| | | Requests help from special education teacher as needed | | | |

| Characteristics of Setting | Check if It Applies | Student's Present Performance Level | Has Mastered Skills | Is Working on Skills | Is Unable to Perform Skills |
|---|---|---|---|---|---|
| G. Socio-Emotional Transition<br>  1. Support provided for socio-emotional/behavioral transition problems<br>  2. Provides transition time from home to school | | Handles emotional difficulties (please list any difficulty presently experiencing):<br>_____ | | | |
| | | Home-to-school transition | | | |
| II. PHYSICAL ENVIRONMENT<br>A. Grouping for Instruction<br>  1. Large group<br>  2. Small group<br>  3. One-to-one<br>  4. Alone | | | | | |
| | | Works well in a large group | | | |
| | | Works well in a small group | | | |
| | | Works well one-to-one | | | |
| | | Works better alone | | | |
| | | Adapts to various group settings | | | |
| B. Seating Arrangement<br>  1. Traditional seating<br>  2. Circular or horseshoe<br>  3. Cubicles/Carrels<br>  4. Other | | Works in traditional arrangement | | | |
| | | Works in circular arrangement | | | |
| | | Works in cubicle/carrel | | | |
| | | Adapts to varied seating arrangements | | | |
| C. Sound<br>  1. No talking allowed<br>  2. Minor distractions (some interaction)<br>  3. Noisy environment (open interaction)<br>  4. Provisions for individual study space with reduced auditory distractions | | Works silently | | | |
| | | Works with minor distractions | | | |
| | | Works with many distractions | | | |
| | | Works in individual study space | | | |
| | | Adapts to various degrees of noise | | | |
| D. Physical Transition<br>  1. Structure provided for physical transitions | | Requires notice/structure for physical transitions | | | |

| Characteristics of Setting | Check if It Applies | Student's Present Performance Level | Has Mastered Skills | Is Working on Skills | Is Unable to Perform Skills |
|---|---|---|---|---|---|
| E. Attendance | | Excessive absenteeism | | | |
| | | Excessive tardies | | | |
| | | Excessive early dismissals | | | |
| | | | | | |
| III. TEACHING TECHNIQUES | | | | | |
| A. Class Structure | | | | | |
| 1. Structured class | | Works well with structure | | | |
| 2. Student requires self-structure | | Imposes self-structure | | | |
| B. Instructional Variables | | | | | |
| 1. Lecture | | Retains material from lectures | | | |
| 2. Explanation | | Comprehends group explanations | | | |
| 3. Audio-visual presentation | | Retains audio-visual presentations | | | |
| 4. Discussion | | Participates in class discussion | | | |
| 5. Asking questions | | Responds to questioning adequately | | | |
| 6. Self-directed study | | Works on independent projects | | | |
| 7. Experiments | | Performs lab experiments | | | |
| 8. Constructing | | Builds projects independently | | | |
| 9. Group work | | Works in small groups | | | |
| 10. Other | | Adapts to varied teaching methods | | | |
| C. Student's Perceptual Style | | Learns best: | | | |
| 1. Visual | | Visually | | | |
| 2. Auditory | | Auditorally | | | |
| 3. Kinesthetic | | Kinesthetically | | | |
| IV. CONTENT | | | | | |
| A. Homework | | | | | |
| 1. Assignments copied from chalkboard/overhead | | Copies accurately from chalkboard/overhead | | | |

| Characteristics of Setting | Check if It Applies | Student's Present Performance Level | Has Mastered Skills | Is Working on Skills | Is Unable to Perform Skills |
|---|---|---|---|---|---|
| 2. Written assignments provided | | Reads written assignments accurately | | | |
| 3. Oral assignment provided | | Follows oral directions | | | |
| 4. Kept in notebook | | Keeps homework in notebook | | | |
| 5. Other requirements (specify) | | Completes homework independently | | | |
| B. Notebooks Required | | Organizes notebook | | | |
| | | Continues to keep notebook | | | |
| | | Brings notebook to class | | | |
| C. Study Guides Given for Test  yes ___  no ___ | | Needs study guide | | | |
| D. Adaptations of Assignments  1. No modifications made in subject matter | | Needs modifications  yes ___  no ___ | | | |
| 2. Some modifications made: (list) | | Requires some modifications: (list) | | | |
| 3. Peer tutors used | | Requires assistance of peer tutor | | | |
| E. Class Procedure  1. Students read aloud | | Reads text aloud | | | |
| 2. Students present projects/reports orally | | Presents materials orally | | | |
| 3. Student panel discussions | | Participates in oral discussions | | | |
| 4. Lab work required | | Works in laboratory setting | | | |
| | | Completes lab reports | | | |
| | | Assembles and stores equipment | | | |
| 5. Other (list) | | Adapts to varied class procedures | | | |
| F. Homework  1. Assignments copied from chalkboard/overhead | | Copies accurately from chalkboard/ overhead | | | |
| 2. Written assignments provided | | Reads written assignments accurately | | | |

| Characteristics of Setting | Check if It Applies | Student's Present Performance Level | Has Mastered Skills | Is Working on Skills | Is Unable to Perform Skills |
|---|---|---|---|---|---|
| 3. Oral assignments provided | | Can follow directions | | | |
| 4. Kept in notebook | | Can keep homework in notebook | | | |
| 5. Other requirements (specify) | | Can complete homework independently | | | |
| G. Academic Transition | | | | | |
| 1. Notice is provided when making academic transition | | Makes academic transitions smoothly | | | |
| 2. Notice is not provided when making academic transition | | | | | |
| V. MEDIA | | | | | |
| A. Equipment Used | | Learns from varied media: | | | |
| 1. Overhead projector | | Overhead projector | | | |
| 2. Filmstrip projector | | Filmstrip projector | | | |
| 3. Tape recorder | | Tape recorder | | | |
| 4. Computer | | Computer | | | |
| 5. Videotape recorder | | Videotape recorder | | | |
| 6. Film/Movies | | Film/Movies | | | |
| 7. Television | | Television | | | |
| 8. Slide projector | | Slide projector | | | |
| 9. Other | | Other | | | |
| B. Materials | | | | | |
| 1. Textbook used | | Reads textbooks at grade level | | | |
| 2. Reading level of text | | Needs test adapted to level | | | |
| 3. Supplementary handouts | | Reads most handouts | | | |
| 4. Other materials (please list) | | Adapts to variety of materials | | | |
| VI. EVALUATION | | | | | |
| A. Test Format Used: | | Takes tests in these formats: | | | |
| 1. True-false | | True-false | | | |
| 2. Matching | | Matching | | | |
| 3. Fill-in-the-blank | | Fill-in-the-blank | | | |
| 4. Multiple choice | | Multiple choice | | | |
| 5. Essay | | Essay | | | |
| 6. Open book | | Open book | | | |
| 7. Other (list) | | Other | | | |

| Characteristics of Setting | Check if It Applies | Student's Present Performance Level | Has Mastered Skills | Is Working on Skills | Is Unable to Perform Skills |
|---|---|---|---|---|---|
| B. Tests Given Orally | | Takes oral tests | | | |
| C. Tests Copied from Board | | Copies tests accurately from board | | | |
| D. Tests are Timed | | Works under time pressure | | | |
| E. Study Guide Provided Prior to Test | | Uses study guide effectively | | | |
| F. Allows Resource Teacher to Administer Tests | | Needs test administered by resource teacher | | | |
| G. Tests are Handwritten | | Reads handwritten tests | | | |
| H. Tests are Typed | | Reads typed tests | | | |
| I. Projects | | Other test modifications needed: (list) | | | |
| J. Other | | | | | |
| K. Grading Systems: | | Works under these systems: | | | |
| 1. Letter grades | | Letter grades | | | |
| 2. Checklist | | Checklist | | | |
| 3. Contract | | Contract | | | |
| 4. Point system | | Point system | | | |
| 5. Pass/Fail | | Pass/Fail | | | |
| 6. Portfolio | | Portfolio | | | |
| 7. Other | | Adapts to varied grading systems | | | |

# INTERVENTION CHECKLIST FOR RELATED ENVIRONMENTS

Student being evaluated: _____

Teacher: _____ Subject: _____

Grade or type of class: _____ Date: _____

Educator completing the observation: _____

*Directions:* The following sources may be used to complete this form:

1. Student Interview

2. Teacher Interview

3. Parent Interview

4. Information from Records

5. Other Appropriate Sources

| Characteristics of Setting | Check if It Applies | Student's Present Performance Level | Has Mastered Skills | Is Working on Skills | Is Unable to Perform Skills |
|---|---|---|---|---|---|
| **SECTION 1 - AREAS COMMON FOR ELEMENTARY/SECONDARY** | | | | | |
| I. TRANSPORTATION | | | | | |
| A. Transportation Type | | Rides bus | | | |
| B. Assistance Needed | | Walks | | | |
| | | Drives | | | |
| | | Rides with parent/ friend/hired driver | | | |
| | | Needs help as follows: | | | |
| | | _____ | | | |
| II. CAFETERIA | | | | | |
| A. Procedures for Purchasing Lunch Ticket/Token Explained/Posted | | Follows correct procedures for ticket/token | | | |
| B. Lunchroom Routine Explained/Posted | | Follows lunch routine: Purchases lunch | | | |
| | | Finds assigned table | | | |
| | | Returns tray | | | |
| C. Students Enter Cafeteria Unsupervised | | Finds cafeteria independently | | | |
| D. Rules for Lunchroom Conduct Explained/Posted | | Understands rules of conduct and follows them independently | | | |
| | | Finds appropriate activity after eating lunch | | | |

| Characteristics of Setting | Check if It Applies | Student's Present Performance Level | Has Mastered Skills | Is Working on Skills | Is Unable to Perform Skills |
|---|---|---|---|---|---|

**SECTION 1 - AREAS COMMON FOR ELEMENTARY/SECONDARY**

| Characteristics of Setting | Check if It Applies | Student's Present Performance Level | Has Mastered Skills | Is Working on Skills | Is Unable to Perform Skills |
|---|---|---|---|---|---|
| E. Appropriate After Lunch Activities Explained/Posted | | Follows instructions of snack machine | | | |
| F. Snack Area Provided | | | | | |
| III. PHYSICAL EDUCATION | | | | | |
| A. Uniform Required | | Purchases appropriate uniform | | | |
| | | Brings clean uniform | | | |
| | | Changes uniform under time pressure | | | |
| B. Showering Required | | Showers independently | | | |
| C. Gym Locker Assigned | | Memorizes lock combination | | | |
| | | Works under time pressure | | | |
| D. Rules of Game Given Orally | | Follows oral game rules | | | |
| E. Notetaking Required of Class Procedures, Rules | | Takes notes adequately | | | |
| F. Activities Organized into Large Groups | | Participates in large group play | | | |
| G. Locker Room Rules Provided | | Follows rules independently | | | |
| H. Handouts Given to Introduce New Units | | Requires handout | | | |
| I. Study Guides Provided for Test | | Requires guide | | | |
| J. Specific Behaviors Required | | | | | |
| 1. Sportsmanship | | Sportsmanship | | | |
| 2. Team player | | Team player | | | |
| IV. ASSEMBLIES/SCHOOL PROGRAMS | | | | | |
| A. No Talking Allowed | | Sits quietly during programs | | | |
| B. Assigned Seating Area | | Finds appropriate seat | | | |
| C. Irregular Scheduling of Programs Followed | | Adapts to interruptions in daily schedule | | | |

| Characteristics of Setting | Check if It Applies | Student's Present Performance Level | Has Mastered Skills | Is Working on Skills | Is Unable to Perform Skills |
|---|---|---|---|---|---|
| V. BETWEEN CLASSES/HALLWAYS | | | | | |
| A. Lockers | | | | | |
| 1. Assigned locker number | | Knows location of locker | | | |
| 2. Lock required | | Memorizes lock combination | | | |
| | | Works lock combination under time pressure | | | |
| 3. Locker area rules explained | | Follows area rules | | | |
| 4. Pay phone available | | Understands rules of pay phone area | | | |
| 5. Building change required | | Changes building independently | | | |
| 6. Older children in halls | | Afraid of others (crowds) | | | |
| 7. Numbers on door easily seen | | Understands room number | | | |
| 8. Specific hall rules required | | Difficulty finding next room (wandering) | | | |
| | | Difficulty pushing/ shoving | | | |
| | | Hides in corners | | | |
| 9. Drinking fountain in halls | | Understands drinking fountain rules | | | |
| B. Movement | | | | | |
| 1. Rules for hallway conduct explained/posted | | Understands oral rules | | | |
| | | Understands written rules | | | |
| 2. Students move from class to class following written schedule | | Requires map of school | | | |
| | | Copies schedule accurately | | | |
| | | Memorizes schedule | | | |
| 3. Arrives to class on time | | Arrives to class on time | | | |
| | | Has difficulty with peers during passing periods | | | |

SECTION 1 - AREAS COMMON FOR ELEMENTARY/SECONDARY

| Characteristics of Setting | Check if It Applies | Student's Present Performance Level | Has Mastered Skills | Is Working on Skills | Is Unable to Perform Skills |
|---|---|---|---|---|---|

**SECTION 1 - AREAS COMMON FOR ELEMENTARY/SECONDARY**

| Characteristics of Setting | Check if It Applies | Student's Present Performance Level | Has Mastered Skills | Is Working on Skills | Is Unable to Perform Skills |
|---|---|---|---|---|---|
| VI. LIBRARY | | | | | |
| A. Procedures for Checking Out and Returning Materials Explained/Posted | | Follows procedures independently | | | |
| B. Finds Appropriate Books/Materials Independently or With Assistance of Teacher or Librarian | | Finds materials independently | | | |
| C. Talking in Low Voices | | Works quietly | | | |
| D. Uses "Browsing Time" According to Explained Expectations | | Understands explained expectations | | | |
| E. Works on Teacher/Librarian Planned Activities | | Works independently | | | |
| F. Exemplifies Appreciation for Literature and Information | | Appreciates litera- ture/ information | | | |
| VII. SCHOOL OFFICES | | Knows how to ask permission to go to appropriate office | | | |
| A. Guidance | | | | | |
| B. Clinic | | | | | |
| C. Principal | | | | | |
| D. Attendance | | Knows how to interact with secretary, etc. | | | |
| | | Goes and returns promptly | | | |
| | | Knows what service each office offers | | | |
| VIII. DRILLS | | | | | |
| A. Fire/Tornado Drills | | Understands rules of drill | | | |
| | | Follows rules independently | | | |
| IX. RESTROOMS | | | | | |
| A. Restrooms | | Needs assistance with rules | | | |
| | | Difficulty with noise level | | | |
| | | Uses soap/towels correctly | | | |
| | | Reads signs | | | |
| | | Dresses independently | | | |

| Characteristics of Setting | Check if It Applies | Student's Present Performance Level | Has Mastered Skills | Is Working on Skills | Is Unable to Perform Skills |
|---|---|---|---|---|---|

**SECTION 1 - AREAS COMMON FOR ELEMENTARY/SECONDARY**

| Characteristics of Setting | Check if It Applies | Student's Present Performance Level | Has Mastered Skills | Is Working on Skills | Is Unable to Perform Skills |
|---|---|---|---|---|---|
| X. TEACHER'S AIDE/SUBSTITUTE | | | | | |
| A. Teacher's Aide/Substitute Teacher in Room | | Works well with aides/substitutes | | | |
| XI. FIELD TRIPS | | | | | |
| A. Behaves Appropriately | | Keeps hands to self | | | |
| | | Attends to guide | | | |
| | | Understands rules | | | |
| XII. COMPUTER LABS | | | | | |
| A. Computer Labs | | Follows rules | | | |
| | | Respects equipment | | | |
| XIII. MUSIC/ART | | | | | |
| A. Students Move to Class Independently | | Moves to nonacademic classes independently | | | |
| B. Rules of Classroom Explained/Posted | | Follows orally presented rules | | | |
| | | Follows written rules | | | |
| C. Grading System Used | | Works best under following system: | | | |
| 1. Letter/numerical grade | | Letter/numerical grade | | | |
| 2. Pass/Fail | | Pass/Fail | | | |
| 3. Other | | Adapts to various grading systems | | | |
| D. Respect for Equipment | | Uses equipment properly | | | |
| XIV. OUTSIDE ON GROUNDS BEFORE & AFTER SCHOOL | | Following rules without supervision | | | |
| | | Stays in designated area | | | |
| XV. SCHOOL SUSPENSION | | | | | |
| A. In-School Suspension | | | | | |
| 1. No talking allowed | | Conforms to "talking rule" | | | |
| 2. Study materials for each subject area required | | Follows rules independently | | | |
| | | Brings materials independently | | | |
| 3. Reporting to in-school suspension and absenteeism | | Understands reporting rules | | | |
| B. Out-of-School Suspension | | | | | |

| Characteristics of Setting | Check if It Applies | Student's Present Performance Level | Has Mastered Skills | Is Working on Skills | Is Unable to Perform Skills |
|---|---|---|---|---|---|

## SECTION 1 - AREAS COMMON FOR ELEMENTARY/SECONDARY

| Characteristics of Setting | Check if It Applies | Student's Present Performance Level | Has Mastered Skills | Is Working on Skills | Is Unable to Perform Skills |
|---|---|---|---|---|---|
| XVI. OTHER AREAS WHERE SERVICES ARE PROVIDED<br>A. Advanced Placement<br>B. Speech and Language<br>C. Occupational/Physical<br>D. Charter I<br>E. Gifted and Talented | | | | | |

## SECTION 2 - AREAS SPECIFIC TO ELEMENTARY LEVEL

| Characteristics of Setting | Check if It Applies | Student's Present Performance Level | Has Mastered Skills | Is Working on Skills | Is Unable to Perform Skills |
|---|---|---|---|---|---|
| I. BEFORE & AFTER SCHOOL PLACEMENT<br>A. Before and After School Placement | | Child in before/after care<br>yes _____<br>no _____<br>Specific skills needed:<br>_____<br>Works best with 1 adult<br>Can adjust to different adults | | | |
| II. SNACK BREAK PROVIDED<br>A. Snack Break Provided | | Adheres to rules required during snack break<br>Requires specific snacks:<br>_____ | | | |
| III. PLAYGROUND<br>A. Interactions Required | | Plays alone<br>Tries to play with others<br>Plays with only one child<br>Has trouble playing | | | |
| B. Required Areas<br>1. Slide<br>2. Play escape<br>3. Monkey bars<br>4. Balance beams<br>5. Fire truck<br>6. Swings<br>7. Jumping stumps | | Ability level<br>1. Slide<br>2. Play escape<br>3. Monkey bars<br>4. Balance beams<br>5. Fire truck<br>6. Swings<br>7. Jumping stumps | | | |

| Characteristics of Setting | Check if It Applies | Student's Present Performance Level | Has Mastered Skills | Is Working on Skills | Is Unable to Perform Skills |
|---|---|---|---|---|---|

## SECTION 2 - AREAS SPECIFIC TO ELEMENTARY LEVEL

| Characteristics of Setting | Check if It Applies | Student's Present Performance Level | Has Mastered Skills | Is Working on Skills | Is Unable to Perform Skills |
|---|---|---|---|---|---|
| C. Rules Required | | Ability level | | | |
| 1. Lining up | | 1. Lining up | | | |
| 2. Playing on equipment | | 2. Playing on equipment | | | |
| 3. Interactions with classmates | | 3. Interactions with classmates | | | |
| 4. Answering questions | | 4. Answering questions | | | |
| 5. Relating problems in complete thought and in sequential order | | 5. Requesting assistance  Relating problems in complete thought and in sequential order | | | |
| 6. Taking turns | | 6. Taking turns | | | |
| 7. Participating in and understanding recess | | 7. Participating in and understanding recess | | | |

## SECTION 3 - AREAS SPECIFIC TO SECONDARY LEVEL

| Characteristics of Setting | Check if It Applies | Student's Present Performance Level | Has Mastered Skills | Is Working on Skills | Is Unable to Perform Skills |
|---|---|---|---|---|---|
| I. TECHNICAL EDUCATION CLASSES | | | | | |
| A. Technical Education Classes | | | | | |
| 1. Please list area(s): _____ | | Has difficulty with following in specific area of _____ . | | | |
| 2. Please list specific areas at shop, restaurant, etc.: _____ | | Please list: | | | |
| II. STUDY HALL REQUIRED | | | | | |
| A. Study Hall Required | | Brings appropriate materials  Works independently | | | |
| III. AFTER-SCHOOL ACTIVITIES | | Participates in the following: | | | |
| A. Activity Type | | Athletics | | | |
| | | Band | | | |
| | | Pep squad | | | |
| | | Cheerleading | | | |
| | | Dance team | | | |
| | | Club meetings | | | |
| B. Needs Assistance: _____ _____ | | Needs assistance: _____ _____ | | | |

# APPENDIX B

## *Organizations and Resources*

Alexander Graham Bell Association
for the Deaf
2000 M Street
Suite 210
Washington, DC 20036
(202) 337-5220 (V/TDD)
**www.agbell.org**

American Academy of Child and
Adolescent Psychiatry
Public Information Office
1615 Wisconsin Avenue, NW
Washington, DC 20016
(202) 966-7300
**www.aacap.org**

American Association on Mental
Retardation (AAMR)
444 N. Capital Street NW
Suite 846
Washington, DC 20001
(202) 387-1968; (800) 424-3688
**www.aamr.org**

American Council of the Blind
Parents
C/o American Council of the Blind
1155 15th St. NW
Suite 1004
Washington, DC 20005
(202) 467-5081; (800) 424-8666
**www.acb.org**

American Foundation for the Blind
11 Penn Plaza
Suite 300
New York, NY 10001
(212) 620-2000; (800) AFBLIND
**www.afb.org**

American Orthopsychiatric
Association
330 7th St., 18th Floor
New York, NY 10001
(212) 564-5930
**www.amerortho.org**

American Psychiatric Association
1400 K St. NW
Washington, DC 20005
(202) 682-6000
**www.psych.org**

American Psychological Association
750 First St. NE
Washington, DC 20002
**www.apa.org**

American Speech-Language-
Hearing Association (ASHA)
10801 Rockville Pike
Rockville, MD 20852
(301) 897-5700 (V/TDD);
(800) 638-8255
**www.asha.org**

Autism Hotline
Autism Services Center
PO Box 507
Huntington, WV 27510-0507
(304) 525-8014

Autism Society of America
7910 Woodmont Ave.
Suite 300
Bethesda, MD 20814
(301) 657-0881

Blind Children's Center
4120 Marathon Street
PO Box 29159
Los Angeles, CA 90029-0159
(213) 664-2153; (800)222-3566

Cancer Information Clearinghouse
National Cancer Institute
9000 Rockville Pike
Bethesda, MD 20892
(800) 4-CANCER
**cancernet.nci.nih.gov**

Council for Children with Behavioral
Disorders, c/o Council for
Exceptional Children (CEC)
1110 N. Glebe Rd
Suite 300
Arlington, VA 22201-5704
(703) 620-3660
**www.cec.sped.org**

Council for Learning Disabilities
(CLD)
PO Box 40303
Overland Park, KS 66204
(913) 492-8755

Division for Children with
Communication Disorders, c/o
Council for Exceptional Children
(CEC)
1110 N. Glebe Rd
Suite 300
Arlington, VA 22201-5704
(703) 620-3660
**www.cec.sped.org**

Division for the Visually
Handicapped, c/o Council for
Exceptional Children (CEC)
1110 N. Glebe Rd
Suite 300
Arlington, VA 22201-5704
(703) 620-3660
**www.cec.sped.org**

Division on Physically Handicapped
c/o Council for Exceptional Children
(CEC)
1110 N. Glebe Rd
Suite 300
Arlington, VA 22201-5704
(703) 620-3660
**www.cec.sped.org**

Easter Seal Society
70 East Lake Street
230 W Monroe
Suite 1800
Chicago, IL 60606
(312) 726-6200; (312) 726-4258
(TDD); (800) 221-6827
**www.easter-seals.org**

Epilepsy Foundation of America
4351 Garden City Drive, Suite 500
Landover, MD 20785-7223
(301) 459-3700
**www.epilepsyfoundation.org**

ERIC Clearinghouse on
Handicapped and Gifted Children,
c/o Council for Exceptional Children
(CEC)
1110 N. Glebe Rd
Suite 300
Arlington, VA 22201-5704
(703) 620-3660
**www.cec.sped.org**

Federation of Families for Children's
Mental Health
1101 King Street, Suite 420
Alexandria, VA 22314
(703) 684-7710
**www.ffcmh.org**

International Dyslexia Association
Chester Building, Suite 382
8600 LaSalle Road
Baltimore, MD 21286
(410) 296-0232; (800) 222-3123
**www.interdys.org**

Learning Disabilities Association of
America (LDA)
4156 Library Road
Pittsburgh, PA 15234
(412) 341-1515; (412) 341-8077
**www.ldaamerica.org**

March of Dimes Birth Defects
Foundation
PO Box 2000
1275 Mamaroneck Avenue
White Plains, NY 10605
(914) 428-7100
**www.modimes.org**

National Alliance for the Mentally Ill
2107 Wilson Boulevard, Suite 300
Arlington, VA 22201
(703) 524-7600
**www.nami.org**

National Association for Parents of
Children with Visual Impairments
PO Box 317
Watertown, MA 02471
(800) 562-6265
**www.spedex.com/napvi**

National Association for the Visually
Handicapped
22 West 21st Street
New York, NY 10010
(212) 889-3141
**www.navh.org**

National Association of the Deaf
814 Thayer Avenue
Silver Spring, MD 20910
(301) 587-1788 (V/TDD)
**www.nad.org**

National Braille Association (NBA)
3 Townline Circle
Rochester, NY 14623
(716) 427-8260

National Braille Press
88 St. Stephen Street
Boston, MA 02115
(617) 266-6160; (800) 548-7323
**www.nbp.com**

National Center for Learning
Disabilities
381 Park Avenue South
New York, NY 10016
(212) 545-9655
**www.ncld.org**

National Down Syndrome Congress
7000 Peachtree Road
Dunwoody Bldg. 5, Suite 100
Atlanta, GA 30328
(800) 232-NDSC
**www.ndsccenter.org**

National Down Syndrome Society
666 Broadway, Suite 810 New York,
NY 10012
(212) 460-9330; (800) 221-4602
**www.ndss.org**

National Eye Institute
National Institutes of Health
U.S. Department of Health and
Human Services
31 Center Drive
Bldg 31, Room 6A-32
MSC 2510
Bethesda, MD 20892
(301) 496-5248
**www.nei.nih.gov**

National Federation of the Blind,
Parents Division, c/o National
Federation of the Blind
1800 Johnson Street
Baltimore, MD 21230
(410) 659-9314
**www.nfb.org**

National Library Services for the
Blind and Physically Handicapped
Library of Congress
1291 Taylor Street, NW
Washington, DC 20542
(202) 707-5100; (800) 424-8567
**www.lcweb.loc.gov/nls**

National Mental Health Association
1021 Prince Street
Alexandria, VA 22314-2971
(703) 684-7722
**www.nmha.org**

National Rehabilitation Information
Center
102 Irving Street, NW
Washington, DC 20010
(202) 877-1000
**www.nrhrehab.org**

National Retinitis Pigmentosa
Foundation
11431-35 Crownhill Dr.
Suite D
Owings Mills, MD 21117
(800) 683-5555
**www.stopblindness.org**

National Society to Prevent
Blindness
500 East Remington Road
Schaumberg, IL 60173
(708) 843-2020; (800) 221-3004
**www.preventblindness.org**

Scottish Rite Foundation
Southern Jurisdiction, U.S.A.
1733 16th Street, NW
Washington, DC 20009-3199
(202) 232-3579
**www.council@srmason-sj.org**

Trace Research and Development
Center on Communication, Control,
and Computer Access for
Handicapped Individuals
University of Wisconsin-Madison
5901 Research Park Blvd.
Madison, WI 53719
(608) 262-6966; (608) 263-5408
(TDD)
**www.trace.wisc.edu**

United Cerebral Palsy Association
1660 L Street NW
Suite 700
Washington, DC 20036
(202) 842-1266; (202) 776-0794;
(800) 872-5827

# APPENDIX C

# *A Lesson Plan for Teaching Personal Development: Self-Control*

# PERSONAL DEVELOPMENT
## Self-Control

### Integration
Language Arts, Writing, Social Studies

### Materials

| | |
|---|---|
| Activity Sheets | Puppets |
| | Paper bags |
| | Construction paper |
| | Yarn |

### Vocabulary

| | | |
|---|---|---|
| hit | kick | push |
| bite | bullying | |

### Objectives

- To recognize current intensity of feelings with regard to own coping limits.
- To identify alternative solutions to problems as a decision-making process.
- To control impulses.
- To use stress-reducing techniques.
- To respect the property of others.
- To deal with feelings in a way that will not be harmful to self or others.
- To accept responsibility for behavior without shifting blame.

### Procedure

1. Introduce vocabulary words.
2. Write down the way a physically aggressive situation may happen.
   Explain to the class how:
   - 1st: A disagreement begins. Two children may want to play separate games.
   - 2nd: One child may accuse the other of cheating.
   - 3rd: Child number one pushes child number two.

- 4th: Child number two pushes child number one back to defend himself or herself.

3. Replay what you just told the class using puppets.

4. Discuss:
   - What caused the problem?
   - What could have happened differently?

5. Replay the situation again using another situation. Ask the students to replay the scene using the puppets.

6. Give each student a chance to choose a correct response to these situations:
   - Someone runs over and pushes you down as you're running to a swing.
   - Someone sticks a foot out to trip you.
   - Someone throws a rock at you on the way to school.
   - While you are having a disagreement with someone in your class, the person's friend comes over, grabs your arm, and starts twisting it.

7. Complete Activity Sheets (numbers 1, 2, 3, and 4).

8. Present Journal Writing Activity.

## Extension Activity

Draw and color a picture of students playing with classmates on the playground in a positive way. Write three words under your picture that tell how the children are getting along.

# ACTIVITY SHEET (NUMBER 1)
## Self-Control

**Grade 1**                                                                 **Lesson 2**

**Name** _____     **Date** _____

Someone sticks a foot out to trip you. Draw a picture of the right thing to do after this happens.

# ACTIVITY SHEET (NUMBER 2)
## Self-Control

| Grade 1 | Lesson 2 |
|---|---|

**Name** _____ **Date** _____

Someone runs over and pushes you down as you're running to a swing. Draw a picture of the right thing to do after this happens.

# ACTIVITY SHEET (NUMBER 3)
## Self-Control

| Grade 1 | Lesson 2 |
|---|---|

**Name** _____ **Date** _____

Someone throws a rock at you on the way to school. Draw a picture of the right thing to do after this happens.

ACTIVITY SHEET (NUMBER 4)

Self-Control

**Grade 1**  Lesson 2

Name _____  **Date** _____

While you are having a disagreement with someone in your class, the person's friend comes over, grabs your arm, and starts twisting it. Draw a picture of what you would do.

**Grade 1**  Lesson 2

Name _____  **Date** _____

Draw a picture about these words:

| hit | kick | push | bite |

Tell the class the opposite way to act instead of the way in your picture.

# PERSONAL DEVELOPMENT
## Self-Control

| Grade 2 | Lesson 2 |
|---------|----------|

**Integration**

Language Arts, Writing, Social Studies

**Materials**

Tongue depressors
Construction paper

**Vocabulary**

| schedule | change | confuse | react |
|----------|--------|---------|-------|
| plans    | expect | routine |       |

**Objectives**

- To tolerate changes in a daily schedule.
- To express concern appropriately.
- To express disappointment in an appropriate manner.
- To respect adult clues that channel behavior toward a more appropriate end.
- To recognize that one has behavioral options in a social situation.

**Procedure**

1. Introduce vocabulary words.
2. Construct puppets out of the tongue depressors and construction paper.
3. Using the students' puppets, act out the following:
   Puppet 1—"Now it's time to do math."
   Puppet 2—"Today we will not be doing math; we have an assembly."
   Puppet 1—"No! I want to do math." (gets very upset)
4. Discuss how getting upset is not a good choice when plans change. Sometimes doing something different can be nice, if you're willing to remain calm.
5. Ask students, "Tell me a time when plans changed and how you reacted."
6. Allow students to show the class by using their puppets to act out the situation.
7. Present Journal Writing Activity.

Extension Activity

Have a crazy, mixed-up day where the schedule is completely changed. Go over the changes at the first of the morning.

Have a mixed-up lunch, where the dessert is served first, etc., and all utensils are mixed up.

# JOURNAL WRITING ACTIVITY
## Self-Control

| Grade 2 | Lesson 2 |
|---|---|

**Name** _____    **Date** _____

If you had to dress like a person from another country for a day, where would you be from? How would you act? What language would you speak?

_____

_____

_____

_____

_____

_____

_____

_____

_____

_____

_____

_____

_____

_____

_____

_____

_____

_____

# PERSONAL DEVELOPMENT
## Self-Control

**Grade 3**                                                    **Lesson 2**

### Integration
Language Arts, Writing, Social Studies

### Materials
Activity Sheets

### Vocabulary
praise        compliment      attitude      proud      comment

### Objectives
- To seek attention through accepted classroom procedures.
- To realize that one's behavior influences how others will treat him or her.
- To decrease the number of competitive or negative statements to peers.
- To accept responsibility for the consequences of one's own behavior.
- To listen to different points of view.
- To show an acceptance of praise.

### Procedure
1. Introduce vocabulary words.
2. Discuss praise as something nice that someone says to you about something you did.
3. List situations where one can expect to receive praise.
4. Ask students to give examples of times they received praise. Ask students:
   - How did you feel?
   - How did you respond?
5. Go over steps to respond to praise:
   - Listen to the compliment.
   - Show pleasure through facial expression and body language.
   - Thank the person for giving praise.
   - Try not to deny praise.
   - Offer praise when appropriate.

6. Read and discuss Activity Sheets Numbers 1 and 2.
7. Complete Activity Sheet Number 3.
8. Present Journal Writing Activity.

### Extension Activity

Divide the class into groups. Role-play situations where students compliment each other.

* Someone praises you for a nice job that you've done on a school project.
* Someone praises you for being helpful.
* Someone praises you for having a good attitude. Students may make suggestions for new examples and role-play more than one.

# ACTIVITY SHEET (NUMBER 1)
## Self-Control

| Grade 3 | Lesson 2 |
|---|---|

**Name** _____    **Date** _____

Tommy, Michelle, and Scott are in Ms. Nelson's class. The children have been working on special paintings about countries all around the world. All the children have worked hard to do a good job.

When Ms. Nelson tells Tommy that he used pretty colors, Tommy says, "I'm great."

When Ms. Nelson tells Michelle that her painting looked just like a castle in Germany, Michelle says, "It's ugly."

Scott is happy that Ms. Nelson likes the way he painted his house. He says, "Thank you!"

# ACTIVITY SHEET (NUMBER 2)
## Self-Control

| Grade 3 | Lesson 2 |
|---------|----------|

**Name** _____  **Date** _____

When someone tells you that you've done a good job or that you look nice, how do you feel?

Chances are that you are glad to hear that someone has noticed you. What else do you feel? You can feel proud, but you can also feel a little uncomfortable.

Let's imagine that Mary has come to school wearing new boots. Her friend, Ann, comments that she likes Mary's boots. Mary likes her boots, too, but she responds, "Oh, they make my feet look big. Maybe I should have gotten black!"

Now Ann has a problem. All she wanted to do was to tell Mary how she felt. She wanted to compliment Mary on her new boots. Now Mary "disagrees" with her. What do you think Ann can say back?

There are times when people feel uncomfortable or embarrassed when they are "praised." It is important that we learn how to accept that praise. Comments like, "Do you really like my boots?" or "I'm glad you like them; it was hard to find a pair I liked" are responses that would be good.

Rejecting or denying the praise only works to make the other person feel awkward. Sometimes a simple "thank you" will do the trick.

# ACTIVITY SHEET (NUMBER 3)
## Self-Control

| **Grade 3** | **Lesson 2** |
|---|---|

**Name** _____  **Date** _____

1. Think of what Mary could have said to Ann to let her know she was glad that Ann complimented her.

   _____

   _____

   _____

2. What have you done when someone has praised you?

   _____

   _____

   _____

3. Did you ever praise someone and wish that you hadn't? Why?

   _____

   _____

   _____

   _____

4. Why do you think teachers praise students?

   _____

   _____

   _____

5. Do you ever praise your parents or your teachers? What have they said to you?

   _____

   _____

   _____

# JOURNAL WRITING ACTIVITY
## Self-Control

**Grade 3**                                          **Lesson 2**

**Name** _____ **Date** _____

Try and think of compliments you could give to certain classmates. List them. Be honest.

_____

_____

_____

_____

_____

_____

_____

_____

_____

_____

_____

_____

_____

_____

_____

_____

_____

_____

_____

_____

_____

_____

_____

_____

_____

_____

_____

_____

# PERSONAL DEVELOPMENT
## Self-Control

**Grade 4**                                                          **Lesson 2**

### Integration
Language Arts, Writing, Social Studies

### Materials
Activity Sheets

### Vocabulary

| | | | |
|---|---|---|---|
| respect | consideration | negative | courteous |
| polite | disrespect | teasing | necessary |

### Objectives
- To recognize current intensity of feelings with regard to own limits.
- To identify alternative solutions to problems as part of a decision-making process.
- To control impulses.
- To use stress-reducing techniques.
- To respect the property of others.
- To accept responsibility for consequences of own behaviors without shifting blame.
- To recognize that one has behavioral options in a social situation.

### Procedure
1. Introduce vocabulary words.
2. Ask students to list the kinds of situations that make people angry when being teased.
3. Read narrative (Activity Sheet Number 1) and discuss ways Mary could ignore those teasing her.
4. Complete Activity Sheet Number 2.
5. Share Activity Sheet with partner or the class.
6. Discuss how many times students "tease" people because they are old. Have students list ways they can show respect to older people.
7. Present Journal Writing Activity.

### Extension Activity
Have students work in groups. Ask them to write down ways they can show their appreciation for differences in our culture. Also, have them list ways that rules in our society show respect.

# ACTIVITY SHEET (NUMBER 1)
## Self-Control

| Grade 4 | Lesson 2 |
| --- | --- |

**Name** _____ **Date** _____

## TEASING

Mary is a student who wears glasses. She is usually calm, but she "blows up" when other children call her "Four Eyes." Mary becomes very upset, so it is not going to be easy for her to stop reacting.

What should Mary do? Should Mary come back with a smart remark? Should Mary simply not pay attention to the remarks? Remember that some students make fun of other students to put on a show. Maybe the student who is doing the teasing doesn't feel very good about himself or herself.

Let's think of some things that Mary could say to make herself feel better. Being funny is really helpful.

"Four eyes are better than one."

"The better to see you, my dear!"

We agree that Mary needs to stop reacting, but it may take her awhile to train herself. These answers will give her time to change what she is now doing.

# ACTIVITY SHEET (NUMBER 2)
## Self-Control

| Grade 4 | Lesson 2 |
|---------|----------|

Name _____     Date _____

1. How can you tell if your teasing becomes "too much"?

   _____

   _____

   _____

2. What should you do if you are doing the teasing and the person becomes angry?

   _____

   _____

   _____

3. Think of a time when someone teased you, and you became very angry. If you can't think of a personal situation, tell of a situation that you know happened to someone else.

   _____

   _____

   _____

4. Write down the dictionary definition of *tease*.

   _____

   _____

   _____

5. Write down the dictionary definition of *respect*.

   _____

   _____

   _____

# JOURNAL WRITING ACTIVITY
## Self-Control

**Grade 4** **Lesson 2**

**Name** _____ **Date** _____

At times students are teased because they are a different color or race. Write how you can show respect for these people.

_____
_____
_____
_____
_____
_____
_____
_____
_____
_____
_____
_____
_____
_____
_____
_____
_____
_____
_____
_____
_____
_____
_____
_____

# PERSONAL DEVELOPMENT
## Self-Control

### Integration
Language Arts, Writing, Social Studies

### Materials
Activity Sheets

### Vocabulary

| | |
|---|---|
| threats | impulsive |
| consequences | negative |
| responsibility | "taking ownership of a problem" |
| option | intimidated |
| rumors | |

### Objectives
- To express concerns appropriately.
- To identify alternative solutions to problems as part of a decision-making process.
- To seek attention through accepted classroom procedures.
- To realize that one's behavior influences how others will treat him or her.
- To predict consequences and evaluate the risk factors in social situations.
- To recognize that one has behavioral options in a social situation.

### Procedure
1. Introduce vocabulary words.
2. Explain the meaning of a threat (someone talking about doing harm).
3. Discuss types of threats. For example:
   - Someone will do something that you won't like.
   - Someone will hurt someone else.
   - Someone will damage another's property.
4. Discuss appropriate responses to a threat. Discuss the importance of thinking before you act. Impulsive behavior may make others mad and may make matters worse. It may make you feel bad later, hurt you, or destroy your chance to do what you decide is best.

5. Complete Activity Sheets (numbers 1, 2, and 3)—steps that are positive ways to deal with threats.

6. Read and discuss the questions and answers. Compare solutions.

7. Present Journal Writing Activity.

## Extension Activity

Role-playing activity: Divide students into groups. Give each group a situation where they are part of the "threat-making" group. They refuse to take responsibility. Have them act out the skit for the class. After the skits, ask students the questions below.

### *Skits*

1. You made excuses in order to avoid a negative consequence.

2. You purposely caused another student to skip class.

3. You kept money you found on someone's desk.

4. You didn't clean the house, and told Mom you didn't have to do it. "It's her job."

5. You decided to copy from someone else's paper because you didn't have time to do your work.

# ACTIVITY SHEET (NUMBER 1)
## Self-Control

| Grade 5 | Lesson 2 |
|---------|----------|

**Name** _____ **Date** _____

Steps that are positive ways to deal with threats:

1. Listen carefully.
2. Stop and consider your options.
3. Move away from the person making the threat.
4. Tell an adult about the threat.

How would you handle the following threats?

1. "I'm going to hit you."

   _____

   _____

   _____

   _____

2. "You'd better give me that or else."

   _____

   _____

   _____

   _____

3. "If you tell Jason what we said, we'll come after you."

   _____

   _____

   _____

   _____

4. "If you don't let me borrow your new sweater, I'll turn the class against you."

_____

_____

_____

_____

5. "If you don't lend me $10.00, I'll start rumors about you."

_____

_____

_____

_____

6. "If you don't give me the answers to your homework, I'll tell the teacher I saw you copy from someone else's paper."

_____

_____

_____

_____

7. "We already have our groups in this school. Besides, you talk funny" (to a new student who speaks a different language).

_____

_____

_____

_____

# ACTIVITY SHEET (NUMBER 2)
## Self-Control

| Grade 5 | Lesson 2 |
|---------|----------|

**Name** _____ **Date** _____

When you control your impulses, you decide on behavior that will make a situation better. Check the responses to threats that will make the situation better.

_____ hitting someone when they say they'll hit you

_____ telling them to go away

_____ laughing at the other student

_____ yelling rude things

_____ asking why they are grumpy

_____ crying

_____ walking away

_____ telling someone not to threaten you

_____ finding an adult

_____ accusing or threatening back

_____ calmly talking about situation

# ACTIVITY SHEET (NUMBER 3)
## Self-Control

**Grade 5**                                                   **Lesson 2**

**Name** _____ **Date** _____

1. List two threatening situations that happened to you sometime at home or school.

   a. _____

   _____

   _____

   _____

   _____

   b. _____

   _____

   _____

   _____

   _____

2. Using one of the examples from above, give advice to someone who is in a threatening situation.

   _____

   _____

   _____

   _____

3. Why do you think some kids threaten others?

   _____

   _____

   _____

   _____

# JOURNAL WRITING ACTIVITY
## Self-Control

| Grade 5 | Lesson 2 |
| --- | --- |

**Name** _____     **Date** _____

You refused to lend a classmate money and he/she organized a group to tease you. They even tried to convince your teacher that you are the troublemaker. What would you do?

_____

_____

_____

_____

_____

_____

_____

_____

_____

_____

_____

_____

_____

_____

_____

_____

_____

_____

_____

_____

_____

_____

_____

# PERSONAL DEVELOPMENT
## Self-Control

**Grade 6**                                                     **Lesson 2**

### Integration
Language Arts, Writing, Social Studies

### Materials
Activity Sheets

### Vocabulary

| | | |
|---|---|---|
| disappointed | sad | angry |
| frustrated | resume | express |
| alternative | expectation | |

### Objectives
- To recognize current intensity of feelings with regard to own coping limits.
- To realize that one's behavior influences how others would treat him or her.
- To use language that is not offensive to others.
- To express disappointment in an appropriate manner.
- To accept constructive criticism.

### Procedure
1. Introduce vocabulary words.
2. Discuss disappointment as the feeling of not having your expectations or hopes met.
3. Give students examples of situations when a person might feel disappointed.
4. Read narratives (Activity Sheets Numbers 1 and 2) and discuss in class.
5. Ask students to give examples of times when they have felt disappointed.
6. Present Journal Writing Activity.

### Extension Activity
Role-play positive responses to being disappointed.

- You were planning to go to a football game and a pizza party, but the game was cancelled because of snow.

- You were planning to spend the weekend with a friend. You weren't allowed to go because your mom became ill.
- Your dad came home with tickets to the football game on the night of your best friend's birthday party.
- You studied hard for a test, but still failed.

   Now write the positive response for each of these situations. Work in groups.

## ACTIVITY SHEET (NUMBER 1)
### Self-Control

| Grade 6 | Lesson 2 |
|---|---|

**Name** _____    **Date** _____

Tom and Bill were best friends. They were in the same class at school. One day the principal announced that there would be a science fair, and that everyone should try to develop a project so that they could enter the fair.

   Tom and Bill decided to make a giant thermometer to show changes in the temperature. They worked every day after school for two weeks, and they were excited about their project. After all, they did it all by themselves.

   When the day of the science fair came, everyone thought the giant thermometer was a great idea. But Tom and Bill did not win a top prize for their project. They did receive Honorable Mention, but they were still very disappointed.

   Discuss:

- feelings that Tom and Bill might have had.
- ways Tom and Bill might respond to these feelings.

# ACTIVITY SHEET (NUMBER 2)
## Self-Control

**Grade 6**                                                              **Lesson 2**

**Name** _____  **Date** _____

## RESPONDING TO DISAPPOINTMENT

Responding appropriately to disappointment can be difficult. Sometimes plans we make to get together with friends have to be changed or cancelled. This change might happen because our friends change their minds or because something comes up at the last minute and they can't make it.

Other times our parents might promise to buy us something or take us somewhere special, and they either forget or just aren't able to do what they had promised—for whatever reason.

There are appropriate ways to deal with this disappointment. We can:

- tell the person involved that we are disappointed.
- make alternative plans and follow through on them.
- tell the person not to make a promise unless that person can and will do what he or she says.

We need to remember, however, that sometimes the unexpected happens. We need to remember that there will be times when things don't go our way or don't happen as we would like for them to happen. We need to work on handling our disappointment at these times in a positive way. Sometimes by doing this we become a good example for others.

Let's think of times when we were disappointed. How did we manage to handle our disappointment?

# JOURNAL WRITING ACTIVITY
## Self-Control

**Grade 6**                                                    **Lesson 2**

**Name** _____     **Date** _____

When your family is faced with a problem or conflict, what do you do to help? When your friend is faced with a problem, what do you do to help?

_____

_____

_____

_____

_____

_____

_____

_____

_____

_____

_____

_____

_____

_____

_____

_____

_____

_____

_____

_____

_____

# PERSONAL DEVELOPMENT
## Self-Control

**Grade 7**                                                        **Lesson 2**

**Integration**

Language Arts, Writing, Social Studies

**Materials**

Activity Sheets

**Vocabulary**

emotions: nervous, worried, angry, exhausted, upset

| | | |
|---|---|---|
| communication | nonverbal | verbal |
| interaction | impulsive | expressions |
| aggression | | |

**Objectives**

- To recognize current intensity of feelings with regard to own coping limits.
- To identify alternative solutions to problems as part of a decision-making process.
- To control impulse.
- To use stress-reducing techniques.
- To respect the property of others.
- To accept responsibility for consequences of own behaviors and without shifting blame.
- To recognize that one has behavioral options in a social situation.

**Procedure**

1. Introduce vocabulary words.
2. Introduce the topic of controlling one's anger. Review vocabulary as necessary.
3. Ask students to list some of the kinds of situations that can make people angry. For example, when they are:
   - being teased or embarrassed.
   - being hit, kicked, etc.
   - being told they can't do something.
   - being ignored.

4. Ask students to list some common reactions to anger. What do people do when they are angry? What are the consequences?

   Some common reactions to anger are:
   - crying.
   - screaming or yelling.
   - hurting someone back.
   - withdrawing to your room.

5. Read and discuss the narrative (Activity Sheet Number 1): THE FIGHT.

6. Discuss the importance of thinking before you act. Impulsive behavior may hurt others, make others mad, make you feel bad later, hurt you, or destroy your chance to do what you decide is best.

7. Read and discuss Activity Sheet Number 2.

8. Complete Activity Sheet Number 3.

9. Present Journal Writing Activity.

## Extension Activity

Have students cut out a newspaper article of someone arrested for negative behavior. Put them on a bulletin board and discuss the negative behavior.

# ACTIVITY SHEET (NUMBER 1)
## Self-Control

| Grade 7 | Lesson 2 |
|---------|----------|

**Name** _____     **Date** _____

## THE FIGHT

On Saturday morning, Mom heard a loud noise upstairs. When she went upstairs she found Dustin, head first, in the clothes hamper. Michelle was nowhere to be seen. Mom pulled Dustin out of the hamper. "What happened?" Mom asked Dustin. "Nothing," said Dustin. "Dangling in the clothes hamper is not nothing," said Mom. "You didn't do it yourself!" "Well, Michelle pushed me and I fell into the hamper." "Why did Michelle push you?" Mom asked. "She just did. I wasn't doing anything and she pushed me," Dustin said.

Just then Michelle appeared. "I pushed him because he hit me." "Why did you hit her, Dustin?" asked Mom. "Because." "That's not a very good reason for hitting. And, pushing Dustin into the clothes hamper was not a good way to react to his hitting you," explained Mom. "Well, what should I do to him?" asked Michelle. "You don't have to do anything to him."

Mom explained that there was a better way to react to hitting besides doing something that could hurt the other person. "Let's say, Michelle, that Dustin hit you again," said Mom. "Telling the person not to hurt you and getting help if he hurts you again is a much better way to react."

"Michelle, what will happen the next time someone hits you?" Mom asked. "I'll tell them I don't like it and to stop. If they don't stop, I'll tell someone." "Good. Dustin, don't hit Michelle again!" said Mom.

Mom told Michelle and Dustin a better way to react to hitting. What was her better way?

# ACTIVITY SHEET (NUMBER 2)
## Self-Control

| Grade 7 | Lesson 2 |
|---------|----------|

**Name** _____     **Date** _____

People have one of the three behaviors below. The assertive behavior is the healthy, positive reaction to situations.

A. *Aggressive Behavior*—forceful, sometimes confused or impulsive.

B. *Assertive Behavior*—firm and straightforward.

C. *Passive Behavior*—lacking direction and often influenced by others.

# ACTIVITY SHEET (NUMBER 3)
## Self-Control

| Grade 7 | Lesson 2 |
|---|---|

**Name** _____    **Date** _____

1. One thing that makes me angry is

   _____

   _____

   _____

   _____

2. When I get angry, I feel

   _____

   _____

   _____

   _____

3. When I get angry, I react by

   _____

   _____

   _____

   _____

4. I need to

   _____

   _____

   _____

   _____

   when I get angry.

# JOURNAL WRITING ACTIVITY
## Self-Control

| Grade 7 | Lesson 2 |
|---------|----------|

**Name** _____ **Date** _____

Write about a time when you saw someone very angry. How did that person react to his or her own anger?

_____

_____

_____

_____

_____

_____

_____

_____

_____

_____

_____

_____

_____

_____

_____

_____

_____

_____

_____

_____

_____

_____

_____

_____

_____

# PERSONAL DEVELOPMENT
## Self-Control

| Grade 8 | Lesson 2 |
| --- | --- |

### Integration
Language Arts, Writing, Social Studies

### Materials
Activity Sheets

### Vocabulary

| | | |
| --- | --- | --- |
| criticism | opinion | fact |
| negative | positive | construction |

### Objectives

- To control impulses.
- To realize that one's behavior influences how others will treat him or her.
- To accept responsibility for consequences of own behavior.
- To adjust his or her behaviors and try again.
- To listen to different points of view.
- To respond positively to criticism or direction.
- To accept constructive criticism.
- To accept responsibility for behavior without shifting blame.
- To accept adult clues that channel behavior toward a more appropriate end.

### Procedure

1. Introduce vocabulary words.
2. Discuss criticism as telling you that you are doing something wrong or that you need to improve something.
3. Discuss the difference between constructive and destructive criticism. Give examples of each.
4. Discuss why one might be criticized.

5. Discuss the feelings that accompany being criticized (angry, hurt, defeated, embarrassed) and the negative ways we sometimes react.

- Stopping the activity that was criticized.
- Showing verbal anger.
- Showing physical anger.

6. Read narrative (Activity Sheet Number 1).
7. Complete Activity Sheets (Numbers 2, 3, and 4).
8. Present Journal Writing Activity.

### Extension Activity

Bring in a newspaper article describing a problem in your community. Divide students into groups and ask them to discuss and then present one side of the problem or the other, or both. Talk about the message of Dr. Martin Luther King, Jr.

## ACTIVITY SHEET (NUMBER 1)
### Self-Control

| Grade 8 | Lesson 2 |
|---|---|

**Name** _____  **Date** _____

To criticize means to judge or to analyze. It means to stress the faults. You may have heard the term *constructive criticism.* Constructive criticism means to offer information to someone so that they may improve on something they have done. When a person offers "constructive criticism," he or she must be very careful to use the right words and to use the correct tone of voice so as not to *offend* the other person.

Oftentimes, however, people criticize others without much concern for how they sound or how the other person might feel. People can criticize how a person looks, what the person does or doesn't do, and sometimes even how the person thinks! Criticism is usually a negative approach taken in attempting to improve someone else.

Does this mean, then, that people should never offer others information about themselves? No, not necessarily. There are times when we appreciate others telling us ways that we might change in order to improve ourselves. What we must keep in mind is that we should be kind in our approach. We must remember that no one is perfect, and that we are not necessarily right all of the time.

What can we do if someone makes a *habit* out of criticizing the things we say or do? A good start would be to calmly tell the person that it's really annoying to be criticized so often. Tell the person who is criticizing that you feel he or she is being *inconsiderate.* Keep in mind that it's a really good idea to let a person know when he or she does things well also.

# ACTIVITY SHEET (NUMBER 2)
## Self-Control

| Grade 8 | Lesson 2 |

**Name** _____  **Date** _____

List three comments that you might consider to be "constructive" criticism.

1. _____

_____

_____

2. _____

_____

_____

3. _____

_____

_____

List three comments that you might consider "malicious" or negative criticism.

1. _____

_____

_____

2. _____

_____

_____

3. _____

_____

_____

What is another word that can be used instead of *criticism?*

_____

# ACTIVITY SHEET (NUMBER 3)
## Self-Control

| Grade 8 | Lesson 2 |

**Name** _____  **Date** _____

## RESPONDING TO BEING CRITICIZED

1.  Think of a situation in which you have been criticized. Write a sentence or two to describe it.

   _____

   _____

   _____

2.  Brainstorm and think of as many negative ways to respond to the criticism as you can.

   _____

   _____

   _____

   _____

3.  Brainstorm and think of as many positive ways to respond to the criticism as you can.

   _____

   _____

   _____

   _____

4.  Write a sentence or two to describe how you would choose to respond in a positive way to the situation you described.

   _____

   _____

   _____

# ACTIVITY SHEET (NUMBER 4)
## Self-Control

**Grade 8**                                                    **Lesson 2**

**Name** _____ **Date** _____

In each situation below, you are being criticized by someone. Write a *positive* response to each criticism.

1. Your teacher tells you that your homework assignments are messy and difficult to read.

   _____

   _____

   _____

   _____

2. Another student at the lunch table tells you to eat with your mouth closed.

   _____

   _____

   _____

   _____

3. Your best friend tells you that you act immature around his or her other friends.

   _____

   _____

   _____

   _____

4. Your mom tells you that your clothes don't match when you are getting ready for school.

   _____

   _____

   _____

   _____

# JOURNAL WRITING ACTIVITY
## Self-Control

| Grade 8 | Lesson 2 |
|---------|----------|

**Name** _____ **Date** _____

Write about a time when you were very angry. How long did it take for you to feel less angry? What or who helped you feel less angry?

_____

_____

_____

_____

_____

_____

_____

_____

_____

_____

_____

_____

_____

_____

_____

_____

_____

_____

_____

_____

_____

_____

_____

_____

# REFERENCES

Affleck, J. Q., Lowenbraun, S., & Archer, A. (1980). *Teaching the mildly handicapped in the regular classroom.* Upper Saddle River, NJ: Merrill/ Prentice Hall.

Algozzine, B., Crews, W. B., & Stoddard, K. (1986). *Analysis of basic skill competencies of learning disabled adolescents.* (ERIC Document Reproduction Service No. ED 191 775)

American Association on Mental Retardation (AAMR). (1992). *Mental Retardation: Definition, classification, and systems of supports.* Washington, DC: American Association on Mental Retardation.

Anastasi, A. (1976). *Psychological testing* (4th ed.). New York: Macmillian.

Anderson, R. M., Greer, J. G., & Odle, S. J. (1978). *Individualizing educational materials for special children in the mainstream.* Baltimore: University Park Press.

Anderson, W., Chitwood, S., & Hayden, D. (1990). *Negotiating the special education maze.* Rockville, MD: Woodbine House.

Arbuthnot, J., & Gordon, D. (1988). Disseminating effective interventions for juvenile delinquents: Cognitively-based sociomoral reasoning development programs. *Journal of Correctional Education, 39*(2), 48–53.

Association for Retarded Citizens (ARC). *The new IDEA: Knowing your rights.*

August, D., & Hakuta, K. *Improving schooling for language minority children: A research agenda.* Washington, DC: National Research Council, National Academy Press.

Battle, D. A., Dicken-Wright, L. L., & Murphy, S. C. (1998). How to empower adolescents: Guidelines for effective self-advocacy. *Teaching Exceptional Children, 30*(3), 28–33.

Bauwens, J., & Houreade, J. J. (1995). *Cooperative teaching: Rebuilding teaching: Rebuilding the schoolhouse for all students.* Austin, TX: Pro-Ed.

Blackorby, J., & Wagner, M. (1996). Longitudinal postschool outcomes of youth with disabilities: Findings from the National Longitudinal Transition Study. *Exceptional Children* [online], *62*(5), 399–413. Available: Northern Light/Special Collection/DG19970923010103950 [1999, July 8]. http://library.northernlight.com/DG19970923010 103950.html?cb=0&sc=0#doc[2000, March 16].

Blalock, G. (1996). Community transition teams as the foundation for transition services for youth with disabilities. *Journal of Learning Disabilities, 29*(2), 148–159.

Blalock, G., & Patton, J. R. (1996). Transition and students with learning disabilities: Creating sound futures. In G. Blalock & J. R. Patton (Eds.), *Transition and students with learning disabilities: Facilitating the movement from school to adult life* (pp. 1–18). Austin, TX: Pro-Ed.

Blasi, A. (1980). Bridging moral cognition and moral action: A critical review of the literature. *Psychological Bulletin, 88,* 1–45.

Bloom, B. S. (Ed.). (1956). *Taxonomy of educational objectives: The classification of educational goals.* Handbook 1: *Cognitive domain.* New York: Longman.

Bloom, B. S. (1968). Learning for mastery. *Evaluation Comment, 1*(2).

Bloom, B. S. (1976). *Human characteristics and school learning.* New York: McGraw-Hill.

Boarman, G. L., & Kirkpatrick, B. S. (1995). The hybrid schedule: Scheduling to the curriculum. *NASSP Bulletin, 79*(571), 42–52.

Bodner, J. R., Clark, G. M., & Mellard, D. F. (1987). *State graduation policies and program practices related to high school special education programs.* Lawrence: University of Kansas, Department of Special Education. (ERIC Document Reproduction Service No. ED 294 347)

Brown, D. (1988). Be a computer tutor for people with learning disabilities. In H. J. Murphy (Ed.), *Proceedings of the fourth annual conference on technology and persons with disabilities* (pp. 91–104). Northridge: California State University.

Brown, J., Lewis, R., & Harcleroad, F. (1977). *AV instruction: Technology, media, and methods* (5th ed.). New York: Macmillan.

Bryk, A. S. (1983). Editor's notes. In A. S. Bryk (Ed.), *New directions for program evaluation: Stakeholder-based evaluation.* Washington, DC: Jossey-Bass.

Buckman, D. C., King, B. B., & Ryan, S. (1995). Block scheduling: A means to improve school climate. *NASSP Bulletin, 79*(571), 19–22.

*Building blocks for elementary career awareness.* (1997). Stillwater, OK: Oklahoma Department of Vocational and Technical Education.

Burdette, P. J., & Crockett, J. B. (1999). *An exploration of consultation approaches and implementation in heterogeneous classrooms. Research to practice in the 21st century.* MRDD, 34(4), 432–452.

Carbo, M., & Hodges, H. (1988, Summer). Learning style strategies can help students at risk. *Teaching Exceptional Children,* 55–58.

Carpenter, D. (1985). Grading handicapped pupils: Review and position statements. *Remedial and Special Education, 6*(4), 54–59.

Cartwright, C. A., Cartwright, G. P., Ward, M., & Willoughby-Herb, S. (1981). *Teachers of special learners.* Belmont, CA: Wadsworth.

Chalfant, J. C., & Pysh, M. (1989). Teacher assistance teams: Five descriptive studies on 96 teams. *Remedial and Special Education, 10*(6), 49–58.

Chandler, M., & Moran, T. (1990). Psychopathy and moral development: A comparative study of delinquent and non-delinquent youth. *Development and Psychopathology, 2*(3), 227–246.

Chang, M. K., Richards, J. S., & Jackson, A. (1996). *Accommodating students with disabilities: A practical guide for the faculty.* Funded by U.S. Department of Education, National Institute on Disability and Rehabilitation Research.

Clark, G. M. (1998). *Assessment for transitions planning.* Austin, TX: Pro-Ed.

Coburn, P., Kelman, P., Roberts, N., Snyder, T. F., Watt, D. H., & Weiner, C. (1982). *Practical guide to computers in education.* Reading, MA: Addison-Wesley.

Coffey, O. (1987). The incarcerated: Much more to be done. *Vocational Education Journal, 62*(2), 30–32.

Cohen, S. B. (1983). Assigning report card grades to the mainstreamed child. *Teaching Exceptional Children, 15*(2), 86–89.

Colby, C. R., Wircenski, J. L., & Parrish, L. H. (1987). *Vocational special needs teacher training curriculum.*

Coles, R. (1997). *The moral intelligence of children: How to raise a moral child.* New York: Random House.

Collier, V. (Fall 1995). "Acquiring a Second Language for School." *Directions in language and education, national clearinghouse for bilingual education.*

Comparison of Key Changes: Previous Regulations 7 34 CFR Parts 300 & 301. (1999). Reston, VA: National Association of State Directors of Special Education.

Cooper, J., Hansen, J., Martorella, P., Morine-Dershimer, G., Sadker, M., Sokolove, S., Shostak, R., Tenbrink, T., & Weber, W. (Eds.). (1977). *Classroom teaching skills: A workbook.* Lexington, MA: Heath.

Cosden, M. A., & Abernathy, T. V. (1990). Microcomputer use in the schools: Teacher roles and instructional options. *Remedial and Special Education, 11*(5), 31–38.

Costa, A. L., & Kallick, B. (2000). *Discovering & exploring: Habits of mind.* Alexandria, Virginia: Association for Supervision and Curriculum Development.

Costa, A. L., & Kallick, B. (2000). *Habits of mind.* Alexandria, VA: Association for Supervision and Curriculum Development.

Council for Exceptional Children. July/Aug. 2000. Bright futures for exceptional learners: An action agenda to achieve quality conditions for teaching and learning for every exceptional learner. *Teaching Exceptional Children, 32*(6), 56–69. [online]. Available: cec.sped.org.

Courtnage, L., & Healy, H. (1984). Interdisciplinary team training: A competency- and procedure-based approach. *Teacher Education and Special Education, 7,* 3–11.

Courtnage, L., & Smith-Davis, F. (1987). Interdisciplinary team training: A national survey of special education teacher training programs. *Exceptional Children, 53,* 451–458.

Cummins, J. et. al. *Schooling and language minority students: A theoretical framework.* Los Angeles, CA: California State University, School of Education, 1994.

Curtis, E., & Dezelsky, M. (1994). *It's my life: Preference-based planning for self-directed goal meetings.* Castle Valley, UT: New Hats, Inc.

D'Alonzo, B. J., D'Alonzo, R. L., & Mauser, A. J. (1979). Developing resource rooms for the handicapped. *Teaching Exceptional Children, 11*(3), 91–96.

Danielson, L. (1999, Fall). Universal design: Ensuring access to the general education curriculum. *Research Connections, 5,* 2–3.

Dardig, J. (1981). Helping teachers integrate handicapped students into the regular classroom. *Educational Horizons, 59,* 124–129.

Dave, R. H. (1970). *Taxonomy of educational objectives: Psychomotor domain.* New Delhi, India: National Institute of Education.

Davies, I. K. (1981). *Instructional techniques.* New York: McGraw-Hill.

deFur, S. H., & Patton, J. R. (Eds.). (1999). *Transition and school-based services: Interdisciplinary perspectives for enhancing the transition process.* Austin, TX: Pro-Ed.

Dewey, J. (1937, April). Democracy and educational administration. *School and Society, 458–459.*

Duffy, P. L., & Wannie, T. W. (1995). *Setting your career and life direction.* Indianapolis, IN: JIST Works, Inc.

Dugdale, R. L. (1910). *The Jukes: A study of crime, pauperism, disease, and heredity.* New York: Putnam.

Dunn, R., Dunn, K., & Price, G. E. (1979). *Learning styles inventory manual.* Lawrence, KS: Price Systems.

Durkin, D. (1984). Is there a match between what elementary teachers do and what basal reader manuals recommend? *Reading Teacher, 37,* 734–745.

Edwards, C. M., Jr. (1993). Restructuring to improve student performance. *NASSP Bulletin, 77*(553), 77–88.

Edwards, C. M., Jr. (1995). Virginia's 4 × 4 high schools: High school, college, and more. *NASSP Bulletin, 79*(571), 23–41.

Elliott, J., Thurlow, M., & Ysseldyke, J. (1996). *Assessment guidelines that maximize the participation of students with disabilities in large-scale assessments: Characteristics and considerations.* National Center for Educational Outcomes, National Association of State Directors of Special Education.

Everson, J. M. (1993). *Youth with disabilities: Strategies for interagency transition programs.* Boston, MA: Andover Medical Publishers.

Farr, J. M. (1996). *The guide for occupational exploration inventory: A self-directed guide to career, learning, and lifestyle options.* Indianapolis, IN: JIST Works, Inc.

Ferrara, S. F. (1984). *Modifications, support, and mainstreaming: Excellence in mainstreaming practices and evaluation.* Paper presented at the annual meeting of the Evaluation Research Society, San Francisco. (ERIC Document Reproduction Service No. ED 257 254)

Feuerstein, R., Rand, Y., Hoffman, M. B., & Miller, R. (1980). *Instrumental enrichment: An intervention program for cognitive modifiability.* Baltimore: University Park Press. In Costa & Kallick, B. *Discovering and Exploring: Habits of Mind.*

Foster-Johnson, L., & Dunlap, G. (1993). Using functional assessment to develop effective, individualized interventions for challenging behaviors. *Teaching Exceptional Children, 25*(3), 44–50.

Friend, M. (1995). *Collaboration team training.* Bowling Green: Northwest Ohio Special Education Regional Resource Center.

Friend, M., & Cook, L. (1992). *Interactions: Collaboration skills for school professionals.* White Plains, NY: Longman.

Friend, M., & Cook, L. (1996). *Interactions: Collaboration skills for school professionals* (2nd ed.). White Plains, New York: Longman.

Fuhrmann, B. S. (1980, August). *Models and methods of assessing learning styles.* Paper presented at a meeting of the Virginia Educational Research Association.

Fuhrmann, B. S., & Grasha, A. F. (1983). *A practical handbook for college teachers.* Boston: Little, Brown.

Furney, K. S., Hasazi, S. B., & DeStefan, L. (1997). Transition policies, practices, and promises: Lessons learned from three states. *Exceptional Children, 63*(3), 343–355.

Gardner, H. (1983). *Frames of mind: The theory of multiple intelligences.* New York: Basic Books.

Gardner, H. (1993). Educating for understanding. *American School Board Journal, 180*(7), 20–24.

Gardner, H. (1999, July). *Multiple intelligences.* Speech delivered at Thinking for a Change Conference, 7th International Thinking Conference, Edmonton, Alberta, Canada.

Gerber, P. J., & Popp, P. A. (1999). Consumer perspectives on the collaborative teaching model. *Remedial and Special Education, 20*(5). Austin, TX: Pro Ed.

Gersten, R., Darch, C., Davis, G., & George, N. (1991). Apprenticeship and intensive training of consulting teachers: A naturalistic study. *Exceptional Children, 57*(3), 226–236.

Gloeckler, T., & Simpson, C. (1988). *Exceptional students in regular classrooms.* Mountain View, CA: Mayfield.

Goddard, H. H. (1912). *The Kallikak family.* New York: Macmillan.

Goldenstein, A. (1990). *Delinquents on delinquency.* Champaign, IL: Research Press.

Good, T., & Brophy, J. (1987). *Looking in classrooms* (4th ed.). New York: Harper & Row.

Good, T. L. (1987). Two decades of research on teacher expectations: Findings and future directions. *Journal of Teacher Education, 38*(4), 32–47.

Greenburg, D. E. (1987). *A special educator's perspective on interfacing special and regular education: A review for administrators.* Reston, VA: Council for Exceptional Children.

Greer, J. G., Friedman, I., & Laycock, V. (1978). Instructional games. In R. M. Anderson, J. G. Greer, & S. Odle (Eds.), *Individualizing educational materials for special children in the mainstream* (pp. 267–293). Baltimore: University Park Press.

Guiding Principles for an Inclusive Accountability System. (1997). Reston, VA: National Association of State Directors of Special Education.

Guilford, J. P., & Hoeptner, R. (1971). *The analysis of intelligence.* New York: McGraw-Hill. In Costa & Kallick, B. *Discovering and Exploring: Habits of Mind.* 4–5.

Guskey, T. R. (1981). Individualizing instruction in the mainstream classroom: A mastery learning approach. *Educational Unlimited, 3*(1), 12–15.

Hackett, B. (1992). *Correctional education: A way to stay out.* Springfield, IL: Illinois State Council on Vocational Education. (ERIC Document Reproduction Service No. ED 357 172)

Hart, V. (1981). *Mainstreaming children with special needs.* White Plains, NY: Longman.

Hayward, B. (1992, April). *Dropout prevention in vocational education: Findings from the first years of the demonstration.* Paper presented at the annual meeting of the American Education Research Association, San Francisco, CA. (ERIC Document Reproduction Service No. ED 348 560)

Heron, T. E., & Harris, K. C. (1987). *The educational consultant.* Austin, TX: Pro-Ed.

Hess, R., Miller, A., Reese, J., & Robinson, G. A. (1987). *Grading-credit-diploma: Accommodation practices for students with mild disabilities.* Des Moines: Iowa State Department of Education, Bureau of Special Education.

Heward, W. L. (1996). *Exceptional children: An introduction to special education* (5th ed.). Englewood Cliffs, NJ: Prentice Hall.

*High Stakes Testing for Students: Unanswered questions and implementations for students with disabilities.* Synthesis Report 26. Minneapolis, MN: University of Minnesota. National Center on Educational Outcomes, 9–10.

Hoover, K. H., & Hollingsworth, P. M. (1975). *Learning and teaching in the elementary school.* Boston: Allyn & Bacon.

Huefner, D. C. (1994). An introduction to section 504 of the Rehabilitation Act. *Utah Special Educator, 14*(4), 10–11.

Huff, A. L. (1995). Flexible block scheduling: It works for us! *NASSP Bulletin, 79*(571), 19–22.

Huff, C. R. (1990). *Gangs in America.* Newbury Park, CA: Sage.

Idol, L. (1988). A rationale and guidelines for establishing special education consultation programs. *Remedial and Special Education, 9*(6), 48–58.

Idol, L., & West, J. F. (1987). Consultation in special education. Part 2: Training and practice. *Journal of Learning Disabilities, 20*(8), 474–494.

Idol, L., Paolucci-Whitcomb, P., & Nevin, A. (1987). *Collaborative consultation.* Austin, TX: Pro-Ed.

Idol-Maestas, L., & Ritter, S. (1985). A follow-up study of resource/consulting teachers: Factors that facilitate and inhibit teacher consultation. *Teacher Education and Special Education, 8*(3), 121–131.

Iowa Department of Education. (1989). *Guidelines for serving at-risk students.* Des Moines: Author.

Jacobsen, D., Eggen, D., & Kauchak, D. (1989). *Methods for teaching.* Upper Saddle River, NJ: Merrill/Prentice Hall.

Jarolimek, J., & Foster, C. (1981). *Teaching and learning in the elementary school* (2nd ed.). New York: Macmillan.

Jenkins, J. R., & Pany, D. (1978). Standardized achievement tests: How useful for special education? *Exceptional Children, 44,* 448–453.

Johnson, D. W., & Johnson, R. T. (1986). Mainstreaming and cooperative learning strategies. *Exceptional Children, 52*(6), 553–561.

Johnson, G. R. (1976). *Analyzing college teaching.* Manchach, TX: Sterling Swift.

Johnson, R. T., Johnson, D. W., & Holubec, E. J. (Eds.). (1987). *Structuring cooperative learning: Lesson plans for teachers* (pp. 55–56). Edina, MN: Interaction.

Jordan, D. R. (1996). *Overcoming dyslexia in children, adolescents, and adults* (2nd ed.). Austin, TX: Pro-Ed.

Kaplan, P. S. (1996). *Pathways for exceptional children: School, home, and culture.* St. Paul, MN: West.

Kaplan, S. W., Kaplan, J. A. B., Madsen, S. K., & Taylor, B. K. (1973). *Change for children.* Pacific Palisades, CA: Goodyear.

Kauffman, J. M., & Pullen, P. L. (1989). An historical perspective: A personal perspective on our history of service to mildly handicapped and at-risk students. *Remedial and Special Education, 10*(6), 12–14.

Kelly, D. (1990, June 26). A call to cut school class size. *USA Today,* p. 1D.

Kelly, L. K. (1979). Student self-scheduling: Is it worth the risks? *NASSP Bulletin, 63*(424), 84–91.

Kindsvatter, R., Wilen, W., & Ishler, M. (1988). *Dynamics of effective teaching.* New York: Longman.

Kjerland, L., Neiss, J., Franke, B., Verdon, C., & Westman, E. (1988, Winter). Team membership: Who's on first? *Impact: Feature Issue on Integrated Education, 1*(2). Minneapolis: University of Minnesota Institute on Community Integration.

Knoff, H. M. (1985). Attitudes toward mainstreaming: A status report and comparison of regular and special educators in New York and Massachusetts. *Psychology in the Schools, 22,* 410–418.

Kozma, C., & Stock, J. C. (1993). What is mental retardation? In R. Smith (Ed.), *Children with mental retardation: A parents' guide* (pp. 1–49). Rockville, MD: Woodbine House.

Krashen, S. (1993) *The power of reading.* Englewood, CO: Libraries Unlimited.

Krashen, S., & Biber, D. (1988). *On course: Bilingual education's success in California.* Sacramento, CA: California Association for Bilingual Education.

Krogstad, R. (1987). An open-ended cycle system in vocational education. *Journal of Correctional Education, 38*(1), 8–10.

Kruse, C. A., & Kruse, G. D. (1995). The master schedule and learning: Improving the quality of education? *NASSP Bulletin, 79*(571), 1–8.

Kurpius, D. (1978). Introduction to the special issue: An overview on consultation. *Personnel and Guidance Journal, 56,* 320–323.

Laham, S. L. (2000). *Working together: A practical guide for facilitators.* Richmond, VA: Judy Wood Publishing Company.

Larson, R., & Wood, J. W. (2001). *Power prompts: Narrative.* With permission.

*The Lau decision and Lau remedies.* (1976). Lansing: Michigan State Board of Education.

Lee, J. F., Jr., & Pruitt, K. W. (1970). Homework assignments: Classroom games or teaching tools? *Clearing House, 1,* 31–35.

Leon, P., Rutherford, R., & Nelson, C. (1991). *Special education in juvenile corrections.* Reston, VA: The Council for Exceptional Children.

Lewis, R. B., & Doorlag, D. H. (1987). *Teaching special students in the mainstream.* Upper Saddle River, NJ: Merrill/Prentice Hall.

Lewis, R. B., & Doorlag, D. H. (1998). *Teaching special students in general education classrooms* (5th ed.). Upper Saddle River, NJ: Prentice Hall.

Long, N. J., & Newman, R. (1980). Managing surface behaviors of children in schools. In N. J. Long, W. Morse, & R. Newman (Eds.), *Conflict in the classroom: The education of emotionally disturbed children* (4th ed.). Belmont, CA: Wadsworth.

Longo, P. (1997, June). Making standards work: *Aligning transition competencies with academic content standards.* Denver, CO: Colorado Department of Education.

Lovitt, T. (1989). Constructing graphic organizers. In *Graphic organizer interactive video packet.* Salt Lake City: Utah Learning Resource Center.

McKenzie, H., Egner, A. N., Knight, M. F., Perelman, P. F., & Miller, L. (1990). The regular education initiative and school reform: Lessons from the mainstream. *Remedial and Special Education, 11*(3), 17–22.

Meers, G. D. (1987). *Handbook of vocational special needs education.* Rockville, MD: Aspen.

Meyen, D., Vergason, H., & Whelan, C. (1993). "In my dreams": A second look at inclusion and programming. *Journal of the Association for Persons with Severe Handicaps, 18,* 296–298.

Miller, M. (1989). *Apprenticeship training in correctional institutions.* Paper presented at the American Vocational Association Convention, Orlando, FL. (ERIC Document Reproduction Service No. ED 315 643)

Munk, D. D., & Bursuck, W. D. (1997–1998). Can grades be helpful? *Education Leadership, 55*(4), 44–47.

Myles, B. S., & Simpson, R. L. (1989). Regular educators' modification preferences for mainstreaming mildly handicapped children. *Journal of Special Education, 22*(4), 479–492.

Nadeau, K. (2000, Nov/Dec.). Girls with AD/HD. *Attention, 7*(1), 48–54.

Nelson, C. M., & Stevens, K. B. (1981). An accountable consultation model for mainstreaming behaviorally disordered children. *Behavior Disorders, 6*(12), 82–91.

Nelson, J., Smith, D., & Dodd, J. (1990). The moral reasoning of juvenile delinquents: A meta-analysis. *Journal of Abnormal Child Psychology, 18*(3), 231–239.

Nelson, J. S., Madhavi, J., Epstein, M. H., & Bursuck, W. D. (2000, January/February). Student preferences for adaptations in classroom testing. *Remedial and Special Education, 21*(1), 41–52.

*1997 state special education outcomes.* (1997). Minneapolis, MN: University of Minnesota, National Center on Educational Outcomes.

O'Leary, E. (1998, February). *Transition: Terms and concepts.* Des Moines, IA: Mountain Plains Regional Resource Center.

Patton, J. R., & Dunn, C. (1998). *Transition from school to young adulthood: Basic concepts and recommended practices.* Austin, TX: Pro-Ed.

Perkins, D. W. (1995). Outsmarting IQ: *The emerging science of learnable intelligence.* New York: The Free Press.

Peterson, N. L. (1987). *Early intervention for handicapped and at-risk children.* Denver: Love.

Phelps, L. A., & Hanley-Maxwell, C. (1997). School to work transitions for youth with disabilities: A review of outcomes and practices. *Review of Educational Research, 67,* 197–226.

Piechowiak, A. B., & Cook, M. B. (1976). *Complete guide to the elementary learning center.* West Nyack, NY: Parker.

Pollard, R., & Kaufman, J. (1994). Successful special populations program characteristics: A qualitative inquiry. *Journal of Instructional Psychology, 21*(2), 148–154.

Pollard, R., Pollard, C., & Meers, G. (1994). Determining effective transition strategies for adjudicated youth with disabilities: A national delphi study. *Journal of Correctional Education, 45*(4), 190–196.

Pugach, M. C., & Johnson, L. J. (1995). Unlocking expertise among classroom teachers through structured dialogue: Extending research on peer collaboration. *Exceptional Children, 62*(2), 101–110.

Purkey, W. (1978). *Inviting school success.* Belmont, CA: Wadsworth.

Quay, H. (1987). Patterns of delinquent behavior. In H. C. Quay (Ed.), *Handbook of juvenile delinquency* (pp. 118–138). New York: Wiley.

Raphael, T. E. (1982). Question-answering strategies for children. *Reading Teacher, 36,* 186–190.

Relic, P. D., Cavallaro, A., Borrelli, M., & Currie, J. H. (1986). *Special education/regular education.* West Hartford, CT: West Hartford Public Schools.

Reporting Educational Results for Students with Disabilities. (1997). National Center on Educational Outcomes, University of Minnesota, 2.

Reynolds, M. C. (1989). An historical perspective: The delivery of special education to mildly disabled and at-risk students. *Remedial and Special Education, 10*(6), 7–11.

Reynolds, M. C., Wang, M. C., & Walberg, H. J. (1987). The necessary restructuring of special and regular education. *Exceptional Children, 53*(5), 391–398.

Robbins, R. L., & Harway, N. I. (1977). Goal setting and reactions to success and failure in children with learning disabilities. *Journal of Learning Disabilities, 10*(6), 356–362.

Rocha, R. M., Wiley, D., & Watson, M. J. (1982). Special subject teachers and the special educator work to mainstream. *Teaching Exceptional Children, 14*(4), 141–145.

Rosenthal, R. (1974). *On the social psychology of the self-fulfilling prophecy: Further evidence of Pygmalion effects and their mediating mechanisms.* New York: MSS Modular.

Rowe, M. B. (1974). Wait time and reward as instructional variables, their influence on language, logic, and fate control. Part 1: Wait time. *Journal of Research on Science Teaching, 11,* 81–94.

Rueda, R., Gallego, M. A., & Moll, L. C. (2000). The least restrictive environment: A place or a concept? *Remedial and Special Education, 21*(2), 70–78.

Rusch, F. R., & Chadsey, J. G. (1998). *Beyond high school: Transition from school to work.* Belmont, CA: Wadsworth Publishing Company.

Rutherford, R. (1988). Correctional special education. *Teaching Exceptional Children, 20*(4), 52–54.

Safran, J., & Safran, S. P. (1985). Organizing communication for the LD teacher. *Academic Therapy, 20*(4), 427–435.

Sagatun, I. (1991). Attributions of delinquency by delinquent minors, their families, and probation officers. *Journal of Offender Rehabilitation, 16*(3), 43–57.

Sage, D. D. (Ed.). (1997). *Inclusion in secondary schools: Bold initiative challenging change.* Port Chester, NY: National Professional Resources, Inc.

Salend, S. J., & Salend, S. M. (1986). Competencies for mainstreaming secondary level learning disabled students. *Journal of Learning Disabilities, 19,* 91–94.

Salend, S. J., & Schliff, J. (1988). The many dimensions of homework. *Academic Therapy, 23*(4), 397–403.

Samuels, S. J. (1984). Basic academic skills. In J. E. Ysseldyke (Ed.), *School psychology: The state of the art.* Minneapolis: National School Psychology In-service Training Network, University of Minnesota.

Schniedewind, N., & Salend, S. J. (1987). Cooperative learning works. *Teaching Exceptional Children, 19*(2), 22–25.

Schulte, A. C., Osborne, S. S., & McKinney, J. D. (1990). Academic outcomes for students with learning disabilities in consultation and resource programs. *Exceptional Children, 57*(2), 162–172.

Showers, B. (1985). Teachers coaching teachers. *Educational Leadership, 42*(7), 63–68.

Silver, H. F., Strong, R. W., & Perini, M. J. (2000). *So each may learn: Integrating learning styles and multiple intelligences.* Alexandria, VA: Association for Supervision and Curriculum Development.

Simpson, R. L. (1980). Modifying the attitudes of regular class students toward the handicapped. *Focus on Exceptional Children, 13*(3), 1–11.

Sitlington, P. L., Clark, G. M., & Kolstoe, O. P. (2000). *Transition education and services for adolescents with disabilities.* Needham Heights, MA: Allyn & Bacon.

Smith, D. D., & Luckasson, R. (1995). *Introduction to special education: Teaching in an age of challenge* (2nd ed.). Needham Heights, MA: Allyn & Bacon.

*Special education teacher responses to the 1997 basic standards testing.* (1997). Minneapolis, MN: NCED.

Spodek, B. (1982). What special educators need to know about regular classrooms. *Educational Forum, 46*(3), 295–307.

Spodek, B., Saracho, O. N., & Lee, R. C. (1984). *Mainstreaming young children.* Belmont, CA: Wadsworth.

Stainback, W., Stainback, S., Courtnage, L., & Jaben, T. (1985). Facilitating mainstreaming by modifying the mainstream. *Exceptional Children, 52*(2), 144–152.

Sternberg, R. J., Taff, B., & Grigorento, E. (1998, May). *Teaching for successful intelligence raises school achievement. Phi Delta Kappa* (79C9), 667–669.

*Success for all.* Baltimore: Johns Hopkins University.

Sulzer-Azaroff, B., & Mayer, G. R. (1977). *Applying behavioral analysis procedures with children and youth.* New York: Holt, Rhinehart, & Winston.

Suydam, M. N. (1985). Individualizing for cooperative learning. *Arithmetic Teacher, 32*(8), 39.

Szymanski, E. M., Hanley-Maxwell, C., & Asselin, S. B. (1992). Systems interface: Vocational rehabilitation, special education, and vocational education. In F. R. Rusch, L. DeStefano, J. Chadsey-Rusch, L. A. Phelps, & E. Szymanski (Eds.), *Transition from school to adult life* (pp. 153–171). Pacific Grove, CA: Brooks/Cole.

Teachers stake out position on big tests. *USA Today,* (2000, July 13). 10D.

Tenbrink, T. (1977). Writing instructional objectives. In J. Cooper, J. Hansen, P. Martorella, G. Morine-Dershimer, D. Sadker, M. Sadker, R. Shostak, S. Sokolove, T. Tenbrink, & W. Weber (Eds.), *Classroom teaching skills: A handbook.* Lexington, MA: Heath.

Thompson, A. C. (1981). Some counterthinking about learning disabilities. *Journal of Learning Disabilities, 14,* 394–396.

Thousand, J. S., & Villa, R. A. (1990). Sharing expertise and responsibilities through teaching teams. In W. Stainback & S. Stainback (Eds.), *Support systems for educating all students in the mainstream.* Baltimore: Brookes.

Thuli, K. K., & Hong, E. (1998). *Employer toolkit.* Washington, DC: National Transition Alliance for Youth with Disabilities, Academy for Educational Development.

Thurlow, M., Elliott, J., Ysseldyke, J., & Erickson, R. (1996). *Questions and answers: Tough questions about accountability systems and students with disabilities.* Synthesis Report 24. Minneapolis, MN: University of Minnesota, National Center on Educational Outcomes.

Tilson, G. P. (1996). The employer partnership in transition for youth with disabilities. *Journal for Vocational Special Needs Education, 18*(3), 88–92.

Tindall, L. W. (1992). Business linkages. In F. R. Rusch, L. DeStefano, J. Chadsey-Rusch, L. A. Phelps, & Symanski (Eds.), *Transition from school to adult life: Models, linkages, and policy* (pp. 321–340). Sycamore, IL: Sycamore Publishing.

*Transition trek: A game for planning life after high school for youth with disabilities.* (1996). Minneapolis, MN: PACER Center, Inc. Developed/written by Committee.

Turnbull, A. P., & Turnbull, H. R. (1986). *Families, professionals, and exceptionality.* Upper Saddle River, NJ: Merrill/Prentice Hall.

Turner, T. (1984). The joy of homework. *Tennessee Education, 14,* 25–33.

U.S. Department of Education. (1998). *To assure the free appropriate public education of all children with disabilities* (twentieth annual report to Congress on the implementation of the Individuals with Disabilities Education Act). Washington, DC: U.S. Government Printing Office.

*The Utah Special Educator,* (1994, April). *14*(6).

Utah State Board of Education. (1992). *Special education rules.* Salt Lake City: Author.

Vasa, S. F. (1981). Alternative procedures for grading handicapped students in the secondary schools. *Education Unlimited, 3*(1), 16–23.

Virginia Department of Education. (1989). *Issues related to graduation and students receiving special education services* (Superintendents' Memo No. 126). Richmond: Author.

Voight, B. C. (1973). *Invitation to learning.* Washington, DC: Acropolis.

Vygotsky, L. (1978). *Mind and society.* Cambridge: Harvard University Press.

Wanner, D. A. (2000). Curriculum for teaching personal development, cultural, awareness &

global respect. *Reaching the hard to teach.* Richmond, VA.

Wehman, P. (1996). *Life beyond the classroom: Transition strategies for young people with disabilities* (2nd ed.). Baltimore, MD: Paul H. Brookes.

Weintraub, F. J., & Ross, J. W. (1980). Policy approaches regarding the impact of graduation requirements on handicapped students. *Exceptional Children, 47*(3), 200–203.

West, E. (1975). *Leading discussions.* Unpublished paper. University of Minnesota.

West, J. F., & Brown, P. (1987). State departments of education policies on consultation in special education: The state of the states. *Remedial and Special Education, 8*(3), 45–51.

West, J. F., & Idol, L. (1990). Collaborative consultation in the education of mildly handicapped and at-risk students. *Remedial and Special Education, 11*(1), 22–31.

Whimbey, A., Wimbey, L. S., & Shaw, L. (1975). *Intelligence can be taught.* New York: Lawrence Earlbaum Associates. In Costa & Kallick, B. *Discovering and Exploring: Habits of Mind.* 6.

Wiatrowski, M., & Anderson, K. (1987). The dimensionality of the social bond. *Journal of Quantitative Criminology, 3*(3), 65–81.

Wiederholt, J. L., & Chamberlain, S. P. (1990). A critical analysis of resource programs. *Remedial and Special Education, 10*(6), 15–37.

Williams, P. A., Alley, R. D., & Henson, K. T. (1999). *Managing secondary classrooms: Principles and strategies for effective management and instruction.* Boston, MA: Allyn & Bacon.

Wimmer, D. (1981). Functional learning curricula in the secondary schools. *Exceptional Children, 47*(8), 610–616.

Wood, J. W. (1987). *Mainstreaming: A practical approach for educators.* Columbus, Ohio: Merrill.

Wood, J. W. (1993). *Mainstreaming: A practical approach for teachers.* Upper Saddle River, NJ: Merrill/Prentice Hall.

Wood, J. W. (1997). *Intervention taxonomy levels.* Richmond, VA: Judy Wood.

Wood, J. W. (2000). *Intervention/transition checklist.* Richmond, VA: Judy Wood.

Wood, J.W., & Lazzari, A. M. (1997). *Exceeding the boundaries: Understanding exceptional learners* (p. 468). Fort Worth, TX: Harcourt Brace.

Wood, J.W., & Reeves, C. K. (1989). Mainstreaming: An overview. In J. W. Wood, *Mainstreaming: A practical approach for teachers.* Upper Saddle River, NJ: Merrill/Prentice Hall.

Wood, J. W., & Wooley, J. A. (1986). Adapting textbooks. *Clearing House, 59,* 332–335.

Wood, J., Womack, S., & Feola, P. (1996). Intervention taxonomy. *Reaching the hard to teach.* Richmond, VA.

Wood, M. (1998). Whose job is it anyway? Educational roles in inclusion. *Exceptional Children, 64*(2), 181–195.

Yinger, R. (1980). A study of teacher planning. *Elementary School Journal, 80*(3), 107–127.

Ysseldyke, J. E., & Algozzine, D. (1982). *Critical issues in special and remedial education.* Boston: Houghton Mifflin.

Zehler, A. (1994). "Working with English Language Learners: Strategies for Elementary and Middle School Teachers." *NCBE program information guide series,* Number 19. (1997) Washington, DC.

## Internet Resources on Bilingual /ESL Programs

Center for Research on Education, Diversity, & Excellence
*http://crede.ucsc.edu/*

Dave's ESL Café
*http://www.pacificnet.net/~sperling/*

English as a Second Language Home Page
*http://www.rong-chang.com/*

Family Literacy Foundation
*http://www.read2kids.org/*

National Association for Bilingual Education
*http://www.nabe.org/*

National Clearinghouse for Bilingual Education
*http://www.ncbe.gwu.edu*

National Clearinghouse for ESL Literacy Education
*http://www.cal.org/ncle/*

Office of Bilingual Education and Minority Language Affairs
*http://www.ed.gov./offices/OBEMLA/*

## Public laws

Americans with Disabilities Act of 1990, PL 101-36.

The Education for All Handicapped Children Act of 1975, PL 94-142.

The Individuals with Disabilities Education Act of 1990, PL 101-476.

The Individuals with Disabilities Education Act Amendments of 1997, PL 105-17.

The School-to-Work Opportunities Act of 1994, PL 103-239.

The Smith-Hughes Act of 1917, PL 347.

The Vocational Education Act Amendments of 1968, PL 90-210.

The Vocational Education Act of 1963, PL 88-210.

Vocational Rehabilitation Act of 1973, PL 93-112.

Washington, DC: US Government Printing Office. [on-line], http://www.access.gpo.gov.

# INDEX